PROGRAMMING:
Visual Logic & Design

Joyce Farrell | Thad Crews | Chip Murphy

Australia • Brazil • Japan • Korea • Mexico • Singapore • Spain • United Kingdom • United States

PROGRAMMING: Visual Logic & Design

Senior Project Development Manager:
Linda deStefano

Market Development Manager:
Heather Kramer

Senior Production/
Manufacturing Manager:
Donna M. Brown

Production Editorial Manager:
Kim Fry

Sr. Rights Acquisition Account Manager:
Todd Osborne

Printed in the United States of America

Programming Logic and Design, Comprehenisve version, Seventh Edition
Joyce Farrell

© 2013 Cengage Learning. All rights reserved.

Some of the product names and company names used in this book have been used for identification purposes only and may be trademarks or registered trademarks of their respective manufacturers and sellers. Unless otherwise credited, all art © Cengage Learning, produced by Integra.
Course Technology, Cengage Learning is an independent entity from the Microsoft Corporation, and not affiliated with Microsoft in any manner.

SA Guide to Working with Visual Logic
Thad Crews | Chip Murphy

© 2009 Cengage Learning. All rights reserved.

ALL RIGHTS RESERVED. No part of this work covered by the copyright herein may be reproduced, transmitted, stored or used in any form or by any means graphic, electronic, or mechanical, including but not limited to photocopying, recording, scanning, digitizing, taping, Web distribution, information networks, or information storage and retrieval systems, except as permitted under Section 107 or 108 of the 1976 United States Copyright Act, without the prior written permission of the publisher.

> For product information and technology assistance, contact us at
> **Cengage Learning Customer & Sales Support, 1-800-354-9706**
> For permission to use material from this text or product,
> submit all requests online at **cengage.com/permissions**
> Further permissions questions can be emailed to
> **permissionrequest@cengage.com**

This book contains select works from existing Cengage Learning resources and was produced by Cengage Learning Custom Solutions for collegiate use. As such, those adopting and/or contributing to this work are responsible for editorial content accuracy, continuity and completeness.

Compilation © 2013 Cengage Learning

ISBN-13: 978-1-285-91593-7

ISBN-10: 1-285-91593-3

Cengage Learning
5191 Natorp Boulevard
Mason, Ohio 45040
USA

Cengage Learning is a leading provider of customized learning solutions with office locations around the globe, including Singapore, the United Kingdom, Australia, Mexico, Brazil, and Japan. Locate your local office at:
international.cengage.com/region.
Cengage Learning products are represented in Canada by Nelson Education, Ltd.
For your lifelong learning solutions, visit **www.cengage.com /custom.**
Visit our corporate website at **www.cengage.com.**

PART I

Programming Logic and Design, Comprehensive

Joyce Farrell

PROGRAMMING LOGIC AND DESIGN

COMPREHENSIVE VERSION

Brief Contents

	Preface	xviii
CHAPTER 1	An Overview of Computers and Programming	1
CHAPTER 2	Elements of High-Quality Programs	37
CHAPTER 3	Understanding Structure	83
CHAPTER 4	Making Decisions	121
CHAPTER 5	Looping	169
CHAPTER 6	Arrays	213
CHAPTER 7	File Handling and Applications	257
CHAPTER 8	Advanced Data Handling Concepts	305
CHAPTER 9	Advanced Modularization Techniques	355
CHAPTER 10	Object-Oriented Programming	407
CHAPTER 11	More Object-Oriented Programming Concepts	449
CHAPTER 12	Event-Driven GUI Programming, Multithreading, and Animation	491
CHAPTER 13	System Modeling with the UML	523
CHAPTER 14	Using Relational Databases	555
APPENDIX A	Understanding Numbering Systems and Computer Codes	601
APPENDIX B	Flowchart Symbols	611
APPENDIX C	Structures	612
APPENDIX D	Solving Difficult Structuring Problems	614

BRIEF CONTENTS

APPENDIX E	Creating Print Charts	**624**
APPENDIX F	Two Variations on the Basic Structures—case and do-while	**626**
	Glossary	**633**
	Index	**653**

Contents

Preface xviii

CHAPTER 1   An Overview of Computers and Programming . 1

    Understanding Computer Systems 2
    Understanding Simple Program Logic 5
    Understanding the Program Development Cycle 7
        Understanding the Problem 8
        Planning the Logic 9
        Coding the Program 10
        Using Software to Translate the Program into Machine Language . 10
        Testing the Program 12
        Putting the Program into Production 13
        Maintaining the Program 13
    Using Pseudocode Statements and Flowchart Symbols 14
        Writing Pseudocode 15
        Drawing Flowcharts 16
        Repeating Instructions 17
    Using a Sentinel Value to End a Program 19
    Understanding Programming and User Environments 22
        Understanding Programming Environments 22
        Understanding User Environments 24
    Understanding the Evolution of Programming Models 25
    Chapter Summary 27
    Key Terms 28
    Review Questions 31
    Exercises 33
        Find the Bugs 35
        Game Zone 35
        Up for Discussion 36

CHAPTER 2 — Elements of High-Quality Programs 37

Declaring and Using Variables and Constants 38
    Understanding Unnamed, Literal Constants and their
        Data Types 38
    Working with Variables 39
    Naming Variables 41
    Assigning Values to Variables 42
    Understanding the Data Types of Variables 43
    Declaring Named Constants 44
Performing Arithmetic Operations 45
Understanding the Advantages of Modularization 48
    Modularization Provides Abstraction 49
    Modularization Allows Multiple Programmers to
        Work on a Problem 50
    Modularization Allows You to Reuse Work 50
Modularizing a Program 51
    Declaring Variables and Constants within Modules 55
    Understanding the Most Common Configuration for Mainline Logic . 57
Creating Hierarchy Charts 61
Features of Good Program Design 63
    Using Program Comments 64
    Choosing Identifiers 66
    Designing Clear Statements 68
    Writing Clear Prompts and Echoing Input 69
    Maintaining Good Programming Habits 71
Chapter Summary 72
Key Terms 73
Review Questions 76
Exercises 79
    Find the Bugs 81
    Game Zone 82
    Up for Discussion 82

CHAPTER 3 — Understanding Structure 83

The Disadvantages of Unstructured Spaghetti Code 84
Understanding the Three Basic Structures 86

Using a Priming Input to Structure a Program 95
Understanding the Reasons for Structure 101
Recognizing Structure 102
Structuring and Modularizing Unstructured Logic 105
Chapter Summary 110
Key Terms 111
Review Questions 112
Exercises 114
   Find the Bugs 118
   Game Zone 118
   Up for Discussion 119

CHAPTER 4 Making Decisions 121

Boolean Expressions and the Selection Structure 122
Using Relational Comparison Operators 126
   Avoiding a Common Error with Relational Operators 129
Understanding *AND* Logic 129
   Nesting *AND* Decisions for Efficiency 132
   Using the *AND* Operator 134
   Avoiding Common Errors in an *AND* Selection 136
Understanding *OR* Logic 138
   Writing *OR* Decisions for Efficiency 140
   Using the *OR* Operator 141
   Avoiding Common Errors in an *OR* Selection 143
Making Selections within Ranges 148
   Avoiding Common Errors When Using Range Checks 150
Understanding Precedence When Combining *AND*
  and *OR* Operators 154
Chapter Summary 157
Key Terms 158
Review Questions 159
Exercises 162
   Find the Bugs 167
   Game Zone 167
   Up for Discussion 168

CONTENTS

CHAPTER 5   Looping **169**

Understanding the Advantages of Looping 170
Using a Loop Control Variable 171
    Using a Definite Loop with a Counter 172
    Using an Indefinite Loop with a Sentinel Value 173
    Understanding the Loop in a Program's Mainline Logic 175
Nested Loops 177
Avoiding Common Loop Mistakes 183
    Mistake: Neglecting to Initialize the Loop Control Variable . . . 183
    Mistake: Neglecting to Alter the Loop Control Variable 185
    Mistake: Using the Wrong Comparison with the Loop Control
        Variable 186
    Mistake: Including Statements Inside the Loop
        that Belong Outside the Loop 187
Using a `for` Loop 192
Common Loop Applications 194
    Using a Loop to Accumulate Totals 194
    Using a Loop to Validate Data 198
    Limiting a Reprompting Loop 200
    Validating a Data Type 202
    Validating Reasonableness and Consistency of Data 203
Chapter Summary 205
Key Terms 205
Review Questions 206
Exercises 209
    Find the Bugs 211
    Game Zone 211
    Up for Discussion 212

CHAPTER 6   Arrays **213**

Storing Data in Arrays 214
    How Arrays Occupy Computer Memory 214
How an Array Can Replace Nested Decisions 216
Using Constants with Arrays 224
    Using a Constant as the Size of an Array 224
    Using Constants as Array Element Values 225
    Using a Constant as an Array Subscript 225

Searching an Array for an Exact Match 226
Using Parallel Arrays 230
   Improving Search Efficiency 234
Searching an Array for a Range Match 237
Remaining within Array Bounds 241
Using a `for` Loop to Process Arrays 244
Chapter Summary 245
Key Terms 246
Review Questions 246
Exercises 249
   Find the Bugs 253
   Game Zone 253
   Up for Discussion 255

CHAPTER 7   File Handling and Applications **257**

Understanding Computer Files 258
   Organizing Files 259
Understanding the Data Hierarchy 260
Performing File Operations 261
   Declaring a File 261
   Opening a File 262
   Reading Data from a File 262
   Writing Data to a File 264
   Closing a File 264
   A Program that Performs File Operations 264
Understanding Sequential Files and Control Break Logic 267
   Understanding Control Break Logic 268
Merging Sequential Files 273
Master and Transaction File Processing 281
Random Access Files 290
Chapter Summary 292
Key Terms 293
Review Questions 295
Exercises 299
   Find the Bugs 302
   Game Zone 302
   Up for Discussion 303

CONTENTS

CHAPTER 8 Advanced Data Handling Concepts 305

Understanding the Need for Sorting Data 306
Using the Bubble Sort Algorithm 307
    Understanding Swapping Values 308
    Understanding the Bubble Sort 309
    Sorting a List of Variable Size 318
    Refining the Bubble Sort to Reduce Unnecessary
       Comparisons 322
    Refining the Bubble Sort to Eliminate Unnecessary
       Passes 324
Sorting Multifield Records 326
    Sorting Data Stored in Parallel Arrays 326
    Sorting Records as a Whole 328
Using the Insertion Sort Algorithm 329
Using Multidimensional Arrays 333
Using Indexed Files and Linked Lists 340
    Using Indexed Files 340
    Using Linked Lists 342
Chapter Summary 345
Key Terms 346
Review Questions 347
Exercises 350
    Find the Bugs 352
    Game Zone 353
    Up for Discussion 354

CHAPTER 9 Advanced Modularization Techniques 355

Using Methods with No Parameters 356
Creating Methods that Require Parameters 358
    Creating Methods that Require Multiple Parameters 364
Creating Methods that Return a Value 366
    Using an IPO Chart 372
Passing an Array to a Method 373
Overloading Methods 380
    Avoiding Ambiguous Methods 383
Using Predefined Methods 386

Method Design Issues: Implementation Hiding, Cohesion,
and Coupling 388
   Understanding Implementation Hiding 388
   Increasing Cohesion 388
   Reducing Coupling 389
Understanding Recursion 390
Chapter Summary 395
Key Terms 396
Review Questions 397
Exercises 400
   Find the Bugs 404
   Game Zone 404
   Up for Discussion 405

CHAPTER 10 Object-Oriented Programming **407**

Principles of Object-Oriented Programming 408
   Classes and Objects 408
   Polymorphism 412
   Inheritance 413
   Encapsulation 414
Defining Classes and Creating Class Diagrams 415
   Creating Class Diagrams 417
   The Set Methods 420
   The Get Methods 421
   Work Methods 422
Understanding Public and Private Access 424
Organizing Classes 428
Understanding Instance Methods 429
Understanding Static Methods 434
Using Objects 436
Chapter Summary 440
Key Terms 440
Review Questions 442
Exercises 445
   Find the Bugs 447
   Game Zone 447
   Up for Discussion 447

CONTENTS

CHAPTER 11 More Object-Oriented Programming Concepts 449

Understanding Constructors 450
    Default Constructors 450
    Nondefault Constructors 453
    Overloading Methods and Constructors 453
Understanding Destructors 456
Understanding Composition 458
Understanding Inheritance 459
    Understanding Inheritance Terminology 462
    Accessing Private Fields and Methods of a Parent Class . . . 465
    Using Inheritance to Achieve Good Software Design 470
An Example of Using Predefined Classes: Creating GUI Objects . 472
Understanding Exception Handling 473
    Drawbacks to Traditional Error-Handling Techniques 473
    The Object-Oriented Exception-Handling Model 475
    Using Built-in Exceptions and Creating Your Own Exceptions . . 477
Reviewing the Advantages of Object-Oriented Programming . . . 479
Chapter Summary 479
Key Terms 480
Review Questions 482
Exercises 485
    Find the Bugs 489
    Game Zone 489
    Up for Discussion 490

CHAPTER 12 Event-Driven GUI Programming, Multithreading, and Animation 491

Understanding Event-Driven Programming 492
User-Initiated Actions and GUI Components 495
Designing Graphical User Interfaces 498
    The Interface Should Be Natural and Predictable 498
    The Interface Should Be Attractive, Easy to Read, and
        Nondistracting 499
    To Some Extent, It's Helpful If the User Can Customize Your
        Applications 500
    The Program Should Be Forgiving 500
    The GUI Is Only a Means to an End 500

Developing an Event-Driven Application	501
Creating Storyboards	502
Defining the Storyboard Objects in an Object Dictionary	502
Defining Connections Between the User Screens	503
Planning the Logic	504
Understanding Threads and Multithreading	509
Creating Animation	512
Chapter Summary	515
Key Terms	516
Review Questions	517
Exercises	520
Find the Bugs	520
Game Zone	521
Up for Discussion	522

CHAPTER 13   System Modeling with the UML   **523**

Understanding System Modeling	524
What Is the UML?	525
Using UML Use Case Diagrams	527
Using UML Class and Object Diagrams	533
Using Other UML Diagrams	537
Sequence Diagrams	537
Communication Diagrams	538
State Machine Diagrams	539
Activity Diagrams	540
Component and Deployment Diagrams	542
Profile Diagrams	544
Diagramming Exception Handling	544
Deciding When to Use the UML and Which UML Diagrams to Use	546
Chapter Summary	547
Key Terms	548
Review Questions	549
Exercises	552
Find the Bugs	553
Game Zone	553
Up for Discussion	554

CONTENTS

CHAPTER 14   Using Relational Databases **555**

    Understanding Relational Database Fundamentals 556
    Creating Databases and Table Descriptions 558
    Identifying Primary Keys 560
    Understanding Database Structure Notation 563
    Working with Records within Tables 564
    Creating Queries 565
    Understanding Relationships between Tables 568
        Understanding One-To-Many Relationships 569
        Understanding Many-To-Many Relationships 569
        Understanding One-To-One Relationships 573
    Recognizing Poor Table Design 574
    Understanding Anomalies, Normal Forms, and Normalization . . 576
        First Normal Form 578
        Second Normal Form 579
        Third Normal Form 582
    Database Performance and Security Issues 585
        Providing Data Integrity 585
        Recovering Lost Data 586
        Avoiding Concurrent Update Problems 586
        Providing Authentication and Permissions 586
        Providing Encryption 587
    Chapter Summary 587
    Key Terms 589
    Review Questions 591
    Exercises 594
        Find the Bugs 598
        Game Zone 598
        Up for Discussion 598

APPENDIX A   Understanding Numbering Systems
                    and Computer Codes **601**

APPENDIX B   Flowchart Symbols **611**

APPENDIX C   Structures **612**

APPENDIX D	Solving Difficult Structuring Problems **614**
APPENDIX E	Creating Print Charts **624**
APPENDIX F	Two Variations on the Basic Structures—`case` and `do-while` **626**

Glossary **633**

Index **653**

Preface

Programming Logic and Design, Comprehensive, Seventh Edition provides the beginning programmer with a guide to developing structured program logic. This textbook assumes no programming language experience. The writing is nontechnical and emphasizes good programming practices. The examples are business examples; they do not assume mathematical background beyond high school business math. Additionally, the examples illustrate one or two major points; they do not contain so many features that students become lost following irrelevant and extraneous details.

The examples in this book have been created to provide students with a sound background in logic, no matter what programming languages they eventually use to write programs. This book can be used in a stand-alone logic course that students take as a prerequisite to a programming course, or as a companion book to an introductory programming text using any programming language.

Organization and Coverage

Programming Logic and Design, Comprehensive, Seventh Edition introduces students to programming concepts and enforces good style and logical thinking. General programming concepts are introduced in Chapter 1. Chapter 2 discusses using data and introduces two important concepts: modularization and creating high-quality programs. It is important to emphasize these topics early so that students start thinking in a modular way and concentrate on making their programs efficient, robust, easy to read, and easy to maintain.

Chapter 3 covers the key concepts of structure, including what structure is, how to recognize it, and most importantly, the advantages to writing structured programs. This chapter's content is unique among programming texts. The early overview of structure presented here gives students a solid foundation in thinking in a structured way.

Chapters 4, 5, and 6 explore the intricacies of decision making, looping, and array manipulation. Chapter 7 provides details of file handling so students can create programs that process a significant amount of data.

In Chapters 8 and 9, students learn more advanced techniques in array manipulation and modularization. Chapters 10 and 11 provide a thorough yet accessible introduction to concepts and terminology used in object-oriented programming. Students learn about classes, objects, instance and static class members, constructors, destructors, inheritance, and the advantages of object-oriented thinking.

Organization and Coverage

Chapter 12 explores additional object-oriented programming issues: event-driven GUI programming, multithreading, and animation. Chapter 13 discusses system design issues and details the features of the Unified Modeling Language. Chapter 14 is a thorough introduction to important database concepts that business programmers should understand.

The first three appendices give students summaries of numbering systems, flowchart symbols, and structures. Additional appendices allow students to gain extra experience with structuring large unstructured programs, creating print charts, and understanding posttest loops and case structures.

Programming Logic and Design combines text explanation with flowcharts and pseudocode examples to provide students with alternative means of expressing structured logic. Numerous detailed, full-program exercises at the end of each chapter illustrate the concepts explained within the chapter, and reinforce understanding and retention of the material presented.

Programming Logic and Design distinguishes itself from other programming logic books in the following ways:

- It is written and designed to be non-language specific. The logic used in this book can be applied to any programming language.
- The examples are everyday business examples; no special knowledge of mathematics, accounting, or other disciplines is assumed.
- The concept of structure is covered earlier than in many other texts. Students are exposed to structure naturally, so they will automatically create properly designed programs.
- Text explanation is interspersed with both flowcharts and pseudocode so students can become comfortable with these logic development tools and understand their interrelationship. Screen shots of running programs also are included, providing students with a clear and concrete image of the programs' execution.
- Complex programs are built through the use of complete business examples. Students see how an application is constructed from start to finish instead of studying only segments of programs.

Features

This text focuses on helping students become better programmers and understand the big picture in program development through a variety of key features. In addition to chapter Objectives, Summaries, and Key Terms, these useful features will help students regardless of their learning style.

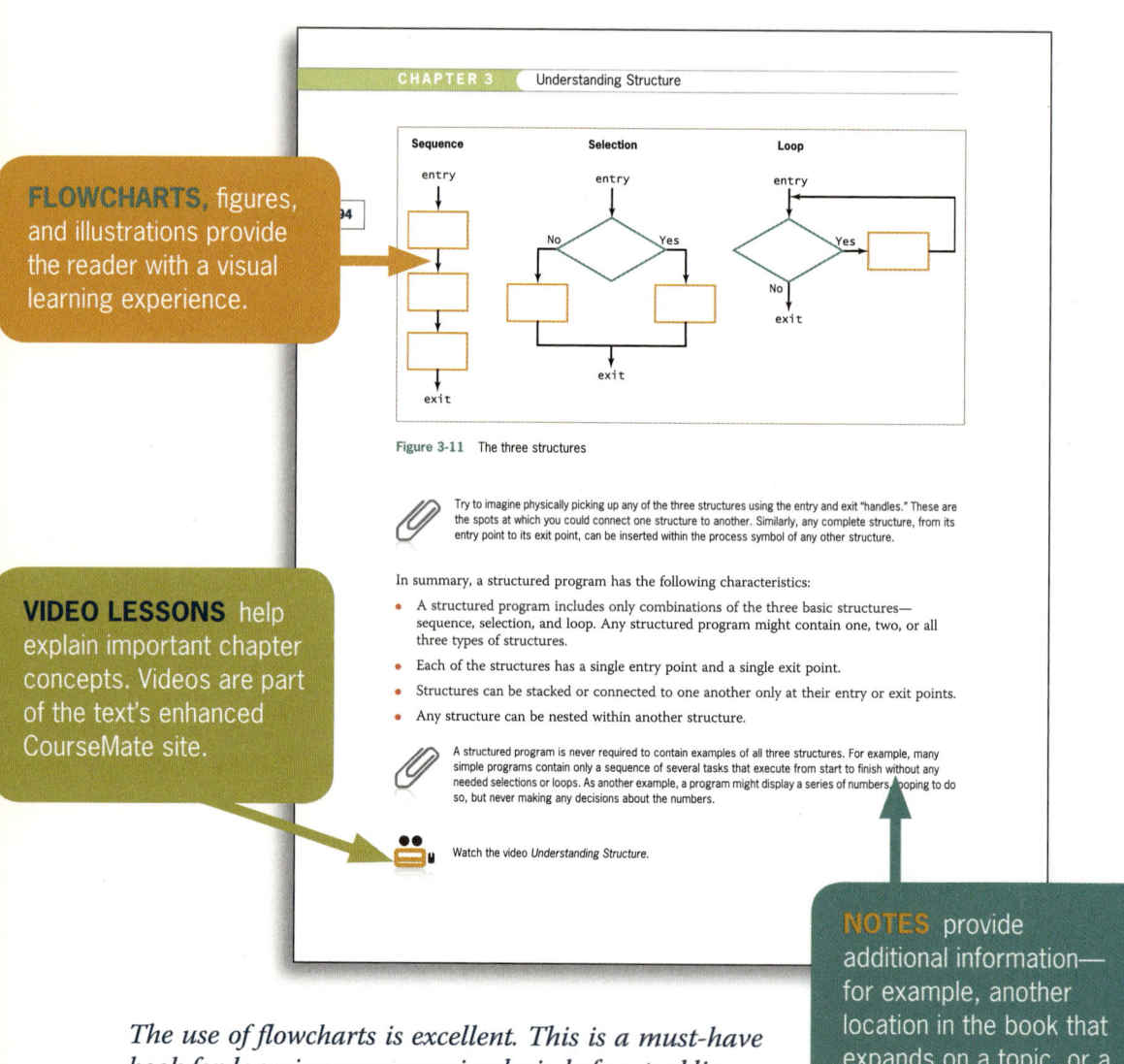

FLOWCHARTS, figures, and illustrations provide the reader with a visual learning experience.

VIDEO LESSONS help explain important chapter concepts. Videos are part of the text's enhanced CourseMate site.

NOTES provide additional information—for example, another location in the book that expands on a topic, or a common error to watch out for.

The use of flowcharts is excellent. This is a must-have book for learning programming logic before tackling the various languages.
—Lori Selby, University of Arkansas at Monticello

TWO TRUTHS & A LIE mini quizzes appear after each chapter section, with answers provided. The quiz contains three statements based on the preceding section of text—two statements are true and one is false. Answers give immediate feedback without "giving away" answers to the multiple-choice questions and programming problems later in the chapter. Students also have the option to take these quizzes electronically through the enhanced CourseMate site.

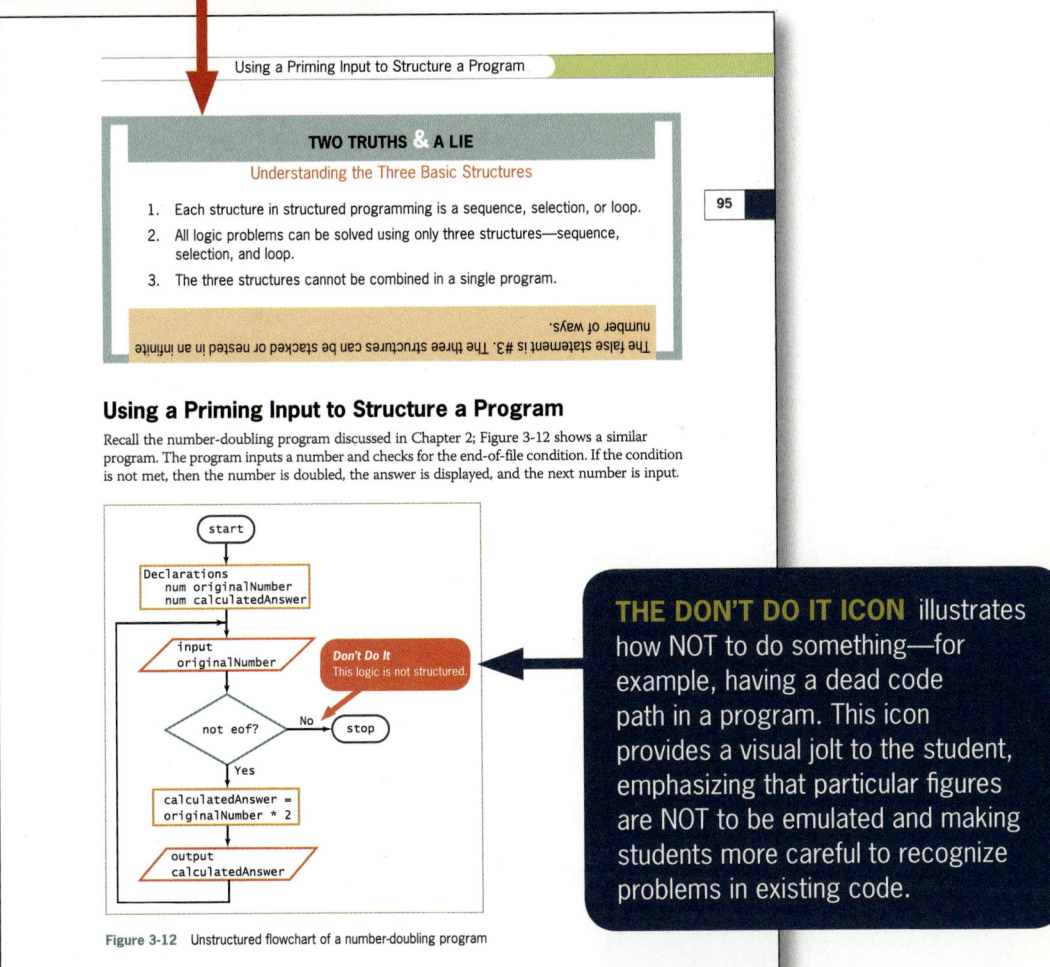

THE DON'T DO IT ICON illustrates how NOT to do something—for example, having a dead code path in a program. This icon provides a visual jolt to the student, emphasizing that particular figures are NOT to be emulated and making students more careful to recognize problems in existing code.

Assessment

The material is very well written, clearly presented, and up to date. All explanations are very solid, and Farrell's language is clean, cogent, and easy to follow.

—**Judy Woodruff, Indiana University-Purdue University Indianapolis**

EXERCISES provide opportunities to practice concepts. These exercises increase in difficulty and allow students to explore logical programming concepts. Each exercise can be completed using flowcharts, pseudocode, or both. In addition, instructors can assign the exercises as programming problems to be coded and executed in a particular programming language.

REVIEW QUESTIONS test student comprehension of the major ideas and techniques presented. Twenty questions follow each chapter.

CHAPTER 3 Understanding Structure

Review Questions

1. Snarled program logic is called _____ code.
   - a. snake
   - b. spaghetti
   - c. string
   - d. gnarly

2. The three structures of structured programming are _____.
   - a. sequence, order, and process
   - b. selection, loop, and iteration
   - c. sequence, selection, and loop
   - d. if, else, and then

3. A sequence structure can contain _____.
   - a. any number of tasks
   - b. exactly three tasks
   - c. no more than three tasks
   - d. only

4. Which of the following is *not* another term for a sel
   - a. decision structure
   - b. if-then-else structure
   - c. dual-
   - d. loop

5. The structure in which you ask a question, and, de some action and then ask the question again, can be except a(n) _____.
   - a. iteration
   - b. loop
   - c. repeti
   - d. if-th

6. Placing a structure within another structure is called
   - a. stacking
   - b. untangling
   - c. buildi
   - d. nestir

7. Attaching structures end to end is called _____
   - a. stacking
   - b. untangling
   - c. buildi
   - d. nestir

8. The statement if age >= 65 then seniorDiscoun a _____.
   - a. sequence
   - b. loop
   - c. dual-
   - d. single

9. The statement while temperature remains below is an example of a _____.
   - a. sequence
   - b. loop
   - c. dual-
   - d. single

Exercises

20. A variable might ho an incorrect value even when it is _____.
    - a. the correct data type
    - b. within a required range
    - c. a constant coded by the programmer
    - d. all of the above

Exercises

1. What is output by each of the pseudocode segments in Figure 5-22?

   a.
   ```
   a = 1
   b = 2
   c = 5
   while a < c
      a = a + 1
      b = b + c
   endwhile
   output a, b, c
   ```

   b.
   ```
   d = 4
   e = 6
   f = 7
   while d > f
      d = d + 1
      e = e - 1
   endwhile
   output d, e, f
   ```

   c.
   ```
   g = 4
   h = 6
   while g < h
      g = g + 1
   endwhile
   output g, h
   ```

   d.
   ```
   j = 2
   k = 5
   n = 9
   while j < k
      m = 6
      while m < n
         output "Goodbye"
         m = m + 1
      endwhile
      j = j + 1
   endwhile
   ```

   e.
   ```
   j = 2
   k = 5
   m = 6
   n = 9
   while j < k
      while m < n
         output "Hello"
         m = m + 1
      endwhile
      j = j + 1
   endwhile
   ```

   f.
   ```
   p = 2
   q = 4
   while p < q
      output "Adios"
      r = 1
      while r < q
         output "Adios"
         r = r + 1
      endwhile
      p = p + 1
   endwhile
   ```

   Figure 5-22 Pseudocode segments for Exercise 1

2. Design the logic for a program that outputs every number from 1 through 20.
3. Design the logic for a program that outputs every number from 1 through 20 along with its value doubled and tripled.
4. Design the logic for a program that outputs every even number from 2 through 100.
5. Design the logic for a program that outputs numbers in reverse order from 25 down to 0.
6. Design the logic for a program that allows a user to enter a number. Display the sum of every number from 1 through the entered number.

DEBUGGING EXERCISES are included with each chapter because examining programs critically and closely is a crucial programming skill. Students can download these exercises at *www.cengagebrain.com* and through the CourseMate available for this text. These files are also available to instructors through the Instructor Resources CD and *login.cengage.com*.

grocery store clerk should follow to check out a customer. Include at least two decisions and two loops.

Find the Bugs

12. Your downloadable files for Chapter 3 include DEBUG03-01.txt, DEBUG03-02.txt, and DEBUG03-03.txt. Each file starts with some comments that describe the problem. Comments are lines that begin with two slashes (//). After the comments, each file contains pseudocode that has one or more bugs you must find and correct.

Game Zone

13. Choose a simple children's game and describe its logic, using a flowchart or pseudocode. For example, you might try to explain Rock, Paper, Scissors; Musical Chairs; Duck, Duck, Goose; the card game War; or the elimination game Eenie, Meenie, Minie, Moe.

14. Choose a television game show such as *Deal or No Deal* or *Jeopardy!* and describe its rules using a structured flowchart or pseudocode.

15. Choose a sport such as baseball or football and describe a limited segment of play period (such as an at-bat in baseball or a possession in football) using a structured flowchart or pseudocode.

GAME ZONE EXERCISES are included at the end of each chapter. Students can create games as an additional entertaining way to understand key programming concepts.

game ends. If the number does not come up within three rolls, the computer wins.

18. Create the logic for the dice game Pig, in which a player can compete with the computer. The object of the game is to be the first to score 100 points. The user and computer take turns "rolling" a pair of dice following these rules:

    - On a turn, each player rolls two dice. If no 1 appears, the dice values are added to a running total for the turn, and the player can choose whether to roll again or pass the turn to the other player. When a player passes, the accumulated turn total is added to the player's game total.
    - If a 1 appears on one of the dice, the player's turn total becomes 0; in other words, nothing more is added to the player's game total for that turn, and it becomes the other player's turn.
    - If a 1 appears on both of the dice, not only is the player's turn over, but the player's entire accumulated total is reset to 0.
    - When the computer does not roll a 1 and can choose whether to roll again, generate a random value from 1 to 2. The computer will then decide to continue when the value is 1 and decide to quit and pass the turn to the player when the value is not 1.

Up for Discussion

19. Suppose you wrote a program that you suspect is in an infinite loop because it keeps running for several minutes with no output and without ending. What would you add to your program to help you discover the origin of the problem?

20. Suppose you know that every employee in your organization has a seven-digit ID number used for logging on to the computer system. A loop would be useful to guess every combination of seven digits in an ID. Are there any circumstances in which you should try to guess another employee's ID number?

21. If every employee in an organization had a seven-digit ID number, guessing all the possible combinations would be a relatively easy programming task. How could you alter the format of employee IDs to make them more difficult to guess?

ESSAY QUESTIONS present personal and ethical issues that programmers must consider. These questions can be used for written assignments or as a starting point for classroom discussion.

Other Features of the Text

This edition of the text includes many features to help students become better programmers and understand the big picture in program development. In this edition, all explanations have been carefully reviewed to provide the clearest possible instruction. Material that previously was included in margin notes has most frequently been incorporated into the main text, giving the pages a more streamlined appearance. All the chapters in this edition contain new programming exercises. All Sixth Edition exercises that have been replaced are available on the Instructor Resources CD and through *login. cengage.com* so instructors can use them as additional assigned exercises or as topics for class discussions.

- **Clear explanations**. The language and explanations in this book have been refined over seven editions, providing the clearest possible explanations of difficult concepts.

- **Emphasis on structure**. More than its competitors, this book emphasizes structure. Chapter 3 provides an early picture of the major concepts of structured programming, giving students an overview of the principles before they are required to consider program details.

- **Emphasis on modularity**. From the second chapter, students are encouraged to write code in concise, easily manageable, and reusable modules. Instructors have found that modularization should be encouraged early to instill good habits and a clearer understanding of structure. This edition uses modularization early, using global variables instead of local passed and returned values, and saves parameter passing for later when the student has become more adept.

- **Methods as black boxes**. The use of methods is consistent with the languages in which the student is likely to have first programming experiences. In particular, this book emphasizes using methods as black boxes, declaring all variables and constants as local to methods, and passing arguments to and receiving returned values from methods as needed.

- **Objectives**. Each chapter begins with a list of objectives so the student knows the topics that will be presented in the chapter. In addition to providing a quick reference to topics covered, this feature provides a useful study aid.

- **Pseudocode**. This book includes numerous examples of pseudocode, which illustrate correct usage of the programming logic and design concepts being taught.

- **Chapter summaries**. Following each chapter is a summary that recaps the programming concepts and techniques covered in the chapter. This feature provides a concise means for students to review and check their understanding of the main points in each chapter.

- **Key terms**. Each chapter lists key terms and their definitions; the list appears in the order the terms are encountered in the chapter. Along with the chapter summary, the list of key terms provides a snapshot overview of a chapter's main ideas. A glossary at the end of the book lists all the key terms in alphabetical order, along with working definitions.

CourseMate

The more you study, the better the results. Make the most of your study time by accessing everything you need to succeed in one place. Read your textbook, review flashcards, watch videos, and take practice quizzes online. CourseMate goes beyond the book to deliver what you need! Learn more at *www.cengage.com/coursemate*.

The *Programming Logic and Design* CourseMate includes:

- **Video Lessons**. Designed and narrated by the author, videos in each chapter explain and enrich important concepts.

- **Two Truths & A Lie** and **Debugging Exercises**. Complete popular exercises from the text online!

- An interactive eBook with highlighting and note-taking, flashcards, quizzing, study games, and more!

Instructors may add CourseMate to the textbook package, or students may purchase CourseMate directly at *www.cengagebrain.com*.

Instructor Resources

The following teaching tools are available to the instructor on a single CD-ROM. Many are also available for download through our Instructor Companion Site at *login.cengage.com*.

- **Electronic Instructor's Manual**. The Instructor's Manual follows the text chapter by chapter to assist in planning and organizing an effective, engaging course. The manual includes learning objectives, chapter overviews, lecture notes, ideas for classroom activities, and abundant additional resources. A sample course syllabus is also available.

- **PowerPoint Presentations**. This text provides PowerPoint slides to accompany each chapter. Slides are included to guide classroom presentation, to make available to students for chapter review, or to print as classroom handouts. Instructors may customize the slides, which include the complete figure files from the text, to best suit their courses.

- **Solutions**. Solutions to review questions and exercises are provided to assist with grading.

- **ExamView®**. This textbook is accompanied by ExamView, a powerful testing software package that allows instructors to create and administer printed, LAN-based, and Internet exams. ExamView includes hundreds of questions that correspond to the text, enabling students to generate detailed study guides that include page references for further review. The computer-based and Internet testing components allow students to take exams at their computers, and the components save the instructor time by grading each exam automatically. These test banks are also available in Blackboard and Angel compatible formats.

Additional Offerings

You have the option to bundle software with your text. Please contact your Cengage Learning sales representative for more information.

- **PAL Guides**. Together with *Programming Logic and Design*, these brief books, or PAL guides, provide an excellent opportunity to learn the fundamentals of programming while gaining exposure to a programming language. Readers will discover how real code behaves within the context of the traditionally language-independent logic and design course. PAL guides are available for C++, Java, and Visual Basic; please contact your sales rep for more information on how to add the PAL guides to your course.

- **Microsoft® Office Visio® Professional 2010**, 60-day version. Visio 2010 is a diagramming program that allows users to create flowcharts and diagrams easily while working through the text, enabling them to visualize concepts and learn more effectively.

- **Visual Logic™ software**. Visual Logic is a simple but powerful tool for teaching programming logic and design without traditional high-level programming language syntax. Visual Logic uses flowcharts to explain the essential programming concepts discussed in this book, including variables, input, assignment, output, conditions, loops, procedures, graphics, arrays, and files. Visual Logic also interprets and executes flowcharts, providing students with immediate and accurate feedback. Visual Logic combines the power of a high-level language with the ease and simplicity of flowcharts.

Acknowledgments

I would like to thank all of the people who helped to make this book a reality, especially Dan Seiter, Development Editor. After seven editions, Dan still finds ways to improve my explanations so that we can create a book of the highest possible quality. Thanks also to Alyssa Pratt, Senior Product Manager; Brandi Shailer, Acquisitions Editor; Catherine DiMassa, Senior Content Project Manager; and Green Pen QA, Technical Editors. I am grateful to be able to work with so many fine people who are dedicated to producing quality instructional materials.

Acknowledgments

I am indebted to the many reviewers who provided helpful and insightful comments during the development of this book, including Linda Cohen, Forsyth Tech; Andrew Hurd, Hudson Valley Community College; George Reynolds, Strayer University; Lori Selby, University of Arkansas at Monticello; and Judy Woodruff, Indiana University–Purdue University Indianapolis.

Thanks, too, to my husband, Geoff, and our daughters, Andrea and Audrey, for their support. This book, as were all its previous editions, is dedicated to them.

–Joyce Farrell

CHAPTER 1

An Overview of Computers and Programming

In this chapter, you will learn about:

- Computer systems
- Simple program logic
- The steps involved in the program development cycle
- Pseudocode statements and flowchart symbols
- Using a sentinel value to end a program
- Programming and user environments
- The evolution of programming models

Understanding Computer Systems

A **computer system** is a combination of all the components required to process and store data using a computer. Every computer system is composed of multiple pieces of hardware and software.

- **Hardware** is the equipment, or the physical devices, associated with a computer. For example, keyboards, mice, speakers, and printers are all hardware. The devices are manufactured differently for large mainframe computers, laptops, and even smaller computers that are embedded into products such as cars and thermostats, but the types of operations performed by different-sized computers are very similar. When you think of a computer, you often think of its physical components first, but for a computer to be useful, it needs more than devices; a computer needs to be given instructions. Just as your stereo equipment does not do much until you provide music, computer hardware needs instructions that control how and when data items are input, how they are processed, and the form in which they are output or stored.

- **Software** is computer instructions that tell the hardware what to do. Software is **programs**, which are instruction sets written by programmers. You can buy prewritten programs that are stored on a disk or that you download from the Web. For example, businesses use word-processing and accounting programs, and casual computer users enjoy programs that play music and games. Alternatively, you can write your own programs. When you write software instructions, you are **programming**. This book focuses on the programming process.

Software can be classified into two broad types:

- **Application software** comprises all the programs you apply to a task, such as word-processing programs, spreadsheets, payroll and inventory programs, and even games.

- **System software** comprises the programs that you use to manage your computer, including operating systems such as Windows, Linux, or UNIX.

This book focuses on the logic used to write application software programs, although many of the concepts apply to both types of software.

Together, computer hardware and software accomplish three major operations in most programs:

- **Input**—Data items enter the computer system and are placed in memory, where they can be processed. Hardware devices that perform input operations include keyboards and mice. **Data items** include all the text, numbers, and other raw material that are entered into and processed by a computer. In business, many of the data items used are facts and figures about such entities as products, customers, and personnel. However, data can also include items such as images, sounds, and a user's mouse movements.

- **Processing**—Processing data items may involve organizing or sorting them, checking them for accuracy, or performing calculations with them. The hardware component that performs these types of tasks is the **central processing unit**, or **CPU**.

Understanding Computer Systems

- **Output**—After data items have been processed, the resulting information usually is sent to a printer, monitor, or some other output device so people can view, interpret, and use the results. Programming professionals often use the term *data* for input items, but use the term **information** for data that has been processed and output. Sometimes you place output on **storage devices**, such as disks or flash media. People cannot read data directly from these storage devices, but the devices hold information for later retrieval. When you send output to a storage device, sometimes it is used later as input for another program.

You write computer instructions in a computer **programming language** such as Visual Basic, C#, C++, or Java. Just as some people speak English and others speak Japanese, programmers write programs in different languages. Some programmers work exclusively in one language, whereas others know several and use the one that is best suited to the task at hand.

The instructions you write using a programming language are called **program code**; when you write instructions, you are **coding the program**.

Every programming language has rules governing its word usage and punctuation. These rules are called the language's **syntax**. Mistakes in a language's usage are **syntax errors**. If you ask, "How the geet too store do I?" in English, most people can figure out what you probably mean, even though you have not used proper English syntax—you have mixed up the word order, misspelled a word, and used an incorrect word. However, computers are not nearly as smart as most people; in this case, you might as well have asked the computer, "Xpu mxv ort dod nmcad bf B?" Unless the syntax is perfect, the computer cannot interpret the programming language instruction at all.

When you write a program, you usually type its instructions using a keyboard. When you type program instructions, they are stored in **computer memory**, which is a computer's temporary, internal storage. **Random access memory**, or **RAM**, is a form of internal, volatile memory. Programs that are currently running and data items that are currently being used are stored in RAM for quick access. Internal storage is **volatile**—its contents are lost when the computer is turned off or loses power. Usually, you want to be able to retrieve and perhaps modify the stored instructions later, so you also store them on a permanent storage device, such as a disk. Permanent storage devices are **nonvolatile**—that is, their contents are persistent and are retained even when power is lost. If you have had a power loss while working on a computer, but were able to recover your work when power was restored, it's not because the work was still in RAM. Your system has been configured to automatically save your work at regular intervals on a nonvolatile storage device.

After a computer program is typed using programming language statements and stored in memory, it must be translated to **machine language** that represents the millions of on/off circuits within the computer. Your programming language statements are called **source code**, and the translated machine language statements are **object code**.

Each programming language uses a piece of software, called a **compiler** or an **interpreter**, to translate your source code into machine language. Machine language is also called **binary language**, and is represented as a series of 0s and 1s. The compiler or interpreter that translates your code tells you if any programming language component has been used incorrectly. Syntax errors are relatively easy to locate and correct because your compiler or interpreter highlights them. If you write a computer program using a language such as C++

but spell one of its words incorrectly or reverse the proper order of two words, the software lets you know that it found a mistake by displaying an error message as soon as you try to translate the program.

Although there are differences in how compilers and interpreters work, their basic function is the same—to translate your programming statements into code the computer can use. When you use a compiler, an entire program is translated before it can execute; when you use an interpreter, each instruction is translated just prior to execution. Usually, you do not choose which type of translation to use—it depends on the programming language. However, there are some languages for which both compilers and interpreters are available.

After a program's source code is successfully translated to machine language, the computer can carry out the program instructions. When instructions are carried out, a program **runs**, or **executes**. In a typical program, some input will be accepted, some processing will occur, and results will be output.

Besides the popular, comprehensive programming languages such as Java and C++, many programmers use **scripting languages** (also called **scripting programming languages** or **script languages**) such as Python, Lua, Perl, and PHP. Scripts written in these languages usually can be typed directly from a keyboard and are stored as text rather than as binary executable files. Scripting language programs are interpreted line by line each time the program executes, instead of being stored in a compiled (binary) form. Still, with all programming languages, each instruction must be translated to machine language before it can execute.

TWO TRUTHS & A LIE

Understanding Computer Systems

In each Two Truths and a Lie section, two of the numbered statements are true, and one is false. Identify the false statement and explain why it is false.

1. Hardware is the equipment, or the devices, associated with a computer. Software is computer instructions.
2. The grammar rules of a computer programming language are its syntax.
3. You write programs using machine language, and translation software converts the statements to a programming language.

The false statement is #3. You write programs using a programming language such as Visual Basic or Java, and a translation program (called a compiler or interpreter) converts the statements to machine language, which is 0s and 1s.

Understanding Simple Program Logic

A program with syntax errors cannot be fully translated and cannot execute. A program with no syntax errors is translatable and can execute, but it still might contain **logical errors** and produce incorrect output as a result. For a program to work properly, you must develop correct **logic**; that is, you must write program instructions in a specific sequence, you must not leave any instructions out, and you must not add extraneous instructions.

Suppose you instruct someone to make a cake as follows:

```
Get a bowl
Stir
Add two eggs
Add a gallon of gasoline
Bake at 350 degrees for 45 minutes
Add three cups of flour
```

Don't Do It
Don't bake a cake like this!

The dangerous cake-baking instructions are shown with a Don't Do It icon. You will see this icon when the book contains an unrecommended programming practice that is used as an example of what *not* to do.

Even though the cake-baking instructions use English language syntax correctly, the instructions are out of sequence, some are missing, and some instructions belong to procedures other than baking a cake. If you follow these instructions, you will not make an edible cake, and you may end up with a disaster. Many logical errors are more difficult to locate than syntax errors—it is easier for you to determine whether *eggs* is spelled incorrectly in a recipe than it is for you to tell if there are too many eggs or if they are added too soon.

Just as baking directions can be provided in Mandarin, Urdu, or Spanish, program logic can be expressed correctly in any number of programming languages. Because this book is not concerned with a specific language, the programming examples could have been written in Visual Basic, C++, or Java. For convenience, this book uses instructions written in English!

After you learn French, you automatically know, or can easily figure out, many Spanish words. Similarly, after you learn one programming language, it is much easier to understand several other languages.

Most simple computer programs include steps that perform input, processing, and output. Suppose you want to write a computer program to double any number you provide. You can write the program in a programming language such as Visual Basic or Java, but if you were to write it using English-like statements, it would look like this:

```
input myNumber
set myAnswer = myNumber * 2
output myAnswer
```

The number-doubling process includes three instructions:

- The instruction to `input myNumber` is an example of an input operation. When the computer interprets this instruction, it knows to look to an input device to obtain a number. When you work in a specific programming language, you write instructions that tell the computer which device to access for input. For example, when a user enters a number as data for a program, the user might click on the number with a mouse, type it from a keyboard, or speak it into a microphone. Logically, however, it doesn't matter which hardware device is used, as long as the computer knows to accept a number. When the number is retrieved from an input device, it is placed in the computer's memory in a variable named `myNumber`. A **variable** is a named memory location whose value can vary—for example, the value of `myNumber` might be 3 when the program is used for the first time and 45 when it is used the next time. In this book, variable names will not contain embedded spaces; for example, the book will use `myNumber` instead of `my Number`.

From a logical perspective, when you input, process, or output a value, the hardware device is irrelevant. The same is true in your daily life. If you follow the instruction "Get eggs for the cake," it does not really matter if you purchase them from a store or harvest them from your own chickens—you get the eggs either way. There might be different practical considerations to getting the eggs, just as there are for getting data from a large database as opposed to getting data from an inexperienced user working at home on a laptop computer. For now, this book is only concerned with the logic of operations, not the minor details.

- The instruction `set myAnswer = myNumber * 2` is an example of a processing operation. In most programming languages, an asterisk is used to indicate multiplication, so this instruction means "Change the value of the memory location `myAnswer` to equal the value at the memory location `myNumber` times two." Mathematical operations are not the only kind of processing operations, but they are very typical. As with input operations, the type of hardware used for processing is irrelevant—after you write a program, it can be used on computers of different brand names, sizes, and speeds.

- In the number-doubling program, the `output myAnswer` instruction is an example of an output operation. Within a particular program, this statement could cause the output to appear on the monitor (which might be a flat-panel plasma screen or a cathode-ray tube), or the output could go to a printer (which could be laser or ink-jet), or the output could be written to a disk or DVD. The logic of the output process is the same no matter what hardware device you use. When this instruction executes, the value stored in memory at the location named `myAnswer` is sent to an output device. (The output value also remains in computer memory until something else is stored at the same memory location or power is lost.)

Watch the video *A Simple Program*.

Computer memory consists of millions of numbered locations where data can be stored. The memory location of myNumber has a specific numeric address, but when you write programs, you seldom need to be concerned with the value of the memory address; instead, you use the easy-to-remember name you created. Computer programmers often refer to memory addresses using hexadecimal notation, or base 16. Using this system, they might use a value like 42FF01A to refer to a memory address. Despite the use of letters, such an address is still a hexadecimal number. Appendix A contains information on this numbering system.

TWO TRUTHS & A LIE

Understanding Simple Program Logic

1. A program with syntax errors can execute but might produce incorrect results.
2. Although the syntax of programming languages differs, the same program logic can be expressed in different languages.
3. Most simple computer programs include steps that perform input, processing, and output.

The false statement is #1. A program with syntax errors cannot execute; a program with no syntax errors can execute, but might produce incorrect results.

Understanding the Program Development Cycle

A programmer's job involves writing instructions (such as those in the doubling program in the preceding section), but a professional programmer usually does not just sit down at a computer keyboard and start typing. Figure 1-1 illustrates the **program development cycle**, which can be broken down into at least seven steps:

1. Understand the problem.
2. Plan the logic.
3. Code the program.
4. Use software (a compiler or interpreter) to translate the program into machine language.
5. Test the program.
6. Put the program into production.
7. Maintain the program.

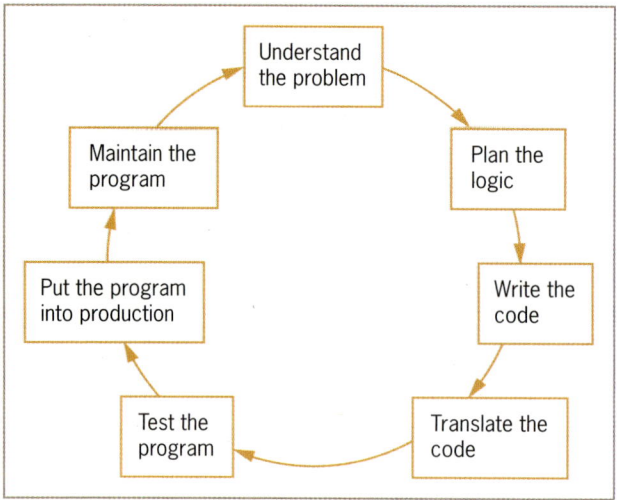

Figure 1-1   The program development cycle

Understanding the Problem

Professional computer programmers write programs to satisfy the needs of others, called **users** or **end users**. Examples of end users include a Human Resources department that needs a printed list of all employees, a Billing department that wants a list of clients who are 30 or more days overdue on their payments, and an Order department that needs a Web site to provide buyers with an online shopping cart. Because programmers are providing a service to these users, programmers must first understand what the users want. When a program runs, you usually think of the logic as a cycle of input-processing-output operations, but when you plan a program, you think of the output first. After you understand what the desired result is, you can plan the input and processing steps to achieve it.

Suppose the director of Human Resources says to a programmer, "Our department needs a list of all employees who have been here over five years, because we want to invite them to a special thank-you dinner." On the surface, this seems like a simple request. An experienced programmer, however, will know that the request is incomplete. For example, you might not know the answers to the following questions about which employees to include:

- Does the director want a list of full-time employees only, or a list of full- and part-time employees together?
- Does she want to include people who have worked for the company on a month-to-month contractual basis over the past five years, or only regular, permanent employees?
- Do the listed employees need to have worked for the organization for five years as of today, as of the date of the dinner, or as of some other cutoff date?
- What about an employee who worked three years, took a two-year leave of absence, and has been back for three years?

The programmer cannot make any of these decisions; the user (in this case, the Human Resources director) must address these questions.

More decisions still might be required. For example:

- What data should be included for each listed employee? Should the list contain both first and last names? Social Security numbers? Phone numbers? Addresses?
- Should the list be in alphabetical order? Employee ID number order? Length-of-service order? Some other order?
- Should the employees be grouped by any criteria, such as department number or years of service?

Several pieces of documentation are often provided to help the programmer understand the problem. **Documentation** consists of all the supporting paperwork for a program; it might include items such as original requests for the program from users, sample output, and descriptions of the data items available for input.

Fully understanding the problem may be one of the most difficult aspects of programming. On any job, the description of what the user needs may be vague—worse yet, users may not really know what they want, and users who think they know frequently change their minds after seeing sample output. A good programmer is often part counselor, part detective!

  Watch the video *The Program Development Cycle, Part 1*.

Planning the Logic

The heart of the programming process lies in planning the program's logic. During this phase of the process, the programmer plans the steps of the program, deciding what steps to include and how to order them. You can plan the solution to a problem in many ways. The two most common planning tools are flowcharts and pseudocode. Both tools involve writing the steps of the program in English, much as you would plan a trip on paper before getting into the car or plan a party theme before shopping for food and favors.

You may hear programmers refer to planning a program as "developing an algorithm." An **algorithm** is the sequence of steps necessary to solve any problem.

  In addition to flowcharts and pseudocode, programmers use a variety of other tools to help in program development. One such tool is an **IPO chart**, which delineates input, processing, and output tasks. Some object-oriented programmers also use **TOE charts**, which list tasks, objects, and events.

The programmer shouldn't worry about the syntax of any particular language during the planning stage, but should focus on figuring out what sequence of events will lead from the available input to the desired output. Planning the logic includes thinking carefully about all the possible data values a program might encounter and how you want the program to handle each scenario. The process of walking through a program's logic on paper before you actually write the program is called **desk-checking**. You will learn more about planning the logic throughout this book; in fact, the book focuses on this crucial step almost exclusively.

Coding the Program

After the logic is developed, only then can the programmer write the source code for a program. Hundreds of programming languages are available. Programmers choose particular languages because some have built-in capabilities that make them more efficient than others at handling certain types of operations. Despite their differences, programming languages are quite alike in their basic capabilities—each can handle input operations, arithmetic processing, output operations, and other standard functions. The logic developed to solve a programming problem can be executed using any number of languages. Only after choosing a language must the programmer be concerned with proper punctuation and the correct spelling of commands—in other words, using the correct *syntax*.

Some experienced programmers can successfully combine logic planning and program coding in one step. This may work for planning and writing a very simple program, just as you can plan and write a postcard to a friend using one step. A good term paper or a Hollywood screenplay, however, needs planning before writing—and so do most programs.

Which step is harder: planning the logic or coding the program? Right now, it may seem to you that writing in a programming language is a very difficult task, considering all the spelling and syntax rules you must learn. However, the planning step is actually more difficult. Which is more difficult: thinking up the twists and turns to the plot of a best-selling mystery novel, or writing a translation of an existing novel from English to Spanish? And who do you think gets paid more, the writer who creates the plot or the translator? (Try asking friends to name any famous translator!)

Using Software to Translate the Program into Machine Language

Even though there are many programming languages, each computer knows only one language—its machine language, which consists of 1s and 0s. Computers understand machine language because they are made up of thousands of tiny electrical switches, each of which can be set in either the on or off state, which is represented by a 1 or 0, respectively.

Languages like Java or Visual Basic are available for programmers because someone has written a translator program (a compiler or interpreter) that changes the programmer's English-like **high-level programming language** into the **low-level machine language** that the computer understands. When you learn the syntax of a programming language, the commands work on any machine on which the language software has been installed. However, your commands then are translated to machine language, which differs in various computer makes and models.

Understanding the Program Development Cycle

If you write a programming statement incorrectly (for example, by misspelling a word, using a word that doesn't exist in the language, or using "illegal" grammar), the translator program doesn't know how to proceed and issues an error message identifying a syntax error. Although making errors is never desirable, syntax errors are not a major concern to programmers, because the compiler or interpreter catches every syntax error and displays a message that notifies you of the problem. The computer will not execute a program that contains even one syntax error.

Typically, a programmer develops logic, writes the code, and compiles the program, receiving a list of syntax errors. The programmer then corrects the syntax errors and compiles the program again. Correcting the first set of errors frequently reveals new errors that originally were not apparent to the compiler. For example, if you could use an English compiler and submit the sentence *The dg chase the cat*, the compiler at first might point out only one syntax error. The second word, *dg*, is illegal because it is not part of the English language. Only after you corrected the word to *dog* would the compiler find another syntax error on the third word, *chase*, because it is the wrong verb form for the subject *dog*. This doesn't mean *chase* is necessarily the wrong word. Maybe *dog* is wrong; perhaps the subject should be *dogs*, in which case *chase* is right. Compilers don't always know exactly what you mean, nor do they know what the proper correction should be, but they do know when something is wrong with your syntax.

 Watch the video *The Program Development Cycle, Part 2*.

When writing a program, a programmer might need to recompile the code several times. An executable program is created only when the code is free of syntax errors. After a program has been translated into machine language, the machine language program is saved and can be run any number of times without repeating the translation step. You only need to retranslate your code if you make changes to your source code statements. Figure 1-2 shows a diagram of this entire process.

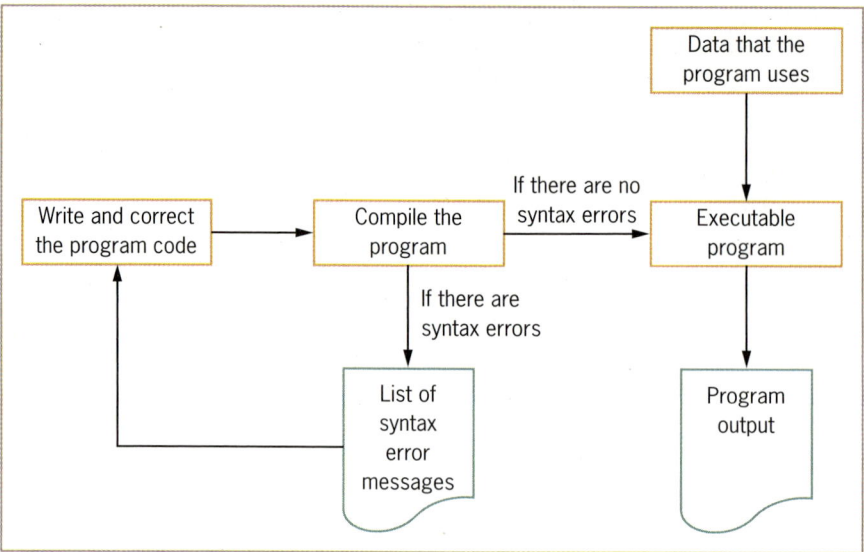

Figure 1-2 Creating an executable program

Testing the Program

A program that is free of syntax errors is not necessarily free of logical errors. A logical error results when you use a syntactically correct statement but use the wrong one for the current context. For example, the English sentence *The dog chases the cat*, although syntactically perfect, is not logically correct if the dog chases a ball or the cat is the aggressor.

Once a program is free of syntax errors, the programmer can test it—that is, execute it with some sample data to see whether the results are logically correct. Recall the number-doubling program:

```
input myNumber
set myAnswer = myNumber * 2
output myAnswer
```

If you execute the program, provide the value 2 as input to the program, and the answer 4 is displayed, you have executed one successful test run of the program.

However, if the answer 40 is displayed, maybe the program contains a logical error. Maybe the second line of code was mistyped with an extra zero, so that the program reads:

```
input myNumber
set myAnswer = myNumber * 20
output myAnswer
```

Don't Do It
The programmer typed 20 instead of 2.

Placing 20 instead of 2 in the multiplication statement caused a logical error. Notice that nothing is syntactically wrong with this second program—it is just as reasonable to multiply a number by 20 as by 2—but if the programmer intends only to double myNumber, then a logical error has occurred.

Understanding the Program Development Cycle

The process of finding and correcting program errors is called **debugging**. You debug a program by testing it using many sets of data. For example, if you write the program to double a number, then enter 2 and get an output value of 4, that doesn't necessarily mean you have a correct program. Perhaps you have typed this program by mistake:

```
input myNumber
set myAnswer = myNumber + 2
output myAnswer
```

Don't Do It
The programmer typed "+" instead of "*".

An input of 2 results in an answer of 4, but that doesn't mean your program doubles numbers—it actually only adds 2 to them. If you test your program with additional data and get the wrong answer—for example, if you enter 7 and get an answer of 9—you know there is a problem with your code.

Selecting test data is somewhat of an art in itself, and it should be done carefully. If the Human Resources department wants a list of the names of five-year employees, it would be a mistake to test the program with a small sample file of only long-term employees. If no newer employees are part of the data being used for testing, you do not really know if the program would have eliminated them from the five-year list. Many companies do not know that their software has a problem until an unusual circumstance occurs—for example, the first time an employee has more than nine dependents, the first time a customer orders more than 999 items at a time, or when the Internet runs out of allocated IP addresses, a problem known as *IPV4 exhaustion*.

Putting the Program into Production

Once the program is thoroughly tested and debugged, it is ready for the organization to use. Putting the program into production might mean simply running the program once, if it was written to satisfy a user's request for a special list. However, the process might take months if the program will be run on a regular basis, or if it is one of a large system of programs being developed. Perhaps data-entry people must be trained to prepare the input for the new program, users must be trained to understand the output, or existing data in the company must be changed to an entirely new format to accommodate this program. **Conversion**, the entire set of actions an organization must take to switch over to using a new program or set of programs, can sometimes take months or years to accomplish.

Maintaining the Program

After programs are put into production, making necessary changes is called **maintenance**. Maintenance can be required for many reasons: for example, because new tax rates are legislated, the format of an input file is altered, or the end user requires additional information not included in the original output specifications. Frequently, your first programming job will require maintaining previously written programs. When you maintain the programs others have written, you will appreciate the effort the original programmer put into writing clear code, using reasonable variable names, and documenting his or her work. When you make changes to existing programs, you repeat the development cycle. That is, you must understand the changes, then plan, code, translate, and test them before putting them into production. If a substantial number of program changes are required, the original program might be retired, and the program development cycle might be started for a new program.

 Watch the video *The Program Development Cycle, Part 3*.

TWO TRUTHS & A LIE

Understanding the Program Development Cycle

1. Understanding the problem that must be solved can be one of the most difficult aspects of programming.
2. The two most commonly used logic-planning tools are flowcharts and pseudocode.
3. Flowcharting a program is a very different process if you use an older programming language instead of a newer one.

The false statement is #3. Despite their differences, programming languages are quite alike in their basic capabilities—each can handle input operations, arithmetic processing, output operations, and other standard functions. The logic developed to solve a programming problem can be executed using any number of languages.

Using Pseudocode Statements and Flowchart Symbols

When programmers plan the logic for a solution to a programming problem, they often use one of two tools: pseudocode (pronounced *sue-doe-code*) or flowcharts.

- **Pseudocode** is an English-like representation of the logical steps it takes to solve a problem. *Pseudo* is a prefix that means *false*, and to *code* a program means to put it in a programming language; therefore, *pseudocode* simply means *false code*, or sentences that appear to have been written in a computer programming language but do not necessarily follow all the syntax rules of any specific language.
- A **flowchart** is a pictorial representation of the same thing.

Writing Pseudocode

You have already seen examples of statements that represent pseudocode earlier in this chapter, and there is nothing mysterious about them. The following five statements constitute a pseudocode representation of a number-doubling problem:

```
start
   input myNumber
   set myAnswer = myNumber * 2
   output myAnswer
stop
```

Using pseudocode involves writing down all the steps you will use in a program. Usually, programmers preface their pseudocode with a beginning statement like start and end it with a terminating statement like stop. The statements between start and stop look like English and are indented slightly so that start and stop stand out. Most programmers do not bother with punctuation such as periods at the end of pseudocode statements, although it would not be wrong to use them if you prefer that style. Similarly, there is no need to capitalize the first word in a sentence, although you might choose to do so. This book follows the conventions of using lowercase letters for verbs that begin pseudocode statements and omitting periods at the end of statements.

Pseudocode is fairly flexible because it is a planning tool, and not the final product. Therefore, for example, you might prefer any of the following:

- Instead of start and stop, some pseudocode developers would use other terms such as begin and end.

- Instead of writing input myNumber, some developers would write get myNumber or read myNumber.

- Instead of writing set myAnswer = myNumber * 2, some developers would write calculate myAnswer = myNumber times 2 or compute myAnswer as myNumber doubled.

- Instead of writing output myAnswer, many pseudocode developers would write display myAnswer, print myAnswer, or write myAnswer.

The point is, the pseudocode statements are instructions to retrieve an original number from an input device and store it in memory where it can be used in a calculation, and then to get the calculated answer from memory and send it to an output device so a person can see it. When you eventually convert your pseudocode to a specific programming language, you do not have such flexibility because specific syntax will be required. For example, if you use the C# programming language and write the statement to output the answer to the monitor, you will code the following:

```
Console.Write(myAnswer);
```

The exact use of words, capitalization, and punctuation are important in the C# statement, but not in the pseudocode statement.

Drawing Flowcharts

Some professional programmers prefer writing pseudocode to drawing flowcharts, because using pseudocode is more similar to writing the final statements in the programming language. Others prefer drawing flowcharts to represent the logical flow, because flowcharts allow programmers to visualize more easily how the program statements will connect. Especially for beginning programmers, flowcharts are an excellent tool to help them visualize how the statements in a program are interrelated.

You can draw a flowchart by hand or use software, such as Microsoft Word and Microsoft PowerPoint, that contains flowcharting tools. You can use several other software programs, such as Visio and Visual Logic, specifically to create flowcharts. When you create a flowchart, you draw geometric shapes that contain the individual statements and that are connected with arrows. (Appendix B contains a summary of all the flowchart symbols you will see in this book.) You use a parallelogram to represent an **input symbol**, which indicates an input operation. You write an input statement in English inside the parallelogram, as shown in Figure 1-3.

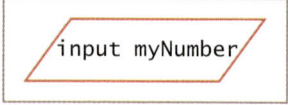

Figure 1-3 Input symbol

Arithmetic operation statements are examples of processing. In a flowchart, you use a rectangle as the **processing symbol** that contains a processing statement, as shown in Figure 1-4.

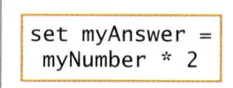

Figure 1-4 Processing symbol

To represent an output statement, you use the same symbol as for input statements—the **output symbol** is a parallelogram, as shown in Figure 1-5. Because the parallelogram is used for both input and output, it is often called the **input/output symbol** or **I/O symbol**.

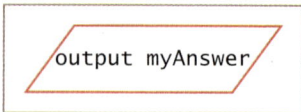

Figure 1-5 Output symbol

Some software programs that use flowcharts (such as Visual Logic) use a left-slanting parallelogram to represent output. As long as the flowchart creator and the flowchart reader are communicating, the actual shape used is irrelevant. This book will follow the most standard convention of using the right-slanting parallelogram for both input and output.

To show the correct sequence of these statements, you use arrows, or **flowlines**, to connect the steps. Whenever possible, most of a flowchart should read from top to bottom or from left to right on a page. That's the way we read English, so when flowcharts follow this convention, they are easier for us to understand.

To be complete, a flowchart should include two more elements: **terminal symbols**, or start/stop symbols, at each end. Often, you place a word like `start` or `begin` in the first terminal symbol and a word like `end` or `stop` in the other. The standard terminal symbol is shaped like a racetrack; many programmers refer to this shape as a lozenge, because it resembles the shape of the medication you might use to soothe a sore throat. Figure 1-6 shows a complete flowchart for the program that doubles a number, and the pseudocode for the same problem.

You can see from the figure that the flowchart and pseudocode statements are the same—only the presentation format differs.

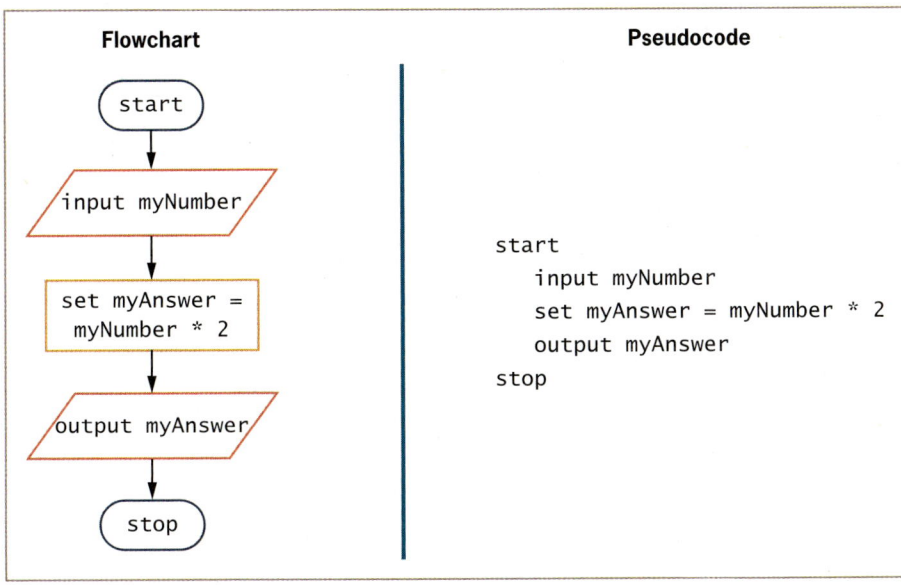

Figure 1-6 Flowchart and pseudocode of program that doubles a number

Programmers seldom create both pseudocode and a flowchart for the same problem. You usually use one or the other. In a large program, you might even prefer to write pseudocode for some parts and to draw a flowchart for others.

When you tell a friend how to get to your house, you might write a series of instructions or you might draw a map. Pseudocode is similar to written, step-by-step instructions; a flowchart, like a map, is a visual representation of the same thing.

Repeating Instructions

After the flowchart or pseudocode has been developed, the programmer only needs to: (1) buy a computer, (2) buy a language compiler, (3) learn a programming language, (4) code the program, (5) attempt to compile it, (6) fix the syntax errors, (7) compile it again, (8) test it with several sets of data, and (9) put it into production.

"Whoa!" you are probably saying to yourself. "This is simply not worth it! All that work to create a flowchart or pseudocode, and *then* all those other steps? For five dollars, I can buy a pocket calculator that will double any number for me instantly!" You are absolutely right. If this were a real computer program, and all it did was double the value of a number, it would not be worth the effort. Writing a computer program would be worthwhile only if you had many numbers (let's say 10,000) to double in a limited amount of time—let's say the next two minutes.

Unfortunately, the program represented in Figure 1-6 does not double 10,000 numbers; it doubles only one. You could execute the program 10,000 times, of course, but that would require you to sit at the computer and run the program over and over again. You would be better off with a program that could process 10,000 numbers, one after the other.

One solution is to write the program shown in Figure 1-7 and execute the same steps 10,000 times. Of course, writing this program would be very time consuming; you might as well buy the calculator.

```
start
   input myNumber
   set myAnswer = myNumber * 2
   output myAnswer
   input myNumber
   set myAnswer = myNumber * 2
   output myAnswer
   input myNumber
   set myAnswer = myNumber * 2
   output myAnswer
   ...and so on for 9,997 more times
```

Don't Do It
You would never want to write such a repetitious list of instructions.

Figure 1-7 Inefficient pseudocode for program that doubles 10,000 numbers

A better solution is to have the computer execute the same set of three instructions over and over again, as shown in Figure 1-8. The repetition of a series of steps is called a **loop**. With this approach, the computer gets a number, doubles it, displays the answer, and then starts again with the first instruction. The same spot in memory, called myNumber, is reused for the second number and for any subsequent numbers. The spot in memory named myAnswer is reused each time to store the result of the multiplication operation. However, the logic illustrated in the flowchart in Figure 1-8 contains a major problem—the sequence of instructions never ends. This programming situation is known as an **infinite loop**—a repeating flow of logic with no end. You will learn one way to handle this problem later in this chapter; you will learn a superior way in Chapter 3.

Using a Sentinel Value to End a Program

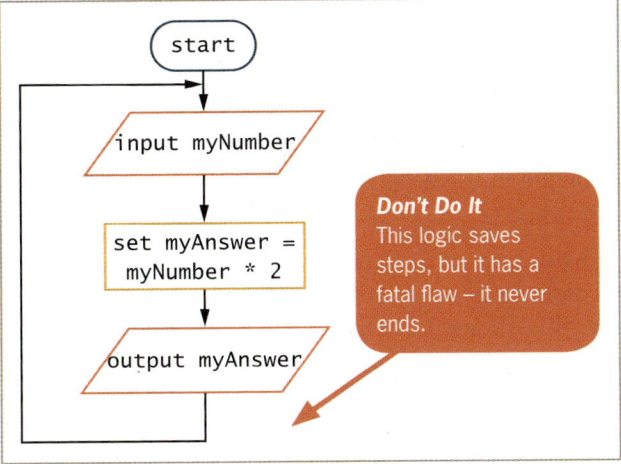

Figure 1-8 Flowchart of infinite number-doubling program

TWO TRUTHS & A LIE

Using Pseudocode Statements and Flowchart Symbols

1. When you draw a flowchart, you use a parallelogram to represent an input operation.
2. When you draw a flowchart, you use a parallelogram to represent a processing operation.
3. When you draw a flowchart, you use a parallelogram to represent an output operation.

The false statement is #2. When you draw a flowchart, you use a rectangle to represent a processing operation.

Using a Sentinel Value to End a Program

The logic in the flowchart for doubling numbers, shown in Figure 1-8, has a major flaw—the program contains an infinite loop. If, for example, the input numbers are being entered at the keyboard, the program will keep accepting numbers and outputting their doubled values forever. Of course, the user could refuse to type any more numbers. But the program cannot progress any further while it is waiting for input; meanwhile, the program is occupying computer memory and tying up operating system resources. Refusing to enter any more numbers is not a practical solution. Another way to end the program is simply to turn off the computer. But again, that's neither the best solution nor an elegant way for the program to end.

A superior way to end the program is to set a predetermined value for myNumber that means "Stop the program!" For example, the programmer and the user could agree that the user will never need to know the double of 0 (zero), so the user could enter a 0 to stop. The program could then test any incoming value contained in myNumber and, if it is a 0, stop the program. Testing a value is also called **making a decision**.

You represent a decision in a flowchart by drawing a **decision symbol**, which is shaped like a diamond. The diamond usually contains a question, the answer to which is one of two mutually exclusive options—often yes or no. All good computer questions have only two mutually exclusive answers, such as yes and no or true and false. For example, "What day of the year is your birthday?" is not a good computer question because there are 366 possible answers. However, "Is your birthday June 24?" is a good computer question because the answer is always either yes or no.

The question to stop the doubling program should be "Is the value of myNumber just entered equal to 0?" or "myNumber = 0?" for short. The complete flowchart will now look like the one shown in Figure 1-9.

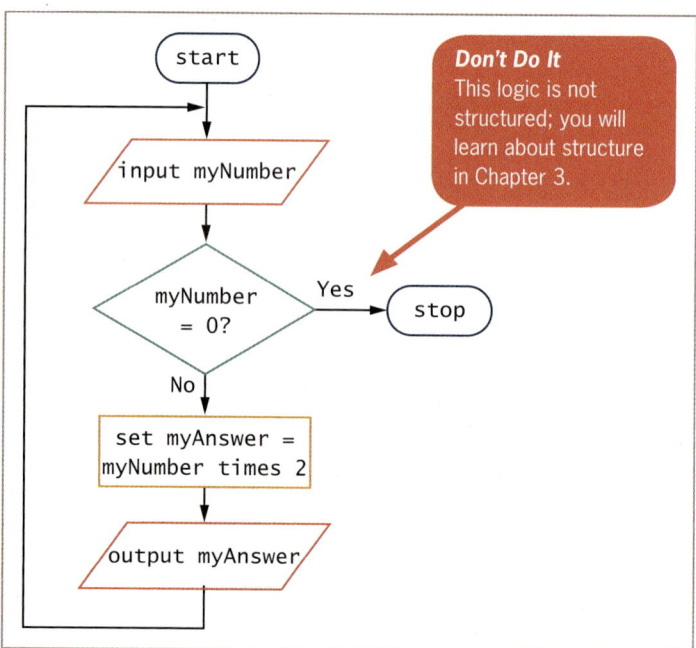

Figure 1-9 Flowchart of number-doubling program with sentinel value of 0

One drawback to using 0 to stop a program, of course, is that it won't work if the user does need to find the double of 0. In that case, some other data-entry value that the user never will need, such as 999 or –1, could be selected to signal that the program should end. A preselected value that stops the execution of a program is often called a **dummy value** because it does not represent real data, but just a signal to stop. Sometimes, such a value is called a **sentinel value** because it represents an entry or exit point, like a sentinel who guards a fortress.

Not all programs rely on user data entry from a keyboard; many read data from an input device, such as a disk. When organizations store data on a disk or other storage device, they do not commonly use a dummy value to signal the end of the file. For one thing, an input record might have hundreds of fields, and if you store a dummy record in every file, you are wasting a large quantity of storage on "nondata." Additionally, it is often difficult to choose sentinel values for fields in a company's data files. Any `balanceDue`, even a zero or a negative number, can be a legitimate value, and any `customerName`, even "ZZ", could be someone's name. Fortunately, programming languages can recognize the end of data in a file automatically, through a code that is stored at the end of the data. Many programming languages use the term **eof** (for *end of file*) to refer to this marker that automatically acts as a sentinel. This book, therefore, uses `eof` to indicate the end of data whenever using a dummy value is impractical or inconvenient. In the flowchart shown in Figure 1-10, the `eof` question is shaded.

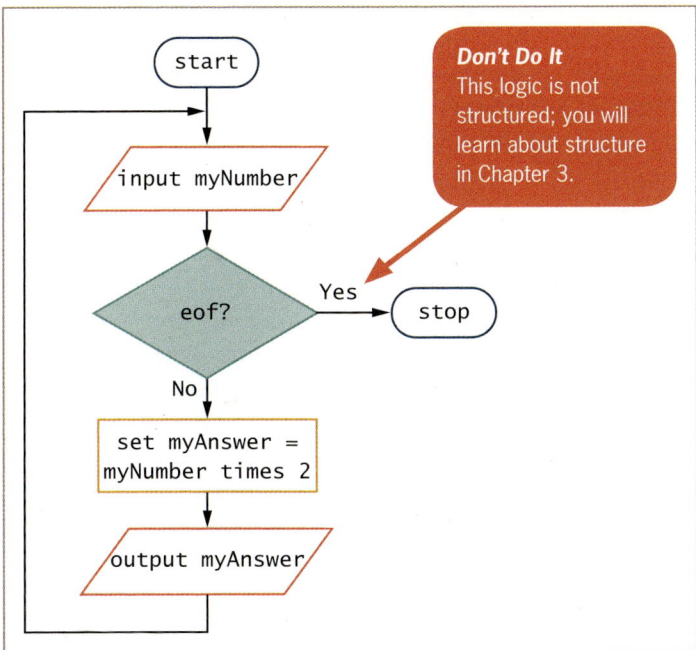

Figure 1-10 Flowchart using `eof`

> **TWO TRUTHS & A LIE**
>
> Using a Sentinel Value to End a Program
>
> 1. A program that contains an infinite loop is one that never ends.
> 2. A preselected value that stops the execution of a program is often called a dummy value or a sentinel value.
> 3. Many programming languages use the term fe (for *file end*) to refer to a marker that automatically acts as a sentinel.
>
> The false statement is #3. The term eof (for *end of file*) is the common term for a file sentinel.

Understanding Programming and User Environments

Many approaches can be used to write and execute a computer program. When you plan a program's logic, you can use a flowchart, pseudocode, or a combination of the two. When you code the program, you can type statements into a variety of text editors. When your program executes, it might accept input from a keyboard, mouse, microphone, or any other input device, and when you provide a program's output, you might use text, images, or sound. This section describes the most common environments you will encounter as a new programmer.

Understanding Programming Environments

When you plan the logic for a computer program, you can use paper and pencil to create a flowchart, or you might use software that allows you to manipulate flowchart shapes. If you choose to write pseudocode, you can do so by hand or by using a word-processing program. To enter the program into a computer so you can translate and execute it, you usually use a keyboard to type program statements into an editor. You can type a program into one of the following:

- A plain text editor
- A text editor that is part of an integrated development environment

A **text editor** is a program that you use to create simple text files. It is similar to a word processor, but without as many features. You can use a text editor such as Notepad that is included with Microsoft Windows. Figure 1-11 shows a C# program in Notepad that accepts a number and doubles it. An advantage to using a simple text editor to type and save a program is that the completed program does not require much disk space for storage. For example, the file shown in Figure 1-11 occupies only 314 bytes of storage.

Understanding Programming and User Environments

```
using System;
public class NumberDoublingProgram
{
    public static void Main()
    {
        int myNumber;
        int myAnswer;
        Console.Write("Please enter a number >> ");
        myNumber = Convert.ToInt32(Console.ReadLine());
        myAnswer = myNumber * 2;
        Console.WriteLine(myAnswer);
    }
}
```

> This line contains a prompt that tells the user what to enter. You will learn more about prompts in Chapter 2.

Figure 1-11   A C# number-doubling program in Notepad

You can use the editor of an **integrated development environment** (**IDE**) to enter your program. An IDE is a software package that provides an editor, compiler, and other programming tools. For example, Figure 1-12 shows a C# program in the **Microsoft Visual Studio IDE**, an environment that contains tools useful for creating programs in Visual Basic, C++, and C#.

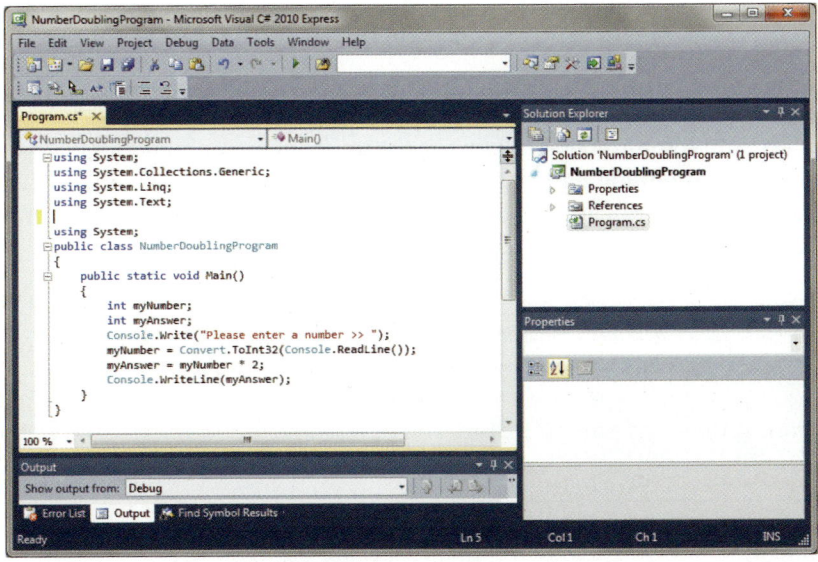

Figure 1-12   A C# number-doubling program in Visual Studio

Using an IDE is helpful to programmers because usually it provides features similar to those you find in many word processors. In particular, an IDE's editor commonly includes such features as the following:

- It uses different colors to display various language components, making elements like data types easier to identify.
- It highlights syntax errors visually for you.
- It employs automatic statement completion; when you start to type a statement, the IDE suggests a likely completion, which you can accept with a keystroke.
- It provides tools that allow you to step through a program's execution one statement at a time so you can more easily follow the program's logic and determine the source of any errors.

When you use the IDE to create and save a program, you occupy much more disk space than when using a plain text editor. For example, the program in Figure 1-12 occupies more than 49,000 bytes of disk space.

Although various programming environments might look different and offer different features, the process of using them is very similar. When you plan the logic for a program using pseudocode or a flowchart, it does not matter which programming environment you will use to write your code, and when you write the code in a programming language, it does not matter which environment you use to write it.

Understanding User Environments

A user might execute a program you have written in any number of environments. For example, a user might execute the number-doubling program from a command line like the one shown in Figure 1-13. A **command line** is a location on your computer screen at which you type text entries to communicate with the computer's operating system. In the program in Figure 1-13, the user is asked for a number, and the results are displayed.

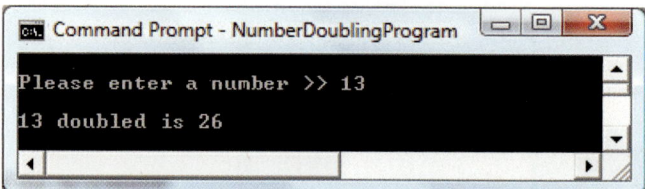

Figure 1-13 Executing a number-doubling program in a command-line environment

Many programs are not run at the command line in a text environment, but are run using a **graphical user interface**, or **GUI** (pronounced *gooey*), which allows users to interact with a program in a graphical environment. When running a GUI program, the user might type input into a text box or use a mouse or other pointing device to select options on the screen. Figure 1-14 shows a number-doubling program that performs exactly the same task as the one in Figure 1-13, but this program uses a GUI.

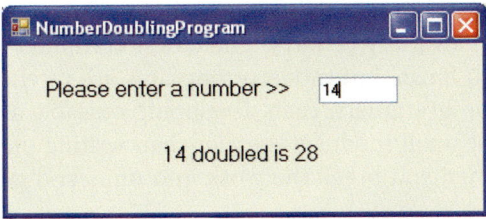

Figure 1-14   Executing a number-doubling program in a GUI environment

A command-line program and a GUI program might be written in the same programming language. (For example, the programs shown in Figures 1-13 and 1-14 were both written using C#.) However, no matter which environment is used to write or execute a program, the logical process is the same. The two programs in Figures 1-13 and 1-14 both accept input, perform multiplication, and perform output. In this book, you will not concentrate on which environment is used to type a program's statements, nor will you care about the type of environment the user will see. Instead, you will be concerned with the logic that applies to all programming situations.

TWO TRUTHS & A LIE

Understanding Programming and User Environments

1. You can type a program into an editor that is part of an integrated development environment, but using a plain text editor provides you with more programming help.
2. When a program runs from the command line, a user types text to provide input.
3. Although GUI and command-line environments look different, the logic of input, processing, and output apply to both program types.

The false statement is #1. An integrated development environment provides more programming help than a plain text editor.

Understanding the Evolution of Programming Models

People have been writing modern computer programs since the 1940s. The oldest programming languages required programmers to work with memory addresses and to memorize awkward codes associated with machine languages. Newer programming languages look much more like natural language and are easier to use, partly because they allow programmers to name variables instead of using unwieldy memory addresses. Also, newer programming languages allow programmers to create self-contained modules or program segments that can be pieced together in a variety of ways. The oldest computer programs were written in one piece, from start to finish, but modern programs are rarely written that way—they are created by teams of programmers, each developing reusable and connectable program procedures. Writing several small modules is easier than writing one large program, and most large tasks are easier when you break the work into units and get other workers to help with some of the units.

Ada Byron Lovelace predicted the development of software in 1843; she is often regarded as the first programmer. The basis for most modern software was proposed by Alan Turing in 1935.

Currently, two major models or paradigms are used by programmers to develop programs and their procedures:

- **Procedural programming** focuses on the procedures that programmers create. That is, procedural programmers focus on the actions that are carried out—for example, getting input data for an employee and writing the calculations needed to produce a paycheck from the data. Procedural programmers would approach the job of producing a paycheck by breaking down the process into manageable subtasks.

- **Object-oriented programming** focuses on objects, or "things," and describes their features (also called attributes) and behaviors. For example, object-oriented programmers might design a payroll application by thinking about employees and paychecks, and by describing their attributes. Employees have names and Social Security numbers, and paychecks have names and check amounts. Then the programmers would think about the behaviors of employees and paychecks, such as employees getting raises and adding dependents and paychecks being calculated and output. Object-oriented programmers would then build applications from these entities.

With either approach, procedural or object oriented, you can produce a correct paycheck, and both models employ reusable program modules. The major difference lies in the focus the programmer takes during the earliest planning stages of a project. For now, this book focuses on procedural programming techniques. The skills you gain in programming procedurally—declaring variables, accepting input, making decisions, producing output, and so on—will serve you well whether you eventually write programs using a procedural approach, an object-oriented approach, or both. The programming language in which you write your source code might determine your approach. You can write a procedural program in any language that supports object orientation, but the opposite is not always true.

Chapter Summary

> ### TWO TRUTHS & A LIE
> #### Understanding the Evolution of Programming Models
>
> 1. The oldest computer programs were written in many separate modules.
> 2. Procedural programmers focus on actions that are carried out by a program.
> 3. Object-oriented programmers focus on a program's objects and their attributes and behaviors.
>
> The false statement is #1. The oldest programs were written in a single piece; newer programs are divided into modules.

Chapter Summary

- Together, computer hardware (physical devices) and software (instructions) accomplish three major operations: input, processing, and output. You write computer instructions in a computer programming language that requires specific syntax; the instructions are translated into machine language by a compiler or interpreter. When both the syntax and logic of a program are correct, you can run, or execute, the program to produce the desired results.

- For a program to work properly, you must develop correct logic. Logical errors are much more difficult to locate than syntax errors.

- A programmer's job involves understanding the problem, planning the logic, coding the program, translating the program into machine language, testing the program, putting the program into production, and maintaining it.

- When programmers plan the logic for a solution to a programming problem, they often use flowcharts or pseudocode. When you draw a flowchart, you use parallelograms to represent input and output operations, and rectangles to represent processing. Programmers also use decisions to control repetition of instruction sets.

- To avoid creating an infinite loop when you repeat instructions, you can test for a sentinel value. You represent a decision in a flowchart by drawing a diamond-shaped symbol that contains a question, the answer to which is either yes or no.

- You can type a program into a plain text editor or one that is part of an integrated development environment. When a program's data values are entered from a keyboard, they can be entered at the command line in a text environment or in a GUI. Either way, the logic is similar.

- Procedural and object-oriented programmers approach problems differently. Procedural programmers concentrate on the actions performed with data. Object-oriented programmers focus on objects and their behaviors and attributes.

Key Terms

A **computer system** is a combination of all the components required to process and store data using a computer.

Hardware is the collection of physical devices that comprise a computer system.

Software consists of the programs that tell the computer what to do.

Programs are sets of instructions for a computer.

Programming is the act of developing and writing programs.

Application software comprises all the programs you apply to a task.

System software comprises the programs that you use to manage your computer.

Input describes the entry of data items into computer memory using hardware devices such as keyboards and mice.

Data items include all the text, numbers, and other information processed by a computer.

Processing data items may involve organizing them, checking them for accuracy, or performing mathematical operations on them.

The **central processing unit**, or **CPU**, is the hardware component that processes data.

Output describes the operation of retrieving information from memory and sending it to a device, such as a monitor or printer, so people can view, interpret, and work with the results.

Information is processed data.

Storage devices are types of hardware equipment, such as disks, that hold information for later retrieval.

Programming languages, such as Visual Basic, C#, C++, Java, or COBOL, are used to write programs.

Program code is the set of instructions a programmer writes in a programming language.

Coding the program is the act of writing programming language instructions.

The **syntax** of a language is its grammar rules.

A **syntax error** is an error in language or grammar.

Computer memory is the temporary, internal storage within a computer.

Random access memory (**RAM**) is temporary, internal computer storage.

Key Terms

Volatile describes storage whose contents are lost when power is lost.

Nonvolatile describes storage whose contents are retained when power is lost.

Machine language is a computer's on/off circuitry language.

Source code is the statements a programmer writes in a programming language.

Object code is translated machine language.

A **compiler** or **interpreter** translates a high-level language into machine language and indicates if you have used a programming language incorrectly.

Binary language is represented using a series of 0s and 1s.

To **run** or **execute** a program is to carry out its instructions.

Scripting languages (also called **scripting programming languages** or **script languages**) such as Python, Lua, Perl, and PHP are used to write programs that are typed directly from a keyboard. Scripting languages are stored as text rather than as binary executable files.

A **logical error** occurs when incorrect instructions are performed, or when instructions are performed in the wrong order.

You develop the **logic** of the computer program when you give instructions to the computer in a specific sequence, without omitting any instructions or adding extraneous instructions.

A **variable** is a named memory location whose value can vary.

The **program development cycle** consists of the steps that occur during a program's lifetime.

Users (or **end users**) are people who employ and benefit from computer programs.

Documentation consists of all the supporting paperwork for a program.

An **algorithm** is the sequence of steps necessary to solve any problem.

An **IPO chart** is a program development tool that delineates input, processing, and output tasks.

A **TOE chart** is a program development tool that lists tasks, objects, and events.

Desk-checking is the process of walking through a program solution on paper.

A **high-level programming language** supports English-like syntax.

A **low-level machine language** is made up of 1s and 0s and does not use easily interpreted variable names.

Debugging is the process of finding and correcting program errors.

Conversion is the entire set of actions an organization must take to switch over to using a new program or set of programs.

Maintenance consists of all the improvements and corrections made to a program after it is in production.

Pseudocode is an English-like representation of the logical steps it takes to solve a problem.

A **flowchart** is a pictorial representation of the logical steps it takes to solve a problem.

An **input symbol** indicates an input operation and is represented by a parallelogram in flowcharts.

A **processing symbol** indicates a processing operation and is represented by a rectangle in flowcharts.

An **output symbol** indicates an output operation and is represented by a parallelogram in flowcharts.

An **input/output symbol** or **I/O symbol** is represented by a parallelogram in flowcharts.

Flowlines, or arrows, connect the steps in a flowchart.

A **terminal symbol** indicates the beginning or end of a flowchart segment and is represented by a lozenge

A **loop** is a repetition of a series of steps.

An **infinite loop** occurs when repeating logic cannot end.

Making a decision is the act of testing a value.

A **decision symbol** is shaped like a diamond and used to represent decisions in flowcharts.

A **dummy value** is a preselected value that stops the execution of a program.

A **sentinel value** is a preselected value that stops the execution of a program.

The term **eof** means *end of file*.

A **text editor** is a program that you use to create simple text files; it is similar to a word processor, but without as many features.

An **integrated development environment** (**IDE**) is a software package that provides an editor, compiler, and other programming tools.

Microsoft Visual Studio IDE is a software package that contains useful tools for creating programs in Visual Basic, C++, and C#.

A **command line** is a location on your computer screen at which you type text entries to communicate with the computer's operating system.

A **graphical user interface**, or **GUI** (pronounced *gooey*), allows users to interact with a program in a graphical environment.

Procedural programming is a programming model that focuses on the procedures that programmers create.

Object-oriented programming is a programming model that focuses on objects, or "things," and describes their features (also called attributes) and behaviors.

Review Questions

1. Computer programs also are known as _____.
   a. hardware
   b. software
   c. data
   d. information

2. The major computer operations include _____.
   a. hardware and software
   b. input, processing, and output
   c. sequence and looping
   d. spreadsheets, word processing, and data communications

3. Visual Basic, C++, and Java are all examples of computer _____.
   a. operating systems
   b. hardware
   c. machine languages
   d. programming languages

4. A programming language's rules are its _____.
   a. syntax
   b. logic
   c. format
   d. options

5. The most important task of a compiler or interpreter is to _____.
   a. create the rules for a programming language
   b. translate English statements into a language such as Java
   c. translate programming language statements into machine language
   d. execute machine language programs to perform useful tasks

6. Which of the following is temporary, internal storage?
   a. CPU
   b. hard disk
   c. keyboard
   d. memory

7. Which of the following pairs of steps in the programming process is in the correct order?
   a. code the program, plan the logic
   b. test the program, translate it into machine language
   c. put the program into production, understand the problem
   d. code the program, translate it into machine language

CHAPTER 1 — An Overview of Computers and Programming

8. A programmer's most important task before planning the logic of a program is to _____ .
    a. decide which programming language to use
    b. code the problem
    c. train the users of the program
    d. understand the problem

9. The two most commonly used tools for planning a program's logic are _____ .
    a. flowcharts and pseudocode
    b. ASCII and EBCDIC
    c. Java and Visual Basic
    d. word processors and spreadsheets

10. Writing a program in a language such as C++ or Java is known as _____ the program.
    a. translating
    b. coding
    c. interpreting
    d. compiling

11. An English-like programming language such as Java or Visual Basic is a _____ programming language.
    a. machine-level
    b. low-level
    c. high-level
    d. binary-level

12. Which of the following is an example of a syntax error?
    a. producing output before accepting input
    b. subtracting when you meant to add
    c. misspelling a programming language word
    d. all of the above

13. Which of the following is an example of a logical error?
    a. performing arithmetic with a value before inputting it
    b. accepting two input values when a program requires only one
    c. dividing by 3 when you meant to divide by 30
    d. all of the above

14. The parallelogram is the flowchart symbol representing _____ .
    a. input
    b. output
    c. both a and b
    d. none of the above

15. In a flowchart, a rectangle represents _____.
    a. input
    b. a sentinel
    c. a question
    d. processing

16. In flowcharts, the decision symbol is a _____.
    a. parallelogram
    b. rectangle
    c. lozenge
    d. diamond

17. The term *eof* represents _____.
    a. a standard input device
    b. a generic sentinel value
    c. a condition in which no more memory is available for storage
    d. the logical flow in a program

18. When you use an IDE instead of a simple text editor to develop a program, _____.
    a. the logic is more complicated
    b. the logic is simpler
    c. the syntax is different
    d. some help is provided

19. When you write a program that will run in a GUI environment as opposed to a command-line environment, _____.
    a. the logic is very different
    b. some syntax is different
    c. you do not need to plan the logic
    d. users are more confused

20. As compared to procedural programming, with object-oriented programming, _____.
    a. the programmer's focus differs
    b. you cannot use some languages, such as Java
    c. you do not accept input
    d. you do not code calculations; they are created automatically

Exercises

1. Match the definition with the appropriate term.
   1. Computer system devices
   2. Another word for *programs*
   3. Language rules
   4. Order of instructions
   5. Language translator

   a. compiler
   b. syntax
   c. logic
   d. hardware
   e. software

2. In your own words, describe the steps to writing a computer program.

3. Match the term with the appropriate shape (see Figure 1-15).

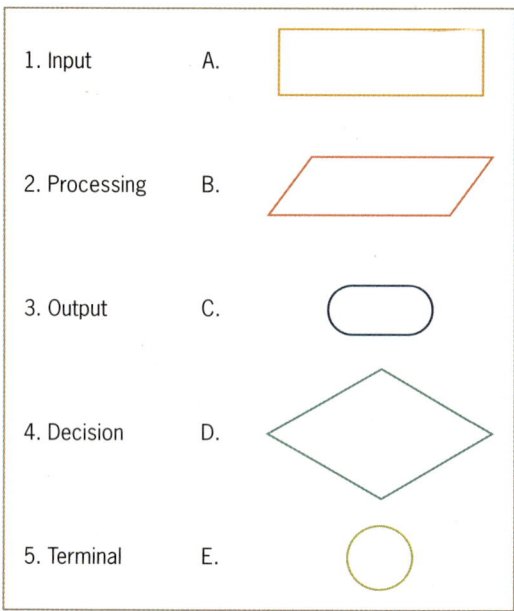

1. Input
2. Processing
3. Output
4. Decision
5. Terminal

A.
B.
C.
D.
E.

Figure 1-15   Identifying shapes

4. Draw a flowchart or write pseudocode to represent the logic of a program that allows the user to enter a value. The program divides the value by 2 and outputs the result.

5. Draw a flowchart or write pseudocode to represent the logic of a program that allows the user to enter a value for one edge of a cube. The program calculates the surface area of one side of the cube, the surface area of the cube, and its volume. The program outputs all the results.

6. Draw a flowchart or write pseudocode to represent the logic of a program that allows the user to enter two values. The program outputs the product of the two values.

7. a. Draw a flowchart or write pseudocode to represent the logic of a program that allows the user to enter values for the width and length of a room's floor in feet. The program outputs the area of the floor in square feet.

   b. Modify the program that computes floor area to compute and output the number of 12-inch square tiles needed to tile the floor.

Exercises

8. a. Draw a flowchart or write pseudocode to represent the logic of a program that allows the user to enter values for the width and length of a wall in feet. The program outputs the area of the wall in square feet.

   b. Modify the program that computes wall area to allow the user to enter the price of a gallon of paint. Assume that a gallon of paint covers 350 square feet of a wall. The program outputs the number of gallons needed and the cost of the job. (For this exercise, assume that you do not need to account for windows or doors, and that you can purchase partial gallons of paint.)

9. Research current rates of monetary exchange. Draw a flowchart or write pseudocode to represent the logic of a program that allows the user to enter a number of dollars and convert it to Euros and Japanese yen.

10. Draw a flowchart or write pseudocode to represent the logic of a program that allows the user to enter values for a salesperson's base salary, total sales, and commission rate. The program computes and outputs the salesperson's pay by adding the base salary to the product of the total sales and commission rate.

Find the Bugs

11. Since the early days of computer programming, program errors have been called bugs. The term is often said to have originated from an actual moth that was discovered trapped in the circuitry of a computer at Harvard University in 1945. Actually, the term *bug* was in use prior to 1945 to mean trouble with any electrical apparatus; even during Thomas Edison's life, it meant an industrial defect. However, the term *debugging* is more closely associated with correcting program syntax and logic errors than with any other type of trouble.

    Your downloadable files for Chapter 1 include DEBUG01-01.txt, DEBUG01-02.txt, and DEBUG01-03.txt. Each file starts with some comments (lines that begin with two slashes) that describe the program. Examine the pseudocode that follows the introductory comments, then find and correct all the bugs.

Game Zone

12. In 1952, A. S. Douglas wrote his University of Cambridge Ph.D. dissertation on human-computer interaction, and created the first graphical computer game—a version of Tic-Tac-Toe. The game was programmed on an EDSAC vacuum-tube mainframe computer. The first computer game is generally assumed to be *Spacewar!*, developed in 1962 at MIT; the first commercially available video game was *Pong*, introduced by Atari in 1972. In 1980, Atari's *Asteroids* and *Lunar Lander* became the first video games to be registered with the U. S. Copyright Office. Throughout the

1980s, players spent hours with games that now seem very simple and unglamorous; do you recall playing *Adventure, Oregon Trail, Where in the World Is Carmen Sandiego?,* or *Myst*?

Today, commercial computer games are much more complex; they require many programmers, graphic artists, and testers to develop them, and large management and marketing staffs are needed to promote them. A game might cost many millions of dollars to develop and market, but a successful game might earn hundreds of millions of dollars. Obviously, with the brief introduction to programming you have had in this chapter, you cannot create a very sophisticated game. However, you can get started.

Mad Libs® is a children's game in which players provide a few words that are then incorporated into a silly story. The game helps children understand different parts of speech because they are asked to provide specific types of words. For example, you might ask a child for a noun, another noun, an adjective, and a past-tense verb. The child might reply with such answers as *table, book, silly,* and *studied*. The newly created Mad Lib might be:

Mary had a little *table*

Its *book* was *silly* as snow

And everywhere that Mary *studied*

The *table* was sure to go.

Create the logic for a Mad Lib program that accepts five words from input, then creates and displays a short story or nursery rhyme that uses them.

Up for Discussion

13. Which is the better tool for learning programming—flowcharts or pseudocode? Cite any educational research you can find.

14. What is the image of the computer programmer in popular culture? Is the image different in books than in TV shows and movies? Would you like that image for yourself?

CHAPTER 2

Elements of High-Quality Programs

In this chapter, you will learn about:

- ◎ Declaring and using variables and constants
- ◎ Performing arithmetic operations
- ◎ The advantages of modularization
- ◎ Modularizing a program
- ◎ Hierarchy charts
- ◎ Features of good program design

Declaring and Using Variables and Constants

As you learned in Chapter 1, data items include all the text, numbers, and other information that are processed by a computer. When you input data items into a computer, they are stored in variables in memory where they can be processed and converted to information that is output.

When you write programs, you work with data in three different forms: literals (or unnamed constants), variables, and named constants.

Understanding Unnamed, Literal Constants and their Data Types

All programming languages support two broad data types; **numeric** describes data that consists of numbers and **string** describes data that is nonnumeric. Most programming languages support several additional data types, including multiple types for numeric values of different sizes and with and without decimal places. Languages such as C++, C#, Visual Basic, and Java distinguish between **integer** (whole number) numeric variables and **floating-point** (fractional) numeric variables that contain a decimal point. (Floating-point numbers are also called **real numbers**.) Thus, in some languages, the values 4 and 4.3 would be stored in different types of numeric variables. Additionally, many languages allow you to distinguish between smaller and larger values that occupy different numbers of bytes in memory. You will learn more about these specialized data types when you study a programming language, but this book uses the two broadest types: numeric and string.

When you use a specific numeric value, such as 43, within a program, you write it using the digits and no quotation marks. A specific numeric value is often called a **numeric constant** (or **literal numeric constant**) because it does not change—a 43 always has the value 43. When you store a numeric value in computer memory, additional characters such as dollar signs and commas are not input or stored. Those characters can be added to output for readability, but they are not part of the number.

A specific text value, or string of characters, such as "Amanda", is a **string constant** (or **literal string constant**). String constants, unlike numeric constants, appear within quotation marks in computer programs. String values are also called **alphanumeric values** because they can contain alphabetic characters as well as numbers and other characters. For example, "$3,215.99 U.S.", including the dollar sign, comma, period, letters, and numbers, is a string. Although strings can contain numbers, numeric values cannot contain alphabetic characters. The numeric constant 43 and the string constant "Amanda" are examples of **unnamed constants**—they do not have identifiers like variables do.

 Watch the video *Declaring Variables and Constants*.

Working with Variables

Variables are named memory locations whose contents can vary or differ over time. For example, in the number-doubling program in Figure 2-1, myNumber and myAnswer are variables. At any moment in time, a variable holds just one value. Sometimes, myNumber holds 2 and myAnswer holds 4; at other times, myNumber holds 6 and myAnswer holds 12. The ability of memory variables to change in value is what makes computers and programming worthwhile. Because one memory location can be used repeatedly with different values, you can write program instructions once and then use them for thousands of separate calculations. *One* set of payroll instructions at your company produces each employee paycheck, and *one* set of instructions at your electric company produces each household's bill.

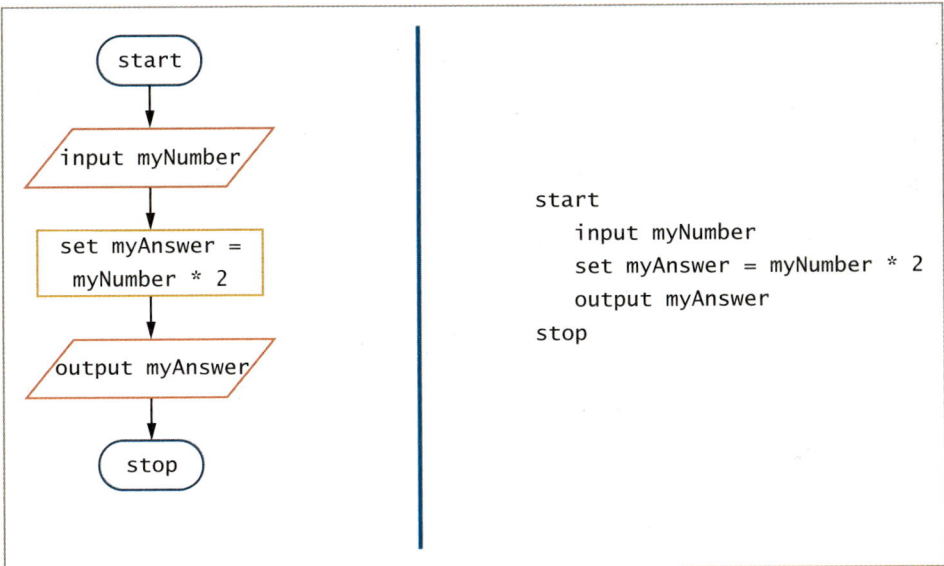

Figure 2-1 Flowchart and pseudocode for the number-doubling program

In most programming languages, before you can use any variable, you must include a declaration for it. A **declaration** is a statement that provides a data type and an identifier for a variable. An **identifier** is a program component's name. A data item's **data type** is a classification that describes the following:

- What values can be held by the item
- How the item is stored in computer memory
- What operations can be performed on the data item

As mentioned earlier, most programming languages support several data types, but in this book, only two data types will be used: num and string.

When you declare a variable, you provide both a data type and an identifier. Optionally, you can declare a starting value for any variable. Declaring a starting value is known as **initializing the variable**. For example, each of the following statements is a valid declaration. Two of the statements include initializations, and two do not:

```
num mySalary
num yourSalary = 14.55
string myName
string yourName = "Juanita"
```

Figure 2-2 shows the number-doubling program from Figure 2-1 with the added declarations shaded. Variables must be declared before they are used in a program for the first time. Some languages require all variables to be declared at the beginning of the program; others allow variables to be declared anywhere as long as they are declared before their first use. This book will follow the convention of declaring all variables together.

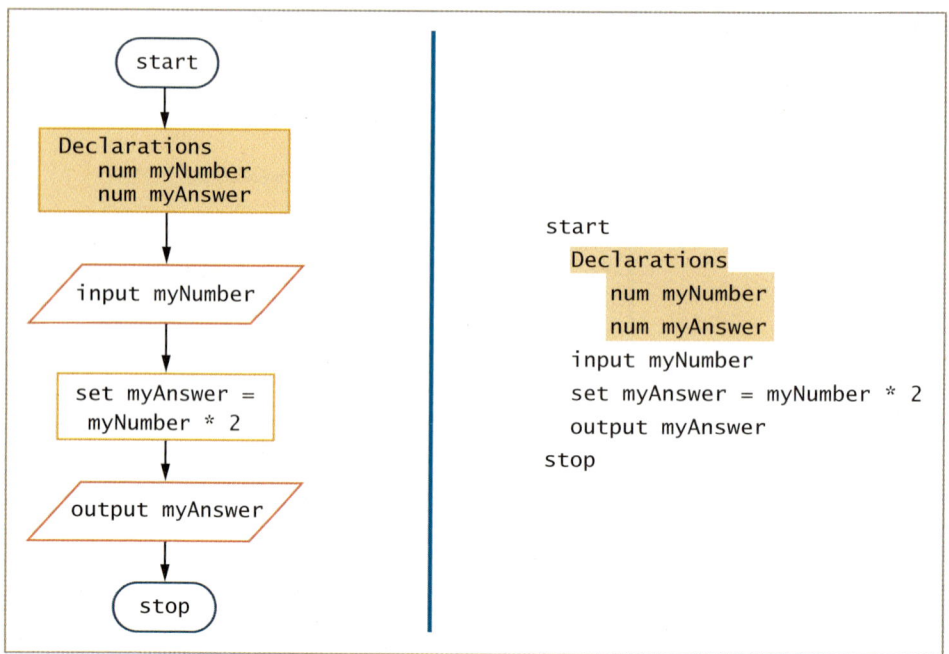

Figure 2-2 Flowchart and pseudocode of number-doubling program with variable declarations

In many programming languages, if you declare a variable and do not initialize it, the variable contains an unknown value until it is assigned a value. A variable's unknown value commonly is called **garbage**. Although some languages use a default value for some variables (such as assigning 0 to any unassigned numeric variable), this book will assume that an unassigned variable holds garbage. In many languages it is illegal to use a garbage-holding variable in an arithmetic statement or to display it as output. Even if you work with a language that allows you to display garbage, it serves no purpose to do so and constitutes a logical error.

When you create a variable without assigning it an initial value (as with myNumber and myAnswer in Figure 2-2), your intention is to assign a value later—for example, by receiving one as input or placing the result of a calculation there.

Naming Variables

The number-doubling example in Figure 2-2 requires two variables: myNumber and myAnswer. Alternatively, these variables could be named userEntry and programSolution, or inputValue and twiceTheValue. As a programmer, you choose reasonable and descriptive names for your variables. The language interpreter then associates the names you choose with specific memory addresses.

Every computer programming language has its own set of rules for creating identifiers. Most languages allow letters and digits within identifiers. Some languages allow hyphens in variable names, such as hourly-wage, and some allow underscores, as in hourly_wage. Some languages allow dollar signs or other special characters in variable names (for example, hourly$); others allow foreign-alphabet characters, such as π or Ω. Each programming language has a few (perhaps 100 to 200) reserved **keywords** that are not allowed as variable names because they are part of the language's syntax. When you learn a programming language, you will learn its list of keywords.

Different languages put different limits on the length of variable names, although in general, the length of identifiers in newer languages is virtually unlimited. In many languages, identifiers are case sensitive, so HoUrLyWaGe, hourlywage, and hourlyWage are three separate variable names. Programmers use multiple conventions for naming variables, often depending on the programming language or standards implemented by their employers. Common conventions include the following:

- **Camel casing** is the convention in which the variable starts with a lowercase letter and any subsequent word begins with an uppercase letter, such as hourlyWage. The variable names in this book are shown using camel casing.
- **Pascal casing** is a convention in which the first letter of a variable name is uppercase, as in HourlyWage.
- **Hungarian notation** is a convention in which a variable's data type is part of the identifier—for example, numHourlyWage or stringLastName.

Adopting a naming convention for variables and using it consistently will help make your programs easier to read and understand.

Even though every language has its own rules for naming variables, you should not concern yourself with the specific syntax of any particular computer language when designing the logic of a program. The logic, after all, works with any language. The variable names used throughout this book follow only three rules:

1. *Variable names must be one word.* The name can contain letters, digits, hyphens, underscores, or any other characters you choose, with the exception of spaces. Therefore, r is a legal variable name, as are rate and interestRate. The variable name interest rate is not allowed because of the space.

2. *Variable names must start with a letter.* Some programming languages allow variable names to start with a nonalphabetic character such as an underscore. Almost all programming languages prohibit variable names that start with a digit. This book follows the most common convention of starting variable names with a letter.

 When you write a program using an editor that is packaged with a compiler in an IDE, the compiler may display variable names in a different color from the rest of the program. This visual aid helps your variable names stand out from words that are part of the programming language.

3. *Variable names should have some appropriate meaning.* This is not a formal rule of any programming language. When computing an interest rate in a program, the computer does not care if you call the variable g, u84, or fred. As long as the correct numeric result is placed in the variable, its actual name doesn't matter. However, it's much easier to follow the logic of a statement like set interestEarned = initialInvestment * interestRate than a statement like set f = i * r or set someBanana = j89 * myFriendLinda. When a program requires changes, which could be months or years after you write the original version, you and your fellow programmers will appreciate clear, descriptive variable names in place of cryptic identifiers. Later in this chapter, you will learn more about selecting good identifiers.

Notice that the flowchart in Figure 2-2 follows the preceding rules for variables: Both variable names, myNumber and myAnswer, are single words without embedded spaces, and they have appropriate meanings. Some programmers name variables after friends or create puns with them, but computer professionals consider such behavior unprofessional and amateurish.

Assigning Values to Variables

When you create a flowchart or pseudocode for a program that doubles numbers, you can include a statement such as the following:

set myAnswer = myNumber * 2

Such a statement is an **assignment statement**. This statement incorporates two actions. First, the computer calculates the arithmetic value of myNumber * 2. Second, the computed value is stored in the myAnswer memory location.

The equal sign is the **assignment operator**. The assignment operator is an example of a **binary operator**, meaning it requires two operands—one on each side. The assignment operator always operates from right to left, which means that it has **right-associativity** or **right-to-left associativity**. This means that the value of the expression to the right of the assignment operator is evaluated first, and then the result is assigned to the operand on the left. The operand to the right of an assignment operator can be a value, a formula, a named constant, or a variable. The operand to the left of an assignment operator must be a name that represents a memory address—the name of the location where the result will be stored.

Declaring and Using Variables and Constants

For example, if you have declared two numeric variables named someNumber and someOtherNumber, then each of the following is a valid assignment statement:

```
set someNumber = 2
set someNumber = 3 + 7
set someOtherNumber = someNumber
set someOtherNumber = someNumber * 5
```

In each case, the expression to the right of the assignment operator is evaluated and stored at the location referenced on the left side. The result to the left of an assignment operator is called an **lvalue**. The *l* is for left. Lvalues are always memory address identifiers.

The following statements, however, are *not* valid:

```
set 2 + 4 = someNumber
set someOtherNumber * 10 = someNumber
```

Don't Do It
The operand to the left of an assignment operator must represent a memory address.

In each of these cases, the value to the left of the assignment operator is not a memory address, so the statements are invalid.

When you write pseudocode or draw a flowchart, it might help you to use the word *set* in assignment statements, as shown in these examples, to emphasize that the left-side value is being set. However, in most programming languages, the word *set* is not used, and assignment statements take the following simpler form:

```
someNumber = 2
someOtherNumber = someNumber
```

Because the abbreviated form is how assignments appear in most languages, it is used for the rest of this book.

Understanding the Data Types of Variables

Computers handle string data differently from the way they handle numeric data. You may have experienced these differences if you have used application software such as spreadsheets or database programs. For example, in a spreadsheet, you cannot sum a column of words. Similarly, every programming language requires that you specify the correct type for each variable, and that you use each type appropriately.

- A **numeric variable** is one that can hold digits and have mathematical operations performed on it. In this book, all numeric variables can hold a decimal point and a sign indicating positive or negative; some programming languages provide specialized numeric types for these options. In the statement myAnswer = myNumber * 2, both myAnswer and myNumber are numeric variables; that is, their intended contents are numeric values, such as 6 and 3, 14.8 and 7.4, or −18 and −9.

- A **string variable** can hold text, such as letters of the alphabet, and other special characters, such as punctuation marks. If a working program contains the statement lastName = "Lincoln", then lastName is a string variable. A string variable also can hold digits either with or without other characters. For example, "235 Main Street" and "86" are both strings. A string like "86" is stored differently than the numeric value 86, and you cannot perform arithmetic with the string.

Type-safety is the feature of programming languages that prevents assigning values of an incorrect data type. You can assign data to a variable only if it is the correct type. If you declare taxRate as a numeric variable and inventoryItem as a string, then the following statements are valid:

    taxRate - 2.5
    inventoryItem = "monitor"

The following are invalid because the type of data being assigned does not match the variable type:

    taxRate = "2.5"
    inventoryItem = 2.5

> **Don't Do It**
> If taxRate is numeric and inventoryItem is a string, then these assignments are invalid.

 Watch the video *Understanding Data Types*.

Declaring Named Constants

Besides variables, most programming languages allow you to create named constants. A **named constant** is similar to a variable, except it can be assigned a value only once. You use a named constant when you want to assign a useful name for a value that will never be changed during a program's execution. Using named constants makes your programs easier to understand by eliminating magic numbers. A **magic number** is an unnamed constant, like 0.06, whose purpose is not immediately apparent.

For example, if a program uses a sales tax rate of 6 percent, you might want to declare a named constant as follows:

    num SALES_TAX_RATE = 0.06

After SALES_TAX_RATE is declared, the following statements have identical meaning:

    taxAmount = price * 0.06
    taxAmount = price * SALES_TAX_RATE

The way in which named constants are declared differs among programming languages. This book follows the convention of using all uppercase letters in constant identifiers, and using underscores to separate words for readability. Using these conventions makes named constants easier to recognize. In many languages a constant must be assigned its value when it is declared, but in some languages a constant can be assigned its value later. In both cases, however, a constant's value cannot be changed after the first assignment. This book follows the convention of initializing all constants when they are declared.

When you declare a named constant, program maintenance becomes easier. For example, if the value of the sales tax changes from 0.06 to 0.07 in the future, and you have declared a named constant SALES_TAX_RATE, you only need to change the value assigned to the named constant at the beginning of the program, then retranslate the program into machine language, and all references to SALES_TAX_RATE are automatically updated. If you used the unnamed literal 0.06 instead, you would have to search for every instance of the value and replace it with the new one. Additionally, if the literal 0.06 was used in other calculations within the program (for example, as a discount rate), you would have to carefully select which instances of the value to alter, and you would be likely to make a mistake.

Sometimes, using unnamed literal constants is appropriate in a program, especially if their meaning is clear to most readers. For example, in a program that calculates half of a value by dividing by two, you might choose to use the unnamed literal 2 instead of incurring the extra time and memory costs of creating a named constant HALF and assigning 2 to it. Extra costs that result from adding variables or instructions to a program are known as **overhead**.

TWO TRUTHS & A LIE

Declaring and Using Variables and Constants

1. A variable's data type describes the kind of values the variable can hold and the types of operations that can be performed with it.

2. If name is a string variable, then the statement set name = "Ed" is valid.

3. The operand to the right of an assignment operator must be a name that represents a memory address.

The false statement is #3. The operand to the left of an assignment operator must be a name that represents a memory address—the name of the location where the result will be stored. Any operand on the right of an assignment operator can be a memory address (a variable) or a constant.

Performing Arithmetic Operations

Most programming languages use the following standard arithmetic operators:

+ (plus sign)—addition

− (minus sign)—subtraction

* (asterisk)—multiplication

/ (slash)—division

Many languages also support additional operators that calculate the remainder after division, raise a number to a higher power, manipulate individual bits stored within a value, and perform other operations.

Each of the standard arithmetic operators is a binary operator; that is, each requires an expression on both sides. For example, the following statement adds two test scores and assigns the sum to a variable named totalScore:

totalScore = test1 + test2

The following adds 10 to totalScore and stores the result in totalScore:

totalScore = totalScore + 10

In other words, this example increases the value of totalScore. This last example looks odd in algebra because it might appear that the value of totalScore and totalScore plus 10 are equivalent. You must remember that the equal sign is the assignment operator, and that the statement is actually taking the original value of totalScore, adding 10 to it, and assigning the result to the memory address on the left of the operator, which is totalScore.

In programming languages, you can combine arithmetic statements. When you do, every operator follows **rules of precedence** (also called the **order of operations**) that dictate the order in which operations in the same statement are carried out. The rules of precedence for the basic arithmetic statements are as follows:

- Expressions within parentheses are evaluated first. If there are multiple sets of parentheses, the expression within the innermost parentheses is evaluated first.
- Multiplication and division are evaluated next, from left to right.
- Addition and subtraction are evaluated next, from left to right.

The assignment operator has a very low precedence. Therefore, in a statement such as d = e * f + g, the operations on the right of the assignment operator are always performed before the final assignment to the variable on the left.

When you learn a specific programming language, you will learn about all the operators that are used in that language. Many programming language books contain a table that specifies the relative precedence of every operator used in the language.

For example, consider the following two arithmetic statements:

firstAnswer = 2 + 3 * 4
secondAnswer = (2 + 3) * 4

After these statements execute, the value of firstAnswer is 14. According to the rules of precedence, multiplication is carried out before addition, so 3 is multiplied by 4, giving 12, and then 2 and 12 are added, and 14 is assigned to firstAnswer. The value of secondAnswer, however, is 20, because the parentheses force the contained addition operation to be performed first. The 2 and 3 are added, producing 5, and then 5 is multiplied by 4, producing 20.

Forgetting about the rules of arithmetic precedence, or forgetting to add parentheses when you need them, can cause logical errors that are difficult to find in programs. For example, the following statement might appear to average two test scores:

average = score1 + score2 / 2

action (watching a video), take care of some other task (for example, making a sandwich), and then return to the main task exactly where you left off.

The process of breaking down a large program into modules is **modularization**; computer scientists also call it **functional decomposition**. You are never required to modularize a large program to make it run on a computer, but there are at least three reasons for doing so:

- Modularization provides abstraction.
- Modularization allows multiple programmers to work on a problem.
- Modularization allows you to reuse work more easily.

Modularization Provides Abstraction

One reason that modularized programs are easier to understand is that they enable a programmer to see the "big picture." **Abstraction** is the process of paying attention to important properties while ignoring nonessential details. Abstraction is selective ignorance. Life would be tedious without abstraction. For example, you can create a list of things to accomplish today:

```
Do laundry
Call Aunt Nan
Start term paper
```

Without abstraction, the list of chores would begin:

```
Pick up laundry basket
Put laundry basket in car
Drive to Laundromat
Get out of car with basket
Walk into Laundromat
Set basket down
Find quarters for washing machine
... and so on.
```

You might list a dozen more steps before you finish the laundry and move on to the second chore on your original list. If you had to consider every small, low-level detail of every task in your day, you would probably never make it out of bed in the morning. Using a higher-level, more abstract list makes your day manageable. Abstraction makes complex tasks look simple.

 Abstract artists create paintings in which they see only the big picture—color and form—and ignore the details. Abstraction has a similar meaning among programmers.

Likewise, some level of abstraction occurs in every computer program. Fifty years ago, a programmer had to understand the low-level circuitry instructions the computer used. But now, newer high-level programming languages allow you to use English-like vocabulary in which one broad statement corresponds to dozens of machine instructions. No matter which high-level programming language you use, if you display a message on the monitor, you are never required to understand how a monitor works to create each pixel on the screen. You write an instruction like `output message` and the details of the hardware operations are handled for you by the operating system.

Modules provide another way to achieve abstraction. For example, a payroll program can call a module named `computeFederalWithholdingTax()`. When you call this module from your program, you use one statement; the module itself might contain dozens of statements. You can write the mathematical details of the module later, someone else can write them, or you can purchase them from an outside source. When you plan your main payroll program, your only concern is that a federal withholding tax will have to be calculated; you save the details for later.

Modularization Allows Multiple Programmers to Work on a Problem

When you dissect any large task into modules, you gain the ability to more easily divide the task among various people. Rarely does a single programmer write a commercial program that you buy. Consider any word-processing, spreadsheet, or database program you have used. Each program has so many options, and responds to user selections in so many possible ways, that it would take years for a single programmer to write all the instructions. Professional software developers can write new programs in weeks or months, instead of years, by dividing large programs into modules and assigning each module to an individual programmer or team.

Modularization Allows You to Reuse Work

If a module is useful and well written, you may want to use it more than once within a program or in other programs. For example, a routine that verifies the validity of dates is useful in many programs written for a business. (For example, a month value is valid if it is not lower than 1 or higher than 12, a day value is valid if it is not lower than 1 or higher than 31 if the month is 1, and so on.) If a computerized personnel file contains each employee's birth date, hire date, last promotion date, and termination date, the date-validation module can be used four times with each employee record. Other programs in an organization can also use the module; these programs might ship customer orders, plan employees' birthday parties, or calculate when loan payments should be made. If you write the date-checking instructions so they are entangled with other statements in a program, they are difficult to extract and reuse. On the other hand, if you place the instructions in their own module, the unit is easy to use and portable to other applications. The feature of modular programs that allows individual modules to be used in a variety of applications is **reusability**.

You can find many real-world examples of reusability. When you build a house, you don't invent plumbing and heating systems; you incorporate systems with proven designs. This certainly reduces the time and effort it takes to build a house. The plumbing and electrical systems you choose are in service in other houses, so they have been tested under a variety of circumstances, increasing their reliability. **Reliability** is the feature of programs that assures you a module has been proven to function correctly. Reliable software saves time and money. If you create the functional components of your programs as stand-alone modules and test them in your current programs, much of the work will already be done when you use the modules in future applications.

> **TWO TRUTHS & A LIE**
>
> Understanding the Advantages of Modularization
>
> 1. Modularization eliminates abstraction, a feature that makes programs more confusing.
> 2. Modularization makes it easier for multiple programmers to work on a problem.
> 3. Modularization allows you to reuse work more easily.
>
> The false statement is #1. Modularization enables abstraction, which allows you to see the big picture.

Modularizing a Program

Most programs consist of a **main program**, which contains the basic steps, or the **mainline logic**, of the program. The main program then accesses modules that provide more refined details.

When you create a module, you include the following:

- A header—The **module header** includes the module identifier and possibly other necessary identifying information.
- A body—The **module body** contains all the statements in the module.
- A `return` statement—The **module return statement** marks the end of the module and identifies the point at which control returns to the program or module that called the module. In most programming languages, if you do not include a `return` statement at the end of a module, the logic will still return. However, this book follows the convention of explicitly including a `return` statement with every module.

Naming a module is similar to naming a variable. The rules for naming modules are slightly different in every programming language, but in this text, module names follow the same general rules used for variable identifiers:

- Module names must be one word and start with a letter.
- Module names should have some meaning.

Although it is not a requirement of any programming language, it frequently makes sense to use a verb as all or part of a module's name, because modules perform some action. Typical module names begin with action words such as `get`, `calculate`, and `display`. When you program in visual languages that use screen components such as buttons and text boxes, the module names frequently contain verbs representing user actions, such as `click` or `drag`.

Additionally, in this text, module names are followed by a set of parentheses. This will help you distinguish module names from variable names. This style corresponds to the way modules are named in many programming languages, such as Java, C++, and C#.

As you learn more about modules in specific programming languages, you will find that you sometimes place variable names within the parentheses of module names. Any variables enclosed in the parentheses contain information you want to send to the module. For now, the parentheses at the end of module names will be empty in this book.

When a main program wants to use a module, it calls the module. A module can call another module, and the called module can call another. The number of chained calls is limited only by the amount of memory available on your computer. In this book, the flowchart symbol used to call a module is a rectangle with a bar across the top. You place the name of the module you are calling inside the rectangle.

Some programmers use a rectangle with stripes down each side to represent a module in a flowchart, and this book uses that convention if a module is external to a program. For example, prewritten, built-in modules that generate random numbers, compute standard trigonometric functions, and sort values often are external to your programs. However, if the module is being created as part of the program, the book uses a rectangle with a single stripe across the top.

In a flowchart, you draw each module separately with its own sentinel symbols. The beginning sentinel contains the name of the module. This name must be identical to the name used in the calling program. The ending sentinel contains `return`, which indicates that when the module ends, the logical progression of statements will exit the module and return to the calling program. Similarly, in pseudocode, you start each module with its name and end with a `return` statement; the module name and `return` statements are vertically aligned and all the module statements are indented between them.

For example, consider the program in Figure 2-3, which does not contain any modules. It accepts a customer's name and balance due as input and produces a bill. At the top of the bill, the company's name and address are displayed on three lines, which are followed by the customer's name and balance due. To display the company name and address, you can simply include three `output` statements in the mainline logic of a program, as shown in Figure 2-3, or you can modularize the program by creating both the mainline logic and a `displayAddressInfo()` module, as shown in Figure 2-4.

Modularizing a Program

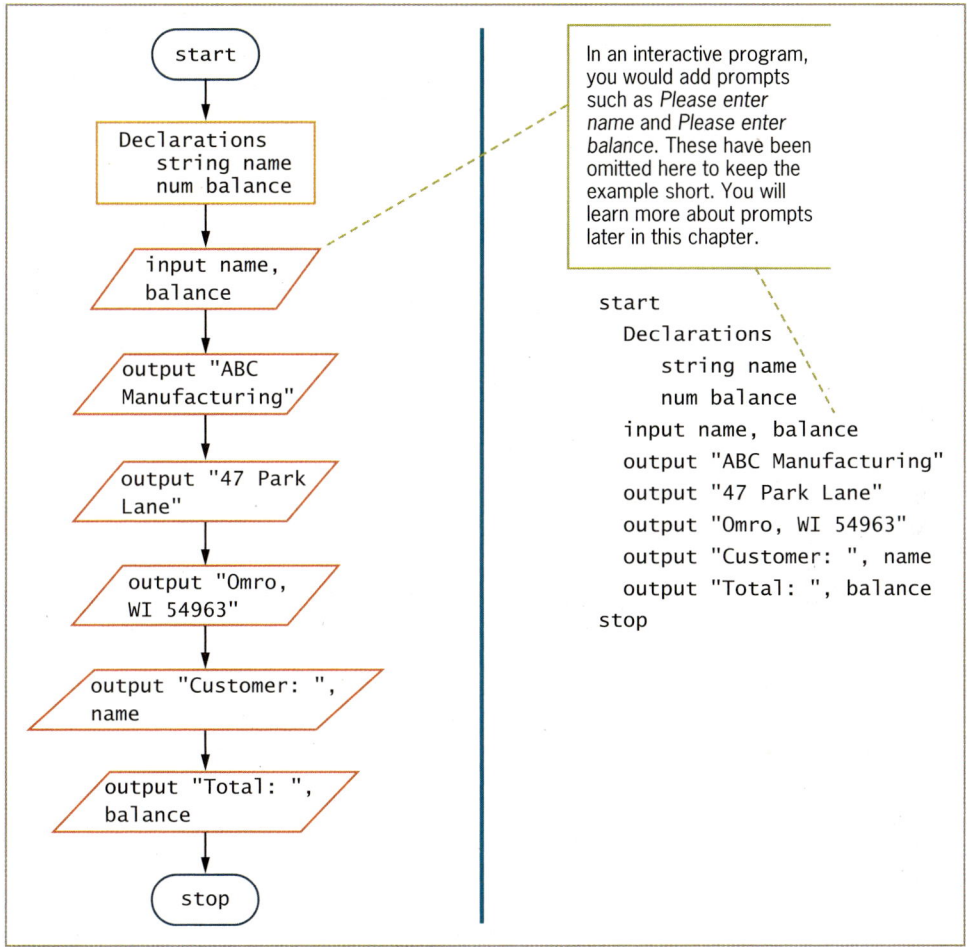

Figure 2-3 Program that produces a bill using only main program

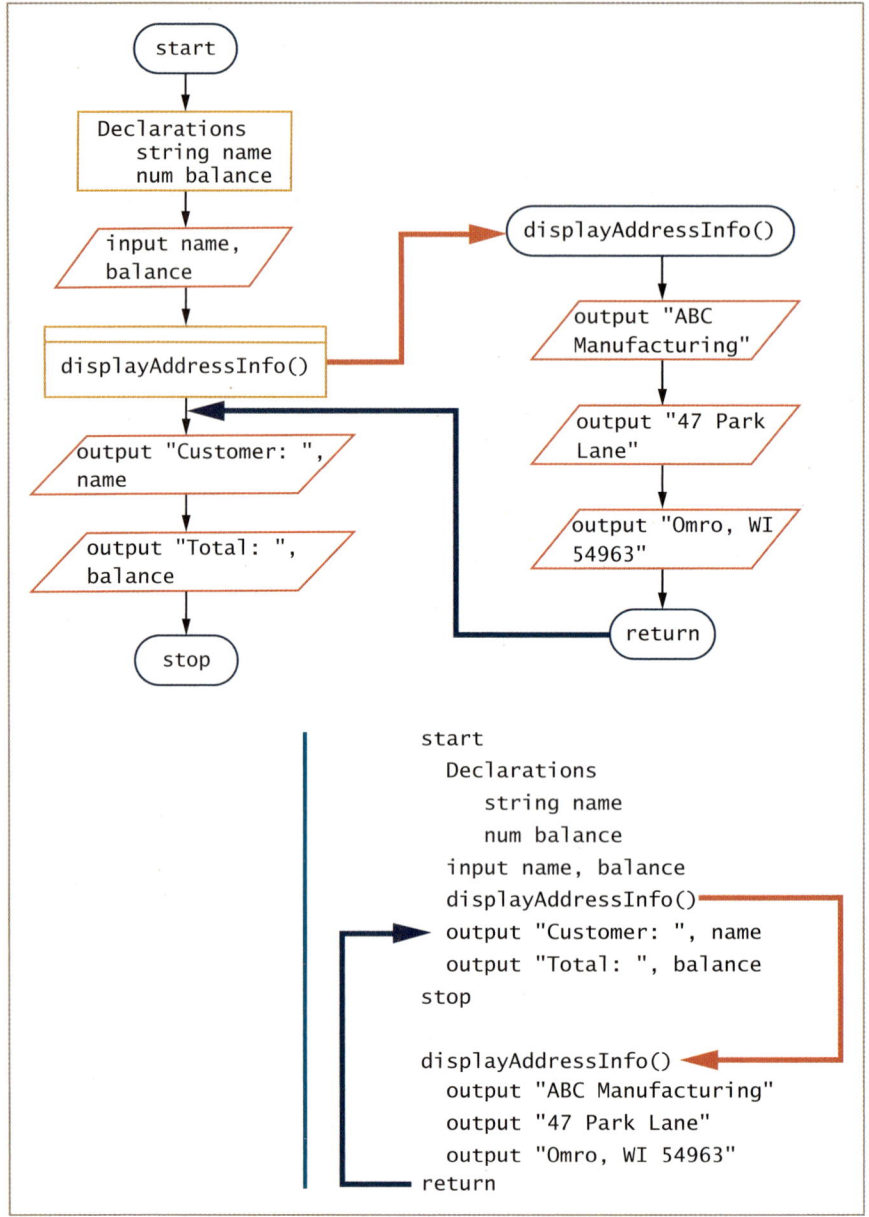

Figure 2-4 Program that produces a bill using main program that calls `displayAddressInfo()` module

When the `displayAddressInfo()` module is called in Figure 2-4, logic transfers from the main program to the `displayAddressInfo()` module, as shown by the large red arrow in both the flowchart and the pseudocode. There, each module statement executes in turn before logical control is transferred back to the main program, where it continues with the statement that follows the module call, as shown by the large blue arrow. Programmers say the statements that are contained in a module have been **encapsulated**.

Neither of the programs in Figures 2-3 and 2-4 is superior to the other in terms of functionality; both perform exactly the same tasks in the same order. However, you may prefer the modularized version of the program for at least two reasons:

- First, the main program remains short and easy to follow because it contains just one statement to call the module, rather than three separate `output` statements to perform the work of the module.
- Second, a module is easily reusable. After you create the address information module, you can use it in any application that needs the company's name and address. In other words, you do the work once, and then you can use the module many times.

A potential drawback to creating modules and moving between them is the overhead incurred. The computer keeps track of the correct memory address to which it should return after executing a module by recording the memory address in a location known as the **stack**. This process requires a small amount of computer time and resources. In most cases, the advantage to creating modules far outweighs the small amount of overhead required.

Determining when to modularize a program does not depend on a fixed set of rules; it requires experience and insight. Programmers do follow some guidelines when deciding how far to break down modules or how much to put in each of them. Some companies may have arbitrary rules, such as "a module's instructions should never take more than a page," or "a module should never have more than 30 statements," or "never have a module with only one statement." Rather than use such arbitrary rules, a better policy is to place together statements that contribute to one specific task. The more the statements contribute to the same job, the greater the **functional cohesion** of the module. A module that checks the validity of a date variable's value, or one that asks a user for a value and accepts it as input, is considered cohesive. A module that checks date validity, deducts insurance premiums, and computes federal withholding tax for an employee would be less cohesive.

Chapter 9 of the comprehensive version of this book provides more information on designing modules for high cohesion. It also explores the topic of *coupling*, which is a measure of how much modules depend on each other.

Watch the video *Modularizing a Program*.

Declaring Variables and Constants within Modules

You can place any statements within modules, including input, processing, and output statements. You also can include variable and constant declarations within modules. For example, you might decide to modify the billing program in Figure 2-4 so it looks like the one

CHAPTER 2   Elements of High-Quality Programs

in Figure 2-5. In this version of the program, three named constants that hold the three lines of company data are declared within the `displayAddressInfo()` module. (See shading.)

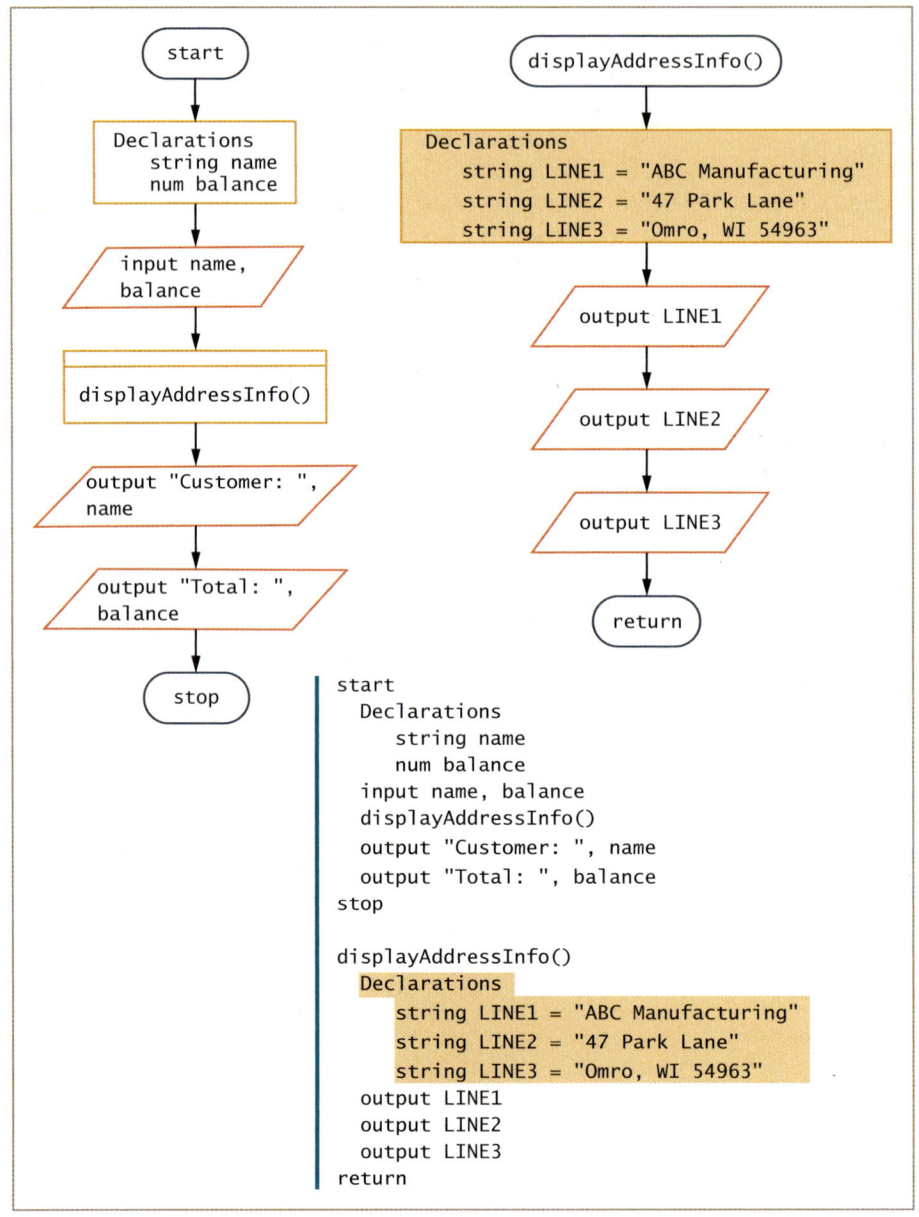

Figure 2-5   The billing program with constants declared within the module

The variables and constants declared in a module are usable only within the module. Programmers say the data items are **visible** only within the module in which they are declared. That means the program only recognizes them there. Programmers say that variables and constants declared within a module are **in scope** only within that module. Programmers also say that variables and constants are **local** to the module in which they are declared. In other words, when the strings LINE1, LINE2, and LINE3 are declared in the displayAddressInfo() module in Figure 2-5, they are not recognized and cannot be used by the main program.

One of the motivations for creating modules is that separate modules are easily reusable in multiple programs. If the displayAddressInfo() module will be used by several programs within the organization, it makes sense that the definitions for its variables and constants must come with it. This makes the modules more **portable**; that is, they are self-contained units that are easily transported.

Besides local variables and constants, you can create global variables and constants. **Global** variables and constants are known to the entire program; they are said to be declared at the **program level**. That means they are visible to and usable in all the modules called by the program. The opposite is not true—variables and constants declared within a module are not usable elsewhere; they are visible only to that module. (For example, in Figure 2-5, the main program variables name and balance are global variables, although in this case they are not used in any modules.) For the most part, this book will use only global variables and constants so that the examples are easier to follow and you can concentrate on the main logic.

Many programmers do not approve of using global variables and constants. They are used here so you can more easily understand modularization before you learn the techniques of sending local variables from one module to another. Chapter 9 of the comprehensive version of this book will describe how you can make every variable local.

Understanding the Most Common Configuration for Mainline Logic

In Chapter 1, you learned that a procedural program contains procedures that follow one another in sequence. The mainline logic of almost every procedural computer program can follow a general structure that consists of three distinct parts:

1. **Housekeeping tasks** include any steps you must perform at the beginning of a program to get ready for the rest of the program. They can include tasks such as variable and constant declarations, displaying instructions to users, displaying report headings, opening any files the program requires, and inputting the first piece of data.

Inputting the first data item is always part of the housekeeping module. You will learn the theory behind this practice in Chapter 3. Chapter 7 covers file handling, including what it means to open and close a file.

2. **Detail loop tasks** do the core work of the program. When a program processes many records, detail loop tasks execute repeatedly for each set of input data until there are no more. For example, in a payroll program, the same set of calculations is executed repeatedly until a check has been produced for each employee.

3. **End-of-job tasks** are the steps you take at the end of the program to finish the application. You can call these finish-up or clean-up tasks. They might include displaying totals or other final messages and closing any open files.

Figure 2-6 shows the relationship of these three typical program parts. Notice how the housekeeping() and endOfJob() tasks are executed just once, but the detailLoop() tasks repeat as long as the eof condition has not been met. The flowchart uses a flowline to show how the detailLoop() module repeats; the pseudocode uses the words while and endwhile to contain statements that execute in a loop. You will learn more about the while and endwhile terms in subsequent chapters; for now, understand that they are a way of expressing repeated actions.

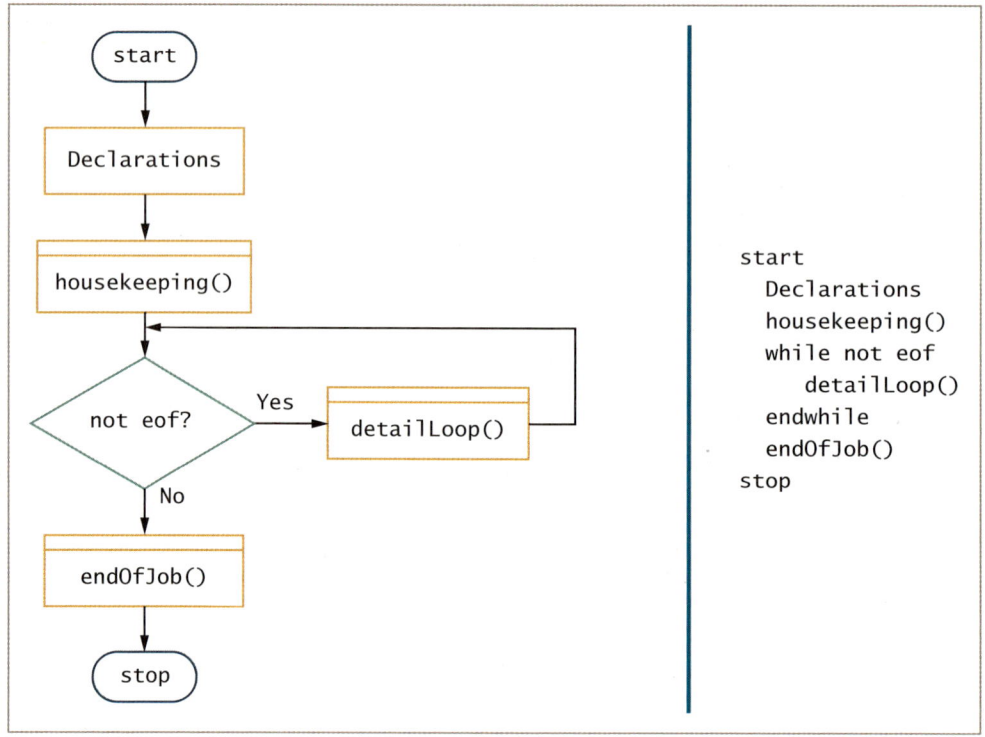

Figure 2-6 Flowchart and pseudocode of mainline logic for a typical procedural program

Modularizing a Program

Many everyday tasks follow the three-module format just described. For example, a candy factory opens in the morning, and the machines are started and filled with ingredients. These housekeeping tasks occur just once at the start of the day. Then, repeatedly during the day, candy is manufactured. This process might take many steps, each of which occurs many times. These are the steps in the detail loop. Then, at the end of the day, the machines are cleaned and shut down. These are the end-of-job tasks.

Not all programs take the format of the logic shown in Figure 2-6, but many do. Keep this general configuration in mind as you think about how you might organize many programs. For example, Figure 2-7 shows a sample payroll report for a small company. A user enters employee names until there are no more to enter, at which point the user enters *XXX*. As long as the entered name is not *XXX*, the user enters the employee's weekly gross pay. Deductions are computed as a flat 25 percent of the gross pay, and the statistics for each employee are output. The user enters another name, and as long as it is not *XXX*, the process continues. Examine the logic in Figure 2-8 to identify the components in the housekeeping, detail loop, and end-of-job tasks. You will learn more about the payroll report program in the next few chapters. For now, concentrate on the big picture of how a typical application works.

Payroll Report

Name	Gross	Deductions	Net
Andrews	1000.00	250.00	750.00
Brown	1400.00	350.00	1050.00
Carter	1275.00	318.75	956.25
Young	1100.00	275.00	825.00

***End of report

Figure 2-7 Sample payroll report

CHAPTER 2 Elements of High-Quality Programs

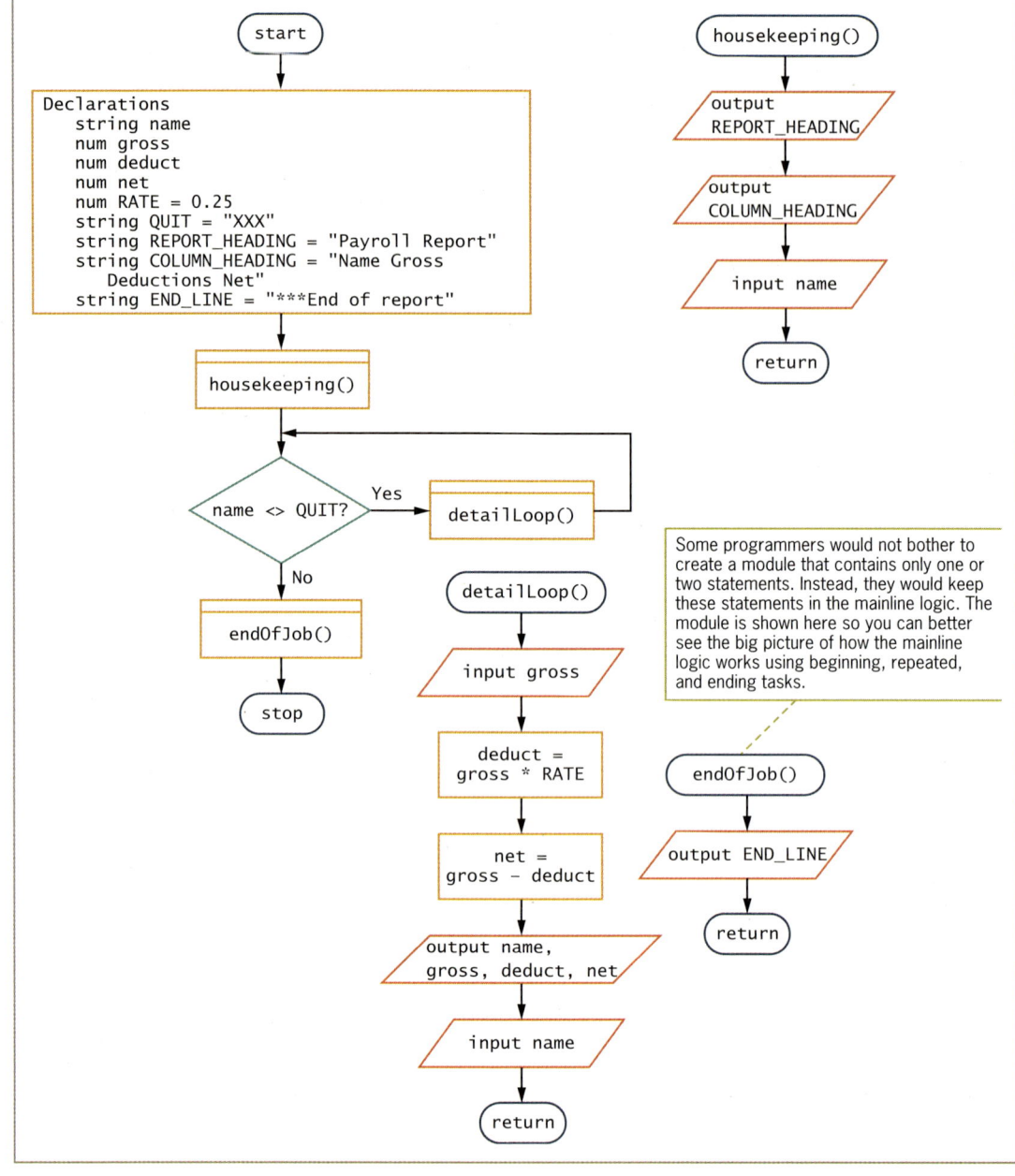

Figure 2-8 Logic for payroll report

Creating Hierarchy Charts

> ### TWO TRUTHS & A LIE
> #### Modularizing a Program
>
> 1. A calling program calls a module's name when it wants to use the module.
> 2. Whenever a main program calls a module, the logic transfers to the module; when the module ends, the program ends.
> 3. Housekeeping tasks include any steps you must perform just once at the beginning of a program to get ready for the rest of the program.
>
> The false statement is #2. When a module ends, the logical flow transfers back to the main calling program and resumes where it left off.

Creating Hierarchy Charts

You may have seen hierarchy charts for organizations, such as the one in Figure 2-9. The chart shows who reports to whom, not when or how often they report.

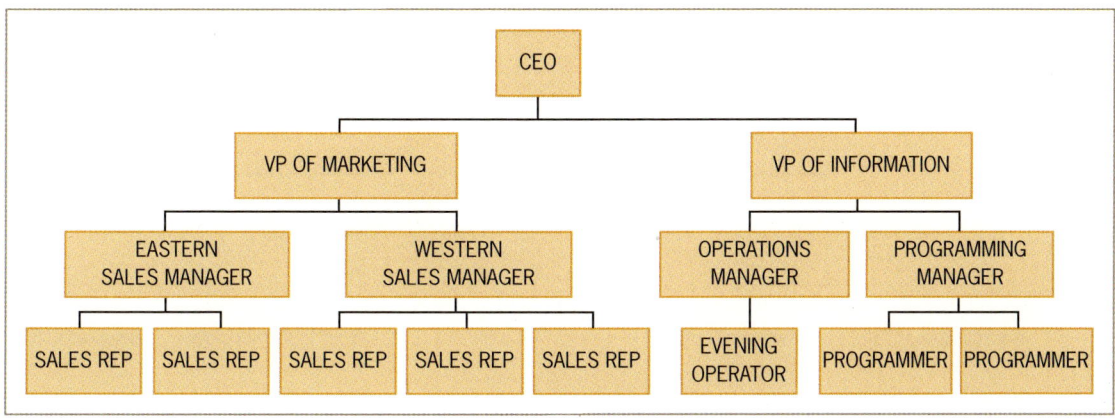

Figure 2-9 An organizational hierarchy chart

When a program has several modules calling other modules, programmers often use a program **hierarchy chart** that operates in a similar manner to show the overall picture of how modules are related to one another. A hierarchy chart does not tell you what tasks are to be performed *within* a module, *when* the modules are called, *how* a module executes, or *why* they are called—that information is in the flowchart or pseudocode. A hierarchy chart tells you only *which* modules exist within a program and *which* modules call others. The hierarchy chart for the program in Figure 2-8 looks like Figure 2-10. It shows that the main module calls three others—housekeeping(), detailLoop(), and endOfJob().

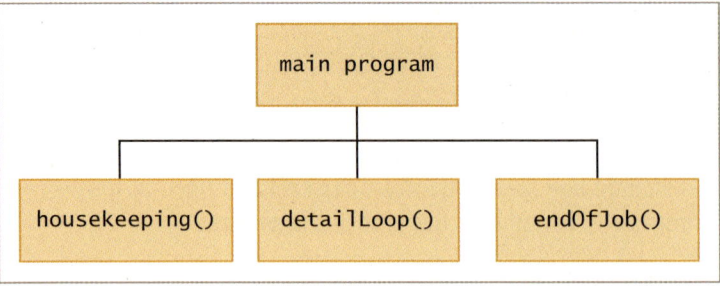

Figure 2-10   Hierarchy chart of payroll report program in Figure 2-8

Figure 2-11 shows an example of a hierarchy chart for the billing program of a mail-order company. The hierarchy chart is for a more complicated program, but like the payroll report chart in Figure 2-10, it supplies module names and a general overview of the tasks to be performed, without specifying any details.

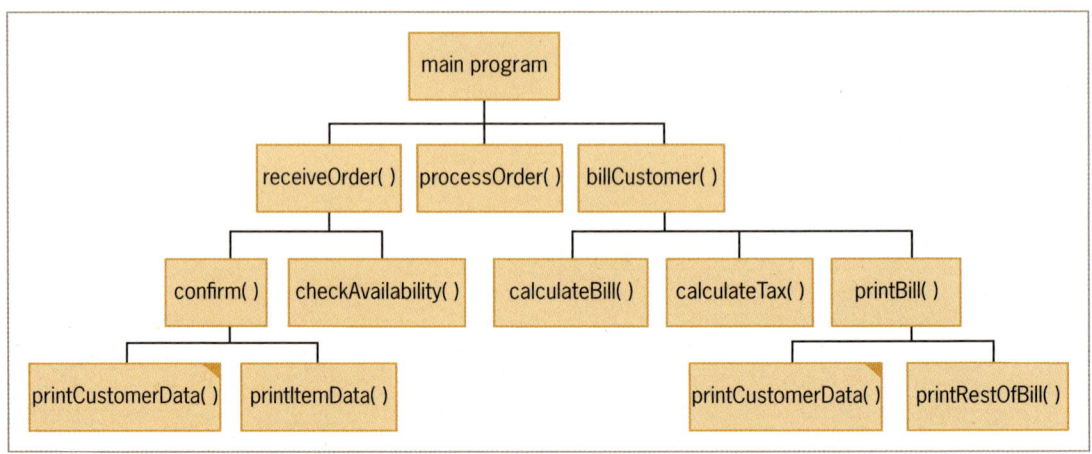

Figure 2-11   Billing program hierarchy chart

Because program modules are reusable, a specific module may be called from several locations within a program. For example, in the billing program hierarchy chart in Figure 2-11, you can see that the printCustomerData() module is used twice. By convention, you blacken a corner of each box that represents a module used more than once. This action alerts readers that any change to this module could have consequences in multiple locations.

Features of Good Program Design

A hierarchy chart can be both a planning tool for developing the overall relationship of program modules before you write them and a documentation tool to help others see how modules are related after a program is written. For example, if a tax law changes, a programmer might be asked to rewrite the `calculateTax()` module in the billing program diagrammed in Figure 2-11. As the programmer changes the `calculateTax()` module, the hierarchy chart shows other dependent modules that might be affected. A hierarchy chart is useful for getting the big picture in a complex program.

Hierarchy charts are used in procedural programming, but other types of diagrams frequently are used in object-oriented environments. Chapter 13 of the comprehensive edition of this book describes the Unified Modeling Language, which is a set of diagrams you use to describe a system.

TWO TRUTHS & A LIE
Creating Hierarchy Charts

1. You can use a hierarchy chart to illustrate modules' relationships.
2. A hierarchy chart tells you what tasks are to be performed within a module.
3. A hierarchy chart tells you only which modules call other modules.

The false statement is #2. A hierarchy chart tells you nothing about tasks performed within a module; it only depicts how modules are related to each other.

Features of Good Program Design

As your programs become larger and more complicated, the need for good planning and design increases. Think of an application you use, such as a word processor or a spreadsheet. The number and variety of user options are staggering. Not only would it be impossible for a single programmer to write such an application, but without thorough planning and design, the components would never work together properly. Ideally, each program module you design needs to work well as a stand-alone component and as an element of larger systems. Just as a house with poor plumbing or a car with bad brakes is fatally flawed, a computer-based application can be highly functional only if each component is designed well. Walking through your program's logic on paper (called desk-checking, as you learned in Chapter 1) is an important step to achieving superior programs. Additionally, you can implement several design features while creating programs that are easier to write and maintain. To create good programs, you should do the following:

- Use program comments where appropriate.
- Choose identifiers thoughtfully.

- Strive to design clear statements within your programs and modules.
- Write clear prompts and echo input.
- Continue to maintain good programming habits as you develop your programming skills.

Using Program Comments

When you write programs, you often might want to insert program comments. **Program comments** are written explanations that are not part of the program logic but that serve as documentation for readers of the program. In other words, they are nonexecuting statements that help readers understand programming statements. Readers might include users who help you test the program and other programmers who might have to modify your programs in the future. Even you, as the program's author, will appreciate comments when you make future modifications and forget why you constructed a statement in a certain way.

The syntax used to create program comments differs among programming languages. This book starts comments in pseudocode with two front slashes. For example, Figure 2-12 contains comments that explain the origins and purposes of variables in a real estate program.

Program comments are a type of **internal documentation**. This term distinguishes them from supporting documents outside the program, which are called **external documentation**. Appendix D discusses other types of documentation.

```
Declarations
   num sqFeet
      // sqFeet is an estimate provided by the seller of the property
   num pricePerFoot
      // pricePerFoot is determined by current market conditions
   num lotPremium
      // lotPremium depends on amenities such as whether lot is waterfront
```

Figure 2-12 Pseudocode that declares variables and includes comments

In a flowchart, you can use an annotation symbol to hold information that expands on what is stored within another flowchart symbol. An **annotation symbol** is most often represented by a three-sided box that is connected to the step it references by a dashed line. Annotation symbols are used to hold comments or sometimes statements that are too long to fit neatly into a flowchart symbol. For example, Figure 2-13 shows how a programmer might use some annotation symbols in a flowchart for a payroll program.

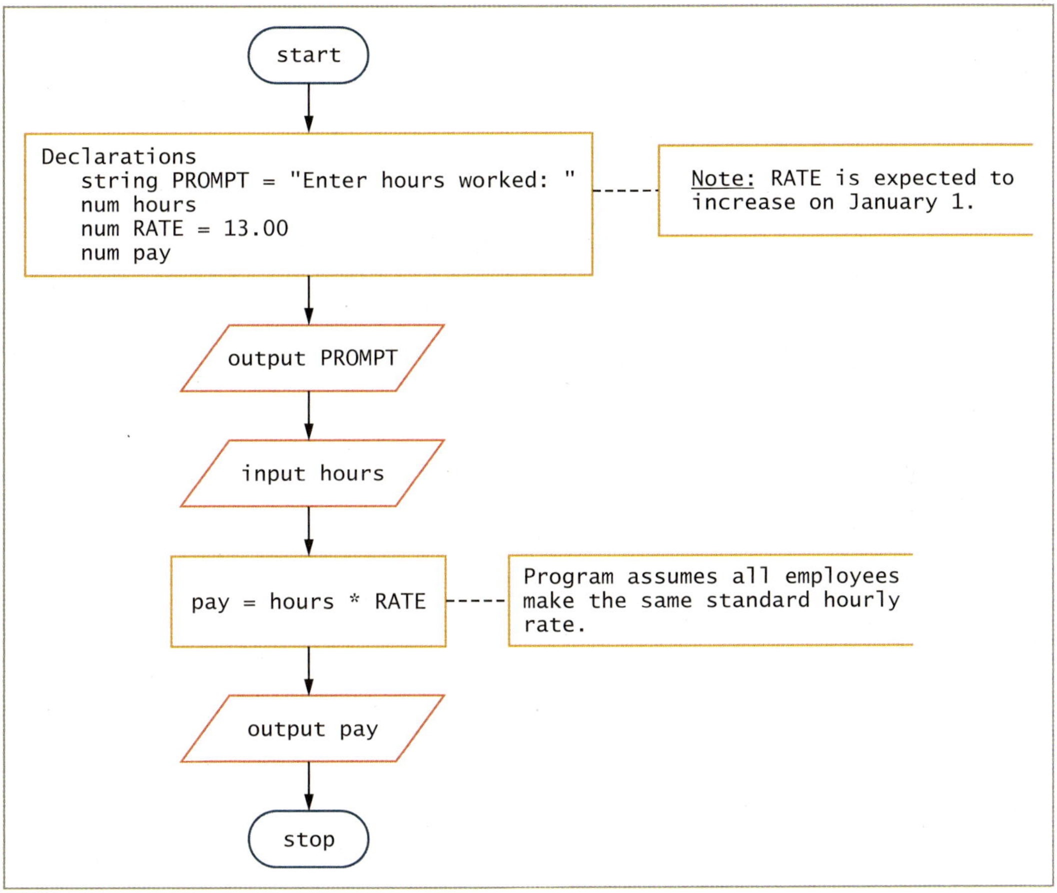

Features of Good Program Design

```
                          ┌─────────┐
                          │  start  │
                          └────┬────┘
                               ▼
┌──────────────────────────────────────────┐         ┌──────────────────────────────┐
│ Declarations                             │         │ Note: RATE is expected to    │
│   string PROMPT = "Enter hours worked: " │-------- │ increase on January 1.       │
│   num hours                              │         └──────────────────────────────┘
│   num RATE = 13.00                       │
│   num pay                                │
└──────────────────┬───────────────────────┘
                   ▼
            ╱ output PROMPT ╱
                   │
                   ▼
            ╱ input hours ╱
                   │
                   ▼
        ┌──────────────────────┐               ┌──────────────────────────────────┐
        │ pay = hours * RATE   │---------------│ Program assumes all employees    │
        └──────────┬───────────┘               │ make the same standard hourly    │
                   │                           │ rate.                            │
                   ▼                           └──────────────────────────────────┘
            ╱ output pay ╱
                   │
                   ▼
               ┌───────┐
               │ stop  │
               └───────┘
```

Figure 2-13   Flowchart that includes annotation symbols

You probably will use comments in your coded programs more frequently than you use them in pseudocode or flowcharts. For one thing, flowcharts and pseudocode are more English-like than the code in some languages, so your statements might be less cryptic. Also, your comments will remain in the program as part of the program documentation, but your planning tools are likely to be discarded once the program goes into production.

Including program comments is not necessary to create a working program, but comments can help you to remember the purpose of variables or to explain complicated calculations. Some students do not like to include comments in their programs because it takes time to type them and they aren't part of the "real" program, but the programs you write in the future probably will require some comments. When you acquire your first programming job and modify a program written by another programmer, you will appreciate well-placed comments that explain complicated sections of the code.

A drawback to comments is that they must be kept current as a program is modified. Outdated comments can provide misleading information about a program's status.

Choosing Identifiers

The selection of good identifiers is an often-overlooked element in program design. When you write programs, you choose identifiers for variables, constants, and modules. You learned the rules for naming variables and modules earlier in this chapter: Each must be a single word with no embedded spaces and must start with a letter. Those simple rules provide a lot of leeway in naming program elements, but not all identifiers are equally good. Choosing good identifiers simplifies your programming job and makes it easier for others to understand your work.

Some general guidelines include the following:

- Although not required in any programming language, it usually makes sense to give a variable or constant a name that is a noun (or a combination of an adjective and noun) because it represents a thing. Similarly, it makes sense to give a module an identifier that is a verb, or a combined verb and noun, because a module takes action.

- Use meaningful names. Creating a data item named `someData` or a module named `firstModule()` makes a program cryptic. Not only will others find it hard to read your programs, but you will forget the purpose of these identifiers even within your own programs. All programmers occasionally use short, nondescriptive names such as `x` or `temp` in a quick program; however, in most cases, data and module names should be meaningful. Programmers refer to programs that contain meaningful names as **self-documenting**. This means that even without further documentation, the program code explains itself to readers.

- Use pronounceable names. A variable name like `pzf` is neither pronounceable nor meaningful. A name that looks meaningful when you write it might not be as meaningful when someone else reads it; for instance, `preparead()` might mean "Prepare ad" to you, but "Prep a read" to others. Look at your names critically to make sure they can be pronounced. Very standard abbreviations do not have to be pronounceable. For example, most businesspeople would interpret `ssn` as a Social Security number.

- Don't forget that not all programmers share your culture. An abbreviation whose meaning seems obvious to you might be cryptic to someone in a different part of the world, or even a different part of your country. For example, you might name a variable `roi` to hold a value for *return on investment*, but a French-speaking person might interpret the meaning as *king*.

- Be judicious in your use of abbreviations. You can save a few keystrokes when creating a module called `getStat()`, but is the module's purpose to find the state in which a city is located, input some statistics, or determine the status of some variables? Similarly, is a variable named `fn` meant to hold a first name, file number, or something else? Abbreviations can also confuse people in different lines of work: AKA might suggest a sorority (Alpha Kappa Alpha) to a college administrator, a registry (American Kennel Association) to a dog breeder, or an alias (also known as) to a police detective.

Features of Good Program Design

To save typing time when you develop a program, you can use a short name like `efn`. After the program operates correctly, you can use a text editor's Search and Replace feature to replace your coded name with a more meaningful name such as `employeeFirstName`.

Many IDEs support an automatic statement-completion feature that saves typing time. After the first time you use a name like `employeeFirstName`, you need to type only the first few letters before the compiler editor offers a list of available names from which to choose. The list is constructed from all the names you have used that begin with the same characters.

- Usually, avoid digits in a name. Zeroes get confused with the letter O, and the lowercase letter *l* is misread as the numeral 1. Of course, use your judgment: `budgetFor2014` probably will not be misinterpreted.

- Use the system your language allows to separate words in long, multiword variable names. For example, if the programming language you use allows dashes or underscores, then use a module name like `initialize-data()` or `initialize_data()`, which is easier to read than `initializedata()`. Another option is to use camel casing to create an identifier such as `initializeData()`. If you use a language that is case sensitive, it is legal but confusing to use variable names that differ only in case. For example, if a single program contains `empName`, `EmpName`, and `Empname`, confusion is sure to follow.

- Consider including a form of the verb *to be*, such as *is* or *are*, in names for variables that are intended to hold a status. For example, use `isFinished` as a string variable that holds a Y or N to indicate whether a file is exhausted. The shorter name `finished` is more likely to be confused with a module that executes when a program is done. (Many languages support a Boolean data type, which you assign to variables meant to hold only true or false. Using a form of *to be* in identifiers for Boolean variables is appropriate.)

- Many programmers follow the convention of naming constants using all uppercase letters, inserting underscores between words for readability. In this chapter you saw examples such as `SALES_TAX_RATE`.

- Organizations sometimes enforce different rules for programmers to follow when naming program components. It is your responsibility to find out the conventions used in your organization and to adhere to them.

Programmers sometimes create a **data dictionary**, which is a list of every variable name used in a program, along with its type, size, and description. When a data dictionary is created, it becomes part of the program documentation.

When you begin to write programs, the process of determining what data variables, constants, and modules you need and what to name them all might seem overwhelming. The design process is crucial, however. When you acquire your first professional programming assignment, the design process might very well be completed already. Most likely, your first assignment will be to write or modify one small member module of a much larger application. The more the original programmers stuck to naming guidelines, the better the original design was, and the easier your job of modification will be.

Designing Clear Statements

In addition to using program comments and selecting good identifiers, you can use the following tactics to contribute to the clarity of the statements within your programs:

- Avoid confusing line breaks.
- Use temporary variables to clarify long statements.

Avoiding Confusing Line Breaks

Some older programming languages require that program statements be placed in specific columns. Most modern programming languages are free-form; you can arrange your lines of code any way you see fit. As in real life, with freedom comes responsibility; when you have flexibility in arranging your lines of code, you must take care to make sure your meaning is clear. With free-form code, programmers are allowed to place two or three statements on a line, or, conversely, to spread a single statement across multiple lines. Both make programs harder to read. All the pseudocode examples in this book use appropriate, clear spacing and line breaks.

Using Temporary Variables to Clarify Long Statements

When you need several mathematical operations to determine a result, consider using a series of temporary variables to hold intermediate results. A **temporary variable** (or a **work variable**) is not used for input or output, but instead is just a working variable that you use during a program's execution. For example, Figure 2-14 shows two ways to calculate a value for a real estate salespersonCommission variable. Each module achieves the same result—the salesperson's commission is based on the square feet multiplied by the price per square foot, plus any premium for a lot with special features, such as a wooded or waterfront lot. However, the second example uses two temporary variables: basePropertyPrice and totalSalePrice. When the computation is broken down into less complicated, individual steps, it is easier to see how the total price is calculated. In calculations with even more computation steps, performing the arithmetic in stages would become increasingly helpful.

```
// Using a single statement to compute commission
salespersonCommission = (sqFeet * pricePerFoot + lotPremium) * commissionRate

// Using multiple statements to compute commission
basePropertyPrice = sqFeet * pricePerFoot
totalSalePrice = basePropertyPrice + lotPremium
salespersonCommission = totalSalePrice * commissionRate
```

Figure 2-14   Two ways of achieving the same salespersonCommission result

Features of Good Program Design

 Programmers might say using temporary variables, like the second example in Figure 2-14, is *cheap*. When executing a lengthy arithmetic statement, even if you don't explicitly name temporary variables, the programming language compiler creates them behind the scenes (although without descriptive names), so declaring them yourself does not cost much in terms of program execution time.

Writing Clear Prompts and Echoing Input

When program input should be retrieved from a user, you almost always want to provide a prompt for the user. A **prompt** is a message that is displayed on a monitor to ask the user for a response and perhaps explain how that response should be formatted. Prompts are used both in command-line and GUI interactive programs.

For example, suppose a program asks a user to enter a catalog number for an item the user is ordering. The following prompt is not very helpful:

Please enter a number.

The following prompt is more helpful:

Please enter a five-digit catalog order number.

The following prompt is even more helpful:

The five-digit catalog order number appears to the right of the item's picture in the catalog. Please enter it now.

When program input comes from a stored file instead of a user, prompts are not needed. However, when a program expects a user response, prompts are valuable. For example, Figure 2-15 shows the flowchart and pseudocode for the beginning of the bill-producing program shown earlier in this chapter. If the input was coming from a data file, no prompt would be required, and the logic might look like the logic in Figure 2-15.

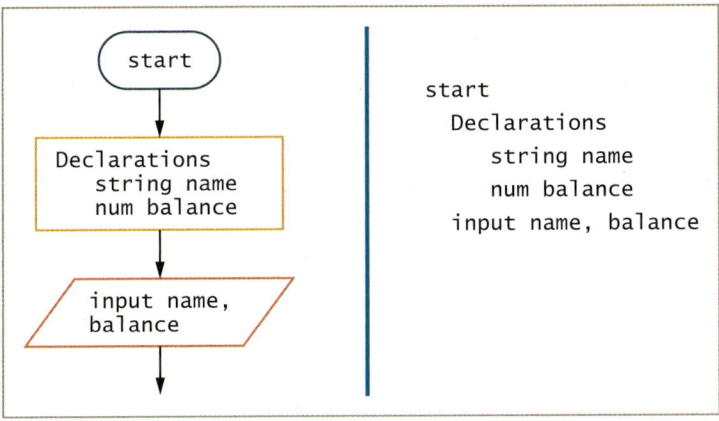

Figure 2-15   Beginning of a program that accepts a name and balance as input

However, if the input was coming from a user, including prompts would be helpful. You could supply a single prompt such as *Please enter a customer's name and balance due*, but inserting more requests into a prompt generally makes it less likely that the user can remember to enter all the parts or enter them in the correct order. It is almost always best to include a separate prompt for each item to be entered. Figure 2-16 shows an example.

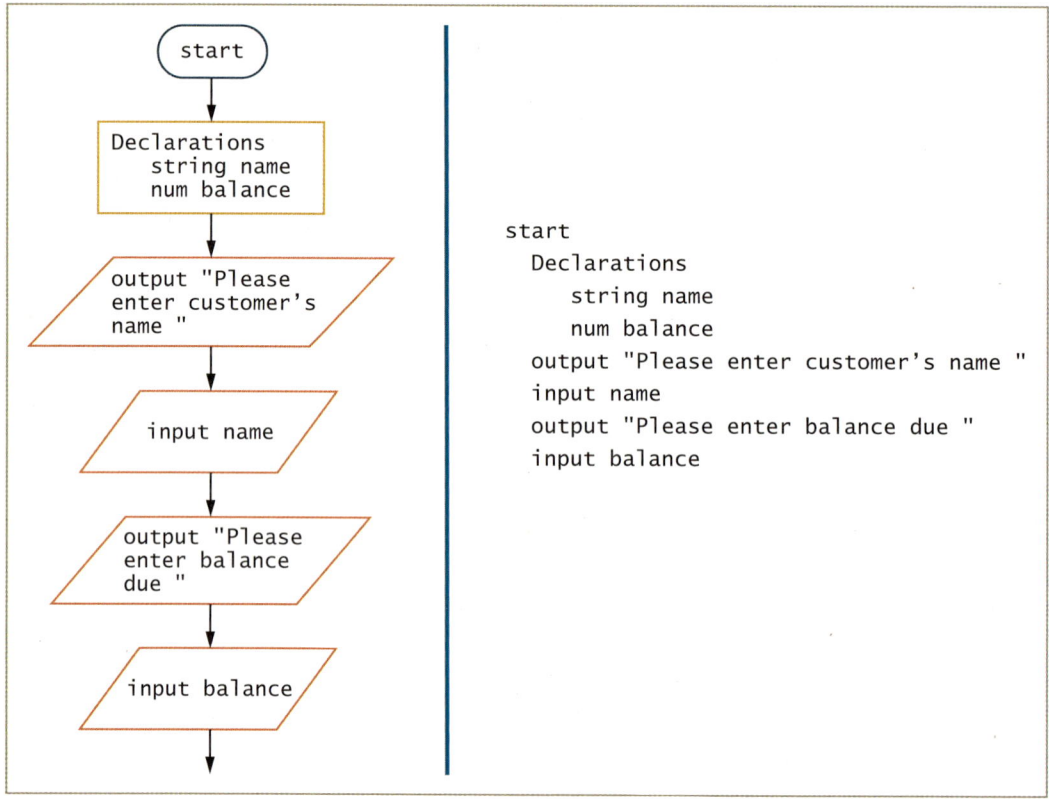

Figure 2-16 Beginning of a program that accepts a name and balance as input and uses a separate prompt for each item

Users also find it helpful when you echo their input. **Echoing input** is the act of repeating input back to a user either in a subsequent prompt or in output. For example, Figure 2-17 shows how the second prompt in Figure 2-16 can be improved by echoing the user's first piece of input data in the second prompt. When a user runs the program that is started in Figure 2-17 and enters *Green* for the customer name, the second prompt will not be *Please enter balance due*. Instead, it will be *Please enter balance due for Green*. For example, if a clerk was about to enter the balance for the wrong customer, the mention of *Green* might be enough to alert the clerk to the potential error.

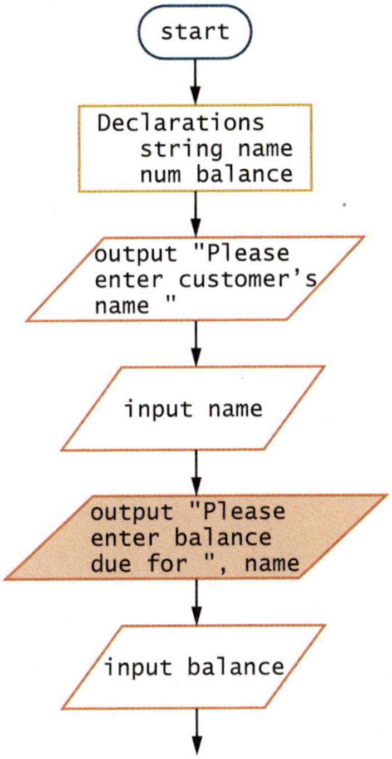

Features of Good Program Design

```
start
   Declarations
      string name
      num balance
   output "Please enter customer's name "
   input name
   output "Please enter balance due for ", name
   input balance
```

Figure 2-17 Beginning of a program that accepts a customer's name and uses it in the second prompt

Notice the space before the quotation mark in the prompt that asks the user for a balance due. The space will appear between *for* and the last name.

Maintaining Good Programming Habits

When you learn a programming language and begin to write lines of program code, it is easy to forget the principles you have learned in this text. Having some programming knowledge and a keyboard at your fingertips can lure you into typing lines of code before you think things through. But every program you write will be better if you plan before you code. Maintaining the habits of first drawing flowcharts or writing pseudocode, as you have learned here, will make your future programming projects go more smoothly. If you desk-check your program logic on paper before coding statements in a programming language, your programs will run correctly sooner. If you think carefully about the variable and module names you choose, and design program statements to be easy to read and use, your programs will be easier to develop and maintain.

TWO TRUTHS & A LIE

Features of Good Program Design

1. A program comment is a message that is displayed on a monitor to ask the user for a response and perhaps explain how that response should be formatted.
2. It usually makes sense to give each variable a name that contains a noun and to give each module a name that contains a verb.
3. Echoing input can help a user to confirm that a data item was entered correctly.

The false statement is #1. A program comment is a written explanation that is not part of the program logic but that serves as documentation for those reading the program. A prompt is a message that is displayed on a monitor to ask the user for a response and perhaps explain how that response should be formatted.

Chapter Summary

- Programs contain data in three different forms: literals (or unnamed constants), variables, and named constants. Each of these types of data can be numeric or string. Variables are named memory locations, the contents of which can vary. A variable declaration includes a data type and an identifier; optionally, it can include an initialization. Every computer programming language has its own set of rules for naming variables; however, all variable names must be written as one word without embedded spaces and should have appropriate meaning. A named constant is similar to a variable, except it can be assigned a value only once.

- Most programming languages use +, −, *, and / as the four standard arithmetic operators. Every operator follows rules of precedence that dictate the order in which operations in the same statement are carried out; multiplication and division always take precedence over addition and subtraction. The rules of precedence can be overridden using parentheses.

- Programmers break down programming problems into smaller, cohesive units called modules, subroutines, procedures, functions, or methods. To execute a module, you call it from another program or module. Any program can contain an unlimited number of modules, and each module can be called an unlimited number of times. Modularization provides abstraction, allows multiple programmers to work on a problem, and makes it easier for you to reuse work.

- When you create a module, you include a header, a body, and a `return` statement. A program or module calls a module's name to execute it. You can place any statements within modules, including declarations, which are local to the module. Global variables and constants are those that are known to the entire program. The mainline logic of almost every procedural computer program can follow a general structure that consists of three distinct parts: housekeeping tasks, detail loop tasks, and end-of-job tasks.

- A hierarchy chart illustrates modules and their relationships; it indicates which modules exist within a program and which modules call others.

- As programs become larger and more complicated, the need for good planning and design increases. You should use program comments where appropriate. Choose identifiers wisely, strive to design clear statements within your programs and modules, write clear prompts and echo input, and continue to maintain good programming habits as you develop your programming skills.

Key Terms

Numeric describes data that consists of numbers.

String describes data that is nonnumeric.

An **integer** is a whole number.

A **floating-point** number is a number with decimal places.

Real numbers are floating-point numbers.

A **numeric constant** (or **literal numeric constant**) is a specific numeric value.

A **string constant** (or **literal string constant**) is a specific group of characters enclosed within quotation marks.

Alphanumeric values can contain alphabetic characters, numbers, and punctuation.

An **unnamed constant** is a literal numeric or string value.

A **declaration** is a statement that provides a data type and an identifier for a variable.

An **identifier** is a program component's name.

A data item's **data type** is a classification that describes what values can be assigned, how the item is stored, and what types of operations can be performed with the item.

Initializing a variable is the act of assigning its first value, often at the same time the variable is created.

Garbage describes the unknown value stored in an unassigned variable.

Keywords comprise the limited word set that is reserved in a language.

CHAPTER 2 Elements of High-Quality Programs

Camel casing is a variable-naming convention in which the initial letter is lowercase, multiple-word variable names are run together, and each new word within the variable name begins with an uppercase letter.

Pascal casing is a variable-naming convention in which the initial letter is uppercase, multiple-word variable names are run together, and each new word within the variable name begins with an uppercase letter.

Hungarian notation is a variable-naming convention in which a variable's data type or other information is stored as part of its name.

An **assignment statement** assigns a value from the right of an assignment operator to the variable or constant on the left of the assignment operator.

The **assignment operator** is the equal sign; it is used to assign a value to the variable or constant on its left.

A **binary operator** is an operator that requires two operands—one on each side.

Right-associativity and **right-to-left associativity** describe operators that evaluate the expression to the right first.

An **lvalue** is the memory address identifier to the left of an assignment operator.

A **numeric variable** is one that can hold digits, have mathematical operations performed on it, and usually can hold a decimal point and a sign indicating positive or negative.

A **string variable** can hold text that includes letters, digits, and special characters such as punctuation marks.

Type-safety is the feature of programming languages that prevents assigning values of an incorrect data type.

A **named constant** is similar to a variable, except that its value cannot change after the first assignment.

A **magic number** is an unnamed constant whose purpose is not immediately apparent.

Overhead describes the extra resources a task requires.

Rules of precedence dictate the order in which operations in the same statement are carried out.

The **order of operations** describes the rules of precedence.

Left-to-right associativity describes operators that evaluate the expression to the left first.

Modules are small program units that you can use together to make a program. Programmers also refer to modules as **subroutines**, **procedures**, **functions**, or **methods**.

To **call a module** is to use the module's name to invoke it, causing it to execute.

Modularization is the process of breaking down a program into modules.

Key Terms

Functional decomposition is the act of reducing a large program into more manageable modules.

Abstraction is the process of paying attention to important properties while ignoring nonessential details.

Reusability is the feature of modular programs that allows individual modules to be used in a variety of applications.

Reliability is the feature of modular programs that assures you a module has been tested and proven to function correctly.

A **main program** runs from start to stop and calls other modules.

The **mainline logic** is the logic that appears in a program's main module; it calls other modules.

The **module header** includes the module identifier and possibly other necessary identifying information.

The **module body** contains all the statements in the module.

The **module return statement** marks the end of the module and identifies the point at which control returns to the program or module that called the module.

Encapsulation is the act of containing a task's instructions in a module.

A **stack** is a memory location in which the computer keeps track of the correct memory address to which it should return after executing a module.

The **functional cohesion** of a module is a measure of the degree to which all the module statements contribute to the same task.

Visible describes the state of data items when a module can recognize them.

In scope describes the state of data that is visible.

Local describes variables that are declared within the module that uses them.

A **portable** module is one that can more easily be reused in multiple programs.

Global describes variables that are known to an entire program.

Global variables are declared at the **program level**.

Housekeeping tasks include steps you must perform at the beginning of a program to get ready for the rest of the program.

Detail loop tasks of a program include the steps that are repeated for each set of input data.

End-of-job tasks hold the steps you take at the end of the program to finish the application.

A **hierarchy chart** is a diagram that illustrates modules' relationships to each other.

Program comments are written explanations that are not part of the program logic but that serve as documentation for those reading the program.

Internal documentation is documentation within a coded program.

External documentation is documentation that is outside a coded program.

An **annotation symbol** contains information that expands on what appears in another flowchart symbol; it is most often represented by a three-sided box that is connected to the step it references by a dashed line.

Self-documenting programs are those that contain meaningful data and module names that describe the programs' purpose.

A **data dictionary** is a list of every variable name used in a program, along with its type, size, and description.

A **temporary variable** (or a **work variable**) is a working variable that you use to hold intermediate results during a program's execution.

A **prompt** is a message that is displayed on a monitor to ask the user for a response and perhaps explain how that response should be formatted.

Echoing input is the act of repeating input back to a user either in a subsequent prompt or in output.

Review Questions

1. What does a declaration provide for a variable?
   a. a name
   b. a data type
   c. both of the above
   d. none of the above

2. A variable's data type describes all of the following *except* _____ .
   a. what values the variable can hold
   b. how the variable is stored in memory
   c. what operations can be performed with the variable
   d. the scope of the variable

3. The value stored in an uninitialized variable is _____ .
   a. garbage
   b. null
   c. compost
   d. its identifier

4. The value 3 is a _____ .
   a. numeric variable
   b. numeric constant
   c. string variable
   d. string constant

Review Questions

5. The assignment operator _____.
    a. is a binary operator
    b. has left-to-right associativity
    c. is most often represented by a colon
    d. two of the above

6. Which of the following is true about arithmetic precedence?
    a. Multiplication has a higher precedence than division.
    b. Operators with the lowest precedence always have left-to-right associativity.
    c. Division has higher precedence than subtraction.
    d. all of the above

7. Which of the following is a term used as a synonym for *module* in some programming languages?
    a. method
    b. procedure
    c. both of these
    d. none of these

8. Which of the following is a reason to use modularization?
    a. Modularization avoids abstraction.
    b. Modularization reduces overhead.
    c. Modularization allows you to more easily reuse your work.
    d. Modularization eliminates the need for syntax.

9. What is the name for the process of paying attention to important properties while ignoring nonessential details?
    a. abstraction
    b. extraction
    c. extinction
    d. modularization

10. Every module has all of the following *except* _____.
    a. a header
    b. local variables
    c. a body
    d. a return statement

11. Programmers say that one module can _____ another, meaning that the first module causes the second module to execute.
    a. declare
    b. define
    c. enact
    d. call

12. The more that a module's statements contribute to the same job, the greater the _____ of the module.
    a. structure
    b. modularity
    c. functional cohesion
    d. size

13. In most modern programming languages, a variable or constant that is declared in a module is _____ in that module.

    a. global
    b. invisible
    c. in scope
    d. undefined

14. Which of the following is *not* a typical housekeeping task?

    a. displaying instructions
    b. printing summaries
    c. opening files
    d. displaying report headings

15. Which module in a typical program will execute the most times?

    a. the housekeeping module
    b. the detail loop
    c. the end-of-job module
    d. It is different in every program.

16. A hierarchy chart tells you _____.

    a. what tasks are to be performed within each program module
    b. when a module executes
    c. which routines call which other routines
    d. all of the above

17. What are nonexecuting statements that programmers place within code to explain program statements in English?

    a. comments
    b. pseudocode
    c. trivia
    d. user documentation

18. Program comments are _____.

    a. required to create a runnable program
    b. a form of external documentation
    c. both of the above
    d. none of the above

19. Which of the following is valid advice for naming variables?

    a. To save typing, make most variable names one or two letters.
    b. To avoid conflict with names that others are using, use unusual or unpronounceable names.
    c. To make names easier to read, separate long names by using underscores or capitalization for each new word.
    d. To maintain your independence, shun the conventions of your organization.

20. A message that asks a user for input is a _____.

    a. comment
    b. prompt
    c. echo
    d. declaration

Exercises

1. Explain why each of the following names does or does not seem like a good variable name to you.

    a. d

    b. dsctamt

    c. discountAmount

    d. discount Amount

    e. discount

    f. discountAmountForEachNewCustomer

    g. discountYear2013

    h. 2013Discountyear

2. If productCost and productPrice are numeric variables, and productName is a string variable, which of the following statements are valid assignments? If a statement is not valid, explain why not.

    a. productCost = 100

    b. productPrice = productCost

    c. productPrice = productName

    d. productPrice = "24.95"

    e. 15.67 = productCost

    f. productCost = $1,345.52

    g. productCost = productPrice - 10

    h. productName = "mouse pad"

    i. productCost + 20 = productPrice

    j. productName = 3-inch nails

    k. productName = 43

    l. productName = "44"

    m. "99" = productName

    n. productName = brush

    o. battery = productName

    p. productPrice = productPrice

    q. productName = productCost

CHAPTER 2   Elements of High-Quality Programs

3. Assume that income = 8 and expense = 6. What is the value of each of the following expressions?

    a. income + expense * 2

    b. income + 4 - expense / 2

    c. (income + expense) * 2

    d. income - 3 * 2 + expense

    e. 4 * ((income - expense) + 2) + 10

4. Draw a typical hierarchy chart for a program that produces a monthly bill for a cell phone customer. Try to think of at least 10 separate modules that might be included. For example, one module might calculate the charge for daytime phone minutes used.

5. a. Draw the hierarchy chart and then plan the logic for a program needed by the sales manager of The Henry Used Car Dealership. The program will determine the profit on any car sold. Input includes the sale price and actual purchase price for a car. The output is the profit, which is the sale price minus the purchase price. Use three modules. The main program declares global variables and calls housekeeping, detail, and end-of-job modules. The housekeeping module prompts for and accepts a sale price. The detail module prompts for and accepts the purchase price, computes the profit, and displays the result. The end-of-job module displays the message *Thanks for using this program*.

    b. Revise the profit-determining program so that it runs continuously for any number of cars. The detail loop executes continuously while the sale price is not 0; in addition to calculating the profit, it prompts the user for and gets the next sale price. The end-of-job module executes after 0 is entered for the sale price.

6. a. Draw the hierarchy chart and then plan the logic for a program that calculates a person's body mass index (BMI). BMI is a statistical measure that compares a person's weight and height. The program uses three modules. The first prompts a user for and accepts the user's height in inches. The second module accepts the user's weight in pounds and converts the user's height to meters and weight to kilograms. Then, it calculates BMI as weight in kilograms times height in meters squared, and displays the results. There are 2.54 centimeters in an inch, 100 centimeters in a meter, 453.59 grams in a pound, and 1,000 grams in a kilogram. Use named constants whenever you think they are appropriate. The last module displays the message *End of job*.

    b. Revise the BMI-determining program to execute continuously until the user enters 0 for the height in inches.

7. Draw the hierarchy chart and design the logic for a program that calculates service charges for Hazel's Housecleaning service. The program contains housekeeping, detail loop, and end-of-job modules. The main program declares any needed global variables and constants and calls the other modules. The housekeeping module

displays a prompt for and accepts a customer's last name. While the user does not enter *ZZZZ* for the name, the detail loop accepts the number of bathrooms and the number of other rooms to be cleaned. The service charge is computed as $40 plus $15 for each bathroom and $10 for each of the other rooms. The detail loop also displays the service charge and then prompts the user for the next customer's name. The end-of-job module, which executes after the user enters the sentinel value for the name, displays a message that indicates the program is complete.

8. Draw the hierarchy chart and design the logic for a program that calculates the projected cost of an automobile trip. Assume that the user's car travels 20 miles per gallon of gas. Design a program that prompts the user for a number of miles driven and a current cost per gallon. The program computes and displays the cost of the trip as well as the cost if gas prices rise by 10 percent. The program accepts data continuously until 0 is entered for the number of miles. Use appropriate modules, including one that displays *End of program* when the program is finished.

9. a. Draw the hierarchy chart and design the logic for a program needed by the manager of the Stengel County softball team, who wants to compute slugging percentages for his players. A slugging percentage is the total bases earned with base hits divided by the player's number of at-bats. Design a program that prompts the user for a player jersey number, the number of bases earned, and the number of at-bats, and then displays all the data, including the calculated slugging average. The program accepts players continuously until 0 is entered for the jersey number. Use appropriate modules, including one that displays *End of job* after the sentinel is entered for the jersey number.

b. Modify the slugging percentage program to also calculate a player's on-base percentage. An on-base percentage is calculated by adding a player's hits and walks, and then dividing by the sum of at-bats, walks, and sacrifice flies. Prompt the user for all the additional data needed, and display all the data for each player.

c. Modify the softball program so that it also computes a gross production average (GPA) for each player. A GPA is calculated by multiplying a player's on-base percentage by 1.8, then adding the player's slugging percentage, and then dividing by four.

Find the Bugs

10. Your downloadable files for Chapter 2 include DEBUG02-01.txt, DEBUG02-02.txt, and DEBUG02-03.txt. Each file starts with some comments that describe the problem. Comments are lines that begin with two slashes (//). Following the comments, each file contains pseudocode that has one or more bugs you must find and correct.

CHAPTER 2 Elements of High-Quality Programs

Game Zone

11. For games to hold your interest, they almost always include some random, unpredictable behavior. For example, a game in which you shoot asteroids loses some of its fun if the asteroids follow the same, predictable path each time you play. Therefore, generating random values is a key component in creating most interesting computer games. Many programming languages come with a built-in module you can use to generate random numbers. The syntax varies in each language, but it is usually something like the following:

    myRandomNumber = random(10)

    In this statement, myRandomNumber is a numeric variable you have declared and the expression random(10) means "call a method that generates and returns a random number between 1 and 10." By convention, in a flowchart, you would place a statement like this in a processing symbol with two vertical stripes at the edges, as shown below.

    ```
    | myRandomNumber = |
    | random(10)       |
    ```

    Create a flowchart or pseudocode that shows the logic for a program that generates a random number, then asks the user to think of a number between 1 and 10. Then display the randomly generated number so the user can see whether his or her guess was accurate. (In future chapters, you will improve this game so that the user can enter a guess and the program can determine whether the user was correct.)

Up for Discussion

12. Many programming style guides are published on the Web. These guides suggest good identifiers, explain standard indentation rules, and identify style issues in specific programming languages. Find style guides for at least two languages (for example, C++, Java, Visual Basic, or C#) and list any differences you notice.

13. What advantages are there to requiring variables to have a data type?

14. As this chapter mentions, some programming languages require that named constants are assigned a value when they are declared; other languages allow a constant's value to be assigned later in a program. Which requirement do you think is better? Why?

15. Would you prefer to write a large program by yourself, or to work on a team in which each programmer produces one or more modules? Why?

16. Extreme programming is a system for rapidly developing software. One of its tenets is that all production code is written by two programmers sitting at one machine. Is this a good idea? Does working this way as a programmer appeal to you? Why or why not?

CHAPTER 3

Understanding Structure

In this chapter, you will learn about:

- The disadvantages of unstructured spaghetti code
- The three basic structures—sequence, selection, and loop
- Using a priming input to structure a program
- The need for structure
- Recognizing structure
- Structuring and modularizing unstructured logic

The Disadvantages of Unstructured Spaghetti Code

Professional business applications usually get far more complicated than the examples you have seen so far in Chapters 1 and 2. Imagine the number of instructions in the computer programs that guide an airplane's flight or audit an income tax return. Even the program that produces your paycheck at work contains many, many instructions. Designing the logic for such a program can be a time-consuming task. When you add several thousand instructions to a program, including several hundred decisions, it is easy to create a complicated mess. The popular name for logically snarled program statements is **spaghetti code**, because the logic is as hard to follow as one noodle through a plate of spaghetti. Not only is spaghetti code confusing, the programs that contain it are prone to error, difficult to reuse, and hard to use as building blocks for larger applications. Programs that use spaghetti code logic are **unstructured programs**; that is, they do not follow the rules of structured logic that you will learn in this chapter. **Structured programs** *do* follow those rules, and eliminate the problems caused by spaghetti code.

For example, suppose that you start a job as a dog washer and that you receive the instructions shown in Figure 3-1. This flowchart is an example of unstructured spaghetti code. A computer program that is structured similarly might "work"—that is, it might produce correct results—but it would be difficult to read and maintain, and its logic would be hard to follow.

The Disadvantages of Unstructured Spaghetti Code

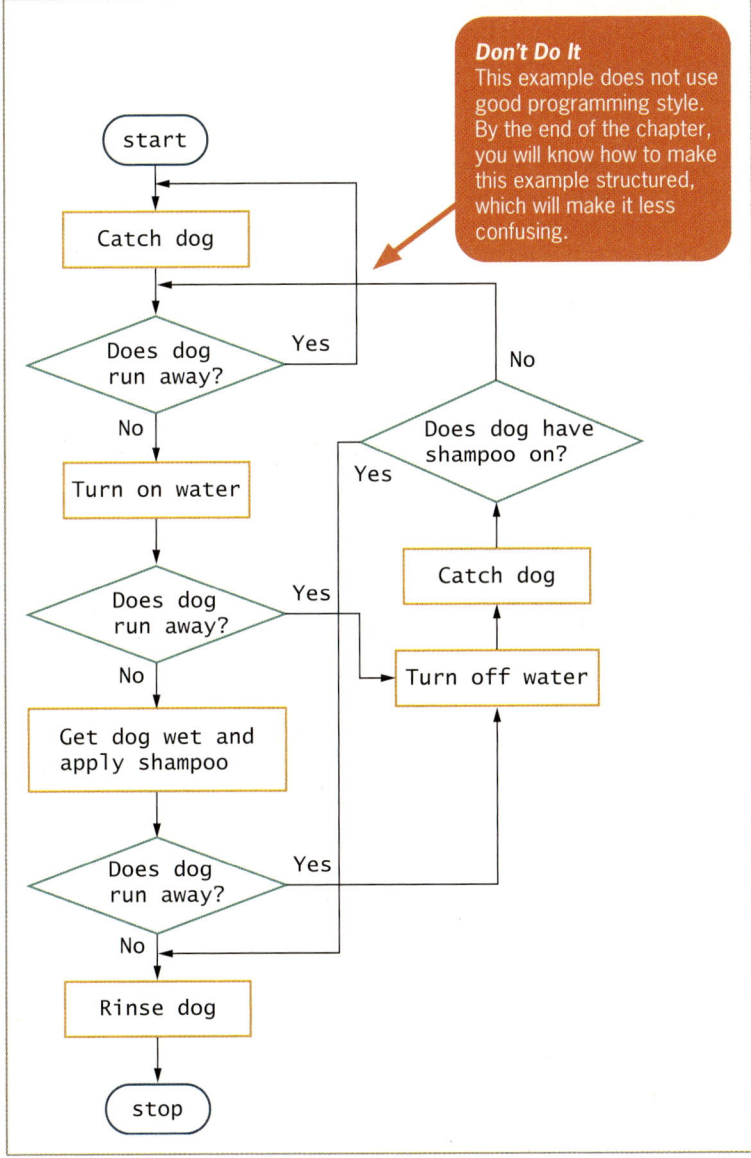

Figure 3-1 Spaghetti code logic for washing a dog

You might be able to follow the logic of the dog-washing procedure in Figure 3-1 for two reasons:
- You probably already know how to wash a dog.
- The flowchart contains a limited number of steps.

However, imagine that you were not familiar with dog washing, or that the process was far more complicated. (For example, imagine you must wash 100 dogs concurrently while applying flea and tick medication, giving them haircuts, and researching their genealogy.) Depicting more complicated logic in an unstructured way would be cumbersome. By the end of this chapter, you will understand how to make the unstructured process in Figure 3-1 clearer and less error-prone.

Software developers say that a program that contains spaghetti code has a shorter life than one with structured code. This means that programs developed using spaghetti code exist as production programs in an organization for less time. Such programs are so difficult to alter that when improvements are required, developers often find it easier to abandon the existing program and start from scratch. This takes extra time and costs more money.

TWO TRUTHS & A LIE

The Disadvantages of Unstructured Spaghetti Code

1. The popular name for logically snarled program statements is spaghetti code.
2. Programs written using spaghetti code cannot produce correct results.
3. Programs written using spaghetti code are more difficult to follow than other programs.

The false statement is #2. Programs written using spaghetti code can produce correct results, but they are more difficult to understand and maintain than programs that use structured techniques.

Understanding the Three Basic Structures

In the mid-1960s, mathematicians proved that any program, no matter how complicated, can be constructed using one or more of only three structures. A **structure** is a basic unit of programming logic; each structure is one of the following:

- sequence
- selection
- loop

With these three structures alone, you can diagram any task, from doubling a number to performing brain surgery. You can diagram each structure with a specific configuration of flowchart symbols.

The first of these three basic structures is a sequence, as shown in Figure 3-2. With a **sequence structure**, you perform an action or task, and then you perform the next action, in order. A sequence can contain any number of tasks, but there is no option to branch off and skip any of the tasks. Once you start a series of actions in a sequence, you must continue step by step until the sequence ends.

As an example, driving directions often are listed as a sequence. To tell a friend how to get to your house from school, you might provide the following sequence, in which one step follows the other and no steps can be skipped:

```
go north on First Avenue for 3 miles
turn left on Washington Boulevard
go west on Washington for 2 miles
stop at 634 Washington
```

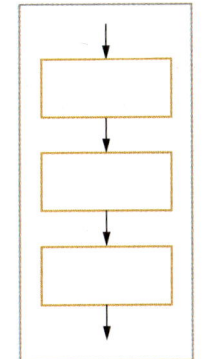

Figure 3-2 Sequence structure

The second of the three structures is a **selection structure** or **decision structure**, as shown in Figure 3-3. With this structure, you ask a question and, depending on the answer, you take one of two courses of action. Then, no matter which path you follow, you continue with the next task. (In other words, a flowchart that describes a selection structure must begin with a decision symbol, and the branches of the decision must join at the bottom of the structure. Pseudocode that describes a selection structure must start with if. Pseudocode uses the **end-structure statement** endif to clearly show where the structure ends.)

Some people call the selection structure an if-then-else because it fits the following statement:

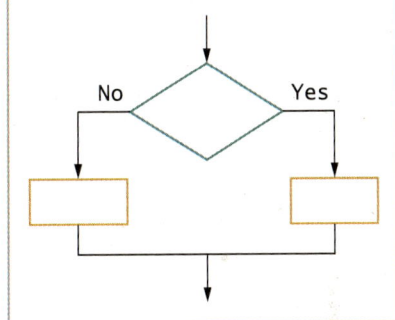

Figure 3-3 Selection structure

```
if someCondition is true then
    do oneProcess
else
    do theOtherProcess
endif
```

For example, you might provide part of the directions to your house as follows:

```
if traffic is backed up on Washington Boulevard then
    continue for 1 block on First Avenue and turn left on Adams Lane
else
    turn left on Washington Boulevard
endif
```

Similarly, a payroll program might include a statement such as:

```
if hoursWorked is more than 40 then
    calculate regularPay and overtimePay
else
    calculate regularPay
endif
```

These if-else examples can also be called **dual-alternative ifs** (or **dual-alternative selections**), because they contain two alternatives—the action taken when the tested condition is true and the action taken when it is false. Note that it is perfectly correct for one branch of the selection to be a "do nothing" branch. In each of the following examples, an action is taken only when the tested condition is true:

```
if it is raining then
    take an umbrella
endif
if employee participates in the dental plan then
    deduct $40 from employee gross pay
endif
```

The previous examples without else clauses are **single-alternative ifs** (or **single-alternative selections**); a diagram of their structure is shown in Figure 3-4. In these cases, you do not take any special action if it is not raining or if the employee does not belong to the dental plan. The case in which nothing is done is often called the **null case**.

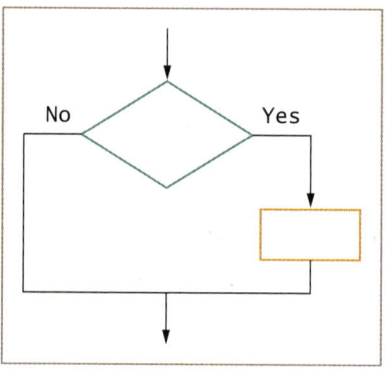

Figure 3-4 Single-alternative selection structure

The last of the three basic structures, shown in Figure 3-5, is a loop. In a **loop structure**, you continue to repeat actions while a condition remains true. The action or actions that occur within the loop are the **loop body**. In the most common type of loop, a condition is evaluated; if the answer is true, you execute the loop body and evaluate the condition again. If the condition is still true, you execute the loop body again and then reevaluate the original condition. This continues until the condition becomes false, and then you exit the structure. (In other words, a flowchart that describes a loop structure always begins with a decision symbol that has a branch that returns to a spot prior to the decision. Pseudocode that describes a loop starts with while and ends with the end-structure statement endwhile.) You may hear programmers refer to looping as **repetition** or **iteration**.

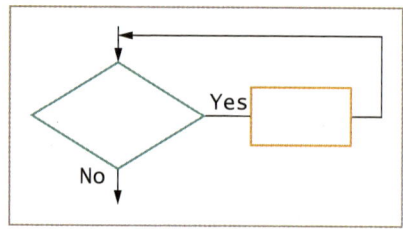

Figure 3-5 Loop structure

Some programmers call this structure a **while…do**, or more simply, a **while loop**, because it fits the following statement:

```
while testCondition continues to be true
    do someProcess
endwhile
```

Understanding the Three Basic Structures

When you provide directions to your house, part of the directions might be:

while the address of the house you are passing remains below 634
    travel forward to the next house
    look at the address on the house
endwhile

You encounter examples of looping every day, as in each of the following:

while you continue to be hungry
    take another bite of food
    determine whether you still feel hungry
endwhile
while unread pages remain in the reading assignment
    read another unread page
    determine whether there are more pages to be read
endwhile

All logic problems can be solved using only these three structures—sequence, selection, and loop. The structures can be combined in an infinite number of ways. For example, you can have a sequence of tasks followed by a selection, or a loop followed by a sequence. Attaching structures end to end is called **stacking structures**. For example, Figure 3-6 shows a structured flowchart achieved by stacking structures, and shows pseudocode that follows the flowchart logic.

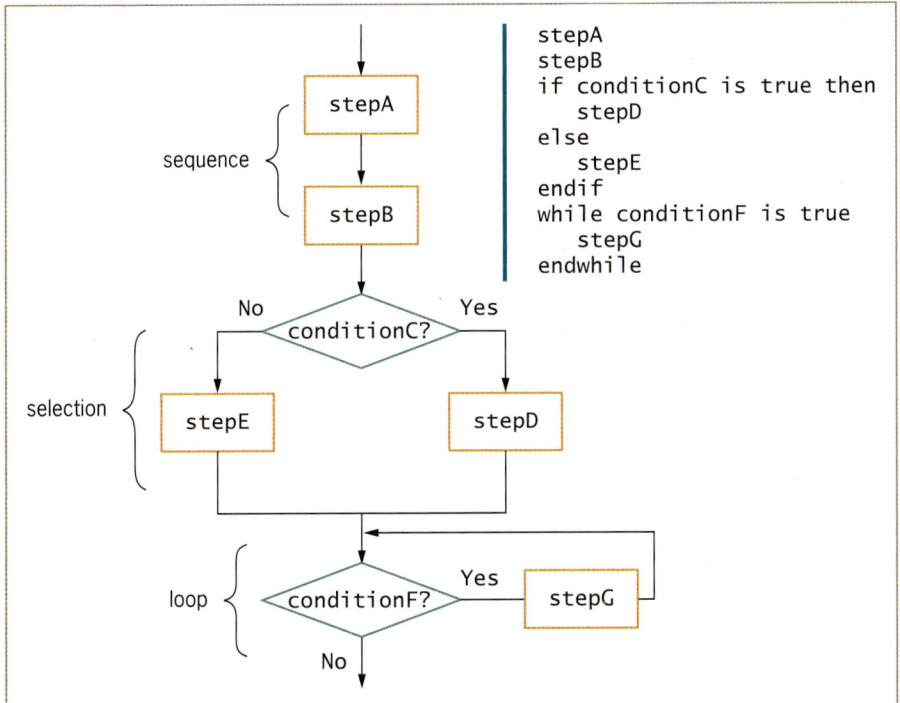

Figure 3-6 Structured flowchart and pseudocode with three stacked structures

Whether you are drawing a flowchart or writing pseudocode, you can use either of the following pairs to represent decision outcomes: *Yes* and *No* or *true* and *false*. This book follows the convention of using *Yes* and *No* in flowchart diagrams and *true* and *false* in pseudocode.

The pseudocode in Figure 3-6 shows a sequence, followed by a selection, followed by a loop. First stepA and stepB execute in sequence. Then a selection structure starts with the test of conditionC. The instruction that follows the if clause (stepD) occurs when its tested condition is true, the instruction that follows else (stepE) occurs when the tested condition is false, and any instructions that follow endif occur in either case. In other words, statements beyond the endif statement are "outside" the decision structure. Similarly, the endwhile statement shows where the loop structure ends. In Figure 3-6, while conditionF continues to be true, stepG continues to execute. If any statements followed the endwhile statement, they would be outside of, and not a part of, the loop.

Besides stacking structures, you can replace any individual steps in a structured flowchart diagram or pseudocode with additional structures. In other words, any sequence, selection, or loop can contain other sequences, selections, or loops. For example, you can have a sequence of three tasks on one side of a selection, as shown in Figure 3-7. Placing a structure within another structure is called **nesting structures**.

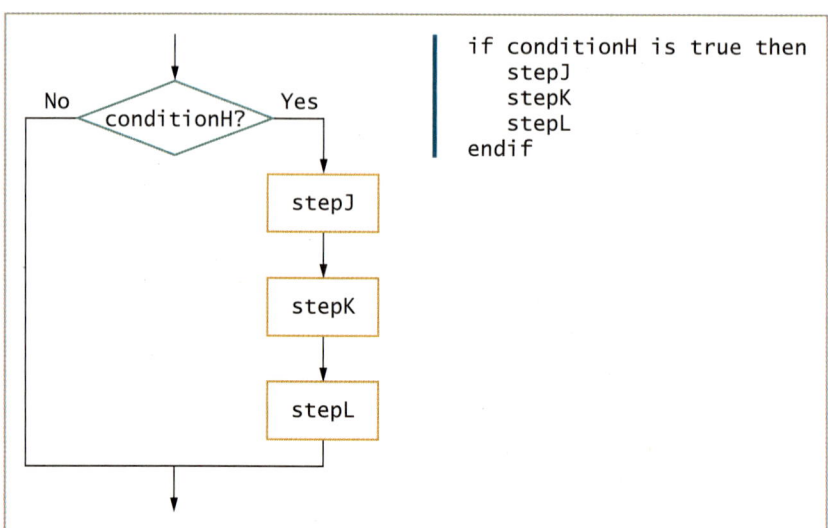

Figure 3-7 Flowchart and pseudocode showing nested structures—a sequence nested within a selection

In the pseudocode for the logic shown in Figure 3-7, the indentation shows that all three statements (stepJ, stepK, and stepL) must execute if conditionH is true. The three statements constitute a **block**, or a group of statements that executes as a single unit.

In place of one of the steps in the sequence in Figure 3-7, you can insert another structure. In Figure 3-8, the process named stepK has been replaced with a loop structure that begins with a test of the condition named conditionM.

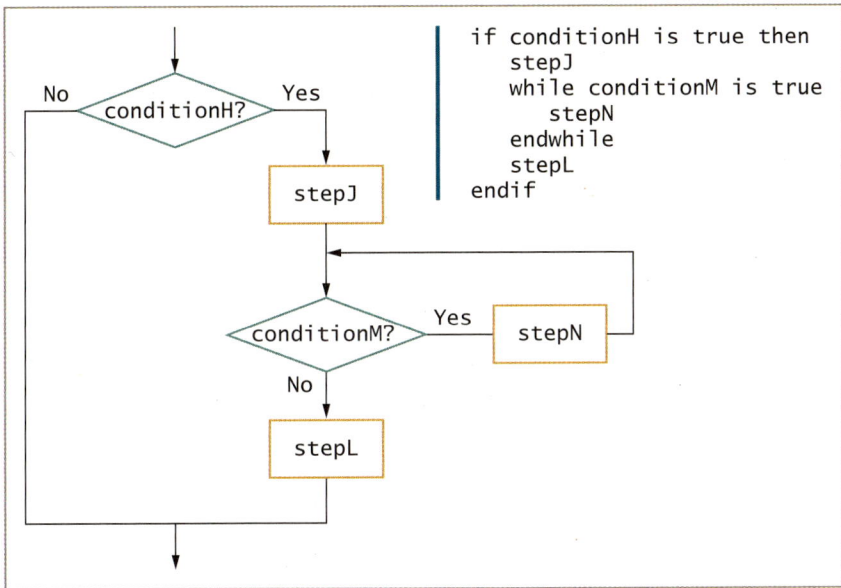

Figure 3-8 Flowchart and pseudocode showing nested structures—a loop nested within a sequence, nested within a selection

In the pseudocode shown in Figure 3-8, notice that if and endif are vertically aligned. This shows that they are all "on the same level." Similarly, stepJ, while, endwhile, and stepL are aligned, and they are evenly indented. In the flowchart in Figure 3-8, you could draw a vertical line through the symbols containing stepJ, the entry and exit points of the while loop, and stepL. The flowchart and the pseudocode represent exactly the same logic.

When you nest structures, the statements that start and end a structure are always on the same level and are always in pairs. Structures cannot overlap. For example, if you have an if that contains a while, then the endwhile statement will come before the endif. On the other hand, if you have a while that contains an if, then the endif statement will come before the endwhile.

There is no limit to the number of levels you can create when you nest and stack structures. For example, Figure 3-9 shows logic that has been made more complicated by replacing stepN with a selection. The structure that performs stepP or stepQ based on the outcome of conditionO is nested within the loop that is controlled by conditionM. In the pseudocode in Figure 3-9, notice how the if, else, and endif that describe the condition selection are aligned with each other and within the while structure that is controlled by conditionM. As before, the indentation used in the pseudocode reflects the logic laid out graphically in the flowchart.

CHAPTER 3   Understanding Structure

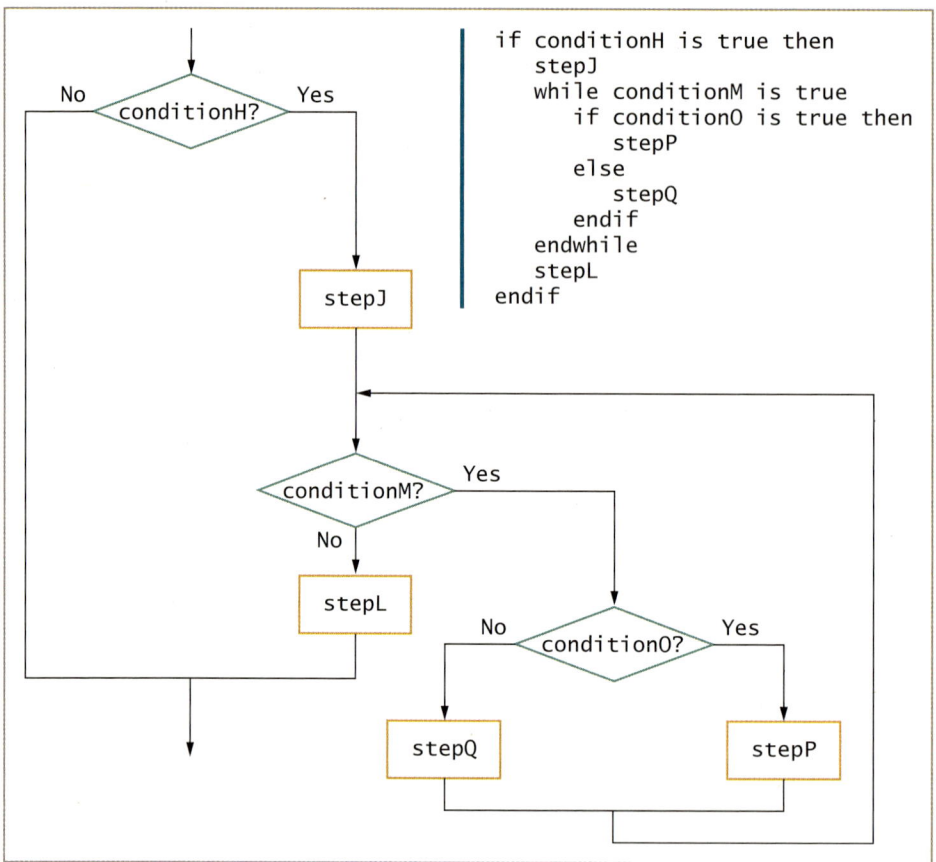

Figure 3-9 Flowchart and pseudocode for a selection within a loop within a sequence within a selection

Many of the preceding examples are generic so that you can focus on the relationships of the shapes without worrying what they do. Keep in mind that generic instructions like **stepA** and generic conditions like **conditionC** can stand for anything. For example, Figure 3-10 shows the process of buying and planting flowers outdoors in the spring after the danger of frost is over. The flowchart and pseudocode structures are identical to the ones in Figure 3-9. In the exercises at the end of this chapter, you will be asked to develop more scenarios that fit the same pattern.

Understanding the Three Basic Structures

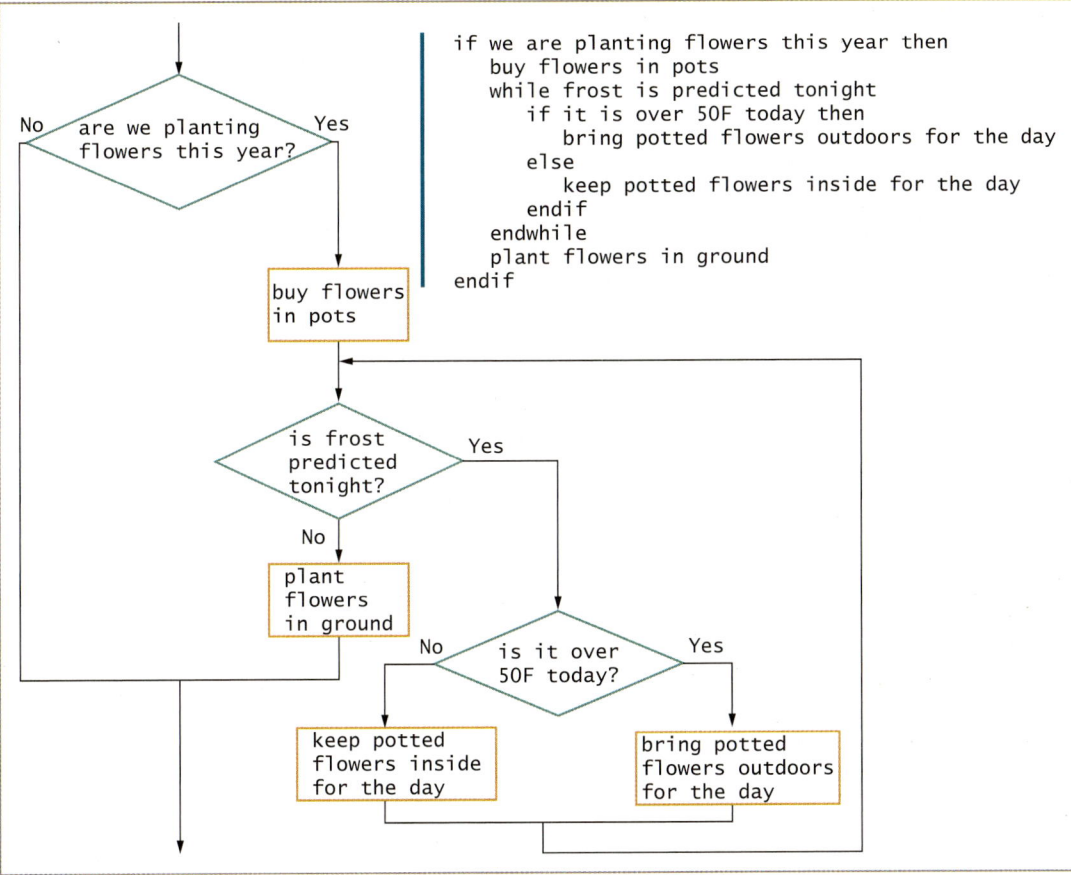

Figure 3-10 The process of buying and planting flowers in the spring

The possible combinations of logical structures are endless, but each segment of a structured program is a sequence, a selection, or a loop. The three structures are shown together in Figure 3-11. Notice that each structure has one entry point and one exit point. One structure can attach to another only at one of these points.

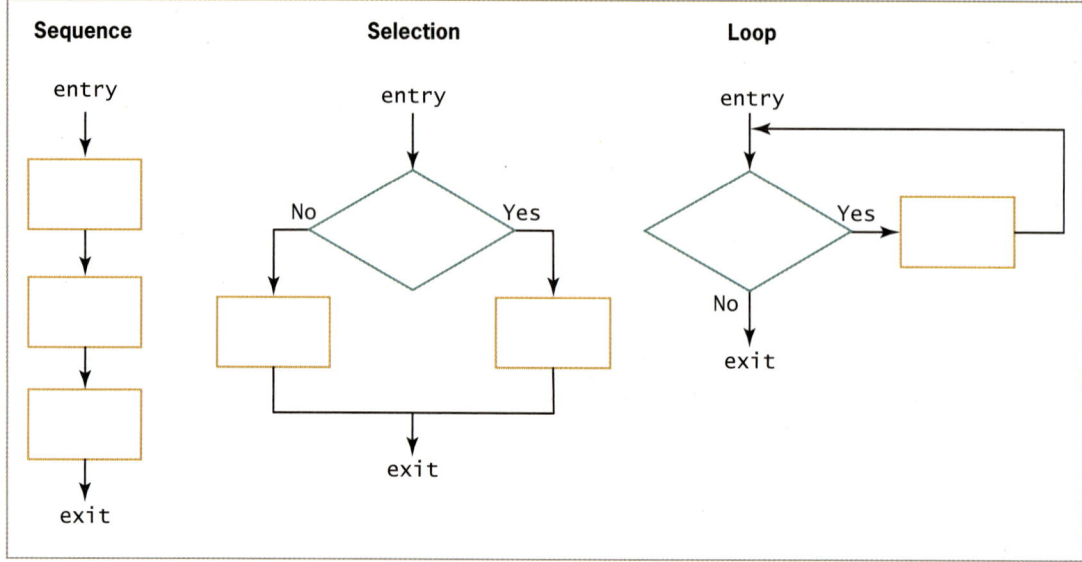

Figure 3-11 The three structures

 Try to imagine physically picking up any of the three structures using the entry and exit "handles." These are the spots at which you could connect one structure to another. Similarly, any complete structure, from its entry point to its exit point, can be inserted within the process symbol of any other structure.

In summary, a structured program has the following characteristics:

- A structured program includes only combinations of the three basic structures—sequence, selection, and loop. Any structured program might contain one, two, or all three types of structures.
- Each of the structures has a single entry point and a single exit point.
- Structures can be stacked or connected to one another only at their entry or exit points.
- Any structure can be nested within another structure.

 A structured program is never required to contain examples of all three structures. For example, many simple programs contain only a sequence of several tasks that execute from start to finish without any needed selections or loops. As another example, a program might display a series of numbers, looping to do so, but never making any decisions about the numbers.

 Watch the video *Understanding Structure*.

Using a Priming Input to Structure a Program

> **TWO TRUTHS & A LIE**
>
> **Understanding the Three Basic Structures**
>
> 1. Each structure in structured programming is a sequence, selection, or loop.
> 2. All logic problems can be solved using only three structures—sequence, selection, and loop.
> 3. The three structures cannot be combined in a single program.
>
> The false statement is #3. The three structures can be stacked or nested in an infinite number of ways.

Using a Priming Input to Structure a Program

Recall the number-doubling program discussed in Chapter 2; Figure 3-12 shows a similar program. The program inputs a number and checks for the end-of-file condition. If the condition is not met, then the number is doubled, the answer is displayed, and the next number is input.

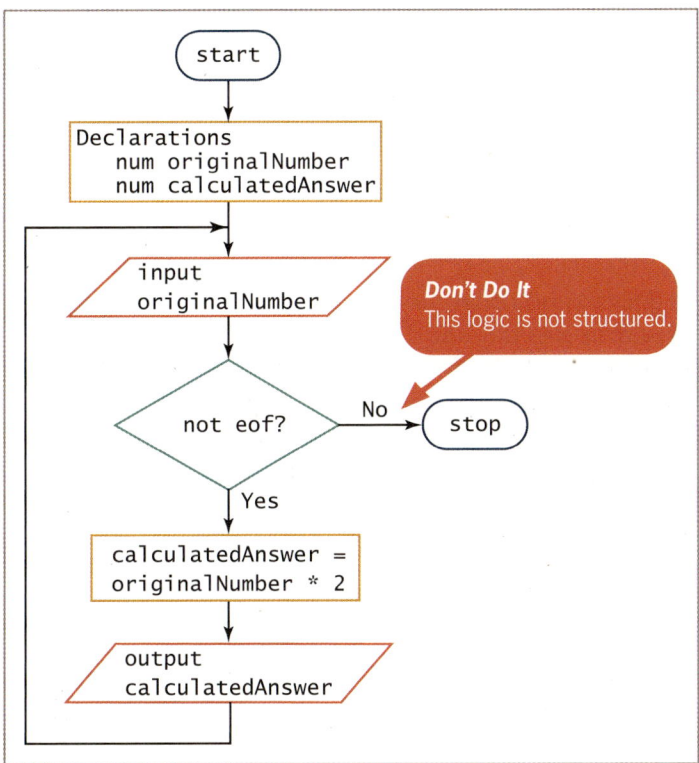

Figure 3-12 Unstructured flowchart of a number-doubling program

Recall from Chapter 1 that this book uses **eof** to represent a generic end-of-data condition when the exact tested parameters are not important to the discussion. In this example, the test is for **not eof?**, because processing will continue while the end of the data has not been reached.

Is the program represented by Figure 3-12 structured? At first, it might be hard to tell. The three allowed structures were illustrated in Figure 3-11, and the flowchart in Figure 3-12 does not look exactly like any of those three shapes. However, because you may stack and nest structures while retaining overall structure, it might be difficult to determine whether a flowchart as a whole is structured. It is easiest to analyze the flowchart in Figure 3-12 one step at a time. The beginning of the flowchart looks like Figure 3-13. Is this portion of the flowchart structured? Yes, it is a sequence of two events.

Adding the next piece of the flowchart looks like Figure 3-14. The sequence is finished; either a selection or a loop is starting. You might not know which one, but you do know the sequence is not continuing because sequences cannot contain questions. With a sequence, each task or step must follow without any opportunity to branch off. So, which type of structure starts with the question in Figure 3-14? Is it a selection or a loop?

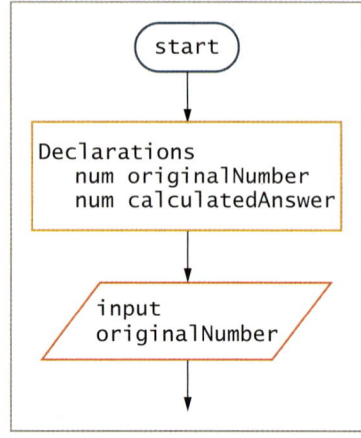

Figure 3-13 Beginning of a number-doubling flowchart

Selection and loop structures differ as follows:

- In a selection structure, the logic goes in one of two directions after the question, and then the flow comes back together; the question is not asked a second time within the structure.

- In a loop, if the answer to the question results in the loop being entered and the loop statements executing, then the logic returns to the question that started the loop. When the body of a loop executes, the question that controls the loop is always asked again.

If the end-of-file condition is not met in the number-doubling problem in the original Figure 3-12, then the result is calculated and output, a new number is obtained, and the logic returns to the question that tests for the end of the file. In other words, while the answer to the **not eof?** question continues to be *Yes*, a body of statements continues to execute. Therefore, the **not eof?** question starts a structure that is more like a loop than a selection.

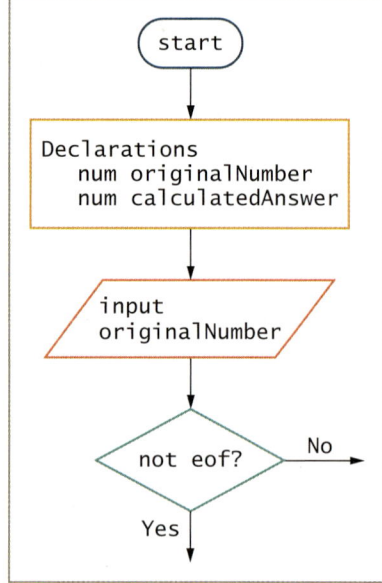

Figure 3-14 Number-doubling flowchart continued

Using a Priming Input to Structure a Program

The number-doubling problem *does* contain a loop, but it is not a structured loop. In a structured loop, the rules are:

1. You ask a question.
2. If the answer indicates you should execute the loop body, then you do so.
3. If you execute the loop body, then you must go right back to repeat the question.

The flowchart in Figure 3-12 asks a question. If the answer is *Yes* (that is, while `not eof?` is true), then the program performs two tasks in the loop body: It does the arithmetic and it displays the results. Doing two things is acceptable because two tasks with no possible branching constitute a sequence, and it is fine to nest a structure within another structure. However, when the sequence ends, the logic does not flow right back to the loop-controlling question. Instead, it goes *above* the question to get another number. For the loop in Figure 3-12 to be a structured loop, the logic must return to the `not eof?` question when the embedded sequence ends.

The flowchart in Figure 3-15 shows the flow of logic returning to the `not eof?` question immediately after the sequence. Figure 3-15 shows a structured flowchart, but it has one major flaw—the flowchart does not do the job of continuously doubling different numbers.

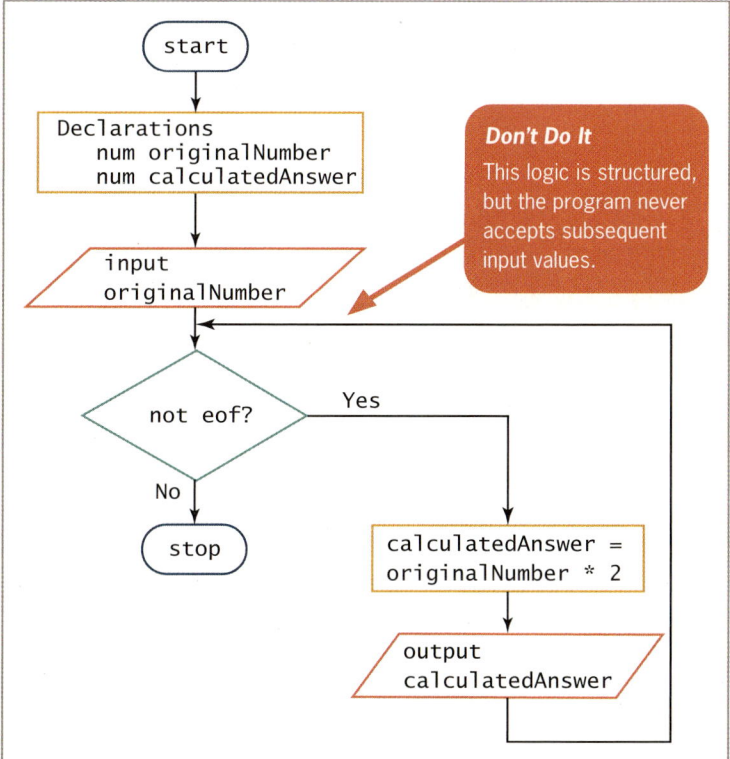

Figure 3-15 Structured, but nonfunctional, flowchart of number-doubling problem

Follow the flowchart through a typical program run, assuming the `eof` condition is an input value of 0. Suppose that when the program starts, the user enters a 9 for the value of `originalNumber`. That is not `eof`, so the number is multiplied by 2, and 18 is displayed as the value of `calculatedAnswer`. Then the question `not eof?` is asked again. The `not eof?` condition must still be true because a new value representing the sentinel (ending) value cannot be entered. The logic never returns to the `input originalNumber` task, so the value of `originalNumber` never changes. Therefore, 9 doubles again and the answer 18 is displayed again. The `not eof?` result is still true, so the same steps are repeated. This goes on *forever*, with the answer 18 being output repeatedly. The program logic shown in Figure 3-15 is structured, but it does not work as intended. Conversely, the program in Figure 3-16 works, but it is not structured because after the tasks execute within a structured loop, the flow of logic must return directly to the loop-controlling question. In Figure 3-16, the logic does not return to this question; instead, it goes "too high" outside the loop to repeat the `input originalNumber` task.

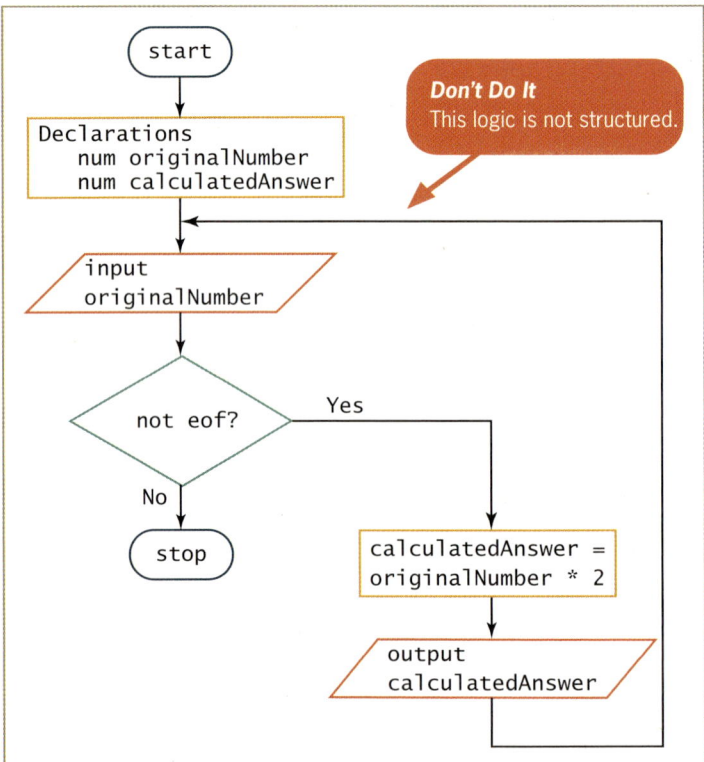

Figure 3-16 Functional but unstructured flowchart

How can the number-doubling problem be both structured and work as intended? Often, for a program to be structured, you must add something extra. In this case, it is a priming input step. A **priming input** or **priming read** is an added statement that gets the first input value in a program. For example, if a program will receive 100 data values as input, you input the first value in a statement that is separate from the other 99. You must do this to keep the program structured.

Consider the solution in Figure 3-17; it is structured *and* it does what it is supposed to do. It contains a shaded, additional `input originalNumber` statement. The program logic contains a sequence and a loop. The loop contains another sequence.

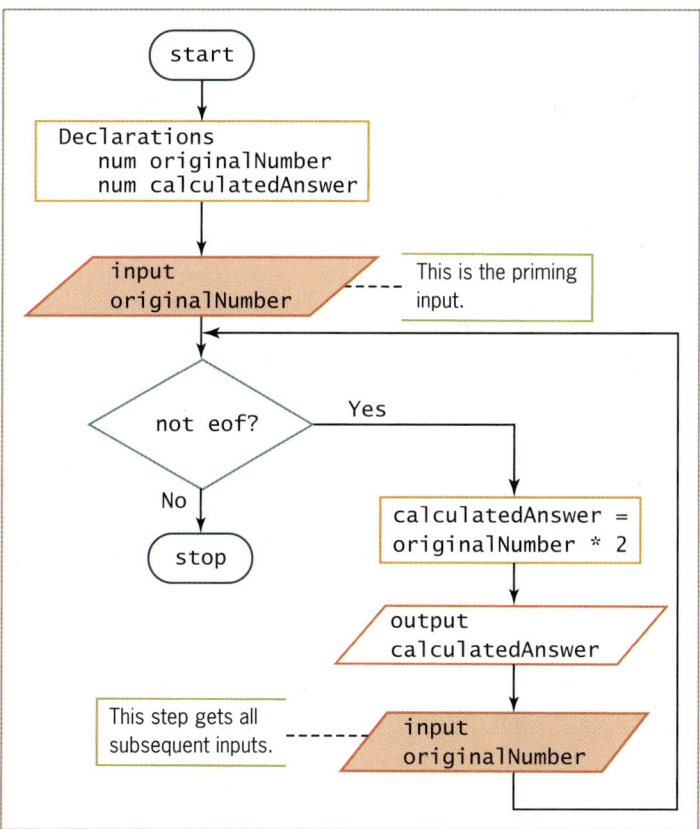

Figure 3-17 Functional, structured flowchart for the number-doubling problem

The additional `input originalNumber` step shown in Figure 3-17 is typical in structured programs. The first of the two input steps is the priming input. The term *priming* comes from the fact that the read is first, or *primary* (it gets the process going, as in "priming the pump"). The purpose of the priming input step is to control the upcoming loop that begins with the `not eof?` question. The last element within the structured loop gets the next, and all subsequent, input values. This is also typical in structured loops—the last step executed within the loop alters the condition tested in the question that begins the loop, which in this case is the `not eof?` question.

CHAPTER 3   Understanding Structure

In Chapter 2, you learned that the group of preliminary tasks that sets the stage for the main work of a program is called the housekeeping section. The priming read is an example of a housekeeping task.

Figure 3-18 shows another way you might attempt to draw the logic for the number-doubling program. At first glance, the figure might seem to show an acceptable solution to the problem—it is structured, contains a single loop with a sequence of three steps within it, and appears to eliminate the need for the priming input statement. When the program starts, the `not eof?` question is asked, and if it is not the end of input data, then the program gets an input number, doubles it, and displays it. Then, if the `not eof?` condition remains true, the program gets another number, doubles it, and displays it. The program might continue while many numbers are input. The last time the `input originalNumber` statement executes, it encounters `eof`, but the program does not stop—instead, it calculates and displays a result one last time. Depending on the language you are using and on the type of input being used, you might receive an error message or you might output garbage. In either case, this last output is extraneous—no value should be doubled and output after the `eof` condition is encountered. As a general rule, an end-of-file test should always come immediately after an input statement because the end-of-file condition will be detected at input. Therefore, the best solution to the number-doubling problem remains the one shown in Figure 3-17—the solution containing the priming input statement.

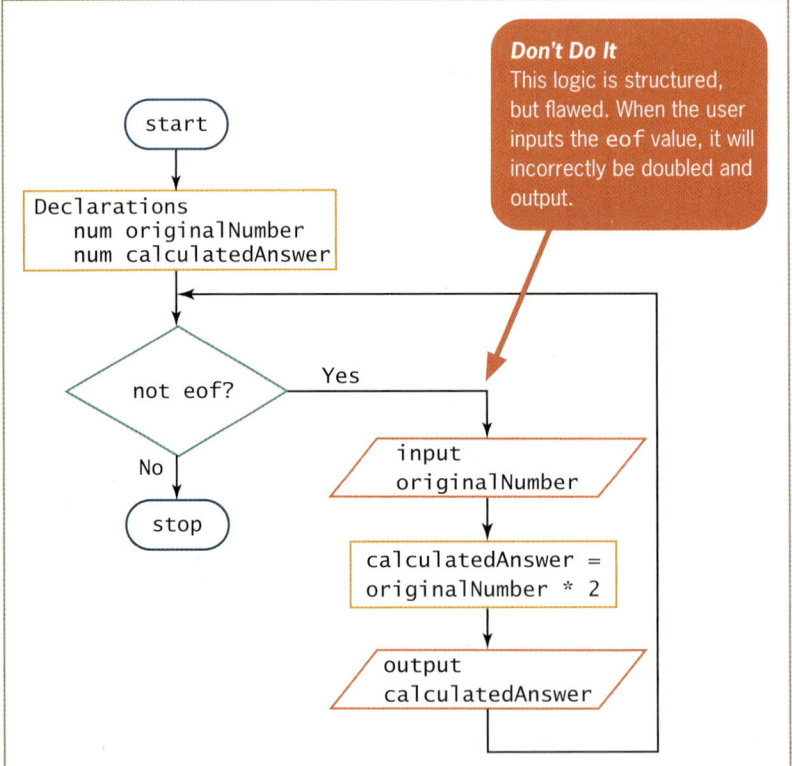

Figure 3-18 Structured but incorrect solution to the number-doubling problem

Understanding the Reasons for Structure

> **TWO TRUTHS & A LIE**
>
> Using a Priming Input to Structure a Program
>
> 1. A priming input is the statement that repeatedly gets all the data that is input in a program.
> 2. A structured program is sometimes longer than an unstructured one.
> 3. A program can be structured yet still be incorrect.
>
> The false statement is #1. A priming input gets the first input.

Understanding the Reasons for Structure

At this point, you may very well be saying, "I liked the original number-doubling program back in Figure 3-12 just fine. I could follow it. Also, the first program had one less step in it, so it was less work. Who cares if a program is structured?"

Until you have some programming experience, it is difficult to appreciate the reasons for using only the three structures—sequence, selection, and loop. However, staying with these three structures is better for the following reasons:

- *Clarity*—The number-doubling program is small. As programs get bigger, they get more confusing if they are not structured.

- *Professionalism*—All other programmers (and programming teachers you might encounter) expect your programs to be structured. It is the way things are done professionally.

- *Efficiency*—Most newer computer languages support structure and use syntax that lets you deal efficiently with sequence, selection, and looping. Older languages, such as assembly languages, COBOL, and RPG, were developed before the principles of structured programming were discovered. However, even programs that use those older languages can be written in a structured form. Newer languages such as C#, C++, and Java enforce structure by their syntax.

 In older languages, you could leave a selection or loop before it was complete by using a "go to" statement. The statement allowed the logic to "go to" any other part of the program whether it was within the same structure or not. Structured programming is sometimes called **goto-less programming**.

- *Maintenance*—You and other programmers will find it easier to modify and maintain structured programs as changes are required in the future.

- *Modularity*—Structured programs can be easily broken down into modules that can be assigned to any number of programmers. The routines are then pieced back together like modular furniture at each routine's single entry or exit point. Additionally, a module often can be used in multiple programs, saving development time in the new project.

TWO TRUTHS & A LIE

Understanding the Reasons for Structure

1. Structured programs are clearer than unstructured programs.
2. You and other programmers will find it easier to modify and maintain structured programs as changes are required in the future.
3. Structured programs are not easily divided into parts, making them less prone to error.

The false statement is #3. Structured programs can be easily broken down into modules that can be assigned to any number of programmers.

Recognizing Structure

When you are beginning to learn about structured program design, it is difficult to detect whether a flowchart of a program's logic is structured. For example, is the flowchart segment in Figure 3-19 structured?

Yes, it is. It has a sequence and a selection structure.

Is the flowchart segment in Figure 3-20 structured?

Yes, it is. It has a loop, and within the loop is a selection.

Is the flowchart segment in the upper-left corner of Figure 3-21 structured?

No, it is not built from the three basic structures. One way to straighten out an unstructured flowchart segment is to use the "spaghetti bowl" method; that is, picture the flowchart as a bowl of spaghetti that you must untangle. Imagine you can grab one piece of pasta at the top of the bowl and start pulling. As you "pull" each symbol out of the tangled mess, you can untangle the separate paths until the entire segment is structured.

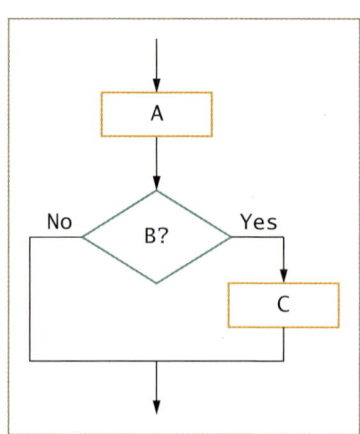

Figure 3-19 Example 1

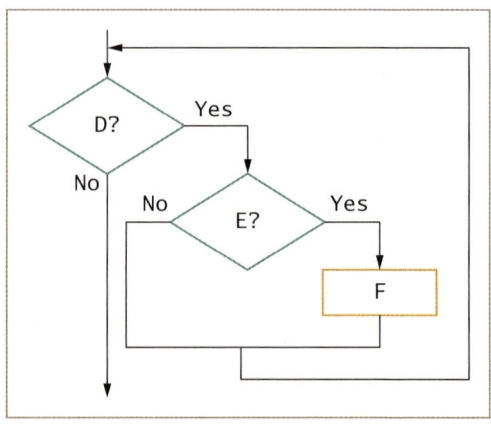

Figure 3-20 Example 2

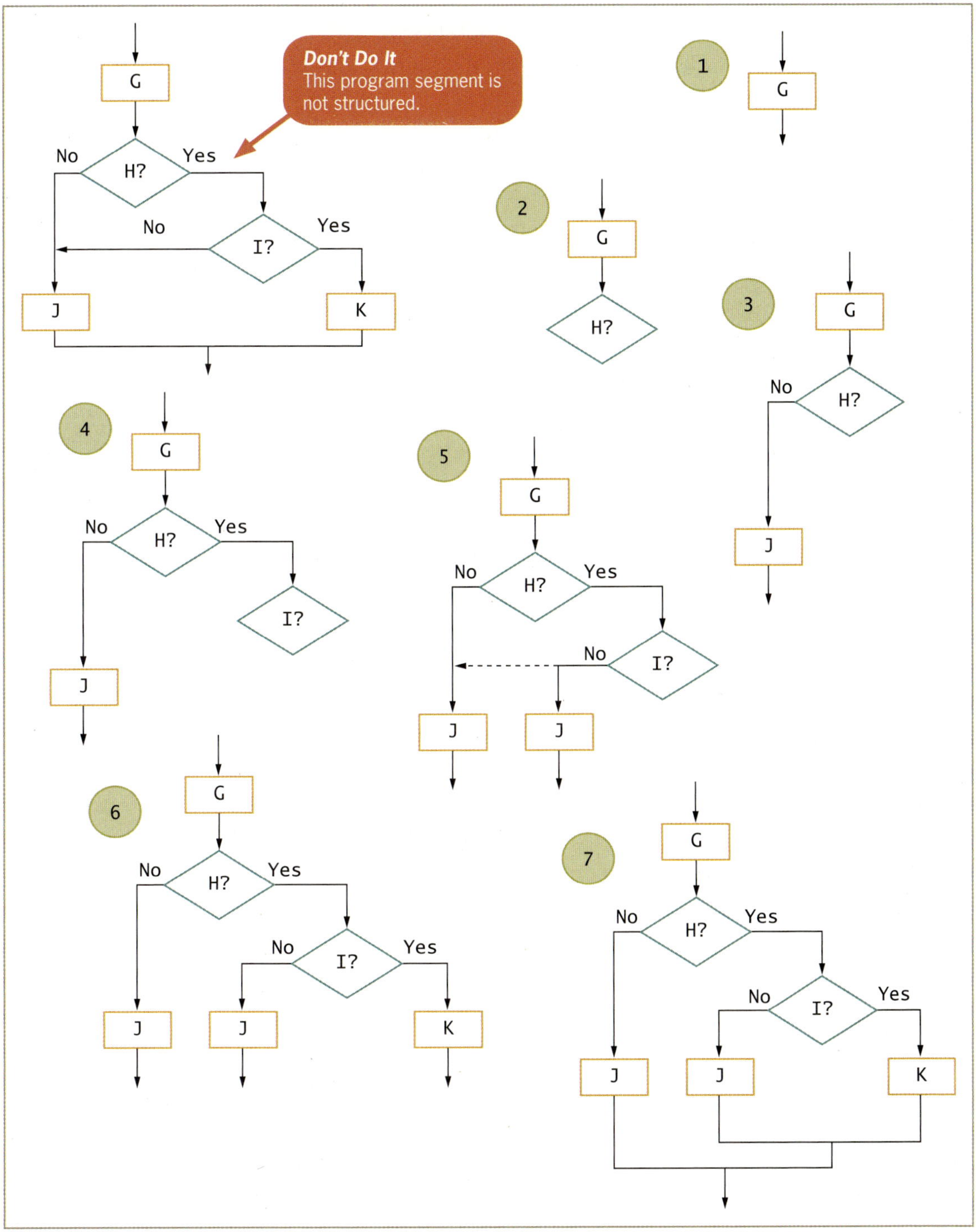

Recognizing Structure

Figure 3-21 Example 3 and process to structure it

Look at the diagram in the upper-left corner of Figure 3-21. If you could start pulling the arrow at the top, you would encounter a procedure box labeled G. (See Figure 3-21, Step 1.) A single process like G is part of an acceptable structure—it constitutes at least the beginning of a sequence structure.

Imagine that you continue pulling symbols from the tangled segment. The next item in the flowchart is a question that tests a condition labeled H, as you can see in Figure 3-21, Step 2. At this point, you know the sequence that started with G has ended. Sequences never have decisions in them, so the sequence is finished; either a selection or a loop is beginning with question H. A loop must return to the loop-controlling question at some later point. You can see from the original logic that whether the answer to H is *Yes* or *No*, the logic never returns to H. Therefore, H begins a selection structure, not a loop structure.

To continue detangling the logic, you would pull up on the flowline that emerges from the left side (the *No* side) of Question H. You encounter J, as shown in Step 3 of Figure 3-21. When you continue beyond J, you reach the end of the flowchart.

Now you can turn your attention to the *Yes* side (the right side) of the condition tested in H. When you pull up on the right side, you encounter Question I. (See Step 4 of Figure 3-21.)

In the original version of the flowchart in Figure 3-21, follow the line on the left side of Question I. The line emerging from the left side of selection I is attached to J, which is outside the selection structure. You might say the I-controlled selection is becoming entangled with the H-controlled selection, so you must untangle the structures by repeating the step that is causing the tangle. (In this example, you repeat Step J to untangle it from the other usage of J.) Continue pulling on the flowline that emerges from J until you reach the end of the program segment, as shown in Step 5 of Figure 3-21.

Now pull on the right side of Question I. Process K pops up, as shown in Step 6 of Figure 3-21; then you reach the end.

At this point, the untangled flowchart has three loose ends. The loose ends of Question I can be brought together to form a selection structure; then the loose ends of Question H can be brought together to form another selection structure. The result is the flowchart shown in Step 7 of Figure 3-21. The entire flowchart segment is structured—it has a sequence followed by a selection inside a selection.

If you want to try structuring a more difficult example of an unstructured program, see Appendix E.

TWO TRUTHS & A LIE
Recognizing Structure

1. Some processes cannot be expressed in a structured format.
2. An unstructured flowchart can achieve correct outcomes.
3. Any unstructured flowchart can be "detangled" to become structured.

The false statement is #1. Any set of instructions can be expressed in a structured format.

Structuring and Modularizing Unstructured Logic

Recall the dog-washing process illustrated in Figure 3-1 at the beginning of this chapter. When you look at it now, you should recognize it as an unstructured process. Can this process be reconfigured to perform precisely the same tasks in a structured way? Of course!

Figure 3-22 demonstrates how you might approach structuring the dog-washing logic. Part 1 of the figure shows the beginning of the process. The first step, *Catch dog*, is a simple sequence. This step is followed by a question. When a question is encountered, the sequence is over, and either a loop or a selection starts. In this case, after the dog runs away, you must catch the dog and determine whether he runs away again, so a loop begins. To create a structured loop like the ones you have seen earlier in this chapter, you can repeat the *Catch dog* process and return immediately to the *Does dog run away?* question.

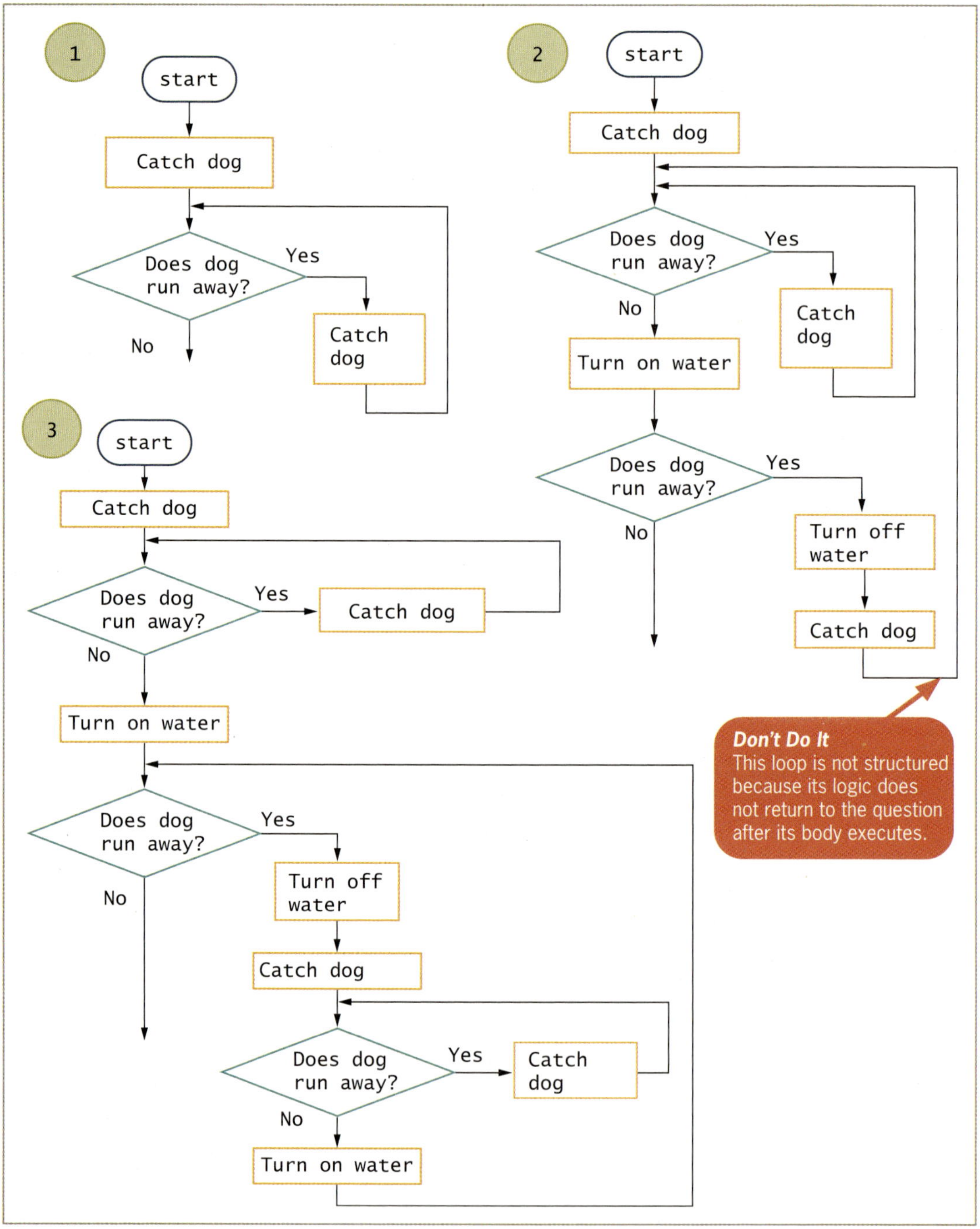

CHAPTER 3   Understanding Structure

Figure 3-22   Steps to structure the dog-washing process

Structuring and Modularizing Unstructured Logic

In the original flowchart in Figure 3-1, you turn on the water when the dog does not run away. This step is a simple sequence, so it can correctly be added after the loop. When the water is turned on, the original logic checks whether the dog runs away after this new development. This starts a loop. In the original flowchart, the lines cross, creating a tangle, so you repeat as many steps as necessary to detangle the lines. After you turn off the water and catch the dog, you encounter the question *Does dog have shampoo on?* Because the logic has not yet reached the shampooing step, there is no need to ask this question; the answer at this point always will be *No*. When one of the logical paths emerging from a question can never be traveled, you can eliminate the question. Part 2 of Figure 3-22 shows that if the dog runs away after you turn on the water, but before you've gotten the dog wet and shampooed him, you must turn the water off, catch the dog, and return to the step that asks whether the dog runs away.

The logic in Part 2 of Figure 3-22 is not structured because the second loop that begins with the question *Does dog run away?* does not immediately return to the loop-controlling question after its body executes. So, to make the loop structured, you can repeat the actions that occur before returning to the loop-controlling question. The flowchart segment in Part 3 of Figure 3-22 is structured; it contains a sequence, a loop, a sequence, and a final, larger loop. This last loop contains its own sequence, loop, and sequence.

After the dog is caught and the water is on, you wet and shampoo the dog. Then, according to the original flowchart in Figure 3-1, you once again check to see whether the dog has run away. If he has, you turn off the water and catch the dog. From this location in the logic, the answer to the *Does dog have shampoo on?* question will always be *Yes*; as before, there is no need to ask a question when there is only one possible answer. So, if the dog runs away, the last loop executes. You turn off the water, continue to catch the dog as he repeatedly escapes, and turn the water on. When the dog is caught at last, you rinse the dog and end the program. Figure 3-23 shows both the complete flowchart and pseudocode.

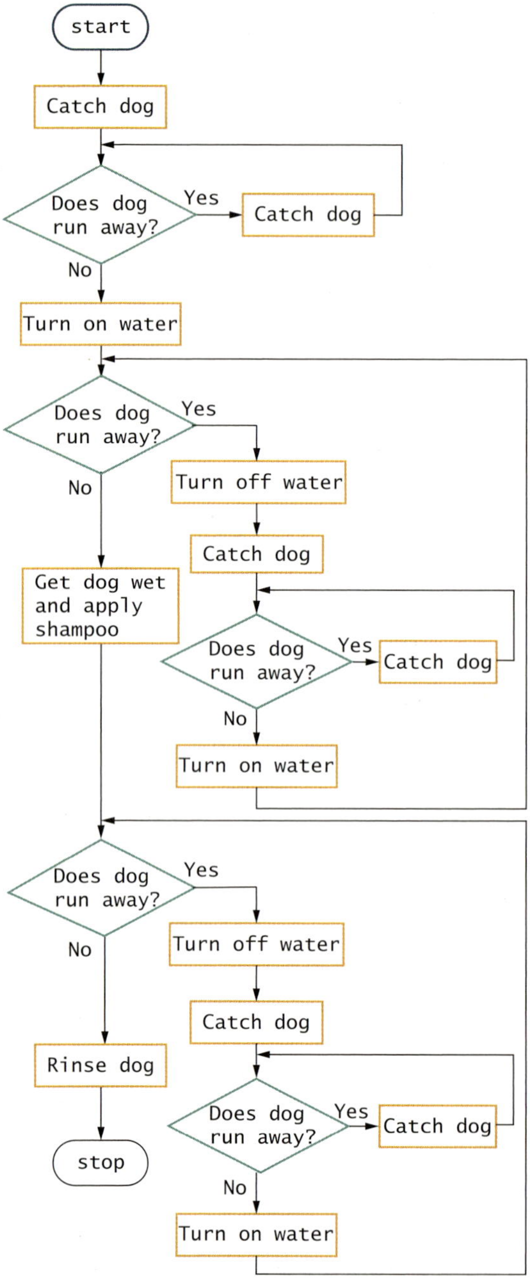

CHAPTER 3   Understanding Structure

```
start
   Catch dog
   while dog runs away
      Catch dog
   endwhile
   Turn on water
   while dog runs away
      Turn off water
      Catch dog
      while dog runs away
         Catch dog
      endwhile
      Turn on water
   endwhile
   Get dog wet and apply shampoo
   while dog runs away
      Turn off water
      Catch dog
      while dog runs away
         Catch dog
      endwhile
      Turn on water
   endwhile
   Rinse dog
stop
```

Figure 3-23   Structured dog-washing flowchart and pseudocode

The flowchart in Figure 3-23 is complete and is structured. It contains alternating sequence and loop structures.

Structuring and Modularizing Unstructured Logic

Figure 3-23 includes three places where the sequence-loop-sequence of catching the dog and turning the water on are repeated. If you wanted to, you could modularize the duplicate sections so that their instruction sets are written once and contained in their own module. Figure 3-24 shows a modularized version of the program; the three module calls are shaded.

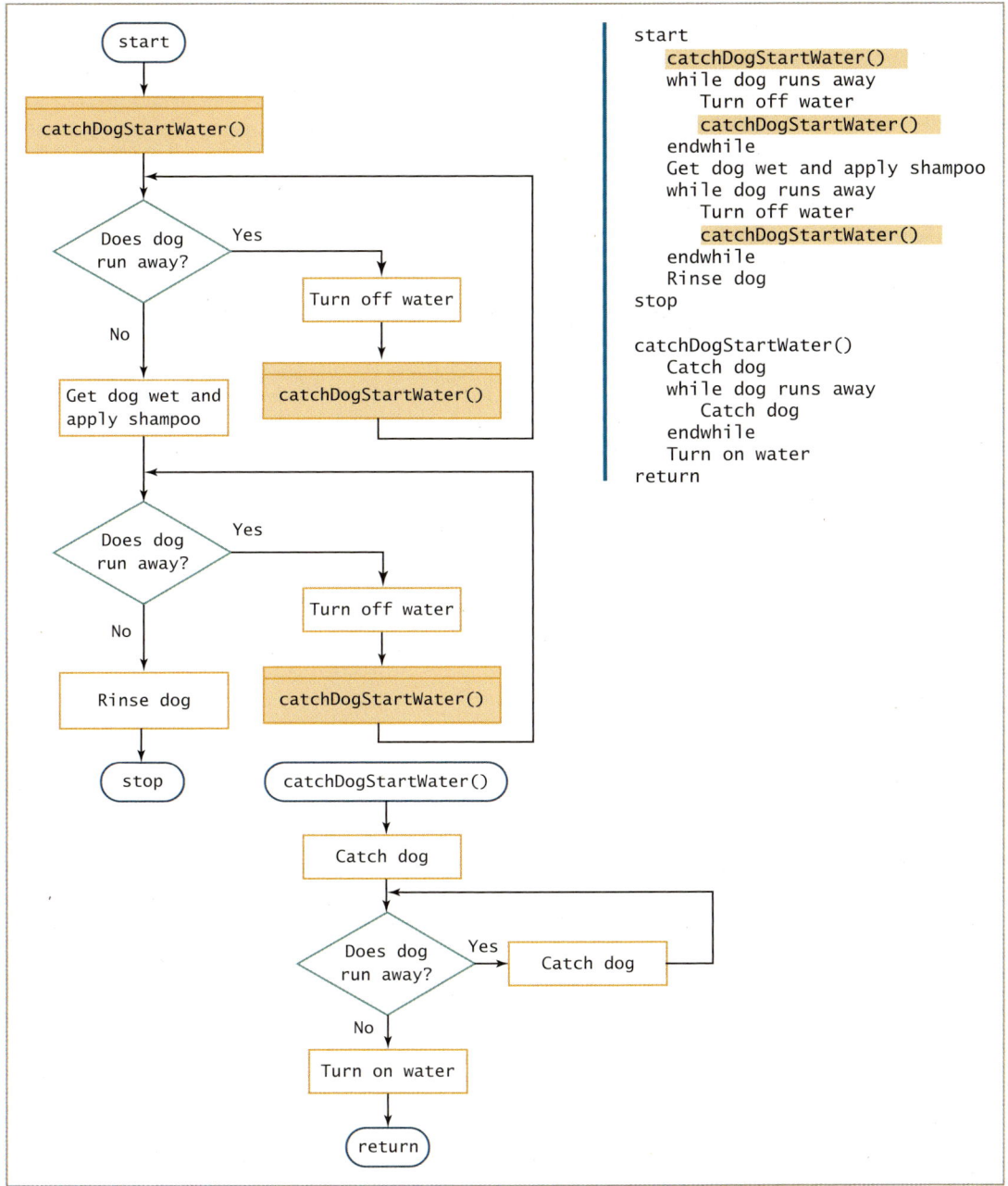

Figure 3-24 Modularized version of the dog-washing program

No matter how complicated it is, any set of steps can always be reduced to combinations of the three basic sequence, selection, and loop structures. These structures can be nested and stacked in an infinite number of ways to describe the logic of any process and to create the logic for every computer program written in the past, present, or future.

For convenience, many programming languages allow two variations of the three basic structures. The `case` structure is a variation of the selection structure and the `do` loop is a variation of the `while` loop. You can learn about these two structures in Appendix F. Even though these extra structures can be used in most programming languages, all logical problems can be solved without them.

Watch the video *Structuring Unstructured Logic*.

TWO TRUTHS & A LIE

Structuring and Modularizing Unstructured Logic

1. When you encounter a question in a logical diagram, a sequence should be ending.
2. In a structured loop, the logic returns to the loop-controlling question after the loop body executes.
3. If a flowchart or pseudocode contains a question to which the answer never varies, you can eliminate the question.

The false statement is #1. When you encounter a question in a logical diagram, either a selection or a loop should start. Any structure might end before the question is encountered.

Chapter Summary

- Spaghetti code is the popular name for unstructured program statements that do not follow the rules of structured logic.
- Clearer programs can be constructed using only three basic structures: sequence, selection, and loop. These three structures can be combined in an infinite number of ways by stacking and nesting them. Each structure has one entry and one exit point; one structure can attach to another only at one of these points.
- A priming input is the statement that gets the first input value prior to starting a structured loop. The last step within the loop gets the next and all subsequent input values.

- Programmers use structured techniques to promote clarity, professionalism, efficiency, and modularity.
- One way to order an unstructured flowchart segment is to imagine it as a bowl of spaghetti that you must untangle.
- Any set of logical steps can be rewritten to conform to the three structures.

Key Terms

Spaghetti code is snarled, unstructured program logic.

Unstructured programs are programs that do *not* follow the rules of structured logic.

Structured programs are programs that do follow the rules of structured logic.

A **structure** is a basic unit of programming logic; each structure is a sequence, selection, or loop.

A **sequence structure** contains a series of steps executed in order. A sequence can contain any number of tasks, but there is no option to branch off and skip any of the tasks.

A **selection structure** or **decision structure** contains a question, and, depending on the answer, takes one of two courses of action before continuing with the next task.

An **end-structure statement** designates the end of a pseudocode structure.

An **if-then-else** is another name for a selection structure.

Dual-alternative ifs (or **dual-alternative selections**) define one action to be taken when the tested condition is true and another action to be taken when it is false.

Single-alternative ifs (or **single-alternative selections**) take action on just one branch of the decision.

The **null case** is the branch of a decision in which no action is taken.

A **loop structure** continues to repeat actions while a test condition remains true.

A **loop body** is the set of actions that occur within a loop.

Repetition and **iteration** are alternate names for a loop structure.

In a **while...do**, or more simply, a **while loop**, a process continues while some condition continues to be true.

Stacking structures is the act of attaching structures end to end.

Nesting structures is the act of placing a structure within another structure.

A **block** is a group of statements that executes as a single unit.

A **priming input** or **priming read** is the statement that reads the first input data record prior to starting a structured loop.

Goto-less programming is a name to describe structured programming, because structured programmers do not use a "go to" statement.

CHAPTER 3 Understanding Structure

Review Questions

1. Snarled program logic is called _____ code.
   a. snake
   b. spaghetti
   c. string
   d. gnarly

2. The three structures of structured programming are _____.
   a. sequence, order, and process
   b. selection, loop, and iteration
   c. sequence, selection, and loop
   d. if, else, and then

3. A sequence structure can contain _____.
   a. any number of tasks
   b. exactly three tasks
   c. no more than three tasks
   d. only one task

4. Which of the following is *not* another term for a selection structure?
   a. decision structure
   b. `if-then-else` structure
   c. dual-alternative `if` structure
   d. loop structure

5. The structure in which you ask a question, and, depending on the answer, take some action and then ask the question again, can be called all of the following except a(n) _____.
   a. iteration
   b. loop
   c. repetition
   d. `if-then-else`

6. Placing a structure within another structure is called _____ the structures.
   a. stacking
   b. untangling
   c. building
   d. nesting

7. Attaching structures end to end is called _____.
   a. stacking
   b. untangling
   c. building
   d. nesting

8. The statement `if age >= 65 then seniorDiscount = "yes"` is an example of a _____.
   a. sequence
   b. loop
   c. dual-alternative selection
   d. single-alternative selection

9. The statement `while temperature remains below 60, leave the furnace on` is an example of a _____.
   a. sequence
   b. loop
   c. dual-alternative selection
   d. single-alternative selection

Review Questions

10. The statement `if age < 13 then movieTicket = 4.00 else movieTicket = 8.50` is an example of a _____.
    a. sequence
    b. loop
    c. dual-alternative selection
    d. single-alternative selection

11. Which of the following attributes do all three basic structures share?
    a. Their flowcharts all contain exactly three processing symbols.
    b. They all have one entry and one exit point.
    c. They all contain a decision.
    d. They all begin with a process.

12. Which is true of stacking structures?
    a. Two incidences of the same structure cannot be stacked adjacently.
    b. When you stack structures, you cannot nest them in the same program.
    c. Each structure has only one point where it can be stacked on top of another.
    d. When you stack structures, the top structure must be a sequence.

13. When you input data in a loop within a program, the input statement that precedes the loop _____.
    a. is the only part of the program allowed to be unstructured
    b. cannot result in `eof`
    c. is called a priming input
    d. executes hundreds or even thousands of times in most business programs

14. A group of statements that executes as a unit is a _____.
    a. block
    b. family
    c. chunk
    d. cohort

15. Which of the following is acceptable in a structured program?
    a. placing a sequence within the true half of a dual-alternative decision
    b. placing a decision within a loop
    c. placing a loop within one of the steps in a sequence
    d. All of these are acceptable.

16. In a selection structure, the structure-controlling question is _____.
    a. asked once at the beginning of the structure
    b. asked once at the end of the structure
    c. asked repeatedly until it is false
    d. asked repeatedly until it is true

17. When a loop executes, the structure-controlling question is _____.
    a. asked exactly once
    b. never asked more than once
    c. asked either before or after the loop body executes
    d. asked only if it is true, and not asked if it is false

18. Which of the following is *not* a reason for enforcing structure rules in computer programs?
    a. Structured programs are clearer to understand than unstructured ones.
    b. Other professional programmers will expect programs to be structured.
    c. Structured programs usually are shorter than unstructured ones.
    d. Structured programs can be broken down into modules easily.

19. Which of the following is *not* a benefit of modularizing programs?
    a. Modular programs are easier to read and understand than nonmodular ones.
    b. If you use modules, you can ignore the rules of structure.
    c. Modular components are reusable in other programs.
    d. Multiple programmers can work on different modules at the same time.

20. Which of the following is true of structured logic?
    a. You can use structured logic with newer programming languages, such as Java and C#, but not with older ones.
    b. Any task can be described using some combination of the three structures.
    c. Structured programs require that you break the code into easy-to-handle modules that each contain no more than five actions.
    d. All of these are true.

Exercises

1. In Figure 3-10, the process of buying and planting flowers in the spring was shown using the same structures as the generic example in Figure 3-9. Use the same logical structure as in Figure 3-9 to create a flowchart or pseudocode that describes some other process you know.

2. Each of the flowchart segments in Figure 3-25 is unstructured. Redraw each segment so that it does the same thing but is structured.

Exercises

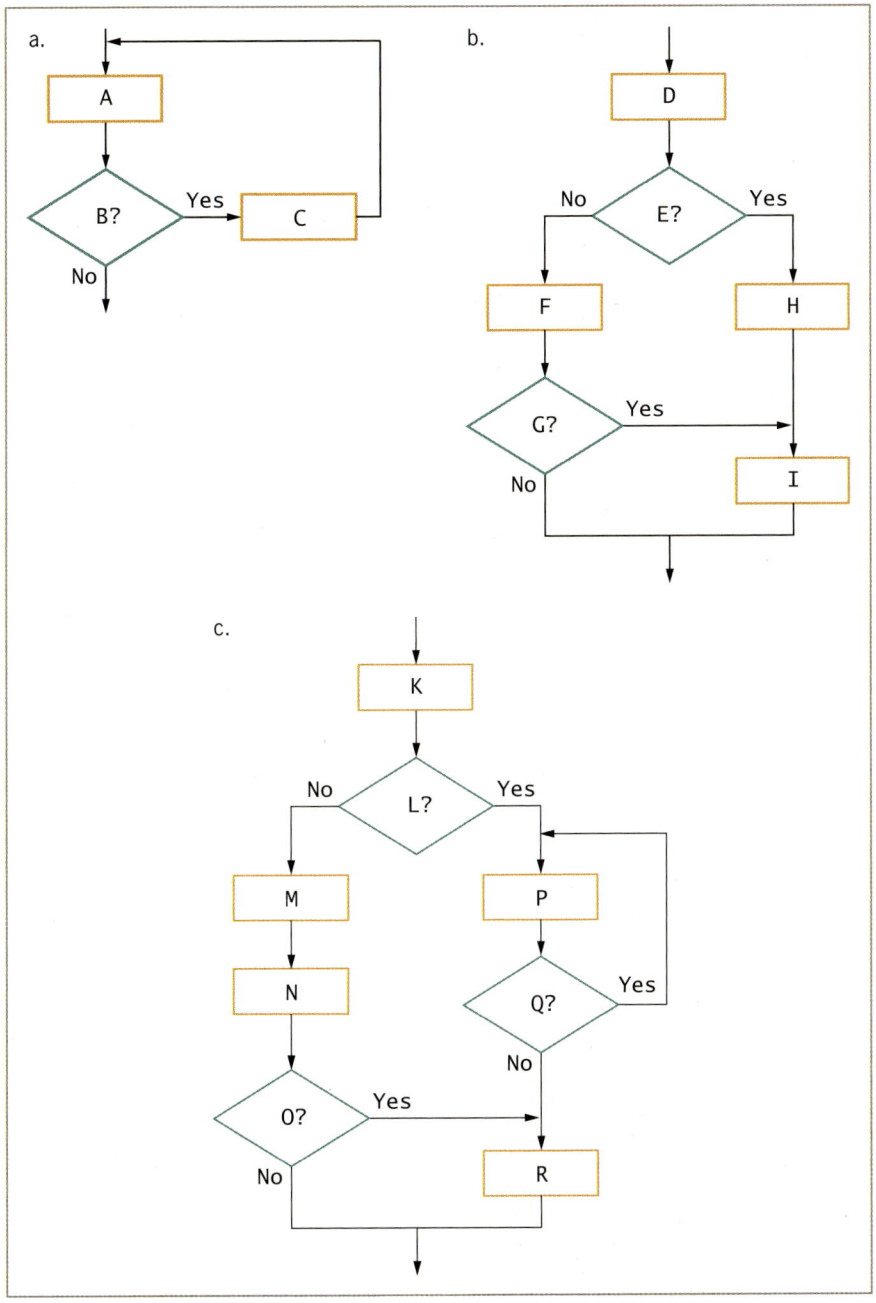

Figure 3-25 Flowcharts for Exercise 2 (continues)

(continued)

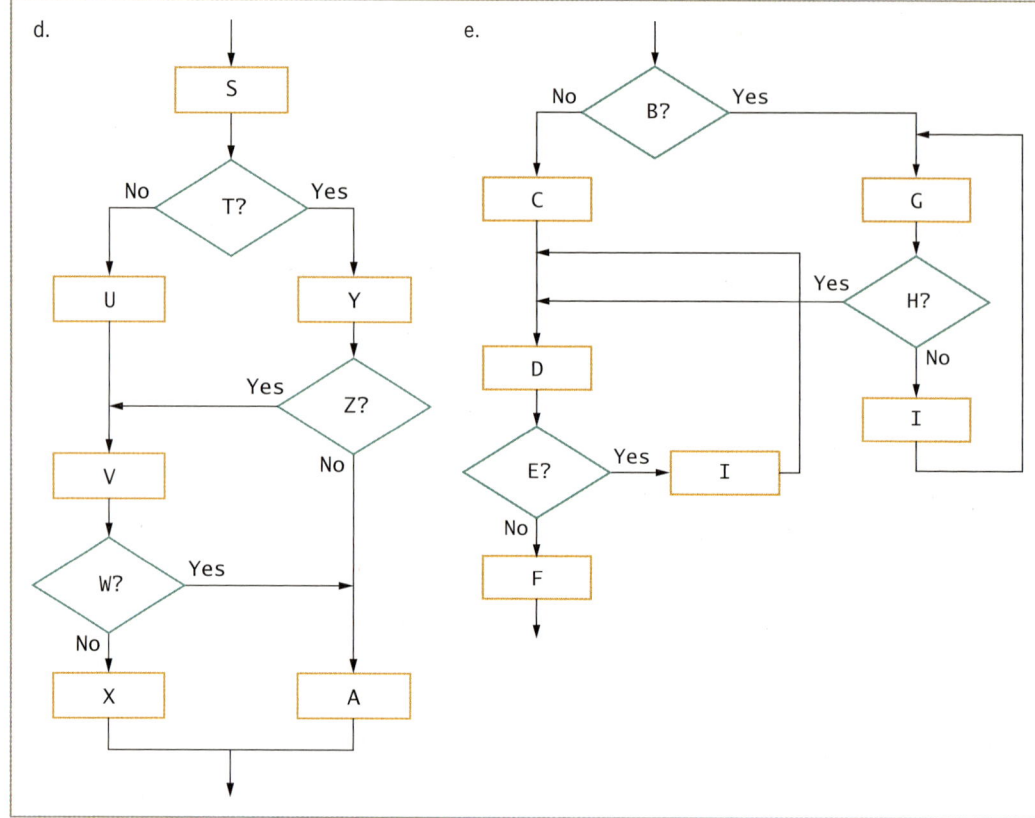

Figure 3-25 Flowcharts for Exercise 2

3. Write pseudocode for each example (a through e) in Exercise 2, making sure your pseudocode is structured but accomplishes the same tasks as the flowchart segment.

4. Assume that you have created a mechanical arm that can hold a pen. The arm can perform the following tasks:

   - Lower the pen to a piece of paper.
   - Raise the pen from the paper.
   - Move the pen 1 inch along a straight line. (If the pen is lowered, this action draws a 1-inch line from left to right; if the pen is raised, this action just repositions the pen 1 inch to the right.)
   - Turn 90 degrees to the right.
   - Draw a circle that is 1 inch in diameter.

   Draw a structured flowchart or write structured pseudocode describing the logic that would cause the arm to draw or write the following. Have a fellow student act as the mechanical arm and carry out your instructions. Don't reveal the desired outcome to your partner until the exercise is complete.

   a. a 1-inch square

   b. a 2-inch by 1-inch rectangle

   c. a string of three beads

   d. a short word (for example, *cat*)

   e. a four-digit number

5. Assume that you have created a mechanical robot that can perform the following tasks:

   - Stand up.
   - Sit down.
   - Turn left 90 degrees.
   - Turn right 90 degrees.
   - Take a step.

   Additionally, the robot can determine the answer to one test condition:

   - Am I touching something?

      a. Place two chairs 20 feet apart, directly facing each other. Draw a structured flowchart or write pseudocode describing the logic that would allow the robot to start from a sitting position in one chair, cross the room, and end up sitting in the other chair. Have a fellow student act as the robot and carry out your instructions.

      b. Draw a structured flowchart or write pseudocode describing the logic that would allow the robot to start from a sitting position in one chair, stand up and circle the chair, cross the room, circle the other chair, return to the first chair, and sit. Have a fellow student act as the robot and carry out your instructions.

6. Draw a structured flowchart or write pseudocode that describes the process of guessing a number between 1 and 100. After each guess, the player is told that the guess is too high or too low. The process continues until the player guesses the correct number. Pick a number and have a fellow student try to guess it following your instructions.

7. Looking up a word in a dictionary can be a complicated process. For example, assume that you want to look up *logic*. You might open the dictionary to a random page and see *juice*. You know this word comes alphabetically before *logic*, so you flip forward and see *lamb*. That is still not far enough, so you flip forward and see *monkey*. You have gone too far, so you flip back, and so on. Draw a structured flowchart or write pseudocode that describes the process of looking up a word in a

dictionary. Pick a word at random and have a fellow student attempt to carry out your instructions.

8. Draw a structured flowchart or write structured pseudocode describing how to find your classroom from the front entrance of the school building. Include at least two decisions and two loops.

9. Draw a structured flowchart or write structured pseudocode describing how to tidy up an apartment. Include at least two decisions and two loops.

10. Draw a structured flowchart or write structured pseudocode describing how to wrap a present. Include at least two decisions and two loops.

11. Draw a structured flowchart or write structured pseudocode describing the steps a grocery store clerk should follow to check out a customer. Include at least two decisions and two loops.

Find the Bugs

12. Your downloadable files for Chapter 3 include DEBUG03-01.txt, DEBUG03-02.txt, and DEBUG03-03.txt. Each file starts with some comments that describe the problem. Comments are lines that begin with two slashes (//). Following the comments, each file contains pseudocode that has one or more bugs you must find and correct.

Game Zone

13. Choose a simple children's game and describe its logic, using a structured flowchart or pseudocode. For example, you might try to explain Rock, Paper, Scissors; Musical Chairs; Duck, Duck, Goose; the card game War; or the elimination game Eenie, Meenie, Minie, Moe.

14. Choose a television game show such as *Deal or No Deal* or *Jeopardy!* and describe its rules using a structured flowchart or pseudocode.

15. Choose a sport such as baseball or football and describe the actions in one limited play period (such as an at-bat in baseball or a possession in football) using a structured flowchart or pseudocode.

Exercises

Up for Discussion

16. Find more information about one of the following people and explain why he or she is important to structured programming: Edsger Dijkstra, Corrado Bohm, Giuseppe Jacopini, and Grace Hopper.

17. Computer programs can contain structures within structures and stacked structures, creating very large programs. Computers also can perform millions of arithmetic calculations in an hour. How can we possibly know the results are correct?

18. Develop a checklist of rules you can use to help you determine whether a flowchart or pseudocode segment is structured.

CHAPTER 4

Making Decisions

In this chapter, you will learn about:

- Boolean expressions and the selection structure
- The relational comparison operators
- AND logic
- OR logic
- Making selections within ranges
- Precedence when combining AND and OR operators

CHAPTER 4 Making Decisions

Boolean Expressions and the Selection Structure

The reason people frequently think computers are smart lies in the ability of computer programs to make decisions. A medical diagnosis program that can decide if your symptoms fit various disease profiles seems quite intelligent, as does a program that can offer different potential vacation routes based on your destination.

Every decision you make in a computer program involves evaluating a **Boolean expression**—an expression whose value can be only true or false. True/false evaluation is natural from a computer's standpoint, because computer circuitry consists of two-state on-off switches, often represented by 1 or 0. Every computer decision yields a true-or-false, yes-or-no, 1-or-0 result. A Boolean expression is used in every selection structure. The selection structure is not new to you—it's one of the basic structures you learned about in Chapter 3. See Figures 4-1 and 4-2.

 Mathematician George Boole (1815–1864) approached logic more simply than his predecessors did, by expressing logical selections with common algebraic symbols. He is considered the founder of mathematical logic, and Boolean (true/false) expressions are named for him.

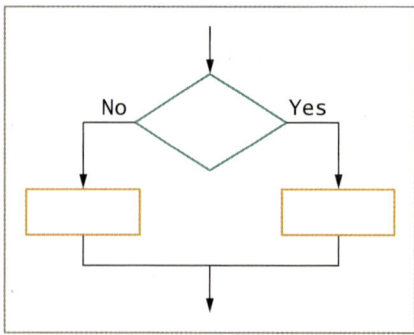

Figure 4-1 The dual-alternative selection structure

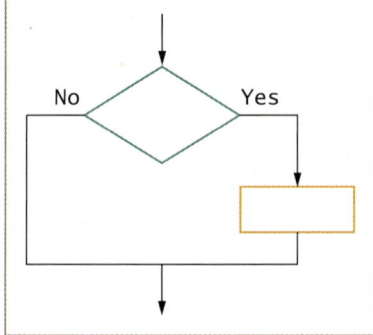

Figure 4-2 The single-alternative selection structure

In Chapter 3 you learned that the structure in Figure 4-1 is a dual-alternative, or binary, selection because an action is associated with each of two possible outcomes: Depending on the answer to the question represented by the diamond, the logical flow proceeds either to the left branch of the structure or to the right. The choices are mutually exclusive; that is, the logic can flow to only one of the two alternatives, never to both.

 This book follows the convention that the two logical paths emerging from a decision are drawn to the right and left of a diamond in a flowchart. Some programmers draw one of the flowlines emerging from the bottom of the diamond. The exact format of the diagram is not as important as the idea that one logical path flows into a selection, and two possible outcomes emerge.

The flowchart segment in Figure 4-2 represents a single-alternative selection in which action is required for only one outcome of the question. This form of the selection structure is called an **if-then**, because no alternative or **else** action is necessary.

Boolean Expressions and the Selection Structure

Figure 4-3 shows the flowchart and pseudocode for an interactive program that computes pay for employees. The program displays the weekly pay for each employee at the same hourly rate ($10.00) and assumes that there are no payroll deductions. The mainline logic calls `housekeeping()`, `detailLoop()`, and `finish()` modules. The `detailLoop()` module contains a typical `if-then-else` decision that determines whether an employee has worked more than a standard workweek (40 hours), and pays one and one-half times the employee's usual hourly rate for hours worked in excess of 40 per week.

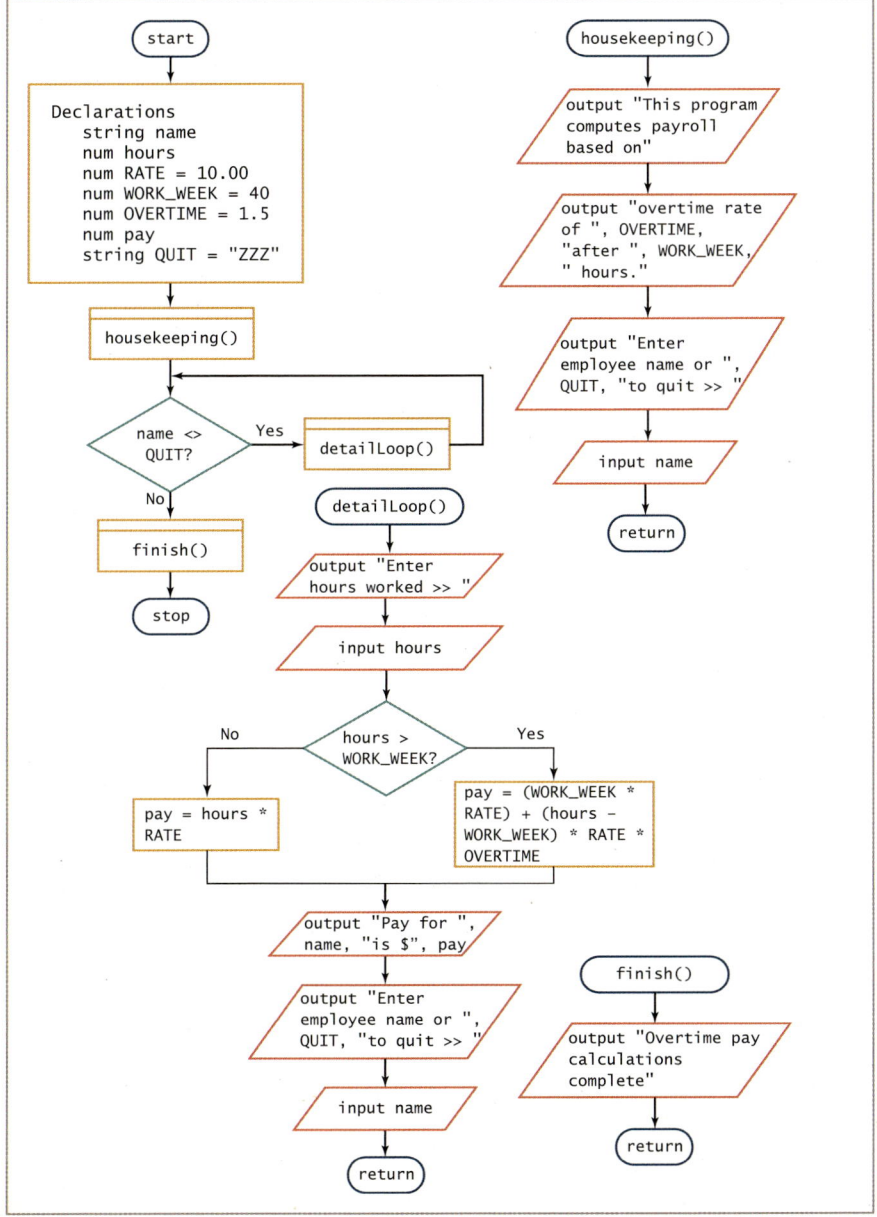

Figure 4-3 Flowchart and pseudocode for overtime payroll program

```
start
   Declarations
      string name
      num hours
      num RATE = 10.00
      num WORK_WEEK = 40
      num OVERTIME = 1.5
      num pay
      string QUIT = "ZZZ"
   housekeeping()
   while name <> QUIT
      detailLoop()
   endwhile
   finish()
stop

housekeeping()
   output "This program computes payroll based on"
   output "overtime rate of ", OVERTIME, "after ", WORK_WEEK, " hours."
   output "Enter employee name or ", QUIT, "to quit >> "
   input name
return

detailLoop()
   output "Enter hours worked >> "
   input hours
   if hours > WORK_WEEK then
      pay = (WORK_WEEK * RATE) + (hours - WORK_WEEK) * RATE * OVERTIME
   else
      pay = hours * RATE
   endif
   output "Pay for ", name, "is $", pay
   output "Enter employee name or ", QUIT, "to quit >> "
   input name
return

finish()
   output "Overtime pay calculations complete"
return
```

Figure 4-3 Flowchart and pseudocode for overtime payroll program (continued)

Throughout this book, many examples are presented in both flowchart and pseudocode form. When you analyze a solution, you might find it easier to concentrate on just one of the two design tools at first. When you understand how the program works using one tool (for example, the flowchart), you can confirm that the solution is identical using the other tool.

Boolean Expressions and the Selection Structure

In the `detailLoop()` module of the program in Figure 4-3, the decision contains two clauses:

- The **if-then clause** is the part of the decision that holds the action or actions that execute when the tested condition in the decision is true. In this example, the clause holds the longer overtime calculation.

- The **else clause** of the decision is the part that executes only when the tested condition in the decision is false. In this example, the clause contains the shorter calculation.

Figure 4-4 shows a typical execution of the program in a command-line environment. Data values are entered for three employees. The first two employees do not work more than 40 hours, so their pay is displayed simply as hours times $10.00. The third employee, however, has worked one hour of overtime, and so makes $15 for the last hour instead of $10.

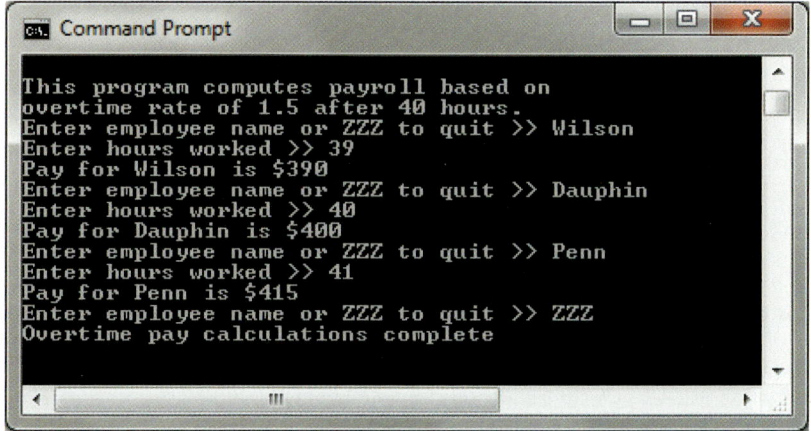

Figure 4-4   Typical execution of the overtime payroll program in Figure 4-3

 Watch the video *Boolean Expressions and Decisions*.

TWO TRUTHS & A LIE

Boolean Expressions and the Selection Structure

1. The `if-then` clause is the part of a decision that executes when a tested condition in a decision is true.
2. The `else` clause is the part of a decision that executes when a tested condition in a decision is true.
3. A Boolean expression is one whose value is true or false.

The false statement is #2. The else clause is the part of a decision that executes when a tested condition in a decision is false.

Using Relational Comparison Operators

Table 4-1 describes the six **relational comparison operators** supported by all modern programming languages. Each of these operators is binary—that is, each requires two operands. When you construct an expression using one of the operators described in Table 4-1, the expression evaluates to true or false. (Notice that some operators are formed using two characters without a space between them.) Usually, both operands in a comparison must be the same data type; that is, you can compare numeric values to other numeric values, and text strings to other strings. Some programming languages allow you to compare a character to a number. If you do, then a single character's numeric code value is used in the comparison. Appendix A contains more information on coding systems. In this book, only operands of the same type will be compared.

Operator	Name	Discussion
=	Equivalency operator	Evaluates as true when its operands are equivalent. Many languages use a double equal sign (==) to avoid confusion with the assignment operator.
>	Greater-than operator	Evaluates as true when the left operand is greater than the right operand.
<	Less-than operator	Evaluates as true when the left operand is less than the right operand.
>=	Greater-than or equal-to operator	Evaluates as true when the left operand is greater than or equivalent to the right operand.
<=	Less-than or equal-to operator	Evaluates as true when the left operand is less than or equivalent to the right operand.
<>	Not-equal-to operator	Evaluates as true when its operands are not equivalent. Some languages use an exclamation point followed by an equal sign to indicate not equal to (!=).

Table 4-1   Relational comparison operators

In any Boolean expression, the two values compared can be either variables or constants. For example, the expression currentTotal = 100? compares a variable, currentTotal, to a numeric constant, 100. Depending on the currentTotal value, the expression is true or false. In the expression currentTotal = previousTotal?, both values are variables, and the result is also true or false depending on the values stored in each of the two variables. Although it's legal, you would never use expressions in which you compare two constants—for example, 20 = 20? or 30 = 40?. Such expressions are **trivial expressions** because each will always evaluate to the same result: true for 20 = 20? and false for 30 = 40?.

Using Relational Comparison Operators

Some languages require special operations to compare strings, but this book will assume that the standard comparison operators work correctly with strings based on their alphabetic values. For example, the comparison "black" < "blue"? would be evaluated as true because "black" precedes "blue" alphabetically. Usually, string variables are not considered to be equal unless they are identical, including the spacing and whether they appear in uppercase or lowercase. For example, "black pen" is not equal to "blackpen", "BLACK PEN", or "Black Pen".

Any decision can be made using combinations of just three types of comparisons: equal, greater than, and less than. You never need the three additional comparisons (greater than or equal, less than or equal, or not equal), but using them often makes decisions more convenient. For example, assume that you need to issue a 10 percent discount to any customer whose age is 65 or greater, and charge full price to other customers. You can use the greater-than-or-equal-to symbol to write the logic as follows:

```
if customerAge >= 65 then
    discount = 0.10
else
    discount = 0
endif
```

As an alternative, if the >= operator did not exist, you could express the same logic by writing:

```
if customerAge < 65 then
    discount = 0
else
    discount = 0.10
endif
```

In any decision for which a >= b is true, then a < b is false. Conversely, if a >= b is false, then a < b is true. By rephrasing the question and swapping the actions taken based on the outcome, you can make the same decision in multiple ways. The clearest route is often to ask a question so the positive or true outcome results in the action that was your motivation for making the test. When your company policy is to "provide a discount for those who are 65 and older," the phrase *greater than or equal to* comes to mind, so it is the most natural to use. Conversely, if your policy is to "provide no discount for those under 65," then it is more natural to use the *less than* syntax. Either way, the same people receive a discount.

Comparing two amounts to decide if they are *not* equal to each other is the most confusing of all the comparisons. Using *not equal to* in decisions involves thinking in double negatives, which can make you prone to including logical errors in your programs. For example, consider the flowchart segment in Figure 4-5.

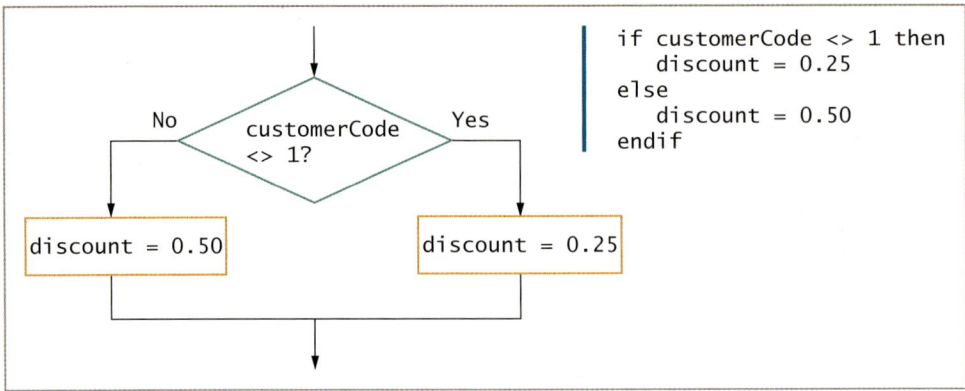

Figure 4-5 Using a negative comparison

In Figure 4-5, if the value of customerCode *is* equal to 1, the logical flow follows the false branch of the selection. If customerCode <> 1 is true, the discount is 0.25; if customerCode <> 1 is not true, it means the customerCode *is* 1, and the discount is 0.50. Even reading the phrase "if customerCode is not equal to 1 is not true" is awkward.

Figure 4-6 shows the same decision, this time asked using positive logic. Making the decision based on what customerCode *is* is clearer than trying to determine what customerCode is *not*.

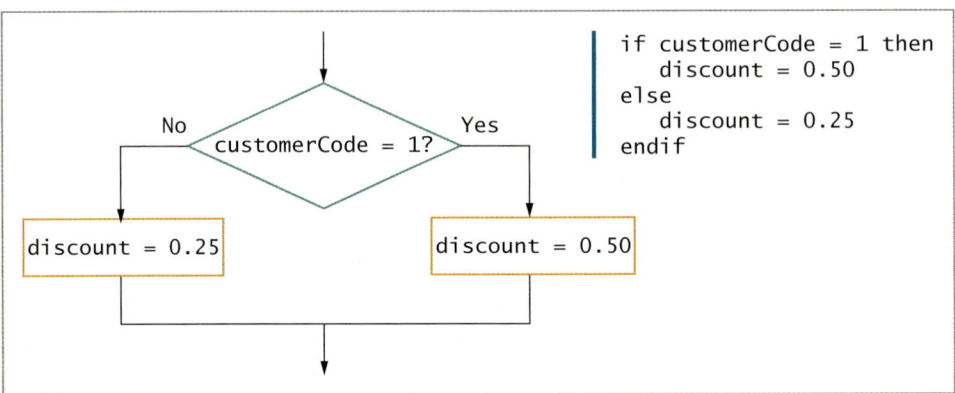

Figure 4-6 Using the positive equivalent of the negative comparison in Figure 4-5

 Although negative comparisons can be awkward to use, your meaning is sometimes clearest when using them. Frequently, this occurs when you use an if without an else, taking action only when some comparison is false. An example would be: if customerZipCode <> LOCAL_ZIP_CODE then total = total + deliveryCharge.

Avoiding a Common Error with Relational Operators

A common error that occurs when programming with relational operators is using the wrong one and missing the boundary or limit required for a selection. If you use the > symbol to make a selection when you should have used >=, all the cases that are equal will go unselected. Unfortunately, people who request programs do not always speak as precisely as a computer. If, for example, your boss says, "Write a program that selects all employees over 65," does she mean to include employees who are 65 or not? In other words, is the comparison age > 65 or age >= 65? Although the phrase *over 65* indicates *greater than 65*, people do not always say what they mean, and the best course of action is to double-check the intended meaning with the person who requested the program—for example, the end user, your supervisor, or your instructor. Similar phrases that can cause misunderstandings are *no more than*, *at least*, and *not under*.

TWO TRUTHS & A LIE

Using Relational Comparison Operators

1. Usually, you can compare only values that are of the same data type.
2. A Boolean expression is defined as one that decides whether two values are equal.
3. In any Boolean expression, the two values compared can be either variables or constants.

The false statement is #2. Although deciding whether two values are equal is a Boolean expression, so is deciding whether one is greater than or less than another. A Boolean expression is one that results in a true or false value.

Understanding *AND* Logic

Often, you need to evaluate more than one expression to determine whether an action should take place. When you ask multiple questions before an outcome is determined, you create a **compound condition**. For example, suppose you work for a cell phone company that charges customers as follows:

- The basic monthly service bill is $30.
- An additional $20 is billed to customers who make more than 100 calls that last for a total of more than 500 minutes.

The logic needed for this billing program includes an **AND decision**—a decision in which two conditions must be true for an action to take place. In this case, both a minimum number of calls must be made *and* a minimum number of minutes must be used before the customer is charged the additional amount. An AND decision can be constructed using a **nested decision**, or a

nested if—that is, a decision within the if-then or else clause of another decision. A series of nested if statements is also called a **cascading if statement**. The flowchart and pseudocode for the program that determines the charges for customers is shown in Figure 4-7.

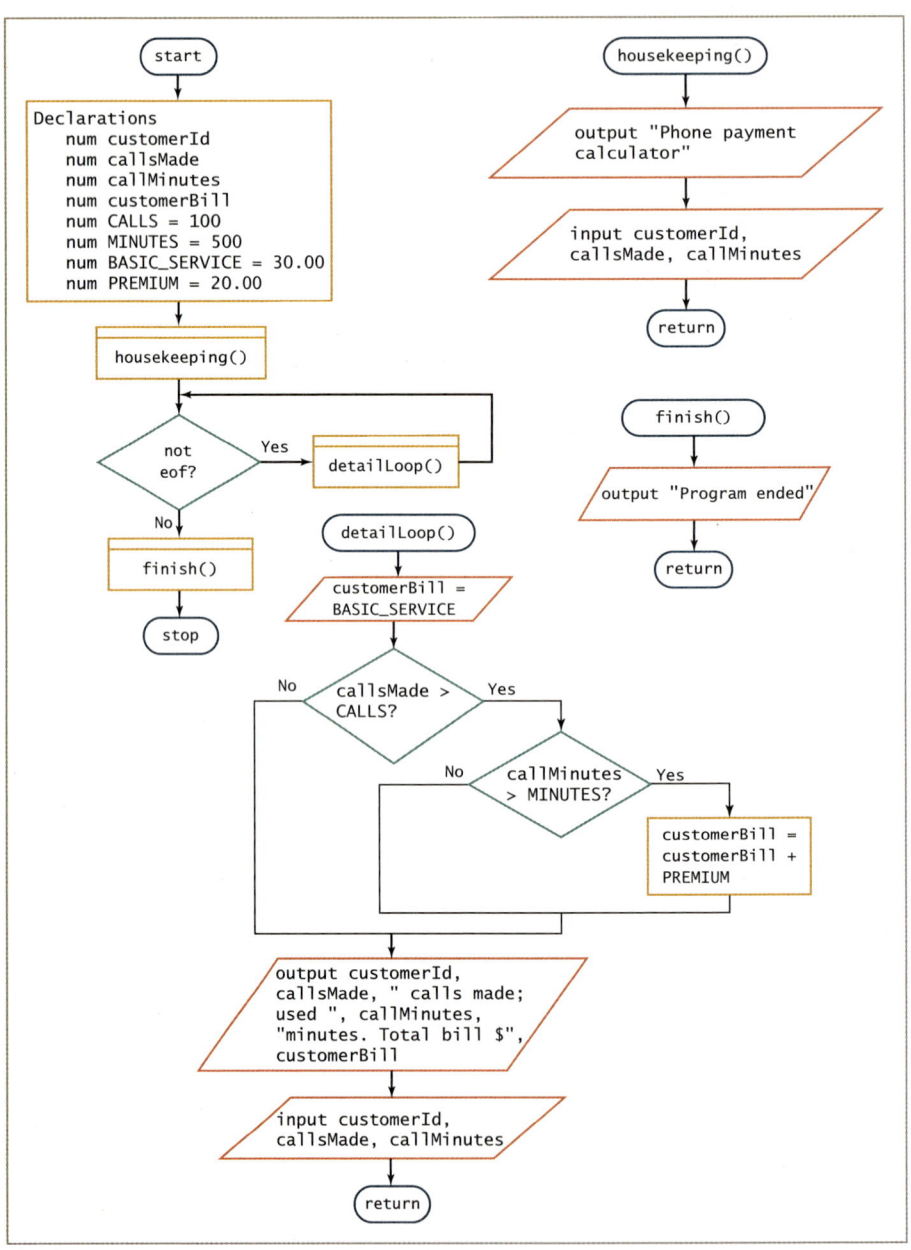

Figure 4-7 Flowchart and pseudocode for cell phone billing program (continues)

(continued)

```
start
    Declarations
        num customerId
        num callsMade
        num callMinutes
        num customerBill
        num CALLS = 100
        num MINUTES = 500
        num BASIC_SERVICE = 30.00
        num PREMIUM = 20.00
    housekeeping()
    while not eof
        detailLoop()
    endwhile
    finish()
stop

housekeeping()
    output "Phone payment calculator"
    input customerId, callsMade, callMinutes
return

detailLoop()
    customerBill = BASIC_SERVICE
    if callsMade > CALLS then
        if callMinutes > MINUTES then
            customerBill = customerBill + PREMIUM
        endif
    endif
    output customerId, callsMade, " calls made; used ",
        callMinutes, " minutes. Total bill $", customerBill
    input customerId, callsMade, callMinutes
return

finish()
    output "Program ended"
return
```

Figure 4-7 Flowchart and pseudocode for cell phone billing program

You first learned about nesting structures in Chapter 3. You can always stack and nest any of the basic structures.

In the cell phone billing program, the customer data is retrieved from a file. This eliminates the need for prompts and keeps the program shorter so you can concentrate on the decision-making process. If this was an interactive program, you would use a prompt before each input statement. Chapter 7 covers file processing and explains a few additional steps you can take when working with files.

In Figure 4-7, the appropriate variables and constants are declared, and then the `housekeeping()` module displays an introductory heading and gets the first set of input data. After control returns to the mainline logic, the `eof` condition is tested, and if data entry is not complete, the `detailLoop()` module executes. In the `detailLoop()` module, the customer's bill is set to the standard fee, and then the nested decision executes. In the nested `if` structure in Figure 4-7, the expression `callsMade > CALLS?` is evaluated first. If this expression is true, only then is the second Boolean expression (`callMinutes > MINUTES?`) evaluated. If that expression is also true, then the $20 premium is added to the customer's bill. If either of the tested conditions is false, the customer's bill value is never altered, retaining the initially assigned value of $30.

Most languages allow you to use a variation of the decision structure called the *case structure* when you must nest a series of decisions about a single variable. Appendix F contains information about the case structure.

Nesting *AND* Decisions for Efficiency

When you nest two decisions, you must choose which of the decisions to make first. Logically, either expression in an AND decision can be evaluated first. However, you often can improve your program's performance by correctly choosing which of two selections to make first.

For example, Figure 4-8 shows two ways to design the nested decision structure that assigns a premium to customers' bills if they make more than 100 cell phone calls and use more than 500 minutes in a billing period. The program can ask about calls made first, eliminate customers who have not made more than the minimum, and ask about the minutes used only for customers who pass (that is, are evaluated as true on) the minimum calls test. Or, the program could ask about the minutes first, eliminate those who do not qualify, and ask about the number of calls only for customers who pass the minutes test. Either way, only customers who exceed both limits must pay the premium. Does it make a difference which question is asked first? As far as the result goes, no. Either way, the same customers pay the premium—those who qualify on the basis of both criteria. As far as program efficiency goes, however, it *might* make a difference which question is asked first.

Understanding AND Logic

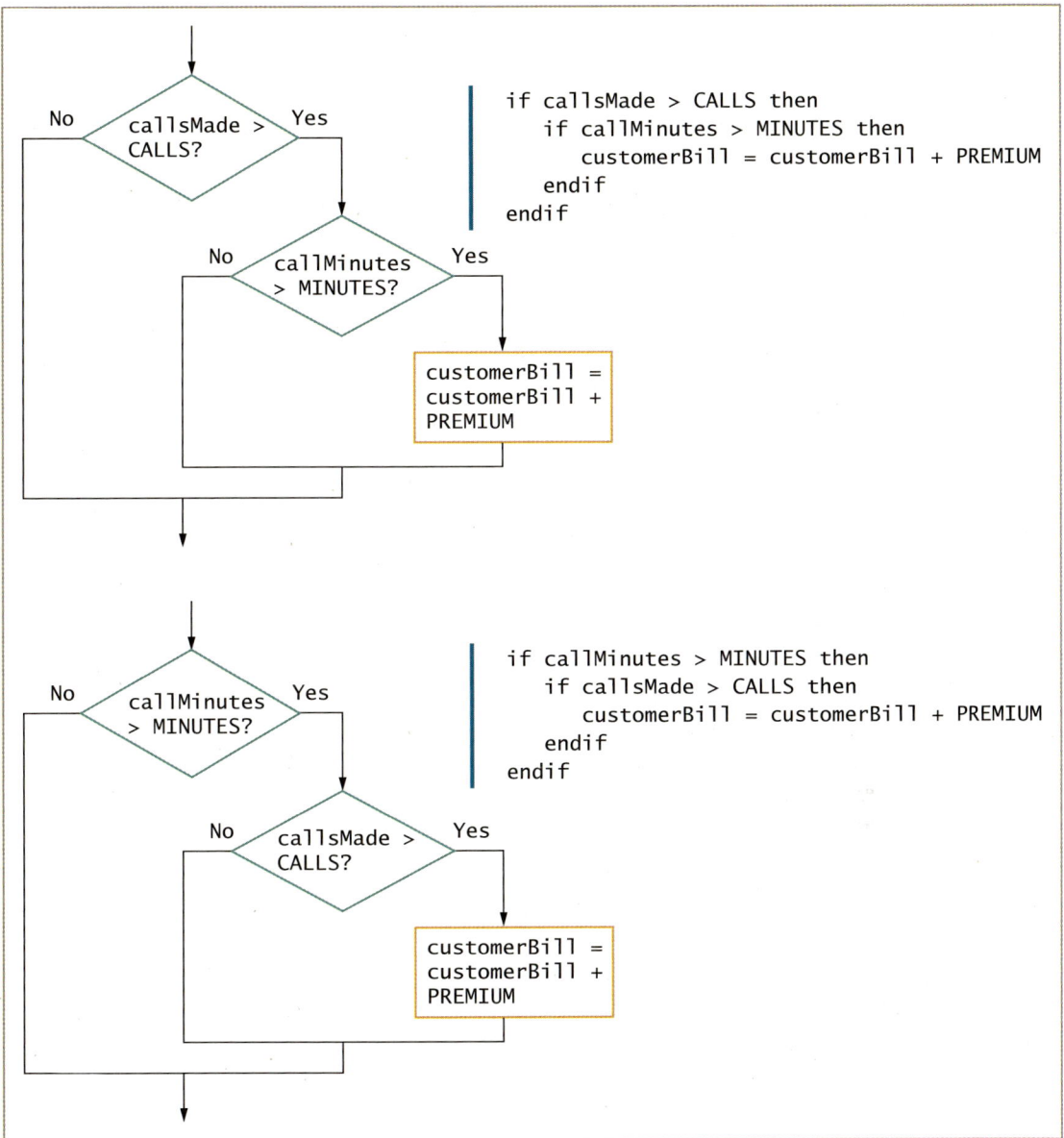

Figure 4-8 Two ways to produce cell phone bills using identical criteria

Assume that you know that out of 1000 cell phone customers, about 90 percent, or 900, make more than 100 calls in a billing period. Assume that you also know that only about half the 1000 customers, or 500, use more than 500 minutes of call time.

If you use the logic shown first in Figure 4-8, and you need to produce 1000 phone bills, the first question, callsMade > CALLS?, will execute 1000 times. For approximately 90 percent of the customers, or 900 of them, the answer is true, so 100 customers are eliminated from the premium assignment, and 900 proceed to the next question about the minutes used. Only about half the customers use more than 500 minutes, so 450 of the 900 pay the premium, and it takes 1900 questions to identify them.

Using the alternate logic shown second in Figure 4-8, the first question, `callMinutes > MINUTES?`, will also be asked 1000 times—once for each customer. Because only about half the customers use the high number of minutes, only 500 will pass this test and proceed to the question for number of calls made. Then, about 90 percent of the 500, or 450 customers, will pass the second test and be billed the premium amount. It takes 1500 questions to identify the 450 premium-paying customers.

Whether you use the first or second decision order in Figure 4-8, the same 450 customers who satisfy both criteria pay the premium. The difference is that when you ask about the number of calls first, the program must ask 400 more questions than when you ask about the minutes used first.

The 400-question difference between the first and second set of decisions doesn't take much time on most computers. But it does take *some* time, and if a corporation has hundreds of thousands of customers instead of only 1000, or if many such decisions have to be made within a program, performance time can be significantly improved by asking questions in the more efficient order.

Often when you must make nested decisions, you have no idea which event is more likely to occur; in that case, you can legitimately ask either question first. However, if you do know the probabilities of the conditions, or can make a reasonable guess, the general rule is: *In an AND decision, first ask the question that is less likely to be true.* This eliminates as many instances of the second decision as possible, which speeds up processing time.

 Watch the video *Writing Efficient Nested Selections*.

Using the AND Operator

Most programming languages allow you to ask two or more questions in a single comparison by using a **conditional AND operator**, or more simply, an **AND operator** that joins decisions in a single statement. For example, if you want to bill an extra amount to cell phone customers who make more than 100 calls that total more than 500 minutes in a billing period, you can use nested decisions, as shown in the previous section, or you can include both decisions in a single statement by writing the following question:

`callsMade > CALLS AND callMinutes > MINUTES?`

When you use one or more AND operators to combine two or more Boolean expressions, each Boolean expression must be true for the entire expression to be evaluated as true. For example, if you ask, "Are you a native-born U.S. citizen and are you at least 35 years old?", the answer to both parts of the question must be *yes* before the response can be a single, summarizing *yes*. If either part of the expression is false, then the entire expression is false.

Understanding AND Logic

The conditional AND operator in Java, C++, and C# consists of two ampersands, with no spaces between them (&&). In Visual Basic, you use the word **And**.

One tool that can help you understand the AND operator is a truth table. **Truth tables** are diagrams used in mathematics and logic to help describe the truth of an entire expression based on the truth of its parts. Table 4-2 shows a truth table that lists all the possibilities with an AND decision. As the table shows, for any two expressions x and y, the expression x AND y? is true only if both x and y are individually true. If either x or y alone is false, or if both are false, then the expression x AND y? is false.

x?	y?	x AND y?
True	True	True
True	False	False
False	True	False
False	False	False

Table 4-2 Truth table for the AND operator

If the programming language you use allows an AND operator, you must realize that the question you place first (to the left of the operator) is the one that will be asked first, and cases that are eliminated based on the first question will not proceed to the second question. In other words, each part of an expression that uses an AND operator is evaluated only as far as necessary to determine whether the entire expression is true or false. This feature is called **short-circuit evaluation**. The computer can ask only one question at a time; even when your pseudocode looks like the first example in Figure 4-9, the computer will execute the logic shown in the second example. Even when you use an AND operator, the computer makes decisions one at a time, and makes them in the order you ask them. If the first question in an AND expression evaluates to false, then the entire expression is false, and the second question is not even tested.

You are never required to use the AND operator because using nested if statements can always achieve the same result. However, using the AND operator often makes your code more concise, less error-prone, and easier to understand.

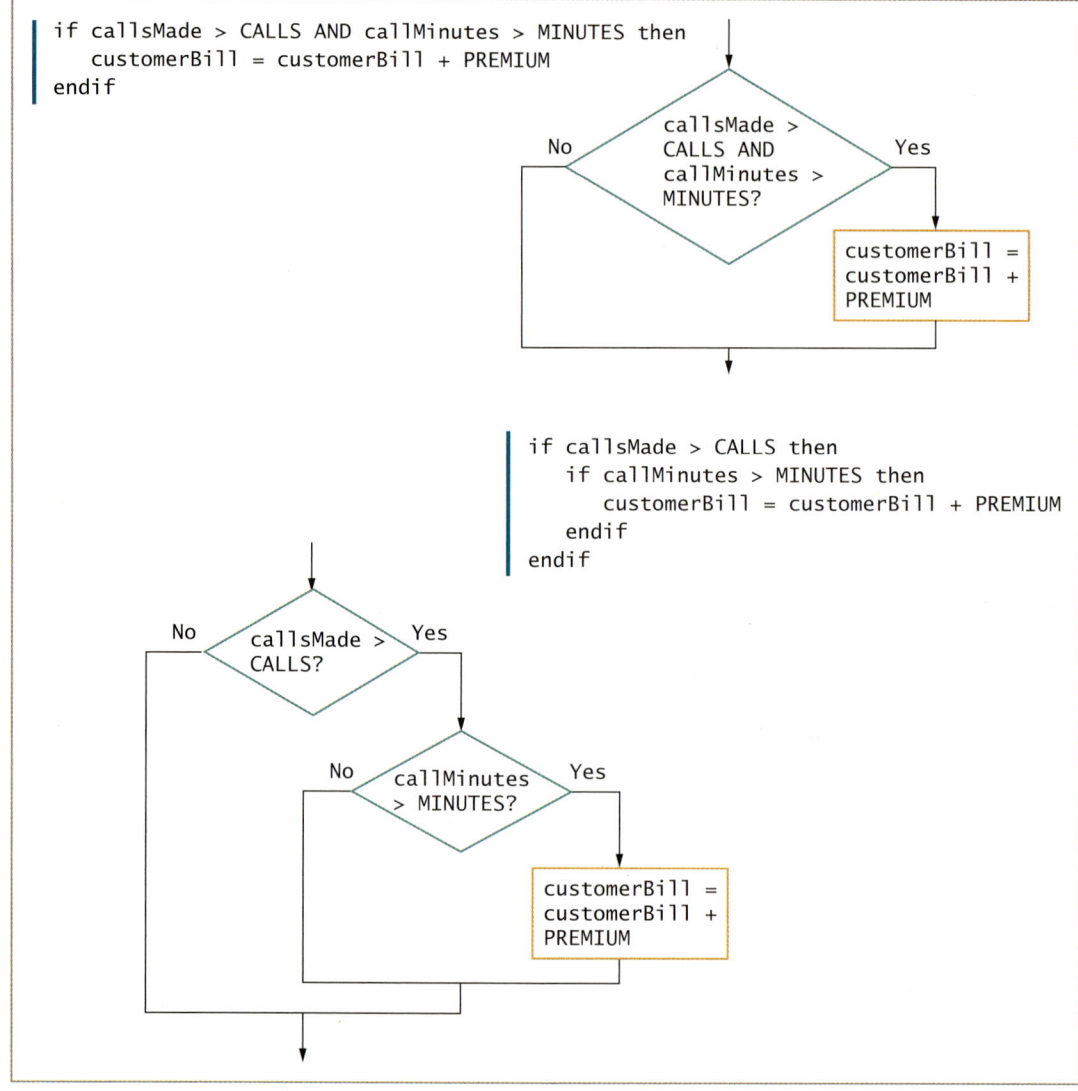

Figure 4-9 Using an AND operator and the logic behind it

Avoiding Common Errors in an *AND* Selection

When you need to satisfy two or more criteria to initiate an event in a program, you must make sure that the second decision is made entirely within the first decision. For example, if a program's objective is to add a $20 premium to the bill of cell phone customers who exceed 100 calls and 500 minutes in a billing period, then the program segment shown in Figure 4-10 contains three different types of logic errors.

Understanding AND Logic

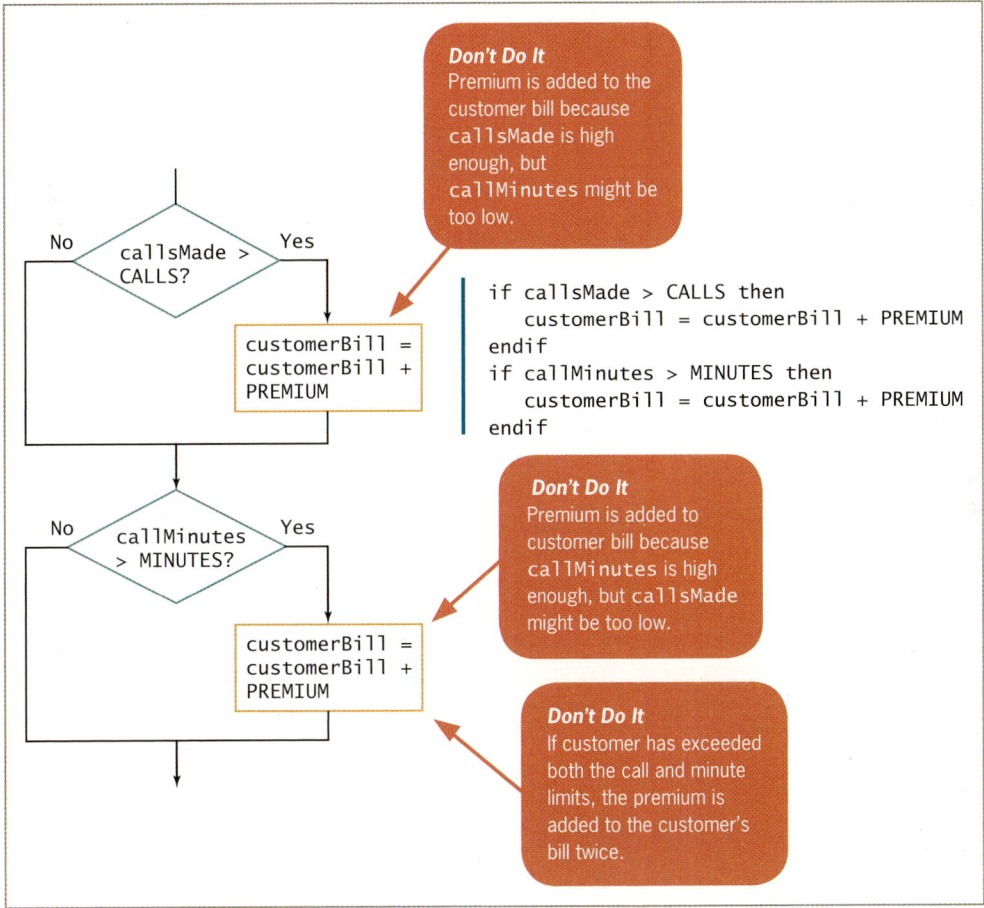

Figure 4-10 Incorrect logic to add a $20 premium to the bills of cell phone customers who meet two criteria

The logic in Figure 4-10 shows that $20 is added to the bill of a customer who makes too many calls. This customer should not necessarily be billed extra—the customer's minutes might be below the cutoff for the $20 premium. In addition, a customer who has made few calls is not eliminated from the second question. Instead, all customers are subjected to the minutes question, and some are assigned the premium even though they might not have passed the criterion for number of calls made. Additionally, any customer who passes both tests has the premium added to his bill twice. For many reasons, the logic shown in Figure 4-10 is *not* correct for this problem.

When you use the AND operator in most languages, you must provide a complete Boolean expression on each side of the operator. In other words, `callMinutes > 100 AND callMinutes < 200` would be a valid expression to find `callMinutes` between 100 and 200. However, `callMinutes > 100 AND < 200` would not be valid because what follows the AND operator (< 200) is not a complete Boolean expression.

For clarity, you can surround each Boolean expression in a compound expression with its own set of parentheses. Use this format if it is clearer to you. For example, you might write the following:

```
if (callMinutes > MINUTES) AND (callsMade > CALLS)
    customerBill = customerBill + PREMIUM
endif
```

TWO TRUTHS & A LIE

Understanding AND Logic

1. When you nest decisions because the resulting action requires that two conditions be true, either decision logically can be made first and the same selections will occur.

2. When two selections are required for an action to take place, you often can improve your program's performance by appropriately choosing which selection to make first.

3. To improve efficiency in a nested selection in which two conditions must be true for some action to occur, you should first ask the question that is more likely to be true.

The false statement is # 3. For efficiency in a nested selection, you should first ask the question that is less likely to be true.

Understanding OR Logic

Sometimes you want to take action when one *or* the other of two conditions is true. This is called an **OR decision** because either one condition *or* some other condition must be met in order for an event to take place. If someone asks, "Are you free for dinner Friday or Saturday?," only one of the two conditions has to be true for the answer to the whole question to be *yes*; only if the answers to both halves of the question are false is the value of the entire expression false.

For example, suppose you want to add $20 to the bills of cell phone customers who either make more than 100 calls or use more than 500 minutes. Figure 4-11 shows the altered `detailLoop()` module of the billing program that accomplishes this objective.

Understanding OR Logic

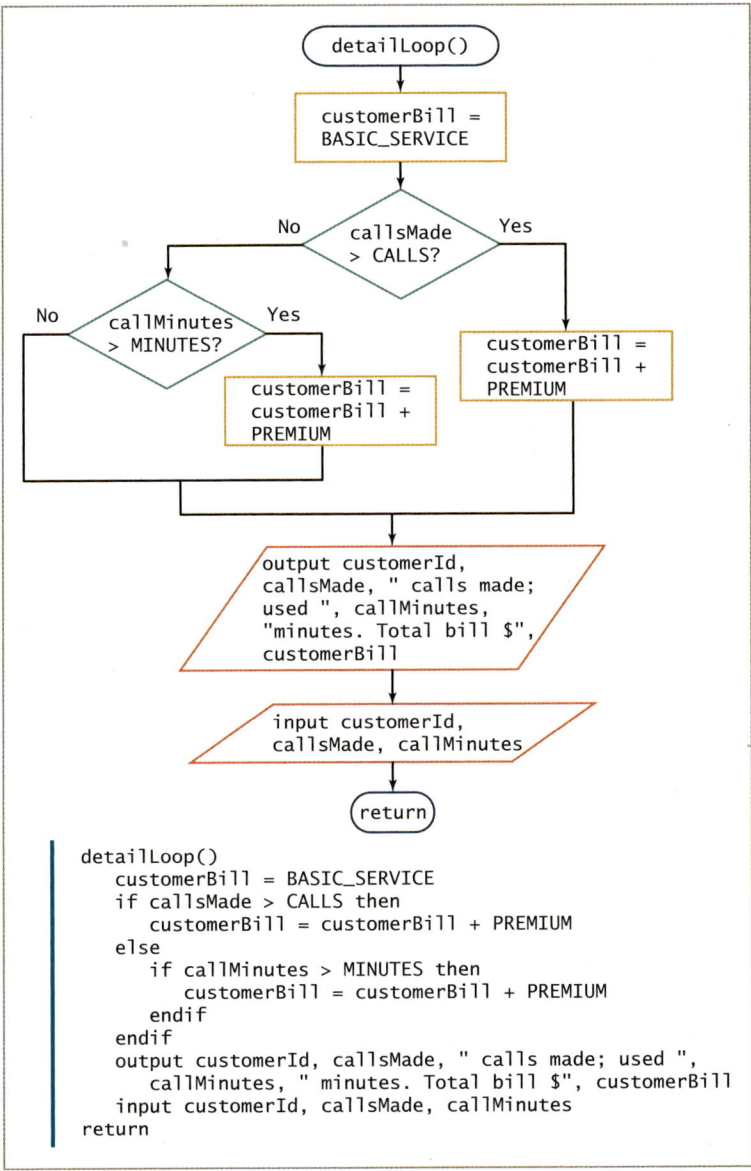

Figure 4-11 Flowchart and pseudocode for cell phone billing program in which a customer must meet one or both of two criteria to be billed a premium

The `detailLoop()` in the program in Figure 4-11 asks the question `callsMade > CALLS?`, and if the result is true, the extra amount is added to the customer's bill. Because making many calls is enough for the customer to incur the premium, there is no need for further questioning. If the customer has not made more than 100 calls, only then does the program need to ask whether `callMinutes > MINUTES` is true. If the customer did not make over 100 calls, but used more than 500 minutes nevertheless, then the premium amount is added to the customer's bill.

Writing OR Decisions for Efficiency

As with an AND selection, when you use an OR selection, you can choose to ask either question first. For example, you can add an extra $20 to the bills of customers who meet one or the other of two criteria using the logic in either part of Figure 4-12.

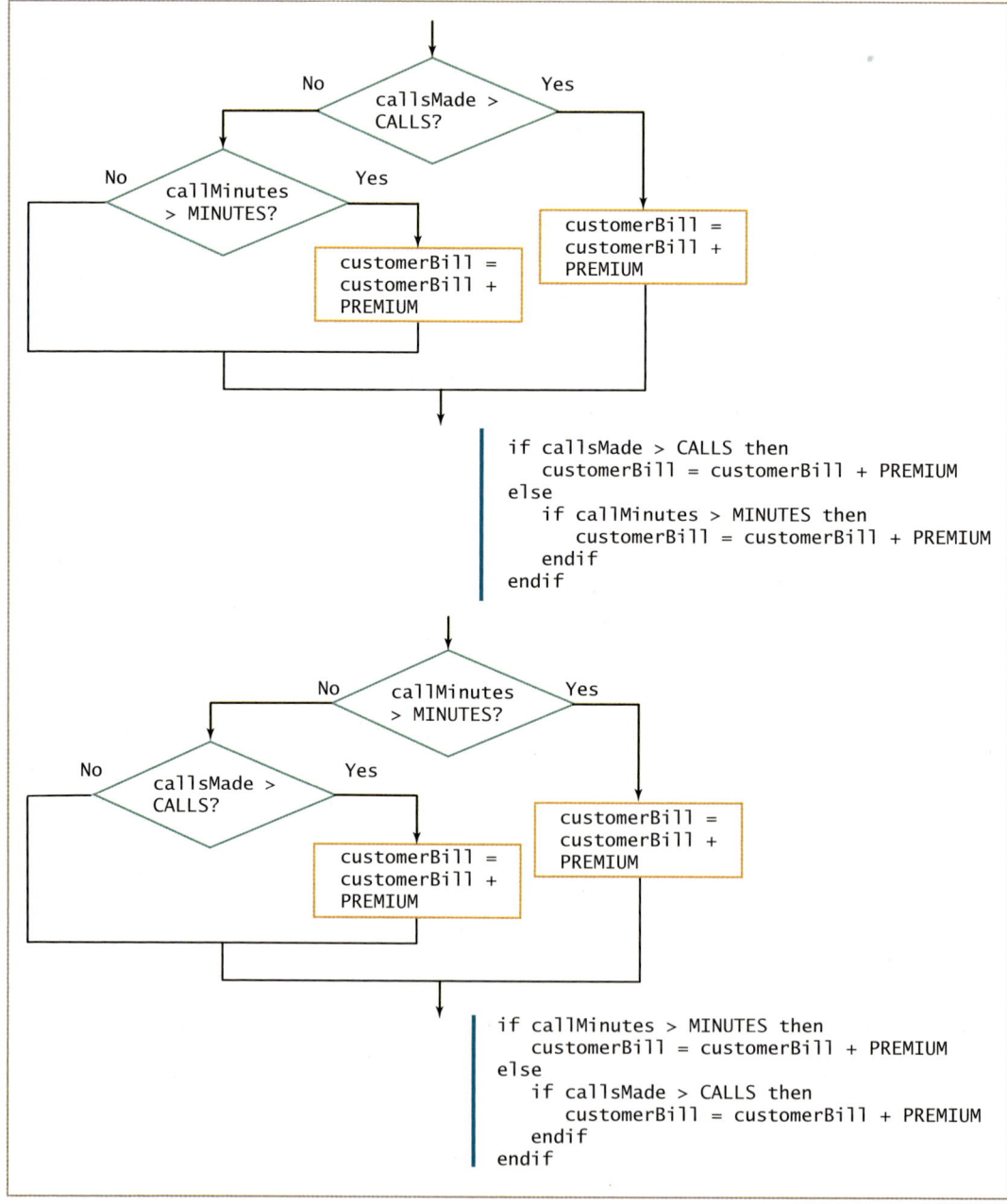

Figure 4-12 Two ways to assign a premium to bills of customers who meet one of two criteria

Understanding OR Logic

You might have guessed that one of these selections is superior to the other when you have some background information about the relative likelihood of each condition being tested. For example, let's say you know that out of 1000 cell phone customers, about 90 percent, or 900, make more than 100 calls in a billing period. You also know that only about half the 1000 customers, or 500, use more than 500 minutes of call time.

When you use the logic shown in the first half of Figure 4-12, you first ask about the calls made. For 900 customers the answer is true, and you add the premium to their bills. Only about 100 sets of customer data continue to the next question regarding the call minutes, where about 50 percent of the 100, or 50, are billed the extra amount. In the end, you have made 1100 decisions to correctly add premium amounts for 950 customers.

If you use the OR logic in the second half of Figure 4-12, you ask about minutes used first—1000 times, once each for 1000 customers. The result is true for 50 percent, or 500 customers, whose bill is increased. For the other 500 customers, you ask about the number of calls made. For 90 percent of the 500, the result is true, so premiums are added for 450 additional people. In the end, the same 950 customers are billed an extra $20—but this approach requires executing 1500 decisions, 400 more decisions than when using the first decision logic.

The general rule is: *In an OR decision, first ask the question that is more likely to be true.* This approach eliminates as many executions of the second decision as possible, and the time it takes to process all the data is decreased. As with the AND situation, in an OR situation, it is more efficient to eliminate as many extra decisions as possible.

Using the OR Operator

If you need to take action when either one or the other of two conditions is met, you can use two separate, nested selection structures, as in the previous examples. However, most programming languages allow you to ask two or more questions in a single comparison by using a **conditional OR operator** (or simply the **OR operator**). For example, you can ask the following question:

callsMade > CALLS OR callMinutes > MINUTES?

As with the AND operator, most programming languages require a complete Boolean expression on each side of the OR operator. When you use the logical OR operator, only one of the listed conditions must be met for the resulting action to take place. Table 4-3 shows the truth table for the OR operator. As you can see in the table, the entire expression x OR y? is false only when x and y each are false individually.

X?	Y?	x OR y?
True	True	True
True	False	True
False	True	True
False	False	False

Table 4-3 Truth table for the OR operator

If the programming language you use supports the OR operator, you still must realize that the question you place first is the question that will be asked first, and cases that pass the test of the first question will not proceed to the second question. As with the AND operator, this feature is called short-circuiting. The computer can ask only one question at a time; even when you write code as shown at the top of Figure 4-13, the computer will execute the logic shown at the bottom.

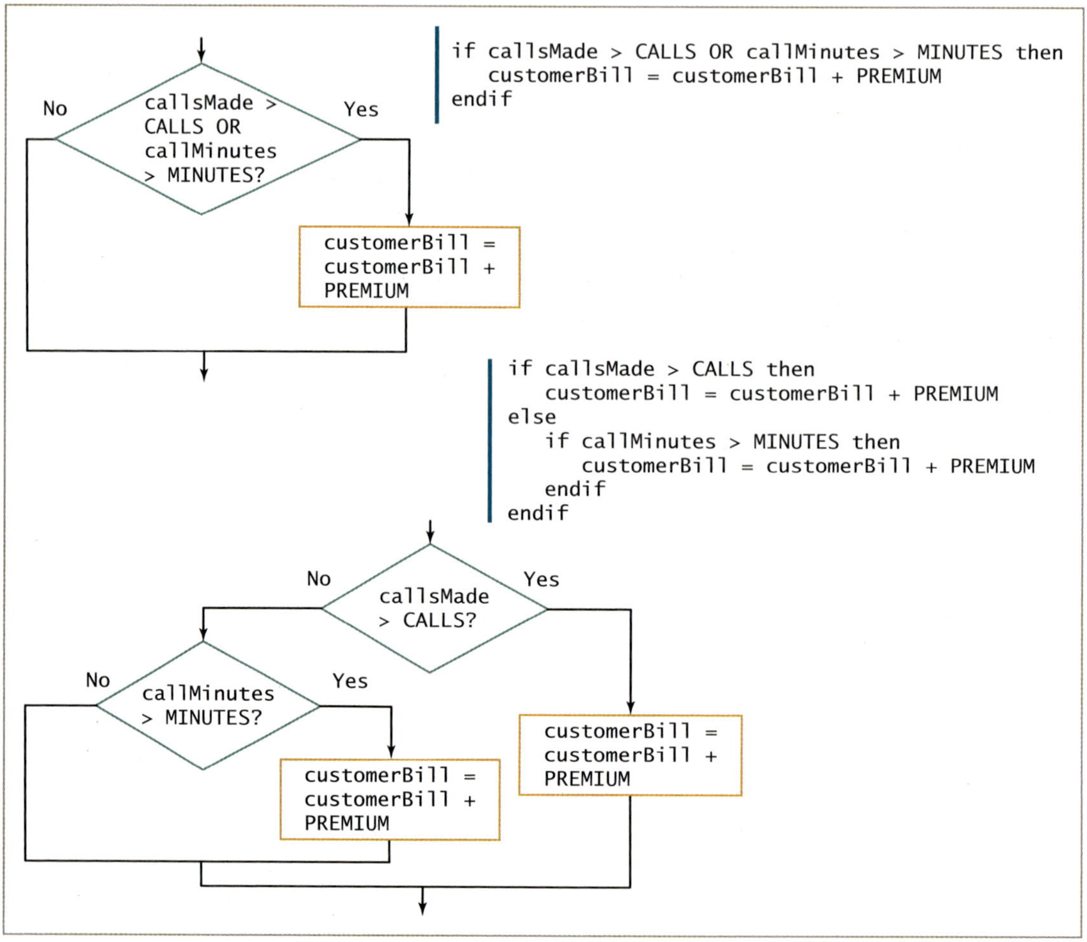

Figure 4-13 Using an OR operator and the logic behind it

C#, C++, C, and Java use the symbol || as the logical OR operator. In Visual Basic, the operator is Or.

Understanding OR Logic

Avoiding Common Errors in an OR Selection

You might have noticed that the assignment statement customerBill = customerBill + PREMIUM appears twice in the decision-making processes in Figures 4-12 and 4-13. When you create a flowchart, the temptation is to draw the logic to look like Figure 4-14. Logically, you might argue that the flowchart in Figure 4-14 is correct because the correct customers are billed the extra $20. However, this flowchart is not structured. The second question is not a self-contained structure with one entry and exit point; instead, the flowline breaks out of the inner selection structure to join the Yes side of the outer selection structure.

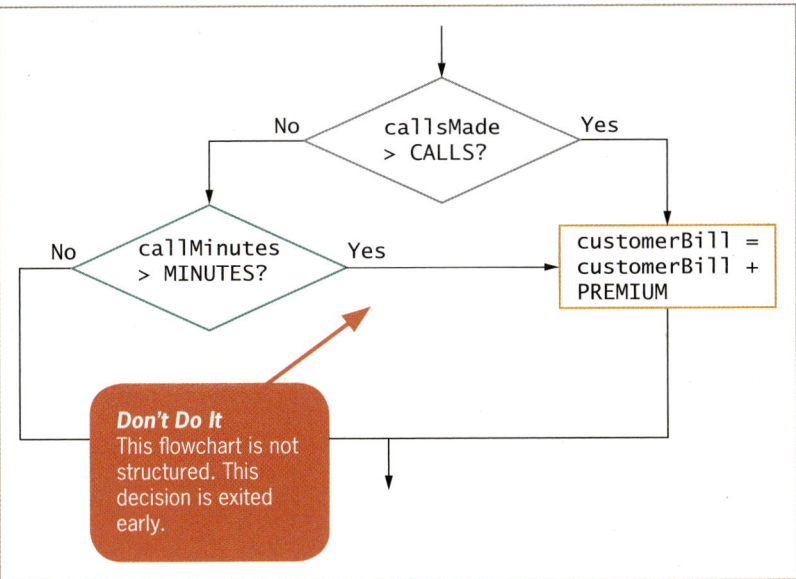

Figure 4-14 Unstructured flowchart for determining customer cell phone bill

The OR selection has additional potential for errors due to the differences in the way people and computers use language. When your boss wants to add an extra amount to the bills of customers who make more than 100 calls *or* use more than 500 minutes, she is likely to say, "Add $20 to the bill of anyone who makes more than 100 calls and to anyone who has used more than 500 minutes." Her request contains the word *and* between two types of people—those who made many calls and those who used many minutes—placing the emphasis on the people. However, each decision you make is about the added $20 for a single customer who has met one criterion *or* the other *or* both. In other words, the OR condition is between each customer's attributes, and not between different customers. Instead of the manager's previous statement, it would be clearer if she said, "Add $20 to the bill of anyone who has made more than 100 calls or has used more than 500 minutes," but you can't count on people to speak like computers. As a programmer, you have the job of clarifying what really is being requested. Often, a casual request for A *and* B logically means a request for A *or* B.

CHAPTER 4   Making Decisions

The way we use English can cause another type of error when you are required to find whether a value falls between two other values. For example, a movie theater manager might say, "Provide a discount to patrons who are under 13 years old and to those who are over 64 years old; otherwise, charge the full price." Because the manager has used the word *and* in the request, you might be tempted to create the decision shown in Figure 4-15; however, this logic will not provide a discounted price for any movie patron. You must remember that every time the decision is made in Figure 4-15, it is made for a single movie patron. If `patronAge` contains a value lower than 13, then it cannot possibly contain a value over 64. Similarly, if `patronAge` contains a value over 64, there is no way it can contain a lesser value. Therefore, no value could be stored in `patronAge` for which both parts of the AND question could be true—and the price will never be set to the discounted price for any patron. Figure 4-16 shows the correct logic.

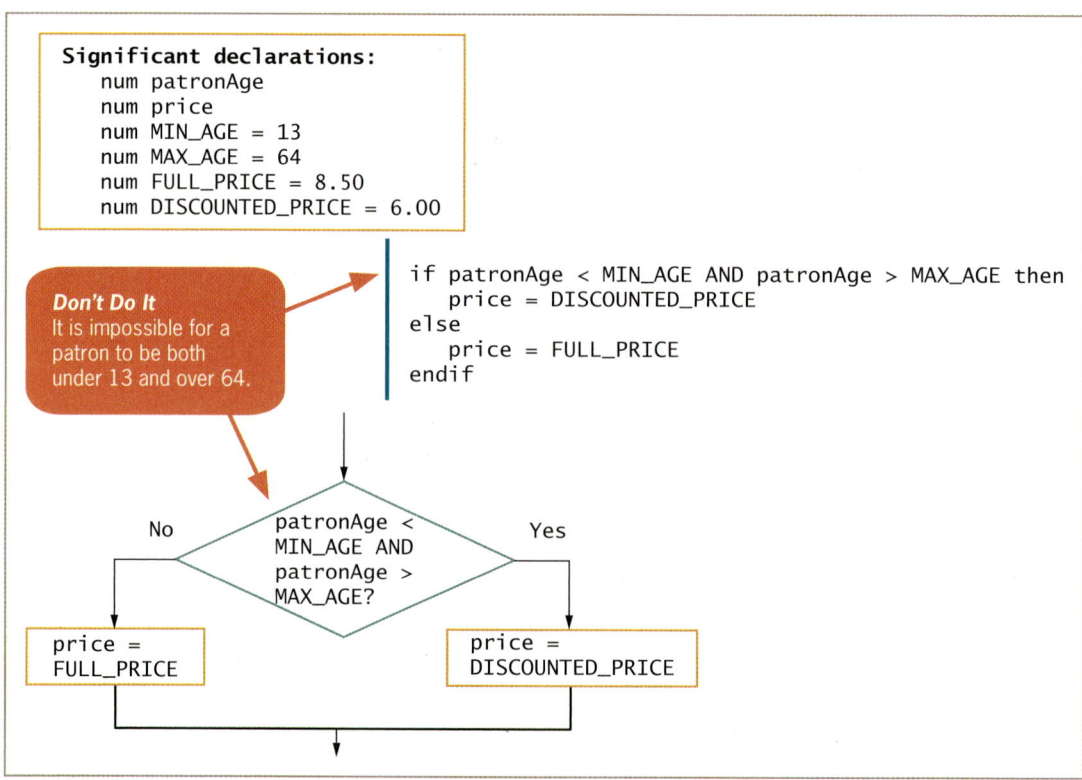

Figure 4-15 Incorrect logic that attempts to provide a discount for young and old movie patrons

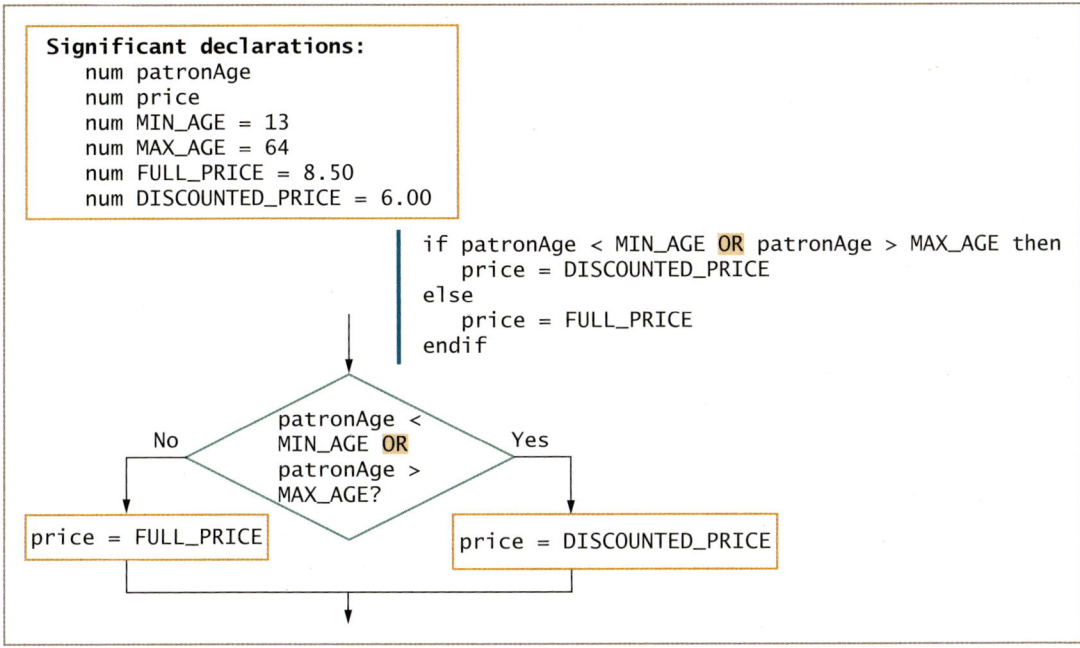

Figure 4-16   Correct logic that provides a discount for young and old movie patrons

A similar error can occur in your logic if the theater manager says something like, "Don't give a discount—that is, do charge full price—if a patron is over 12 or under 65." Because the word *or* appears in the request, you might plan your logic to resemble Figure 4-17. No patron ever receives a discount, because every patron is either over 12 or under 65. Remember, in an OR decision, only one of the conditions needs to be true for the entire expression to be evaluated as true. So, for example, because a patron who is 10 is under 65, the full price is charged, and because a patron who is 70 is over 12, the full price also is charged. Figure 4-18 shows the correct logic for this decision.

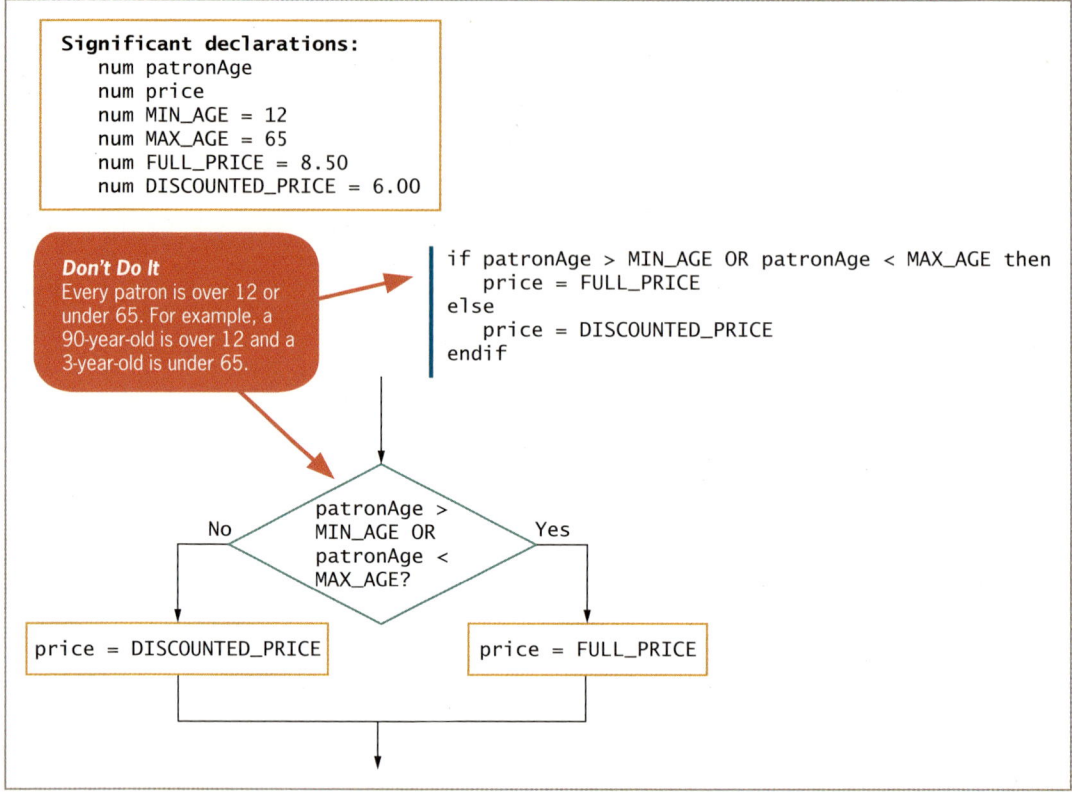

Figure 4-17 Incorrect logic that attempts to charge full price for patrons whose age is over 12 and under 65

Understanding OR Logic

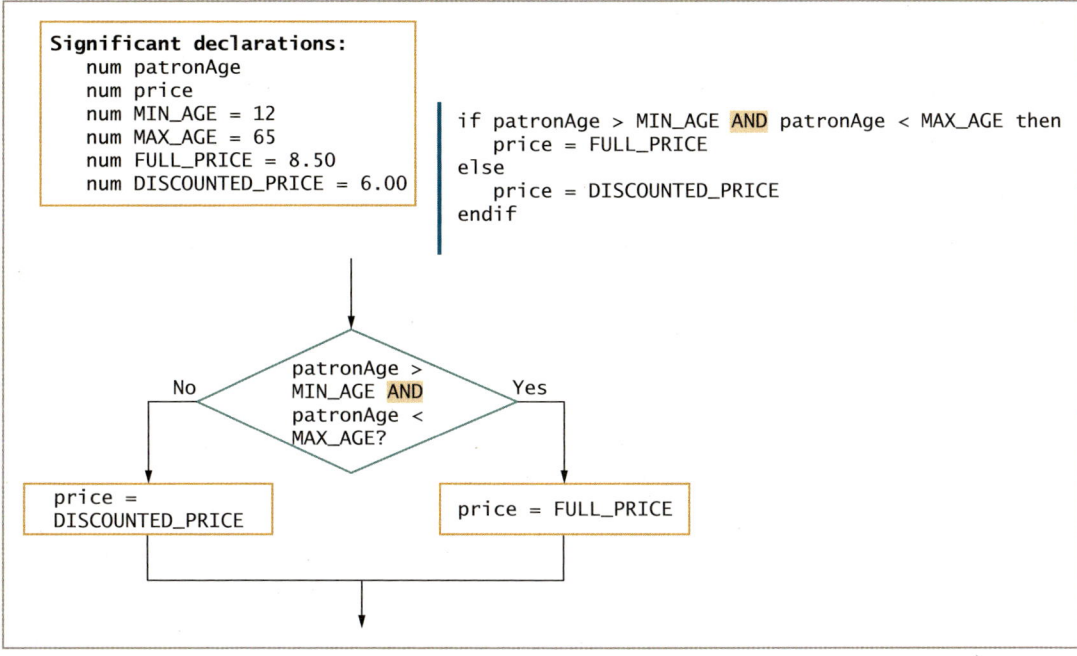

Figure 4-18 Correct logic that charges full price for patrons whose age is over 12 and under 65

 Besides AND and OR operators, most languages support a NOT operator. You use the **logical NOT operator** to reverse the meaning of a Boolean expression. For example, the statement `if NOT (age < 21) output "OK"` outputs *OK* when `age` is greater than or equal to 21. The NOT operator is unary instead of binary—that is, you do not use it between two expressions, but you use it in front of a single expression. In C++, Java, and C#, the exclamation point is the symbol used for the NOT operator. In Visual Basic, the operator is `Not`.

 Watch the video *Looking in Depth at AND and OR Decisions*.

TWO TRUTHS & A LIE

Understanding OR Logic

1. In an OR selection, two or more conditions must be met in order for an event to take place.
2. When you use an OR selection, you can choose to ask either question first and still achieve a usable program.
3. The general rule is: In an OR decision, first ask the question that is more likely to be true.

The false statement is #1. In an OR selection, only one of two conditions must be met in order for an event to take place.

CHAPTER 4　Making Decisions

Making Selections within Ranges

You often need to take action when a variable falls within a range of values. For example, suppose your company provides various customer discounts based on the number of items ordered, as shown in Figure 4-19.

Items Ordered	Discount Rate (%)
0 to 10	0
11 to 24	10
25 to 50	15
51 or more	20

Figure 4-19　Discount rates based on items ordered

When you write the program that determines a discount rate based on the number of items, you could make hundreds of decisions, such as itemQuantity = 1?, itemQuantity = 2?, and so on. However, it is more convenient to find the correct discount rate by using a range check.

When you use a **range check**, you compare a variable to a series of values that mark the limiting ends of ranges. To perform a range check, make comparisons using either the lowest or highest value in each range of values. For example, to find each discount rate listed in Figure 4-19, you can use one of the following techniques:

- Make comparisons using the low ends of the ranges.

  - You can ask: Is itemQuantity less than 11? If not, is it less than 25? If not, is it less than 51? (If it's possible the value is negative, you would also check for a value less than 0 and take appropriate action if it is.)

  - You can ask: Is itemQuantity greater than or equal to 51? If not, is it greater than or equal to 25? If not, is it greater than or equal to 11? (If it's possible the value is negative, you would also check for a value greater than or equal to 0 and take appropriate action if it is not.)

- Make comparisons using the high ends of the ranges.

  - You can ask: Is itemQuantity greater than 50? If not, is it greater than 24? If not, is it greater than 10? (If there is a maximum allowed value for itemQuantity, you would also check for a value greater than that limit and take appropriate action if it is.)

  - You can ask: Is itemQuantity less than or equal to 10? If not, is it less than or equal to 24? If not, is it less than or equal to 50? (If there is a maximum allowed value for itemQuantity, you would also check for a value less than or equal to that limit and

Making Selections within Ranges

Figure 4-20 shows the flowchart and pseudocode that represent the logic for a program that determines the correct discount for each order quantity. In the decision-making process, `itemsOrdered` is compared to the high end of the lowest-range group (RANGE1). If `itemsOrdered` is less than or equal to that value, then you know the correct discount, DISCOUNT1; if not, you continue checking. If `itemsOrdered` is less than or equal to the high end of the next range (RANGE2), then the customer's discount is DISCOUNT2; if not, you continue checking, and the customer's discount eventually is set to DISCOUNT3 or DISCOUNT4. In the pseudocode in Figure 4-20, notice how each associated `if`, `else`, and `endif` aligns vertically.

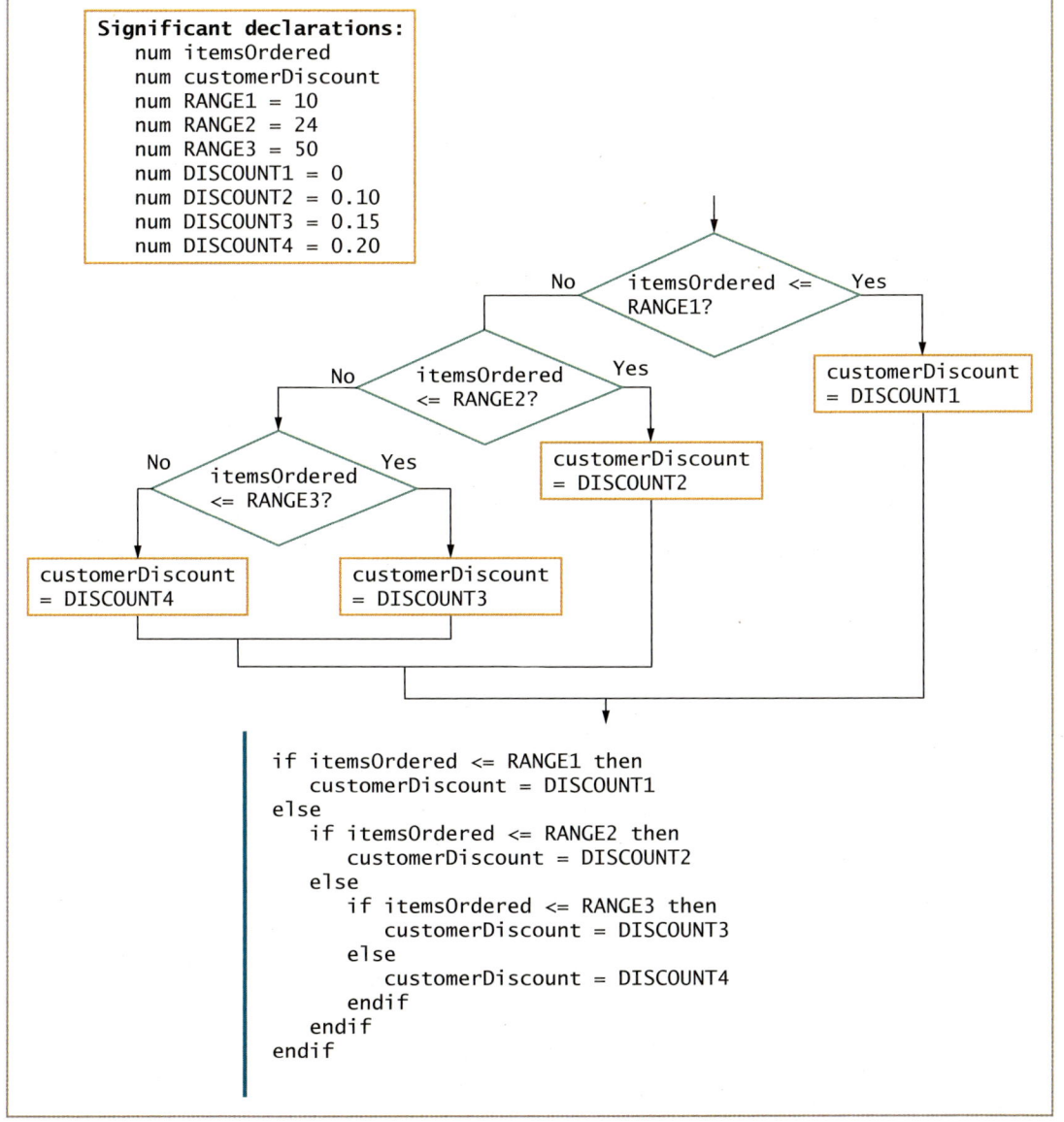

Figure 4-20 Flowchart and pseudocode of logic that selects correct discount based on items

In computer memory, a percent sign (%) is not stored with a numeric value that represents a percentage. Instead, the mathematical equivalent is stored. For example, 15% is stored as 0.15.

For example, consider an order for 30 items. The expression `itemsOrdered <= RANGE1` evaluates as false, so the `else` clause of the decision executes. There, `itemsOrdered <= RANGE2` also evaluates to false, so its `else` clause executes. The expression `itemsOrdered <= RANGE3` is true, so `customerDiscount` becomes `DISCOUNT3`, which is 0.15. Walk through the logic with other values for `itemsOrdered` and verify for yourself that the correct discount is applied each time.

Avoiding Common Errors When Using Range Checks

When new programmers perform range checks, they are prone to including logic that has too many decisions, entailing more work than is necessary.

Figure 4-21 shows a program segment that contains a range check in which the programmer has asked one question too many—the shaded question in the figure. If you know that `itemsOrdered` is not less than or equal to `RANGE1`, not less than or equal to `RANGE2`, and not less than or equal to `RANGE3`, then `itemsOrdered` must be greater than `RANGE3`. Asking whether `itemsOrdered` is greater than `RANGE3` is a waste of time; no customer order can ever travel the logical path on the far left of the flowchart. You might say such a path is a **dead** or **unreachable path**, and that the statements written there constitute dead or unreachable code. Although a program that contains such logic will execute and assign the correct discount to customers who order more than 50 items, providing such a path is inefficient.

Making Selections within Ranges

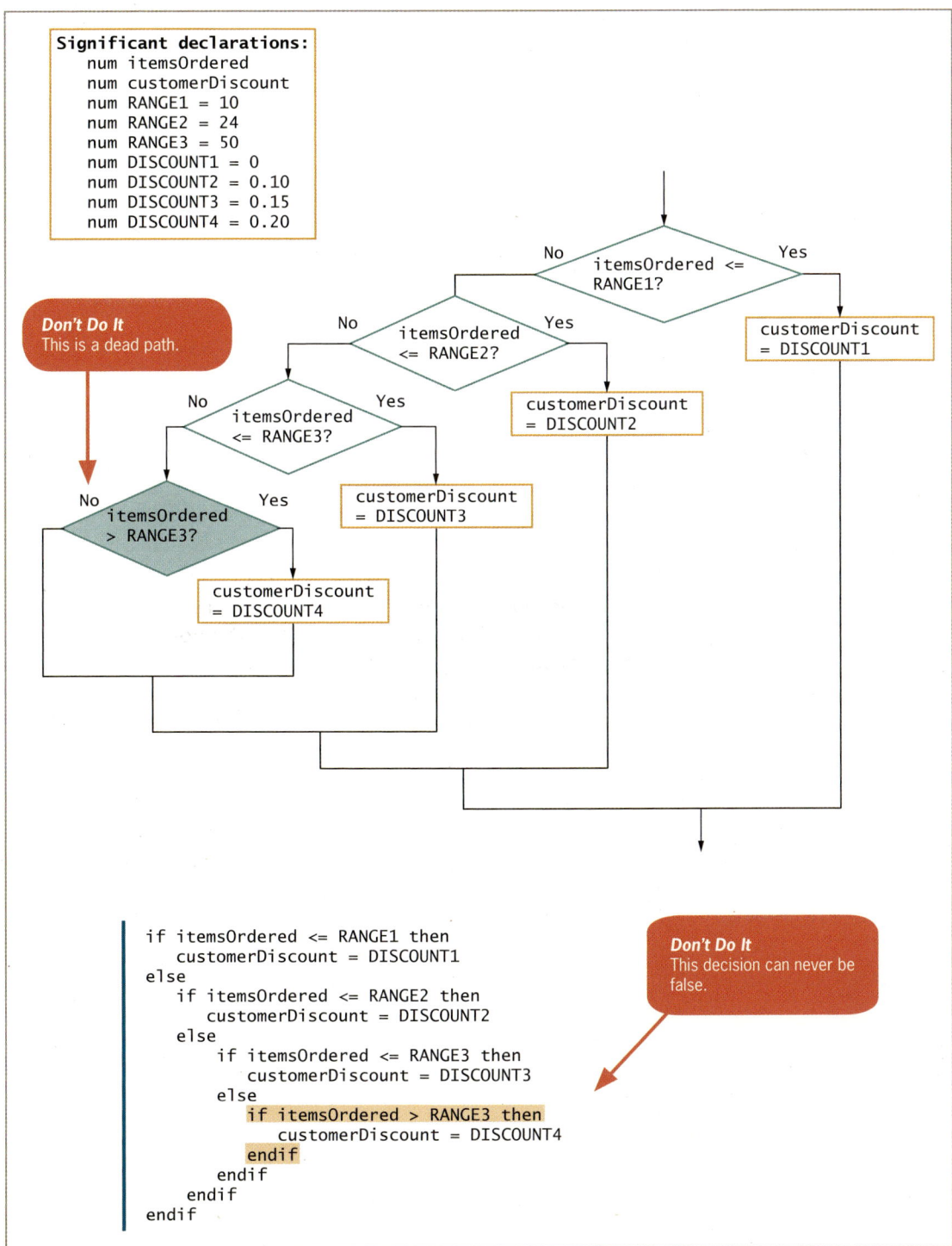

Figure 4-21 Inefficient range selection including unreachable path

In Figure 4-21, it is easier to see the useless path in the flowchart than in the pseudocode representation of the same logic. However, when you use an `if` without an `else`, you are doing nothing when the question's answer is false.

When you ask questions of human beings, you sometimes already know the answers. For example, a good trial lawyer seldom asks a question in court if the answer will be a surprise. With computer logic, however, such questions are an inefficient waste of time.

Another error that programmers make when writing the logic to perform a range check also involves asking unnecessary questions. You should never ask a question if there is only one possible answer or outcome. Figure 4-22 shows an inefficient range selection that asks two unneeded questions. In the figure, if `itemsOrdered` is less than or equal to `RANGE1`, `customerDiscount` is set to `DISCOUNT1`. If `itemsOrdered` is not less than or equal to `RANGE1`, then it must be greater than `RANGE1`, so the next decision (shaded in the figure) is unnecessary. The computer logic will never execute the shaded decision unless `itemsOrdered` is already greater than `RANGE1`—that is, unless the logic follows the false branch of the first selection. If you use the logic in Figure 4-22, you are wasting computer time asking a question that has previously been answered. The same logic applies to the second shaded decision in Figure 4-22. Beginning programmers sometimes justify their use of unnecessary questions as "just making really sure." Such caution is unnecessary when writing computer logic.

Making Selections within Ranges

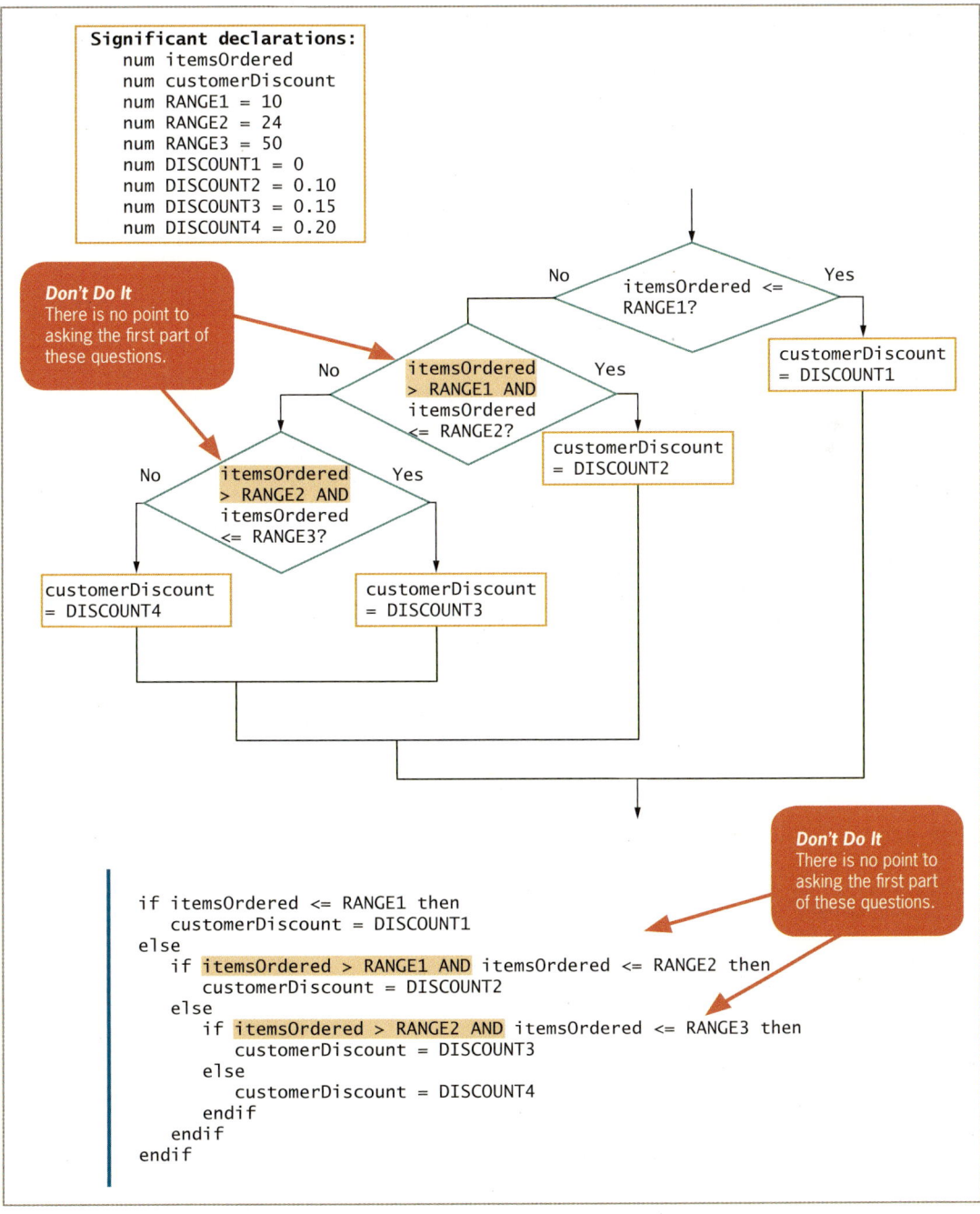

Figure 4-22 Inefficient range selection including unnecessary questions

> **TWO TRUTHS & A LIE**
>
> Making Selections within Ranges
>
> 1. When you perform a range check, you compare a variable to every value in a series of ranges.
>
> 2. You can perform a range check by making comparisons using the lowest value in each range of values you are using.
>
> 3. You can perform a range check by making comparisons using the highest value in each range of values you are using.
>
> The false statement is #1. When you use a range check, you compare a variable to a series of values that represent the ends of ranges. Depending on your logic, you can use either the high or low end of each range.

Understanding Precedence When Combining AND and OR Operators

Most programming languages allow you to combine as many AND and OR operators in an expression as you need. For example, assume that you need to achieve a score of at least 75 on each of three tests to pass a course. You can declare a constant MIN_SCORE equal to 75 and test the multiple conditions with a statement like the following:

```
if score1 >= MIN_SCORE AND score2 >= MIN_SCORE AND score3 >= MIN_SCORE then
   classGrade = "Pass"
else
   classGrade = "Fail"
endif
```

On the other hand, if you need to pass only one of three tests to pass a course, then the logic is as follows:

```
if score1 >= MIN_SCORE OR score2 >= MIN_SCORE OR score3 >= MIN_SCORE then
   classGrade = "Pass"
else
   classGrade = "Fail"
endif
```

The logic becomes more complicated when you combine AND and OR operators within the same statement. When you do, the AND operators take **precedence**, meaning the Boolean values of their expressions are evaluated first.

For example, consider a program that determines whether a movie theater patron can purchase a discounted ticket. Assume that discounts are allowed for children and senior

Understanding Precedence When Combining AND and OR

citizens who attend G-rated movies. The following code looks reasonable, but it produces incorrect results because the expression that contains the AND operator (see shading) evaluates before the one that contains the OR operator.

```
if age <= 12 OR age >= 65 AND rating = "G" then
    output "Discount applies"
endif
```

Don't Do It
The AND evaluates first, which is not the intention.

For example, assume that a movie patron is 10 years old and the movie rating is R. The patron should not receive a discount (or be allowed to see the movie!).

However, within the `if` statement, the part of the expression that contains the AND operator, age >= 65 AND rating = "G", is evaluated first. For a 10-year-old and an R-rated movie, the question is false (on both counts), so the entire `if` statement becomes the equivalent of the following:

```
if age <= 12 OR aFalseExpression then
    output "Discount applies"
endif
```

Because the patron is 10, age <= 12 is true, so the original `if` statement becomes the equivalent of:

```
if aTrueExpression OR aFalseExpression then
    output "Discount applies"
endif
```

The combination true OR false evaluates as true. Therefore, the string "Discount applies" is output when it should not be.

Many programming languages allow you to use parentheses to correct the logic and force the OR expression to be evaluated first, as shown in the following pseudocode:

```
if (age <= 12 OR age >= 65) AND rating = "G" then
    output "Discount applies"
endif
```

With the added parentheses, if the patron's **age** is 12 or under OR the **age** is 65 or over, the expression is evaluated as:

```
if aTrueExpression AND rating = "G" then
    output "Discount applies"
endif
```

In this statement, when the age value qualifies a patron for a discount, then the rating value must also be acceptable before the discount applies. This was the original intention.

You can use the following techniques to avoid confusion when mixing AND and OR operators:

- You can use parentheses to override the default order of operations.
- You can use parentheses for clarity even though they do not change what the order of operations would be without them. For example, if a customer should be between 12 and 19 or have a school ID to receive a high school discount, you can use the expression `(age > 12 AND age < 19) OR validId = "Yes"`, even though the evaluation would be the same without the parentheses.
- You can use nesting `if` statements instead of using AND and OR operators. With the flowchart and pseudocode shown in Figure 4-23, it is clear which movie patrons receive the discount. In the flowchart, you can see that the OR is nested entirely within the Yes branch of the `rating = "G"?` selection. Similarly, in the pseudocode in Figure 4-23, you can see by the alignment that if the rating is not G, the logic proceeds directly to the last `endif` statement, bypassing any checking of `age` at all.

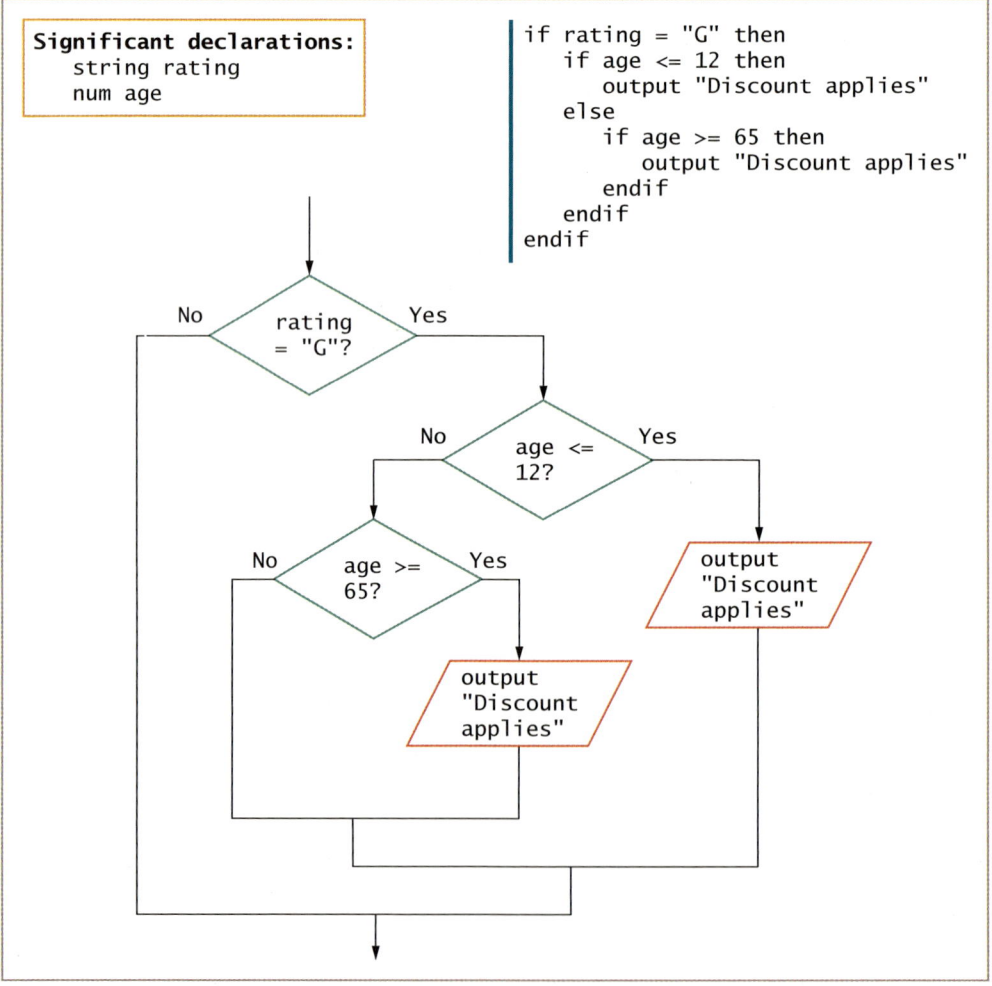

Figure 4-23 Nested decisions that determine movie patron discount

TWO TRUTHS & A LIE

Understanding Precedence When Combining AND and OR Operators

1. Most programming languages allow you to combine as many AND and OR operators in an expression as you need.
2. When you combine AND and OR operators, the OR operators take precedence, meaning their Boolean values are evaluated first.
3. You always can avoid the confusion of mixing AND and OR decisions by nesting `if` statements instead of using AND and OR operators.

The false statement is #2. When you combine AND and OR operators, the AND operators take precedence, meaning the Boolean values of their expressions are evaluated first.

Chapter Summary

- Computer program decisions are made by evaluating Boolean expressions. You can use `if-then-else` or `if-then` structures to choose between two possible outcomes.

- You can use relational comparison operators to compare two operands of the same type. The standard comparison operators are =, >, <, >=, <=, and <>.

- In an AND decision, two conditions must be true for a resulting action to take place. An AND decision requires a nested decision or the use of an AND operator. In an AND decision, the most efficient approach is to start by asking the question that is less likely to be true.

- In an OR decision, at least one of two conditions must be true for a resulting action to take place. In an OR decision, the most efficient approach is to start by asking the question that is more likely to be true. Most programming languages allow you to ask two or more questions in a single comparison by using a conditional OR operator.

- To perform a range check, make comparisons with either the lowest or highest value in each range of comparison values. Common errors that occur when programmers perform range checks include asking unnecessary and previously answered questions.

- When you combine AND and OR operators in an expression, the AND operators take precedence, meaning their Boolean values are evaluated first.

Key Terms

A **Boolean expression** is one that represents only one of two states, usually expressed as true or false.

An **if-then** decision structure contains a tested Boolean expression and an action that is taken only when the expression is true.

An **if-then clause** of a decision holds the action that results when the Boolean expression in the decision is true.

The **else clause** of a decision holds the action or actions that execute only when the Boolean expression in the decision is false.

Relational comparison operators are the symbols that express Boolean comparisons. Examples include =, >, <, >=, <=, and <>.

A **trivial expression** is one that always evaluates to the same value.

A **compound condition** is constructed when you need to ask multiple questions before determining an outcome.

An **AND decision** contains two or more decisions; all conditions must be true for an action to take place.

A **nested decision**, or a **nested if**, is a decision within either the if-then or else clause of another decision.

A **cascading if statement** is a series of nested if statements.

A **conditional AND operator** (or, more simply, an **AND operator**) is a symbol that you use to combine decisions so that two or more conditions must be true for an action to occur.

Truth tables are diagrams used in mathematics and logic to help describe the truth of an entire expression based on the truth of its parts.

Short-circuit evaluation is a logical feature in which expressions in each part of a larger expression are evaluated only as far as necessary to determine the final outcome.

An **OR decision** contains two or more decisions; if at least one condition is met, the resulting action takes place.

A **conditional OR operator** (or, more simply, an **OR operator**) is a symbol that you use to combine decisions when any one condition can be true for an action to occur.

The **logical NOT operator** is a symbol that reverses the meaning of a Boolean expression.

When you use a **range check**, you compare a variable to a series of values that mark the limiting ends of ranges.

A **dead** or **unreachable path** is a logical path that can never be traveled.

Precedence is the quality of an operation that determines the order in which it is evaluated.

Review Questions

1. The selection statement `if quantity > 100 then discountRate = RATE` is an example of a _____.
   a. dual-alternative selection
   b. single-alternative selection
   c. structured loop
   d. all of the above

2. The selection statement `if dayOfWeek = "Sunday" then price = LOWER_PRICE else price = HIGHER_PRICE` is an example of a _____.
   a. dual-alternative selection
   b. single-alternative selection
   c. unary selection
   d. all of the above

3. All selection statements must have _____.
   a. a `then` clause
   b. an `else` clause
   c. both a. and b.
   d. none of the above

4. An expression like `amount < 10?` is a(n) _____ expression.
   a. Gregorian
   b. Edwardian
   c. Machiavellian
   d. Boolean

5. Usually, you compare only variables that have the same _____.
   a. type
   b. size
   c. name
   d. value

6. Symbols such as `>` and `<` are known as _____ operators.
   a. arithmetic
   b. sequential
   c. relational comparison
   d. scripting accuracy

7. If you could use only three relational comparison operators, you could get by with _____.
   a. greater than, less than, and greater than or equal to
   b. equal to, less than, and greater than
   c. less than, less than or equal to, and not equal to
   d. equal to, not equal to, and less than

8. If `a > b` is false, then which of the following is always true?
   a. `a <= b`
   b. `a < b`
   c. `a = b`
   d. `a >= b`

CHAPTER 4 Making Decisions

9. Usually, the most difficult comparison operator to work with is _____.
   a. equal to
   b. greater than
   c. less than
   d. not equal to

10. Which of the lettered choices is equivalent to the following decision?

    ```
    if x > 10 then
       if y > 10 then
          output "X"
       endif
    endif
    ```

    a. if x > 10 OR y > 10 then output "X"
    b. if x > 10 AND x > y then output "X"
    c. if y > x then output "X"
    d. if x > 10 AND y > 10 then output "X"

11. The Midwest Sales region of Acme Computer Company consists of five states—Illinois, Indiana, Iowa, Missouri, and Wisconsin. About 50 percent of the regional customers reside in Illinois, 20 percent in Indiana, and 10 percent in each of the other three states. Suppose you have input records containing Acme customer data, including state of residence. To most efficiently select and display all customers who live in the Midwest Sales region, you would ask first about residency in _____.
    a. Illinois
    b. Indiana
    c. Either Iowa, Missouri, or Wisconsin—it does not matter which one of these three is first.
    d. Any of the five states—it does not matter which one is first.

12. The Boffo Balloon Company makes helium balloons. Large balloons cost $13.00 a dozen, medium-sized balloons cost $11.00 a dozen, and small balloons cost $8.60 a dozen. About 60 percent of the company's sales are of the smallest balloons, 30 percent are medium, and large balloons constitute only 10 percent of sales. Customer order records include customer information, quantity ordered, and size. To write a program that makes the most efficient determination of an order's price based on size ordered, you should ask first whether the size is _____.
    a. large
    b. medium
    c. small
    d. It does not matter.

Review Questions

13. The Boffo Balloon Company makes helium balloons in three sizes, 12 colors, and with a choice of 40 imprinted sayings. As a promotion, the company is offering a 25 percent discount on orders of large, red balloons imprinted with the string "Happy Valentine's Day". To most efficiently select the orders to which a discount applies, you would use _____.

   a. nested if statements using OR logic
   b. nested if statements using AND logic
   c. three completely separate unnested if statements
   d. Not enough information is given.

14. In the following pseudocode, what percentage raise will an employee in Department 5 receive?

    ```
    if department < 3 then
       raise = SMALL_RAISE
    else
       if department < 5 then
          raise = MEDIUM_RAISE
       else
          raise = BIG_RAISE
       endif
    endif
    ```

    a. SMALL_RAISE
    b. MEDIUM_RAISE
    c. BIG_RAISE
    d. impossible to tell

15. In the following pseudocode, what percentage raise will an employee in Department 8 receive?

    ```
    if department < 5 then
       raise = SMALL_RAISE
    else
       if department < 14 then
          raise = MEDIUM_RAISE
       else
          if department < 9 then
             raise = BIG_RAISE
          endif
       endif
    endif
    ```

    a. SMALL_RAISE
    b. MEDIUM_RAISE
    c. BIG_RAISE
    d. impossible to tell

Making Decisions

16. In the following pseudocode, what percentage raise will an employee in Department 10 receive?

    ```
    if department < 2 then
       raise = SMALL_RAISE
    else
       if department < 6 then
          raise = MEDIUM_RAISE
       else
          if department < 10 then
             raise = BIG_RAISE
          endif
       endif
    endif
    ```

    a. SMALL_RAISE
    b. MEDIUM_RAISE
    c. BIG_RAISE
    d. impossible to tell

17. When you use a range check, you compare a variable to the _____ value in the range.

    a. lowest
    b. middle
    c. highest
    d. lowest or highest

18. If sales = 100, rate = 0.10, and expenses = 50, which of the following expressions is true?

    a. sales >= expenses AND rate < 1
    b. sales < 200 OR expenses < 100
    c. expenses = rate OR sales = rate
    d. two of the above

19. If a is true, b is true, and c is false, which of the following expressions is true?

    a. a OR b AND c
    b. a AND b AND c
    c. a AND b OR c
    d. two of the above

20. If d is true, e is false, and f is false, which of the following expressions is true?

    a. e OR f AND d
    b. f AND d OR e
    c. d OR e AND f
    d. two of the above

Exercises

1. Assume that the following variables contain the values shown:

   ```
   numberBig = 300        numberMedium = 100      numberSmall = 5
   wordBig = "Elephant"   wordMedium = "Horse"    wordSmall = "Bug"
   ```

Exercises

For each of the following Boolean expressions, decide whether the statement is true, false, or illegal.

a. numberBig = numberSmall?

b. numberBig > numberSmall?

c. numberMedium < numberSmall?

d. numberBig = wordBig?

e. numberBig = "Big"?

f. wordMedium = "Medium"?

g. wordBig = "Elephant"?

h. numberMedium <= numberBig / 3?

i. numberBig >= 200?

j. numberBig >= numberMedium + numberSmall?

k. numberBig > numberMedium AND numberBig < numberSmall?

l. numberBig = 100 OR numberBig > numberSmall?

m. numberBig < 10 OR numberSmall > 10?

n. numberBig = 30 AND numberMedium = 100 OR numberSmall = 100?

2. Mortimer Life Insurance Company wants several lists of salesperson data. Design a flowchart or pseudocode for the following:

   a. A program that accepts a salesperson's ID number and number of policies sold in the last month, and displays the data only if the salesperson is a high performer—a person who sells more than 25 policies in the month.

   b. A program that accepts salesperson data continuously until a sentinel value is entered and displays a list of high performers.

3. ShoppingBay is an online auction service that requires several reports. Design a flowchart or pseudocode for the following:

   a. A program that accepts auction data as follows: ID number, item description, length of auction in days, and minimum required bid. Display data for an auction if the minimum required bid is over $100.00.

   b. A program that continuously accepts auction data until a sentinel value is entered and displays a list of all data for auctions in which the minimum required bid is over $100.00.

   c. A program that continuously accepts auction data and displays data for every auction in which the minimum bid is $0.00 and the length of the auction is one day or less.

d. A program that continuously accepts auction data and displays data for every auction in which the length is between 7 and 30 days inclusive.

e. A program that prompts the user for a maximum required bid, and then continuously accepts auction data and displays data for every auction in which the minimum bid is less than or equal to the amount entered by the user.

4. The Dash Cell Phone Company charges customers a basic rate of $5 per month to send text messages. Additional rates are as follows:

- The first 60 messages per month, regardless of message length, are included in the basic bill.
- An additional five cents is charged for each text message after the 60th message, up to 180 messages.
- An additional 10 cents is charged for each text message after the 180th message.
- Federal, state, and local taxes add a total of 12 percent to each bill.

Design a flowchart or pseudocode for the following:

a. A program that accepts the following data about one customer's bill: customer area code (three digits), customer phone number (seven digits), and number of text messages sent. Display all the data, including the month-end bill both before and after taxes are added.

b. A program that continuously accepts data about text messages until a sentinel value is entered, and displays all the details.

c. A program that continuously accepts data about text messages until a sentinel value is entered, and displays details only about customers who send more than 100 text messages.

d. A program that continuously accepts data about text messages until a sentinel value is entered, and displays details only about customers whose total bill with taxes is over $20.

e. A program that prompts the user for a three-digit area code from which to select bills. Then the program continuously accepts text message data until a sentinel value is entered, and displays data only for messages sent from the specified area code.

5. The Drive-Rite Insurance Company provides automobile insurance policies for drivers. Design a flowchart or pseudocode for the following:

a. A program that accepts insurance policy data, including a policy number, customer last name, customer first name, age, premium due date (month, day, and year), and number of driver accidents in the last three years. If an entered policy number is not between 1000 and 9999 inclusive, set the policy number to 0. If the month is not between 1 and 12 inclusive, or the day is not correct for the month (for example, not between 1 and 31 for January or 1 and 29 for

February), set the month, day, and year to 0. Display the policy data after any revisions have been made.

b. A program that continuously accepts policy holders' data until a sentinel value has been entered, and displays the data for any policy holder over 35 years old.

c. A program that accepts policy holders' data and displays the data for any policy holder who is at least 21 years old.

d. A program that accepts policy holders' data and displays the data for any policy holder no more than 30 years old.

e. A program that accepts policy holders' data and displays the data for any policy holder whose premium is due no later than March 15 any year.

f. A program that accepts policy holders' data and displays the data for any policy holder whose premium is due up to and including January 1, 2014.

g. A program that accepts policy holders' data and displays the data for any policy holder whose premium is due by April 27, 2013.

h. A program that accepts policy holders' data and displays the data for anyone who has a policy number between 1000 and 4000 inclusive, whose policy comes due in April or May of any year, and who has had fewer than three accidents.

6. The Barking Lot is a dog day care center. Design a flowchart or pseudocode for the following:

a. A program that accepts data for an ID number of a dog's owner, and the name, breed, age, and weight of the dog. Display a bill containing all the input data as well as the weekly day care fee, which is $55 for dogs under 15 pounds, $75 for dogs from 15 to 30 pounds inclusive, $105 for dogs from 31 to 80 pounds inclusive, and $125 for dogs over 80 pounds.

b. A program that continuously accepts dogs' data until a sentinel value is entered, and displays billing data for each dog.

c. A program that continuously accepts dogs' data until a sentinel value is entered, and displays billing data for dog owners who owe more than $100.

7. Mark Daniels is a carpenter who creates personalized house signs. He wants an application to compute the price of any sign a customer orders, based on the following factors:

- The minimum charge for all signs is $30.

- If the sign is made of oak, add $15. No charge is added for pine.

- The first six letters or numbers are included in the minimum charge; there is a $3 charge for each additional character.

CHAPTER 4 Making Decisions

- Black or white characters are included in the minimum charge; there is an additional $12 charge for gold-leaf lettering.

Design a flowchart or pseudocode for the following:

a. A program that accepts data for an order number, customer name, wood type, number of characters, and color of characters. Display all the entered data and the final price for the sign.

b. A program that continuously accepts sign order data and displays all the relevant information for oak signs with five white letters.

c. A program that continuously accepts sign order data and displays all the relevant information for pine signs with gold-leaf lettering and more than 10 characters.

8. Black Dot Printing is attempting to organize carpools to save energy. Each input record contains an employee's name and town of residence. Ten percent of the company's employees live in Wonder Lake; 30 percent live in the adjacent town of Woodstock. Black Dot wants to encourage employees who live in either town to drive to work together. Design a flowchart or pseudocode for the following:

a. A program that accepts an employee's data and displays it with a message that indicates whether the employee is a candidate for the carpool.

b. A program that continuously accepts employee data until a sentinel value is entered, and displays a list of all employees who are carpool candidates.

9. Amanda Cho, a supervisor in a retail clothing store, wants to acknowledge high-achieving salespeople. Design a flowchart or pseudocode for the following:

a. A program that continuously accepts each salesperson's first and last names, the number of shifts worked in a month, number of transactions completed this month, and the dollar value of those transactions. Display each salesperson's name with a productivity score, which is computed by first dividing dollars by transactions and dividing the result by shifts worked. Display three asterisks after the productivity score if it is 50 or higher.

b. A program that accepts each salesperson's data and displays the name and a bonus amount. The bonuses will be distributed as follows:

- If the productivity score is 30 or less, the bonus is $25.
- If the productivity score is 31 or more and less than 80, the bonus is $50.
- If the productivity score is 80 or more and less than 200, the bonus is $100.
- If the productivity score is 200 or higher, the bonus is $200.

c. Modify Exercise 9b to reflect the following new fact, and have the program execute as efficiently as possible:

- Sixty percent of employees have a productivity score greater than 200.

Exercises

Find the Bugs

10. Your downloadable files for Chapter 4 include DEBUG04-01.txt, DEBUG04-02.txt, and DEBUG04-03.txt. Each file starts with some comments that describe the problem. Comments are lines that begin with two slashes (//). Following the comments, each file contains pseudocode that has one or more bugs you must find and correct.

Game Zone

11. In Chapter 2, you learned that many programming languages allow you to generate a random number between 1 and a limiting value named `LIMIT` by using a statement similar to `randomNumber = random(LIMIT)`. Create the logic for a guessing game in which the application generates a random number and the player tries to guess it. Display a message indicating whether the player's guess was correct, too high, or too low. (After you finish Chapter 5, you will be able to modify the application so that the user can continue to guess until the correct answer is entered.)

12. Create a lottery game application. Generate three random numbers, each between 0 and 9. Allow the user to guess three numbers. Compare each of the user's guesses to the three random numbers and display a message that includes the user's guess, the randomly determined three digits, and the amount of money the user has won, as shown in Table 4-4.

Matching Numbers	Award ($)
Any one matching	10
Two matching	100
Three matching, not in order	1000
Three matching in exact order	1,000,000
No matches	0

Table 4-4 Awards for matching numbers in lottery game

Make certain that your application accommodates repeating digits. For example, if a user guesses 1, 2, and 3, and the randomly generated digits are 1, 1, and 1, do not give the user credit for three correct guesses—just one.

Up for Discussion

13. Computer programs can be used to make decisions about your insurability as well as the rates you will be charged for health and life insurance policies. For example, certain preexisting conditions may raise your insurance premiums considerably. Is it ethical for insurance companies to access your health records and then make insurance decisions about you? Explain your answer.

14. Job applications are sometimes screened by software that makes decisions about a candidate's suitability based on keywords in the applications. Is such screening fair to applicants? Explain your answer.

15. Medical facilities often have more patients waiting for organ transplants than there are available organs. Suppose you have been asked to write a computer program that selects which candidates should receive an available organ. What data would you want on file to be able to use in your program, and what decisions would you make based on the data? What data do you think others might use that you would choose not to use?

CHAPTER 5

Looping

In this chapter, you will learn about:

- ◎ The advantages of looping
- ◎ Using a loop control variable
- ◎ Nested loops
- ◎ Avoiding common loop mistakes
- ◎ Using a `for` loop
- ◎ Common loop applications

CHAPTER 5 Looping

Understanding the Advantages of Looping

Although making decisions is what makes computers seem intelligent, looping makes computer programming both efficient and worthwhile. When you use a loop, one set of instructions can operate on multiple, separate sets of data. Using fewer instructions results in less time required for design and coding, fewer errors, and shorter compile time.

Recall the loop structure that you learned about in Chapter 3; it looks like Figure 5-1. As long as a Boolean expression remains true, the body of a `while` loop executes.

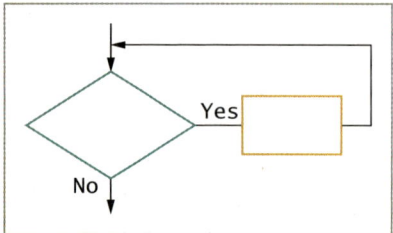

Figure 5-1 The loop structure

You have already learned that many programs use a loop to control repetitive tasks. For example, Figure 5-2 shows the basic structure of many business programs. After some housekeeping tasks are completed, the detail loop repeats once for every data record that must be processed.

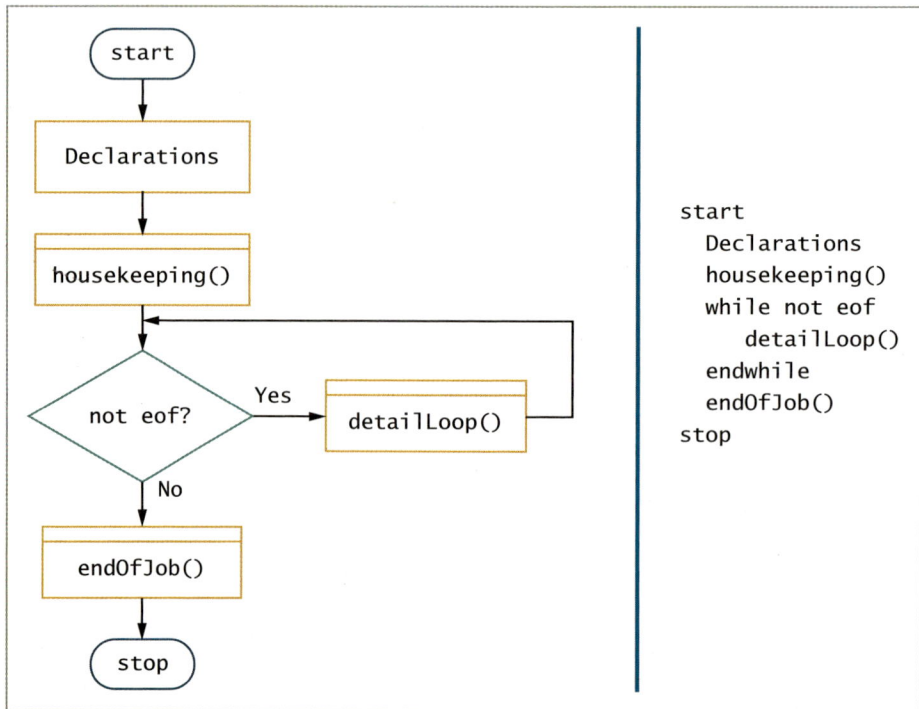

Figure 5-2 The mainline logic common to many business programs

For example, Figure 5-2 might represent the mainline logic of a typical payroll program. The first employee's data would be entered in the `housekeeping()` module, and while the `eof` condition is not met, the `detailLoop()` module would perform such tasks as determining regular and overtime pay and deducting taxes, insurance premiums, charitable contributions, union dues, and other items. Then, after the employee's paycheck is output, the next employee's data would be entered, and the `detailLoop()` module would repeat. The advantage to having a computer produce payroll checks is that the calculation instructions need to be written only once and can be repeated indefinitely.

 Watch the video *A Quick Introduction to Loops*.

TWO TRUTHS & A LIE

Understanding the Advantages of Looping

1. When you use a loop, you can write one set of instructions that operates on multiple, separate sets of data.
2. A major advantage of having a computer perform complicated tasks is the ability to repeat them.
3. A loop is a structure that branches in two logical paths before continuing.

The false statement is #3. A loop is a structure that repeats actions while some condition continues.

Using a Loop Control Variable

You can use a `while` loop to execute a body of statements continuously as long as some condition continues to be true. The body of a loop might contain any number of statements, including method calls, decisions, and other loops. To make a `while` loop end correctly, you should declare a **loop control variable** to manage the number of repetitions a loop performs. Three separate actions should occur:

- The loop control variable is initialized before entering the loop.
- The loop control variable is tested, and if the result is true, the loop body is entered.
- The loop control variable is altered within the body of the loop so that the `while` expression eventually evaluates as false.

If you omit any of these actions or perform them incorrectly, you run the risk of creating an infinite loop. Once your logic enters the body of a structured loop, the entire loop body must execute. Your program can leave a structured loop only at the comparison that tests the loop control variable. Commonly, you can control a loop's repetitions in one of two ways:

- Use a counter to create a definite, counter-controlled loop.
- Use a sentinel value to create an indefinite loop.

Using a Definite Loop with a Counter

Figure 5-3 shows a loop that displays *Hello* four times. The variable count is the loop control variable. This loop is a **definite loop** because it executes a definite, predetermined number of times—in this case, four. The loop is a **counted loop**, or **counter-controlled loop**, because the program keeps track of the number of loop repetitions by counting them.

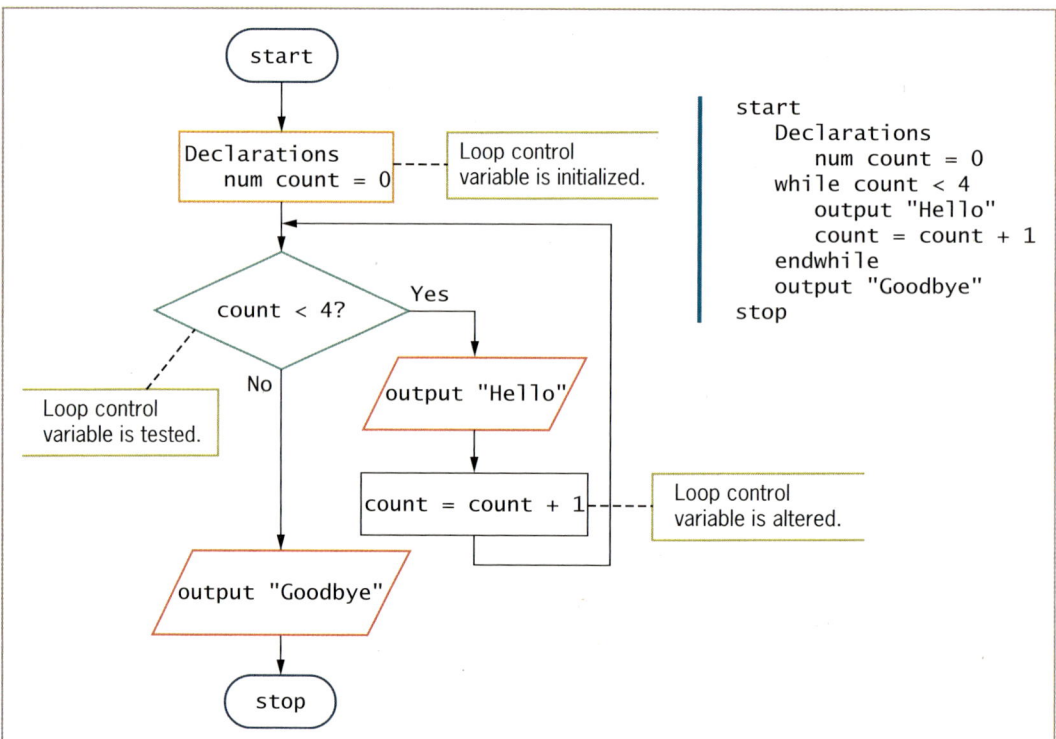

Figure 5-3 A counted while loop that outputs *Hello* four times

The loop in Figure 5-3 executes as follows:

- The loop control variable, count, is initialized to 0.
- The while expression compares count to 4.
- The value of count is less than 4, and so the loop body executes. The loop body shown in Figure 5-3 consists of two statements that display *Hello* and then add 1 to count.

Using a Loop Control Variable

- The next time `count` is evaluated, its value is 1, which is still less than 4, so the loop body executes again. *Hello* is displayed a second time and `count` becomes 2, *Hello* is displayed a third time and `count` becomes 3, then *Hello* is displayed a fourth time and `count` becomes 4. Now when the expression `count < 4?` evaluates, it is `false`, so the loop ends.

Within a loop's body, you can change the value of the loop control variable in a number of ways. For example:

- You might simply assign a new value to the loop control variable.
- You might retrieve a new value from an input device.
- You might **increment**, or increase, the loop control variable, as in the logic in Figure 5-3.
- You might reduce, or **decrement**, the loop control variable. For example, the loop in Figure 5-3 could be rewritten so that `count` is initialized to 4, and reduced by 1 on each pass through the loop. The loop should then continue while `count` remains greater than 0.

The terms *increment* and *decrement* usually refer to small changes; often the value used to increase or decrease the loop control variable is 1. However, loops are also controlled by adding or subtracting values other than 1. For example, to display company profits at five-year intervals for the next 50 years, you would want to add 5 to a loop control variable during each iteration.

Because you frequently need to increment a variable, many programming languages contain a shortcut operator for incrementing. You will learn about these shortcut operators when you study a programming language that uses them.

Watch the video *Looping*.

The looping logic shown in Figure 5-3 uses a counter. A **counter** is any numeric variable you use to count the number of times an event has occurred. In everyday life, people usually count things starting with 1. Many programmers prefer starting their counted loops with a variable containing 0 for two reasons:

- In many computer applications, numbering starts with 0 because of the 0-and-1 nature of computer circuitry.
- When you learn about arrays in Chapter 6, you will discover that array manipulation naturally lends itself to 0-based loops.

Using an Indefinite Loop with a Sentinel Value

Often, the value of a loop control variable is not altered by arithmetic, but instead is altered by user input. For example, perhaps you want to keep performing some task while the user indicates a desire to continue. In that case, you do not know when you write the program whether the loop will be executed two times, 200 times, or at all. This type of loop is an **indefinite loop**.

CHAPTER 5   Looping

Consider an interactive program that displays *Hello* repeatedly as long as the user wants to continue. The loop is indefinite because each time the program executes, the loop might be performed a different number of times. The program appears in Figure 5-4.

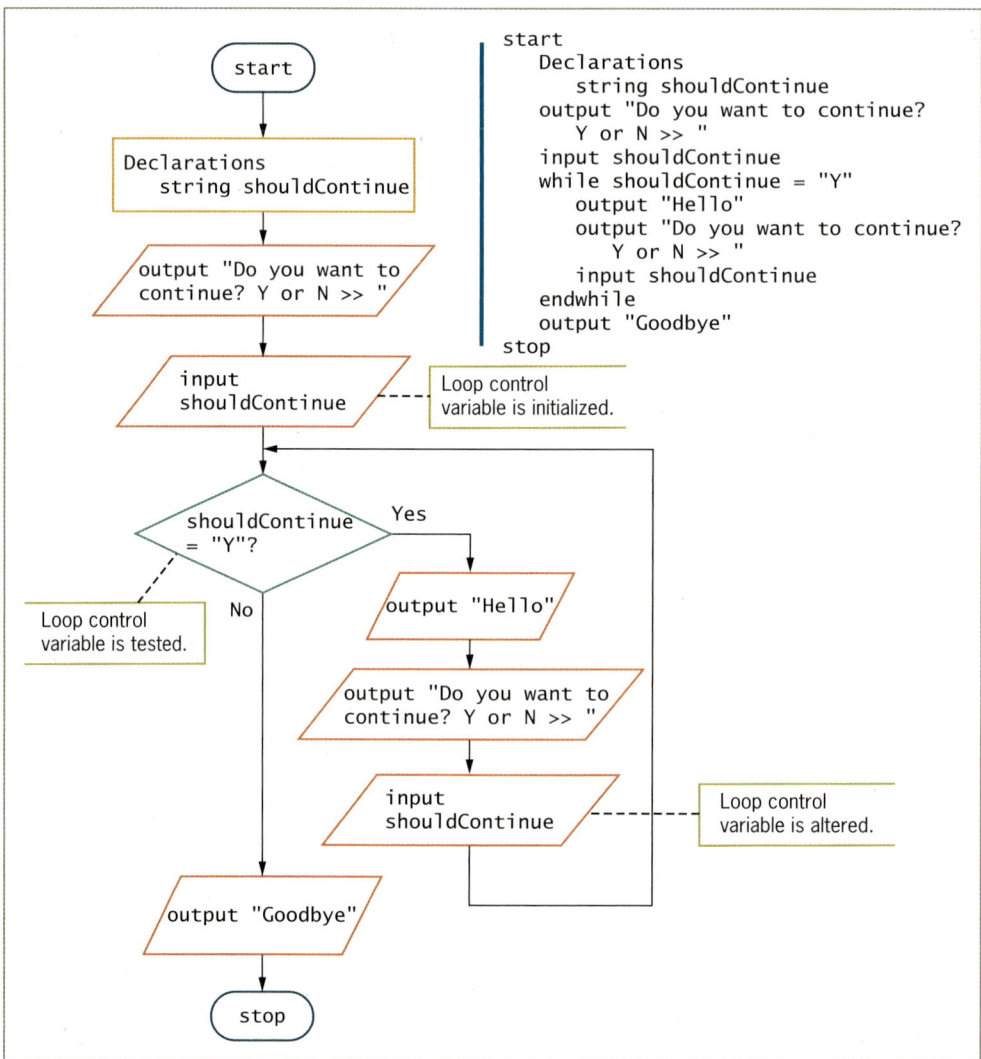

Figure 5-4   An indefinite `while` loop that displays *Hello* as long as the user wants to continue

In the program in Figure 5-4, the loop control variable is `shouldContinue`. The program executes as follows:

- The first `input shouldContinue` statement in the application in Figure 5-4 is a priming input statement. In this statement, the loop control variable is initialized by the user's first response.
- The `while` expression compares the loop control variable to the sentinel value *Y*.

Using a Loop Control Variable

- If the user has entered Y, then *Hello* is output and the user is asked whether the program should continue. In this step, the value of `shouldContinue` might change.
- At any point, if the user enters any value other than Y, the loop ends. In most programming languages, comparisons are case sensitive, so any entry other than Y, including *y*, will end the loop.

Figure 5-5 shows how the program might look when it is executed at the command line and in a GUI environment. The screens in Figure 5-5 show programs that perform exactly the same tasks using different environments. In each environment, the user can continue choosing to see *Hello* messages, or can choose to quit the program and display *Goodbye*.

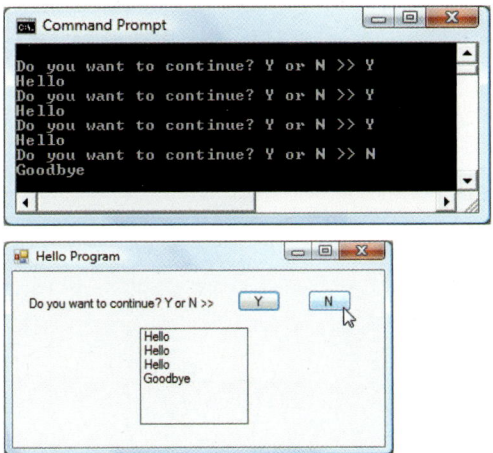

Figure 5-5 Typical executions of the program in Figure 5-4 in two environments

Understanding the Loop in a Program's Mainline Logic

The flowchart and pseudocode segments in Figure 5-4 contain three steps that should occur in every properly functioning loop:

1. You must provide a starting value for the variable that will control the loop.
2. You must test the loop control variable to determine whether the loop body executes.
3. Within the loop, you must alter the loop control variable.

In Chapter 2 you learned that the mainline logic of many business programs follows a standard outline that consists of housekeeping tasks, a loop that repeats, and finishing tasks. The three crucial steps that occur in any loop also occur in standard mainline logic. Figure 5-6 shows the flowchart for the mainline logic of the payroll program that you saw in Figure 2-8. In Figure 5-6, the three loop-controlling steps are highlighted. In this case, the three steps—initializing, testing, and altering the loop control variable—are in different modules. However, the steps all occur in the correct places, showing that the mainline logic uses a standard and correct loop.

CHAPTER 5 Looping

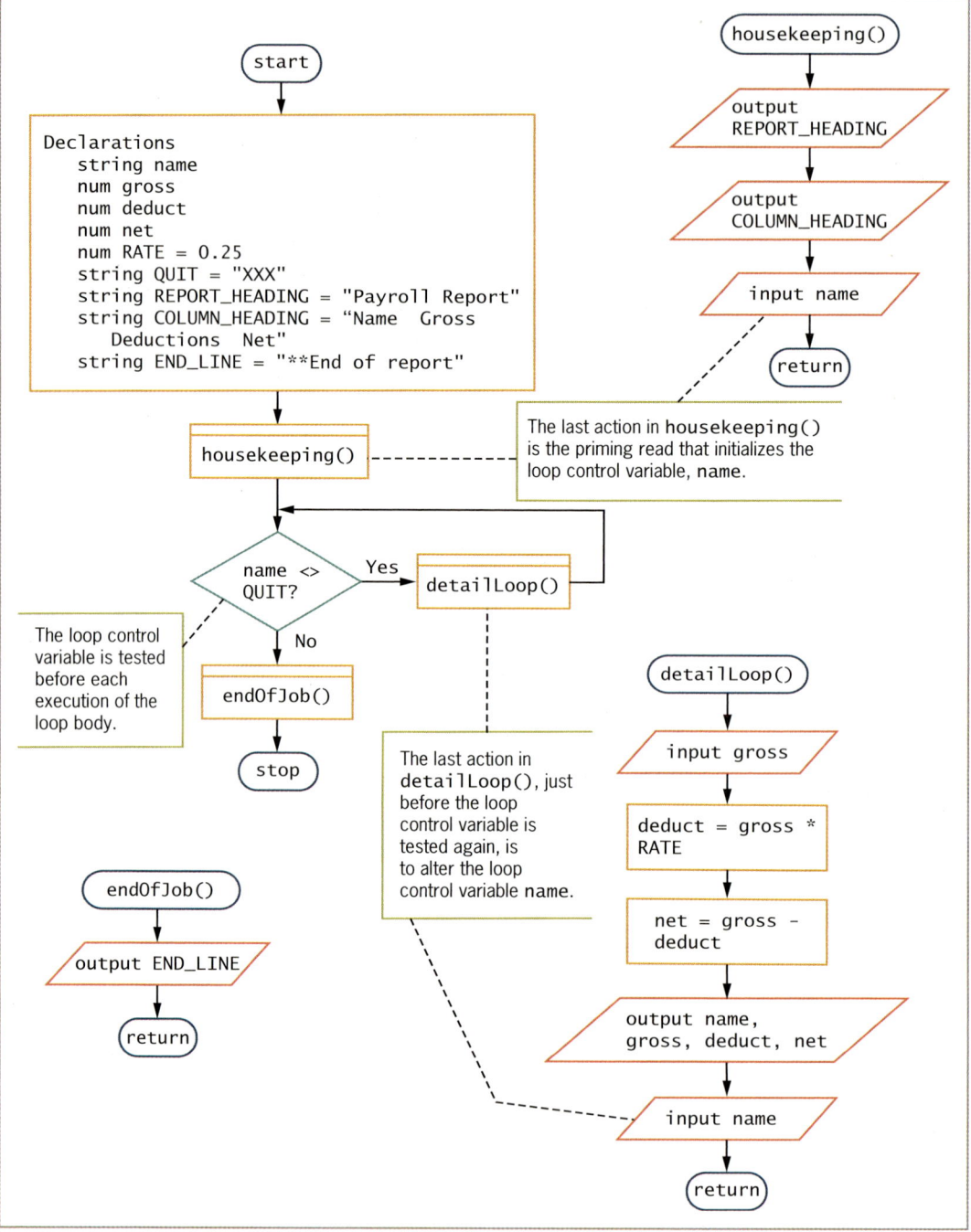

Figure 5-6 A payroll program showing how the loop control variable is used

> **TWO TRUTHS & A LIE**
>
> Using a Loop Control Variable
>
> 1. To make a `while` loop execute correctly, a loop control variable must be set to 0 before entering the loop.
> 2. To make a `while` loop execute correctly, a loop control variable should be tested before entering the loop body.
> 3. To make a `while` loop execute correctly, the body of the loop must take some action that alters the value of the loop control variable.
>
> The false statement is #1. A loop control variable must be initialized, but not necessarily to 0.

Nested Loops

Program logic gets more complicated when you must use loops within loops, or **nested loops**. When one loop appears inside another, the loop that contains the other loop is called the **outer loop**, and the loop that is contained is called the **inner loop**. You need to create nested loops when the values of two or more variables repeat to produce every combination of values. Usually, when you create nested loops, each loop has its own loop control variable.

For example, suppose you want to write a program that produces quiz answer sheets like the ones shown in Figure 5-7. Each answer sheet has a unique heading followed by five parts with three questions in each part, and you want a fill-in-the-blank line for each question. You could write a program that uses 63 separate output statements to produce three sheets (each sheet contains 21 printed lines), but it is more efficient to use nested loops.

CHAPTER 5 Looping

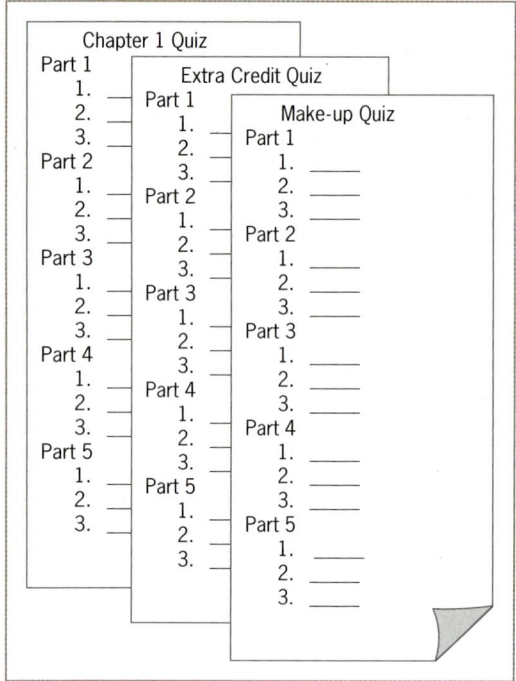

Figure 5-7 Quiz answer sheets

Figure 5-8 shows the logic for the program that produces answer sheets. Three loop control variables are declared for the program:

- quizName controls the detailLoop() module that is called from the mainline logic.
- partCounter controls the outer loop within the detailLoop() module; it keeps track of the answer sheet parts.
- questionCounter controls the inner loop in the detailLoop() module; it keeps track of the questions and answer lines within each part section on each answer sheet.

Five named constants are also declared. Three of these constants (QUIT, PARTS, and QUESTIONS) hold the sentinel values for each of the three loops in the program. The other two hold the text that will be output (the word *Part* that precedes each part number, and the period-space-underscore combination that forms a fill-in line for each question).

When the program starts, the housekeeping() module executes and the user enters the name to be output at the top of the first quiz. If the user enters the QUIT value, the program ends immediately, but if the user enters anything else, such as *Make-up Quiz*, then the detailLoop() module executes.

In the detailLoop() the quiz name is output at the top of the answer sheet. Then partCounter is initialized to 1. The partCounter variable is the loop control variable for the outer loop in this module. The outer loop continues while `partCounter` is less than or equal to `PARTS`. The last statement in the outer loop adds 1 to `partCounter`. In other words, the outer loop will execute when `partCounter` is 1, 2, 3, 4, and 5.

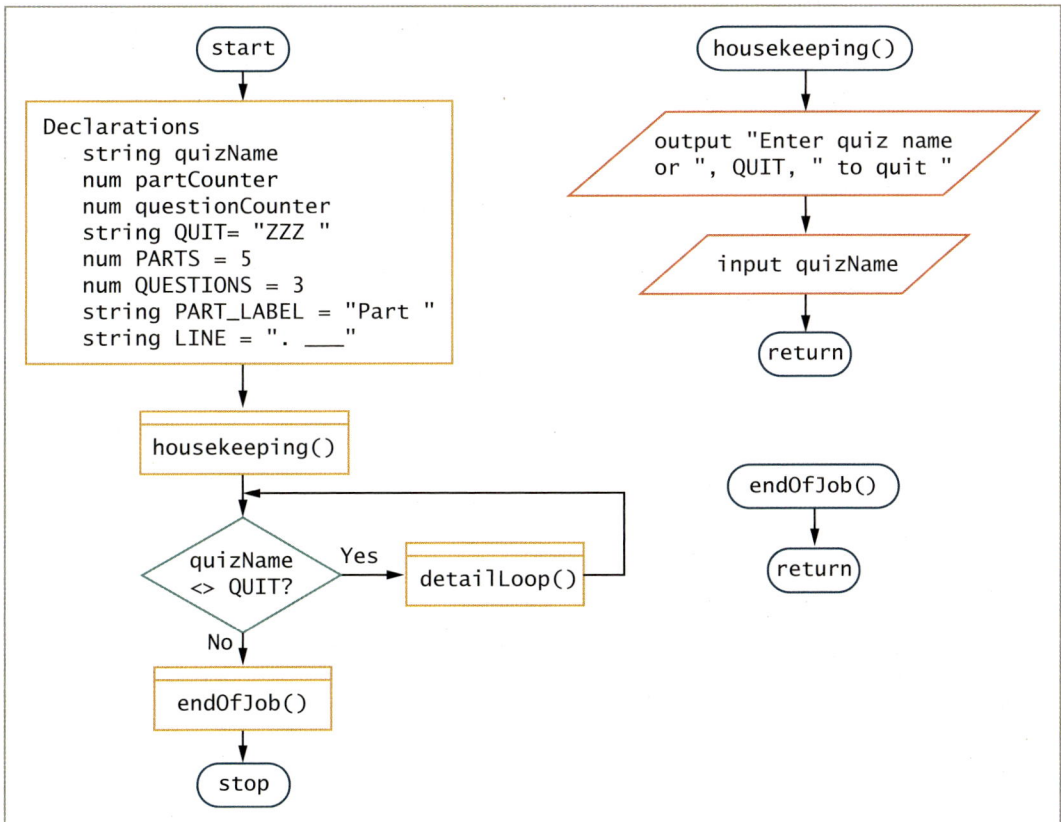

Figure 5-8 Flowchart and pseudocode for `AnswerSheet` program (continues)

(continued)

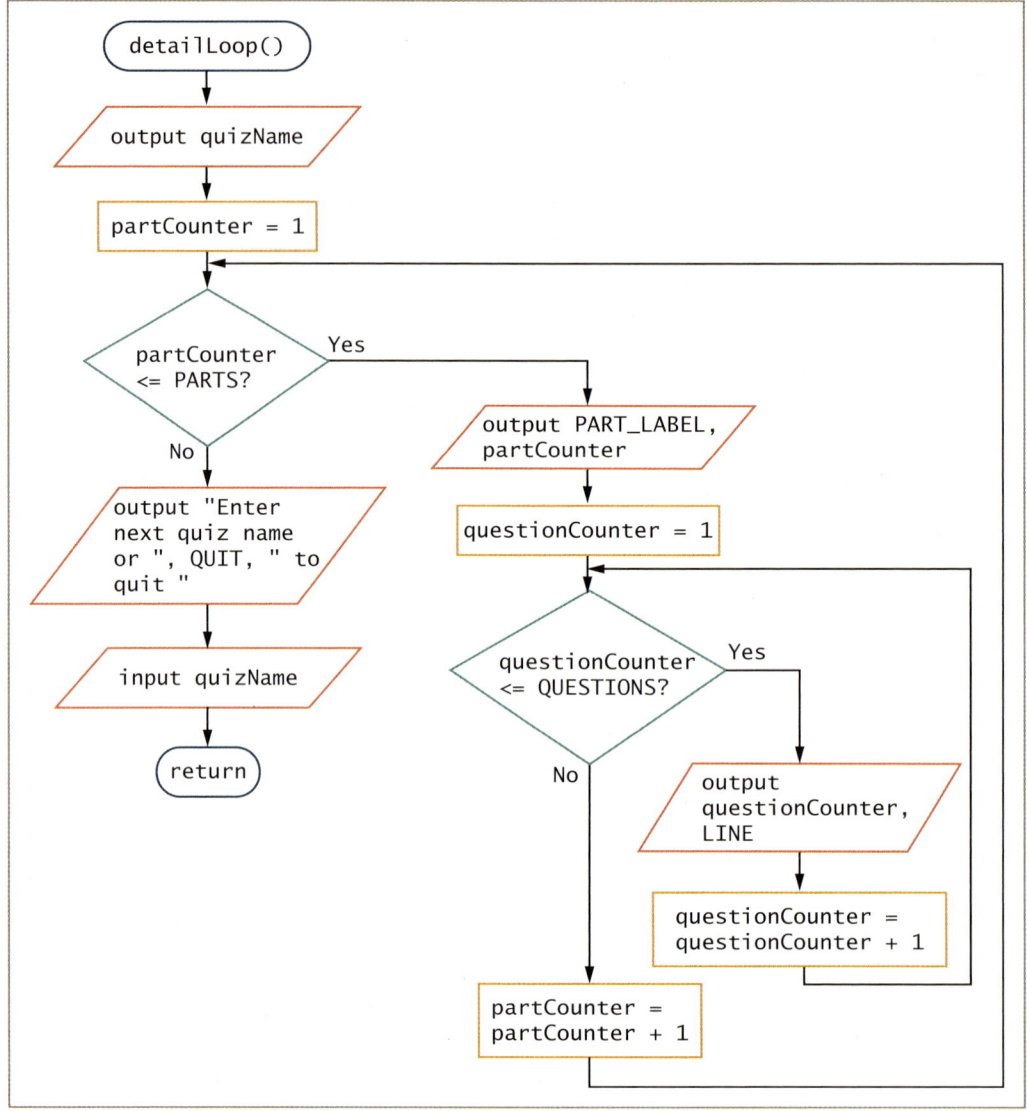

Figure 5-8 Flowchart and pseudocode for `AnswerSheet` program (continues)

(continued)

```
start
   Declarations
      string quizName
      num partCounter
      num questionCounter
      string QUIT = "ZZZ "
      num PARTS = 5
      num QUESTIONS = 3
      string PART_LABEL = "Part "
      string LINE = ". _____"
   housekeeping()
   while quizName <> QUIT
      detailLoop()
   endwhile
   endOfJob()
stop

housekeeping()
   output "Enter quiz name or ", QUIT, " to quit "
   input quizName
return

detailLoop()
   output quizName
   partCounter = 1
   while partCounter <= PARTS
      output PART_LABEL, partCounter
      questionCounter = 1
      while questionCounter <= QUESTIONS
         output questionCounter, LINE
         questionCounter = questionCounter + 1
      endwhile
      partCounter = partCounter + 1
   endwhile
   output "Enter next quiz name or ", QUIT, " to quit "
   input quizName
return

endOfJob()
return
```

Figure 5-8 Flowchart and pseudocode for AnswerSheet program

In Figure 5-8, some output (the user prompt) would be sent to one output device, such as a monitor. Other output (the quiz sheet) would be sent to another output device, such as a printer. The statements needed to send output to separate devices differs among languages. Chapter 7 provides more details.

The endOfJob() module is included in the program in Figure 5-8, even though it contains no statements, so that the mainline logic contains all the parts you have learned. An empty module that acts as a placeholder is called a **stub**.

In the outer loop in the `detailLoop()` module in Figure 5-8, the word *Part* and the current `partCounter` value are output. Then the following steps execute:

- The loop control variable for the inner loop is initialized by setting `questionCounter` to 1.
- The loop control variable `questionCounter` is evaluated by comparing it to `QUESTIONS`, and while `questionCounter` does not exceed `QUESTIONS`, the loop body executes: The value of `questionCounter` is output, followed by a period and a fill-in-the-blank line.
- At the end of the loop body, the loop control variable is altered by adding 1 to `questionCounter` and the `questionCounter` comparison is made again.

In other words, when `partCounter` is 1, the part heading is output and underscore lines are output for questions 1, 2, and 3. Then `partCounter` becomes 2, the part heading is output, and underscore lines are created for another set of questions 1, 2, and 3. Then `partCounter` becomes 3, 4, and 5 in turn, and three underscore lines are created for each part.

In the program in Figure 5-8, it is important that `questionCounter` is reset to 1 within the outer loop, just before entering the inner loop. If this step was omitted, Part 1 would contain questions 1, 2, and 3, but subsequent parts would be empty.

 Watch the video *Nested Loops*.

TWO TRUTHS & A LIE

Nested Loops

1. When one loop is nested inside another, the loop that contains the other loop is called the outer loop.
2. You need to create nested loops when the values of two or more variables repeat to produce every combination of values.
3. The number of times a loop executes always depends on a constant.

The false statement is #3. The number of times a loop executes can depend on a constant or a value that varies.

Avoiding Common Loop Mistakes

Programmers make the following common mistakes with loops:

- Neglecting to initialize the loop control variable
- Neglecting to alter the loop control variable
- Using the wrong comparison with the loop control variable
- Including statements inside the loop that belong outside the loop

The following sections explain these common mistakes in more detail.

Mistake: Neglecting to Initialize the Loop Control Variable

Failing to initialize a loop's control variable is a mistake. For example, consider the program in Figure 5-9. It prompts the user for a name, and while the value of **name** continues not to be the sentinel value *ZZZ*, it outputs a greeting that uses the name and asks for the next name. This program works correctly.

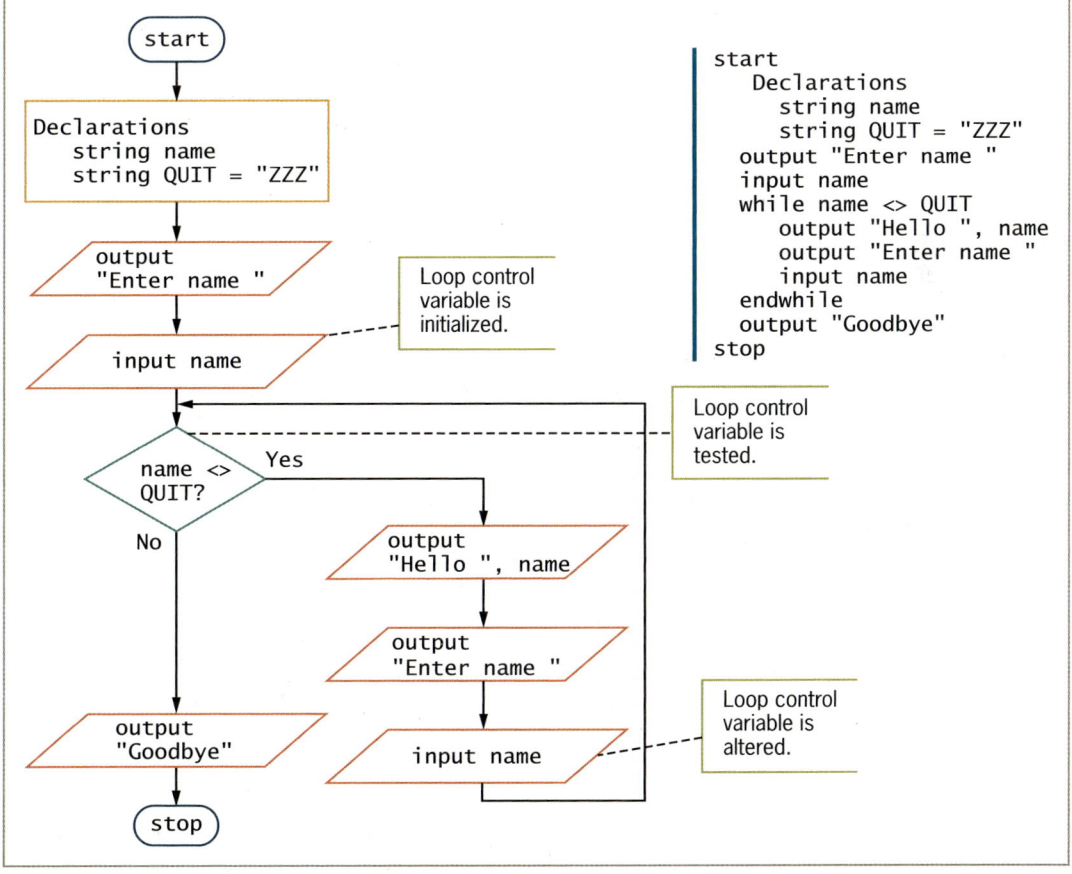

Figure 5-9 Correct logic for greeting program

Figure 5-10 shows an incorrect program in which the loop control variable is not assigned a starting value. If the name variable is not set to a starting value, then when the eof condition is tested, there is no way to predict whether it will be true. If the user does not enter a value for name, the garbage value originally held by that variable might or might not be ZZZ. So, one of two scenarios follows:

- Most likely, the uninitialized value of name is not ZZZ, so the first greeting output will include garbage—for example, *Hello 12BGr5*.
- By a remote chance, the uninitialized value of name *is* ZZZ, so the program ends immediately before the user can enter any names.

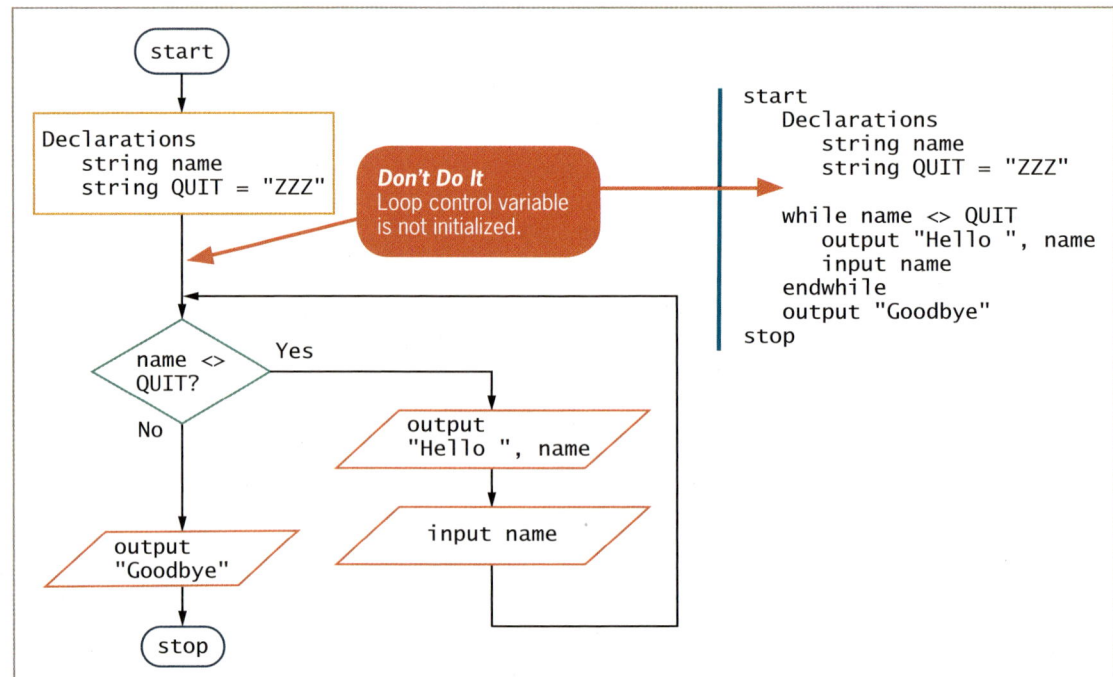

Figure 5-10 Incorrect logic for greeting program because the loop control variable initialization is missing

Avoiding Common Loop Mistakes

Mistake: Neglecting to Alter the Loop Control Variable

Different sorts of errors will occur if you fail to alter a loop control variable within the loop. For example, in the program in Figure 5-9 that accepts and displays names, you create such an error if you don't accept names within the loop. Figure 5-11 shows the resulting incorrect logic.

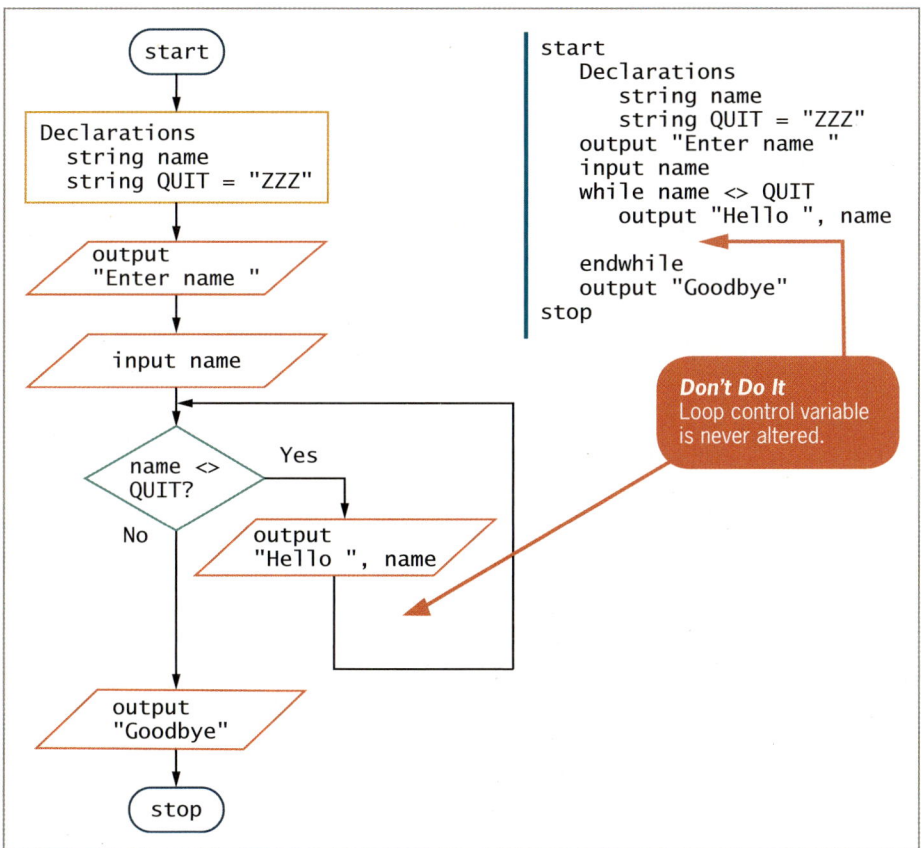

Figure 5-11 Incorrect logic for greeting program because the loop control variable is not altered

If you remove the `input name` instruction from the end of the loop in the program, no name is ever entered after the first one. For example, assume that when the program starts, the user enters *Fred*. The name will be compared to the sentinel value, and the loop will be entered. After a greeting is output for Fred, no new name is entered, so when the logic returns to the loop-controlling question, the `name` will still not be *ZZZ*, and greetings for Fred will continue to be output infinitely. You never want to create a loop that cannot terminate.

CHAPTER 5 Looping

Mistake: Using the Wrong Comparison with the Loop Control Variable

Programmers must be careful to use the correct comparison in the statement that controls a loop. A comparison is correct only when the appropriate operands and operator are used. For example, although only one keystroke differs between the original greeting program in Figure 5-9 and the one in Figure 5-12, the original program correctly produces named greetings and the second one does not.

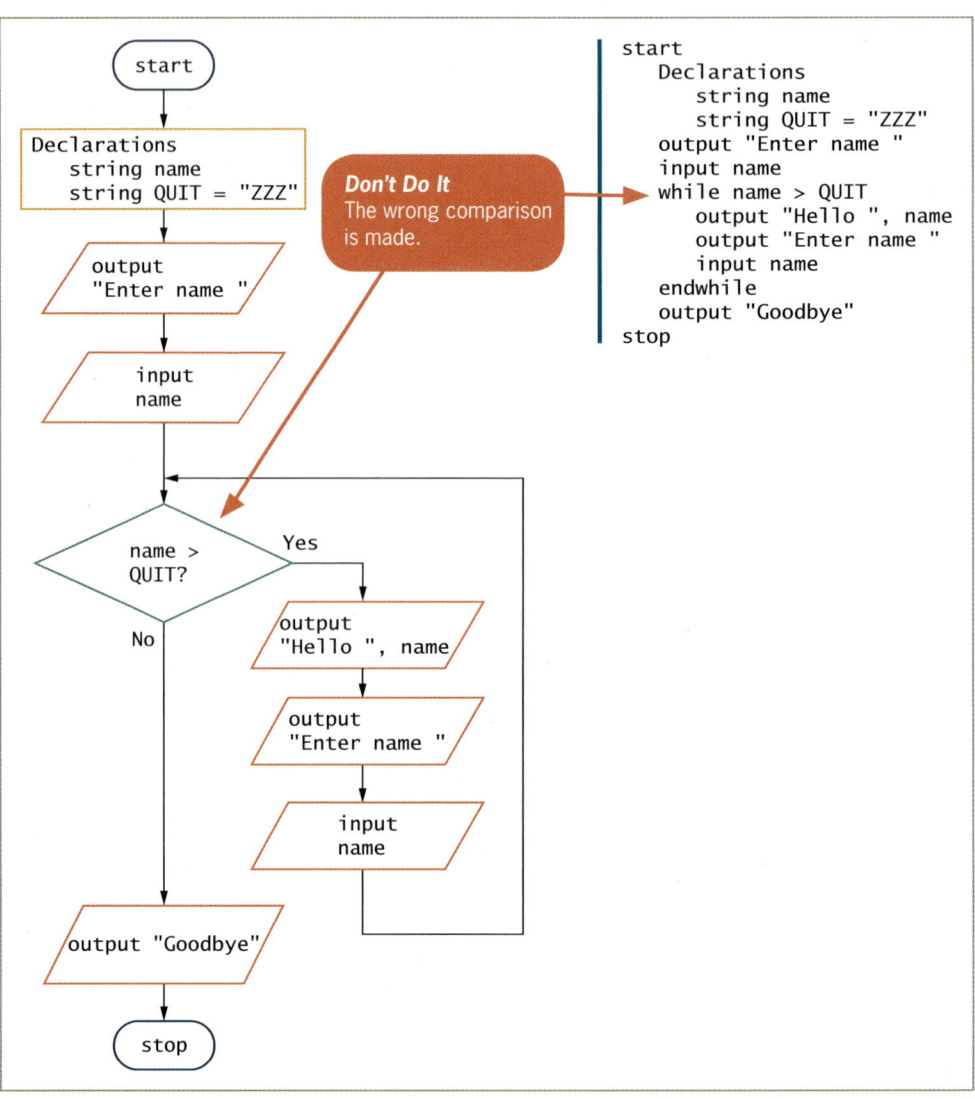

Figure 5-12 Incorrect logic for greeting program because the wrong test is made with the loop control variable

In Figure 5-12, a greater-than comparison (>) is made instead of a not-equal-to (<>) comparison. Suppose that when the program executes, the user enters *Fred* as the first name. In most programming languages, when the comparison between *Fred* and *ZZZ* is made, the values are compared alphabetically. *Fred* is not greater than *ZZZ*, so the loop is never entered, and the program ends.

Using the wrong comparison can have serious effects. For example, in a counted loop, if you use <= instead of < to compare a counter to a sentinel value, the program will perform one loop execution too many. If the loop only displays greetings, the error might not be critical, but if such an error occurred in a loan company application, each customer might be charged a month's additional interest. If the error occurred in an airline's application, it might overbook a flight. If the error occurred in a pharmacy's drug-dispensing application, each patient might receive one extra (and possibly harmful) unit of medication.

Mistake: Including Statements Inside the Loop that Belong Outside the Loop

Suppose that you write a program for a store manager who wants to discount every item he sells by 30 percent. The manager wants 100 new price label stickers for each item. The user enters a price, the new discounted price is calculated, 100 stickers are printed, and the next price is entered. Figure 5-13 shows a program that performs the job inefficiently because the same value, `newPrice`, is calculated 100 separate times for each `price` that is entered.

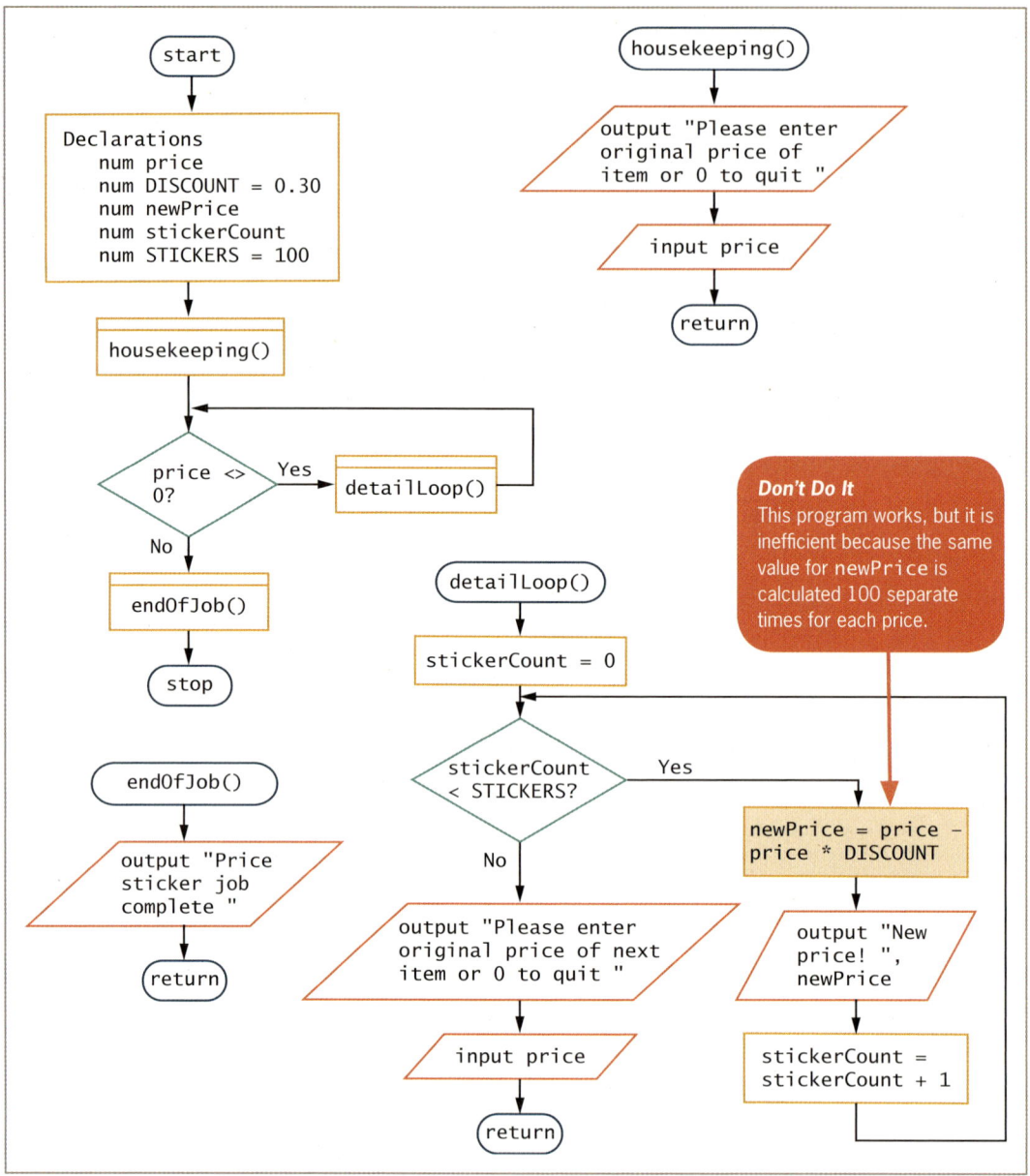

Figure 5-13 Inefficient way to produce 100 discount price stickers for differently priced items (continues)

Avoiding Common Loop Mistakes

(continued)

```
start
   Declarations
      num price
      num DISCOUNT = 0.30
      num newPrice
      num stickerCount
      num STICKERS = 100
   housekeeping()
   while price <> 0
      detailLoop()
   endwhile
   endOfJob()
stop

housekeeping()
   output "Please enter original price of item or 0 to quit "
   input price
return

detailLoop()
   stickerCount = 0
   while stickerCount < STICKERS
      newPrice = price - price * DISCOUNT
      output "New price! ", newPrice
      stickerCount = stickerCount + 1
   endwhile
   output "Please enter original price of
      next item or 0 to quit "
   input price
return

endOfJob()
   output "Price sticker job complete"
return
```

Don't Do It
This program works, but it is inefficient because the same value for newPrice is calculated 100 separate times for each price.

Figure 5-13 Inefficient way to produce 100 discount price stickers for differently priced items

Figure 5-14 shows the same program, in which the newPrice value that is output on the sticker is calculated only once per new price; the calculation has been moved to a better location. The programs in Figures 5-13 and 5-14 do the same thing, but the second program does it more efficiently. As you become more proficient at programming, you will recognize many opportunities to perform the same tasks in alternate, more elegant, and more efficient ways.

When you describe people or events as elegant, you mean they possess a refined gracefulness. Similarly, programmers use the term *elegant* to describe programs that are well designed and easy to understand and maintain.

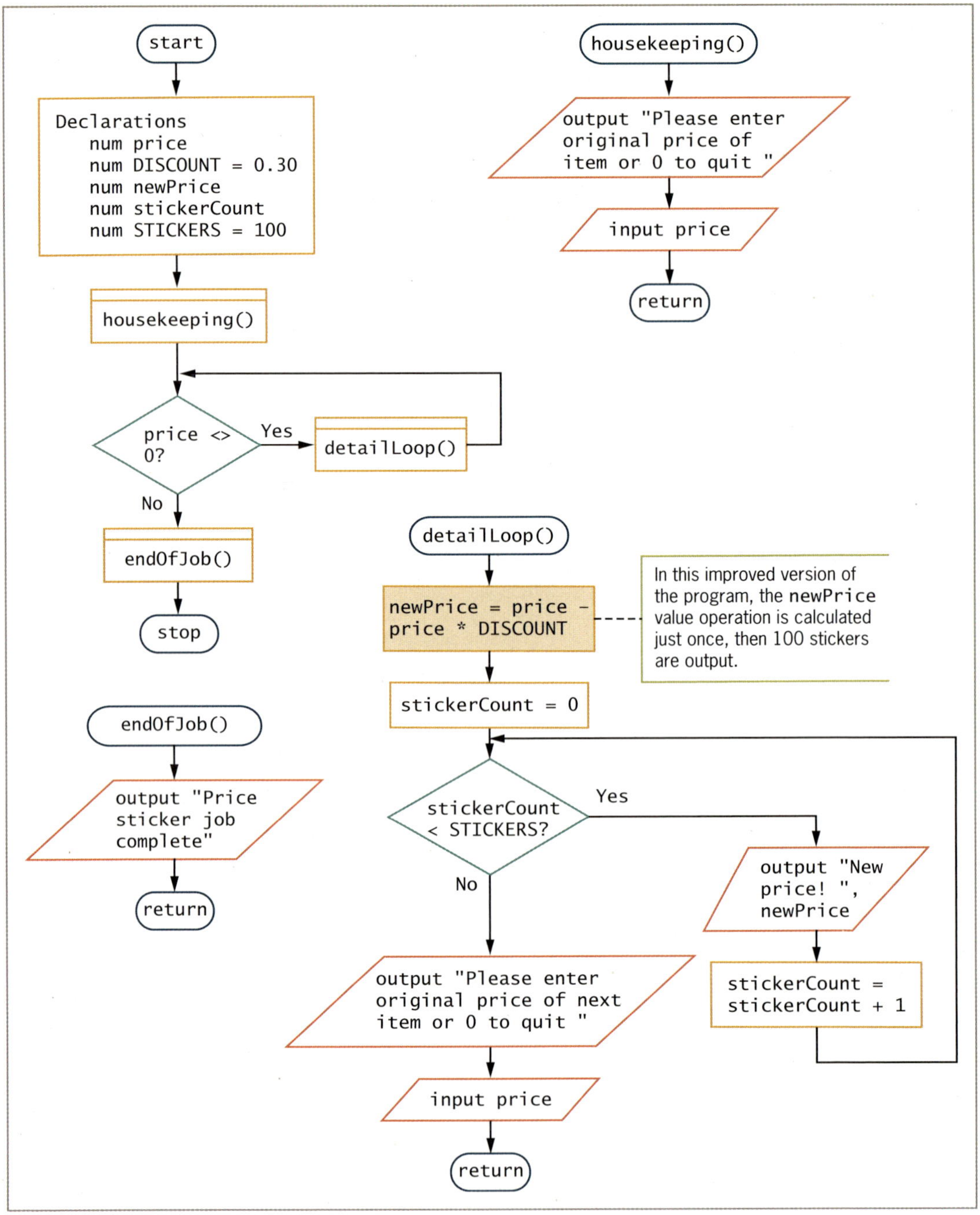

CHAPTER 5   Looping

Figure 5-14   Improved discount sticker-making program (continues)

(continued)

```
start
    Declarations
        num price
        num DISCOUNT = 0.30
        num newPrice
        num stickerCount
        num STICKERS = 100
    housekeeping()
    while price <> 0
        detailLoop()
    endwhile
    endOfJob()
stop

housekeeping()
    output "Please enter original price of item or 0 to quit "
    input price
return

detailLoop()
    newPrice = price - price * DISCOUNT
    stickerCount = 0
    while stickerCount < STICKERS
        output "New price! ", newPrice
        stickerCount = stickerCount + 1
    endwhile
    output "Please enter original price of next item or 0 to quit "
    input price
return

endOfJob()
    output "Price sticker job complete"
return
```

> In this improved version of the program, the newPrice value operation is calculated just once, then 100 stickers are output.

Figure 5-14 Improved discount sticker-making program

TWO TRUTHS & A LIE

Avoiding Common Loop Mistakes

1. In a loop, neglecting to initialize the loop control variable is a mistake.
2. In a loop, neglecting to alter the loop control variable is a mistake.
3. In a loop, comparing the loop control variable using >= or <= is a mistake.

The false statement is #3. Many loops are created correctly using <= or >=.

Using a for Loop

Every high-level programming language contains a `while` statement that you can use to code any loop, including both indefinite and definite loops. In addition to the `while` statement, most computer languages support a `for` statement. You usually use the **for statement**, or **for loop**, with definite loops—those that will loop a specific number of times—when you know exactly how many times the loop will repeat. The `for` statement provides you with three actions in one compact statement. In a `for` statement, a loop control variable is:

- Initialized
- Evaluated
- Altered

The `for` statement takes a form similar to the following:

```
for loopControlVariable = initialValue to finalValue step stepValue
    do something
endfor
```

The amount by which a `for` loop control variable changes is often called a **step value**. The step value can be positive or negative; that is, it can increment or decrement.

For example, to display *Hello* four times, you can write either of the sets of statements in Figure 5-15.

```
count = 0                       for count = 0 to 3 step 1
while count <= 3                    output "Hello"
    output "Hello"              endfor
    count = count + 1
endwhile
```

Figure 5-15 Comparable `while` and `for` statements that each output *Hello* four times

The code segments in Figure 5-15 each accomplish the same tasks:

- The variable `count` is initialized to 0.
- The `count` variable is compared to the limit value 3; while `count` is less than or equal to 3, the loop body executes.
- As the last statement in the loop execution, the value of `count` increases by 1. After the increase, the comparison to the limit value is made again.

The `for` loop simply expresses the same logic in a more compact form than the `while` statement. You never are required to use a `for` statement for any loop; a `while` statement can always be used instead. However, when a loop's execution is based on a loop control variable progressing from a known starting value to a known ending value in equal steps, the `for` loop

Using a for Loop

provides you with a convenient shorthand. It is easy for others to read, and because the loop control variable's initialization, testing, and alteration are all performed in one location, you are less likely to leave out one of these crucial elements.

Although for loops are commonly used to control execution of a block of statements a fixed number of times, the programmer doesn't need to know the starting, ending, or step value for the loop when the program is written. For example, any of the values might be entered by the user, or might be the result of a calculation.

The for loop is particularly useful when processing arrays. You will learn about arrays in Chapter 6.

In Java, C++, and C#, a for loop that displays 21 values (0 through 20) might look similar to the following:
```
for(count = 0; count <= 20; count++)
{
    output count
}
```
The three actions (initialization, comparison, and altering of the loop control variable) are separated by semicolons within a set of parentheses that follow the keyword for. The expression count++ adds 1 to count. The block of statements that depends on the loop sits between a pair of curly braces.

Both the while loop and the for loop are examples of pretest loops. In a **pretest loop**, the loop control variable is tested before each iteration. That means the loop body might never execute because the question controlling the loop might be false the first time it is asked. Most languages allow you to use a variation of the looping structure known as a **posttest loop**, which tests the loop control variable after each iteration. In a posttest loop, the loop body executes at least one time because the loop control variable is not tested until after one iteration. Appendix F contains information about posttest loops.

Some books and flowchart programs use a symbol that looks like a hexagon to represent a for loop in a flowchart. However, no special symbols are needed to express a for loop's logic. A for loop is simply a code shortcut, so this book uses standard flowchart symbols to represent initializing the loop control variable, testing it, and altering it.

CHAPTER 5   Looping

> **TWO TRUTHS & A LIE**
> Using a **for** Loop
>
> 1. The for statement provides you with three actions in one compact statement: initializing, evaluating, and altering a loop control variable.
> 2. A for statement body always executes at least one time.
> 3. In most programming languages, you can provide a for loop with any step value.
>
> The false statement is #2. A for statement body might not execute depending on the initial value of the loop control variable.

Common Loop Applications

Although every computer program is different, many techniques are common to a variety of applications. Loops, for example, are frequently used to accumulate totals and to validate data.

Using a Loop to Accumulate Totals

Business reports often include totals. The supervisor who requests a list of employees in the company dental plan is often as interested in the number of participating employees as in who they are. When you receive your telephone bill each month, you usually check the total as well as charges for the individual calls.

Assume that a real estate broker wants to see a list of all properties sold in the last month as well as the total value for all the properties. A program might accept sales data that includes the street address of each property sold and its selling price. The data records might be entered by a clerk as each sale is made, and stored in a file until the end of the month; then they can be used in a monthly report. Figure 5-16 shows an example of such a report.

```
MONTH-END SALES REPORT

Address            Price

287 Acorn St       150,000
12 Maple Ave       310,000
8723 Marie Ln       65,500
222 Acorn St       127,000
29 Bahama Way      450,000

Total            1,102,500
```

Figure 5-16   Month-end real estate sales report

To create the sales report, you must output the address and price for each property sold and add its value to an accumulator. An **accumulator** is a variable that you use to gather or accumulate values, and is very similar to a counter that you use to count loop iterations. However, usually you add just one to a counter, whereas you add some other value to an accumulator. If the real estate broker wants to know how many listings the company holds, you *count* them. When the broker wants to know the total real estate value, you *accumulate* it.

To accumulate total real estate prices, you declare a numeric variable such as accumPrice and initialize it to 0. As you get data for each real estate transaction, you output it and add its value to the accumulator accumPrice, as shown shaded in Figure 5-17.

CHAPTER 5 Looping

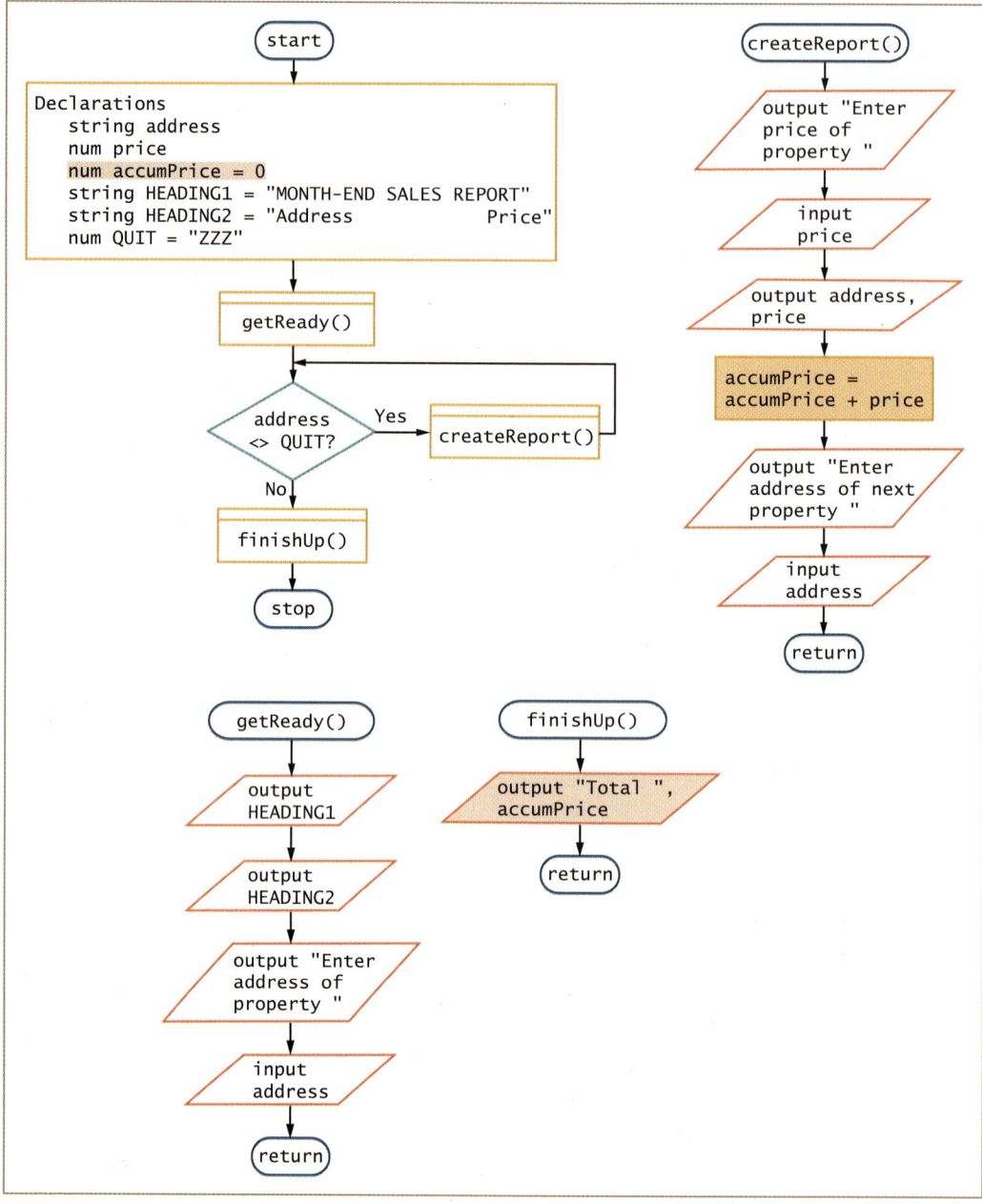

Figure 5-17 Flowchart and pseudocode for real estate sales report program (continues)

Common Loop Applications

(continued)

```
start
   Declarations
      string address
      num price
      num accumPrice = 0
      string HEADING1 = "MONTH-END SALES REPORT"
      string HEADING2 = "Address         Price"
      num QUIT = "ZZZ"
   getReady()
   while address <> QUIT
      createReport()
   endwhile
   finishUp()
stop

getReady()
   output HEADING1
   output HEADING2
   output "Enter address of property "
   input address
return

createReport()
   output "Enter price of property "
   input price
   output address, price
   accumPrice = accumPrice + price
   output "Enter address of next property "
   input address
return

finishUp()
   output "Total ", accumPrice
return
```

Figure 5-17 Flowchart and pseudocode for real estate sales report program

Some programming languages assign 0 to a variable you fail to initialize explicitly, but many do not—when you try to add a value to an uninitialized variable, they either issue an error message or let you incorrectly start with an accumulator that holds garbage. The safest and clearest course of action is to assign the value 0 to accumulators before using them.

After the program in Figure 5-17 gets and displays the last real estate transaction, the user enters the sentinel value and loop execution ends. At that point, the accumulator will hold the grand total of all the real estate values. The program displays the word *Total* and the accumulated value `accumPrice`. Then the program ends.

CHAPTER 5 Looping

Figure 5-17 highlights the three actions you usually must take with an accumulator:

- Accumulators are initialized to 0.
- Accumulators are altered, usually once for every data set processed.
- At the end of processing, accumulators are output.

After outputting the value of `accumPrice`, new programmers often want to reset it to 0. Their argument is that they are "cleaning up after themselves." Although you can take this step without harming the execution of the program, it serves no useful purpose. You cannot set `accumPrice` to 0 in anticipation of having it ready for the next program, or even for the next time you execute the same program. Variables exist only during an execution of the program, and even if a future application happens to contain a variable named `accumPrice`, the variable will not necessarily occupy the same memory location as this one. Even if you run the same application a second time, the variables might occupy different physical memory locations from those during the first run. At the beginning of any method, it is the programmer's responsibility to initialize all variables that must start with a specific value. There is no benefit to changing a variable's value when it will never be used again during the current execution.

Some business reports are **summary reports**—they contain only totals with no data for individual records. In the example in Figure 5-17, suppose that the broker did not care about details of individual sales, but only about the total for all transactions. You could create a summary report by omitting the step that outputs `address` and `price` from the `createReport()` module. Then you could simply output `accumPrice` at the end of the program.

Using a Loop to Validate Data

When you ask a user to enter data into a computer program, you have no assurance that the data will be accurate. Incorrect user entries are by far the most common source of computer errors. The programs you write will be improved if you employ **defensive programming**, which means trying to prepare for all possible errors before they occur. Loops are frequently used to **validate data**—that is, to make sure it is meaningful and useful. For example, validation might ensure that a value is the correct data type or that it falls within an acceptable range.

Suppose that part of a program you are writing asks a user to enter a number that represents his or her birth month. If the user types a number lower than 1 or greater than 12, you must take some sort of action. For example:

- You could display an error message and stop the program.
- You could choose to assign a default value for the month (for example, 1) before proceeding.
- You could reprompt the user for valid input.

Common Loop Applications

If you choose this last course of action, you could then take at least two approaches. You could use a selection, and if the month is invalid, you could ask the user to reenter a number, as shown in Figure 5-18.

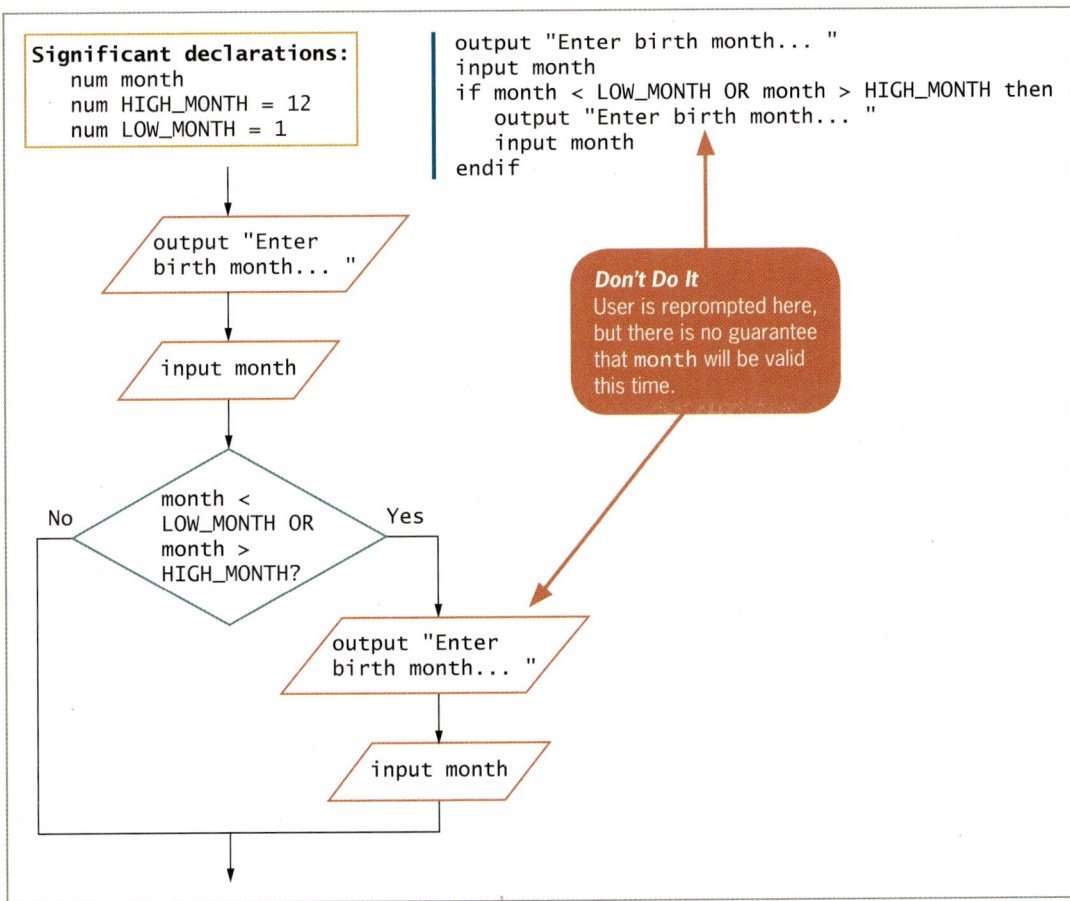

Figure 5-18 Reprompting a user once after an invalid month is entered

The problem with the logic in Figure 5-18 is that the user still might not enter valid data on the second attempt. Of course, you could add a third decision, but you still couldn't control what the user enters.

The superior solution is to use a loop to continuously prompt a user for a month until the user enters it correctly. Figure 5-19 shows this approach.

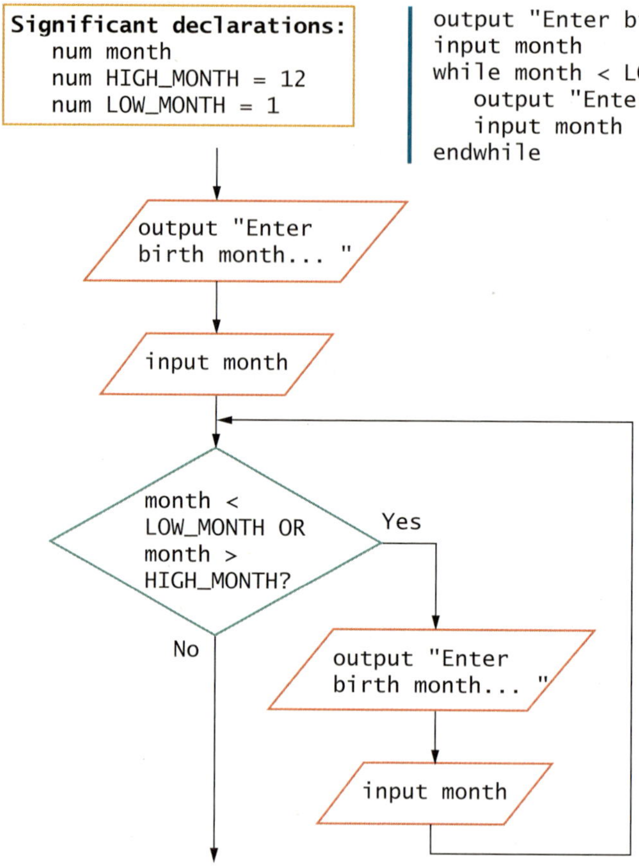

CHAPTER 5 Looping

```
Significant declarations:
   num month
   num HIGH_MONTH = 12
   num LOW_MONTH = 1
```

```
output "Enter birth month... "
input month
while month < LOW_MONTH OR month > HIGH_MONTH
     output "Enter birth month... "
     input month
endwhile
```

output "Enter birth month... "

input month

month < LOW_MONTH OR month > HIGH_MONTH?   Yes

No

output "Enter birth month... "

input month

Figure 5-19   Reprompting a user continuously after an invalid month is entered

Most languages provide a built-in way to check whether an entered value is numeric. When you rely on user input, you frequently accept each piece of input data as a string and then attempt to convert it to a number. The procedure for accomplishing numeric checks varies slightly in different programming languages.

Of course, data validation doesn't prevent all errors; just because a data item is valid does not mean that it is correct. For example, a program can determine that 5 is a valid birth month, but not that your birthday actually falls in month 5. Programmers employ the acronym **GIGO** for *garbage in, garbage out*. It means that if your input is incorrect, your output is worthless.

Limiting a Reprompting Loop

Reprompting a user is a good way to ensure valid data, but it can be frustrating to a user if it continues indefinitely. For example, suppose the user must enter a valid birth month, but has used another application in which January was month 0, and keeps entering 0 no matter how many times you repeat the prompt. One helpful addition to the program would be to use the limiting values as part of the prompt. In other words, instead of the statement output "Enter birth month... ", the following statement might be more useful:

output "Enter birth month between ", LOW_MONTH, ", and " HIGH_MONTH, "..."

Still, the user might not understand the prompt or not read it carefully, so you might want to employ the tactic used in Figure 5-20, in which the program maintains a count of the number of reprompts. In this example, a constant named ATTEMPTS is set to 3. While a count of the user's attempts at correct data entry remains below this limit, and the user enters invalid data, the user continues to be reprompted. If the user exceeds the limited number of allowed attempts, the loop ends. The next action depends on the application. If count equals ATTEMPTS after the data-entry loop ends, you might want to force the invalid data to a default value. **Forcing** a data item means you override incorrect data by setting the variable to a specific value. For example, you might decide that if a month value does not fall between 1 and 12, you will force the month to 0 or 99, which indicates to users that no valid value exists. In a different application, you might just choose to end the program. In an interactive, Web-based program, you might choose to have a customer service representative start a chat session with the user to offer help.

Programs that frustrate users can result in lost revenue for a company. For example, if a company's Web site is difficult to navigate, users might give up and not do business with the organization.

CHAPTER 5   Looping

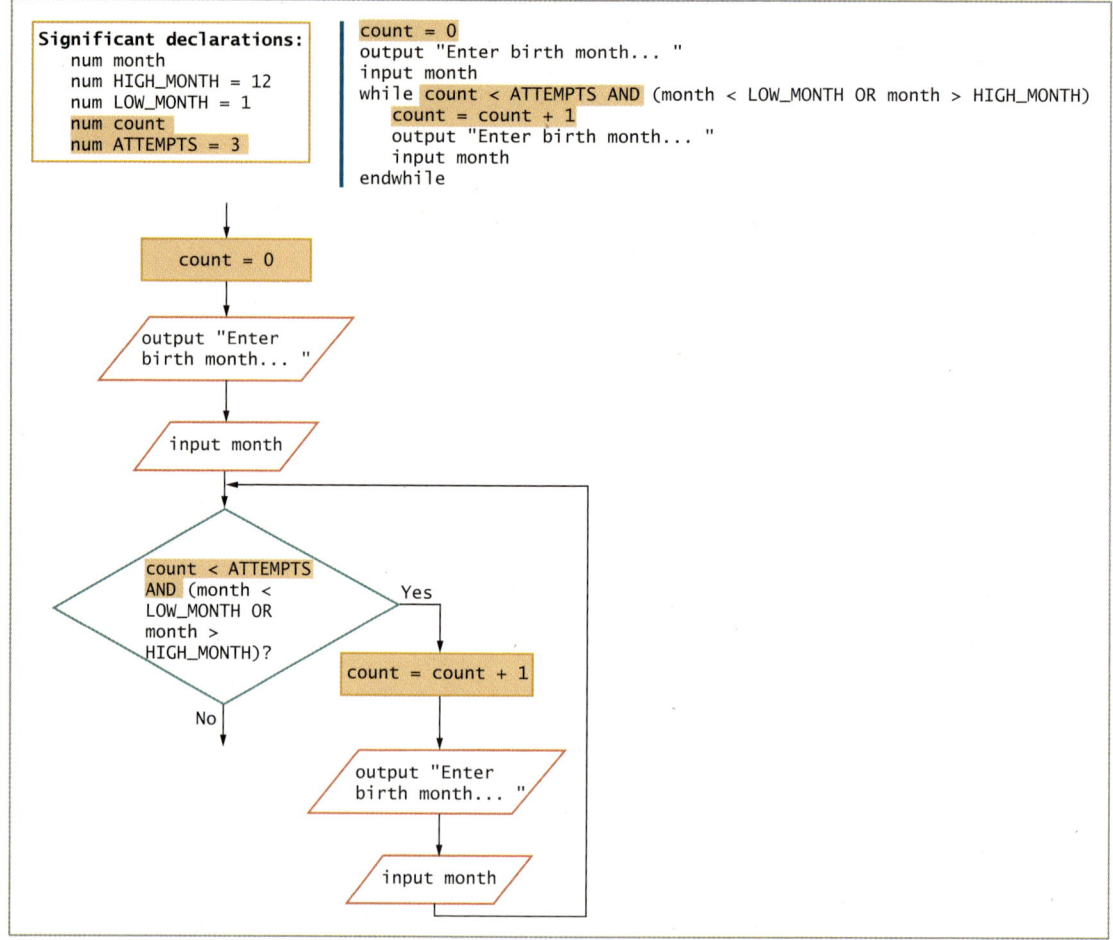

Figure 5-20   Limiting user reprompts

Validating a Data Type

The data you use within computer programs is varied. It stands to reason that validating data requires a variety of methods. For example, some programming languages allow you to check data items to make sure they are the correct data type. Although this technique varies from language to language, you can often make a statement like the one shown in Figure 5-21. In this program segment, `isNumeric()` represents a call to a module; it is used to check whether the entered employee `salary` falls within the category of numeric data. You check to ensure that a value is numeric for many reasons—an important one is that only numeric values can be used correctly in arithmetic statements. A module such as `isNumeric()` is most often provided with the language translator you use to write your programs. Such a method operates as a black box; in other words, you can use the method's results without understanding its internal statements.

Common Loop Applications

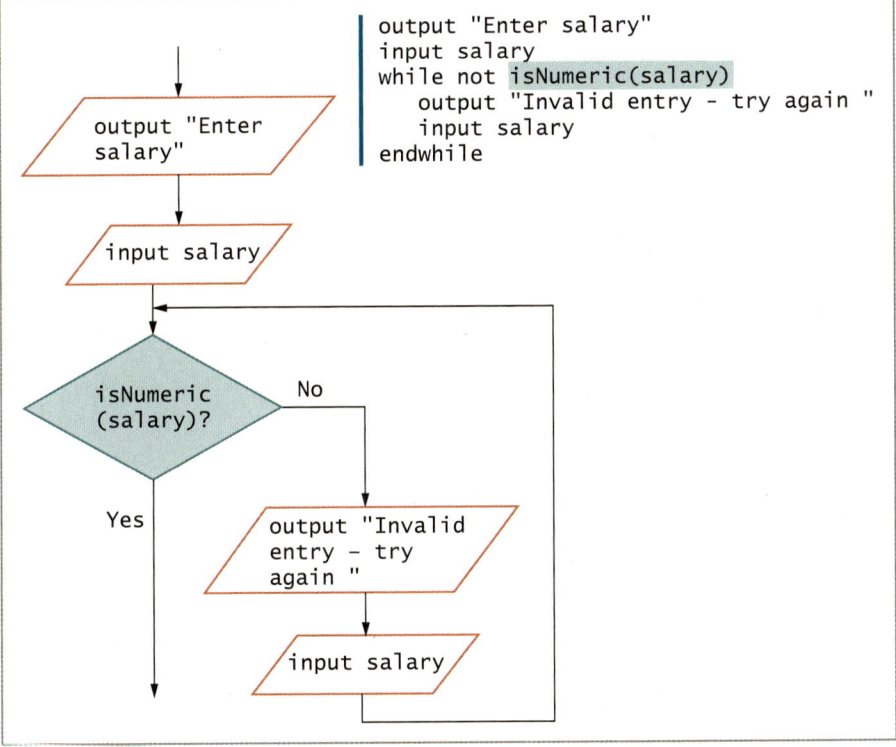

Figure 5-21 Checking data for correct type

Besides allowing you to check whether a value is numeric, some languages contain methods such as isChar(), which checks whether a value is a character data type; isWhitespace(), which checks whether a value is a nonprinting character, such as a space or tab; and isUpper(), which checks whether a value is a capital letter.

In many languages, you accept all user data as a string of characters, and then use built-in methods to attempt to convert the characters to the correct data type for your application. When the conversion methods succeed, you have useful data. When the conversion methods fail because the user has entered the wrong data type, you can take appropriate action, such as issuing an error message, reprompting the user, or forcing the data to a default value.

Validating Reasonableness and Consistency of Data

Data items can be the correct type and within range, but still be incorrect. You have experienced this problem yourself if anyone has ever misspelled your name or overbilled you. The data might have been the correct type—for example, alphabetic letters were used in your name—but the name itself was incorrect. Many data items cannot be checked for reasonableness; for example, the names Catherine, Katherine, and Kathryn are equally reasonable, but only one spelling is correct for a particular woman.

However, many data items can be checked for reasonableness. If you make a purchase on May 3, 2013, then the payment cannot possibly be due prior to that date. Perhaps within your organization, you cannot make more than $20.00 per hour if you work in Department 12. If your zip code is 90201, your state of residence cannot be New York. If your store's cash on hand was $3000 when it closed on Tuesday, the amount should not be different when the store opens on Wednesday. If a customer's title is *Ms.*, the customer's gender should be *F*. Each of these examples involves comparing two data items for reasonableness or consistency. You should consider making as many such comparisons as possible when writing your own programs.

Frequently, testing for reasonableness and consistency involves using additional data files. For example, to check that a user has entered a valid county of residence for a state, you might use a file that contains every county name within every state in the United States, and check the user's county against those contained in the file.

Good defensive programs try to foresee all possible inconsistencies and errors. The more accurate your data, the more useful information you will produce as output from your programs.

When you become a professional programmer, you want your programs to work correctly as a source of professional pride. On a more basic level, you do not want to be called in to work at 3:00 a.m. when the overnight run of your program fails because of errors you created.

TWO TRUTHS & A LIE

Common Loop Applications

1. An accumulator is a variable that you use to gather or accumulate values.
2. An accumulator typically is initialized to 0.
3. An accumulator is typically reset to 0 after it is output.

The false statement is #3. There is typically no need to reset an accumulator after it is output.

Chapter Summary

- A loop contains one set of instructions that operates on multiple, separate sets of data.
- Three steps must occur in every loop: You must initialize a loop control variable, compare the variable to some value that controls whether the loop continues or stops, and alter the variable that controls the loop.
- When you must use loops within loops, you use nested loops. When nesting loops, you must maintain two individual loop control variables and alter each at the appropriate time.
- Common mistakes that programmers make when writing loops include neglecting to initialize the loop control variable, neglecting to alter the loop control variable, using the wrong comparison with the loop control variable, and including statements inside the loop that belong outside the loop.
- Most computer languages support a `for` statement or `for` loop that you can use with definite loops when you know how many times a loop will repeat. The `for` statement uses a loop control variable that it automatically initializes, evaluates, and alters.
- Loops are used in many applications—for example, to accumulate totals in business reports. Loops also are used to ensure that user data entries are valid by continuously reprompting the user.

Key Terms

A **loop control variable** is a variable that determines whether a loop will continue.

A **definite loop** is one for which the number of repetitions is a predetermined value.

A **counted loop**, or **counter-controlled loop**, is a loop whose repetitions are managed by a counter.

To **increment** a variable is to add a constant value to it, frequently 1.

To **decrement** a variable is to decrease it by a constant value, frequently 1.

A **counter** is any numeric variable you use to count the number of times an event has occurred.

An **indefinite loop** is one for which you cannot predetermine the number of executions.

Nested loops occur when a loop structure exists within another loop structure.

An **outer loop** contains another when loops are nested.

An **inner loop** is contained within another when loops are nested.

A **stub** is a method without statements that is used as a placeholder.

A **for statement**, or **for loop**, can be used to code definite loops. It contains a loop control variable that it automatically initializes, evaluates, and alters.

A **step value** is a number you use to increase a loop control variable on each pass through a loop.

A **pretest loop** tests its loop control variable before each iteration, meaning that the loop body might never execute.

A **posttest loop** tests its loop control variable after each iteration, meaning that the loop body executes at least one time.

An **accumulator** is a variable that you use to gather or accumulate values.

A **summary report** lists only totals, without individual detail records.

Defensive programming is a technique with which you try to prepare for all possible errors before they occur.

To **validate data** is to ensure that data items are meaningful and useful. For example, you ensure that values are the correct data type or that they fall within an acceptable range.

GIGO (garbage in, garbage out) means that if your input is incorrect, your output is worthless.

Forcing a data item means you override incorrect data by setting it to a specific value.

Review Questions

1. The structure that allows you to write one set of instructions that operates on multiple, separate sets of data is the _____.

   a. sequence
   b. selection
   c. loop
   d. case

2. The loop that frequently appears in a program's mainline logic _____.

   a. always depends on whether a variable equals 0
   b. works correctly based on the same logic as other loops
   c. is an unstructured loop
   d. is an example of an infinite loop

3. Which of the following is *not* a step that must occur with every correctly working loop?

   a. Initialize a loop control variable before the loop starts.
   b. Set the loop control value equal to a sentinel during each iteration.
   c. Compare the loop control value to a sentinel during each iteration.
   d. Alter the loop control variable during each iteration.

Review Questions

4. The statements executed within a loop are known collectively as the _____.
   a. loop body
   b. loop controls
   c. sequences
   d. sentinels

5. A counter keeps track of _____.
   a. the number of times an event has occurred
   b. the number of machine cycles required by a segment of a program
   c. the number of loop structures within a program
   d. the number of times software has been revised

6. Adding 1 to a variable is also called _____ it.
   a. digesting
   b. resetting
   c. decrementing
   d. incrementing

7. Which of the following is a definite loop?
   a. a loop that executes as long as a user continues to enter valid data
   b. a loop that executes 1000 times
   c. both of the above
   d. none of the above

8. Which of the following is an indefinite loop?
   a. a loop that executes exactly 10 times
   b. a loop that follows a prompt that asks a user how many repetitions to make and uses the value to control the loop
   c. both of the above
   d. none of the above

9. When you decrement a variable, you _____.
   a. set it to 0
   b. reduce it by one-tenth
   c. subtract a value from it
   d. remove it from a program

10. When two loops are nested, the loop that is contained by the other is the _____ loop.
    a. captive
    b. unstructured
    c. inner
    d. outer

11. When loops are nested, _____.
    a. they typically share a loop control variable
    b. one must end before the other begins
    c. both must be the same type—definite or indefinite
    d. none of the above

12. Most programmers use a `for` loop _____.
    a. for every loop they write
    b. when a loop will not repeat
    c. when a loop must repeat many times
    d. when they know the exact number of times a loop will repeat

13. A report that lists only totals, with no details about individual records, is a(n) _____ report.
    a. accumulator
    b. final
    c. summary
    d. detailless

14. Typically, the value added to a counter variable is _____.
    a. 0
    b. 1
    c. 10
    d. different in each iteration

15. Typically, the value added to an accumulator variable is _____.
    a. 0
    b. 1
    c. the same for each iteration
    d. different in each iteration

16. After an accumulator or counter variable is displayed at the end of a program, it is best to _____.
    a. delete the variable from the program
    b. reset the variable to 0
    c. subtract 1 from the variable
    d. none of the above

17. When you _____, you make sure data items are the correct type and fall within the correct range.
    a. validate data
    b. employ offensive programming
    c. use object orientation
    d. count loop iterations

18. Overriding a user's entered value by setting it to a predetermined value is known as _____.
    a. forcing
    b. accumulating
    c. validating
    d. pushing

19. To ensure that a user's entry is the correct data type, frequently you _____.
    a. prompt the user to verify that the type is correct
    b. use a method built into the programming language
    c. include a statement at the beginning of the program that lists the data types allowed
    d. all of the above

20. A variable might hold an incorrect value even when it is _____.
    a. the correct data type
    b. within a required range
    c. a constant coded by the programmer
    d. all of the above

Exercises

1. What is output by each of the pseudocode segments in Figure 5-22?

a.
```
a = 1
b = 2
c = 5
while a < c
    a = a + 1
    b = b + c
endwhile
output a, b, c
```

b.
```
d = 4
e = 6
f = 7
while d > f
    d = d + 1
    e = e - 1
endwhile
output d, e, f
```

c.
```
g = 4
h = 6
while g < h
    g = g + 1
endwhile
output g, h
```

d.
```
j = 2
k = 5
n = 9
while j < k
    m = 6
    while m < n
        output "Goodbye"
        m = m + 1
    endwhile
    j = j + 1
endwhile
```

e.
```
j = 2
k = 5
m = 6
n = 9
while j < k
    while m < n
        output "Hello"
        m = m + 1
    endwhile
    j = j + 1
endwhile
```

f.
```
p = 2
q = 4
while p < q
    output "Adios"
    r = 1
    while r < q
        output "Adios"
        r = r + 1
    endwhile
    p = p + 1
endwhile
```

Figure 5-22   Pseudocode segments for Exercise 1

2. Design the logic for a program that outputs every number from 1 through 20.
3. Design the logic for a program that outputs every number from 1 through 20 along with its value doubled and tripled.
4. Design the logic for a program that outputs every even number from 2 through 100.
5. Design the logic for a program that outputs numbers in reverse order from 25 down to 0.
6. Design the logic for a program that allows a user to enter a number. Display the sum of every number from 1 through the entered number.

7. a. Design an application for the Homestead Furniture Store that gets sales transaction data, including an account number, customer name, and purchase price. Output the account number and name, then output the customer's payment each month for the next 12 months. Assume that there is no finance charge, that the customer makes no new purchases, and that the customer pays off the balance with equal monthly payments.

   b. Modify the Homestead Furniture Store application so it executes continuously for any number of customers until a sentinel value is supplied for the account number.

8. a. Design an application for Domicile Designs that gets sales transaction data, including an account number, customer name, and purchase price. The store charges 1.25 percent interest on the balance due each month. Output the account number and name, then output the customer's projected balance each month for the next 12 months. Assume that when the balance reaches $25 or less, the customer can pay off the account. At the beginning of every month, 1.25 percent interest is added to the balance, and then the customer makes a payment equal to 7 percent of the current balance. Assume that the customer makes no new purchases.

   b. Modify the Domicile Designs application so it executes continuously for any number of customers until a sentinel value is supplied for the account number.

9. Yabe Online Auctions requires its sellers to post items for sale for a six-week period during which the price of any unsold item drops 12 percent each week. For example, an item that costs $10.00 during the first week costs 12 percent less, or $8.80, during the second week. During the third week, the same item is 12 percent less than $8.80, or $7.74. Design an application that allows a user to input prices until an appropriate sentinel value is entered. Program output is the price of each item during each week, one through six.

10. Mr. Roper owns 20 apartment buildings. Each building contains 15 units that he rents for $800 per month each. Design the application that would output 12 payment coupons for each of the 15 apartments in each of the 20 buildings. Each coupon should contain the building number (1 through 20), the apartment number (1 through 15), the month (1 through 12), and the amount of rent due.

11. Design a retirement planning calculator for Skulling Financial Services. Allow a user to enter a number of working years remaining in the user's career and the annual amount of money the user can save. Assume that the user earns three percent simple interest on savings annually. Program output is a schedule that lists each year number in retirement starting with year 0 and the user's savings at the start of that year. Assume that the user spends $50,000 per year in retirement and then earns three percent interest on the remaining balance. End the list after 40 years, or when the user's balance is 0 or less, whichever comes first.

12. Ellison Private Elementary School has three classrooms in each of nine grades, kindergarten (grade 0) through grade 8, and allows parents to pay tuition over the nine-month school year. Design the application that outputs nine tuition payment coupons for each of the 27 classrooms. Each coupon should contain the grade

number (0 through 8), the classroom number (1 through 3), the month (1 through 9), and the amount of tuition due. Tuition for kindergarten is $80 per month. Tuition for the other grades is $60 per month times the grade level.

13. a. Design a program for the Hollywood Movie Rating Guide, which can be installed in a kiosk in theaters. Each theater patron enters a value from 0 to 4 indicating the number of stars that the patron awards to the guide's featured movie of the week. If a user enters a star value that does not fall in the correct range, reprompt the user continuously until a correct value is entered. The program executes continuously until the theater manager enters a negative number to quit. At the end of the program, display the average star rating for the movie.

   b. Modify the movie-rating program so that a user gets three tries to enter a valid rating. After three incorrect entries, the program issues an appropriate message and continues with a new user.

14. The Café Noir Coffee Shop wants some market research on its customers. When a customer places an order, a clerk asks for the customer's zip code and age. The clerk enters that data as well as the number of items the customer orders. The program operates continuously until the clerk enters a 0 for zip code at the end of the day. When the clerk enters an invalid zip code (more than 5 digits) or an invalid age (defined as less than 10 or more than 110), the program reprompts the clerk continuously. When the clerk enters fewer than 1 or more than 12 items, the program reprompts the clerk two more times. If the clerk enters a high value on the third attempt, the program accepts the high value, but if the clerk enters a value of less than 1 on the third attempt, an error message is displayed and the order is not counted. At the end of the program, display a count of the number of items ordered by customers from the same zip code as the coffee shop (54984), and a count from other zip codes. Also display the average customer age as well as counts of the number of items ordered by customers under 30 and by customers 30 and older.

Find the Bugs

15. Your downloadable files for Chapter 5 include DEBUG05-01.txt, DEBUG05-02.txt, and DEBUG05-03.txt. Each file starts with some comments that describe the problem. Comments are lines that begin with two slashes (//). Following the comments, each file contains pseudocode that has one or more bugs you must find and correct.

Game Zone

16. In Chapter 2, you learned that in many programming languages you can generate a random number between 1 and a limiting value named LIMIT by using a statement similar to randomNumber = random(LIMIT). In Chapter 4, you created

the logic for a guessing game in which the application generates a random number and the player tries to guess it. Now, create the guessing game itself. After each guess, display a message indicating whether the player's guess was correct, too high, or too low. When the player eventually guesses the correct number, display a count of the number of guesses that were required.

17. Create the logic for a game that simulates rolling two dice by generating two numbers between 1 and 6 inclusive. The player chooses a number between 2 and 12 (the lowest and highest totals possible for two dice). The player then "rolls" two dice up to three times. If the number chosen by the user comes up, the user wins and the game ends. If the number does not come up within three rolls, the computer wins.

18. Create the logic for the dice game Pig, in which a player can compete with the computer. The object of the game is to be the first to score 100 points. The user and computer take turns "rolling" a pair of dice following these rules:

- On a turn, each player rolls two dice. If no 1 appears, the dice values are added to a running total for the turn, and the player can choose whether to roll again or pass the turn to the other player. When a player passes, the accumulated turn total is added to the player's game total.

- If a 1 appears on one of the dice, the player's turn total becomes 0; in other words, nothing more is added to the player's game total for that turn, and it becomes the other player's turn.

- If a 1 appears on both of the dice, not only is the player's turn over, but the player's entire accumulated total is reset to 0.

- When the computer does not roll a 1 and can choose whether to roll again, generate a random value from 1 to 2. The computer will then decide to continue when the value is 1 and decide to quit and pass the turn to the player when the value is not 1.

Up for Discussion

19. Suppose you wrote a program that you suspect is in an infinite loop because it keeps running for several minutes with no output and without ending. What would you add to your program to help you discover the origin of the problem?

20. Suppose you know that every employee in your organization has a seven-digit ID number used for logging on to the computer system. A loop would be useful to guess every combination of seven digits in an ID. Are there any circumstances in which you should try to guess another employee's ID number?

21. If every employee in an organization had a seven-digit ID number, guessing all the possible combinations would be a relatively easy programming task. How could you alter the format of employee IDs to make them more difficult to guess?

CHAPTER 6

Arrays

In this chapter, you will learn about:
- Storing data in arrays
- How an array can replace nested decisions
- Using constants with arrays
- Searching an array for an exact match
- Using parallel arrays
- Searching an array for a range match
- Remaining within array bounds
- Using a `for` loop to process arrays

CHAPTER 6 Arrays

Storing Data in Arrays

An **array** is a series or list of values in computer memory. Usually, all the values in an array have something in common; for example, they might represent a list of employee ID numbers or prices for items sold in a store.

Whenever you require multiple storage locations for objects, you can use a real-life counterpart of a programming array. If you store important papers in a series of file folders and label each folder with a consecutive letter of the alphabet, then you are using the equivalent of an array. If you keep receipts in a stack of shoe boxes and label each box with a month, you are also using the equivalent of an array. Similarly, when you plan courses for the next semester at your school by looking down a list of course offerings, you are using an array.

The arrays discussed in this chapter are single-dimensional arrays, which are similar to lists. Arrays with multiple dimensions are covered in Chapter 8 of the Comprehensive version of this book.

Each of these real-life arrays helps you organize objects or information. You *could* store all your papers or receipts in one huge cardboard box, or find courses if they were printed randomly in one large book. However, using an organized storage and display system makes your life easier in each case. Using a programming array will accomplish the same results for your data.

How Arrays Occupy Computer Memory

When you declare an array, you declare a structure that contains multiple data items; each data item is one **element** of the array. Each element has the same data type, and each element occupies an area in memory next to, or contiguous to, the others. You can indicate the number of elements an array will hold—the **size of the array**—when you declare the array along with your other variables and constants. For example, you might declare an uninitialized, three-element numeric array named `someVals` as follows:

```
num someVals[3]
```

Each array element is differentiated from the others with a unique **subscript**, also called an **index**, which is a number that indicates the position of a particular item within an array. All array elements have the same group name, but each individual element also has a unique subscript indicating how far away it is from the first element. Therefore, any array's subscripts are always a sequence of integers. For example, a five-element array uses subscripts 0 through 4, and a ten-element array uses subscripts 0 through 9. In all languages, subscript values must be sequential integers (whole numbers). In most modern languages, such as Visual Basic, Java, C++, and C#, the first array element is accessed using subscript 0, and this book follows that convention.

To use an array element, you place its subscript within parentheses or square brackets (depending on the programming language) after the group name. This book will use square brackets to hold array subscripts so that you don't mistake array names for method names. Many newer programming languages such as C++, Java, and C# also use the bracket notation.

After you declare an array, you can assign values to some or all of the elements individually. Providing array values sometimes is called **populating the array**. The following code shows a three-element array declaration, followed by three separate statements that populate the array:

```
Declarations
    num someVals[3]
someVals[0] = 25
someVals[1] = 36
someVals[2] = 47
```

Figure 6-1 shows an array named someVals that contains three elements, so the elements are someVals[0], someVals[1], and someVals[2]. The array elements have been assigned the values 25, 36, and 47, respectively. The element someVals[0] is zero numbers away from the beginning of the array. The element someVals[1] is one number away from the beginning of the array and someVals[2] is two numbers away.

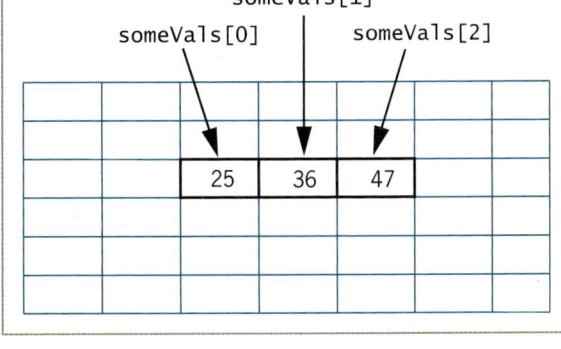

Figure 6-1 Appearance of a three-element array in computer memory

If appropriate, you can declare and initialize array elements in one statement. Most programming languages use a statement similar to the following to declare a three-element array and assign values to it:

num someVals[3] = 25, 36, 47

When you use a list of values to initialize an array, the first value you list is assigned to the first array element (element 0), and the subsequent values are assigned to the remaining elements in order. Many programming languages allow you to initialize an array with fewer starting values than there are array elements declared, but no language allows you to initialize an array using more starting values than positions available. When starting values are supplied for an array in this book, each element will be provided with a value.

After an array has been declared and appropriate values have been assigned to specific elements, you can use an individual element in the same way you would use any other data item of the same type. For example, you can input values to array elements and you can output the values, and if the elements are numeric, you can perform arithmetic with them.

 Watch the video *Understanding Arrays*.

CHAPTER 6   Arrays

> **TWO TRUTHS & A LIE**
>
> Storing Data in Arrays
>
> 1. In an array, each element has the same data type.
> 2. Each array element is accessed using a subscript, which can be a number or a string.
> 3. Array elements always occupy adjacent memory locations.
>
> The false statement is #2. An array subscript must be a number. It can be a named constant, an unnamed constant, or a variable.

How an Array Can Replace Nested Decisions

Consider an application requested by a company's human resources department to produce statistics on employees' claimed dependents. The department wants a report that lists the number of employees who have claimed 0, 1, 2, 3, 4, or 5 dependents. (Assume that you know that no employees have more than five dependents.) For example, Figure 6-2 shows a typical report.

Without using an array, you could write the application that produces counts for the six categories of dependents (0 through 5) by using a series of decisions. Figure 6-3 shows the pseudocode and flowchart for the decision-making part of such an application. Although this logic works, its length and complexity are unnecessary once you understand how to use an array.

Dependents	Count
0	43
1	35
2	24
3	11
4	5
5	7

Figure 6-2 Typical Dependents report

How an Array Can Replace Nested Decisions

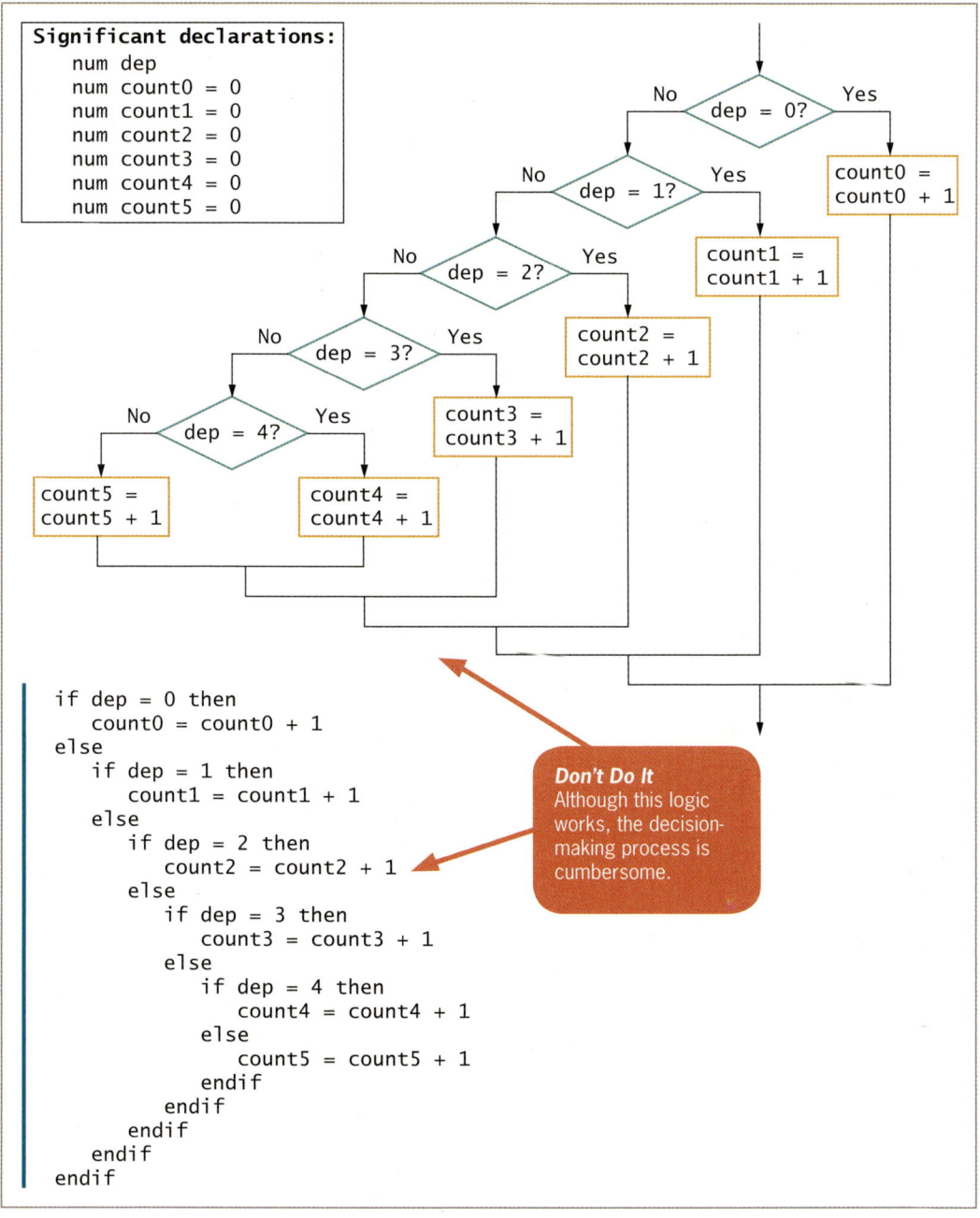

Figure 6-3 Flowchart and pseudocode of decision-making process using a series of decisions—the hard way

The decision-making process in Figure 6-3 accomplishes its purpose, and the logic is correct, but the process is cumbersome and certainly not recommended. Follow the logic here so that you understand how the application works. In the next pages, you will see how to make the application more elegant.

In Figure 6-3, the variable dep is compared to 0. If it is 0, 1 is added to count0. If it is not 0, then dep is compared to 1. Based on the result, 1 is added to count1 or dep is compared to 2, and so on. Each time the application executes this decision-making process, 1 ultimately is added to one of the six variables that acts as a counter. The dependent-counting logic in Figure 6-3 works, but even with only six categories of dependents, the decision-making process is unwieldy. What if the number of dependents might be any value from 0 to 10, or 0 to 20? With either of these scenarios, the basic logic of the program would remain the same; however, you would need to declare many additional variables to hold the counts, and you would need many additional decisions.

Using an array provides an alternate approach to this programming problem and greatly reduces the number of statements you need. When you declare an array, you provide a group name for a number of associated variables in memory. For example, the six dependent count accumulators can be redefined as a single array named count. The individual elements become count[0], count[1], count[2], count[3], count[4], and count[5], as shown in the revised decision-making process in Figure 6-4.

The shaded statement in Figure 6-4 shows that when dep is 0, 1 is added to count[0]. You can see similar statements for the rest of the count elements; when dep is 1, 1 is added to count[1], when dep is 2, 1 is added to count[2], and so on. When the dep value is 5, this means it was not 1, 2, 3, or 4, so 1 is added to count[5]. In other words, 1 is added to one of the elements of the count array instead of to an individual variable named count0, count1, count2, count3, count4, or count5. Is this version a big improvement over the original in Figure 6-3? Of course it isn't. You still have not taken advantage of the benefits of using the array in this application.

How an Array Can Replace Nested Decisions

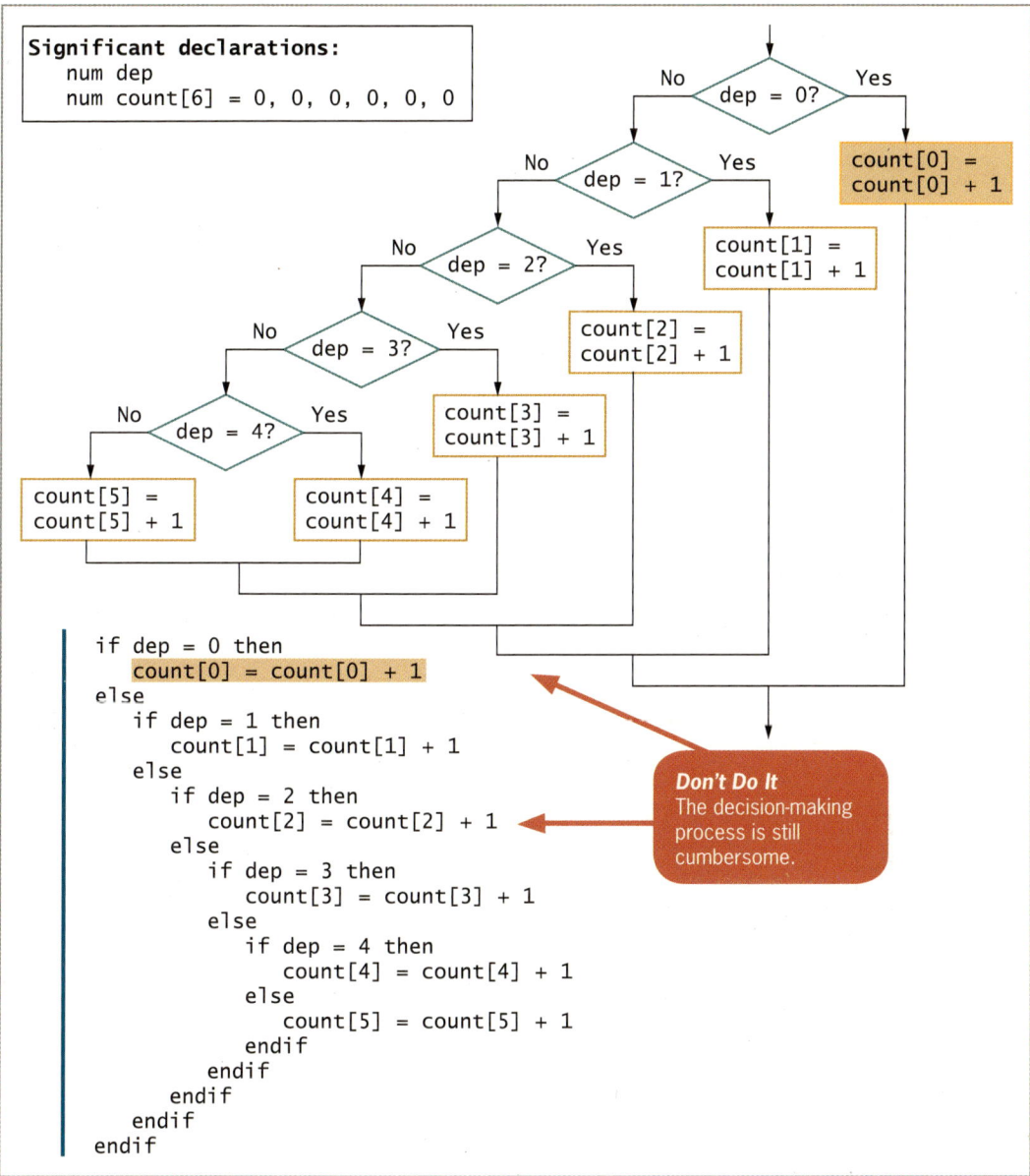

Figure 6-4 Flowchart and pseudocode of decision-making process—but still the hard way

The true benefit of using an array lies in your ability to use a variable as a subscript to the array, instead of using a literal constant such as 0 or 5. Notice in the logic in Figure 6-4 that within each decision, the value compared to **dep** and the constant that is the subscript in the resulting *Yes* process are always identical. That is, when **dep** is 0, the subscript used to add 1 to the **count** array is 0; when **dep** is 1, the subscript used for the **count** array is 1, and so on. Therefore, you can just use **dep** as a subscript to the array. You can rewrite the decision-making process as shown in Figure 6-5.

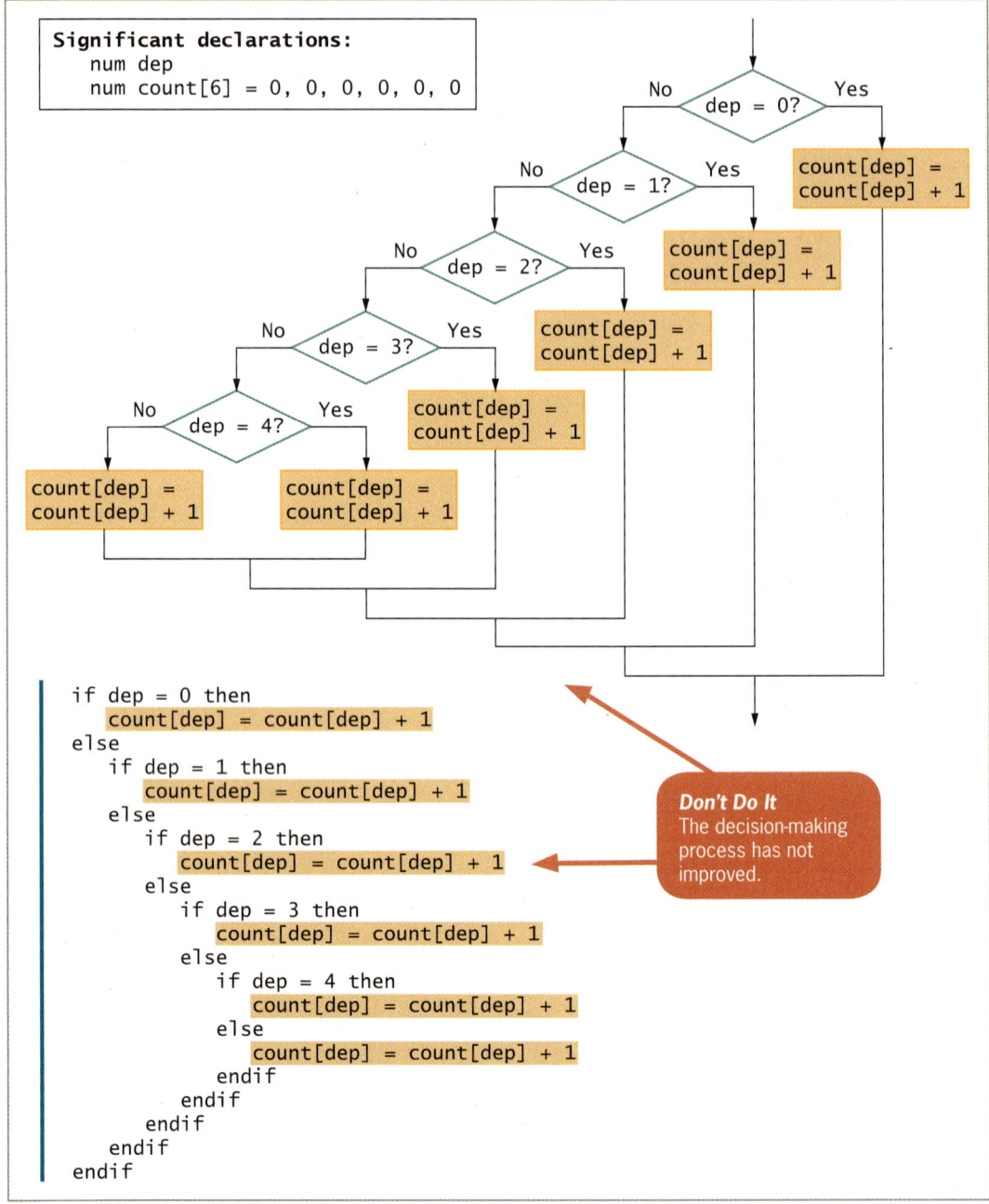

Figure 6-5 Flowchart and pseudocode of decision-making process using an array—but still a hard way

How an Array Can Replace Nested Decisions

The code segment in Figure 6-5 looks no more efficient than the one in Figure 6-4. However, notice the shaded statements in Figure 6-5—the process that occurs after each decision is exactly the same. In each case, no matter what the value of dep is, you always add 1 to count[dep]. If you always will take the same action no matter what the answer to a question is, there is no need to ask the question. Instead, you can rewrite the decision-making process as shown in Figure 6-6.

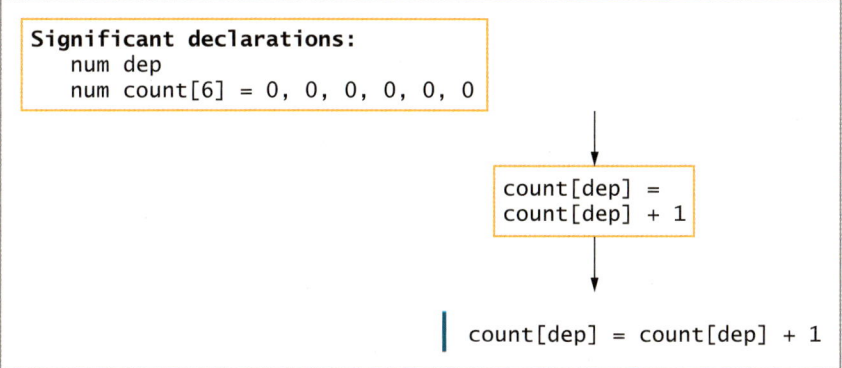

Figure 6-6 Flowchart and pseudocode of efficient decision-making process using an array

The single statement in Figure 6-6 eliminates the *entire* decision-making process that was the original highlighted section in Figure 6-5! When dep is 2, 1 is added to count[2]; when dep is 4, 1 is added to count[4], and so on. *Now* you have significantly improved the original logic. What's more, this process does not change whether there are 20, 30, or any other number of possible categories. To use more than five accumulators, you would declare additional count elements in the array, but the categorizing logic would remain the same as it is in Figure 6-6.

Figure 6-7 shows an entire program that takes advantage of the array to produce the report that shows counts for dependent categories. Variables and constants are declared and, in the getReady() module, a first value for dep is entered into the program. In the countDependents() module, 1 is added to the appropriate element of the count array and the next value is input. The loop in the mainline logic in Figure 6-7 is an indefinite loop; it continues as long as the user does not enter the sentinel value. When data entry is complete, the finishUp() module displays the report. First, the heading is output, then dep is reset to 0, and then each dep and count[dep] are output in a loop. The first output statement contains 0 (as the number of dependents) and the value stored in count[0]. Then, 1 is added to dep and the same set of instructions is used again to display the counts for each number of dependents. The loop in the finishUp() module is a definite loop; it executes precisely six times.

CHAPTER 6   Arrays

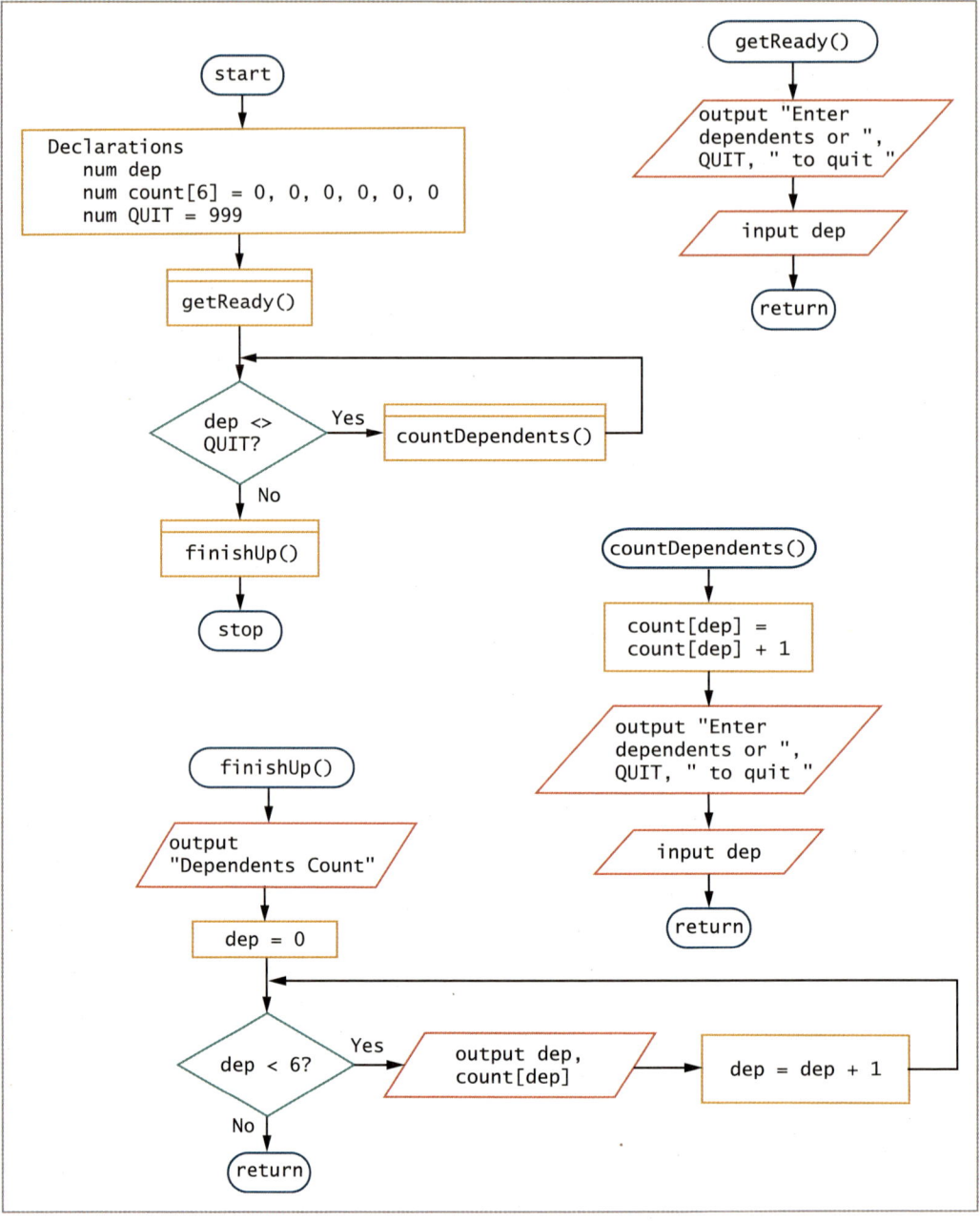

Figure 6-7 Flowchart and pseudocode for Dependents report program (*continues*)

How an Array Can Replace Nested Decisions

(continued)

```
start
    Declarations
        num dep
        num count[6] = 0, 0, 0, 0, 0, 0
        num QUIT = 999
    getReady()
    while dep <> QUIT
        countDependents()
    endwhile
    finishUp()
stop

getReady()
    output "Enter dependents or ", QUIT, " to quit "
    input dep
return

countDependents()
    count[dep] = count[dep] + 1
    output "Enter dependents or ", QUIT, " to quit "
    input dep
return

finishUp()
    output "Dependents Count"
    dep = 0
    while dep < 6
        output dep, count[dep]
        dep = dep + 1
    endwhile
return
```

Figure 6-7 Flowchart and pseudocode for Dependents report program

The dependent-counting program would have *worked* if it contained a long series of decisions and output statements, but the program is easier to write when you use an array and access its values using the number of dependents as a subscript. Additionally, the new program is more efficient, easier for other programmers to understand, and easier to maintain. Arrays are never mandatory, but often they can drastically cut down on your programming time and make your logic easier to understand.

Learning to use arrays properly can make many programming tasks far more efficient and professional. When you understand how to use arrays, you will be able to provide elegant solutions to problems that otherwise would require tedious programming steps.

 Watch the video *Accumulating Values in an Array*.

TWO TRUTHS & A LIE

How an Array Can Replace Nested Decisions

1. You can use an array to replace a long series of decisions.
2. You experience a major benefit of arrays when you use an unnamed numeric constant as a subscript as opposed to using a variable.
3. The process of displaying every element in a 10-element array is basically no different from displaying every element in a 100-element array.

The false statement is #2. You experience a major benefit of arrays when you use a variable as a subscript as opposed to using a constant.

Using Constants with Arrays

In Chapter 2, you learned that named constants hold values that do not change during a program's execution. When working with arrays, you can use constants in several ways:

- To hold the size of an array
- As the array values
- As a subscript

Using a Constant as the Size of an Array

The program in Figure 6-7 still contains one minor flaw. Throughout this book you have learned to avoid *magic numbers*—that is, unnamed constants. As the totals are output in the loop at the end of the program in Figure 6-7, the array subscript is compared to the constant 6. The program can be improved if you use a named constant instead. Using a named constant makes your code easier to modify and understand. In most programming languages you can take one of two approaches:

- You can declare a named numeric constant such as `ARRAY_SIZE = 6`. Then you can use this constant every time you access the array, always making sure any subscript you use remains less than the constant value.
- In many languages, a constant that represents the array size is automatically provided for each array you create. For example, in Java, after you declare an array named `count`, its size is stored in a field named `count.length`. In both C# and Visual Basic, the array size is `count.Length`, with an uppercase *L*.

Using Constants as Array Element Values

Sometimes the values stored in arrays should be constants because they are not changed during program execution. For example, suppose that you create an array that holds names for the months of the year. Don't confuse the array identifier with its contents—the convention in this book is to use all uppercase letters in constant identifiers, but not necessarily in array values. The array can be declared as follows:

```
string MONTH[12] = "January", "February", "March", "April",
    "May", "June", "July", "August", "September", "October",
    "November", "December"
```

Using a Constant as an Array Subscript

Occasionally you will want to use an unnamed numeric constant as a subscript to an array. For example, to display the first value in an array named salesArray, you might write a statement that uses an unnamed literal constant as follows:

```
output salesArray[0]
```

You might also have occasion to use a named constant as a subscript. For example, if salesArray holds sales values for each of 20 states covered by your company, and Indiana is state 5, you could output the value for Indiana as follows:

```
output salesArray[5]
```

However, if you declare a named constant as num INDIANA = 5, then you can display the same value using this statement:

```
output salesArray[INDIANA]
```

An advantage to using a named constant in this case is that the statement becomes self-documenting—anyone who reads your statement more easily understands that your intention is to display the sales value for Indiana.

TWO TRUTHS & A LIE

Using Constants with Arrays

1. If you create a named constant equal to an array size, you can use it as a subscript to the array.

2. If you create a named constant equal to an array size, you can use it as a limit against which to compare subscript values.

3. When you declare an array in Java, C#, and Visual Basic, a constant that represents the array size is automatically provided.

The false statement is #1. If the constant is equal to the array size, then it is larger than any valid array subscript.

Searching an Array for an Exact Match

In the dependent-counting application in this chapter, the array's subscript variable conveniently held small whole numbers—the number of dependents allowed was 0 through 5—and the **dep** variable directly accessed the array. Unfortunately, real life doesn't always happen in small integers. Sometimes you don't have a variable that conveniently holds an array position; sometimes you have to search through an array to find a value you need.

Consider a mail-order business in which customers place orders that contain a name, address, item number, and quantity ordered. Assume that the item numbers from which a customer can choose are three-digit numbers, but perhaps they are not consecutively numbered 001 through 999. For example, let's say that you offer six items: 106, 108, 307, 405, 457, and 688, as shown in the shaded VALID_ITEM array declaration in Figure 6-8. (The array is declared as constant because the item numbers do not change during program execution.) When a customer orders an item, a clerical worker can tell whether the order is valid by looking down the list and manually verifying that the ordered item number is on it. In a similar fashion, a computer program can use a loop to test the ordered item number against each VALID_ITEM, looking for an exact match. When you search through a list from one end to the other, you are performing a **linear search**.

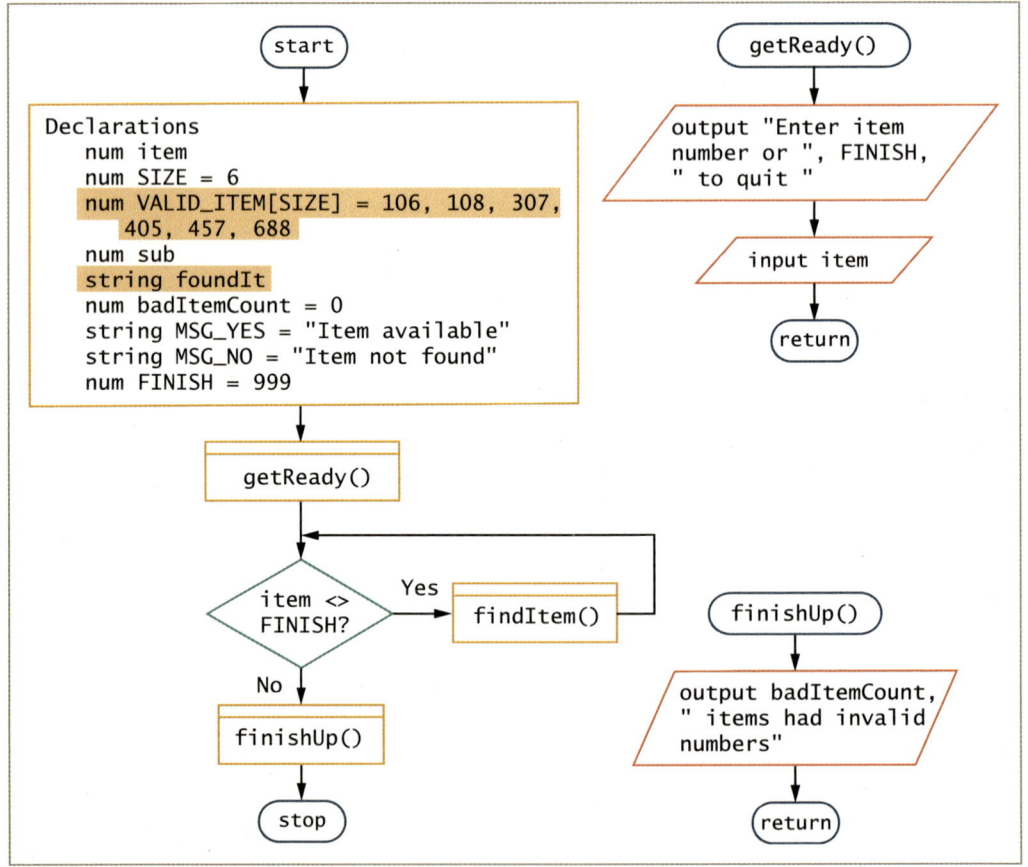

Figure 6-8 Flowchart and pseudocode for program that verifies item availability (*continues*)

(continued)

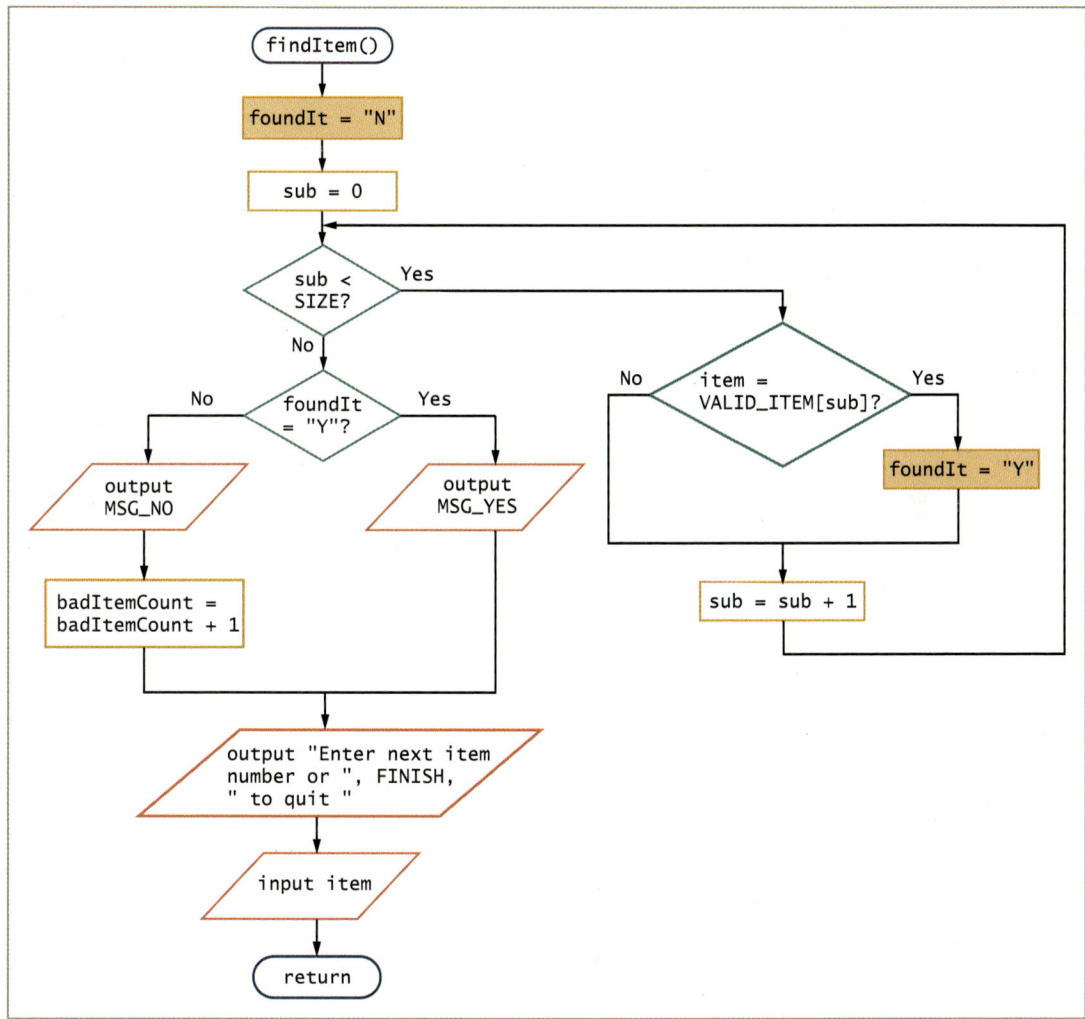

Figure 6-8 Flowchart and pseudocode for program that verifies item availability *(continues)*

(continued)

```
start
   Declarations
      num item
      num SIZE = 6
      num VALID_ITEM[SIZE] = 106, 108, 307,
         405, 457, 688
      num sub
      string foundIt
      num badItemCount = 0
      string MSG_YES = "Item available"
      string MSG_NO = "Item not found"
      num FINISH = 999
   getReady()
   while item <> FINISH
      findItem()
   endwhile
   finishUp()
stop

getReady()
   output "Enter item number or ", FINISH, " to quit "
   input item
return

findItem()
   foundIt = "N"
   sub = 0
   while sub < SIZE
      if item = VALID_ITEM[sub] then
         foundIt = "Y"
      endif
      sub = sub + 1
   endwhile
   if foundIt = "Y" then
      output MSG_YES
   else
      output MSG_NO
      badItemCount = badItemCount + 1
   endif
   output "Enter next item number or ", FINISH, " to quit "
   input item
return

finishUp()
   output badItemCount, " items had invalid numbers"
return
```

Figure 6-8 Flowchart and pseudocode for program that verifies item availability

Searching an Array for an Exact Match

To determine if an ordered item number is valid, you could use a series of six decisions to compare the number to each of the six allowed values. However, the superior approach shown in Figure 6-8 is to create an array that holds the list of valid item numbers and then to search through the array for an exact match to the ordered item. If you search through the entire array without finding a match for the item the customer ordered, it means the ordered item number is not valid.

The `findItem()` module in Figure 6-8 takes the following steps to verify that an item number exists:

- A flag variable named `foundIt` is set to "N". A **flag** is a variable that is set to indicate whether some event has occurred. In this example, *N* indicates that the item number has not yet been found in the list. (See the first shaded statement in the `findItem()` method in Figure 6-8.)

- A subscript, `sub`, is set to 0. This subscript will be used to access each VALID_ITEM element.

- A loop executes, varying `sub` from 0 through one less than the size of the array. Within the loop, the customer's ordered item number is compared to each item number in the array. If the customer-ordered item matches any item in the array, the flag variable is assigned "Y". (See the last shaded statement in the `findItem()` method in Figure 6-8.) After all six valid item numbers have been compared to the ordered item, if the customer item matches none of them, then the flag variable `foundIt` will still hold the value "N".

- If the flag variable's value is "Y" after the entire list has been searched, it means that the item is valid and an appropriate message is displayed, but if the flag has not been assigned "Y", the item was not found in the array of valid items. In this case, an error message is output and 1 is added to a count of bad item numbers.

As an alternative to using the string `foundIt` variable in the method in Figure 6-8, you might prefer to use a numeric variable that you set to 1 or 0. Most programming languages also support a Boolean data type that you can use for `foundIt`; when you declare a variable to be Boolean, you can set its value to true or false.

TWO TRUTHS & A LIE

Searching an Array for an Exact Match

1. Only whole numbers can be stored in arrays.
2. Only whole numbers can be used as array subscripts.
3. A flag is a variable that indicates whether some event has occurred.

The false statement is #1. Whole numbers can be stored in arrays, but so can many other objects, including strings and numbers with decimal places.

Using Parallel Arrays

When you accept an item number into a mail-order company program, you usually want to accomplish more than simply verifying the item's existence. For example, you might want to determine the name, price, or available quantity of the ordered item. Tasks like these can be completed efficiently using parallel arrays. **Parallel arrays** are two or more arrays in which each element in one array is associated with the element in the same relative position in the other array. Although any array can contain just one data type, each array in a set of parallel arrays might be a different type.

Suppose that you have a list of item numbers and their associated prices. One array named VALID_ITEM contains six elements; each element is a valid item number. Its parallel array also has six elements. The array is named VALID_PRICE; each element is a price of an item. Each price in the VALID_PRICE array is conveniently and purposely in the same position as the corresponding item number in the VALID_ITEM array. Figure 6-9 shows how the parallel arrays might look in computer memory.

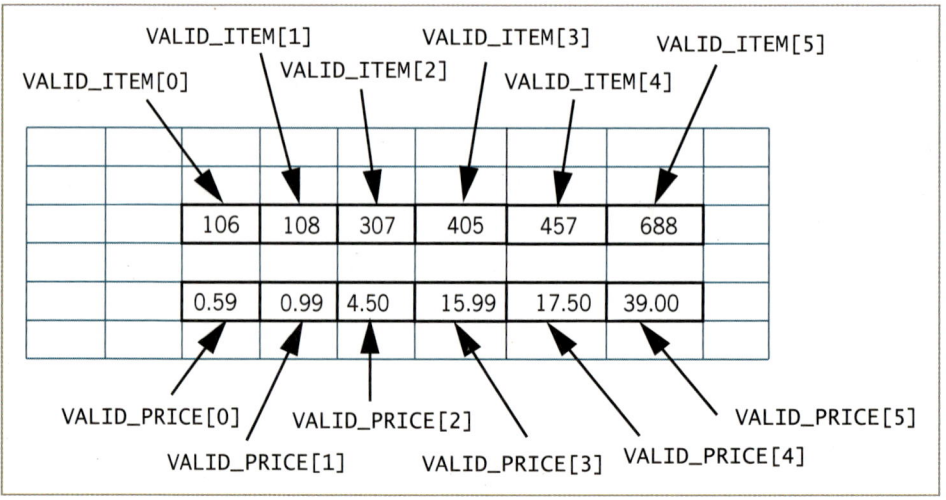

Figure 6-9 Parallel arrays in memory

When you use parallel arrays:

- Two or more arrays contain related data.
- A subscript relates the arrays. That is, elements at the same position in each array are logically related.

Figure 6-10 shows a program that declares parallel arrays. The VALID_PRICE array is shaded; each element in it corresponds to a valid item number.

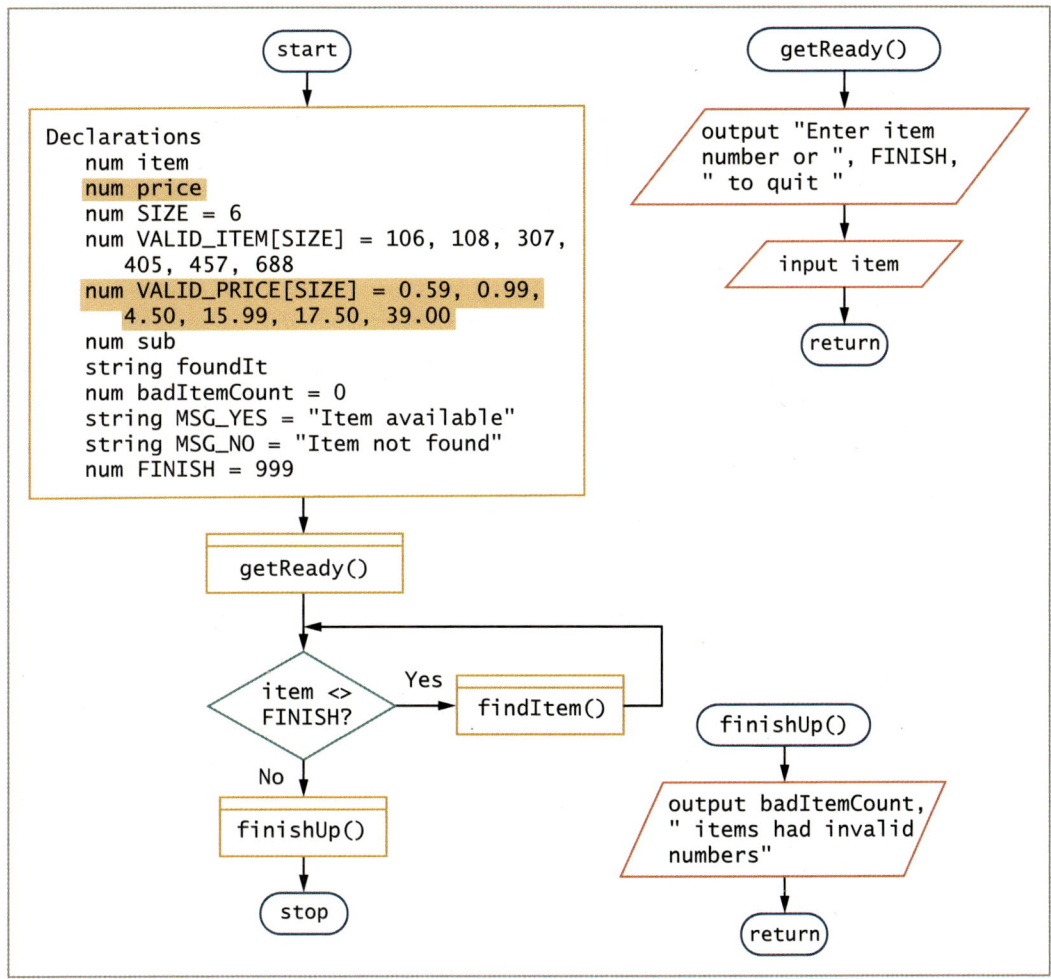

Figure 6-10 Flowchart and pseudocode of program that finds an item price using parallel arrays (continues)

(continued)

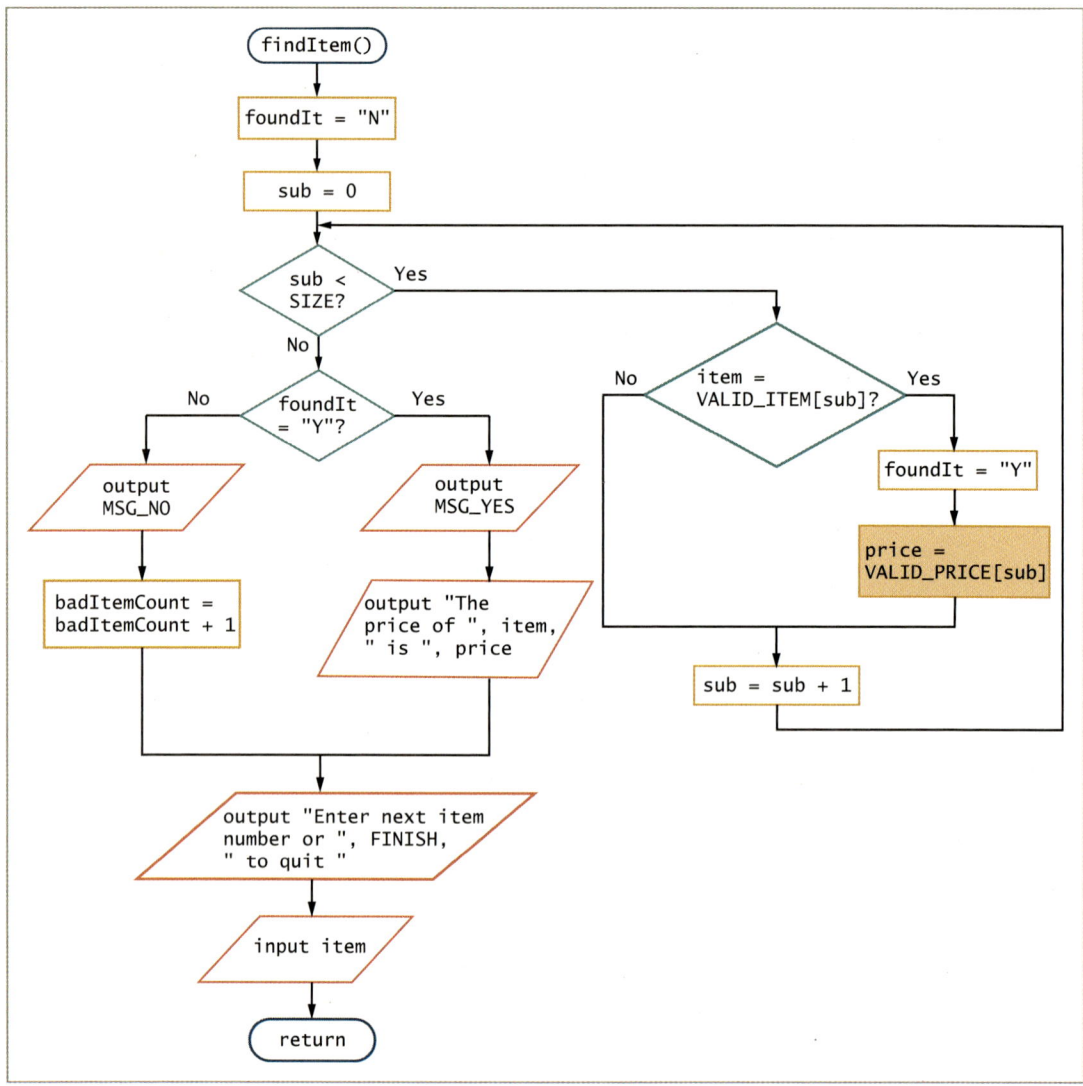

Figure 6-10 Flowchart and pseudocode of program that finds an item price using parallel arrays (*continues*)

(continued)

```
start
   Declarations
      num item
      num price
      num SIZE = 6
      num VALID_ITEM[SIZE] = 106, 108, 307,
         405, 457, 688
      num VALID_PRICE[SIZE] = 0.59, 0.99,
         4.50, 15.99, 17.50, 39.00
      num sub
      string foundIt
      num badItemCount = 0
      string MSG_YES = "Item available"
      string MSG_NO = "Item not found"
      num FINISH = 999
   getReady()
   while item <> FINISH
      findItem()
   endwhile
   finishUp()
stop

getReady()
   output "Enter item number or ", FINISH, " to quit "
   input item
return

findItem()
   foundIt = "N"
   sub = 0
   while sub < SIZE
      if item = VALID_ITEM[sub] then
         foundIt = "Y"
         price = VALID_PRICE[sub]
      endif
      sub = sub + 1
   endwhile
   if foundIt = "Y" then
      output MSG_YES
      output "The price of ", item, " is ", price
   else
      output MSG_NO
      badItemCount = badItemCount + 1
   endif
   output "Enter next item number or ", FINISH, " to quit "
   input item
return

finishUp()
   output badItemCount, " items had invalid numbers"
return
```

Figure 6-10 Flowchart and pseudocode of program that finds an item price using parallel arrays

Some programmers object to using a cryptic variable name for a subscript, such as sub in Figure 6-10, because such names are not descriptive. These programmers would prefer a name like priceIndex. Others approve of short names when the variable is used only in a limited area of a program, as it is used here, to step through an array. Programmers disagree on many style issues like this one. As a programmer, it is your responsibility to find out what conventions are used among your peers in an organization.

As the program in Figure 6-10 receives a customer's order, it looks through each of the VALID_ITEM values separately by varying the subscript sub from 0 to the number of items available. When a match for the item number is found, the program pulls the corresponding parallel price out of the list of VALID_PRICE values and stores it in the price variable. (See shaded statements in Figure 6-10.)

The relationship between an item's number and its price is an **indirect relationship**. That means you don't access a price directly by knowing the item number. Instead, you determine the price by knowing an item number's array position. Once you find a match for the ordered item number in the VALID_ITEM array, you know that the price of the item is in the same position in the other array, VALID_PRICE. When VALID_ITEM[sub] is the correct item, VALID_PRICE[sub] must be the correct price, so sub links the parallel arrays.

Parallel arrays are most useful when value pairs have an indirect relationship. If values in your program have a direct relationship, you probably don't need parallel arrays. For example, if items were numbered 0, 1, 2, 3, and so on consecutively, you could use the item number as a subscript to the price array instead of using a parallel array to hold item numbers. Even if the items were numbered 200, 201, 202, and so on consecutively, you could subtract a constant value (200) from each and use that as a subscript instead of using a parallel array.

Suppose that a customer orders item 457. Walk through the logic yourself to see if you come up with the correct price per item, $17.50. Then, suppose that a customer orders item 458. Walk through the logic and see whether the appropriate *Item not found* message is displayed.

Improving Search Efficiency

The mail-order program in Figure 6-10 is still a little inefficient. When a customer orders item 106 or 108, a match is found on the first or second pass through the loop, and continuing to search provides no further benefit. However, even after a match is made, the program in Figure 6-10 continues searching through the item array until sub reaches the value SIZE. One way to stop the search when the item has been found and foundIt is set to "Y" is to change the loop-controlling question. Instead of simply continuing the loop while the number of comparisons does not exceed the highest allowed array subscript, you should continue the loop while the searched item is not found *and* the number of comparisons has not exceeded the maximum. Leaving the loop as soon as a match is found improves the program's efficiency. The larger the array, the more beneficial it becomes to exit the searching loop as soon as you find the desired value.

Figure 6-11 shows the improved version of the findItem() module with the altered loop-controlling question shaded.

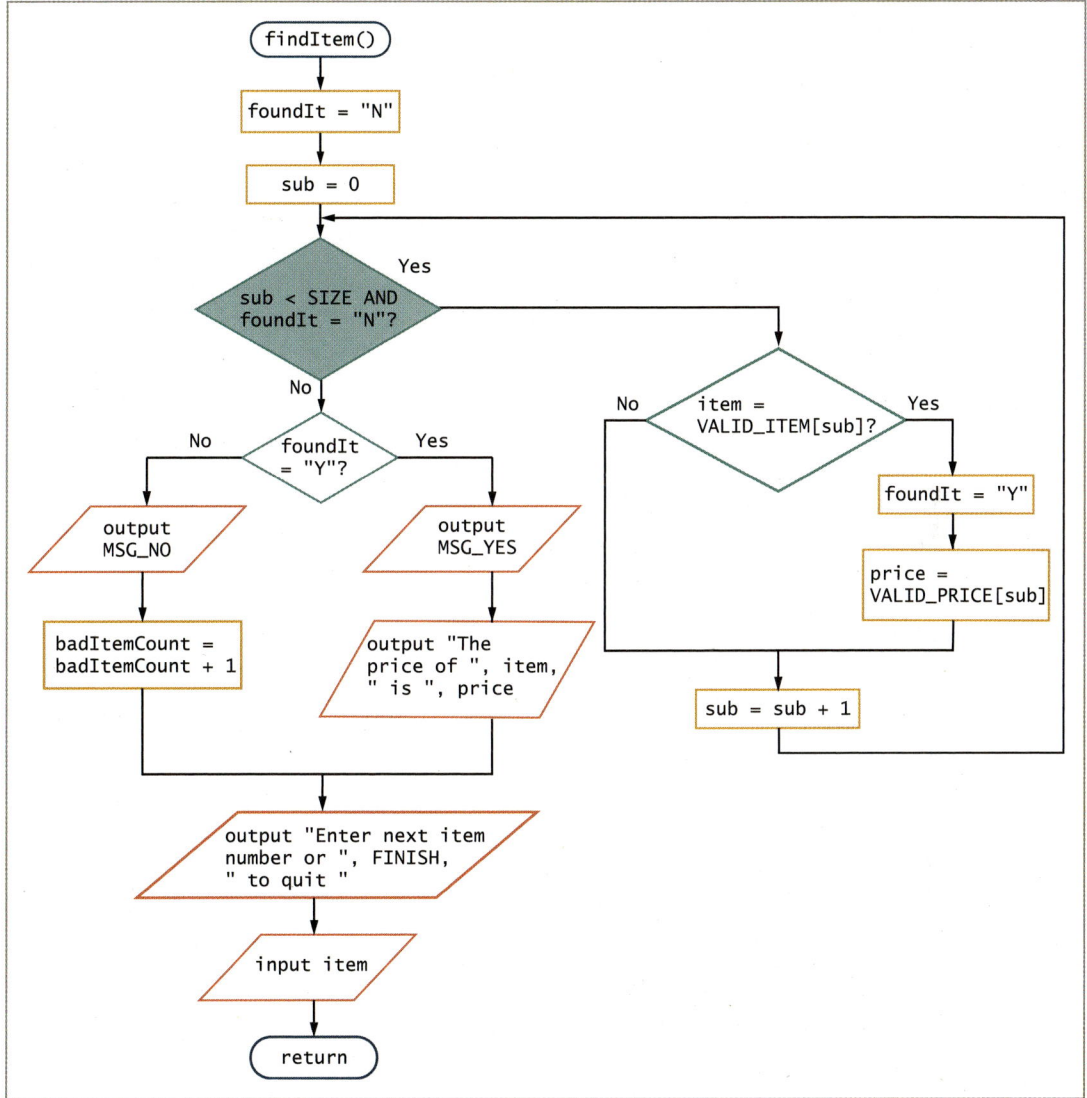

Figure 6-11 Flowchart and pseudocode of the module that finds an item price and exits the loop as soon as it is found (*continues*)

(continued)

```
findItem()
   foundIt = "N"
   sub = 0
   while sub < SIZE AND foundIt = "N"
      if item = VALID_ITEM[sub] then
         foundIt = "Y"
         price = VALID_PRICE[sub]
      endif
      sub = sub + 1
   endwhile
   if foundIt = "Y" then
      output MSG_YES
      output "The price of ", item, " is ", price
   else
      output MSG_NO
      badItemCount = badItemCount + 1
   endif
   output "Enter next item number or ", FINISH, " to quit "
   input item
return
```

Figure 6-11 Flowchart and pseudocode of the module that finds an item price and exits the loop as soon as it is found

Notice that the price-finding program offers the greatest efficiency when the most frequently ordered items are stored at the beginning of the array, so that only the seldom-ordered items require many loops before finding a match. Often, you can improve search efficiency by rearranging array elements.

 As you study programming, you will learn other search techniques. For example, a **binary search** starts looking in the middle of a sorted list, and then determines whether it should continue higher or lower.

 Watch the video *Using Parallel Arrays*.

Searching an Array for a Range Match

> **TWO TRUTHS & A LIE**
>
> **Using Parallel Arrays**
>
> 1. Parallel arrays must be the same data type.
> 2. Parallel arrays usually contain the same number of elements.
> 3. You can improve the efficiency of searching through parallel arrays by using an early exit.
>
> The false statement is #1. Parallel arrays do not need to be the same data type. For example, you might look up a name in a string array to find each person's age in a parallel numeric array.

Searching an Array for a Range Match

Customer order item numbers need to match available item numbers exactly to determine the correct price of an item. Sometimes, however, programmers want to work with ranges of values in arrays. In Chapter 4, you learned that a range of values is any series of values—for example, 1 through 5 or 20 through 30.

Suppose that a company decides to offer quantity discounts when a customer orders multiple items, as shown in Figure 6-12.

Quantity	Discount %
0–8	0
9–12	10
13–25	15
26 or more	20

You want to be able to read in customer order data and determine a discount percentage based on the quantity ordered. For example, if a customer has ordered 20 items, you want to be able to output *Your discount is 15 percent*. One ill-advised approach might be to set up an array with as many elements as any customer might ever order, and store the appropriate discount for each possible number, as shown in Figure 6-13. This array is set up to contain the discount for 0 items, 1 item, 2 items, and so on. This approach has at least three drawbacks:

Figure 6-12 Discounts on orders by quantity

- It requires a very large array that uses a lot of memory.
- You must store the same value repeatedly. For example, each of the first nine elements receives the same value, 0, and each of the next four elements receives the same value, 10.
- How do you know you have enough array elements? Is a customer order quantity of 75 items enough? What if a customer orders 100 or 1000 items? No matter how many elements you place in the array, there's always a chance that a customer will order more.

```
numeric DISCOUNT[76]
   = 0, 0, 0, 0, 0, 0, 0, 0, 0,
     0.10, 0.10, 0.10, 0.10,
     0.15, 0.15, 0.15, 0.15, 0.15,
     0.15, 0.15, 0.15, 0.15, 0.15,
     0.15, 0.15, 0.15,
     0.20, 0.20, 0.20, 0.20, 0.20,
     0.20, 0.20, 0.20, 0.20, 0.20,
     0.20, 0.20, 0.20, 0.20, 0.20,
     0.20, 0.20, 0.20, 0.20, 0.20,
     0.20, 0.20, 0.20, 0.20, 0.20,
     0.20, 0.20, 0.20, 0.20, 0.20,
     0.20, 0.20, 0.20, 0.20, 0.20,
     0.20, 0.20, 0.20, 0.20, 0.20,
     0.20, 0.20, 0.20, 0.20, 0.20,
     0.20, 0.20, 0.20, 0.20, 0.20
```

Don't Do It
Although this array is usable, it is repetitious, prone to error, and difficult to use.

Figure 6-13 Usable—but inefficient—discount array

A better approach is to create two parallel arrays, each with four elements, as shown in Figure 6-14. Each discount rate is listed once in the DISCOUNT array, and the low end of each quantity range is listed in the QUAN_LIMIT array.

```
num DISCOUNT[4]   =  0, 0.10, 0.15, 0.20
num QUAN_LIMIT[4] =  0,    9,   13,   26
```

Figure 6-14 Parallel arrays to use for determining discount

To find the correct discount for any customer's ordered quantity, you can start with the *last* quantity range limit (QUAN_LIMIT[3]). If the quantity ordered is at least that value, 26, the loop is never entered and the customer gets the highest discount rate (DISCOUNT[3], or 20 percent). If the quantity ordered is not at least QUAN_LIMIT[3]—that is, if it is less than 26—then you reduce the subscript and check to see if the quantity is at least QUAN_LIMIT[2], or 13. If so, the customer receives DISCOUNT[2], or 15 percent, and so on. Figure 6-15 shows a program that accepts a customer's quantity ordered and determines the appropriate discount rate.

Searching an Array for a Range Match

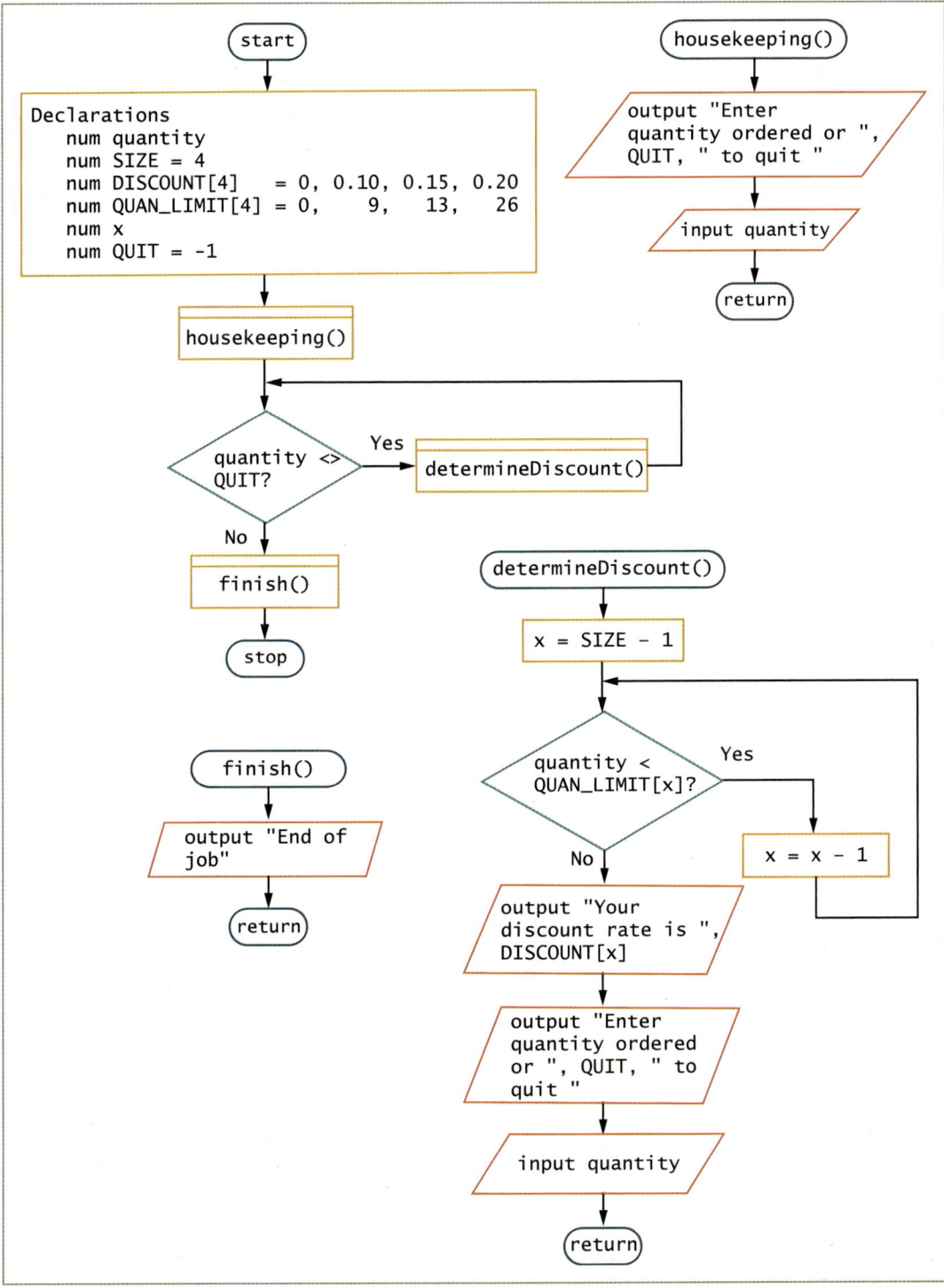

Figure 6-15 Program that determines discount rate (*continues*)

(continued)

```
start
   Declarations
      num quantity
      num SIZE = 4
      num DISCOUNT[4]   =   0, 0.10, 0.15, 0.20
      num QUAN_LIMIT[4] = 0,      9,   13,   26
      num x
      num QUIT = -1
   housekeeping()
   while quantity <> QUIT
      determineDiscount()
   endwhile
   finish()
stop

housekeeping()
   output "Enter quantity ordered or ", QUIT, " to quit "
   input quantity
return

determineDiscount()
   x = SIZE - 1
   while quantity < QUAN_LIMIT[x]
      x = x - 1
   endwhile
   output "Your discount rate is ", DISCOUNT[x]
   output "Enter quantity ordered or ", QUIT, " to quit "
   input quantity
return

finish()
   output "End of job"
return
```

Figure 6-15 Program that determines discount rate

An alternate approach to the one taken in Figure 6-15 is to store the high end of every range in an array. Then you start with the *lowest* element and check for values *less than or equal to* each array element value.

When using an array to store range limits, you use a loop to make a series of comparisons that would otherwise require many separate decisions. The program that determines customer discount rates in Figure 6-15 requires fewer instructions than one that does not use an array, and modifications to the program will be easier to make in the future.

> **TWO TRUTHS & A LIE**
>
> **Searching an Array for a Range Match**
>
> 1. To help locate a range within which a value falls, you can store the highest value in each range in an array.
> 2. To help locate a range within which a value falls, you can store the lowest value in each range in an array.
> 3. When using an array to store range limits, you use a series of comparisons that would otherwise require many separate loop structures.
>
> The false statement is #3. When using an array to store range limits, you use a loop to make a series of comparisons that would otherwise require many separate decisions.

Remaining within Array Bounds

Every array has a finite size. You can think of an array's size in one of two ways—either by the number of elements in the array or by the number of bytes in the array. Arrays are always composed of elements of the same data type, and elements of the same data type always occupy the same number of bytes of memory, so the number of bytes in an array is always a multiple of the number of elements in an array. For example, in Java, integers occupy 4 bytes of memory, so an array of 10 integers occupies exactly 40 bytes.

For a complete discussion of bytes and how they measure computer memory, read Appendix A.

In every programming language, when you access data stored in an array you must use a subscript containing a value that accesses memory occupied by the array. The subscript is actually multiplied by the size of the data type in bytes, and that value is added to the address of the array to find the address of the appropriate element. So, if the subscript is too large or too small, the program will attempt to access an address that is not part of the array's space.

A common error by beginning programmers is to forget that array subscripts start with 0. If you assume that an array's first subscript is 1, you will always be "off by one" in your array manipulation. For example, if you try to manipulate a 10-element array using subscripts 1 through 10, you will commit two errors: You will fail to access the first element that uses subscript 0, and you will attempt to access an extra element at position 10 when the highest usable subscript is 9.

For example, examine the program in Figure 6-16. The method accepts a numeric value for monthNum and displays the name associated with that month. The logic in Figure 6-16 makes a questionable assumption: that every number entered by the user is a valid month number.

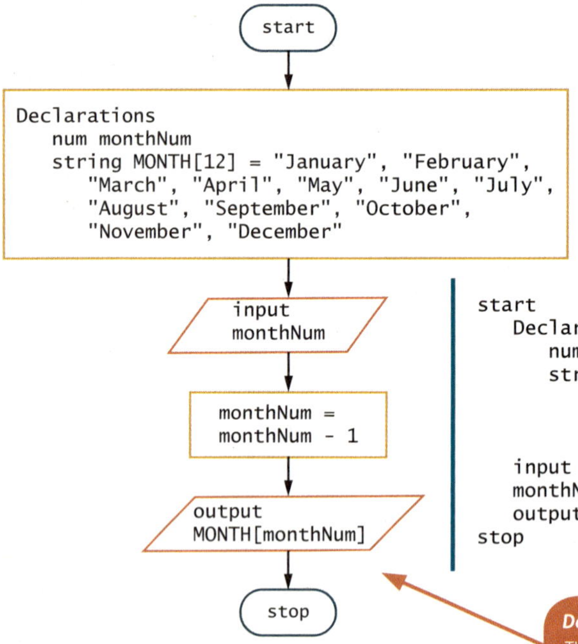

```
                          start
                            |
    Declarations
       num monthNum
       string MONTH[12] = "January", "February",
          "March", "April", "May", "June", "July",
          "August", "September", "October",
          "November", "December"
                            |
                        input
                        monthNum
                            |
                        monthNum =
                        monthNum - 1
                            |
                        output
                        MONTH[monthNum]
                            |
                         stop
```

```
start
   Declarations
      num monthNum
      string MONTH[12] = "January", "February",
         "March", "April", "May", "June", "July",
         "August", "September", "October",
         "November", "December"
   input monthNum
   monthNum = monthNum - 1
   output MONTH[monthNum]
stop
```

Don't Do It
The subscript monthNum might be out of bounds for the MONTH array.

Figure 6-16 Determining the month string from a user's numeric entry

In the program in Figure 6-16, notice that 1 is subtracted from monthNum before it is used as a subscript. Although January is the first month in the year, its name occupies the location in the array with the 0 subscript. With values that seem naturally to start with 1, like month numbers, some programmers would prefer to create a 13-element array and simply never use the zero-position element. That way, each "natural" month number would be the correct value to access its data without subtracting. Other programmers dislike wasting memory by creating an extra, unused array element. Although workable programs can be created with or without the extra array element, professional programmers should follow the conventions and preferences of their colleagues and managers.

In Figure 6-16, if the user enters a number that is too small or too large, one of two things will happen depending on the programming language you use. When you use a subscript value that is negative or higher than the highest allowed subscript:

Remaining within Array Bounds

- Some programming languages will stop execution of the program and issue an error message.
- Other programming languages will not issue an error message but will access a value in a memory location that is outside the area occupied by the array. That area might contain garbage, or worse, it accidentally might contain the name of an incorrect month.

Either way, a logical error occurs. When you use a subscript that is not within the range of acceptable subscripts, it is said to be **out of bounds**. Users enter incorrect data frequently; a good program should be able to handle the mistake and not allow the subscript to be out of bounds.

A user might enter an invalid number or might not enter a number at all. In Chapter 5, you learned that many languages have a built-in method with a name like `isNumeric()` that can test for such mistakes.

You can improve the program in Figure 6-16 by adding a test that ensures the subscript used to access the array is within the array bounds. If you find that the input value is not between 1 and 12 inclusive, you might take one of the following approaches:

- Display an error message and end the program.
- Use a default value for the month. For example, when an entered month is invalid, you might want to assume that it is December.
- Continuously reprompt the user for a new value until it is valid.

The way you handle an invalid month depends on the requirements of your program as spelled out by your user, supervisor, or company policy.

TWO TRUTHS & A LIE

Remaining within Array Bounds

1. Elements in an array frequently are different data types, so calculating the amount of memory the array occupies is difficult.
2. If you attempt to access an array with a subscript that is too small, some programming languages will stop execution of the program and issue an error message.
3. If you attempt to access an array with a subscript that is too large, some programming languages access an incorrect memory location outside the array bounds.

The false statement is #1. Array elements are always the same data type, and elements of the same data type always occupy the same number of bytes of memory, so the number of bytes in an array is always a multiple of the number of elements in an array.

Using a for Loop to Process Arrays

In Chapter 5, you learned about the `for` loop—a loop that, in a single statement, initializes a loop control variable, compares it to a limit, and alters it. The `for` loop is a particularly convenient tool when working with arrays because you frequently need to process every element of an array from beginning to end. As with a `while` loop, when you use a `for` loop, you must be careful to stay within array bounds, remembering that the highest usable array subscript is one less than the size of the array. Figure 6-17 shows a `for` loop that correctly displays all of a company's department names that are stored in an array declared as `DEPTS`. Notice that `dep` is incremented through one less than the number of departments because with a five-item array, the subscripts you can use are 0 through 4.

```
start
   Declarations
      num dep
      num SIZE = 5
      string DEPTS[SIZE] = "Accounting", "Personnel",
         "Technical", "Customer Service", "Marketing"
   for dep = 0 to SIZE - 1 step 1
      output DEPTS[dep]
   endfor
stop
```

Figure 6-17 Pseudocode that uses a `for` loop to display an array of department names

The loop in Figure 6-17 is slightly inefficient because, as it executes five times, the subtraction operation that deducts 1 from `SIZE` occurs each time. Five subtraction operations do not consume much computer power or time, but in a loop that processes thousands or millions of array elements, the program's efficiency would be compromised. Figure 6-18 shows a superior solution. A new constant called `ARRAY_LIMIT` is calculated once, then used repeatedly in the comparison operation to determine when to stop cycling through the array.

```
start
   Declarations
      num dep
      num SIZE = 5
      num ARRAY_LIMIT = SIZE - 1
      string DEPTS[SIZE] = "Accounting", "Personnel",
         "Technical", "Customer Service", "Marketing"
   for dep = 0 to ARRAY_LIMIT step 1
      output DEPTS[dep]
   endfor
stop
```

Figure 6-18 Pseudocode that uses a more efficient `for` loop to output department names

TWO TRUTHS & A LIE

Using a `for` Loop to Process Arrays

1. The `for` loop is a particularly convenient tool when working with arrays.
2. You frequently need to process every element of an array from beginning to end.
3. Not being concerned with array bounds is one advantage to using a `for` loop to process array elements.

The false statement is #3. As with a `while` loop, when you use a `for` loop, you must be careful to stay within array bounds.

Chapter Summary

- An array is a named series or list of values in computer memory, all of which have the same data type but are differentiated with subscripts. Each array element occupies an area in memory next to, or contiguous to, the others.

- You often can use a variable as a subscript to an array, which allows you to replace multiple nested decisions with many fewer statements.

- Constants can be used to hold an array's size or to represent its values. Using a named constant for an array's size makes the code easier to understand and less likely to contain an error. Array values are declared as constant when they should not change during program execution.

- Searching through an array to find a value you need involves initializing a subscript, using a loop to test each array element, and setting a flag when a match is found.

- With parallel arrays, each element in one array is associated with the element in the same relative position in the other array.

- When you need to compare a value to a range of values in an array, you can store either the low- or high-end value of each range for comparison.

- When you access data stored in an array, it is important to use a subscript containing a value that accesses memory occupied by the array. When you use a subscript that is not within the defined range of acceptable subscripts, your subscript is said to be out of bounds.

- The `for` loop is a particularly convenient tool when working with arrays because you frequently need to process every element of an array from beginning to end.

Key Terms

An **array** is a series or list of values in computer memory, all of which have the same name but are differentiated with special numbers called subscripts.

An **element** is a single data item in an array.

The **size of the array** is the number of elements it can hold.

A **subscript**, also called an **index**, is a number that indicates the position of a particular item within an array.

Populating an array is the act of assigning values to the array elements.

A **linear search** is a search through a list from one end to the other.

A **flag** is a variable that indicates whether some event has occurred.

In **parallel arrays**, each element in one array is associated with the element in the same relative position in the other array(s).

An **indirect relationship** describes the relationship between parallel arrays in which an element in the first array does not directly access its corresponding value in the second array.

A **binary search** is one that starts in the middle of a sorted list, and then determines whether it should continue higher or lower to find a target value.

Out of bounds describes an array subscript that is not within the range of acceptable subscripts for the array.

Review Questions

1. A subscript is a(n) _____ .

    a. element in an array
    b. alternate name for an array
    c. number that represents the highest value stored within an array
    d. number that indicates the position of an array element

2. Each variable in an array must have the same _____ as the others.

    a. data type
    b. subscript
    c. value
    d. memory location

3. Each data item in an array is called a(n) _____ .

    a. data type
    b. subscript
    c. component
    d. element

Review Questions

4. The subscripts of any array are always _____.
   a. integers
   b. fractions
   c. characters
   d. strings of characters

5. Suppose that you have an array named `number`, and two of its elements are `number[1]` and `number[4]`. You know that _____.
   a. the two elements hold the same value
   b. the array holds exactly four elements
   c. there are exactly two elements between those two elements
   d. the two elements are at the same memory location

6. Suppose that you want to write a program that inputs customer data and displays a summary of the number of customers who owe more than $1000 each, in each of 12 sales regions. Customer data variables include `name`, `zipCode`, `balanceDue`, and `regionNumber`. At some point during record processing, you would add 1 to an array element whose subscript would be represented by _____.
   a. `name`
   b. `zipCode`
   c. `balanceDue`
   d. `regionNumber`

7. The most useful type of subscript for manipulating arrays is a _____.
   a. numeric constant
   b. variable
   c. character
   d. filename

8. A program contains a seven-element array that holds the names of the days of the week. At the start of the program, you display the day names using a subscript named `dayNum`. You display the same array values again at the end of the program, where you _____ as a subscript to the array.
   a. must use `dayNum`
   b. can use `dayNum`, but can also use another variable
   c. must not use `dayNum`
   d. must use a numeric constant instead of a variable

9. Suppose that you have declared an array as follows: `num values[4] = 0, 0, 0, 0`. Which of the following is an allowed operation?
   a. `values[2] = 17`
   b. `input values[0]`
   c. `values[3] = values[0] + 10`
   d. all of the above

10. Filling an array with values during a program's execution is known as _____ the array.
    a. executing
    b. colonizing
    c. populating
    d. declaring

11. Using an array can make a program _____.
    a. easier to understand
    b. illegal in some modern languages
    c. harder to maintain
    d. all of the above

12. A _____ is a variable that can be set to indicate whether some event has occurred.
    a. subscript
    b. banner
    c. counter
    d. flag

13. What do you call two arrays in which each element in one array is associated with the element in the same relative position in the other array?
    a. cohesive arrays
    b. parallel arrays
    c. hidden arrays
    d. perpendicular arrays

14. In most modern programming languages, the highest subscript you should use with a 12-element array is _____.
    a. 10
    b. 11
    c. 12
    d. 13

15. Parallel arrays _____.
    a. frequently have an indirect relationship
    b. never have an indirect relationship
    c. must be the same data type
    d. must not be the same data type

16. Each element in a seven-element array can hold _____ value(s).
    a. one
    b. seven
    c. at least seven
    d. an unlimited number of

17. After the annual dog show in which the Barkley Dog Training Academy awards points to each participant, the academy assigns a status to each dog based on the criteria in Table 6-1.

Points Earned	Level of Achievement
0–5	Good
6–7	Excellent
8–9	Superior
10	Unbelievable

Table 6-1 Barkley Dog Training Academy achievement levels

The academy needs a program that compares a dog's points earned with the grading scale, so that each dog can receive a certificate acknowledging the appropriate level of achievement. Of the following, which set of values would be most useful for the contents of an array used in the program?

    a. 0, 6, 9, 10

    b. 5, 7, 8, 10

    c. 5, 7, 9, 10

    d. any of the above

18. When you use a subscript value that is negative or higher than the number of elements in an array, _____.

    a. execution of the program stops and an error message is issued

    b. a value in a memory location that is outside the area occupied by the array will be accessed

    c. a value in a memory location that is outside the area occupied by the array will be accessed, but only if the value is the correct data type

    d. the resulting action depends on the programming language used

19. In every array, a subscript is out of bounds when it is _____.

    a. negative

    b. 0

    c. 1

    d. 999

20. You can access every element of an array using a _____.

    a. `while` loop

    b. `for` loop

    c. both of the above

    d. none of the above

Exercises

1. a. Design the logic for a program that allows a user to enter 15 numbers, then displays them in the reverse order of entry.

   b. Modify the reverse-display program so that the user can enter any amount of numbers up to 15 until a sentinel value is entered.

2. a. Design the logic for a program that allows a user to enter 15 numbers, then displays each number and its difference from the numeric average of the numbers entered.

   b. Modify the program in Exercise 2a so that the user can enter any amount of numbers up to 15 until a sentinel value is entered.

3. a. Registration workers at a conference for authors of children's books have collected data about conference participants, including the number of books each author has written and the target age of their readers. The participants have written from 1 to 40 books each, and target readers' ages range from 0 through 16. Design a program that continuously accepts the number of

books written until a sentinel value is entered, and then displays a list of how many participants have written each number of books (1 through 40).

b. Modify the author registration program so that a target age for each author's audience is input until a sentinel value is entered. The output is a count of the number of books written for each of the following age groups: under 3, 3 through 7, 8 through 10, 11 through 13, and 14 and older.

4. a. The Downdog Yoga Studio offers five types of classes, as shown in Table 6-2. Design a program that accepts a number representing a class and then displays the name of the class.

   b. Modify the Downdog Yoga Studio program so that numeric class requests can be entered continuously until a sentinel value is entered. Then display each class number, name, and a count of the number of requests for each class.

Class Number	Class Name
1	Yoga 1
2	Yoga 2
3	Children's Yoga
4	Prenatal Yoga
5	Senior Yoga

Table 6-2 Downdog Yoga Studio classes

5. a. Watson Elementary School contains 30 classrooms numbered 1 through 30. Each classroom can contain any number of students up to 35. Each student takes an achievement test at the end of the school year and receives a score from 0 through 100. Write a program that accepts data for each student in the school—student ID, classroom number, and score on the achievement test. Design a program that lists the total points scored for each of the 30 classrooms.

   b. Modify the Watson Elementary School program so that the average of the test scores is output for each classroom, rather than total scores for each classroom.

6. The Jumpin' Jive coffee shop charges $2.00 for a cup of coffee and offers the add-ins shown in Table 6-3.

   Design the logic for an application that allows a user to enter ordered add-ins continuously until a sentinel value is entered. After each item, display its price or the message *Sorry, we do not carry that* as output. After all items have been entered, display the total price for the order.

Product	Price ($)
Whipped cream	0.89
Cinnamon	0.25
Chocolate sauce	0.59
Amaretto	1.50
Irish whiskey	1.75

Table 6-3 Add-in list for Jumpin' Jive coffee shop

7. Design the application logic for a company that wants a report containing a breakdown of payroll by department. Input includes each employee's department number, hourly salary, and number of hours worked. The output is a list of the

seven departments in the company and the total gross payroll (rate times hours) for each department. The department names are shown in Table 6-4.

8. Design a program that computes pay for employees. Allow a user to continuously input employees' names until an appropriate sentinel value is entered. Also input each employee's hourly wage and hours worked. Compute each employee's gross pay (hours times rate), withholding tax percentage (based on Table 6-5), withholding tax amount, and net pay (gross pay minus withholding tax). Display all the results for each employee. After the last employee has been entered, display the sum of all the hours worked, the total gross payroll, the total withholding for all employees, and the total net payroll.

9. Countrywide Tours conducts sightseeing trips for groups from its home base in Iowa. Create an application that continuously accepts tour data, including a three-digit tour number; the numeric month, day, and year values representing the tour start date; the number of travelers taking the tour; and a numeric code that represents the destination. As data is entered for each tour, verify that the month, day, year, and destination code are valid; if any of these is not valid, continue to prompt the user until valid data is entered. The valid destination codes are shown in Table 6-6.

Design the logic for an application that outputs each tour number, validated start date, destination code, destination name, number of travelers, gross total price for the tour, and price for the tour after discount. The gross total price is the tour price per guest

Department Number	Department Name
1	Personnel
2	Marketing
3	Manufacturing
4	Computer Services
5	Sales
6	Accounting
7	Shipping

Table 6-4 Department numbers and names

Weekly Gross Pay ($)	Withholding Percentage (%)
0.00–300.00	10
300.01–550.00	13
550.01–800.00	16
800.01 and up	20

Table 6-5 Withholding percentage based on gross pay

Code	Destination	Price per Person ($)
1	Chicago	300.00
2	Boston	480.00
3	Miami	1050.00
4	San Francisco	1300.00

Table 6-6 Countrywide Tours codes and prices

times the number of travelers. The final price includes a discount for each person in larger tour groups, based on Table 6-7.

Number of Tourists	Discount per Tourist ($)
1–5	0
6–12	75
13–20	125
21–50	200
51 and over	300

Table 6-7 Countrywide Tours discounts

10. a. *Daily Life Magazine* wants an analysis of the demographic characteristics of its readers. The marketing department has collected reader survey records containing the age, gender, marital status, and annual income of readers. Design an application that allows a user to enter reader data and, when data entry is complete, produces a count of readers by age groups as follows: under 20, 20–29, 30–39, 40–49, and 50 and older.

   b. Modify the *Daily Life Magazine* program so that it produces a count of readers by gender within age group—that is, under-20 females, under-20 males, and so on.

   c. Modify the *Daily Life Magazine* program so that it produces a count of readers by income groups as follows: under $30,000, $30,000–$49,999, $50,000–$69,999, and $70,000 and up.

11. Glen Ross Vacation Property Sales employs seven salespeople, as shown in Table 6-8.

    When a salesperson makes a sale, a record is created, including the date, time, and dollar amount of the sale. The time is expressed in hours and minutes, based on a 24-hour clock. The sale amount is expressed in whole dollars. Salespeople earn a commission that differs for each sale, based on the rate schedule in Table 6-9.

    Design an application that produces each of the following:

    a. A list of each salesperson number, name, total sales, and total commissions

    b. A list of each month of the year as both a number and a word (for example, *01 January*), and the total sales for the month for all salespeople

ID Number	Salesperson Name
103	Darwin
104	Kratz
201	Shulstad
319	Fortune
367	Wickert
388	Miller
435	Vick

Table 6-8 Glen Ross salespeople

Sale Amount ($)	Commission Rate (%)
0–50,999	4
51,000–125,999	5
126,000–200,999	6
201,000 and up	7

Table 6-9 Glen Ross commission schedule

Exercises

c. A list of total sales as well as total commissions earned by all salespeople for each of the following time frames, based on hour of the day: 00–05, 06–12, 13–18, and 19–23

12. Design an application in which the number of days for each month in the year is stored in an array. (For example, January has 31 days, February has 28, and so on. Assume that the year is not a leap year.) Prompt a user to enter a birth month and day, and continue to prompt until the day entered is in range for the month. Compute the day's numeric position in the year. (For example, February 2 is day 33.) Then, using parallel arrays, find and display the traditional Zodiac sign for the date. For example, the sign for February 2 is Aquarius.

Find the Bugs

13. Your downloadable files for Chapter 6 include DEBUG06-01.txt, DEBUG06-02.txt, and DEBUG06-03.txt. Each file starts with some comments that describe the problem. Comments are lines that begin with two slashes (//). Following the comments, each file contains pseudocode that has one or more bugs you must find and correct.

Game Zone

14. Create the logic for a Magic 8 Ball game in which the user enters a question such as *What does my future hold?* The computer randomly selects one of eight possible vague answers, such as *It remains to be seen.*

15. Create the logic for an application that contains an array of 10 multiple-choice questions related to your favorite hobby. Each question contains three answer choices. Also create a parallel array that holds the correct answer to each question—A, B, or C. Display each question and verify that the user enters only A, B, or C as the answer—if not, keep prompting the user until a valid response is entered. If the user responds to a question correctly, display *Correct!*; otherwise, display *The correct answer is* and the letter of the correct answer. After the user answers all the questions, display the number of correct and incorrect answers.

16. a. Create the logic for a dice game. The application randomly "throws" five dice for the computer and five dice for the player. After each random throw, store the results in an array. The application displays all the values, which can be from 1 to 6 inclusive for each die. Decide the winner based on the following

hierarchy of die values. Any higher combination beats a lower one; for example, five of a kind beats four of a kind.

- Five of a kind
- Four of a kind
- Three of a kind
- A pair

For this game, the numeric dice values do not count. For example, if both players have three of a kind, it's a tie, no matter what the values of the three dice are. Additionally, the game does not recognize a full house (three of a kind plus two of a kind). Figure 6-19 shows how the game might be played in a command-line environment.

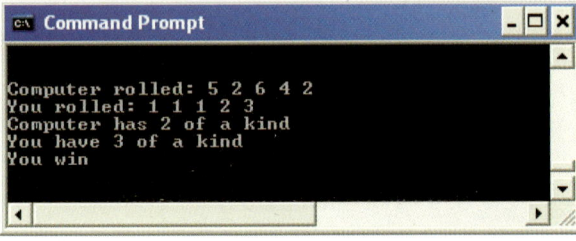

Figure 6-19 Typical execution of the dice game

b. Improve the dice game so that when both players have the same number of matching dice, the higher value wins. For example, two 6s beats two 5s.

17. Design the logic for the game Hangman, in which the user guesses letters in a hidden word. Store the letters of a word in an array of characters. Display a dash for each missing letter. Allow the user to continuously guess a letter until all the letters in the word are guessed correctly. As the user enters each guess, display the word again, filling in the guessed letter if it was correct. For example, if the hidden word is *computer*, first display a series of eight dashes: ————————.
After the user guesses *p*, the display becomes ---*p*----. Make sure that when a user makes a correct guess, all the matching letters are filled in. For example, if the word is *banana* and the user guesses *a*, all three *a* characters should be filled in.

18. Create two parallel arrays that represent a standard deck of 52 playing cards. One array is numeric and holds the values 1 through 13 (representing Ace, 2 through 10, Jack, Queen, and King). The other array is a string array that holds suits (Clubs, Diamonds, Hearts, and Spades). Create the arrays so that all 52 cards are represented. Then, create a War card game that randomly selects two cards (one for the player and one for the computer) and declares a winner or a tie based on the numeric value of the two cards. The game should last for 26 rounds and use a full deck with no repeated cards. For this game, assume that the lowest card is the Ace. Display the values of the player's and computer's cards, compare their values, and determine the winner. When all the cards in the deck are exhausted, display a count of the number of times the player wins, the number of times the computer wins, and the number of ties.

Exercises

Here are some hints:

- Start by creating an array of all 52 playing cards.
- Select a random number for the deck position of the player's first card and assign the card at that array position to the player.
- Move every higher-positioned card in the deck "down" one to fill in the gap. In other words, if the player's first random number is 49, select the card at position 49 (both the numeric value and the string), move the card that was in position 50 to position 49, and move the card that was in position 51 to position 50. Only 51 cards remain in the deck after the player's first card is dealt, so the available-card array is smaller by one.
- In the same way, randomly select a card for the computer and "remove" the card from the deck.

Up for Discussion

19. A train schedule is an everyday, real-life example of an array. Identify at least four more.

20. Every element in an array always has the same data type. Why is this necessary?

CHAPTER 7

File Handling and Applications

In this chapter, you will learn about:

- Computer files
- The data hierarchy
- Performing file operations
- Sequential files and control break logic
- Merging files
- Master and transaction file processing
- Random access files

CHAPTER 7 File Handling and Applications

Understanding Computer Files

In Chapter 1, you learned that computer memory, or random access memory (RAM), is volatile, temporary storage. When you write a program that stores a value in a variable, you are using temporary storage; the value you store is lost when the program ends or the computer loses power.

Permanent, nonvolatile storage, on the other hand, is not lost when a computer loses power. When you write a program and save it to a disk, you are using permanent storage.

When discussing computer storage, *temporary* and *permanent* refer to volatility, not length of time. For example, a *temporary* variable might exist for several hours in a very large program or one that runs in an infinite loop, but a *permanent* piece of data might be saved and then deleted by a user within a few seconds. Because you can erase data from files, some programmers prefer the term *persistent storage* to permanent storage. In other words, you can remove data from a file stored on a device such as a disk drive, so it is not technically permanent. However, the data remains in the file even when the computer loses power, so, unlike in RAM, the data persists.

A **computer file** is a collection of data stored on a nonvolatile device in a computer system. Files exist on **permanent storage devices**, such as hard disks, DVDs, USB drives, and reels of magnetic tape. The two broad categories of files are:

- **Text files**, which contain data that can be read in a text editor because the data has been encoded using a scheme such as ASCII or Unicode. Text files might include facts and figures used by business programs, such as a payroll file that contains employee numbers, names, and salaries. The programs in this chapter will use text files.
- **Binary files**, which contain data that has not been encoded as text. Examples include images and music.

Although their contents vary, files have many common characteristics, as follows:

- Each file has a name. The name often includes a dot and a file extension that describes the type of the file. For example, the extension *.txt* indicates a plain text file, *.dat* is a common extension for a data file, and *.jpg* is used as an extension on image files in Joint Photographic Experts Group format.
- Each file has specific times associated with it—for example, its creation time and the time it was last modified.
- Each file occupies space on a section of a storage device; that is, each file has a size. Sizes are measured in bytes. A **byte** is a small unit of storage; for example, in a simple text file, a byte holds only one character. Because a byte is so small, file sizes usually are expressed in **kilobytes** (thousands of bytes), **megabytes** (millions of bytes), or **gigabytes** (billions of bytes). Appendix A contains more information on bytes and how file sizes are expressed.

Figure 7-1 shows how some files look when you view them in Microsoft Windows.

Understanding Computer Files

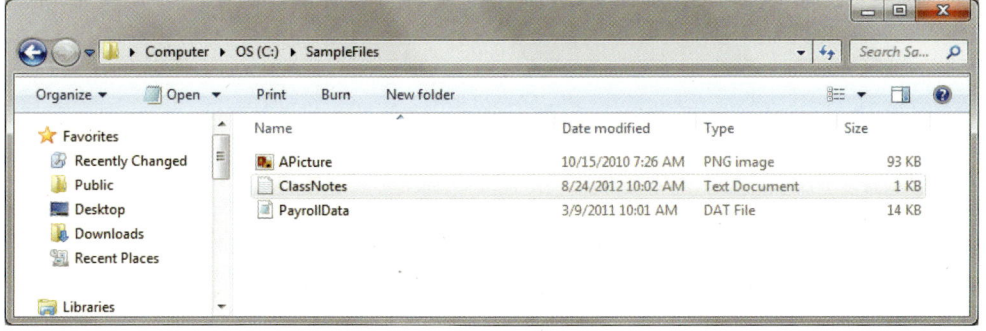

Figure 7-1 Three stored files and their attributes

 Watch the video *Understanding Files*.

Organizing Files

Computer files on a storage device are the electronic equivalent of paper files stored in file cabinets. With a paper file, the easiest way to store a document is to toss it into a file cabinet drawer without a folder. However, for better organization, most office clerks place paper documents in folders—and most computer users organize their files into folders or directories. **Directories** and **folders** are organization units on storage devices; each can contain multiple files as well as additional directories. The combination of the disk drive plus the complete hierarchy of directories in which a file resides is its **path**. For example, in the Windows operating system, the following line would be the complete path for a file named PayrollData.dat on the C drive in a folder named SampleFiles within a folder named Logic:

`C:\Logic\SampleFiles\PayrollData.dat`

 The terms *directory* and *folder* are used synonymously to mean an entity that organizes files. *Directory* is the more general term; the term *folder* came into use in graphical systems. For example, Microsoft began calling directories *folders* with the introduction of Windows 95.

> **TWO TRUTHS & A LIE**
>
> Understanding Computer Files
>
> 1. Temporary storage is volatile.
> 2. Computer files exist on permanent storage devices, such as RAM.
> 3. A file's path is the hierarchy of folders in which it is stored.
>
> The false statement is #2. Computer files exist on permanent storage devices, such as hard disks, DVDs, USB drives, and reels of magnetic tape.

Understanding the Data Hierarchy

When businesses store data items on computer systems, they are often stored in a framework called the **data hierarchy** that describes the relationships between data components. The data hierarchy consists of the following:

- **Characters** are letters, numbers, and special symbols, such as *A*, *7*, and *$*. Anything you can type from the keyboard in one keystroke is a character, including seemingly "empty" characters such as spaces and tabs. Computers also recognize characters you cannot enter from a standard keyboard, such as foreign-alphabet characters like φ or Σ. Characters are made up of smaller elements called bits, but just as most human beings can use a pencil without caring whether atoms are flying around inside it, most computer users store characters without thinking about these bits.

- **Fields** are data items that represent a single attribute of a record and are composed of one or more characters. Fields include items such as `lastName`, `middleInitial`, `streetAddress`, or `annualSalary`.

- **Records** are groups of fields that go together for some logical reason. A random name, address, and salary aren't very useful, but if they're *your* name, *your* address, and *your* salary, then that's your record. An inventory record might contain fields for item number, color, size, and price; a student record might contain an ID number, grade point average, and major.

- **Files** are groups of related records. The individual records of each student in your class might go together in a file called Students.dat. Similarly, records of each person at your company might be in a file called Personnel.dat. Some files can have just a few records. For example, a student file for a college seminar might have only 10 records. Others, such as the file of credit card holders for a major department store chain or policy holders of a large insurance company, can contain thousands or even millions of records.

A **database** holds groups of files or **tables** that together serve the information needs of an organization. Database software establishes and maintains relationships between fields in these tables, so that users can pull related data items together in a format that allows businesspeople to make managerial decisions efficiently. Chapter 14 of the comprehensive version of this text covers database creation.

> **TWO TRUTHS & A LIE**
>
> Understanding the Data Hierarchy
>
> 1. In the data hierarchy, a field is a single data item, such as `lastName`, `streetAddress`, or `annualSalary`.
> 2. In the data hierarchy, fields are grouped together to form a record; records are groups of fields that go together for some logical reason.
> 3. In the data hierarchy, related records are grouped together to form a field.
>
> The false statement is #3. Related records form a file.

Performing File Operations

To use data files in your programs, you need to understand several file operations:

- Declaring a file
- Opening a file
- Reading from a file
- Writing to a file
- Closing a file

Declaring a File

Most languages support several types of files, but one way of categorizing files is by whether they can be used for input or for output. Just as variables and constants have data types such as `num` and `string`, each file has a data type that is defined in the language you are using. For example, a file's type might be `InputFile`. Just like variables and constants, files are declared by giving each a data type and an identifier. As examples, you might declare two files as follows:

```
InputFile employeeData
OutputFile updatedData
```

The `InputFile` and `OutputFile` types are capitalized in this book because their equivalents are capitalized in most programming languages. This approach helps to distinguish these complex types from simple types such as `num` and `string`. The identifiers given to files, such as `employeeData` and `updatedData`, are internal to the program, just as variable names are. To make a program read a file's data from a storage device, you also need to associate the program's internal filename with the operating system's name for the file. Often, this association is accomplished when you open the file.

Opening a File

In most programming languages, before an application can use a data file, it must **open the file**. Opening a file locates it on a storage device and associates a variable name within your program with the file. For example, if the identifier `employeeData` has been declared as type `InputFile`, then you might make a statement similar to the following:

```
open employeeData "EmployeeData.dat"
```

This statement associates the file named EmployeeData.dat on the storage device with the program's internal name `employeeData`. Usually, you also can specify a more complete path when the data file is not in the same directory as the program, as in the following:

```
open employeeData "C:\CompanyFiles\CurrentYear\EmployeeData.dat"
```

Reading Data from a File

Before you can use stored data within a program, you must load the data into computer memory. You never use the data values that are stored on a storage device directly. Instead, you use a copy that is transferred into memory. When you copy data from a file on a storage device into RAM, you **read from the file**.

Especially when data items are stored on a hard disk, their location might not be clear to you—data just seems to be "in the computer." To a casual computer user, the lines between permanent storage and temporary memory are often blurred because many newer programs automatically save data for you periodically without asking your permission. However, at any moment in time, the version of a file in memory might differ from the version that was last saved to a storage device.

If data items have been stored in a file and a program needs them, you can write separate programming statements to input each field, as in the following example:

```
input name from employeeData
input address from employeeData
input payRate from employeeData
```

Most languages also allow you to write a single statement in the following format:

```
input name, address, payRate from employeeData
```

Performing File Operations

 Most programming languages provide a way for you to use a group name for record data, as in the following statement:

`input EmployeeRecord from employeeData`

When this format is used, you need to define the separate fields that compose an `EmployeeRecord` when you declare the variables for the program.

You usually do not want to input several items in a single statement when you read data from a keyboard, because you want to prompt the user for each item separately as you input it. However, when you retrieve data from a file, prompts are not needed. Instead, each item is retrieved in sequence and stored in memory at the appropriate named location.

 The way a program knows how much data to input for each variable differs among programming languages. In many languages, a delimiter such as a comma is stored between data fields. In other languages, the amount of data retrieved depends on the data types of the variables in the input statement.

Figure 7-2 shows how an input statement works. When the input statement executes, each field is copied and placed in the appropriate variable in computer memory. Nothing on the disk indicates a field name associated with any of the data; the variable names exist within the program only. For example, another program could use the same file as input and call the fields `surname`, `street`, and `salary`.

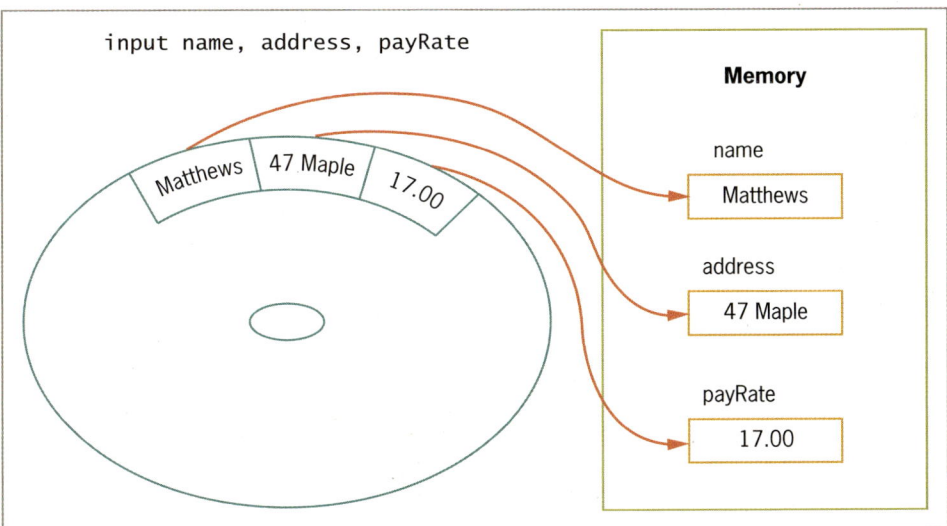

Figure 7-2 Reading three data items from a storage device into memory

 In some languages, you must specify the length of each field that is read from a data file. In other languages, the length of each field is determined by its data type.

When you read data from a file, you must read all the fields that are stored even though you might not want to use all of them. For example, suppose that you want to read an employee data file that contains names, addresses, and pay rates for each employee, and you want to output a list of names. Even though you are not concerned with the address or pay rate fields, you must read them into your program for each employee before you can get to the name for the next employee.

Writing Data to a File

When you store data in a computer file on a persistent storage device, you **write to the file**. This means you copy data from RAM to the file. When you write data to a file, you write the contents of the fields using a statement such as the following:

`output name, address, payRate to employeeData`

When you write data to a file, you usually do not include explanations that make data easier for humans to interpret; you just write facts and figures. For example, you do not include column headings or write explanations such as *The pay rate is*, nor do you include commas, dollar signs, or percent signs in numeric values. Those embellishments are appropriate for output on a monitor or on paper, but not for storage.

Closing a File

When you finish using a file, the program should **close the file**—a closed file is no longer available to your application. Failing to close an input file (a file from which you are reading data) usually does not present serious consequences; the data still exists in the file. However, if you fail to close an output file (a file to which you are writing data), the data might not be saved correctly and might become inaccessible. You should always close every file you open, and you should close the file as soon as you no longer need it. When you leave a file open for no reason, you use computer resources, and your computer's performance suffers. Also, particularly within a network, another program might be waiting to use the file.

In most programming languages, if you read data from a keyboard or write it to the display monitor, you do not need to open or close the device. The keyboard and monitor are the **default input and output devices**, respectively.

A Program that Performs File Operations

Figure 7-3 contains a program that opens two files, reads employee data from the input file, alters the employee's pay rate, writes the updated record to an output file, and closes the files. The statements that use the files are shaded. The convention in this book is to place file open and close statements in parallelograms in flowcharts, because they are operations closely related to input and output.

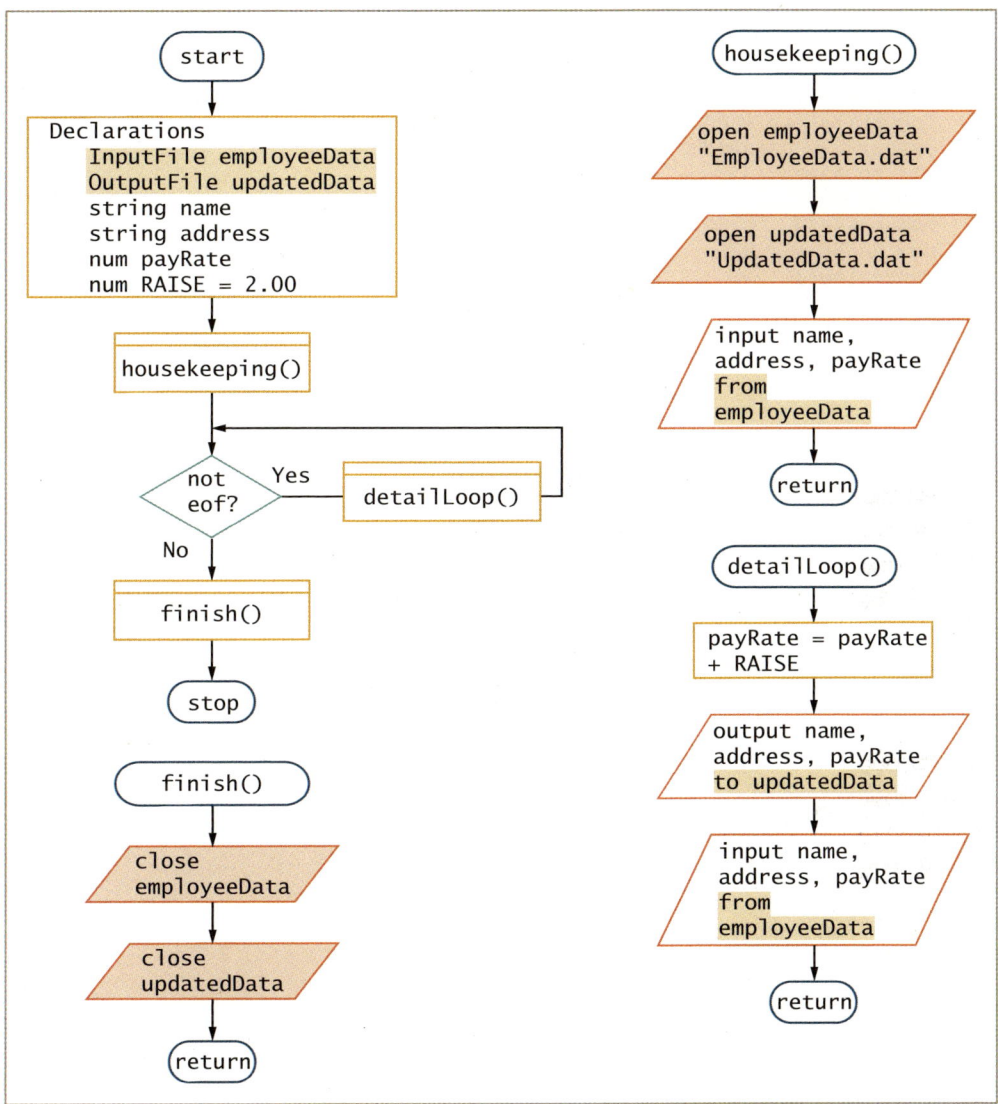

Figure 7-3 Flowchart and pseudocode for program that uses files (*continues*)

(continued)

```
start
    Declarations
        InputFile employeeData
        OutputFile updatedData
        string name
        string address
        num payRate
        num RAISE = 2.00
    housekeeping()
    while not eof
        detailLoop()
    endwhile
    finish()
stop

housekeeping()
    open employeeData "EmployeeData.dat"
    open updatedData "UpdatedData.dat"
    input name, address, payRate from employeeData
return

detailLoop()
    payRate = payRate + RAISE
    output name, address, payRate to updatedData
    input name, address, payRate from employeeData
return

finish()
    close employeeData
    close updatedData
return
```

Figure 7-3 Flowchart and pseudocode for program that uses files

In the program in Figure 7-3, each employee's data is read into memory. Then the `payRate` variable in memory is increased by $2.00. The value of the pay rate on the input storage device is not altered. After the employee's pay rate is increased, the name, address, and newly altered pay rate values are stored in the output file. When processing is complete, the input file retains the original data and the output file contains the revised data. Many organizations would keep the original file as a backup file. A **backup file** is a copy that is kept in case values need to be restored to their original state. The backup copy is called a **parent file** and the newly revised copy is a **child file**.

 Logically, the verbs *print*, *write*, and *display* mean the same thing—all produce output. However, in conversation, programmers usually reserve the word *print* for situations in which they mean *produce hard copy output*. Programmers are more likely to use *write* when talking about sending records to a data file and *display* when sending records to a monitor. In some programming languages, there is no difference in the verb used for output regardless of the hardware; you simply assign different output devices (such as printers, monitors, and disk drives) as needed to programmer-named objects that represent them.

Understanding Sequential Files and Control Break Logic

 Watch the video *File Operations*.

Throughout this book you have been encouraged to think of input as basically the same process, whether it comes from a user typing interactively at a keyboard or from a stored file on a disk or other media. The concept remains valid for this chapter, which discusses applications that commonly use stored file data. While data used by an application could be entered on a keyboard during program execution, this chapter assumes that data items have been entered, validated, and sorted earlier in another application, and then processed as input from files to achieve the results.

Sorting is the process of placing records in order by the value in a specific field or fields. Files can be sorted manually before they are saved, or a program can sort them. You can learn about sorting techniques in Chapter 8 of the comprehensive version of this book; in this chapter, it is assumed that the record sorting process has already been accomplished.

TWO TRUTHS & A LIE
Performing File Operations

1. You give a file an internal name in a program and then associate it with the operating system's name for the file.
2. When you read from a file, you copy values from memory to a storage device.
3. If you fail to close an input file, usually no serious consequences will occur; the data still exists in the file.

The false statement is #2. When you read from a file, you copy values from a storage device into memory. When you write to a file, you copy values from memory to a storage device.

Understanding Sequential Files and Control Break Logic

A **sequential file** is a file in which records are stored one after another in some order. Frequently, records in a sequential file are organized based on the contents of one or more fields. Examples of sequential files include:

- A file of employees stored in order by ID number
- A file of parts for a manufacturing company stored in order by part number
- A file of customers for a business stored in alphabetical order by last name

Understanding Control Break Logic

A **control break** is a temporary detour in the logic of a program. In particular, programmers use a **control break program** when a change in a value initiates special actions or processing. You usually write control break programs to organize output for programs that handle data records organized logically in groups based on the value in a field or fields. As you read records, you examine the same field in each record, and when you encounter a record that contains a different value from the ones that preceded it, you perform a special action. For example, you might generate a report that lists all company clients in order by state of residence, with a count of clients after each state's client list. See Figure 7-4 for an example of a **control break report** that breaks after each change in state.

```
Company Clients by State of Residence

Name            City              State

Albertson       Birmingham        Alabama
Davis           Birmingham        Alabama
Lawrence        Montgomery        Alabama
                                  Count for Alabama    3

Smith           Anchorage         Alaska
Young           Anchorage         Alaska
Davis           Fairbanks         Alaska
Mitchell        Juneau            Alaska
Zimmer          Juneau            Alaska
                                  Count for Alaska     5

Edwards         Phoenix           Arizona
                                  Count for Arizona    1
```

Figure 7-4 A control break report with totals after each state

Other examples of control break reports produced by control break programs could include:

- All employees listed in order by department number, with a new page started for each department
- All books for sale in a bookstore listed in order by category (such as reference or self-help), with a count following each category of book
- All items sold in order by date of sale, with a different ink color for each new month

Each of these reports shares two traits:

- The records used in each report are listed in order by a specific variable: state, department, category, or date.
- When that variable changes, the program takes special action: it starts a new page, prints a count or total, or switches ink color.

Understanding Sequential Files and Control Break Logic

To generate a control break report, your input records must be organized in sequential order based on the field that will cause the breaks. In other words, to write a program that produces a report of customers by state, like the one in Figure 7-4, the records must be grouped by state before you begin processing. Frequently, this grouping will mean placing the records in alphabetical order by state, although they could just as easily be ordered by population, governor's name, or any other factor, as long as all of one state's records are together.

With some newer languages, such as SQL, the details of control breaks are handled automatically. Still, understanding how control break programs work improves your competence as a programmer.

Suppose that you have an input file that contains client names, cities, and states, and you want to produce a report like the one in Figure 7-4. The basic logic of the program works like this:

- Each time you read a client's record from the input file, you determine whether the client resides in the same state as the previous client.
- If so, you simply output the client's data, add 1 to a counter, and read another record, without any special processing. If there are 20 clients in a state, these steps are repeated 20 times in a row—read a client's data, count it, and output it.
- Eventually you will read a record for a client who is not in the same state. At that point, before you output the data for the first client in the new state, you must output the count for the previous state. You also must reset the counter to 0 so it is ready to start counting customers in the next state. Then you can proceed to handle client records for the new state, and you continue to do so until the next time you encounter a client from a different state.

This type of program contains a **single-level control break**, a break in the logic of the program (in this case, pausing or detouring to output a count) that is based on the value of a single variable (in this case, the state). The technique you must use to "remember" the old state so you can compare it with each new client's state is to create a special variable, called a **control break field**, to hold the previous state. As you read each new record, comparing the new and old state values determines when it is time to output the count for the previous state.

Figure 7-5 shows the mainline logic and getReady() module for a program that produces the report in Figure 7-4. In the mainline logic, the control break variable oldState is declared in the shaded statement. In the getReady() module, the report headings are output, the file is opened, and the first record is read into memory. Then, the state value in the first record is copied to the oldState variable. (See shading.) Note that it would be incorrect to initialize oldState when it is declared. When you declare the variables at the beginning of the main program, you have not yet read the first record; therefore, you don't know what the value of the first state will be. You might assume that it is *Alabama* because that is the first state alphabetically, and you might be right, but perhaps in this data set the first state is *Alaska* or even *Wyoming*. You are assured of storing the correct first state value if you copy it from the first input record.

CHAPTER 7 File Handling and Applications

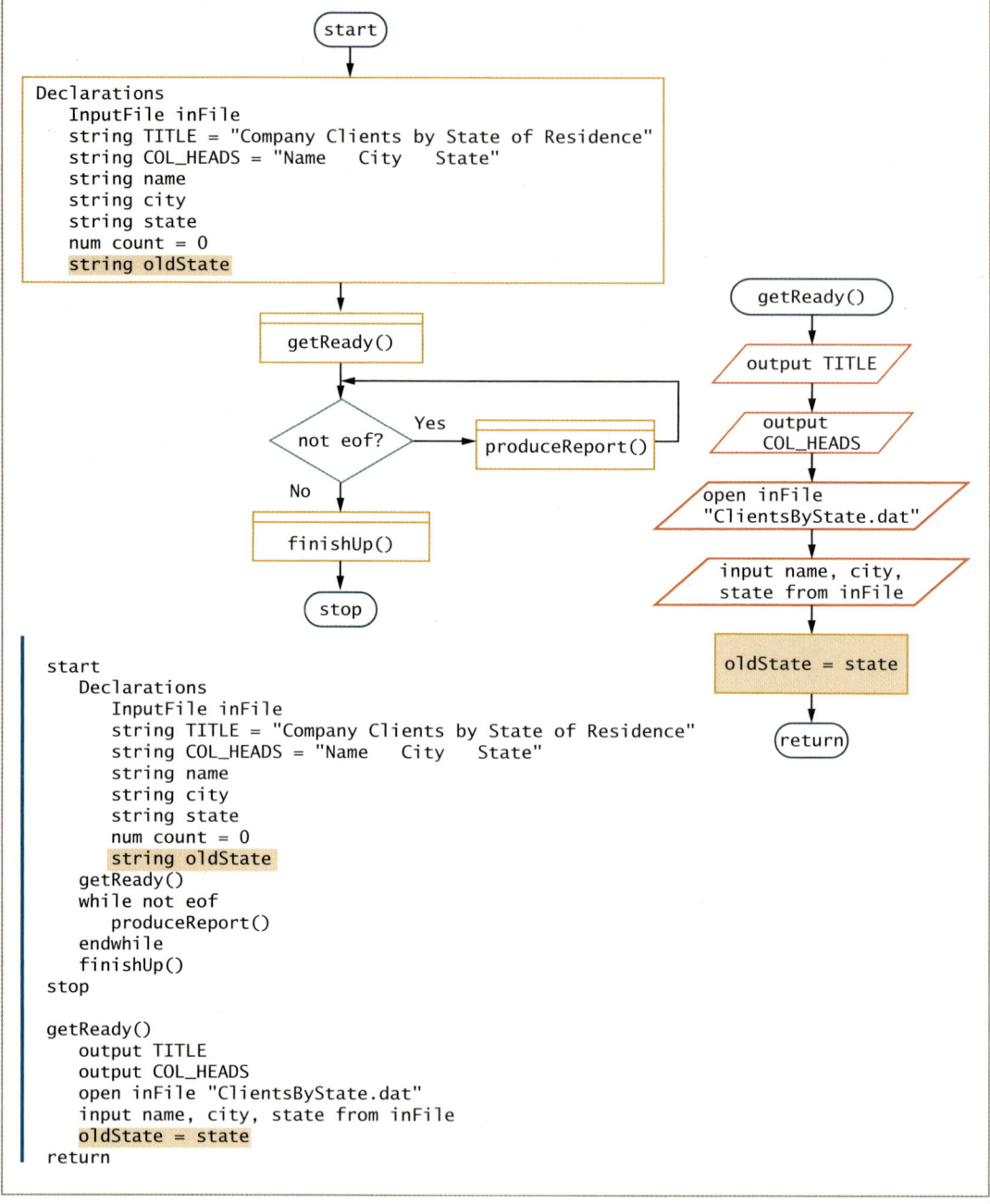

Figure 7-5 Mainline logic and `getReady()` module for the program that produces clients by state report

Within the `produceReport()` module in Figure 7-6, the first task is to check whether `state` holds the same value as `oldState`. For the first record, on the first pass through this method, the values are equal (because you set them to be equal right after getting the first input record in the `getReady()` module). Therefore, you proceed by outputting the first client's data, adding 1 to `count`, and inputting the next record.

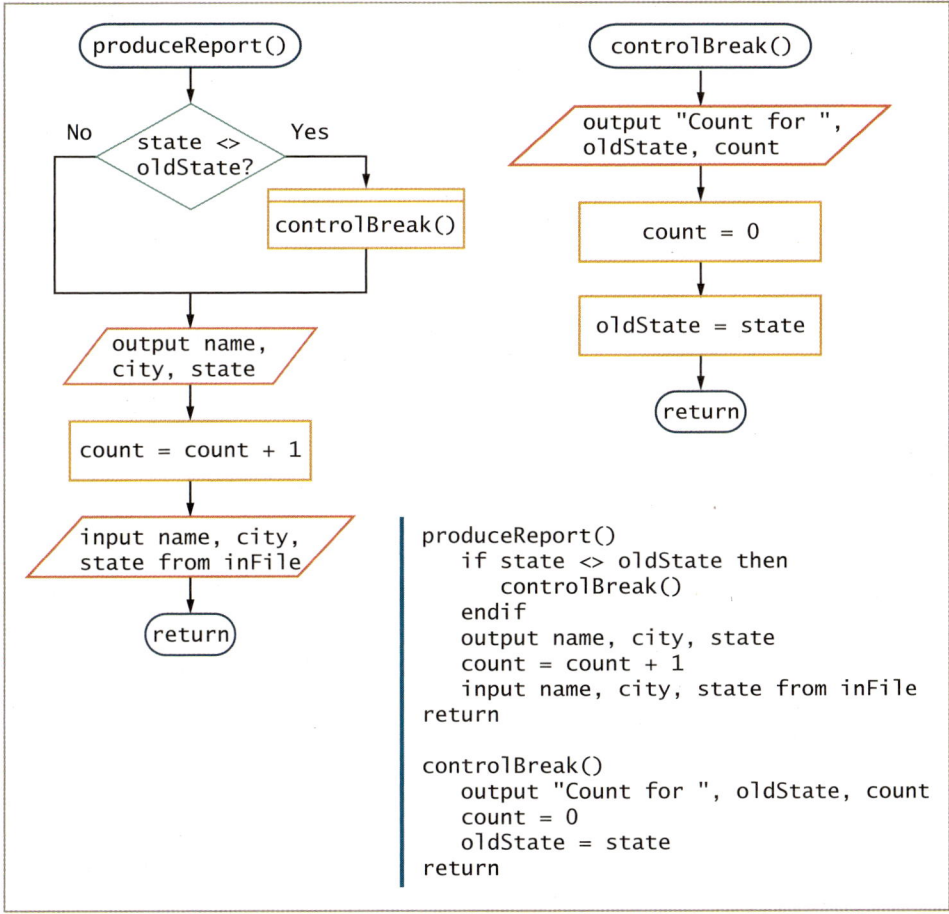

Figure 7-6 The `produceReport()` and `controlBreak()` modules for the program that produces clients by state

As long as each new record holds the same `state` value, you continue outputting, counting, and inputting, never pausing to output the count. Eventually, you will read in a client whose state is different from the previous one. That's when the control break occurs. Whenever a new state differs from the old one, three tasks must be performed:

- The count for the previous state must be output.
- The count must be reset to 0 so it can start counting records for the new state.
- The control break field must be updated.

When the produceReport() module receives a client record for which state is not the same as oldState, you cause a break in the normal flow of the program. The new client record must "wait" while the count for the just-finished state is output and count and the control break field oldState acquire new values.

The produceReport() module continues to output client names, cities, and states until the end of file is reached; then the finishUp() module executes. As shown in Figure 7-7, the module that executes after processing the last record in a control break program must complete any required processing for the last group that was handled. In this case, the finishUp() module must display the count for the last state that was processed. After the input file is closed, the logic can return to the main program, where the program ends.

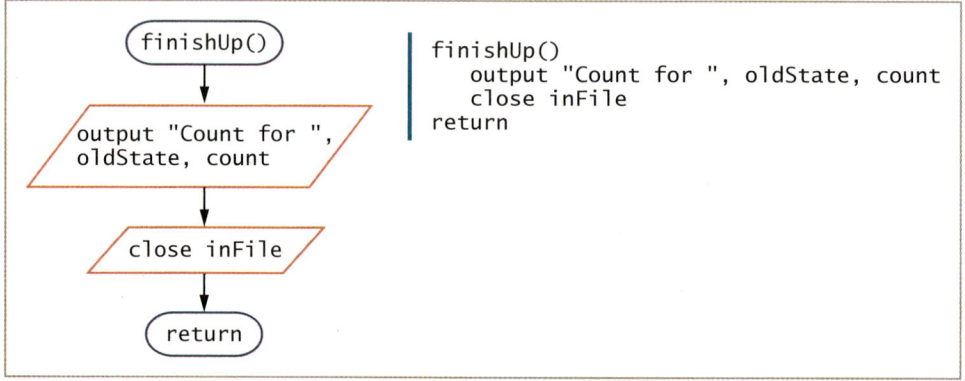

Figure 7-7 The finishUp() module for the program that produces clients by state report

 Watch the video *Control Break Logic*.

TWO TRUTHS & A LIE

Understanding Sequential Files and Control Break Logic

1. In a control break program, a change in the value of a variable initiates special actions or processing.
2. When a control break variable changes, the program takes special action.
3. To generate a control break report, your input records must be organized in sequential order based on the first field in the record.

The false statement is #3. Your input records must be organized in sequential order based on the field that will cause the breaks.

Merging Sequential Files

Businesses often need to merge two or more sequential files. **Merging files** involves combining two or more files while maintaining the sequential order. For example:

- Suppose that you have a file of current employees in ID number order and a file of newly hired employees, also in ID number order. You need to merge these two files into one combined file before running this week's payroll program.

- Suppose that you have a file of parts manufactured in the Northside factory in part-number order and a file of parts manufactured in the Southside factory, also in part-number order. You need to merge these two files into one combined file, creating a master list of available parts.

- Suppose that you have a file that lists last year's customers in alphabetical order and another file that lists this year's customers in alphabetical order. You want to create a mailing list of all customers in order by last name.

Before you can easily merge files, two conditions must be met:

- Each file must contain the same record layout.

- Each file used in the merge must be sorted in the same order based on the same field. **Ascending order** describes records in order from lowest to highest values; **descending order** describes records in order from highest to lowest values.

For example, suppose that your business has two locations, one on the East Coast and one on the West Coast, and each location maintains a customer file in alphabetical order by customer name. Each file contains fields for name and customer balance. You can call the fields in the East Coast file eastName and eastBalance, and the fields in the West Coast file westName and westBalance. You want to merge the two files, creating one combined file containing records for all customers. Figure 7-8 shows some sample data for the files; you want to create a merged file like the one shown in Figure 7-9.

East Coast File		West Coast File	
eastName	eastBalance	westName	westBalance
Able	100.00	Chen	200.00
Brown	50.00	Edgar	125.00
Dougherty	25.00	Fell	75.00
Hanson	300.00	Grand	100.00
Ingram	400.00		
Johnson	30.00		

mergedName	mergedBalance
Able	100.00
Brown	50.00
Chen	200.00
Dougherty	25.00
Edgar	125.00
Fell	75.00
Grand	100.00
Hanson	300.00
Ingram	400.00
Johnson	30.00

Figure 7-8 Sample data contained in two customer files

Figure 7-9 Merged customer file

The mainline logic for a program that merges two files is similar to the main logic you've used before in other programs: It contains preliminary, housekeeping tasks; a detail module that repeats until the end of the program; and some clean-up, end-of-job tasks. However, most programs you have studied processed records until an eof condition was met, either because an input data file reached its end or because a user entered a sentinel value in an interactive program. In a program that merges two input files, checking for eof in only one of them is insufficient. Instead, the program can check a flag variable with a name such as areBothAtEnd. For example, you might initialize a string variable areBothAtEnd to "N", but change its value to "Y" after you have encountered eof in both input files. (If the language you use supports a Boolean data type, you can use the values true and false instead of strings.)

Figure 7-10 shows the mainline logic for a program that merges the files shown in Figure 7-8. After the getReady() module executes, the shaded question that sends the logic to the finishUp() module tests the areBothAtEnd variable. When it holds "Y", the program ends.

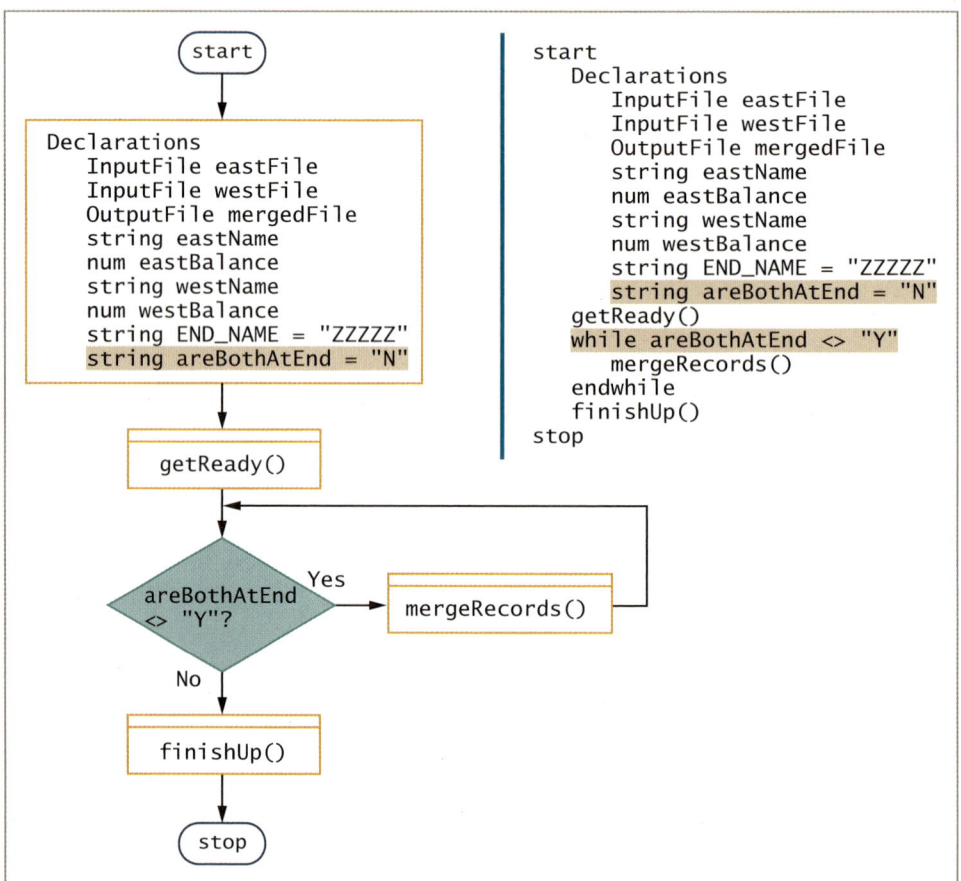

Figure 7-10 Mainline logic of a program that merges files

The getReady() module is shown in Figure 7-11. It opens three files—the input files for the east and west customers, and an output file in which to place the merged records. The program then reads one record from each input file. If either file has reached its end, the END_NAME constant is assigned to the variable that holds the file's customer name. The

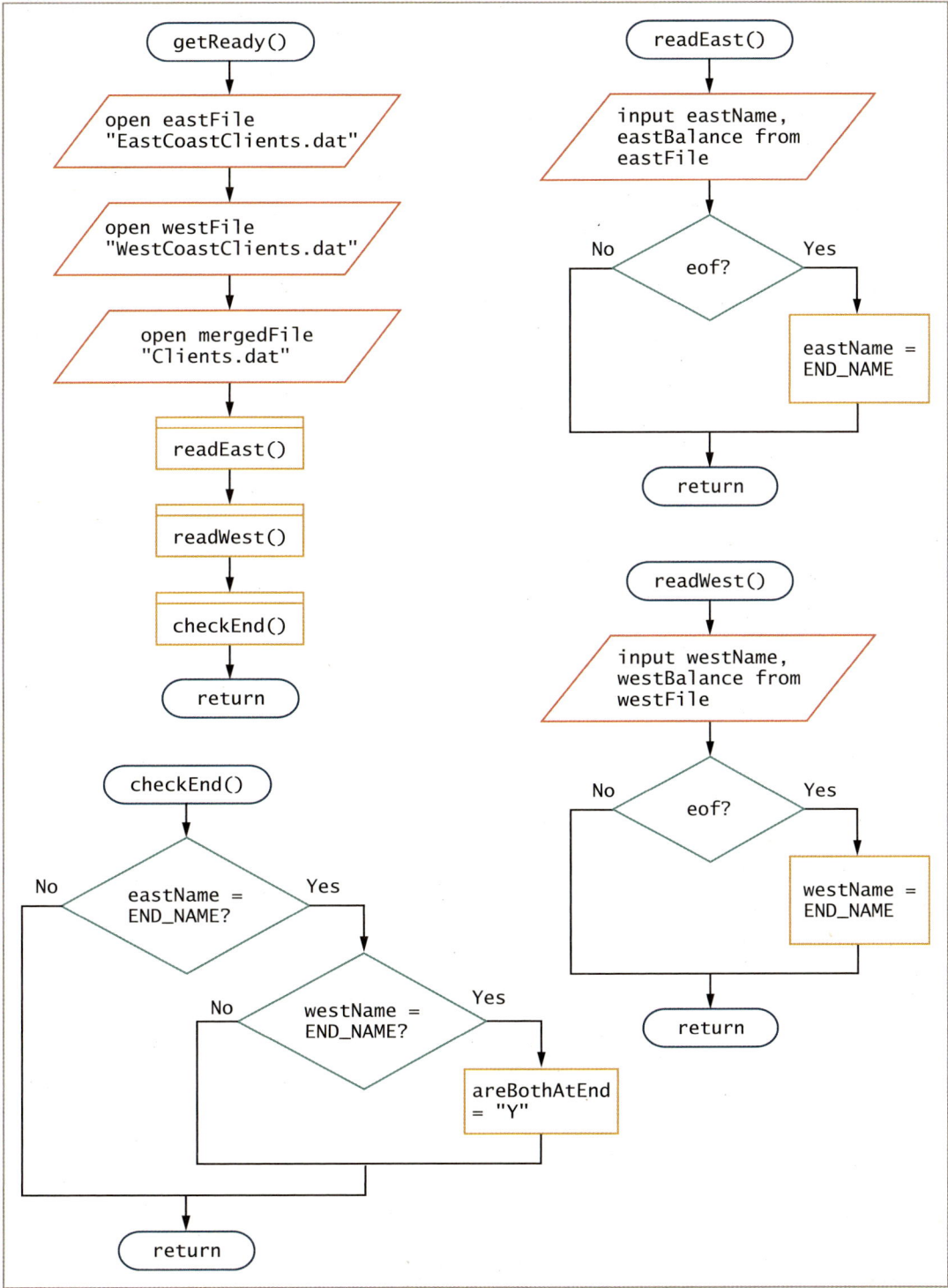

Figure 7-11 The `getReady()` module for a program that merges files, and the methods it calls (*continues*)

(continued)

```
getReady()
    open eastFile "EastCoastClients.dat"
    open westFile "WestCoastClients.dat"
    open mergedFile "Clients.dat"
    readEast()
    readWest()
    checkEnd()
return

readEast()
    input eastName, eastBalance from eastFile
    if eof then
        eastName = END_NAME
    endif
return

readWest()
    input westName, westBalance from westFile
    if eof then
        westName = END_NAME
    endif
return

checkEnd()
    if eastName = END_NAME then
        if westName = END_NAME then
            areBothAtEnd = "Y"
        endif
    endif
return
```

Figure 7-11 The `getReady()` module for a program that merges files, and the methods it calls

getReady() module then checks to see whether both files are finished (admittedly, a rare occurrence in the getReady() portion of the program's execution) and sets the areBothAtEnd flag variable to "Y" if they are. Assuming that at least one record is available, the logic then enters the mergeRecords() module.

When you begin the mergeRecords() module in the program using the files shown in Figure 7-8, two records—one from eastFile and one from westFile—are sitting in the memory of the computer. One of these records needs to be written to the new output file first. Which one? Because the two input files contain records stored in alphabetical order, and you want the new file to store records in alphabetical order, you first output the input record that has the lower alphabetical value in the name field. Therefore, the process begins as shown in Figure 7-12.

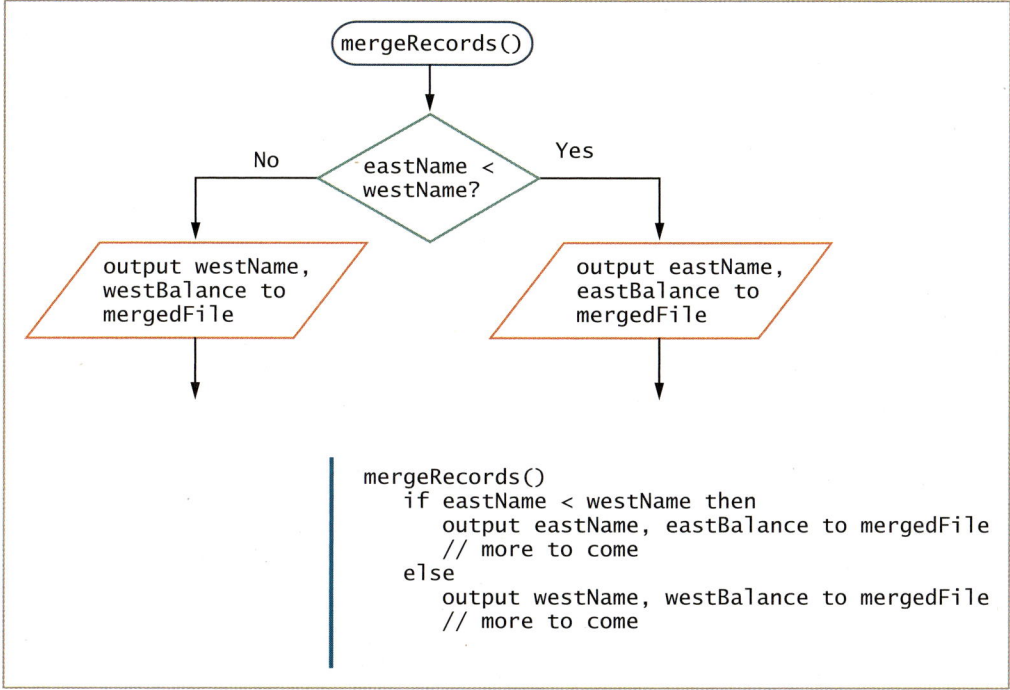

Figure 7-12   Start of merging process

Using the sample data from Figure 7-8, you can see that the *Able* record from the East Coast file should be written to the output file, while Chen's record from the West Coast file waits in memory. The `eastName` value *Able* is alphabetically lower than the `westName` value *Chen*.

After you write Able's record, should Chen's record be written to the output file next? Not necessarily. It depends on the next `eastName` following Able's record in `eastFile`. When data records are read into memory from a file, a program typically does not "look ahead" to determine the values stored in the next record. Instead, a program usually reads the record into memory before making decisions about its contents. In this program, you need to read the next `eastFile` record into memory and compare it to *Chen*. Because in this case the next record in `eastFile` contains the name *Brown*, another `eastFile` record is written; no `westFile` records are written yet.

After the first two `eastFile` records, is it Chen's turn to be written now? You really don't know until you read another record from `eastFile` and compare its name value to *Chen*. Because this record contains the name *Dougherty*, it is indeed time to write Chen's record. After Chen's record is written, should you now write Dougherty's record? Until you read the next record from `westFile`, you don't know whether that record should be placed before or after Dougherty's record.

Therefore, the merging method proceeds like this: compare two records, write the record with the lower alphabetical name, and read another record from the *same* input file. See Figure 7-13.

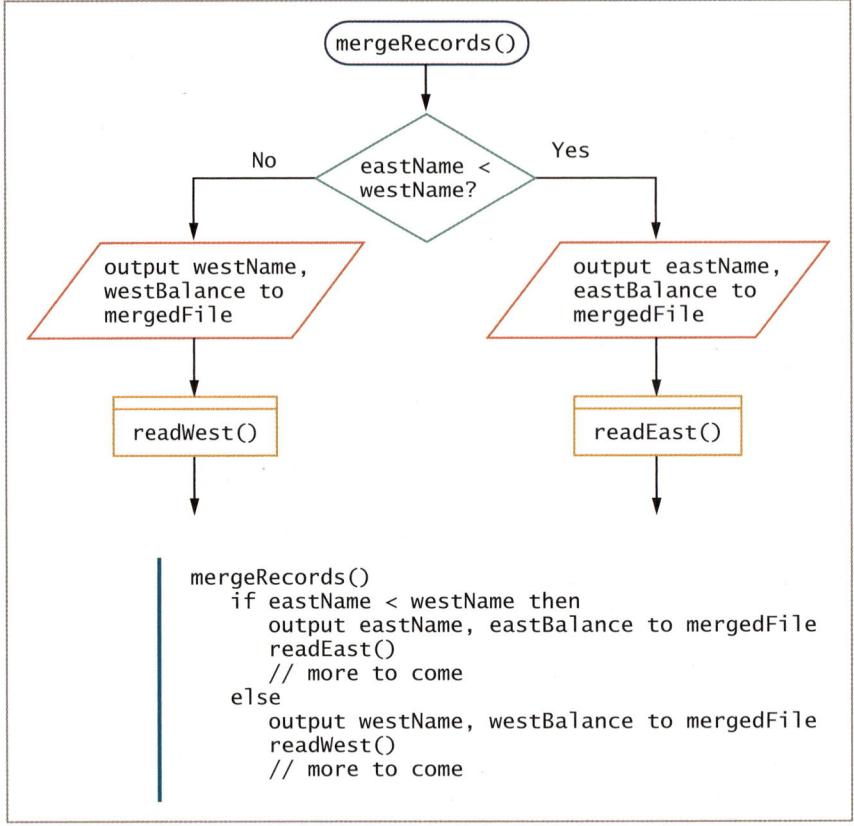

Figure 7-13 Continuation of merging process

Recall the names from the two original files in Figure 7-8, and walk through the processing steps.

1. Compare *Able* and *Chen*. Write Able's record. Read Brown's record from `eastFile`.
2. Compare *Brown* and *Chen*. Write Brown's record. Read Dougherty's record from `eastFile`.
3. Compare *Dougherty* and *Chen*. Write Chen's record. Read Edgar's record from `westFile`.
4. Compare *Dougherty* and *Edgar*. Write Dougherty's record. Read Hanson's record from `eastFile`.
5. Compare *Hanson* and *Edgar*. Write Edgar's record. Read Fell's record from `westFile`.
6. Compare *Hanson* and *Fell*. Write Fell's record. Read Grand's record from `westFile`.
7. Compare *Hanson* and *Grand*. Write Grand's record. Read from `westFile`, encountering `eof`. This causes `westName` to be set to `END_NAME`.

What happens when you reach the end of the West Coast file? Is the program over? It shouldn't be because records for Hanson, Ingram, and Johnson all need to be included in the new output file, and none of them are written yet. Because the `westName` field is set to `END_NAME`, and `END_NAME` has a very high alphabetic value (*ZZZZZ*), each subsequent `eastName` will be lower than the value of `westName`, and the rest of the `eastName` file will be processed. With a different set of data, the `eastFile` might have ended first. In that case, `eastName` would be set to `END_NAME`, and each subsequent `westFile` record would be processed.

Figure 7-14 shows the complete `mergeRecords()` module and the `finishUp()` module.

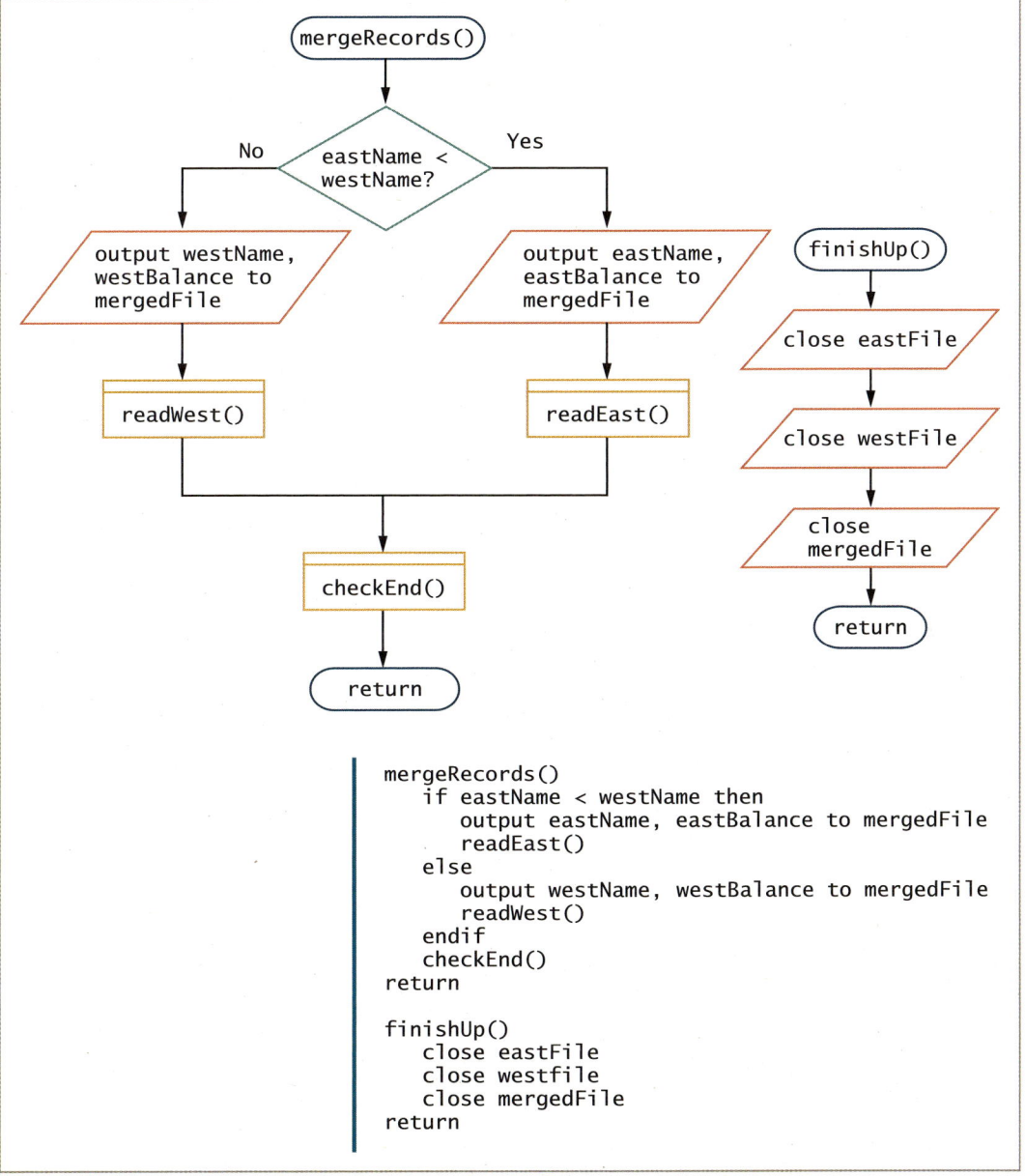

Figure 7-14   The `mergeRecords()` and `finishUp()` modules for the file-merging program

As the value for END_NAME, you might choose to use 10 or 20 Zs instead of only five. Although it is unlikely that a person will have the last name ZZZZZ, you should make sure that the high value you choose is actually higher than any legitimate value.

After Grand's record is processed, `westFile` is read and `eof` is encountered, so `westName` gets set to END_NAME. Now, when you enter the loop again, `eastName` and `westName` are compared, and `eastName` is still *Hanson*. The `eastName` value (*Hanson*) is lower than the `westName` value (*ZZZZZ*), so the data for `eastName`'s record is written to the output file, and another `eastFile` record (*Ingram*) is read.

The complete run of the file-merging program now executes the first six of the seven steps listed previously, and then proceeds as shown in Figure 7-14 and as follows, starting with a modified Step 7:

7. Compare *Hanson* and *Grand*. Write Grand's record. Read from `westFile`, encountering `eof` and setting `westName` to *ZZZZZ*.

8. Compare *Hanson* and *ZZZZZ*. Write Hanson's record. Read Ingram's record.

9. Compare *Ingram* and *ZZZZZ*. Write Ingram's record. Read Johnson's record.

10. Compare *Johnson* and *ZZZZZ*. Write Johnson's record. Read from `eastFile`, encountering `eof` and setting `eastName` to *ZZZZZ*.

11. Now that both names are *ZZZZZ*, set the flag `areBothAtEnd` equal to "Y".

When the `areBothAtEnd` flag variable equals "Y", the loop is finished, the files are closed, and the program ends.

If two names are equal during the merge process—for example, when there is a Hanson record in each file—then both Hansons will be included in the final file. When `eastName` and `westName` match, `eastName` is not lower than `westName`, so you write the `westFile` Hanson record. After you read the next `westFile` record, `eastName` will be lower than the next `westName`, and the `eastFile` Hanson record will be output. A more complicated merge program could check another field, such as first name, when last-name values match.

You can merge any number of files. To merge more than two files, the logic is only slightly more complicated; you must compare the key fields from all the files before deciding which file is the next candidate for output.

Watch the video *Merging Files*.

> **TWO TRUTHS & A LIE**
>
> **Merging Sequential Files**
>
> 1. A sequential file is a file in which records are stored one after another in some order. Most frequently, the records are stored based on the contents of one or more fields within each record.
>
> 2. Merging files involves combining two or more files while maintaining the sequential order.
>
> 3. Before you can easily merge files, each file must contain the same number of records.
>
> The false statement is #3. Before you can easily merge files, each file must contain the same record layout and each file used in the merge must be sorted in the same order based on the same field.

Master and Transaction File Processing

In the last section, you learned how to merge related sequential files in which each record in each file contained the same fields. Some related sequential files, however, do not contain the same fields. Instead, some related files have a master-transaction relationship. A **master file** holds complete and relatively permanent data; a **transaction file** holds more temporary data. For example, a master customer file might hold customers' names, addresses, and phone numbers, and a customer transaction file might contain data that describes each customer's most recent purchase.

Commonly, you gather transactions for a period of time, store them in a file, and then use them one by one to update matching records in a master file. You **update the master file** by making appropriate changes to the values in its fields based on the recent transactions. For example, a file containing transaction purchase data for a customer might be used to update each balance due field in a customer record master file.

Here are a few other examples of files that have a master-transaction relationship:

- A library maintains a master file of all patrons and a transaction file with information about each book or other items checked out.

- A college maintains a master file of all students and a transaction file for each course registration.

CHAPTER 7 File Handling and Applications

- A telephone company maintains a master file for every telephone line (number) and a transaction file with information about every call.

When you update a master file, you can take two approaches:

- You can actually change the information in the master file. When you use this approach, the information that existed in the master file prior to the transaction processing is lost.

- You can create a copy of the master file, making the changes in the new version. Then, you can store the previous, parent version of the master file for a period of time, in case there are questions or discrepancies regarding the update process. The updated, child version of the file becomes the new master file used in subsequent processing. This approach is used in a program later in this chapter.

When a child file is updated, it becomes a parent, and its parent becomes a grandparent. Individual organizations create policies concerning the number of generations of backup files they will save before discarding them. The terms *parent* and *child* refer to file backup generations, but they are used for a different purpose in object-oriented programming. When you base a class on another using inheritance, the original class is the parent and the derived class is the child. You can learn about these concepts in Chapters 10 and 11 of the comprehensive version of this book.

The logic you use to perform a match between master and transaction file records is similar to the logic you use to perform a merge. As with a merge, you must begin with both files sorted in the same order on the same field. Figure 7-15 shows the mainline logic for a program that matches files. The master file contains a customer number, name, and a field that holds the total dollar amount of all purchases the customer has made previously. The transaction file holds data for sales, including a transaction number, the number of the customer who made the transaction, and the amount of the transaction.

Master and Transaction File Processing

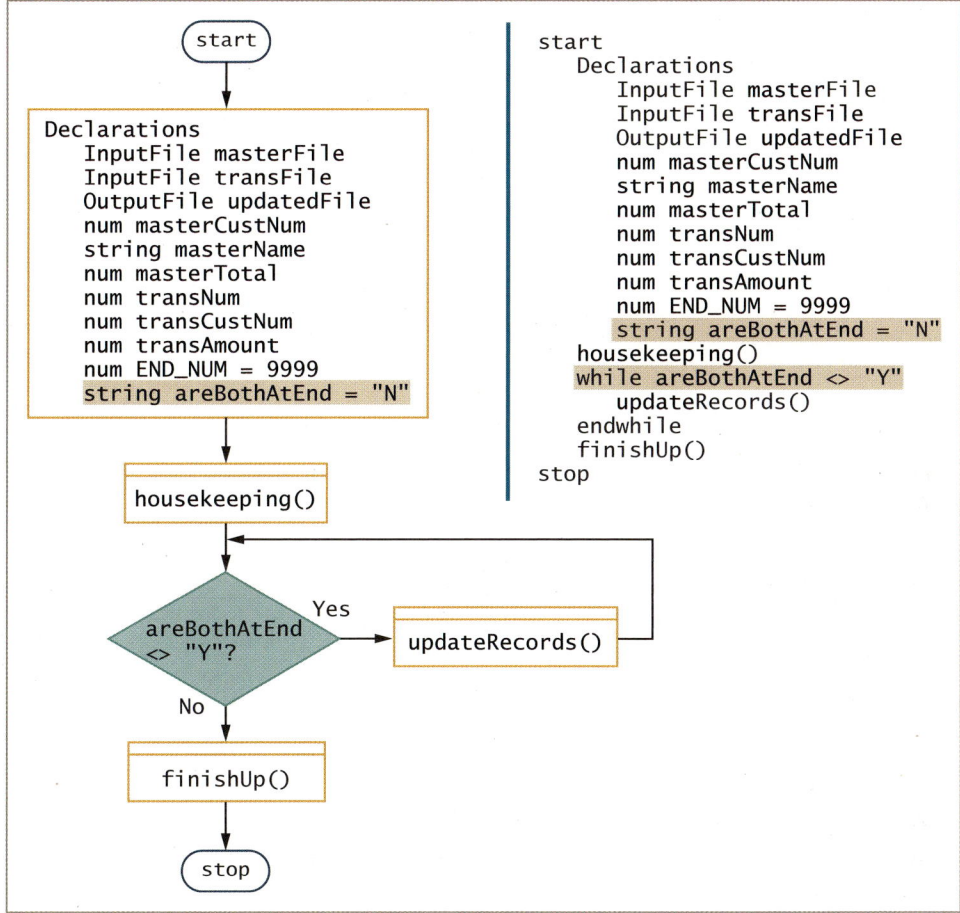

Figure 7-15 The mainline logic for the master-transaction program

Figure 7-16 contains the `housekeeping()` module for the program, and the modules it calls. These modules are very similar to their counterparts in the file-merging program earlier in the chapter. When the program begins, one record is read from each file. When any file ends, the field used for matching is set to a high value, 9999, and when both files end, a flag variable is set so the mainline logic can test for the end of processing. In the file-merging program presented earlier in this chapter, you placed the string "ZZZZZ" in the customer name field at the end of the file because string fields were being compared. In this example, because you are using numeric fields (customer numbers), you can store 9999 in them at the end of the file. The assumption is that 9999 is higher than any valid customer number.

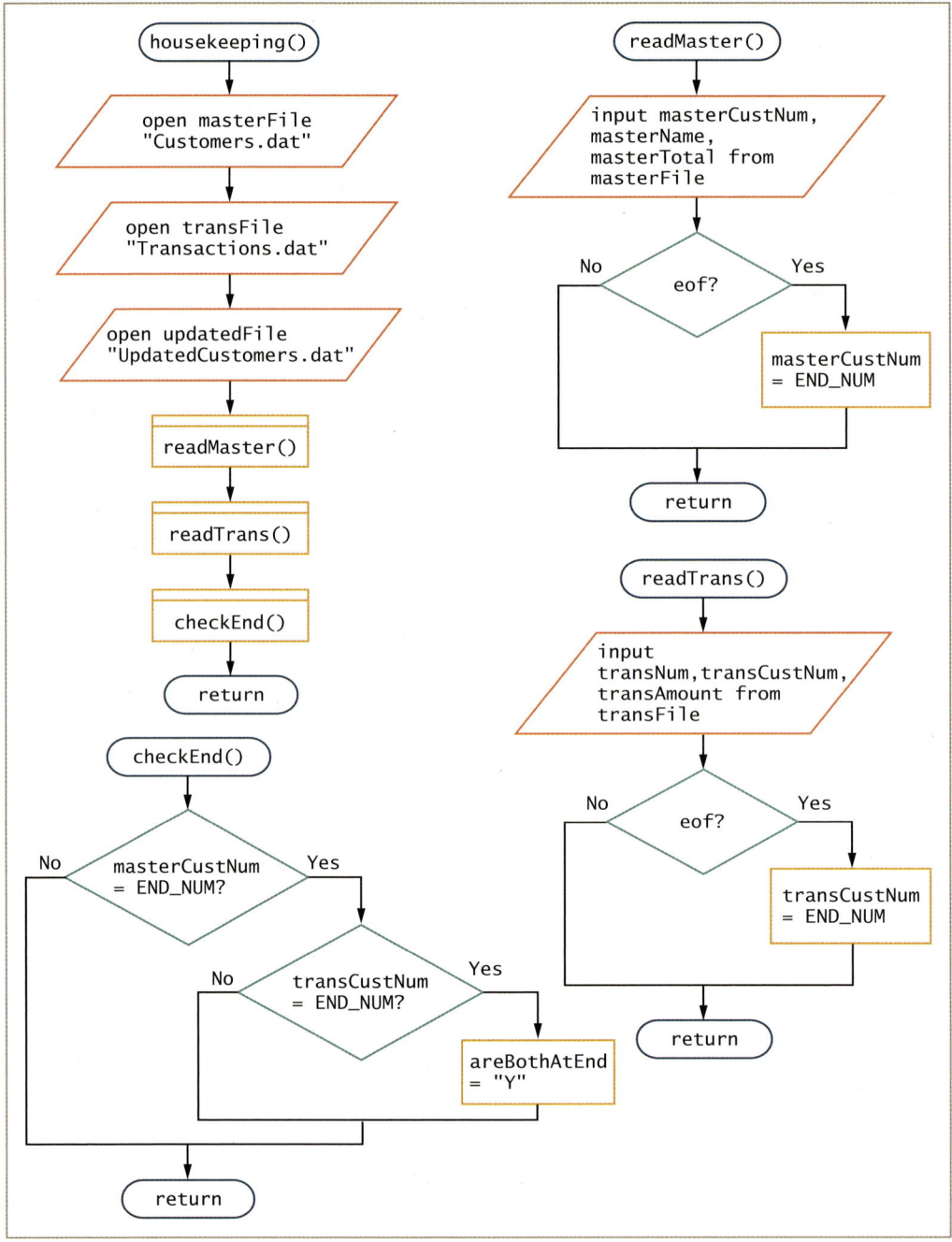

Figure 7-16 The `housekeeping()` module for the master-transaction program, and the modules it calls (*continues*)

(continued)

```
housekeeping()
   open masterFile "Customers.dat"
   open transFile "Transactions.dat"
   open updatedFile "UpdatedCustomers.dat"
   readMaster()
   readTrans()
   checkEnd()
return

readMaster()
   input masterCustNum, masterName, masterTotal from masterFile
   if not eof then
      masterCustNum = END_NUM
   endif
return

readTrans()
   input transNum, transCustNum, transAmount from transFile
   if not eof then
      transCustNum = END_NUM
   endif
return

checkEnd()
   if masterCustNum = END_NUM then
      if transCustNum = END_NUM then
         areBothAtEnd = "Y"
      endif
   endif
return
```

Figure 7-16 The `housekeeping()` module for the master-transaction program, and the modules it calls

Imagine that you will update master file records by hand instead of using a computer program, and imagine that each master and transaction record is stored on a separate piece of paper. The easiest way to accomplish the update is to sort all the master records by customer number and place them in a stack, and then sort all the transactions by customer number (not transaction number) and place them in another stack. You then would examine the first transaction and look through the master records until you found a match. Any master records without transactions would be placed in a "completed" stack without changes. When a transaction matched a master record, you would correct the master record using the new transaction amount, and then go on to the next transaction. Of course, if there is no matching master record for a transaction, then you would realize an error had occurred, and you would probably set the transaction aside before continuing. The `updateRecords()` module works exactly the same way.

In the file-merging program presented earlier in this chapter, your first action in the program's detail loop was to determine which file held the record with the lower value; then, you wrote that record. In a matching program, you are trying to determine not only whether one file's comparison field is larger than another's; it's also important to know if they are *equal*. In this example, you want to update the master file record's masterTotal field only if the transaction record transCustNum field contains an exact match for the customer number in the master file record. Therefore, you compare masterCustNum from the master file and transCustNum from the transaction file. Three possibilities exist:

- The transCustNum value equals masterCustNum. In this case, you add transAmount to masterTotal and then write the updated master record to the output file. Then, you read in both a new master record and a new transaction record.

- The transCustNum value is higher than masterCustNum. This means a sale was not recorded for that customer. That's all right; not every customer makes a transaction every period, so you simply write the original customer record with exactly the same information it contained when input. Then, you get the next customer record to see if this customer made the transaction currently under examination.

- The transCustNum value is lower than masterCustNum. This means you are trying to apply a transaction for which no master record exists, so there must be an error, because a transaction should always have a master record. You can handle this error in a variety of ways; here, you will write an error message to an output device before reading the next transaction record. A human operator can then read the message and take appropriate action.

The logic used here assumes that there can be only one transaction per customer. In the exercises at the end of this chapter, you will develop the logic for a program in which the customer can have multiple transactions.

Whether transCustNum was higher than, lower than, or equal to masterCustNum, after reading the next transaction or master record (or both), you check whether both masterCustNum and transCustNum have been set to 9999. When both are 9999, you set the areBothAtEnd flag to "Y".

Figure 7-17 shows the updateRecords() module that carries out the logic of the file-matching process. Figure 7-18 shows some sample data you can use to walk through the logic for this program.

Master and Transaction File Processing

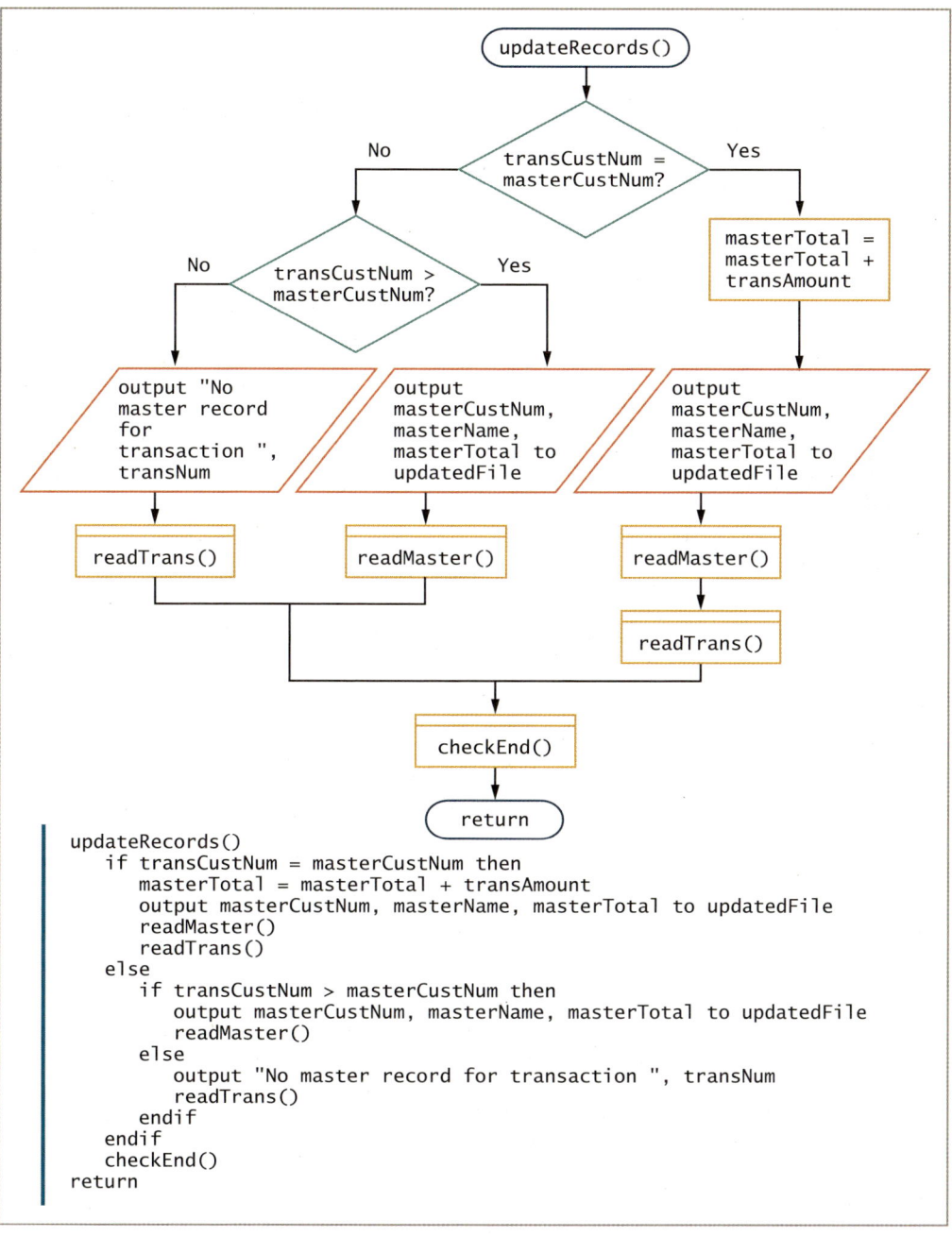

Figure 7-17 The `updateRecords()` module for the master-transaction program

CHAPTER 7   File Handling and Applications

Master File		Transaction File	
masterCustNum	masterTotal	transCustNum	transAmount
100	1000.00	100	400.00
102	50.00	105	700.00
103	500.00	108	100.00
105	75.00	110	400.00
106	5000.00		
109	4000.00		
110	500.00		

Figure 7-18   Sample data for the file-matching program

The program proceeds as follows:

1. Read customer 100 from the master file and customer 100 from the transaction file. Customer numbers are equal, so 400.00 from the transaction file is added to 1000.00 in the master file, and a new master file record is written with a 1400.00 total sales figure. Then, read a new record from each input file.

2. The customer number in the master file is 102 and the customer number in the transaction file is 105, so there are no transactions today for customer 102. Write the master record exactly the way it came in, and read a new master record.

3. Now, the master customer number is 103 and the transaction customer number is still 105. This means customer 103 has no transactions, so you write the master record as is and read a new one.

4. Now, the master customer number is 105 and the transaction number is 105. Because customer 105 had a 75.00 balance and now has a 700.00 transaction, the new total sales figure for the master file is 775.00, and a new master record is written. Read one record from each file.

5. Now, the master number is 106 and the transaction number is 108. Write customer record 106 as is, and read another master.

6. Now, the master number is 109 and the transaction number is 108. An error has occurred. The transaction record indicates that you made a sale to customer 108, but there is no master record for customer number 108. Either the transaction is incorrect (there is an error in the transaction's customer number) or the transaction is correct but you have failed to create a master record. Either way, write an error message so that a clerk is notified and can handle the problem. Then, get a new transaction record.

7. Now, the master number is 109 and the transaction number is 110. Write master record 109 with no changes and read a new one.

Master and Transaction File Processing

8. Now, the master number is 110 and the transaction number is 110. Add the 400.00 transaction to the previous 500.00 balance in the master file, and write a new master record with 900.00 in the `masterTotal` field. Read one record from each file.

9. Because both files are finished, end the job. The result is a new master file in which some records contain exactly the same data they contained going in, but others (for which a transaction has occurred) have been updated with a new total sales figure. The original master and transaction files that were used as input can be saved for a period of time as backups.

Figure 7-19 shows the `finishUp()` module for the program. After all the files are closed, the updated master customer file contains all the customer records it originally contained, and each holds a current total based on the recent group of transactions.

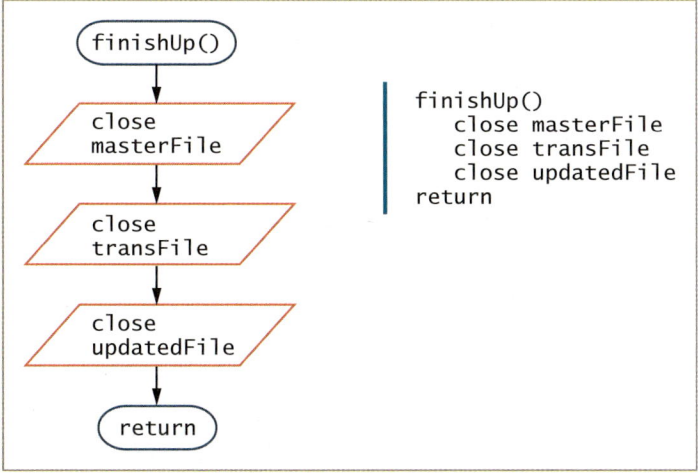

Figure 7-19   The `finishUp()` module for the master-transaction program

---

TWO TRUTHS & A LIE

Master and Transaction File Processing

1. You use a master file to hold temporary data related to transaction file records.
2. You use a transaction file to hold data that is used to update a master file.
3. The saved version of a master file is the parent file; the updated version is the child file.

The false statement is #1. You use a master file to hold relatively permanent data.

Random Access Files

The examples of files that have been written to and read from in this chapter are sequential access files, which means that you access the records in sequential order from beginning to end. For example, if you wrote an employee record with an ID number 234, and then you created a second record with an ID number 326, you would see when you retrieved the records that they remain in the original data-entry order. Businesses store data in sequential order when they use the records for **batch processing**, or processing that involves performing the same tasks with many records, one after the other. For example, when a company produces paychecks, the records for the pay period are gathered in a batch and the checks are calculated and printed in sequence. It really doesn't matter whose check is produced first because none are distributed to employees until all have been printed. Batch processing usually implies some delay in processing. That is, records are gathered over a period of time and then processed together later. For example, when a company produces paychecks, the records might be gathered every day for two weeks before processing occurs.

 Besides indicating a system that works with many records, the term *batch processing* can also mean a system in which you issue many operating system commands as a group.

For many applications, sequential access is inefficient. These applications, known as **real-time** applications, require that a record be accessed immediately while a client is waiting. A program in which the user makes direct requests is an **interactive program**. For example, if a customer telephones a department store with a question about a monthly bill, the customer service representative does not need or want to access every customer account in sequence. With tens of thousands of account records to read, it would take too long to access the customer's record. Instead, customer service representatives require **random access files**, files in which records can be located in any order. Files in which records must be accessed immediately are also called **instant access files**. Because they enable you to locate a particular record directly (without reading all of the preceding records), random access files are also called **direct access files**. You can declare a random access file with a statement similar to the following:

`RandomFile customerFile`

You associate this name with a stored file in the same manner that you associate an identifier with sequential input and output files. You also can use read, write, and close operations with a random access file. However, with random access files you have the additional capability to find a record directly. For example, you might be able to use a statement similar to the following to find customer number 712 on a random access file:

`seek record 712`

This feature is particularly useful in random access processing. Consider a business with 20,000 customer accounts. When the customer who has the 14,607th record in the file acquires a new telephone number, it is convenient to access the 14,607th record directly, writing the new telephone number to the file in the location where the old number was previously stored.

TWO TRUTHS & A LIE

Random Access Files

1. A batch program usually uses instant access files.
2. In a real-time application, a record is accessed immediately while a client is waiting.
3. An interactive program usually uses random access files.

The false statement is #1. A batch program usually uses sequential files; interactive programs use random, instant access files.

CHAPTER 7: File Handling and Applications

Chapter Summary

- A computer file is a collection of data stored on a nonvolatile device in a computer system. Although the contents of files differ, each file occupies space on a section of a storage device, and each has a name and specific times associated with it. Computer files are organized in directories or folders. A file's complete list of directories is its path.

- Data items in a file usually are stored in a hierarchy. Characters are letters, numbers, and special symbols, such as *A*, *7*, and *$*. Fields are data items that represent a single attribute of a record and are composed of one or more characters. Records are groups of fields that go together for some logical reason. Files are groups of related records.

- When you use a data file in a program, you must declare the file and open it; opening a file associates an internal program identifier with the name of a physical file on a storage device. When you read from a file, the data is copied into memory. When you write to a file, the data is copied from memory to a storage device. When you are done with a file, you close it.

- A sequential file is a file in which records are stored one after another in some order. A control break program is one that reads a sequential file and performs special processing based on a change in one or more fields in each record in the file.

- Merging files involves combining two or more files while maintaining the sequential order.

- Some related sequential files are master files that hold relatively permanent data, and transaction files that hold more temporary data. Commonly, you gather transactions for a period of time, store them in a file, and then use them one by one to update matching records in a master file.

- Real-time, interactive applications require random access files in which records can be located in any order. Files in which records must be accessed immediately are also called instant access files and direct access files.

Key Terms

A **computer file** is a collection of data stored on a nonvolatile device in a computer system.

Permanent storage devices hold nonvolatile data; examples include hard disks, DVDs, USB drives, and reels of magnetic tape.

Text files contain data that can be read in a text editor.

Binary files contain data that has not been encoded as text.

A **byte** is a small unit of storage; for example, in a simple text file, a byte holds only one character.

A **kilobyte** is approximately 1000 bytes.

A **megabyte** is a million bytes.

A **gigabyte** is a billion bytes.

Directories are organization units on storage devices; each can contain multiple files as well as additional directories. In a graphic system, directories are often called *folders*.

Folders are organization units on storage devices; each can contain multiple files as well as additional folders. Folders are graphic directories.

A file's **path** is the combination of its disk drive and the complete hierarchy of directories in which the file resides.

The **data hierarchy** is a framework that describes the relationships between data components. The data hierarchy contains characters, fields, records, and files.

Characters are letters, numbers, and special symbols, such as *A*, *7*, and *$*.

Fields are data items that represent a single attribute of a record and are composed of one or more characters.

Records are groups of fields that go together for some logical reason.

Files are groups of related records.

A **database** holds groups of files and provides methods for easy retrieval and organization.

Tables are files in a database.

Opening a file locates it on a storage device and associates a variable name within your program with the file.

Reading from a file copies data from a file on a storage device into RAM.

Writing to a file copies data from RAM to persistent storage.

Closing a file makes it no longer available to an application.

Default input and output devices are those that do not require opening. Usually they are the keyboard and monitor, respectively.

A **backup file** is a copy that is kept in case values need to be restored to their original state.

A **parent file** is a copy of a file before revision.

A **child file** is a copy of a file after revision.

Sorting is the process of placing records in order by the value in a specific field or fields.

A **sequential file** is a file in which records are stored one after another in some order.

A **control break** is a temporary detour in the logic of a program.

A **control break program** is one in which a change in the value of a variable initiates special actions or processing.

A **control break report** is a form of output that includes special processing after each group of records.

A **single-level control break** is a break in the logic of a program to perform special processing based on the value of a single variable.

A **control break field** holds a value that causes special processing in a control break program.

Merging files involves combining two or more files while maintaining the sequential order.

Ascending order describes records placed in order from lowest to highest based on the value in a field.

Descending order describes records placed in order from highest to lowest based on the value in some field.

A **master file** holds complete and relatively permanent data.

A **transaction file** holds temporary data that you use to update a master file.

To **update a master file** involves making changes to the values in its fields based on transactions.

Batch processing involves performing the same tasks with many records, one after the other.

Real-time applications require that a record be accessed immediately while a client is waiting.

In an **interactive program**, the user makes direct requests, as opposed to one in which input comes from a file.

In **random access files**, records can be located in any order.

Instant access files are random access files in which records must be accessed immediately.

Direct access files are random access files.

Review Questions

1. Random access memory is _____.

   a. permanent
   b. volatile
   c. persistent
   d. continual

2. Which is true of text files?

   a. Text files contain data that can be read in a text editor.
   b. Text files commonly contain images and music.
   c. both of the above
   d. none of the above

3. Every file on a storage device has a _____.

   a. name
   b. size
   c. both of the above
   d. none of the above

4. Which of the following is true regarding the data hierarchy?

   a. Files contain records.
   b. Characters contain fields.
   c. Fields contain files.
   d. Fields contain records.

5. The process of _____ a file locates it on a storage device and associates a variable name within your program with the file.

   a. opening
   b. closing
   c. declaring
   d. defining

6. When you write to a file, you _____.

   a. move data from a storage device to memory
   b. copy data from a storage device to memory
   c. move data from memory to a storage device
   d. copy data from memory to a storage device

7. Unlike when you print a report, when a program's output is a data file, you do not _____.

   a. include headings or other formatting
   b. open the files
   c. include all the fields represented as input
   d. all of the above

8. When you close a file, it _____.

   a. is no longer available to the program
   b. cannot be reopened
   c. becomes associated with an internal identifier
   d. ceases to exist

Review Questions

9. A file in which records are stored one after another in some order is a(n) _____ file.
   a. temporal
   b. sequential
   c. random
   d. alphabetical

10. When you combine two or more sorted files while maintaining their sequential order based on a field, you are _____ the files.
    a. tracking
    b. collating
    c. merging
    d. absorbing

11. A control break occurs when a program _____.
    a. takes one of two alternate courses of action for every record
    b. ends prematurely, before all records have been processed
    c. pauses to perform special processing based on the value of a field
    d. passes logical control to a module contained within another program

12. Which of the following is an example of a control break report?
    a. a list of all customers of a business in zip code order, with a count of the number of customers who reside in each zip code
    b. a list of all students in a school, arranged in alphabetical order, with a total count at the end of the report
    c. a list of all employees in a company, with a "Retain" or "Dismiss" message following each employee record
    d. a list of medical clinic patients who have not seen a doctor for at least two years

13. A control break field _____.
    a. always is output prior to any group of records on a control break report
    b. always is output after any group of records on a control break report
    c. never is output on a report
    d. causes special processing to occur

14. Whenever a control break occurs during record processing in any control break program, you must _____.
    a. declare a control break field
    b. set the control break field to 0
    c. update the value in the control break field
    d. output the control break field

15. Assume that you are writing a program to merge two files named FallStudents and SpringStudents. Each file contains a list of students enrolled in a programming logic course during the semester indicated, and each file is sorted in student ID number order. After the program compares two records and subsequently writes a Fall student to output, the next step is to _____.
    a. read a SpringStudents record
    b. read a FallStudents record
    c. write a SpringStudents record
    d. write another FallStudents record

16. When you merge records from two or more sequential files, the usual case is that the records in the files _____.
    a. contain the same data
    b. have the same format
    c. are identical in number
    d. are sorted on different fields

17. A file that holds more permanent data than a transaction file is a _____ file.
    a. master
    b. primary
    c. key
    d. mega-

18. A transaction file is often used to _____ another file.
    a. augment
    b. remove
    c. verify
    d. update

19. The saved version of a file that does not contain the most recently applied transactions is known as a _____ file.

   a. master
   b. child
   c. parent
   d. relative

20. Random access files are used most frequently in all of the following except _____.

   a. interactive programs
   b. batch processing
   c. real-time applications
   d. programs requiring direct access

Exercises

Your downloadable files for Chapter 7 include one or more comma-delimited sample data files for each exercise in this section and the Game Zone section. You might want to use these files in any of several ways:

- You can look at the file contents to better understand the types of data each program uses.
- You can use the file contents as sample data when you desk-check the logic of your flowcharts or pseudocode.
- You can use the files as input files if you implement the solutions in a programming language and write programs that accept file input.
- You can use the data as guides for entering appropriate values if you implement the solutions in a programming language and write interactive programs.

   1. The Vernon Hills Mail Order Company often sends multiple packages per order. For each customer order, output a mailing label for each box to be mailed. The mailing labels contain the customer's complete name and address, along with a box number in the form *Box 9 of 9*. For example, an order that requires three boxes produces three labels: *Box 1 of 3*, *Box 2 of 3*, and *Box 3 of 3*. Design an application that reads records that contain a customer's title (for example, *Mrs.*), first name, last name, street address, city, state, zip code, and number of boxes. The application must read the records until `eof` is encountered and produce enough mailing labels for each order.

2. The Cupid Matchmaking Service maintains two files—one for male clients and another for female clients. Each file contains a client ID, last name, first name, and address. Each file is in client ID number order. Design the logic for a program that merges the two files into one file containing a list of all clients, maintaining ID number order.

3. Laramie Park District has files of participants in its summer and winter programs this year. Each file is in participant ID number order and contains additional fields for first name, last name, age, and class taken (for example, *Beginning Swimming*).

   a. Design the logic for a program that merges the files for summer and winter programs to create a list of the first and last names of all participants for the year.

   b. Modify the program so that if a participant has more than one record, you output the participant's name only once.

   c. Modify the program so that if a participant has more than one record, you output the name only once, but you also output a count of the total number of classes the participant has taken.

4. The Apgar Medical group keeps a patient file for each doctor in the office. Each record contains the patient's first and last name, home address, and birth year. The records are sorted in ascending birth year order. Two doctors, Dr. Best and Dr. Cushing, have formed a partnership. Design the logic that produces a merged list of their patients in ascending order by birth year.

5. The Martin Weight Loss Clinic maintains two patient files—one for male clients and one for female clients. Each record contains the name of a patient and current total weight loss in pounds. Each file is in descending weight loss order. Design the logic that merges the two files to produce one combined file in order by weight loss.

Exercises

6. a. The Curl Up and Dye Beauty Salon maintains a master file that contains a record for each of its clients. Fields in the master file include the client's ID number, first name, last name, and total amount spent this year. Every week, a transaction file is produced. It contains a customer's ID number, the service received (for example, *Manicure*), and the price paid. Each file is sorted in ID number order. Design the logic for a program that matches the master and transaction file records and updates the total paid for each client by adding the current week's price paid to the cumulative total. Not all clients purchase services each week. The output is the updated master file and an error report that lists any transaction records for which no master record exists.

   b. Modify the program to output a coupon for a free haircut each time a client exceeds $750 in services. The coupon, which contains the client's name and an appropriate congratulatory message, is output during the execution of the update program when a client total surpasses $750.

7. a. The Timely Talent Temporary Help Agency maintains an employee master file that contains an employee ID number, last name, first name, address, and hourly rate for each temporary worker. The file has been sorted in employee ID number order. Each week, a transaction file is created with a job number, address, customer name, employee ID, and hours worked for every job filled by Timely Talent workers. The transaction file is also sorted in employee ID order. Design the logic for a program that matches the master and transaction file records, and output one line for each transaction, indicating job number, employee ID number, hours worked, hourly rate, and gross pay. Assume that each temporary worker works at most one job per week; output one line for each worker who has worked that week.

   b. Modify the help agency program so that any temporary worker can work any number of separate jobs in a week. Print one line for each job that week.

   c. Modify the help agency program so that it accumulates the worker's total pay for all jobs in a week and outputs one line per worker.

Find the Bugs

8. Your downloadable files for Chapter 7 include DEBUG07-01.txt, DEBUG07-02.txt, and DEBUG07-03.txt. Each file starts with some comments that describe the problem. Comments are lines that begin with two slashes (//). Following the comments, each file contains pseudocode that has one or more bugs you must find and correct.

Game Zone

9. The International Rock Paper Scissors Society holds regional and national championships. Each region holds a semifinal competition in which contestants play 500 games of Rock Paper Scissors. The top 20 competitors in each region are invited to the national finals. Assume that you are provided with files for the East, Midwest, and Western regions. Each file contains the following fields for the top 20 competitors: last name, first name, and number of games won. The records in each file are sorted in alphabetical order. Merge the three files to create a file of the top 60 competitors who will compete in the national championship.

10. In the Game Zone section of Chapter 5, you designed a guessing game in which the application generates a random number and the player tries to guess it. After each guess, you displayed a message indicating whether the player's guess was correct, too high, or too low. When the player eventually guessed the correct number, you displayed a score that represented a count of the number of required guesses. Modify the game so that when it starts, the player enters his or her name. After a player plays the game exactly five times, save the best (lowest) score from the five games to a file. If the player's name already exists in the file, update the record with the new lowest score. If the player's name does not already exist in the file, create a new record for the player. After the file is updated, display all the best scores stored in the file.

Exercises

Up for Discussion

11. Suppose that you are hired by a police department to write a program that matches arrest records with court records detailing the ultimate outcome or verdict for each case. You have been given access to current files so that you can test the program. Your friend works in the personnel department of a large company and must perform background checks on potential employees. (The job applicants sign a form authorizing the check.) Police records are open to the public and your friend could look up police records at the courthouse, but it would take many hours per week. As a convenience, should you provide your friend with outcomes of any arrest records of job applicants?

12. Suppose that you are hired by a clinic to match a file of patient office visits with patient master records to print various reports. While working with the confidential data, you notice the name of a friend's fiancé. Should you tell your friend that the fiancé is seeking medical treatment? Does the type of treatment affect your answer?

CHAPTER 8

Advanced Data Handling Concepts

In this chapter, you will learn about:

- The need for sorting data
- The bubble sort algorithm
- Sorting multifield records
- The insertion sort algorithm
- Multidimensional arrays
- Indexed files and linked lists

CHAPTER 8   Advanced Data Handling Concepts

Understanding the Need for Sorting Data

When you store data records, they exist in some type of order; that is, one record is first, another second, and so on. When records are in **sequential order**, they are arranged one after another on the basis of the value in a particular field. Examples include employee records stored in numeric order by Social Security number or department number, or in alphabetical order by last name or department name. Even if the records are stored in a random order—for example, the order in which a clerk felt like entering them—they still are *in order*, although probably not the order desired for processing or viewing. Such data records need to be sorted, or placed in order, based on the contents of one or more fields. You can sort data either in ascending order, arranging records from lowest to highest value within a field, or in descending order, arranging records from highest to lowest value.

The sorting process usually is reserved for a relatively small number of data items. If thousands of customer records are stored, and they frequently need to be accessed in order based on different fields (alphabetical order by customer name one day, zip code order the next), the records would probably not be sorted at all, but would be indexed or linked. You learn about indexing and linking later in this chapter.

Here are some examples of occasions when you would need to sort records:

- A college stores student records in ascending order by student ID number, but the registrar wants to view the data in descending order by credit hours earned so he can contact students who are close to graduation.

- A department store maintains customer records in ascending order by customer number, but at the end of a billing period, the credit manager wants to contact customers whose balances are 90 or more days overdue. The manager wants to list these overdue customers in descending order by the amount owed, so the customers with the largest debt can be contacted first.

- A sales manager keeps records for her salespeople in alphabetical order by last name, but she needs to list the annual sales figure for each salesperson so she can determine the median annual sale amount.

The **median** value in a list is the value of the middle item when the values are listed in order. The median is not the same as the arithmetic average, or **mean**. The median is often used as a statistic because it represents a more typical case—half the values are below it and half are above it. Unlike the median, the mean is skewed by a few very high or low values.

- A store manager wants to create a control break report in which individual sales are listed in order in groups by their department. As you learned in Chapter 7, when you create a control break report, the records must have been sorted in order by the control break field.

When computers sort data, they always use numeric values to make comparisons between values. This is clear when you sort records by fields such as a numeric customer ID or balance due. However, even alphabetic sorts are numeric, because computer data is stored as a number using a series of 0s and 1s. Ordinary computer users seldom think about the

Using the Bubble Sort Algorithm

numeric codes behind the letters, numbers, and punctuation marks they enter from their keyboards or see on a monitor. However, they see the consequence of the values behind letters when they see data sorted in alphabetical order. In every popular computer coding scheme, *B* is numerically one greater than *A*, and *y* is numerically one less than *z*. Unfortunately, your system dictates whether *A* is represented by a number that is greater or smaller than the number representing *a*. Therefore, to obtain the most useful and accurate list of alphabetically sorted records, either a company's data-entry personnel should be consistent in the use of capitalization, or the programmer should convert all the data to use consistent capitalization. Because *A* is always less than *B*, alphabetic sorts are ascending sorts.

 The most popular coding schemes include ASCII, Unicode, and EBCDIC. In each code, a number represents a specific computer character. Appendix A contains additional information about these codes.

As a professional programmer, you might never have to write a program that sorts data, because organizations can purchase prewritten, "canned" sorting programs. Additionally, many popular language compilers come with built-in methods that can sort data for you. However, it is beneficial to understand the sorting process so that you can write a special-purpose sort when needed. Understanding the sorting process also improves your array-manipulating skills.

TWO TRUTHS & A LIE

Understanding the Need for Sorting Data

1. When you sort data in ascending order, you arrange records from lowest to highest based on the value in a specific field.
2. Normal alphabetical order, in which *A* precedes *B*, is descending order.
3. When computers sort data, they use numeric values to make comparisons, even when string values are compared.

The false statement is #2. Normal alphabetical order is ascending.

Using the Bubble Sort Algorithm

One of the simplest sorting techniques to understand is a bubble sort. You can use a bubble sort to arrange data items in either ascending or descending order. In a **bubble sort**, items in a list are compared with each other in pairs. When an item is out of order, it swaps values with the item below it. With an ascending bubble sort, after each adjacent pair of items in a list has been compared once, the largest item in the list will have "sunk" to the bottom. After many passes through the list, the smallest items rise to the top like bubbles in a carbonated drink. A bubble sort is sometimes called a **sinking sort**.

When you learn a method like sorting, programmers say you are learning an algorithm. An **algorithm** is a list of instructions that accomplish a task. In this section, you will learn about the bubble sort algorithm for sorting a list of simple values; later in this chapter you will learn more about how multifield records are sorted. To understand the bubble sort algorithm, you first must learn about swapping values.

Understanding Swapping Values

A central concept to many sorting algorithms, including the bubble sort, is the idea of swapping values. When you **swap values** stored in two variables, you exchange their values; you set the first variable equal to the value of the second, and the second variable equal to the value of the first. However, there is a trick to swapping any two values. Assume that you have declared two variables as follows:

```
num score1 = 90
num score2 = 85
```

You want to swap the values so that score1 is 85 and score2 is 90. If you first assign score1 to score2 using a statement such as score2 = score1, both score1 and score2 hold 90 and the value 85 is lost. Similarly, if you first assign score2 to score1 using a statement such as score1 = score2, both variables hold 85 and the value 90 is lost.

To correctly swap two values, you create a temporary variable to hold a copy of one of the scores so it doesn't get lost. Then, you can accomplish the swap as shown in Figure 8-1. First, the value in score2, 85, is assigned to a temporary holding variable named temp. Then, the score1 value, 90, is assigned to score2. At this point, both score1 and score2 hold 90. Then, the 85 in temp is assigned to score1. Therefore, after the swap process, score1 holds 85 and score2 holds 90.

Using the Bubble Sort Algorithm

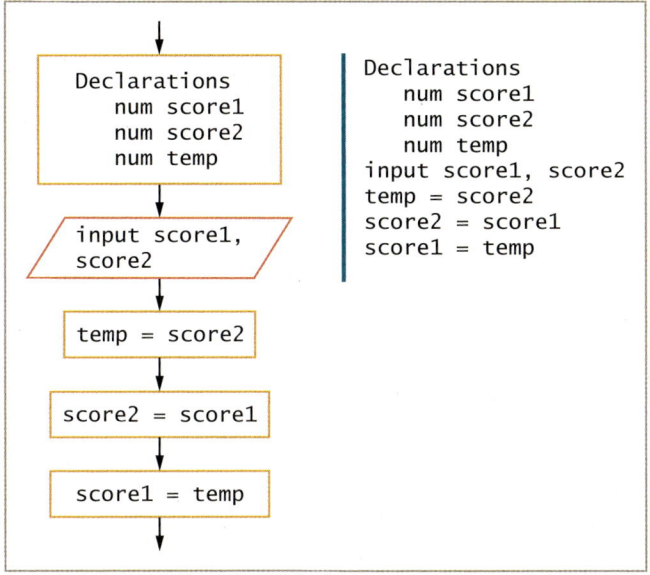

Figure 8-1   Program segment that swaps two values

In Figure 8-1, you can accomplish identical results by assigning score1 to temp, assigning score2 to score1, and finally assigning temp to score2.

   Watch the video *Swapping Values*.

Understanding the Bubble Sort

Assume that you want to sort five student test scores in ascending order. Figure 8-2 shows a program in which a constant is declared to hold an array's size, and then the array is declared to hold five scores. (The other variables and constants, which are shaded in the figure, will be discussed in the next paragraphs when they are used.) The program calls three main procedures—one to input the five scores, one to sort them, and the final one to display the sorted result.

CHAPTER 8 Advanced Data Handling Concepts

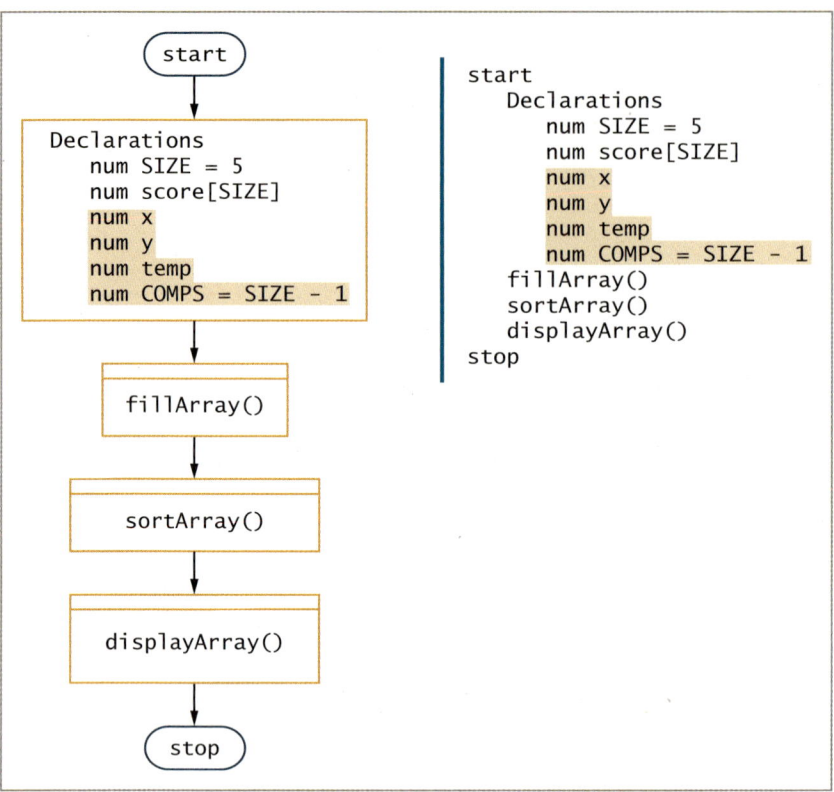

Figure 8-2 Mainline logic for program that accepts, sorts, and displays scores

Figure 8-3 shows the `fillArray()` method. Within the method, a subscript, x, is initialized to 0 and each array element is filled in turn. After a user enters five scores, control returns to the main program.

Using the Bubble Sort Algorithm

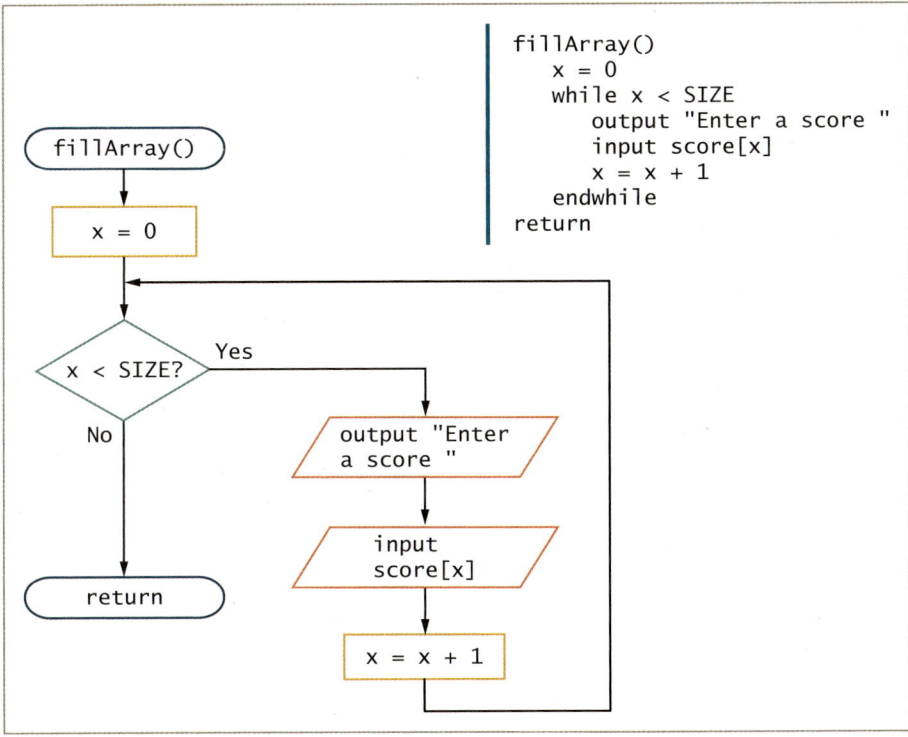

Figure 8-3 The `fillArray()` method

The `sortArray()` method in Figure 8-4 sorts the array elements by making a series of comparisons of adjacent element values and swapping them if they are out of order. To begin sorting this list of scores, you compare the first two scores, `score[0]` and `score[1]`. If they are out of order—that is, if `score[0]` is larger than `score[1]`—you want to reverse their positions, or swap their values.

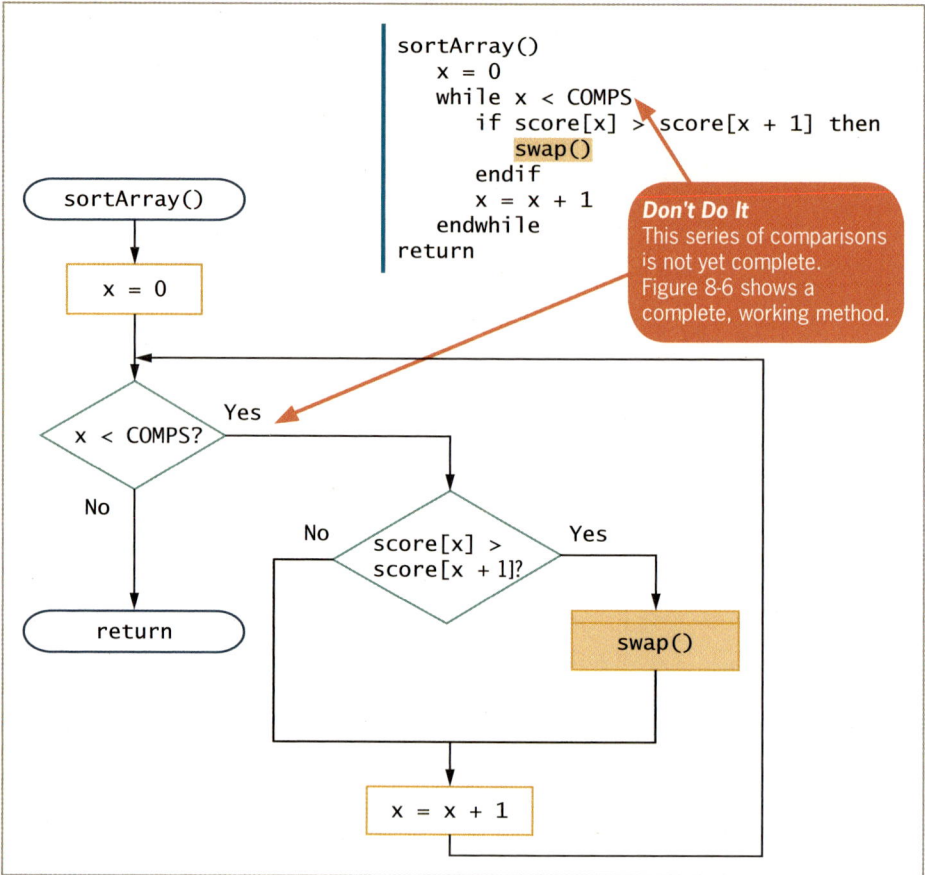

Figure 8-4 The incomplete sortArray() method

For example, assume that the five entered scores are:

score[0] = 90
score[1] = 85
score[2] = 65
score[3] = 95
score[4] = 75

In this list, score[0] is 90 and score[1] is 85; you want to exchange the values of the two elements so that the smaller value ends up earlier in the array. You call the swap() method, which places the scores in slightly better order than they were originally. Figure 8-5 shows the swap() method. This module switches any two adjacent elements in the score array.

Using the Bubble Sort Algorithm

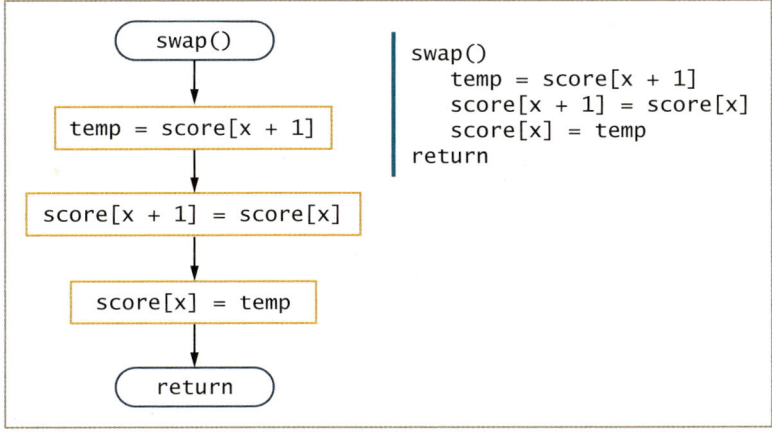

Figure 8-5 The swap() method

In Figure 8-4, the number of comparisons made is based on the value of the constant named COMPS, which was initialized to the value of SIZE - 1. That is, for an array of size 5, the COMPS constant will be 4. Therefore, the following comparisons are made:

score[0] > score[1]?
score[1] > score[2]?
score[2] > score[3]?
score[3] > score[4]?

Each element in the array is compared to the element that follows it. When x becomes COMPS, the while loop ends. If the loop continued when x became equal to COMPS, then the next comparison would be score[4] > score[5]?. This would cause an error because the highest allowed subscript in a five-element array is 4. You must execute the decision score[x] > score[x + 1]? four times—when x is 0, 1, 2, and 3.

For an ascending sort, you need to perform the swap() method whenever any given element of the score array has a value greater than the next element. For any x, if the xth element is not greater than the element at position x + 1, the swap should not take place. For example, when score[x] is 90 and score[x + 1] is 85, a swap should occur. On the other hand, when score[x] is 65 and score[x + 1] is 95, then no swap should occur.

For a descending sort in which you want to end up with the highest value first, you would write the decision so that you perform the switch when score[x] is *less than* score[x + 1].

As a complete example of how this application works using an ascending sort, suppose that you have these original scores:

score[0] = 90
score[1] = 85
score[2] = 65
score[3] = 95
score[4] = 75

The logic of the `sortArray()` method proceeds like this:

1. Set x to 0.
2. The value of x is less than 4 (COMPS), so enter the loop.
3. Compare `score[x]`, 90, to `score[x + 1]`, 85. The two scores are out of order, so they are switched.

   The list is now:

   ```
   score[0] = 85
   score[1] = 90
   score[2] = 65
   score[3] = 95
   score[4] = 75
   ```

4. After the swap, add 1 to x, so x is 1.
5. Return to the top of the loop. The value of x is less than 4, so enter the loop a second time.
6. Compare `score[x]`, 90, to `score[x + 1]`, 65. These two values are out of order, so swap them.

   Now the result is:

   ```
   score[0] = 85
   score[1] = 65
   score[2] = 90
   score[3] = 95
   score[4] = 75
   ```

7. Add 1 to x, so x is now 2.
8. Return to the top of the loop. The value of x is less than 4, so enter the loop.
9. Compare `score[x]`, 90, to `score[x + 1]`, 95. These values are in order, so no switch is made.
10. Add 1 to x, making it 3.
11. Return to the top of the loop. The value of x is less than 4, so enter the loop.
12. Compare `score[x]`, 95, to `score[x + 1]`, 75. These two values are out of order, so switch them.

    Now the list is as follows:

    ```
    score[0] = 85
    score[1] = 65
    score[2] = 90
    score[3] = 75
    score[4] = 95
    ```

13. Add 1 to x, making it 4.
14. Return to the top of the loop. The value of x is 4, so do not enter the loop again.

Using the Bubble Sort Algorithm

When x reaches 4, every element in the list has been compared with the one adjacent to it. The highest score, 95, has "sunk" to the bottom of the list. However, the scores still are not in order. They are in slightly better ascending order than they were when the process began, because the largest value is at the bottom of the list, but they are still out of order. You need to repeat the entire procedure so that 85 and 65 (the current score[0] and score[1] values) can switch places, and 90 and 75 (the current score[2] and score[3] values) can switch places. Then, the scores will be 65, 85, 75, 90, and 95. You will have to go through the list yet again to swap 85 and 75.

As a matter of fact, if the scores had started in the worst possible order (95, 90, 85, 75, 65), the comparison process would have to take place four times. In other words, you would have to pass through the list of values four times, making appropriate swaps, before the numbers would appear in perfect ascending order. You need to place the loop in Figure 8-4 within another loop that executes four times.

Figure 8-6 shows the complete logic for the sortArray() module. The module uses a loop control variable named y to cycle through the list of scores four times. (The initialization, comparison, and alteration of this loop control variable are shaded in the figure.) With an array of five elements, it takes four comparisons to work through the array once, comparing each pair, and it takes four sets of those comparisons to ensure that every element in the entire array is in sorted order. In the sortArray() method in Figure 8-6, x must be reset to 0 for each new value of y so that the comparisons always start at the top of the list.

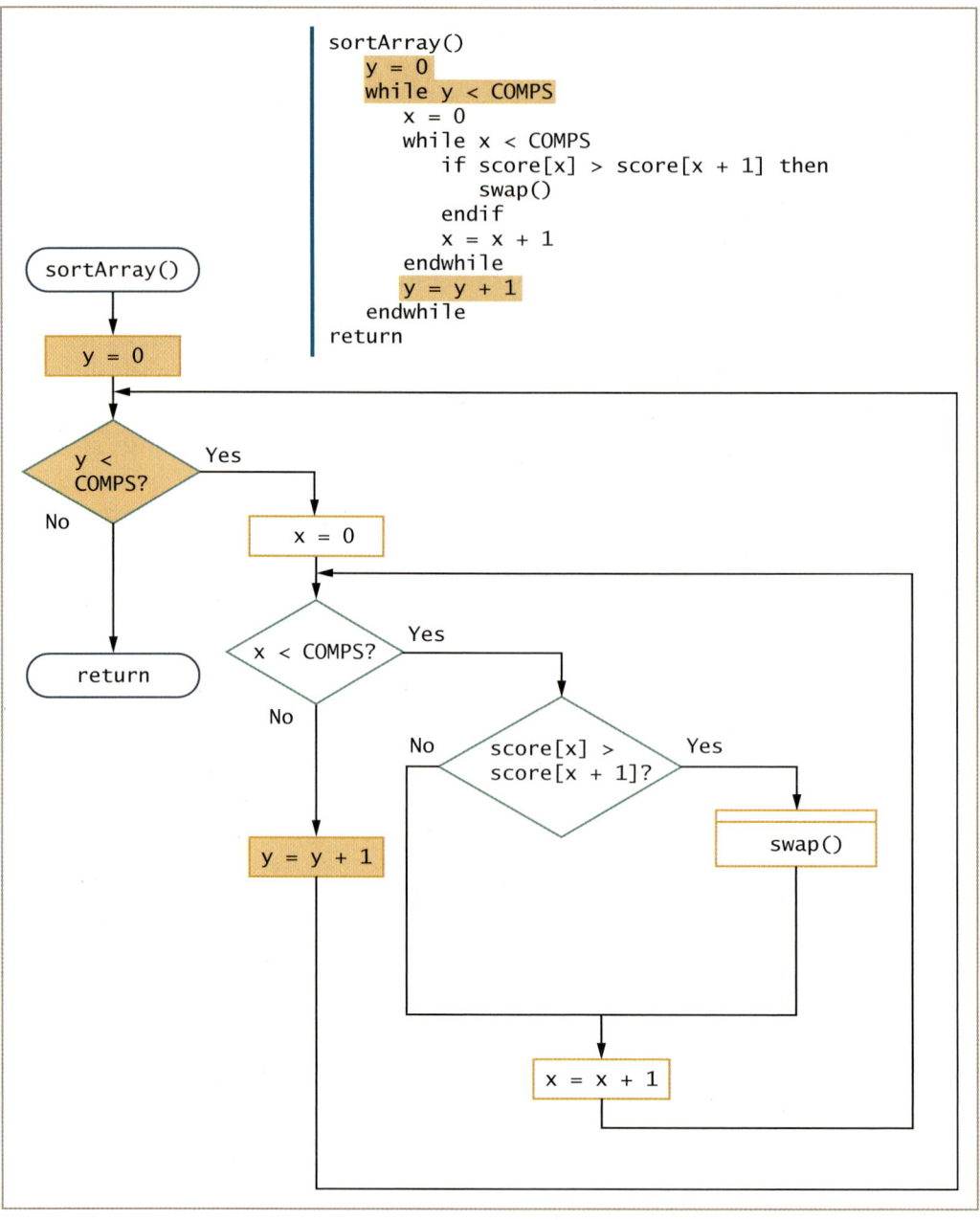

Figure 8-6　The completed sortArray() method

Using the Bubble Sort Algorithm

When you sort the elements in an array this way, you use nested loops—an inner loop that swaps out-of-order pairs, and an outer loop that goes through the list multiple times. The general rules for making comparisons with the bubble sort are:

- The greatest number of pair comparisons you need to make during each loop is *one less* than the number of elements in the array. You use an inner loop to make the pair comparisons.

- The number of times you need to process the list of values is *one less* than the number of elements in the array. You use an outer loop to control the number of times you walk through the list.

As an example, if you want to sort a 10-element array, you make nine pair comparisons on each of nine rotations through the loop, executing a total of 81 score comparison statements.

The last method called by the score-sorting program in Figure 8-2 is the one that displays the sorted array contents. Figure 8-7 shows this method.

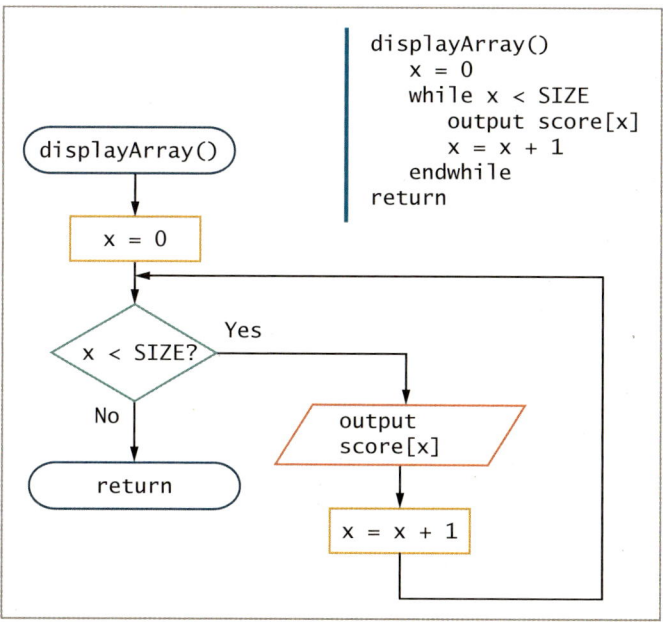

Figure 8-7 The `displayArray()` method

 Watch the video *The Bubble Sort*.

Sorting a List of Variable Size

In the score-sorting program in the previous section, a SIZE constant was initialized to the number of elements to be sorted at the start of the program. At times, however, you don't want to create such a value because you might not know how many array elements will hold valid values. For example, on one program run you might want to sort only three or four scores, and on another run you might want to sort 20. In other words, what if the size of the list to be sorted might vary? Rather than sorting a fixed number of array elements, you can count the input scores and then sort just that many.

To keep track of the number of elements stored in an array, you can create the application shown in Figure 8-8. As in the original version of the program, you call the fillArray() method, and when you input each score, you increase x by 1 to place each new score into a successive element of the score array. After you input one score value and place it in the first element of the array, x is 1. After a second score is input and placed in score[1], x is 2, and so on. After you reach the end of input, x holds the number of scores that have been placed in the array, so you can store x in numberOfEls, and compute comparisons as numberOfEls - 1. With this approach, it doesn't matter if there are not enough score values to fill the array. The sortArray() and displayArray() methods use comparisons and numberOfEls instead of COMPS and SIZE to process the array. For example, if 35 scores are input, numberOfEls will be set to 35 in the fillArray() module, and when the program sorts, it will use 34 as a cutoff point for the number of pair comparisons to make. The sorting program will never make pair comparisons on array elements 36 through 100—those elements will just "sit there," never being involved in a comparison or swap.

Using the Bubble Sort Algorithm

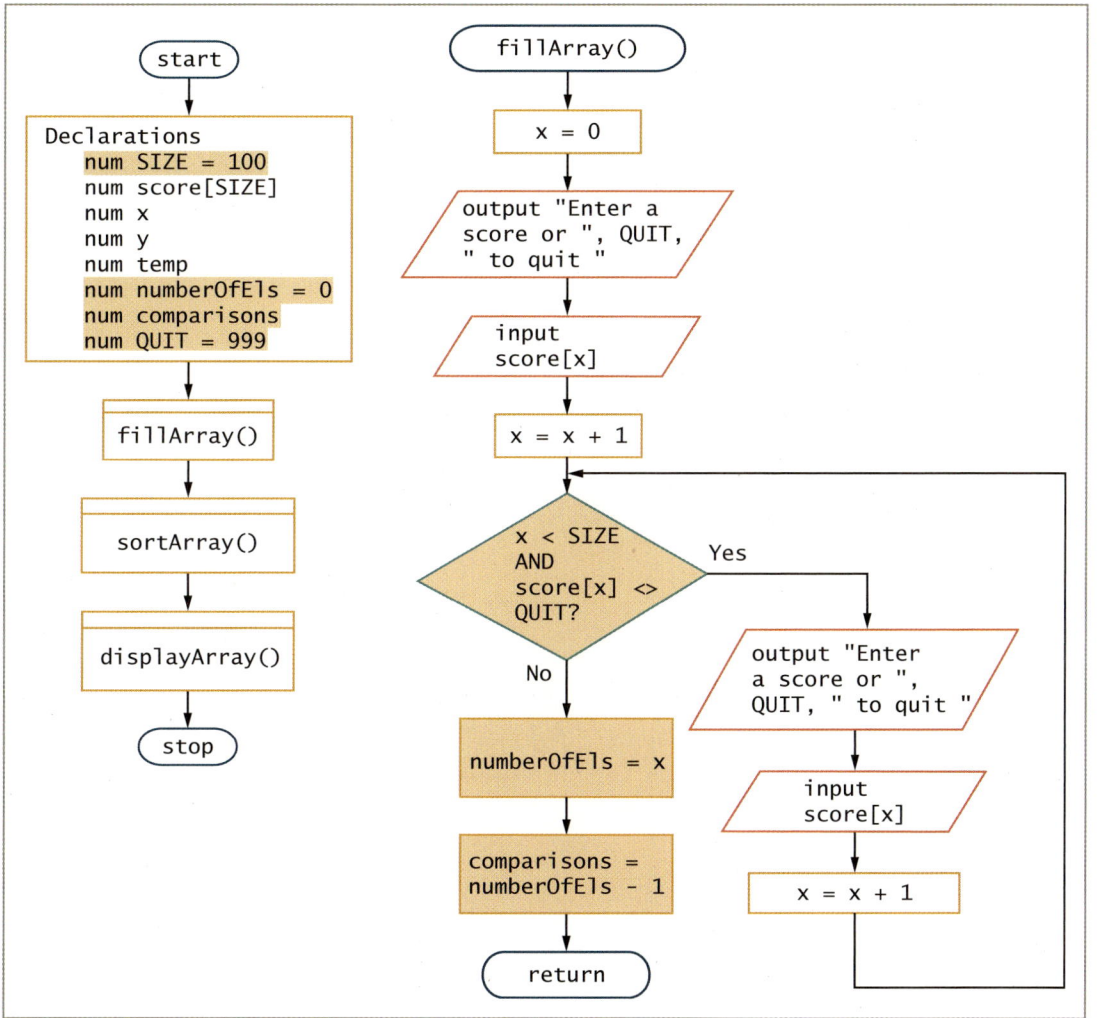

Figure 8-8 Score-sorting application in which number of elements to sort can vary

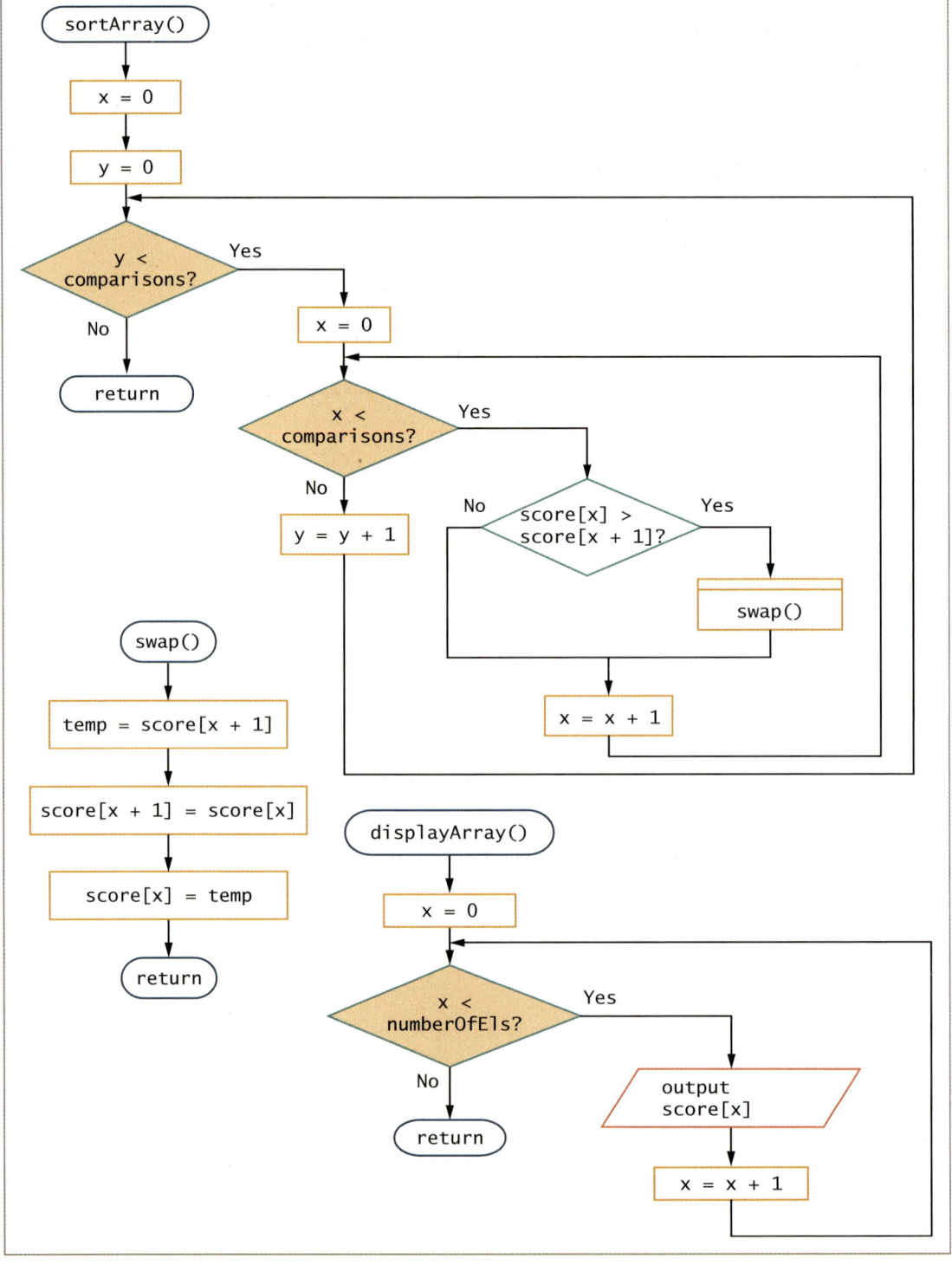

Figure 8-8 Score-sorting application in which number of elements to sort can vary (continued)

Using the Bubble Sort Algorithm

```
start
   Declarations
      num SIZE = 100
      num score[SIZE]
      num x
      num y
      num temp
      num numberOfEls = 0
      num comparisons
      num QUIT = 999
   fillArray()
   sortArray()
   displayArray()
stop

fillArray()
   x = 0
   output "Enter a score or ", QUIT, " to quit "
   input score[x]
   x = x + 1
   while x < SIZE AND score[x] <> QUIT
      output "Enter a score or ", QUIT, " to quit "
      input score[x]
      x = x + 1
   endwhile
   numberOfEls = x
   comparisons = numberOfEls - 1
return

sortArray()
   x = 0
   y = 0
   while y < comparisons
      x = 0
      while x < comparisons
         if score[x] > score[x + 1] then
            swap()
         endif
         x = x + 1
      endwhile
      y = y + 1
   endwhile
return

swap()
   temp = score[x + 1]
   score[x + 1] = score[x]
   score[x] = temp
return

displayArray()
   x = 0
   while x < numberOfEls
      output score[x]
      x = x + 1
   endwhile
return
```

Figure 8-8 Score-sorting application in which number of elements to sort can vary (continued)

> In the `fillArray()` method in Figure 8-8, notice that a priming read has been added to the method. If the user enters the QUIT value at the first input, then the number of elements to be sorted will be 0.

When you count the input values and use the `numberOfEls` variable, it does not matter if there are not enough scores to fill the array. However, an error occurs if you attempt to store more values than the array can hold. When you don't know how many elements will be stored in an array, you must overestimate the number of elements you declare.

Refining the Bubble Sort to Reduce Unnecessary Comparisons

You can make additional improvements to the bubble sort created in the previous sections. As illustrated in Figure 8-8, when you perform the sorting module for a bubble sort, you pass through a list, making comparisons and swapping values if two adjacent values are out of order. If you are performing an ascending sort and you have made one pass through the list, the largest value is guaranteed to be in its correct final position at the bottom of the list. Similarly, the second-largest element is guaranteed to be in its correct second-to-last position after the second pass through the list, and so on. If you continue to compare every element pair on every pass through the list, you are comparing elements that are already guaranteed to be in their final correct position. In other words, after the first pass through the list, you no longer need to check the bottom element; after the second pass, you don't need to check the two bottom elements.

On each pass through the array, you can afford to stop your pair comparisons one element sooner. You can avoid comparing the values that are already in place by creating a new variable, `pairsToCompare`, and setting it equal to the value of `numberOfEls` - 1. On the first pass through the list, every pair of elements is compared, so `pairsToCompare` *should* equal `numberOfEls` - 1. In other words, with five array elements to sort, four pairs are compared, and with 50 elements to sort, 49 pairs are compared. On each subsequent pass through the list, `pairsToCompare` should be reduced by 1; for example, after the first pass is completed, it is not necessary to check the bottom element. See Figure 8-9 to examine the use of the `pairsToCompare` variable.

Using the Bubble Sort Algorithm

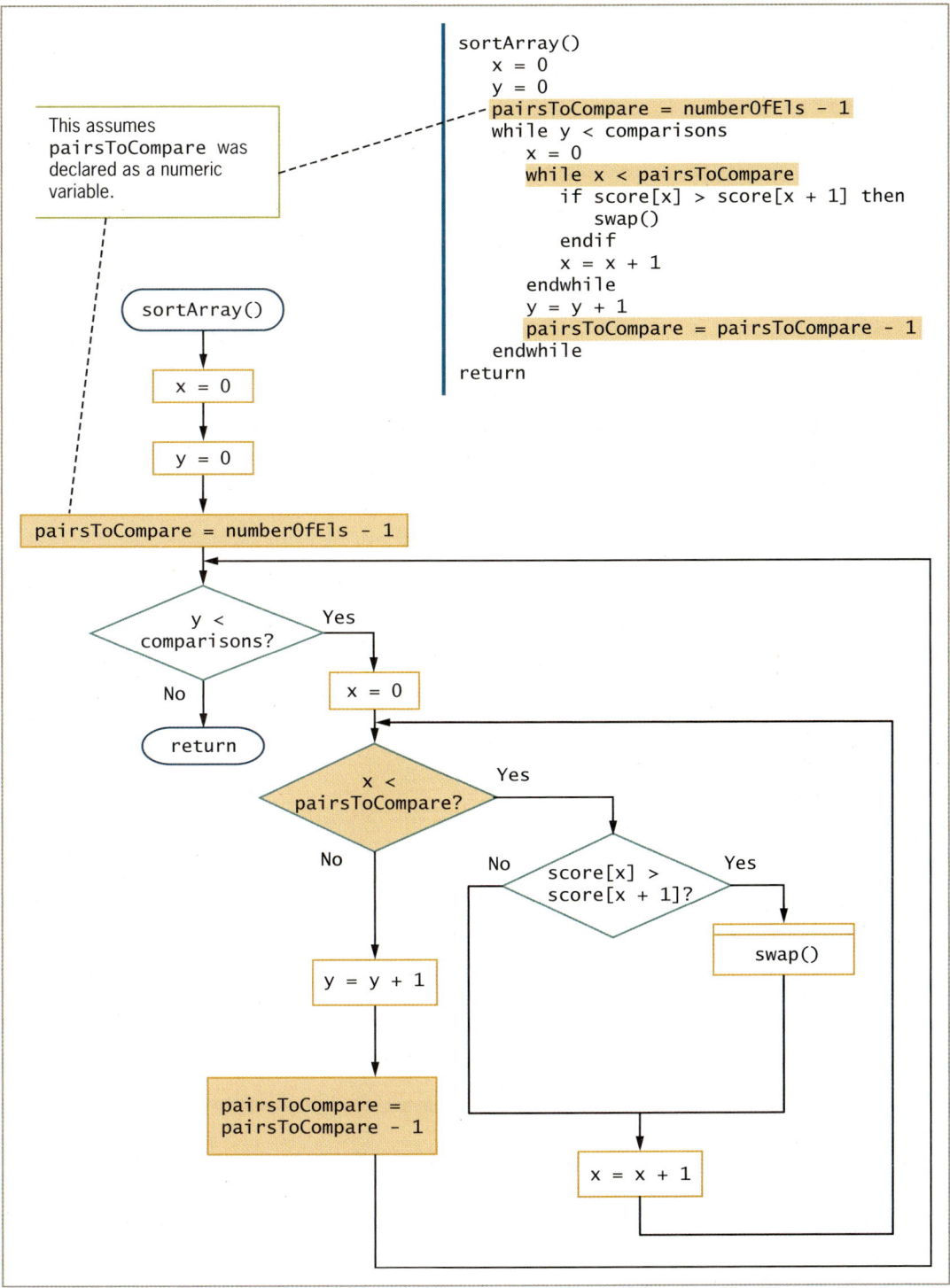

Figure 8-9 Flowchart and pseudocode for `sortArray()` method using `pairsToCompare` variable

Refining the Bubble Sort to Eliminate Unnecessary Passes

You could also improve the bubble sort module in Figure 8-9 by reducing the number of passes through the array. If array elements are badly out of order or in reverse order, many passes through the list are required to place it in order; it takes one fewer pass than the value in numberOfEls to complete all the comparisons and swaps needed to sort the list. However, when the array elements are in order or nearly in order to start, all the elements might be correctly arranged after only a few passes through the list. All subsequent passes result in no swaps. For example, assume that the original scores are as follows:

```
score[0] = 65
score[1] = 75
score[2] = 85
score[3] = 90
score[4] = 95
```

The bubble sort module in Figure 8-9 would pass through the array list four times, making four sets of pair comparisons. It would always find that each score[x] is *not* greater than the corresponding score[x + 1], so no switches would ever be made. The scores would end up in the proper order, but they *were* in the proper order in the first place; therefore, a lot of time would be wasted.

A possible remedy is to add a flag variable set to a "continue" value on any pass through the list in which any pair of elements is swapped (even if just one pair), and which holds a different "finished" value when no swaps are made—that is, when all elements in the list are already in the correct order. For example, you can create a variable named didSwap and set it to "No" at the start of each pass through the list. You can change its value to "Yes" each time the swap() module is performed (that is, each time a switch is necessary).

If you make it through the entire list of pairs without making a switch, the didSwap flag will *not* have been set to "Yes", meaning that no swap has occurred and that the array elements must already be in the correct order. This situation might occur on the first or second pass through the array list, or it might not occur until a much later pass. Once the array elements are in the correct order, you can stop making passes through the list.

Figure 8-10 illustrates a module that sorts scores and uses a didSwap flag. At the beginning of the sortArray() module, initialize didSwap to "Yes" before entering the comparison loop the first time. Then, immediately set didSwap to "No". When a switch occurs—that is, when the swap() module executes—set didSwap to "Yes".

Using the Bubble Sort Algorithm

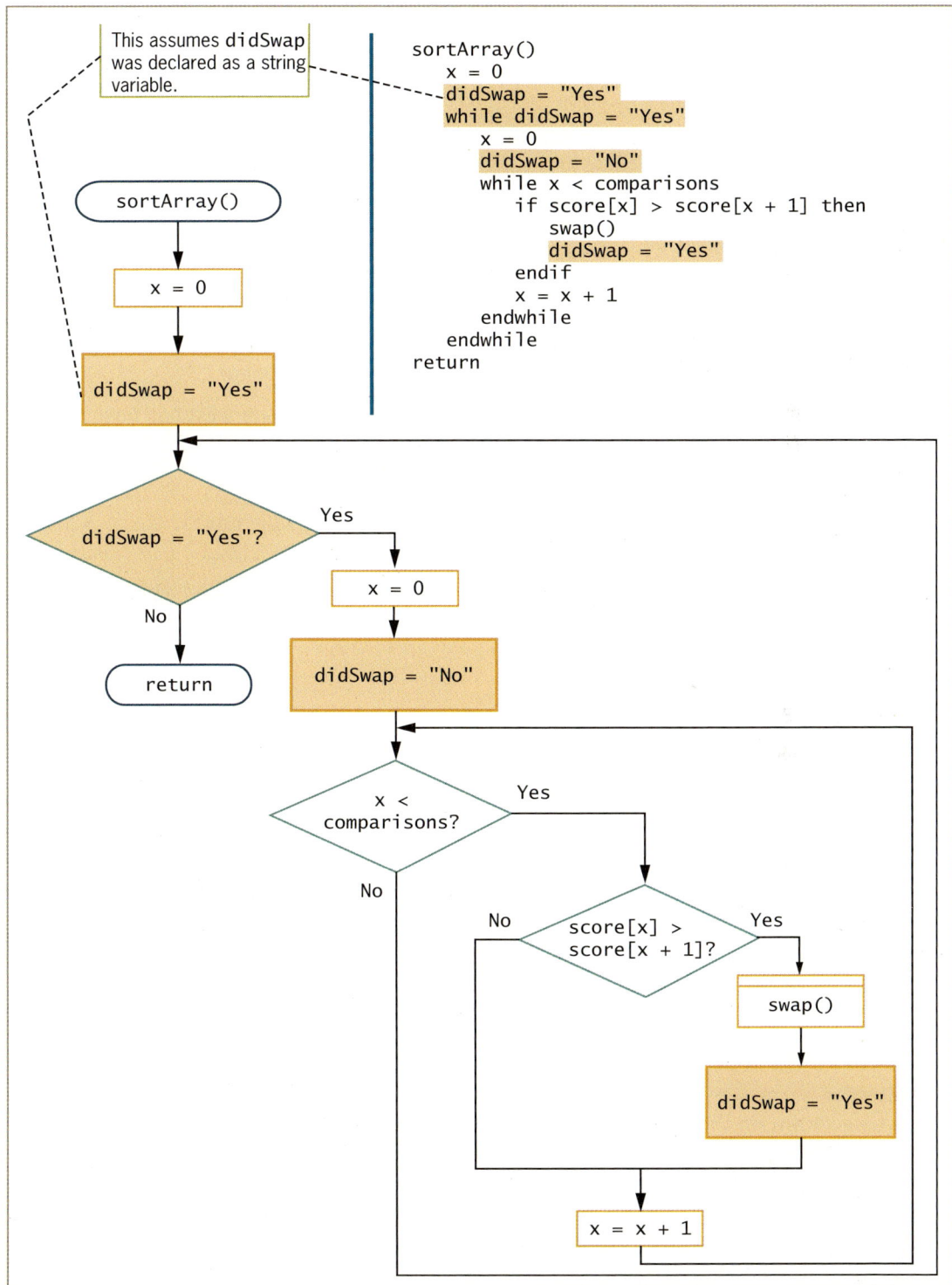

With the addition of the flag variable in Figure 8-10, you no longer need the variable y, which was keeping track of the number of passes through the list. Instead, you keep going through the list until you can make a complete pass without any switches.

TWO TRUTHS & A LIE

Using the Bubble Sort Algorithm

1. You can use a bubble sort to arrange records in ascending or descending order.
2. In a bubble sort, items in a list are compared with each other in pairs, and when an item is out of order, it swaps values with the item below it.
3. With any bubble sort, after each adjacent pair of items in a list has been compared once, the largest item in the list will have "sunk" to the bottom.

The false statement is #3. Statement #3 is true of an ascending bubble sort. However, with a descending bubble sort, the smallest item in the list will have "sunk" to the bottom after each adjacent pair of items has been compared once.

Sorting Multifield Records

The bubble sort algorithm is useful for sorting a list of values, such as a list of test scores in ascending order or a list of names in alphabetical order. Records, however, are most frequently composed of multiple fields. When you want to sort records, you need to make sure data that belongs together stays together. When you sort records, two approaches you can take are to place related data items in parallel arrays and to sort records as a whole.

Sorting Data Stored in Parallel Arrays

Suppose that you have parallel arrays containing student names and test scores, like the arrays shown in Figure 8-11. Each student's name appears in the same relative position in the name array as his or her test score appears in the score array. Further suppose that you want to sort the student names and their scores in alphabetical order. If you use a sort algorithm on the name array to place the names in alphabetical order, the name that starts in position 3, *Anna*, should end up in position 0. If you also neglect to rearrange the score array, Anna's name will no longer be in the same relative position as her score, which is 85. Notice that you don't want to sort the score values. If you did, score[2], 60, would move to position 0, and that is not Anna's score. Instead, when you sort the names, you want to make sure that each corresponding score is moved to the same position as the name to which it belongs.

Sorting Multifield Records

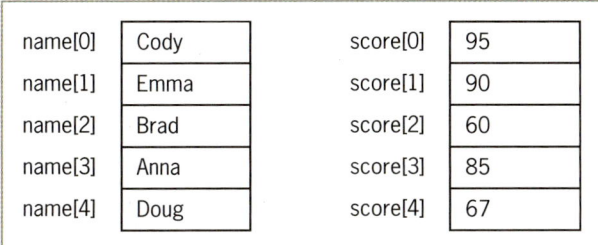

Figure 8-11 Appearance of name and score arrays in memory

Figure 8-12 shows the swap() module for a program that sorts name array values in alphabetical order and moves score array values correspondingly. This version of the swap() module uses two temporary variables—a string named tempName and a numeric variable named tempScore. The swap() method executes whenever two names in positions x and x + 1 are out of order. Besides swapping the names in positions x and x + 1, the module also swaps the scores in the same positions. Therefore, each student's score always moves along with its student's name.

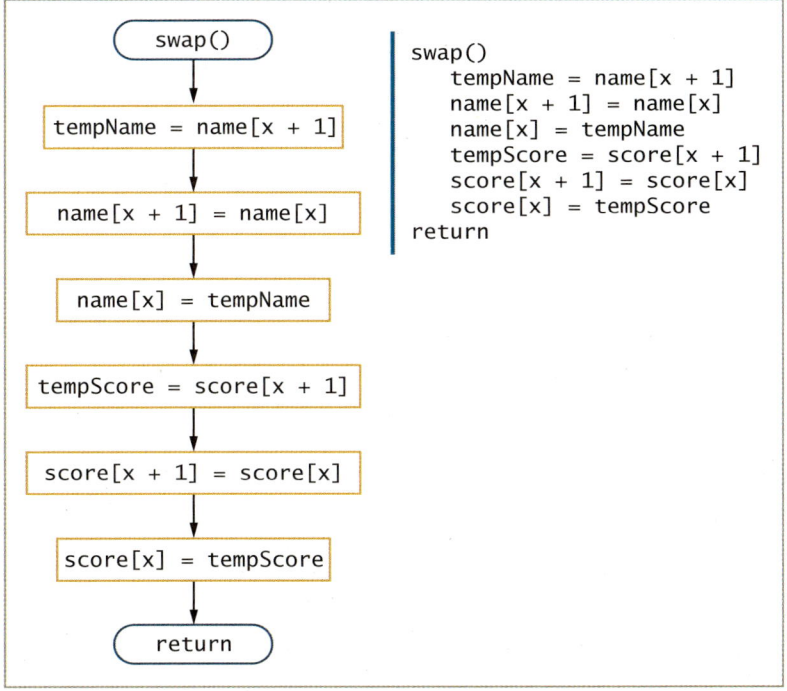

Figure 8-12 The swap() method for a program that sorts student names and retains their correct scores

CHAPTER 8 — Advanced Data Handling Concepts

Sorting Records as a Whole

In most modern programming languages, you can create group items that can be manipulated more easily than single data items. (You first learned about such group names in Chapter 7.) Creating a group name for a set of related data fields is beneficial when you want to move related data items together, as when you sort records with multiple fields. These group items are sometimes called *structures*, but more frequently are created as *classes*. Chapters 10 and 11 provide much more detail on creating classes, but for now, understand that you can create a group item with syntax similar to the following:

```
class StudentRecord
    string name
    num score
endClass
```

To sort student records using the group name, you could do the following:

- Define a class named `StudentRecord`, as shown in the preceding code.

- Define what *greater than* means for a `StudentRecord`. For example, to sort records by student name, you would define *greater than* to compare `name` values, not `score` values. The process for creating this definition varies among programming languages.

- Use a sort algorithm that swaps `StudentRecord` items, including both `names` and `scores`, whenever two `StudentRecords` are out of order.

TWO TRUTHS & A LIE

Sorting Multifield Records

1. To sort related parallel arrays, you must sort each in the same order—either ascending or descending.

2. When you sort related parallel arrays and swap values in one array, you must make sure that all associated arrays make the same relative swap.

3. Most modern programming languages allow you to create a group name for associated fields in a record.

The false statement is #1. To sort related parallel arrays successfully, you must make sure all items in each array are swapped in a synchronized manner. You do not want to sort the arrays separately.

Using the Insertion Sort Algorithm

The bubble sort works well and is relatively easy to understand and manipulate, but many other sorting algorithms have been developed. For example, when you use an **insertion sort**, you look at each list element one at a time. If an element is out of order relative to any of the items earlier in the list, you move each earlier item down one position and then insert the tested element. The insertion sort is similar to the technique you would most likely use to sort a group of objects manually. For example, if a list contains the values 2, 3, 1, and 4, and you want to place them in ascending order using an insertion sort, you test the values 2 and 3, but you do not move them because they are in order. However, when you test the third value in the list, 1, you move both 2 and 3 to later positions and insert 1 at the first position.

Figure 8-13 shows the logic that performs an ascending insertion sort using a five-element array named score. Assume that a constant named SIZE has been set to 5, and that the five scores in the array are as follows:

```
score[0] = 90
score[1] = 85
score[2] = 65
score[3] = 95
score[4] = 75
```

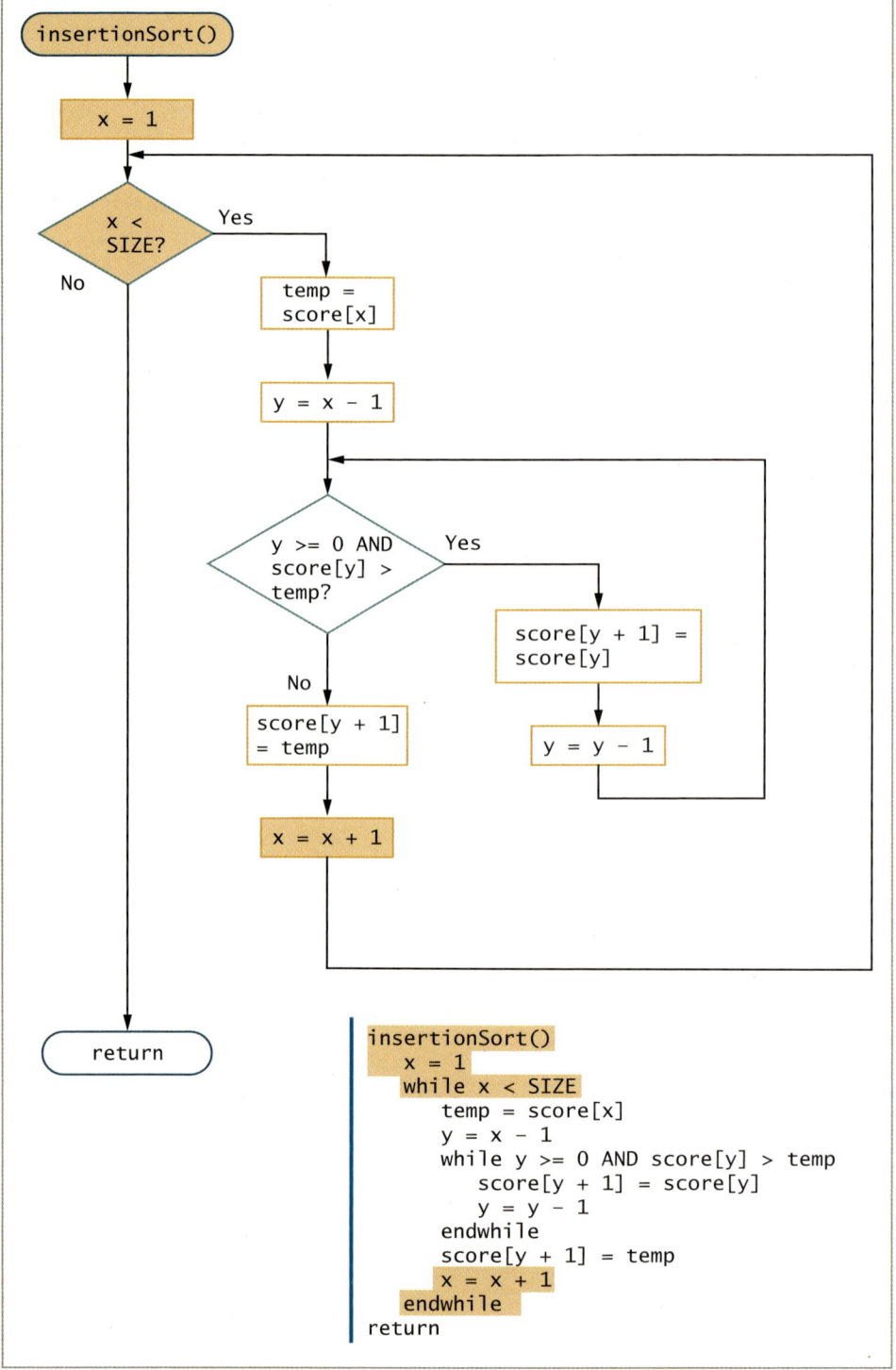

Figure 8-13 Flowchart and pseudocode for the `insertionSort()` method

Using the Insertion Sort Algorithm

The shaded outer loop varies a loop control variable x from 1 through one less than the size of the array. The logic proceeds as follows:

First x is set to 1, and then the unshaded section in the center of Figure 8-13 executes.

1. The value of `temp` is set to `score[1]`, which is 85, and y is set to 0.
2. Because y is greater than or equal to 0 and `score[y]` (90) is greater than `temp`, the inner loop is entered. (If you were performing a descending sort, then you would ask whether `score[y]` was less than `temp`.)
3. The value of `score[1]` becomes 90 and y is decremented, making it −1, so y is no longer greater than or equal to 0, and the inner loop ends.
4. Then `score[0]` is set to `temp`, which is 85.

After these steps, 90 was moved down one position and 85 was inserted in the first position, so the array values are in slightly better order than they were originally. The values are as follows:

```
score[0] = 85
score[1] = 90
score[2] = 65
score[3] = 95
score[4] = 75
```

Now, in the outer loop, x becomes 2. The logic in the unshaded portion of Figure 8-13 proceeds as follows:

1. The value of `temp` becomes 65, and y is set to 1.
2. The value of y is greater than or equal to 0, and `score[y]` (90) is greater than `temp`, so the inner loop is entered.
3. The value of `score[2]` becomes 90 and y is decremented, making it 0, so the loop executes again.
4. The value of `score[1]` becomes 85 and y is decremented, making it −1, so the loop ends.
5. Then `score[0]` becomes 65.

After these steps, the array values are in better order than they were originally, because 65 and 85 now both come before 90:

```
score[0] = 65
score[1] = 85
score[2] = 90
score[3] = 95
score[4] = 75
```

Now, x becomes 3. The logic in Figure 8-13 proceeds to work on the new list as follows:

1. The value of `temp` becomes 95, and y is set to 2.
2. For the loop to execute, y must be greater than or equal to 0, which it is, and `score[y]` (90) must be greater than `temp`, which it is *not*. So, the inner loop does not execute.
3. Therefore, `score[2]` is set to 90, which it already was. In other words, no changes are made.

Now, x is increased to 4. The logic in Figure 8-13 proceeds as follows:

1. The value of `temp` becomes 75, and y is set to 3.
2. The value of y is greater than or equal to 0, and `score[y]` (95) is greater than `temp`, so the inner loop is entered.
3. The value of `score[4]` becomes 95 and y is decremented, making it 2, so the loop executes again.
4. The value of `score[3]` becomes 90 and y is decremented, making it 1, so the loop executes again.
5. The value of `score[2]` becomes 85 and y is decremented, making it 0; `score[y]` (65) is no longer greater than `temp` (75), so the inner loop ends. In other words, the scores 85, 90, and 95 are each moved down one position, but score 65 is left in place.
6. Then `score[1]` becomes 75.

   After these steps, all the array values have been rearranged in ascending order as follows:

   ```
   score[0] = 65
   score[1] = 75
   score[2] = 85
   score[3] = 90
   score[4] = 95
   ```

Watch the video *The Insertion Sort*.

Many sorting algorithms exist in addition to the bubble sort and insertion sort. You might want to investigate the logic used by the *selection sort, cocktail sort, gnome sort,* and *quick sort*.

TWO TRUTHS & A LIE

Using the Insertion Sort Algorithm

1. When you use an insertion sort, you look at each list element one at a time and move items down if the tested element should be inserted before them.
2. You can create an ascending list using an insertion sort, but not a descending one.
3. The insertion sort is similar to the technique you would most likely use to sort a group of objects manually.

The false statement is #2. You can create both ascending and descending lists using an insertion sort.

Using Multidimensional Arrays

In Chapter 6, you learned that an array is a series or list of values in computer memory, all of which have the same name and data type but are differentiated with special numbers called subscripts. Usually, all the values in an array have something in common; for example, they might represent a list of employee ID numbers or a list of prices for items sold in a store. A subscript, also called an index, is a number that indicates the position of a particular item within an array.

An array whose elements you can access using a single subscript is a **one-dimensional** or **single-dimensional array**. The array has only one dimension because its data can be stored in a table that has just one dimension—height. If you know the vertical position of a one-dimensional array's element, you can find its value.

For example, suppose that you own an apartment building and charge five different rent amounts for apartments on different floors (including floor 0, the basement), as shown in Table 8-1.

You could declare the following array to hold the rent values:

num RENT_BY_FLOOR[5] = 350, 400, 475, 600, 1000

The location of any rent value in Table 8-1 depends on only a single variable—the floor of the building. So, when you create a single-dimensional array to hold rent values, you need just one subscript to identify the row.

Floor	Rent ($)
0	350
1	400
2	475
3	600
4	1000

Table 8-1 Rent schedule based on floor

Sometimes, however, locating a value in an array depends on more than one variable. If you must represent values in a table or grid that contains rows and columns instead of a single list, then you might want to use a **two-dimensional array**. A two-dimensional array contains two dimensions: height and width. That is, the location of any element depends on two factors. For example, if an apartment's rent depends on two variables—both the floor of the building and the number of bedrooms—then you want to create a two-dimensional array.

As an example of how useful two-dimensional arrays can be, assume that you own an apartment building with five floors, and that each of the floors has studio apartments (with no bedroom) and one- and two-bedroom apartments. Table 8-2 shows the rental amounts.

Floor	Studio Apartment	1-bedroom Apartment	2-bedroom Apartment
0	350	390	435
1	400	440	480
2	475	530	575
3	600	650	700
4	1000	1075	1150

Table 8-2 Rent schedule based on floor and number of bedrooms

To determine a tenant's rent, you need to know two pieces of information: the floor where the tenant lives and the number of bedrooms in the apartment. Each element in a two-dimensional array requires two subscripts to reference it—one subscript to determine the row and a second to determine the column. Thus, the 15 rent values for a two-dimensional array based on Table 8-2 would be arranged in five rows and three columns and defined as follows:

```
num RENT_BY_FLOOR_AND_BDRMS[5][3]= {350, 390, 435},
                                   {400, 440, 480},
                                   {475, 530, 575},
                                   {600, 650, 700},
                                   {1000, 1075, 1150}
```

Using Multidimensional Arrays

Figure 8-14 shows how the one- and two-dimensional rent arrays might appear in computer memory.

A Single-Dimensional Array

num RENT_BY_FLOOR[5] =
350, 400, 475, 600, 1000

350
400
475
600
1000

A Two-Dimensional Array

num RENT_BY_FLOOR_AND_BDRMS[5][3] =
    {350, 390, 435},
    {400, 440, 480},
    {475, 530, 575},
    {600, 650, 700},
    {1000, 1075, 1150}

350	390	435
400	440	480
475	530	575
600	650	700
1000	1075	1150

Figure 8-14 One- and two-dimensional arrays in memory

When you declare a one-dimensional array, you use a set of square brackets after the array type and name. To declare a two-dimensional array, many languages require you to use two sets of brackets after the array type and name. For each element in the array, the first square bracket holds the number of rows and the second one holds the number of columns. In other words, the two dimensions represent the array's height and its width.

 Instead of two sets of brackets to indicate a position in a two-dimensional array, some languages use a single set of brackets but separate the subscripts with commas. Therefore, the elements in row 1, column 2 would be RENT_BY_FLOOR_AND_BDRMS[1, 2].

In the RENT_BY_FLOOR_AND_BDRMS array declaration, the values that are assigned to each row are enclosed in braces to help you picture the placement of each number in the array. The first row of the array holds the three rent values 350, 390, and 435 for floor 0; the second row holds 400, 440, and 480 for floor 1; and so on.

You access a two-dimensional array value using two subscripts, in which the first subscript represents the row and the second one represents the column. For example, some of the values in the array are as follows:

- RENT_BY_FLOOR_AND_BDRMS[0][0] is 350
- RENT_BY_FLOOR_AND_BDRMS[0][1] is 390
- RENT_BY_FLOOR_AND_BDRMS[0][2] is 435
- RENT_BY_FLOOR_AND_BDRMS[4][0] is 1000
- RENT_BY_FLOOR_AND_BDRMS[4][1] is 1075
- RENT_BY_FLOOR_AND_BDRMS[4][2] is 1150

If you declare two variables to hold the floor number and bedroom count as num floor and num bedrooms, any tenant's rent is RENT_BY_FLOOR_AND_BDRMS[floor][bedrooms].

When mathematicians use a two-dimensional array, they often call it a **matrix** or a **table**. You may have used a spreadsheet, which is a two-dimensional array in which you need to know a row number and a column letter to access a specific cell.

Figure 8-15 shows a program that continuously displays rents for apartments based on renter requests for floor location and number of bedrooms. Notice that although significant setup is required to provide all the values for the rents, the basic program is extremely brief and easy to follow. (You could improve the program in Figure 8-15 by making sure the values for floor and bedrooms are within range before using them as array subscripts.)

Using Multidimensional Arrays

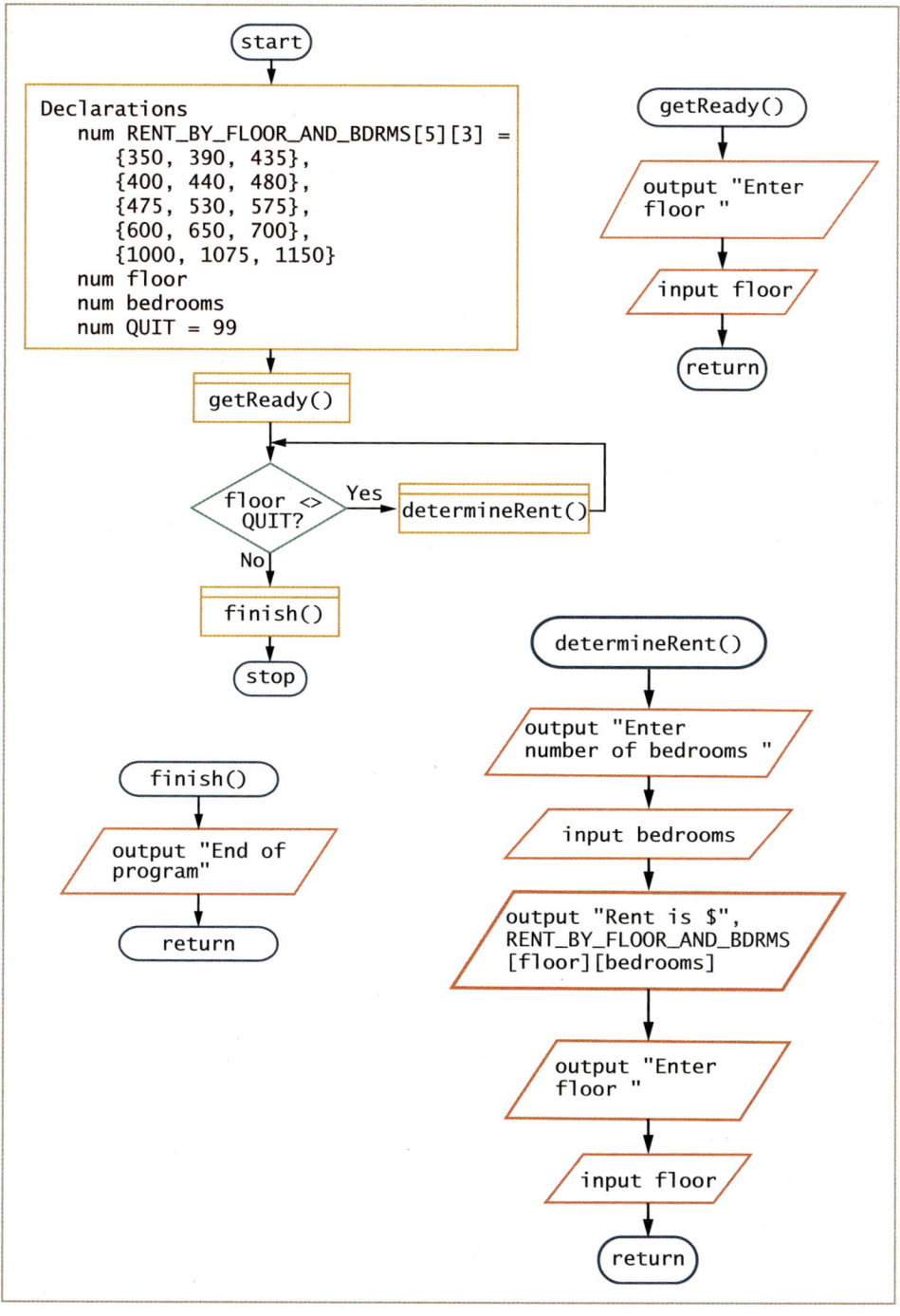

Figure 8-15 A program that determines rents

```
start
    Declarations
        num RENT_BY_FLOOR_AND_BDRMS[5][3] = {350, 390, 435},
                                            {400, 440, 480},
                                            {475, 530, 575},
                                            {600, 650, 700},
                                            {1000, 1075, 1150}
        num floor
        num bedrooms
        num QUIT = 99
    getReady()
    while floor <> QUIT
        determineRent()
    endwhile
    finish()
stop

getReady()
    output "Enter floor "
    input floor
return

determineRent()
    output "Enter number of bedrooms "
    input bedrooms
    output "Rent is $", RENT_BY_FLOOR_AND_BDRMS[floor][bedrooms]
    output "Enter floor "
    input floor
return

finish()
    output "End of program"
return
```

Figure 8-15 A program that determines rents (continued)

 Watch the video *Two-Dimensional Arrays*.

Two-dimensional arrays are never actually *required* in order to achieve a useful program. The same 15 categories of rent information could be stored in three separate single-dimensional arrays of five elements each, and you could use a decision to determine which array to access. Of course, don't forget that even one-dimensional arrays are never required to solve a problem. You could also declare 15 separate rent variables and make 15 separate decisions to determine the rent.

Besides one- and two-dimensional arrays, many programming languages also support **three-dimensional arrays**. For example, if you own a multistory apartment building with different numbers of bedrooms available in apartments on each floor, you can use a two-dimensional array to store the rental fees, but if you own several apartment buildings, you might want to employ a third dimension to store the building number. For example, if a three-dimensional array is stored on paper, you might need to know an element's row, column, and page to access it, as shown in Figure 8-16.

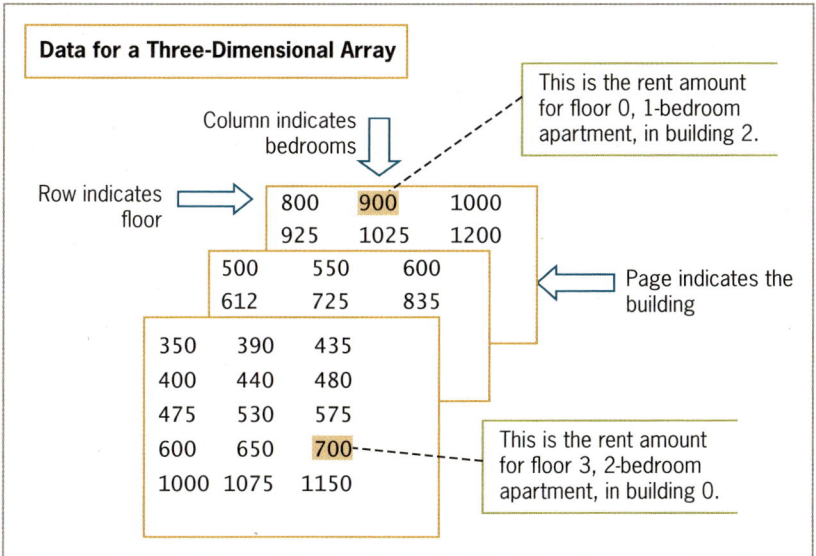

Figure 8-16 Picturing a three-dimensional array

If you declare a three-dimensional array named RENT_BY_3_FACTORS, then you can use an expression such as RENT_BY_3_FACTORS[floor][bedrooms][building], which refers to a specific rent figure for an apartment whose floor and bedroom numbers are stored in the floor and bedrooms variables, and whose building number is stored in the building variable. Specifically, RENT_BY_3_FACTORS[0][1][2] refers to a one-bedroom apartment on floor 0 of building 2.

 Both two- and three-dimensional arrays are examples of **multidimensional arrays**, which are arrays that have more than one dimension. Some languages allow many dimensions. For example, in C# and Visual Basic, an array can have 32 dimensions. However, it's usually hard for people to keep track of more than three dimensions.

TWO TRUTHS & A LIE

Using Multidimensional Arrays

1. In every multidimensional array, the location of any element depends on two factors.
2. For each element in a two-dimensional array, the first subscript represents the row number and the second one represents the column.
3. Multidimensional arrays are never actually *required* in order to achieve a useful program.

The false statement is #1. In a two-dimensional array, the location of any element depends on two factors, but in a three-dimensional array, it depends on three factors, and so on.

Using Indexed Files and Linked Lists

Sorting a list of five or even 100 scores does not require significant computer resources. However, many data files contain thousands of records, and each record might contain dozens of data fields. Sorting large numbers of data records requires considerable time and computer memory. When a large data file needs to be processed in ascending or descending order based on a particular field, the most efficient approach is usually to store and access records based on their logical order rather than sorting and accessing them in their physical order. **Physical order** refers to a "real" order for storage; an example would be writing the names of 10 friends, each one on a separate index card. You can arrange the cards alphabetically by the friends' last names, chronologically by age of the friendship, or randomly by throwing the cards in the air and picking them up as you find them. Whichever way you do it, the records still follow each other in *some* order. In addition to their current physical order, you can think of the cards as having a **logical order**; that is, a virtual order, based on any criterion you choose—from the tallest friend to the shortest, from the one who lives farthest away to the closest, and so on. Sorting the cards in a new physical order can take a lot of time; using the cards in their logical order without physically rearranging them is often more efficient.

Using Indexed Files

A common method of accessing records in logical order requires using an index. Using an index involves identifying a key field for each record. A record's **key field** is the field whose contents make the record unique among all records in a file. For example, multiple employees can have the same last name, first name, salary, or street address, but each employee possesses a unique employee identification number, so an ID number field might make a good key field for a personnel file. Similarly, a product number makes a good key field in an inventory file.

As pages in a book have numbers, computer memory and storage locations have **addresses**. In Chapter 1, you learned that every variable has a numeric address in computer memory; likewise, every data record on a disk has a numeric address where it is stored. You can store records in any physical order on the disk, but when you **index** records, you store a list of key fields paired with the storage address for the corresponding data record. Then you can use the index to find the records in order based on their addresses.

When you use an index, you can store records on a **random-access storage device**, such as a disk, from which records can be accessed in any order. Each record can be placed in any physical location on the disk, and you can use the index as you would use an index in the back of a book. If you pick up a 600-page American history book because you need some facts about Betsy Ross, you do not want to start on page one and work your way through the book. Instead, you turn to the index, discover that Betsy Ross is mentioned on page 418, and go directly to that page. As a programmer, you do not need to determine a record's exact physical address in order to use it. A computer's operating system takes care of locating available storage for your records.

 Chapter 7 contains a discussion of random access files.

You can picture an index based on ID numbers by looking at the index in Figure 8-17. The index is stored on a portion of the disk. The address in the index refers to other scattered locations on the disk.

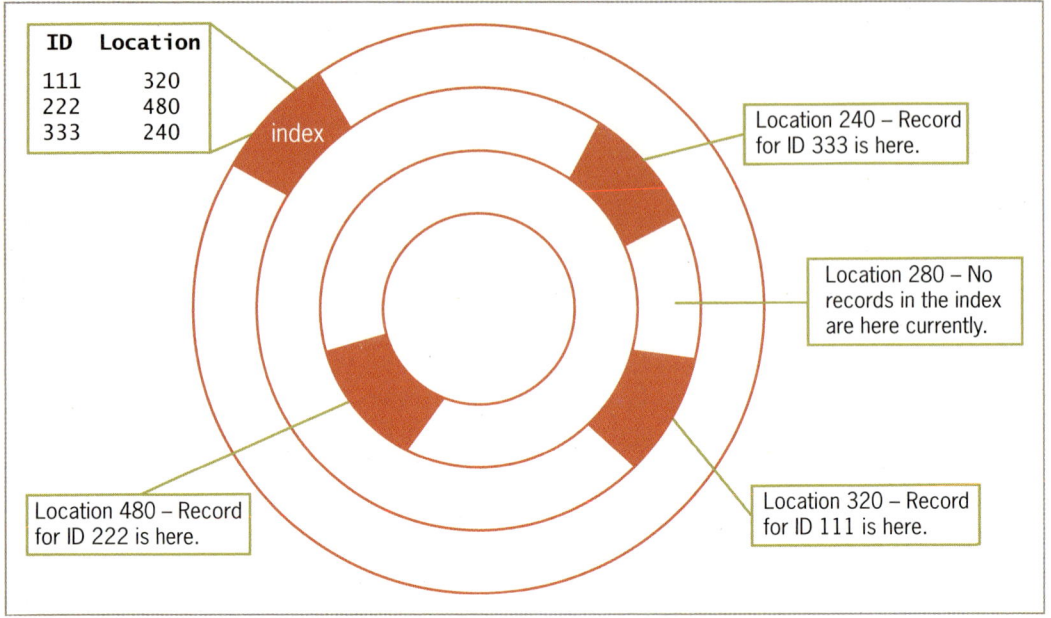

Figure 8-17　An index on a disk that associates ID numbers with disk addresses

When you want to access the data for employee 333, you tell your computer to look through the ID numbers in the index, find a match, and then proceed to the memory location specified. Similarly, when you want to process records in order based on ID number, you tell your system to retrieve records at the locations in the index in sequence. Thus, employee 111 may have been hired last and the record may be stored at the highest physical address on the disk, but if the employee record has the lowest ID number, it will be accessed first during any ordered processing.

When a record is removed from an indexed file, it does not have to be physically removed. Its reference can simply be deleted from the index, and then it will not be part of any further processing.

 Watch the video *Using an Indexed File*.

Using Linked Lists

Another way to access records in a desired order, even though they might not be physically stored in that order, is to create a linked list. In its simplest form, creating a **linked list** involves creating one extra field in every record of stored data. This extra field holds the physical address of the next logical record. For example, a record that holds a customer's ID, name, and phone number might contain the following fields:

idNum
name
phoneNum
nextCustAddress

Every time you use a record, you access the next record based on the address held in the nextCustAddress field.

Every time you add a new record to a linked list, you search through the list for the correct logical location of the new record. For example, assume that customer records are stored at the addresses shown in Table 8-3 and that they are linked in customer ID order. Notice that the addresses of the records are not shown in sequential order. The records are shown in their logical order by idNum.

Address	idNum	name	phoneNum	nextCustAddress of Record
0000	111	Baker	234-5676	7200
7200	222	Vincent	456-2345	4400
4400	333	Silvers	543-0912	6000
6000	444	Donovan	328-8744	eof

Table 8-3 Sample linked customer list

You can see from Table 8-3 that each customer record contains a nextCustAddress field that stores the address of the next customer who follows in customer ID number order (and not necessarily in address order). For any individual customer, the next logical customer's address might be physically distant.

Examine the file shown in Table 8-3, and suppose that a new customer is acquired with number *245* and the name *Newberg*. Also suppose that the computer operating system finds an available storage location for Newberg's data at address 8400. In this case, the procedure to add Newberg to the list is:

1. Create a variable named currentAddress to hold the address of the record in the list you are examining. Store the address of the first record in the list, 0000, in this variable.

2. Compare the new customer Newberg's ID, 245, with the current (first) record's ID, 111 (in other words, the ID at address 0000). The value 245 is higher than 111, so you save the first customer's address—0000, the address you are currently examining—in a variable you can name saveAddress. The saveAddress variable always holds the address you just finished examining. The first customer record contains a link to the address of the next logical customer—7200. Store 7200 in the currentAddress variable.

3. Examine the second customer record, the one that physically exists at the address 7200, which is currently held in the currentAddress variable.

4. Compare Newberg's ID, 245, with the ID stored in the record at currentAddress, 222. The value 245 is higher, so save the current address, 7200, in saveAddress and store its nextCustAddress address field, 4400, in the currentAddress variable.

5. Compare Newberg's ID, 245, with 333, which is the ID at currentAddress (4400). Up to this point, 245 had been higher than each ID tested, but this time the value 245 is lower, so customer 245 should logically precede customer 333. Set the nextCustAddress field in Newberg's record (customer 245) to 4400, which is the address of customer 333 and the address stored in currentAddress. This means that in any future processing, Newberg's record will logically be followed by the record containing 333. Also set the nextCustAddress field of the record located at saveAddress (7200, customer 222, Vincent, who logically preceded Newberg) to the new customer Newberg's address, 8400. The updated list appears in Table 8-4.

Address	idNum	name	phoneNum	nextCustAddress of Record
0000	111	Baker	234-5676	7200
7200	222	Vincent	456-2345	8400
8400	245	Newberg	222-9876	4400
4400	333	Silvers	543-0912	6000
6000	444	Donovan	328-8744	eof

Table 8-4 Updated customer list

As with indexing, when removing records from a linked list, the records do not need to be physically deleted from the medium on which they are stored. If you need to remove customer 333 from the preceding list, all you need to do is change Newberg's nextCustAddress field to the value in Silvers' nextCustAddress field, which is Donovan's address: 6000. In other words, the value of 6000 is obtained not by knowing to which record Newberg should point, but by knowing to which record Silvers previously pointed. When Newberg's record points to Donovan, Silvers' record is then bypassed during any further processing that uses the links to travel from one record to the next.

More sophisticated linked lists store *two* additional fields with each record. One field stores the address of the next record, and the other field stores the address of the *previous* record so that the list can be accessed either forward or backward.

 Watch the video *Using a Linked List*.

> **TWO TRUTHS & A LIE**
>
> **Using Indexed Files and Linked Lists**
>
> 1. When a large data file needs to be processed in order based on a particular field, the most efficient approach is usually to sort the records.
> 2. A record's key field contains a value that makes the record unique among all records in a file.
> 3. Creating a linked list requires you to create one extra field for every record; this extra field holds the physical address of the next logical record.
>
> The false statement is #1. The most efficient approach is usually to store and access records based on their logical order rather than sorting and accessing them in their physical order.

Chapter Summary

- Frequently, data items need to be sorted. When you sort data, you can sort either in ascending order, arranging records from lowest to highest value, or in descending order, arranging records from highest to lowest value.

- In a bubble sort, items in a list are compared with each other in pairs. When an item is out of order, it swaps values with the item below it. With an ascending bubble sort, after each adjacent pair of items in a list has been compared once, the largest item in the list will have "sunk" to the bottom; after many passes through the list, the smallest items rise to the top. The bubble sort algorithm can be improved to sort varying numbers of values and to eliminate unnecessary comparisons.

- When you sort records, two possible approaches are to place related data items in parallel arrays and to sort records as a whole.

- When you use an insertion sort, you look at each list element one at a time. If an element is out of order relative to any of the items earlier in the list, you move each earlier item down one position and then insert the tested element.

- Two-dimensional arrays have both rows and columns of values. You must use two subscripts when you access an element in a two-dimensional array. Many languages support arrays with even more dimensions.

- You can use an index or linked list to access data records in a logical order that differs from their physical order. Using an index involves identifying a physical address and key field for each record. Creating a linked list involves creating an extra field within every record to hold the physical address of the next logical record.

CHAPTER 8   Advanced Data Handling Concepts

Key Terms

Sequential order describes the arrangement of records when they are stored one after another on the basis of the value in a particular field.

The **median** value in a list is the value in the middle position when the values are sorted.

The **mean** value in a list is the arithmetic average.

A **bubble sort** is a sort in which you arrange list elements in either ascending or descending order by comparing items in pairs; when an item is out of order, it swaps values with the item below it.

A **sinking sort** is another name for a bubble sort.

An **algorithm** is a list of instructions that accomplish a task.

To **swap values** is to exchange the values of two variables.

An **insertion sort** is a sort in which you look at each list element one at a time; if an element is out of order relative to any of the items earlier in the list, you move each earlier item down one position and then insert the tested element.

A **one-dimensional** or **single-dimensional array** is a list accessed using a single subscript.

Two-dimensional arrays have both rows and columns of values; you must use two subscripts when you access an element in a two-dimensional array.

Matrix and **table** are terms used by mathematicians to describe a two-dimensional array.

Three-dimensional arrays are arrays in which each element is accessed using three subscripts.

Multidimensional arrays are lists with more than one dimension.

A list's **physical order** is the order in which it is actually stored.

A list's **logical order** is the order in which you use it, even though it is not necessarily stored in that physical order.

The **key field** of a record contains a value that makes the record unique among all records in a file.

Addresses identify computer memory and storage locations.

When you **index** records, you store a list of key fields paired with the storage address for the corresponding data record.

A **random-access storage device**, such as a disk, is one from which records can be accessed in any order.

A **linked list** contains an extra field in every record of stored data; this extra field holds the physical address of the next logical record.

Review Questions

1. Employee records stored in order from highest-paid to lowest-paid have been sorted in _____ order.

   a. ascending
   b. descending
   c. staggered
   d. recursive

2. Student records stored in alphabetical order by last name have been sorted in _____ order.

   a. ascending
   b. descending
   c. staggered
   d. recursive

3. When computers sort data, they always _____.

   a. place items in ascending order
   b. use a bubble sort
   c. use numeric values when making comparisons
   d. begin the process by locating the position of the lowest value

4. Which of the following code segments correctly swaps the values of variables named x and y?

   a. ```
      x = y
      y = temp
      x = temp
      ```
   b. ```
      temp = x
      x = y
      y = temp
      ```
   c. ```
      x = y
      temp = x
      y = temp
      ```
   d. ```
      temp = x
      y = x
      x = temp
      ```

5. Which type of sort compares list items in pairs, swapping any two adjacent values that are out of order?

   a. bubble sort
   b. indexed sort
   c. insertion sort
   d. selection sort

6. To sort a list of eight values using a bubble sort, the greatest number of times you would have to pass through the list making comparisons is _____.

   a. six
   b. seven
   c. eight
   d. nine

7. To completely sort a list of eight values using a bubble sort, the greatest possible number of required pair comparisons is _____.

   a. seven
   b. eight
   c. 49
   d. 64

8. When you do not know how many items need to be sorted in a program, you can create an array that has _____.
   a. variable-sized elements
   b. at least as many elements as the number you predict you will need
   c. at least one element less than the number you predict you will need
   d. You cannot sort items if you do not know the number of items when you write the program.

9. In a bubble sort, on each pass through the list that must be sorted, you can stop making pair comparisons _____.
   a. one comparison sooner
   b. two comparisons sooner
   c. one comparison later
   d. two comparisons later

10. When performing a bubble sort on a list of 10 values, you can stop making passes through the list of values as soon as _____ on a single pass through the list.
    a. no swaps are made
    b. exactly one swap is made
    c. no more than nine swaps are made
    d. no more than 10 swaps are made

11. The bubble sort is _____.
    a. the most efficient sort
    b. a relatively fast sort compared to others
    c. a relatively easy sort to understand
    d. all of the above

12. Data stored in a table that can be accessed using row and column numbers is stored as a _____ array.
    a. single-dimensional
    b. two-dimensional
    c. three-dimensional
    d. nondimensional

13. A two-dimensional array declared as num myArray[6][7] has _____ columns.
    a. 5
    b. 6
    c. 7
    d. 8

14. In a two-dimensional array declared as num myArray[6][7], the highest row number is _____.
    a. 5
    b. 6
    c. 7
    d. 8

15. If you access a two-dimensional array with the expression `output myArray[2][5]`, the output value will be _____ .

    a. 0
    b. 2
    c. 5
    d. impossible to tell from the information given

16. Three-dimensional arrays _____ .

    a. are supported in many modern programming languages
    b. always contain at least nine elements
    c. are used only in object-oriented languages
    d. all of the above

17. Student records are stored in ID number order, but accessed by grade-point average for a report. Grade-point average order is a(n) _____ order.

    a. imaginary
    b. physical
    c. logical
    d. illogical

18. When you store a list of key fields paired with the storage address for the corresponding data record, you are creating _____ .

    a. a directory
    b. a three-dimensional array
    c. a linked list
    d. an index

19. When a record in an indexed file is not needed for further processing, _____ .

    a. its first character must be replaced with a special character, indicating it is a deleted record
    b. its position must be retained, but its fields must be replaced with blanks
    c. it must be physically removed from the file
    d. the record can stay in place physically, but its reference is removed from the index

20. With a linked list, every record _____ .

    a. is stored in sequential order
    b. contains a field that holds the address of another record
    c. contains a code that indicates the record's position in an imaginary list
    d. is stored in a physical location that corresponds to a key field

Exercises

1. Design an application that accepts 10 numbers and displays them in descending order.

2. Design an application that accepts eight friends' first names and displays them in alphabetical order.

3. a. Professor Zak allows students to drop the two lowest scores on the 10 100-point quizzes she gives during the semester. Design an application that accepts a student name and 10 quiz scores. Output the student's name and total points for the student's eight highest-scoring quizzes.

    b. Modify the application in Exercise 3a so that the student's mean and median scores on the eight best quizzes are displayed.

4. The Keen Knife Company has 12 salespeople. Write a program into which a clerk can enter each salesperson's monthly sales goal and actual monthly sales in dollars, and determine the mean and median values of each of the two monthly amounts.

5. The village of Marengo conducted a census and collected records that contain household data, including the number of occupants in each household. The exact number of household records has not yet been determined, but you know that Marengo has fewer than 300 households. Develop the logic for a program that allows a user to enter each household size and determine the mean and median household size in Marengo.

6. a. The Palmertown Elementary School has 30 classrooms. The children in the school donate used books to sell at an annual fundraising book fair. Write a program that accepts each teacher's name and the number of books donated by that teacher's classroom. Display the names of the four teachers whose classrooms donated the most books.

    b. Modify the book donation program so that, besides the teacher's name and number of books donated, the program also accepts the number of students in each classroom. Display the names of the teachers whose classrooms had the four highest ratios of book donations per pupil.

7. *The Daily Trumpet* newspaper accepts classified advertisements in 15 categories such as *Apartments for Rent* and *Pets for Sale*. Develop the logic for a program that accepts classified advertising data, including category code (an integer 1 through 15) and number of words in the ad. Store these values in parallel arrays. Then sort the arrays so that records are in ascending order by category. The output lists each category, the number of ads in each category, and the total number of words in the ads in each category.

8. The MidAmerica Bus Company charges fares to passengers based on the number of travel zones they cross. Additionally, discounts are provided for multiple passengers traveling together. Ticket fares are shown in Table 8-5.

Exercises

		Zones Crossed		
Passengers	0	1	2	3
1	7.50	10.00	12.00	12.75
2	14.00	18.50	22.00	23.00
3	20.00	21.00	32.00	33.00
4	25.00	27.50	36.00	37.00

Table 8-5 Bus fares

Develop the logic for a program that accepts the number of passengers and zones crossed as input. The output is the ticket charge.

9. In golf, par represents a standard number of strokes a player needs to complete a hole. Instead of using an absolute score, players can compare their scores on a hole to the par figure. Families can play nine holes of miniature golf at the Family Fun Miniature Golf Park. So that family members can compete fairly, the course provides a different par for each hole based on the player's age. The par figures are shown in Table 8-6.

					Holes				
Age	1	2	3	4	5	6	7	8	9
4 and under	8	8	9	7	5	7	8	5	8
5–7	7	7	8	6	5	6	7	5	6
8–11	6	5	6	5	4	5	5	4	5
12–15	5	4	4	4	3	4	3	3	4
16 and over	4	3	3	3	2	3	2	3	3

Table 8-6 Golf par values

   a. Develop the logic for a program that accepts a player's name, age, and nine-hole score as input. Display the player's name and score on each of the nine holes, with one of the phrases *Over par*, *Par*, or *Under par* next to each score.

   b. Modify the program in Exercise 9a so that, at the end of the golfer's report, the total score is displayed. Include the player's total score in relation to par for the entire course.

10. Building Block Day Care Center charges varying weekly rates depending on the age of the child and the number of days per week the child attends, as shown in Table 8-7. Develop the logic for a program that continuously accepts child care data and displays the appropriate weekly rate.

	Days Per Week				
Age in Years	1	2	3	4	5
0	30.00	60.00	88.00	115.00	140.00
1	26.00	52.00	70.00	96.00	120.00
2	24.00	46.00	67.00	89.00	110.00
3	22.00	40.00	60.00	75.00	88.00
4 or more	20.00	35.00	50.00	66.00	84.00

Table 8-7 Day care rates

11. Executive Training School offers typing classes. Each final exam evaluates a student's typing speed and the number of typing errors made. Develop the logic for a program that produces a summary table of each examination's results. Each row represents the number of students whose typing speed falls within the following ranges of words per minute: 0–19, 20–39, 40–69, and 70 or more. Each column represents the number of students who made different numbers of typing errors—0 through 6 or more.

12. HappyTunes is an application for downloading music files. Each time a file is purchased, a transaction record is created that includes the music genre and price paid. The available genres are *Classical, Easy Listening, Jazz, Pop, Rock,* and *Other*. Develop an application that accepts input data for each transaction and displays a report that lists each of the music genres, along with a count of the number of downloads in each of the following price categories:

    - Over $10.00
    - $6.00 through $9.99
    - $3.00 through $5.99
    - Under $3.00

Find the Bugs

13. Your downloadable files for Chapter 8 include DEBUG08-01.txt, DEBUG08-02.txt, and DEBUG08-03.txt. Each file starts with some comments that describe the problem. Comments are lines that begin with two slashes (//). Following the comments, each file contains pseudocode that has one or more bugs you must find and correct.

Exercises

Game Zone

14. In the Game Zone section of Chapter 6, you designed the logic for a quiz that contains multiple-choice questions about a topic of your choice. (Each question had three answer options.) Now, modify the program so it allows the user to retake the quiz up to four additional times or until the user achieves a perfect score, whichever comes first. At the end of all the quiz attempts, display a recap of the user's scores.

15. In the Game Zone section of Chapter 5, you designed a guessing game in which the application generates a random number and the player tries to guess it. After each guess, you displayed a message indicating whether the player's guess was correct, too high, or too low. When the player eventually guessed the correct number, you displayed a score that represented a count of the number of required guesses. Now, modify that program to allow a player to replay the game as many times as he likes, up to 20 times. When the player is done, display the scores from highest to lowest, and display the mean and median scores.

16. a. Create a TicTacToe game. In this game, two players alternate placing Xs and Os into a grid until one player has three matching symbols in a row, either horizontally, vertically, or diagonally. Create a game that displays a three-by-three grid containing the digits 1 through 9, similar to the first window shown in Figure 8-18. When the user chooses a position by typing a number, place an X in the appropriate spot. For example, after the user chooses 3, the screen looks like the second window in Figure 8-18. Generate a random number for the position where the computer will place an O. Do not allow the player or the computer to place a symbol where one has already been placed. When either the player or computer has three symbols in a row, declare a winner. If all positions have been used and no one has three symbols in a row, declare a tie.

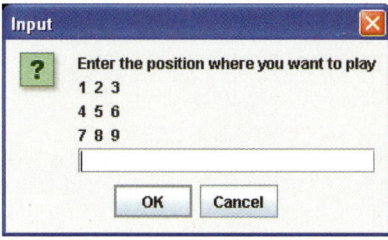 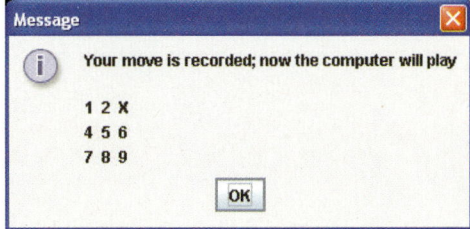

Figure 8-18   A TicTacToe game

b. In the TicTacToe game in Exercise 16a, the computer's selection is chosen randomly. Improve the game so that when the computer has two Os in any row, column, or diagonal, it selects the winning position for its next move rather than selecting a position randomly.

CHAPTER 8 Advanced Data Handling Concepts

 ## Up for Discussion

17. Now that you are becoming comfortable with arrays, you can see that programming is a complex subject. Should all literate people understand how to program? If so, how much programming should they understand?

18. What are language standards? At this point in your study of programming, what do they mean to you?

19. This chapter discusses sorting data. Suppose that a large hospital hires you to write a program that displays lists of potential organ recipients. The hospital's doctors will consult this list if they have an organ that can be transplanted. The hospital administrators instruct you to sort potential recipients by last name and display them sequentially in alphabetical order. If more than 10 patients are waiting for a particular organ, the first 10 patients are displayed; a doctor can either select one or move on to view the next set of 10 patients. You worry that this system gives an unfair advantage to patients with last names that start with A, B, C, and D. Should you write and install the program? If you do not, many transplant opportunities will be missed while the hospital searches for another programmer to write the program. Are there different criteria you would want to use to sort the patients?

CHAPTER 9

Advanced Modularization Techniques

In this chapter, you will learn about:

◎ Methods with no parameters
◎ Methods that require parameters
◎ Methods that return a value
◎ Passing arrays to methods
◎ Overloading methods
◎ Using predefined methods
◎ Method design issues, including implementation hiding, cohesion, and coupling
◎ Recursion

Using Methods with No Parameters

In object-oriented programming languages such as Java and C#, modules are most often called *methods*. In Chapter 2, you learned about many features of methods and much of the vocabulary associated with them. For example:

- A **method** is a program module that contains a series of statements that carry out a task; you can invoke or call a method from another program or method.

- Any program can contain an unlimited number of methods, and each method can be called an unlimited number of times.

- The rules for naming methods are different in every programming language, but they often are similar to the language's rules for variable names. In this text, method names are followed by a set of parentheses.

- A method must include a **method header** (also called the declaration or definition), which contains identifying information about the method.

- A method includes a **method body**. The body contains the method's **implementation**—the statements that carry out the method's tasks.

- A **method return statement** returns control to the calling method after a method executes. Although methods with multiple `return` statements are allowed in many programming languages, that style is not recommended. Structured programming requires that a method should contain only one `return` statement—the last statement in the method.

- Variables and constants can be declared within a method. A data item declared in a method is **local** to that method, meaning it is in scope, or recognized only within that method.

- The opposite of local is global. When a data item is known to all of a program's modules, it is a **global** data item. In general, programmers prefer local data items because when data is contained within the method that uses it, the method is more portable and less prone to error. In Chapter 2, you learned that when a method is described as *portable*, it can easily be moved to another application and used there.

Figure 9-1 shows a program that allows a user to enter a preferred language (English or Spanish) and then, using the chosen language, asks the user to enter his or her weight. The program then calculates the user's weight on the moon as 16.6 percent of the user's weight on Earth. The main program contains two variables and a constant, all of which are declared in the main program. The program calls the `displayInstructions()` method, which contains its own local variable and constants that are invisible to the main program. The method prompts the user for a language indicator and displays a prompt in the selected language. Figure 9-2 shows a typical program execution in a command-line environment.

Using Methods with No Parameters

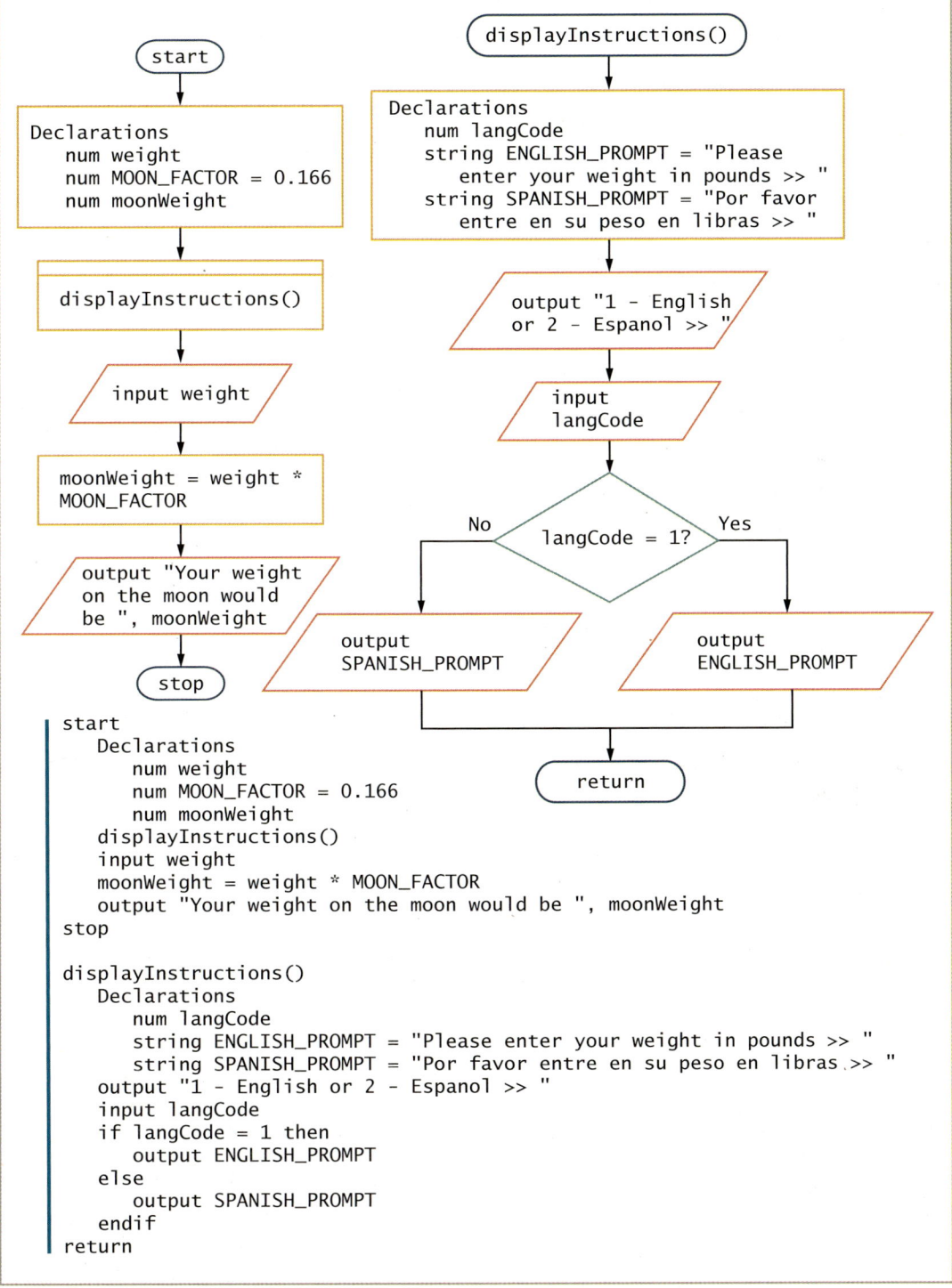

Figure 9-1   A program that calculates the user's weight on the moon

CHAPTER 9   Advanced Modularization Techniques

 In Chapter 2, you learned that this book uses a rectangle with a horizontal stripe across the top to represent a method call statement in a flowchart. Some programmers prefer to use a rectangle with two vertical stripes at the sides, and you should use that convention if your organization prefers it. This book reserves the shape with two vertical stripes to represent a method from a library that is external to the program.

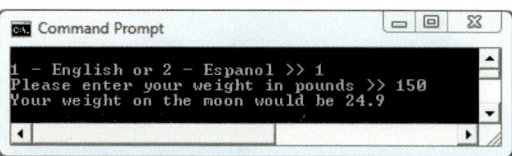

Figure 9-2   Output of moon weight calculator program in Figure 9-1

In Figure 9-1, the main program and the called method each contain only data items that are needed at the local level. However, sometimes two or more parts of a program require access to the same data. When methods must share data, you can pass the data into methods and return data out of them. In this chapter, you will learn that when you call a method from a program or other method, you should know three things:

- The name of the called method
- What type of information to send to the method, if any
- What type of return data to expect from the method, if any

TWO TRUTHS & A LIE

Using Methods with No Parameters

1. A program can contain an unlimited number of methods, but each method can be called once.
2. A method includes a header and a body.
3. Variables and constants are in scope within, or local to, only the method in which they are declared.

The false statement is #1. Each method can be called an unlimited number of times.

Creating Methods that Require Parameters

Some methods require information to be sent in from the outside. When you pass a data item into a method from a calling program, it is called an **argument to the method**, or more simply, an argument. When the method receives the data item, it is called a **parameter to the method**, or more simply, a parameter.

Creating Methods that Require Parameters

Parameter and *argument* are closely related terms. A calling method sends an argument to a called method. A called method accepts the value as its parameter.

If a method could not receive parameters, you would have to write an infinite number of methods to cover every possible situation. As a real-life example, when you make a restaurant reservation, you do not need to employ a different method for every date of the year at every possible time of day. Rather, you can supply the date and time as information to the person who carries out the method. The method that records the reservation is carried out in the same manner, no matter what date and time are supplied. If you design a `square()` method that squares numeric values, you should supply the method with a parameter that represents the value to be squared, rather than developing a `square1()` method that squares the value 1, a `square2()` method that squares the value 2, and so on. To call a `square()` method that accepts a parameter, you might write a statement like `square(17)` or `square(86)` and let the method use whatever argument you send.

When you write the declaration for a method that can receive a parameter, you must include the following items within the method declaration's parentheses:

- The type of the parameter
- A local name for the parameter

The types and names of parameters are the method's **parameter list**. A method's name and parameter list constitute the method's **signature**.

For example, suppose that you decide to improve the moon weight program in Figure 9-1 by making the final output more user-friendly and adding the explanatory text in the chosen language. It makes sense that if the user can request a prompt in a specific language, the user would want to see the output explanation in the same language. However, in Figure 9-1, the `langCode` variable is local to the `displayInstructions()` method and therefore cannot be used in the main program. You could rewrite the program by taking several approaches:

- You could rewrite the program without including any methods. That way, you could prompt the user for a language preference and display the prompt and the result in the appropriate language. This approach would work, but you would not be taking advantage of the benefits provided by modularization. Those benefits include making the main program more streamlined and abstract, and making the `displayInstructions()` method a self-contained unit that can easily be transported to other programs—for example, applications that might determine a user's weight on Saturn or Mars.

- You could retain the `displayInstructions()` method, but make at least the `langCode` variable global by declaring it outside of any methods. If you took this approach, you would lose some of the portability of the `displayInstructions()` method because everything it used would no longer be contained within the method.

- You could retain the `displayInstructions()` method as is with its own local declarations, but add a section to the main program that also asks the user for a preferred language to display the result. The disadvantage to this approach is that the user must answer the same question twice during one execution of the program.

- You could store the variable that holds the language code in the main program so that it could be used to determine the result language. You could also retain the `displayInstructions()` method, but pass the language code to it so the prompt would appear in the appropriate language. This is the best choice, and is illustrated in Figures 9-3 and 9-4.

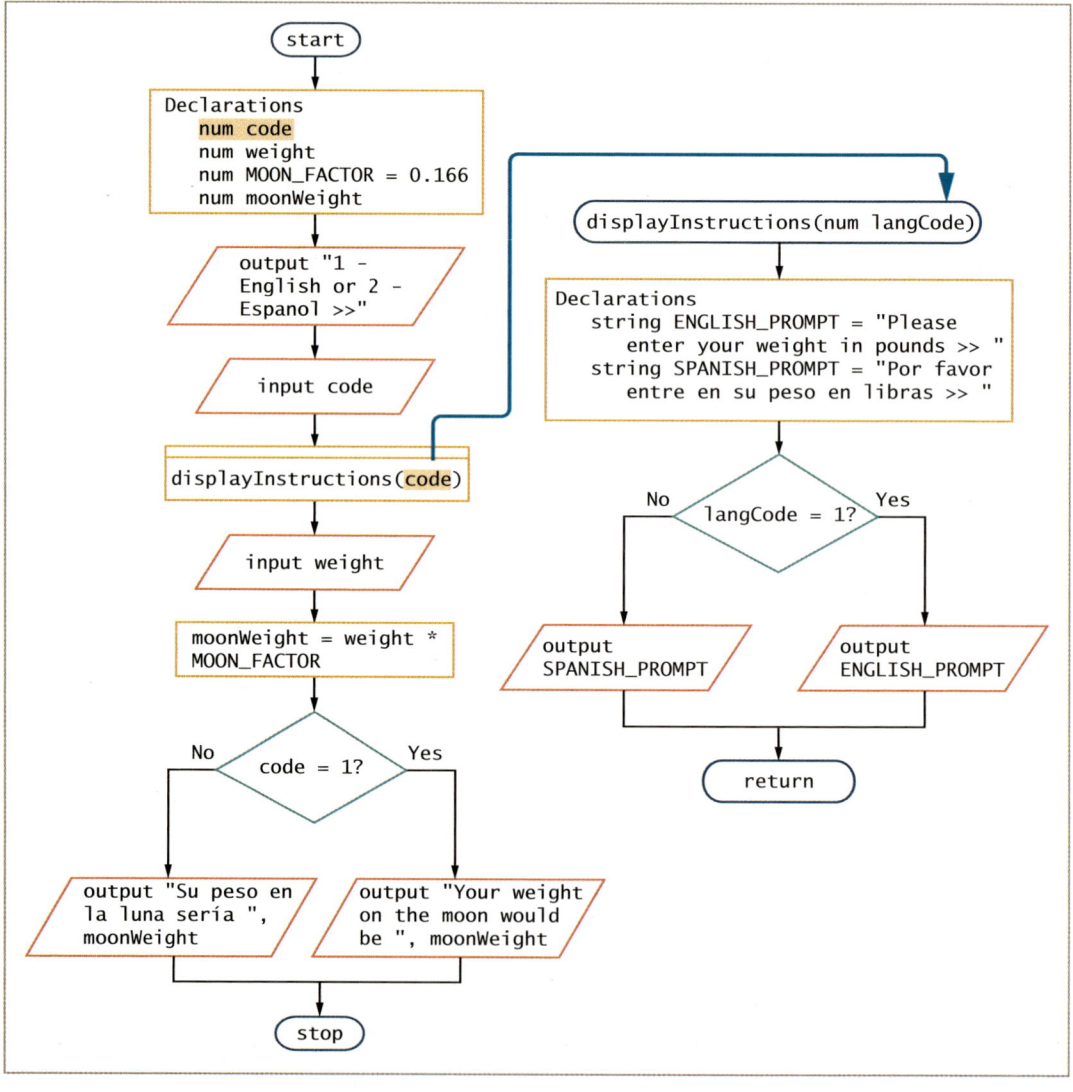

Figure 9-3 Moon weight program that passes an argument to a method

Creating Methods that Require Parameters

```
start
   Declarations
      num code
      num weight
      num MOON_FACTOR = 0.166
      num moonWeight
   output "1 - English or 2 - Espanol >>"
   input code
   displayInstructions(code)
   input weight
   moonWeight = weight * MOON_FACTOR
   if code = 1 then
      output "Your weight on the moon would be ", moonWeight
   else
      output "Su peso en la luna seria ", moonWeight
   endif
stop

displayInstructions(num langCode)
   Declarations
      string ENGLISH_PROMPT = "Please enter your weight in pounds >> "
      string SPANISH_PROMPT = "Por favor entre en su peso en libras >> "
   if langCode = 1 then
      output ENGLISH_PROMPT
   else
      output SPANISH_PROMPT
   endif
return
```

Figure 9-3 Moon weight program that passes an argument to a method (continued)

Figure 9-4 Typical execution of moon weight program in Figure 9-3

In the main program in Figure 9-3, a numeric variable named **code** is declared and the user is prompted for a value. The value then is passed to the `displayInstructions()` method. The value of the language code is stored in two places in memory:

- The main method stores the code in the variable **code** and passes it to `displayInstructions()` as an argument.

- The `displayInstructions()` method accepts the parameter as `langCode`. Within the method, `langCode` takes on the value that **code** had in the main program.

You can think of the parentheses in a method declaration as a funnel into the method; parameters listed there hold values that are "dropped in" to the method.

A variable passed into a method is **passed by value**; that is, a copy of its value is sent to the method and stored in a new memory location accessible to the method. The `displayInstructions()` method could be called using any numeric value as an argument, whether it is a variable, a named constant, or a literal constant. If the value used as an argument in the method call is a variable, it might possess the same identifier as the parameter declared in the method header, or it might possess a different identifier. Within a method, the passed variable is simply a temporary placeholder; it makes no difference what name the variable "goes by" in the calling program.

Each time a method executes, any parameter variables listed as parameters in the method header are redeclared—that is, new memory locations are reserved and named. When the method ends at the `return` statement, the locally declared parameter variables cease to exist. For example, Figure 9-5 shows a program that declares a variable, assigns a value to it, displays it, and sends it to a method. Within the method, the parameter is displayed, altered, and displayed again. When control returns to the main program, the original variable is displayed one last time. As the execution in Figure 9-6 shows, even though the variable in the method was altered, the original variable in the main program retains its starting value because it never was altered; it occupies a different memory address from the variable in the method.

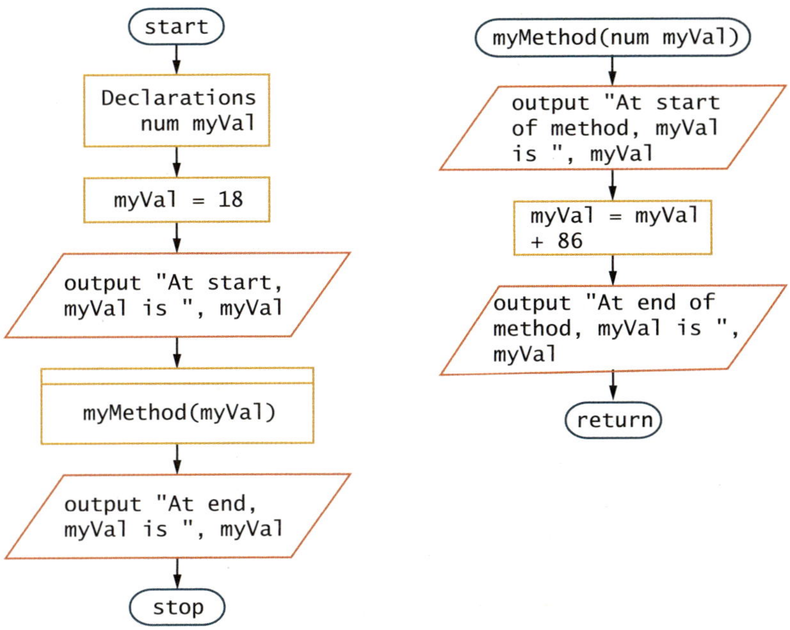

Creating Methods that Require Parameters

```
start
    Declarations
        num myVal
    myVal = 18
    output "At start, myVal is ", myVal
    myMethod(myVal)
    output "At end, myVal is ", myVal
stop

myMethod(num myVal)
    output "At start of method, myVal is ", myVal
    myVal = myVal + 86
    output "At end of method, myVal is ", myVal
return
```

Figure 9-5 A program that calls a method in which the argument and parameter have the same identifier

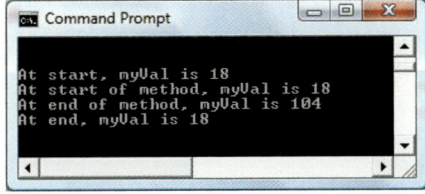

Figure 9-6 Execution of the program in Figure 9-5

CHAPTER 9 Advanced Modularization Techniques

 Watch the video *Methods with a Parameter*.

Creating Methods that Require Multiple Parameters

You create and use a method with multiple parameters by doing the following:

- You list the arguments within the method call, separated by commas.
- You list a data type and local identifier for each parameter within the method header's parentheses, separating each declaration with a comma. Even if multiple parameters are the same data type, the type must be repeated with each parameter.

 The arguments sent to a method in a method call are its **actual parameters**. The variables in the method declaration that accept the values from the actual parameters are **formal parameters**.

For example, suppose that you want to create a computeTax() method that calculates a tax on any value passed into it. You can create a method to which you pass two values—the amount to be taxed as well as a rate by which to tax it. Figure 9-7 shows a method that accepts two such parameters.

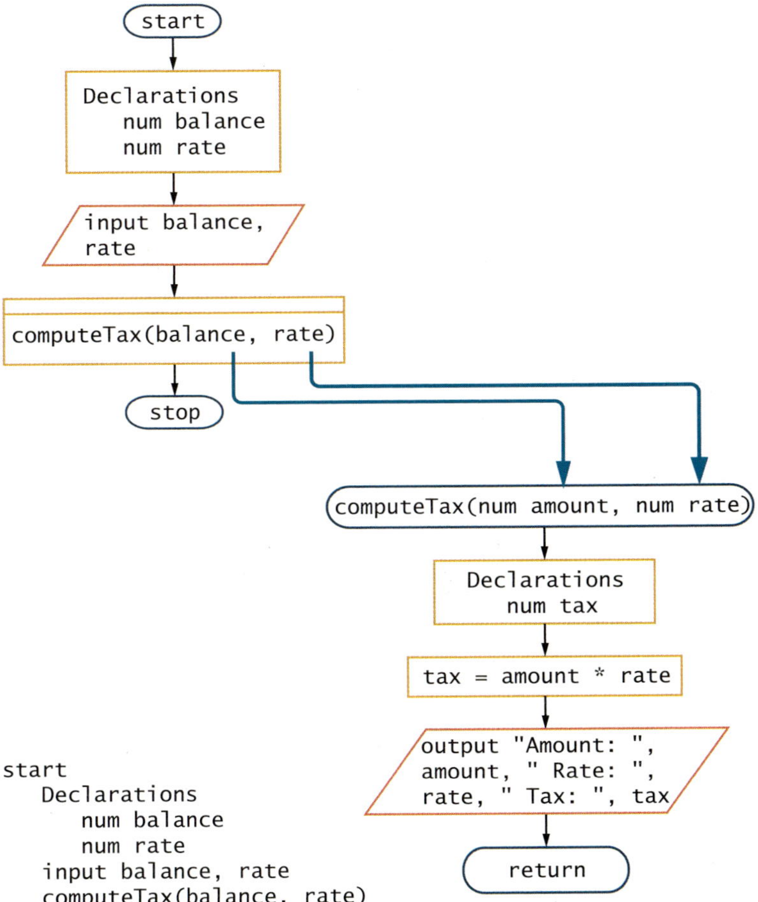

Creating Methods that Require Parameters

```
start
   Declarations
      num balance
      num rate
   input balance, rate
   computeTax(balance, rate)
stop

computeTax(num amount, num rate)
   Declarations
      num tax
   tax = amount * rate
   output "Amount: ", amount, " Rate: ", rate, " Tax: ", tax
return
```

Figure 9-7 A program that calls a `computeTax()` method that requires two parameters

In Figure 9-7, notice that one of the arguments to the method has the same name as the corresponding method parameter, and the other has a different name from its corresponding parameter. Each could have the same identifier as its counterpart, or all could be different. Each identifier is local to its own method.

In Figure 9-7, two parameters (`num amount` and `num rate`) appear within the parentheses in the method header. A comma separates each parameter, and each requires its own declared type (in this case, both are numeric) as well as its own identifier. When multiple values are passed to a method, they are accepted by the parameters in the order in which they are passed. You can write a method so that it takes any number of parameters in any order. However, when you call a method, the arguments you send to the method must match in order—both in number and in type—the parameters listed in the method declaration. A call of `computeTax(rate, balance)` instead of `computeTax(balance, rate)` would result in incorrect values being displayed in the output statement.

If method arguments are the same type—for example, two numeric arguments—passing them to a method in the wrong order results in a logical error; the program will compile and execute, but produce incorrect results. If a method expects arguments of diverse types—for example, a number and a string—then passing arguments in the wrong order is a syntax error, and the program will not compile.

 Watch the video *Methods with Multiple Parameters*.

TWO TRUTHS & A LIE

Creating Methods that Require Parameters

1. A value sent to a method from a calling program is a parameter.
2. When you write the declaration for a method that can receive parameters, you must include a data type for each parameter even if multiple parameters are the same type.
3. When a variable is used as an argument in a method call, it can have the same identifier as the parameter in the method header.

The false statement is #1. A calling method sends an argument; when the method receives the value, it is a parameter.

Creating Methods that Return a Value

A variable declared within a method ceases to exist when the method ends—it goes out of scope. When you want to retain a value that exists when a method ends, you can return the value from the method to the calling method. When a method returns a value, the method must have a **return type** that matches the data type of the returned value. A return type can be any type, which includes `num` and `string`, as well as other types specific to the programming language you are using. A method can also return nothing, in which case the return type is `void`, and the method is a **void method**. (The term *void* means "nothing" or "empty.") A method's return type is known more succinctly as a **method's type**, which is listed in front of the method name when it is defined. Previously, this book has not included return types for methods because all the methods have been void. From this point forward, a return type is included with every method.

Along with an identifier and parameter list, a return type is part of a method's declaration. Some programmers claim a method's return type is part of its signature, but this is not the case. Only the method name and parameter list constitute the signature.

For example, a method that returns the number of hours an employee has worked might have the following header:

`num getHoursWorked()`

This method returns a numeric value, so its type is `num`.

When a method returns a value, you usually want to use the returned value in the calling method, although this is not required. For example, Figure 9-8 shows how a program might use the value returned by the `getHoursWorked()` method. A variable named `hours` is declared in the main program. The `getHoursWorked()` method call is part of an assignment statement. When the method is called, the logical control is transferred to the `getHoursWorked()` method, which contains a variable named `workHours`. A value is obtained for this variable, which is returned to the main program where it is assigned to `hours`. After logical control returns to the main program from the `getHoursWorked()` method, the method's local variable `workHours` no longer exists. However, its value has been stored in the main program where, as `hours`, it can be displayed and used in a calculation.

As an example of when you might call a method but not use its returned value, consider a method that gets a character from the keyboard and returns its value to the calling program. In some applications, you would want to use the value of the returned characters. However, in other applications, you might want to tell the user to press any key. Then, you could call the method to accept the character from the keyboard, but you would not care which key was pressed or which key value was returned.

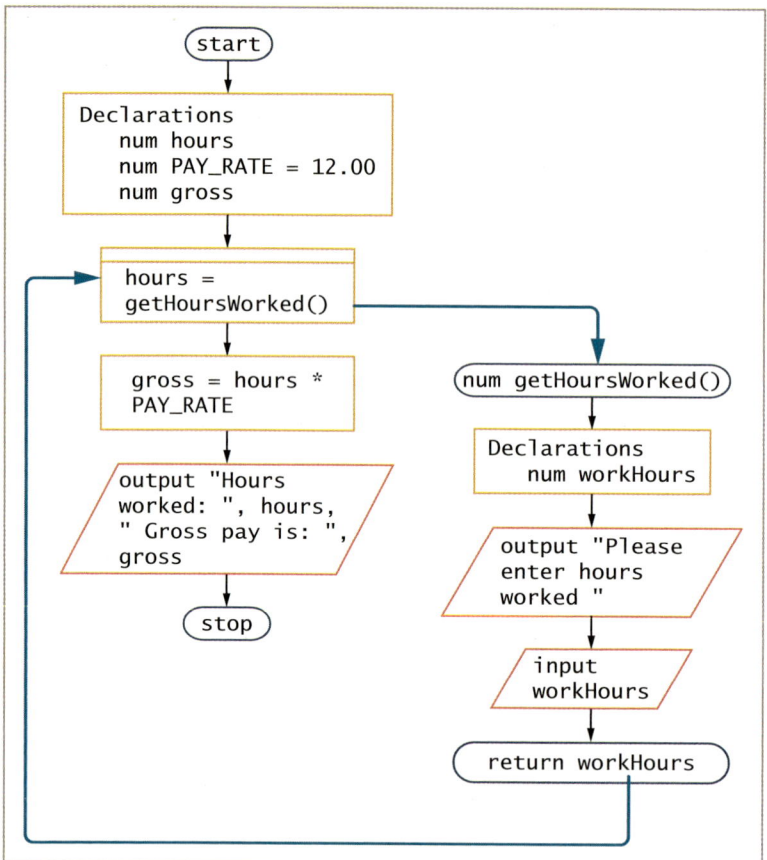

Figure 9-8 A payroll program that calls a method that returns a value

In Figure 9-8, notice the return type **num** that precedes the method name in the `getHoursWorked()` method header. A method's declared return type must match the type of value used in the **return** statement; if it does not, the program will not compile. A numeric value is correctly included in the **return** statement—the last statement in the `getHoursWorked()` method. When you place a value in a **return** statement, the value is sent from the called method back to the calling method.

A method's **return** statement can return one value at most. The returned value can be a variable or a constant. The value can be a simple data type or a more complex type. For example, in Chapter 10 you will learn to create objects, which are more complex data types.

You are not required to assign a method's return value to a variable to use the value. Instead, you can use a method's returned value directly, without storing it. You use a method's value in the same way you would use any variable of the same type. For example, you can output a return value in a statement such as the following:

```
output "Hours worked is ", getHoursWorked()
```

Because `getHoursWorked()` returns a numeric value, you can use the method call `getHoursWorked()` in the same way that you would use any simple numeric value. Figure 9-9 shows an example of a program that uses a method's return value directly without storing it. The value of the shaded `workHours` variable returned from the method is used directly in the calculation of `gross` in the main program.

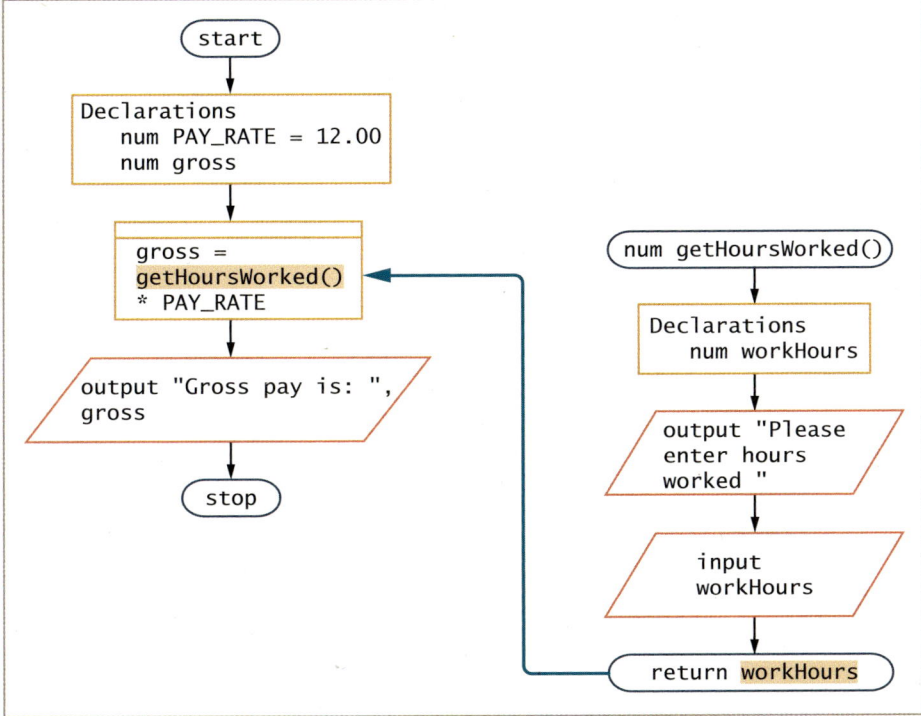

Figure 9-9 A program that uses a method's returned value without storing it

When a program needs to use a method's returned value in more than one place, it makes sense to store the returned value in a variable instead of calling the method multiple times. A program statement that calls a method requires more computer time and resources than a statement that does not call any outside methods. Programmers use the term **overhead** to describe any extra time and resources required by an operation.

As mentioned earlier, in most programming languages you technically are allowed to include multiple `return` statements in a method, but this book does not recommend the practice for most business programs. For example, consider the `findLargest()` method in Figure 9-10. The method accepts three parameters and returns the largest of the values. Although this method works correctly and you might see this technique used, its style is awkward and not structured. In Chapter 3, you learned that structured logic requires each structure to contain one entry point and one exit point. The `return` statements in Figure 9-10 violate this convention by leaving decision structures before they are complete. Figure 9-11 shows the superior and recommended way to handle the problem. In Figure 9-11, the largest value is stored in a variable. Then, when the nested decision structure is complete, the stored value is returned in the last method statement.

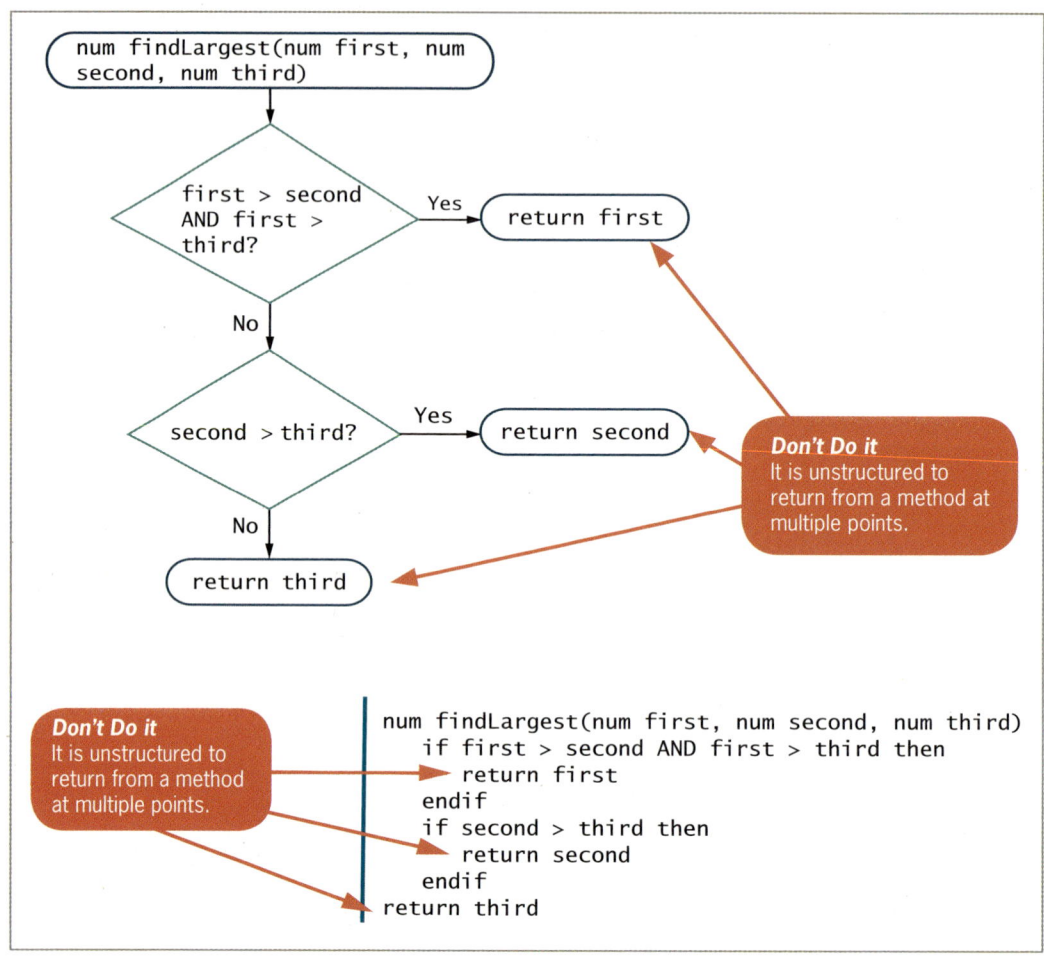

Figure 9-10 Unstructured approach to returning one of several values

Creating Methods that Return a Value

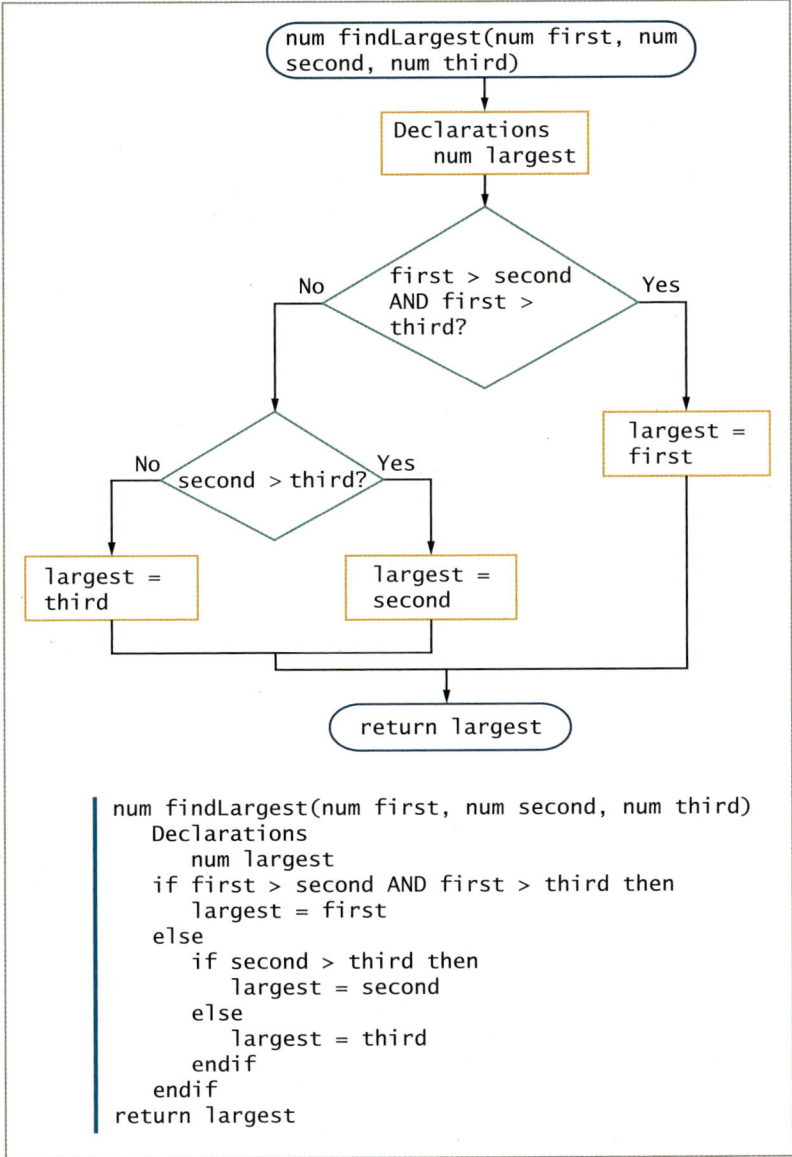

Figure 9-11 Recommended, structured approach to returning one of several values

When you want to use a method, you should know four things:
- What the method does in general, but not necessarily how it carries out tasks internally
- The method's name
- The method's required parameters, if any
- The method's return type, so that you can use any returned value appropriately

CHAPTER 9 — Advanced Modularization Techniques

Using an IPO Chart

When designing methods to use within larger programs, some programmers find it helpful to use an **IPO chart**, a tool that identifies and categorizes each item needed within the method as pertaining to input, processing, or output. For example, consider a method that finds the smallest of three numeric values. When you think about designing this method, you can start by placing each of its components in one of the three processing categories, as shown in Figure 9-12.

Input	Processing	Output
First value Second value Third value	If the first value is smaller than each of the other two, save it as the smallest value; otherwise, if the second value is smaller than the third, save it as the smallest value; otherwise, save the third value as the smallest value	Smallest value

Figure 9-12 IPO chart for the method that finds the smallest of three numeric values

The IPO chart in Figure 9-12 provides an overview of the processing steps involved in the method. Like a flowchart or pseudocode, an IPO chart is just another tool to help you plan the logic of your programs. Many programmers create an IPO chart only for specific methods in their programs and as an alternative to flowcharting or writing pseudocode. IPO charts provide an overview of input to the method, the processing steps that must occur, and the result.

This book emphasizes creating flowcharts and pseudocode, but you can find many more examples of IPO charts on the Web.

TWO TRUTHS & A LIE

Creating Methods that Return a Value

1. The return type for a method can be any type, which includes numeric, character, and string, as well as other more specific types that exist in the programming language you are using.

2. A method's return type must be the same type as one of the method's parameters.

3. You are not required to use a method's returned value.

The false statement is #2. The return type of a method can be any type. The return type must match the type of value in the method's return statement. A method's return type is not required to match any of the method's parameters.

Passing an Array to a Method

In Chapter 6, you learned that you can declare an array to create a list of elements, and that you can use any individual array element in the same manner you would use any single variable of the same type. For example, suppose that you declare a numeric array as follows:

`num someNums[12]`

You can subsequently output `someNums[0]` or perform arithmetic with `someNums[11]`, just as you would for any simple variable that is not part of an array. Similarly, you can pass a single array element to a method in exactly the same manner you would pass a variable or constant.

Consider the program shown in Figure 9-13. This program creates an array of four numeric values and then outputs them. Next, the program calls a method named `tripleTheValue()` four times, passing each of the array elements in turn. The method outputs the passed value, multiplies it by 3, and outputs it again. Finally, back in the calling program, the four numbers are output again. Figure 9-14 shows an execution of this program in a command-line environment.

CHAPTER 9   Advanced Modularization Techniques

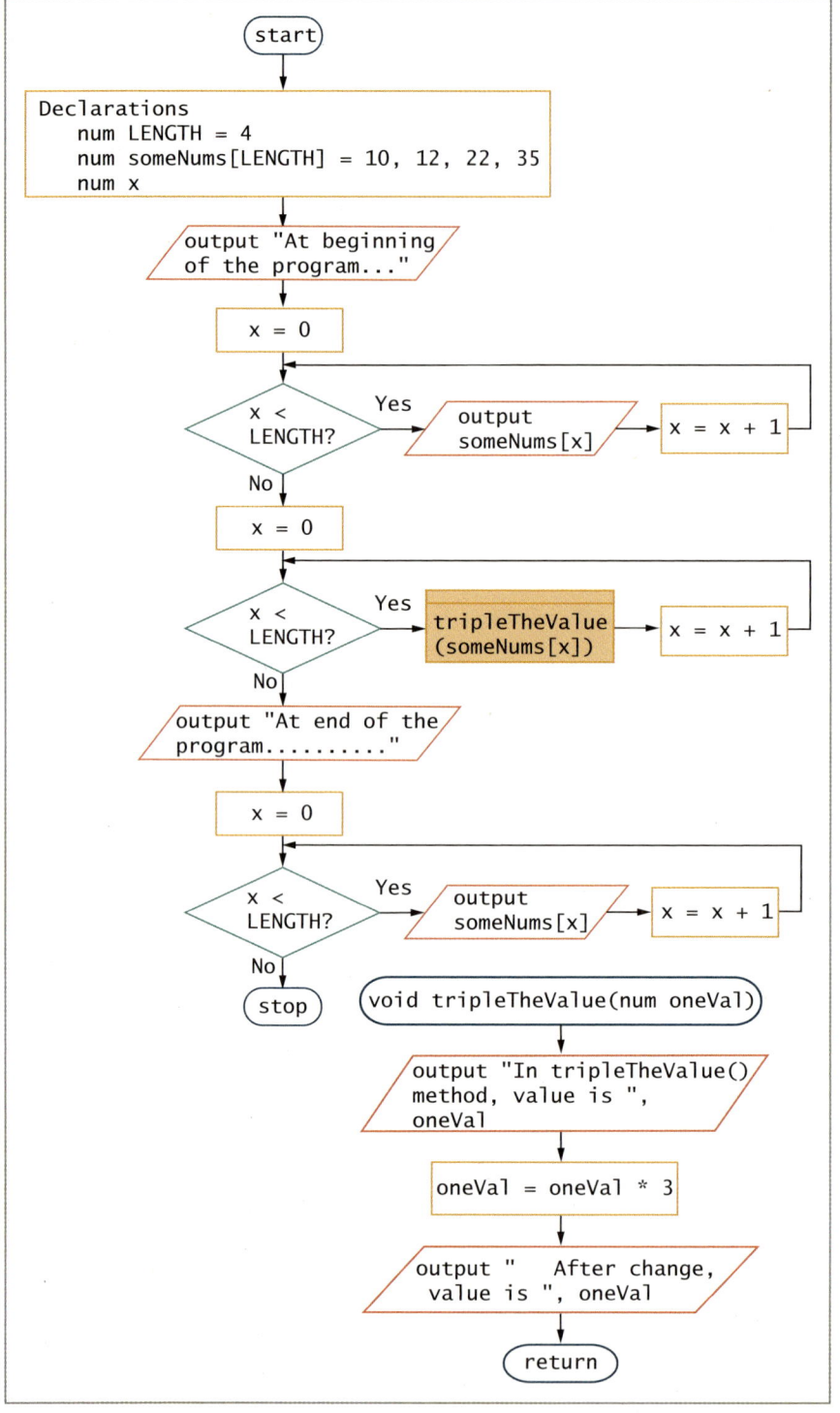

Figure 9-13   PassArrayElement program

Passing an Array to a Method

```
start
    Declarations
        num LENGTH = 4
        num someNums[LENGTH] = 10, 12, 22, 35
        num x
    output "At beginning of the program..."
    x = 0
    while x < LENGTH
        output someNums[x]
        x = x + 1
    endwhile
    x = 0
    while x < LENGTH
        tripleTheValue(someNums[x])
        x = x + 1
    endwhile
    output "At end of the program.........."
    x = 0
    while x < LENGTH
        output someNums[x]
        x = x + 1
    endwhile
stop

void tripleTheValue(num oneVal)
    output "In tripleTheValue() method, value is ", oneVal
    oneVal = oneVal * 3
    output "    After change, value is ", oneVal
return
```

Figure 9-13 PassArrayElement program (continued)

```
At beginning of the program...   10    12    22    35
In tripleTheValue() method, value is 10
    After change, value is 30
In tripleTheValue() method, value is 12
    After change, value is 36
In tripleTheValue() method, value is 22
    After change, value is 66
In tripleTheValue() method, value is 35
    After change, value is 105
At end of the program..........   10    12    22    35
```

Figure 9-14 Output of PassArrayElement program

As you can see in Figure 9-14, the program displays the four original values, then passes each value to the `tripleTheValue()` method, where it is displayed, multiplied by 3, and displayed again. After the method executes four times, the logic returns to the main program where the four values are displayed again, showing that they are unchanged by the new assignments within `tripleTheValue()`. The `oneVal` variable is local to the `tripleTheValue()` method;

therefore, any changes to it are not permanent and are not reflected in the array declared in the main program. Each `oneVal` variable in the `tripleTheValue()` method holds only a copy of the array element passed into the method, and the `oneVal` variable that holds each newly assigned, larger value exists only while the `tripleTheValue()` method is executing. In all respects, a single array element acts just like any single variable of the same type would.

Instead of passing a single array element to a method, you can pass an entire array as an argument. You can indicate that a method parameter must be an array by placing square brackets after the data type in the method's parameter list. When you pass an array to a method, changes you make to array elements within the method are permanent; that is, they are reflected in the original array that was sent to the method. Arrays, unlike simple built-in types, are **passed by reference**; the method receives the actual memory address of the array and has access to the actual values in the array elements.

The name of an array represents a memory address, and the subscript used with an array name represents an offset from that address.

 Simple nonarray variables usually are passed to methods by value. Many programming languages provide the means to pass variables by reference as well as by value. The syntax to accomplish this differs among the languages that allow it; you will learn this technique when you study a specific language.

The program shown in Figure 9-15 creates an array of four numeric values. After the numbers are output, the entire array is passed to a method named `quadrupleTheValues()`. Within the method header, the parameter is declared as an array by using square brackets after the parameter type. Within the method, the numbers are output, which shows that they retain their values from the main program upon entering the method. Then the array values are multiplied by 4. Even though `quadrupleTheValues()` returns nothing to the calling program, when the program displays the array for the last time within the mainline logic, all of the values have been changed to their new quadrupled values. Figure 9-16 shows an execution of the program. Because arrays are passed by reference, the `quadrupleTheValues()` method "knows" the address of the array declared in the calling program and makes its changes directly to the original array that was declared in the calling program.

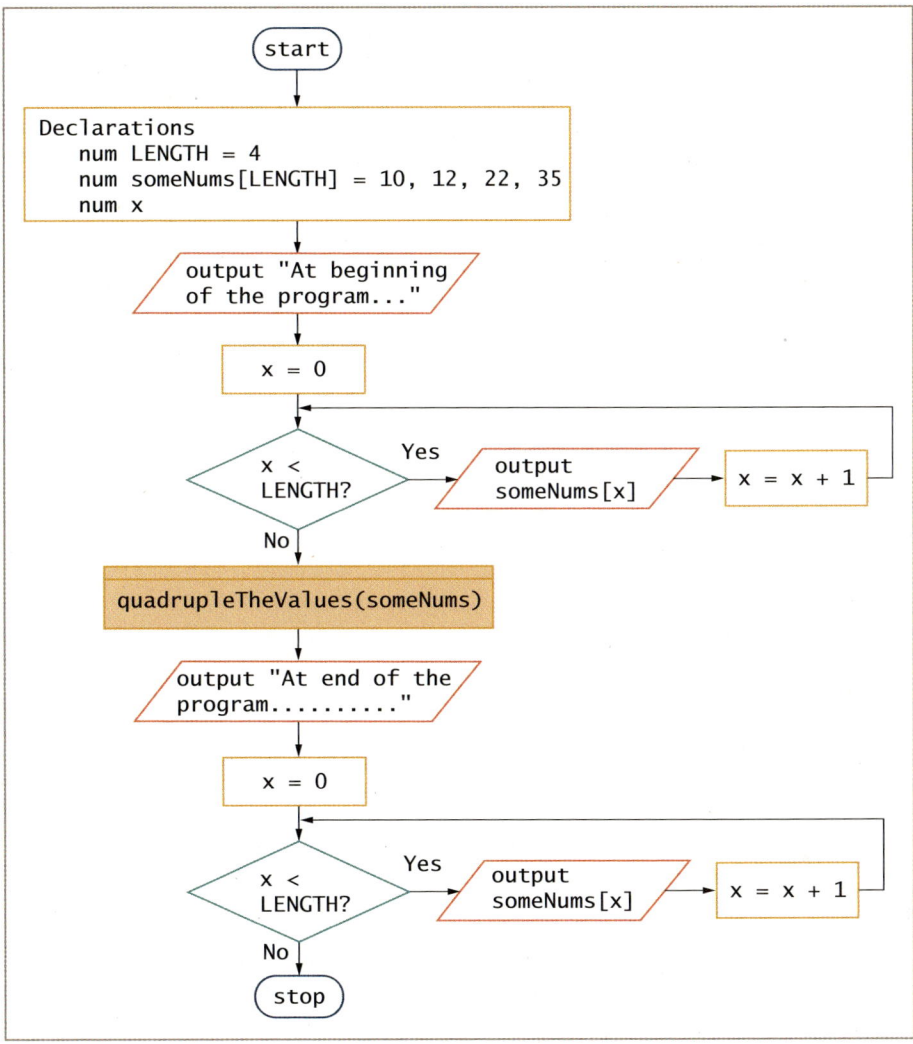

Figure 9-15 PassEntireArray program

CHAPTER 9   Advanced Modularization Techniques

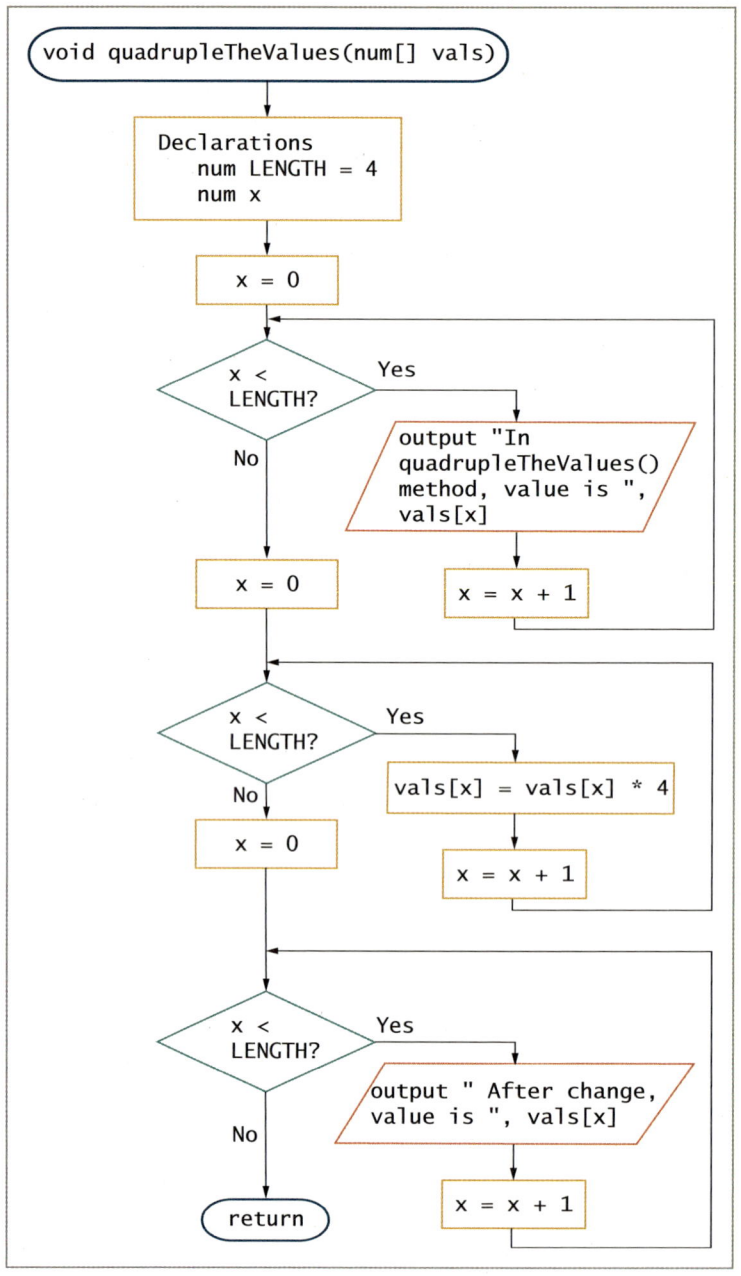

Figure 9-15   PassEntireArray program (continued)

Passing an Array to a Method

```
start
   Declarations
      num LENGTH = 4
      num someNums[LENGTH] = 10, 12, 22, 35
      num x
   output "At beginning of the program..."
   x = 0
   while x < LENGTH
      output someNums[x]
      x = x + 1
   endwhile
   quadrupleTheValues(someNums)
   output "At end of the program.........."
   x = 0
   while x < LENGTH
      output someNums[x]
      x = x + 1
   endwhile
stop

void quadrupleTheValues(num[] vals)
   Declarations
      num LENGTH = 4
      num x
   x = 0
   while x < LENGTH
      output "In quadrupleTheValues() method, value is ", vals[x]
      x = x + 1
   endwhile
   x = 0
   while x < LENGTH
      vals[x] = vals[x] * 4
      x = x + 1
   endwhile
   x = 0
   while x < LENGTH
      output "     After change, value is ", vals[x]
      x = x + 1
   endwhile
return
```

Figure 9-15 `PassEntireArray` program (continued)

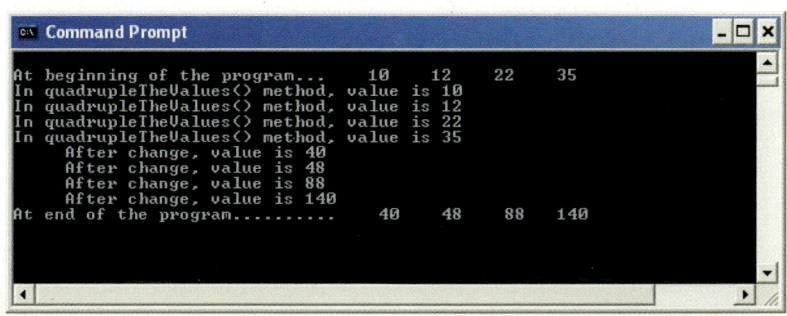

CHAPTER 9 Advanced Modularization Techniques

When an array is a method parameter, the square brackets in the method header remain empty and do not hold a size. The array name that is passed is a memory address that indicates the start of the array. Depending on the language you are working in, you can control the values you use for a subscript to the array in different ways. In some languages, you might also want to pass a constant that indicates the array size to the method. In other languages, you can access the automatically created length field for the array. Either way, the array size itself is never implied when you use the array name. The array name only indicates the starting point from which subscripts will be used.

TWO TRUTHS & A LIE
Passing an Array to a Method

1. You can pass an entire array as a method's argument.
2. You can indicate that a method parameter must be an array by placing square brackets after the data type in the method's parameter list.
3. Arrays, unlike simple built-in types, are passed by value; the method receives a copy of the original array.

The false statement is #3. Arrays, unlike simple built-in types, are passed by reference; the method receives the actual memory address of the array and has access to the actual values in the array elements.

Overloading Methods

In programming, **overloading** involves supplying diverse meanings for a single identifier. When you use the English language, you frequently overload words. When you say *break a window*, *break bread*, *break the bank*, and *take a break*, you describe four very different actions that use different methods and produce different results. However, anyone who speaks English well comprehends your meaning because *break* is understood in the context of the discussion.

In most programming languages, some operators are overloaded. For example, a + between two values indicates addition, but a single + to the left of a value means the value is positive. The + sign has different meanings based on the arguments used with it.

Overloading a method is an example of **polymorphism**—the ability of a method to act appropriately according to the context. Literally, *polymorphism* means "many forms."

When you **overload a method**, you write multiple methods with a shared name but different parameter lists. When you call an overloaded method, the language translator understands

Overloading Methods

which version of the method to use based on the arguments used. For example, suppose that you create a method to output a message and the amount due on a customer bill, as shown in Figure 9-17. The method receives a numeric parameter that represents the customer's balance and produces two lines of output. Assume that you also need a method that is similar to `printBill()`, except the new method applies a discount to the customer bill. One solution to this problem would be to write a new method with a different name—for example, `printBillWithDiscount()`. A downside to this approach is that a programmer who uses your methods must remember the names of each slightly different version. It is more natural for your method's clients to use a single well-designed method name for the task of printing bills, but to be able to provide different arguments as appropriate. In this case, you can overload the `printBill()` method so that, in addition to the version that takes a single numeric argument, you can create a version that takes two numeric arguments—one that represents the balance and one that represents the discount rate. Figure 9-17 shows the two versions of the `printBill()` method.

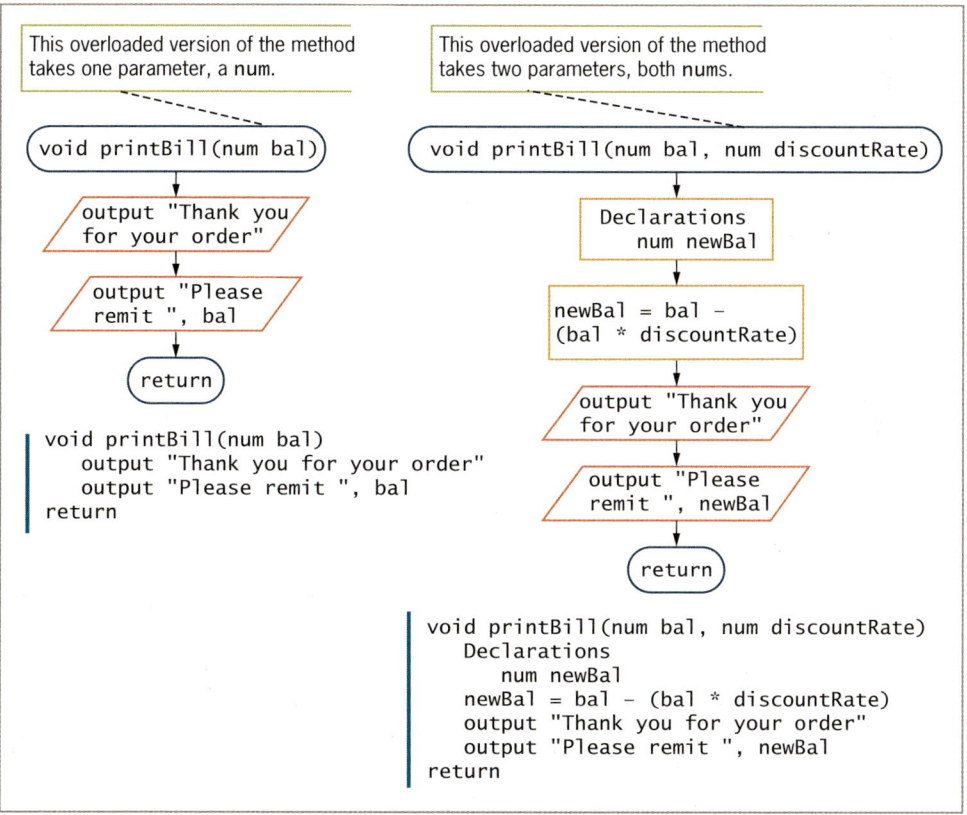

Figure 9-17 Two overloaded versions of the `printBill()` method

If both versions of `printBill()` are included in a program and you call the method using a single numeric argument, as in `printBill(custBalance)`, the first version of the method in

CHAPTER 9   Advanced Modularization Techniques

Figure 9-17 executes. If you use two numeric arguments in the call, as in `printBill(custBalance, rate)`, the second version of the method executes.

If it suited your needs, you could provide more versions of the `printBill()` method, as shown in Figure 9-18. The first version accepts a numeric parameter that holds the customer's balance, and a string parameter that holds an additional message that can be customized for the bill recipient and displayed on the bill. For example, if a program makes a method call such as the following, this version of `printBill()` will execute:

`printBill(custBal, "Due in 10 days")`

The second version of the method in Figure 9-18 accepts three parameters, providing a balance, discount rate, and customized message. For example, the following method call would use this version of the method:

`printBill(balanceDue, discountRate, specialMessage)`

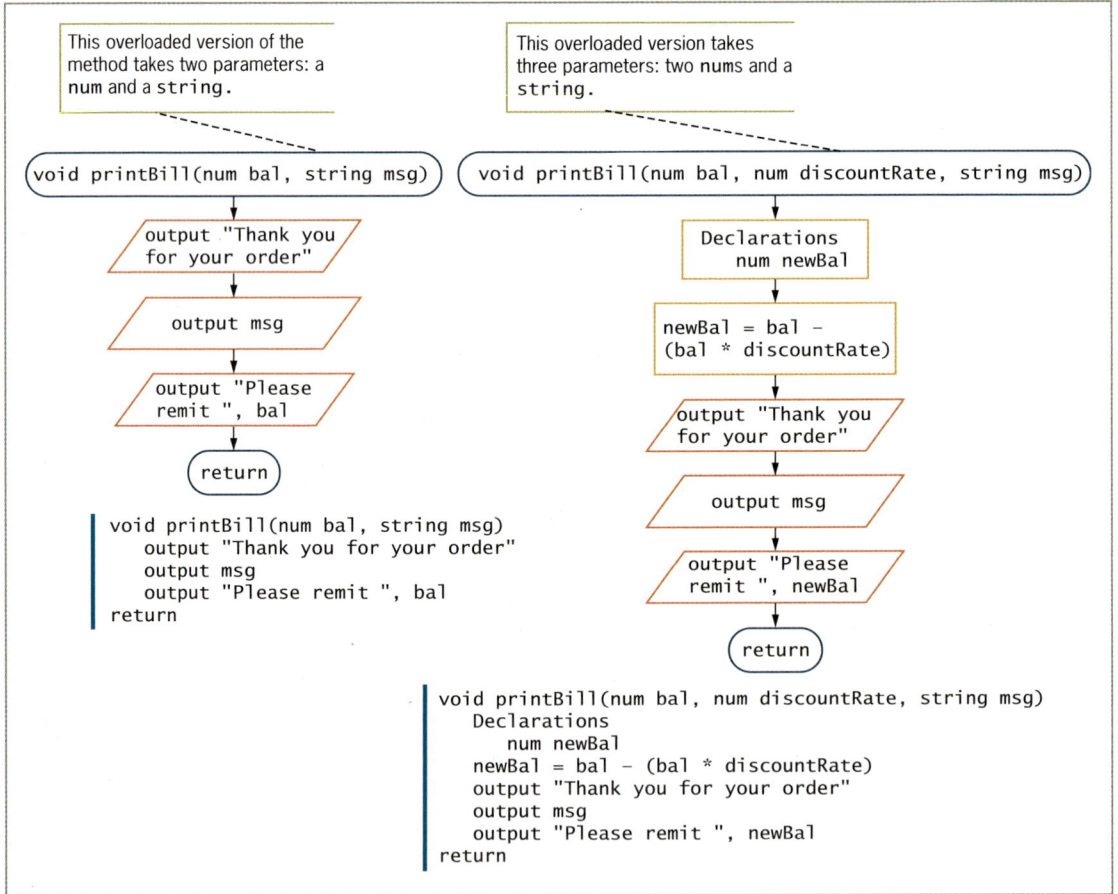

Figure 9-18   Two additional overloaded versions of the `printBill()` method

Overloading Methods

Overloading methods is never required in a program. Instead, you could create multiple methods with unique identifiers such as `printBill()` and `printBillWithDiscountAndMessage()`. Overloading methods does not reduce your work when creating a program; you need to write each method individually. The advantage is provided to your method's clients; those who use your methods need to remember just one appropriate name for all related tasks.

In many programming languages, the `output` statement is actually an overloaded method that you call. Using a single name such as `output`, whether you want to output a number, a `string`, or any combination of the two, is convenient.

Even if you write two or more overloaded versions of a method, many program clients will use just one version. For example, suppose that you develop a bill-creating program that contains all four versions of the `printBill()` method just discussed, and then sell it to different companies. An organization that adopts your program and its methods might only want to use one or two versions of the method. You probably own many devices for which only some of the features are meaningful to you; for example, some people who own microwave ovens only use the *Popcorn* button or never use *Defrost*.

Avoiding Ambiguous Methods

When you overload a method, you run the risk of creating **ambiguous methods**—a situation in which the compiler cannot determine which method to use. Every time you call a method, the compiler decides whether a suitable method exists; if so, the method executes, and if not, you receive an error message. For example, suppose that you write two versions of a `printBill()` method, as shown in the program in Figure 9-19. One version of the method is intended to accept a customer balance and a discount rate, and the other is intended to accept a customer balance and a discount amount expressed in dollars.

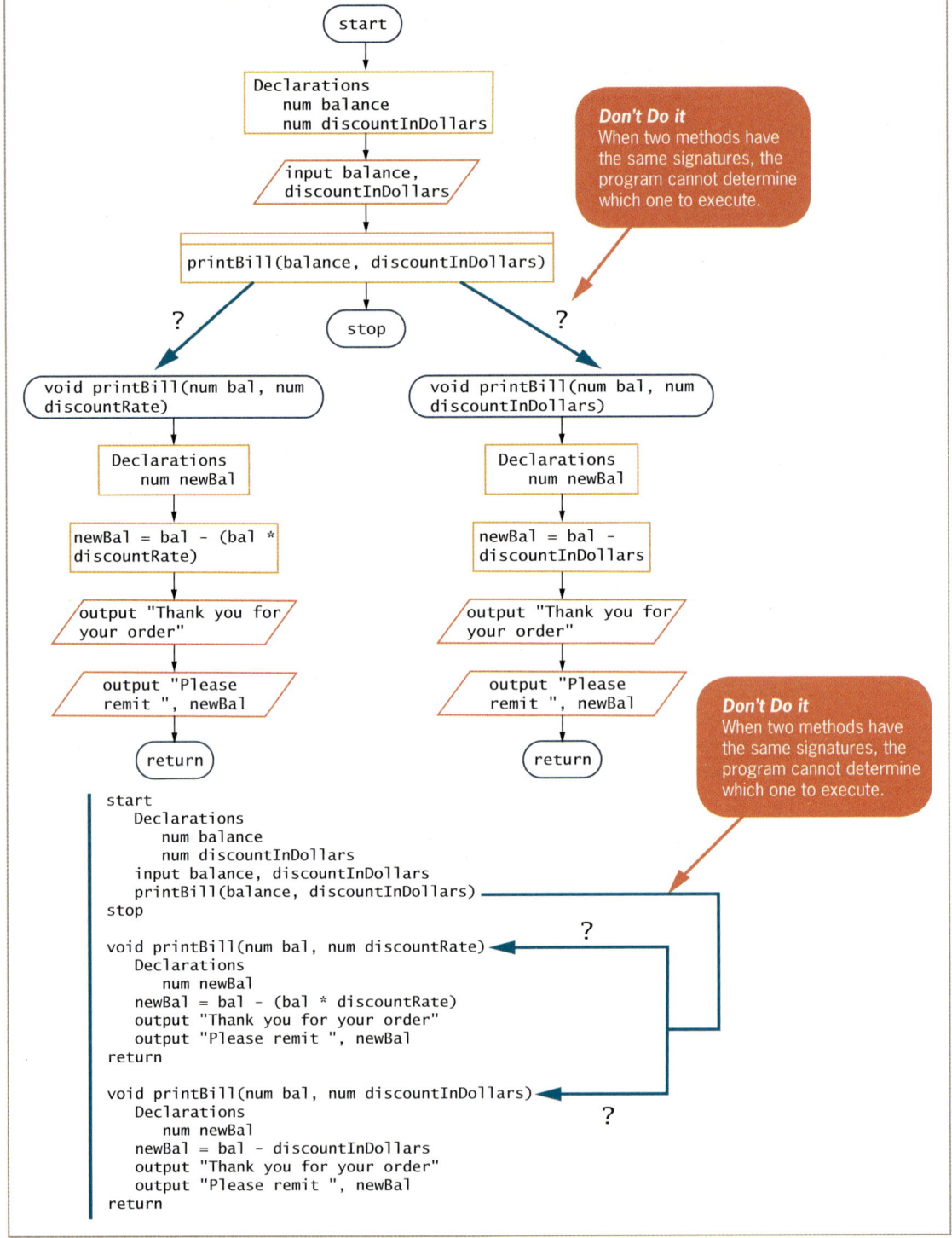

Figure 9-19 Program that contains ambiguous method call

Overloading Methods

Each of the two versions of `printBill()` in Figure 9-19 is a valid method on its own. However, when the two versions exist in the same program, a problem arises. When the main program calls `printBill()` using two numeric arguments, the compiler cannot determine which version to call. You might think that the version of the method with a parameter named `discountInDollars` would execute, because the method call uses the identifier `discountInDollars`. However, the compiler determines which version of a method to call based on argument data types only, not their identifiers. Because both versions of the `printBill()` method could accept two numeric parameters, the compiler cannot determine which version to execute, so an error occurs and program execution stops.

An overloaded method is not ambiguous on its own—it becomes ambiguous only if you make a method call that matches multiple method signatures. In many languages, a program with potentially ambiguous methods will run without problems if you don't make any method calls that match more than one method.

Methods can be overloaded correctly by providing different parameter lists for methods with the same name. Methods with identical names that have identical parameter lists but different return types are not overloaded—they are ambiguous. For example, the following two method headers create ambiguity.

```
string aMethod(num x)
num aMethod(num y)
```

The compiler determines which version of a method to call based on parameter lists, not return types. When the method call `aMethod(17)` is made, the compiler will not know which of the two methods to execute because both possible choices take a numeric argument.

All the popular object-oriented programming languages support multiple numeric data types. For example, Java, C#, C++, and Visual Basic all support integer (whole number) data types that are different from floating-point (decimal place) data types. Many languages have even more specialized numeric types, such as signed and unsigned. Methods that accept different specific types are correctly overloaded.

Watch the video *Overloading Methods*.

CHAPTER 9   Advanced Modularization Techniques

TWO TRUTHS & A LIE

Overloading Methods

1. In programming, overloading involves supplying diverse meanings for a single identifier.

2. When you overload a method, you write multiple methods with different names but identical parameter lists.

3. Methods can be overloaded correctly by providing different parameter lists for methods with the same name.

The false statement is #2. When you overload a method, you write methods with a shared name but different parameter lists.

Using Predefined Methods

All modern programming languages contain many methods that have already been written for programmers. Predefined methods might originate from several sources:

- Some prewritten methods are built into a language. For example, methods that perform input and output are usually predefined.

- When you work on a program in a team, each programmer might be assigned specific methods to create, and your methods will interact with methods written by others.

- If you work for a company, many standard methods may already have been written and you will be required to use them. For example, the company might have a standard method that displays its logo.

Predefined methods save you time and effort. For example, in most languages, displaying a message on the screen involves using a built-in method. When you want to display *Hello* on the command prompt screen in C#, you write the following:

`Console.WriteLine("Hello");`

In Java, you write:

`System.out.println("Hello");`

In these statements, you can recognize `WriteLine()` and `println()` as method names because they are followed by parentheses; the parentheses hold an argument that represents the message to display. If these methods were not prewritten, you would have to know the low-level details of how to manipulate pixels on a screen to get the characters to display. Instead, by using the prewritten methods, you can concentrate on the higher-level task of displaying a useful and appropriate message.

In C#, the convention is to begin method names with an uppercase letter. In Java, method names conventionally begin with a lowercase letter. The `WriteLine()` and `println()` methods follow their respective language's convention. The `WriteLine()` and `println()` methods are both overloaded in their respective languages. For example, if you pass a string to either method, the version of the method that accepts a string parameter executes, but if you pass a number, another version that accepts a numeric parameter executes.

Most programming languages also contain a variety of mathematical methods, such as those that compute a square root or the absolute value of a number. Other methods retrieve the current date and time from the operating system or select a random number to use in a game application. These methods were written as a convenience for you—computing a square root and generating random numbers are complicated tasks, so it is convenient to have methods already written, tested, and available when you need them. The names of the methods that perform these functions differ among programming languages, so you need to research the language's documentation to use them. For example, many of a language's methods are described in introductory programming language textbooks, and you can also find language documentation online.

Whether you want to use a predefined method or any other method, you should know the following four details:

- What the method does in general—for example, compute a square root.
- The method's name—for example, it might be `sqrt()`.
- The method's required parameters—for example, a square root method might require a single numeric parameter. There might be multiple overloaded versions of the method from which you can choose.
- The method's return type—for example, a square root method most likely returns a numeric value that is the square root of the argument passed to the method.

You do not need to know how the method is implemented—that is, how the instruction statements are written within it. Like all methods, you can use built-in methods without worrying about their low-level implementation details.

TWO TRUTHS & A LIE

Using Predefined Methods

1. The name of a method that performs a specific function (such as generating a random number) is likely to be the same in various programming languages.

2. When you want to use a predefined method, you should know what the method does in general, along with its name, required parameters, and return type.

3. When you want to use a predefined method, you do not need to know how the method works internally to be able to use the method effectively.

The false statement is #1. Methods that perform standard functions are likely to have different names in various languages.

Method Design Issues: Implementation Hiding, Cohesion, and Coupling

To design effective methods, you should consider several program qualities:

- You should employ implementation hiding; that is, a method's client should not need to understand a method's internal mechanisms.
- You should strive to increase cohesion.
- You should strive to reduce coupling.

Understanding Implementation Hiding

An important principle of modularization is the notion of **implementation hiding**, the encapsulation of method details. That is, when a program makes a request to a method, it doesn't know the details of how the method is executed. For example, when you make a restaurant reservation, you do not need to know how the reservation is actually recorded at the restaurant—perhaps it is written in a book, marked on a large chalkboard, or entered into a computerized database. The implementation details don't concern you as a patron, and if the restaurant changes its methods from one year to the next, the change does not affect your use of the reservation method—you still call and provide your name, a date, and a time. With well-written methods, using implementation hiding means that a method that calls another must know only the following:

- The name of the called method
- What type of information to send to the method
- What type of return data to expect from the method

In other words, the calling method needs to understand only the **interface to the method** that is called. The interface is the only part of a method with which the method's **client** (or method's caller) interacts. The program does *not* need to know how the method works internally. Additionally, if you substitute a new, improved method implementation but the interface to the method does not change, you won't need to make changes in any methods that call the altered method.

Programmers refer to hidden implementation details as existing in a **black box**—you can examine what goes in and what comes out, but not the details of how the method works inside.

Increasing Cohesion

When you begin to design computer programs, it is difficult to decide how much to put into a method. For example, a process that requires 40 instructions can be contained in a single 40-instruction method, two 20-instruction methods, five 8-instruction methods, or many other combinations. In most programming languages, any of these combinations is allowed; you can write a program that executes and produces correct results no matter how you divide the individual steps into methods. However, placing too many or too few instructions in a single method makes a program harder to follow and reduces flexibility.

Method Design Issues: Implementation Hiding, Cohesion, and Coupling

To help determine the appropriate division of tasks among methods, you want to analyze each method's **cohesion**, which refers to how the internal statements of a method serve to accomplish the method's purpose. In highly cohesive methods, all the operations are related, or "go together." Such methods are **functionally cohesive**—all their operations contribute to the performance of a single task. Functionally cohesive methods usually are more reliable than those that have low cohesion; they are considered stronger, and they make programs easier to write, read, and maintain.

For example, consider a method that calculates gross pay. The method receives parameters that define a worker's pay rate and number of hours worked. The method computes gross pay and displays it. The cohesion of this method is high because each of its instructions contributes to one task—computing gross pay. If you can write a sentence describing what a method does using only two words—for example, *Compute gross*, *Cube value*, or *Display record*—the method is probably functionally cohesive.

You might work in a programming environment that has a rule such as *No method will be longer than can be printed on one page* or *No method will have more than 30 lines of code*. The rule maker is trying to achieve more cohesion, but such rules are arbitrary. A two-line method could have low cohesion and—although less likely—a 40-line method might have high cohesion. Because good, functionally cohesive methods perform only one task, they tend to be short. However, the issue is not size. If it takes 20 statements to perform one task within a method, the method is still cohesive.

Most programmers do not consciously make decisions about cohesiveness for each method they write. Rather, they develop a "feel" for what types of tasks belong together, and for which subsets of tasks should be diverted to their own methods.

Reducing Coupling

Coupling is a measure of the strength of the connection between two program methods; it expresses the extent to which information is exchanged by methods. Coupling is either tight or loose, depending on how much one method relies on information from another. **Tight coupling**, which occurs when methods depend on each other excessively, makes programs more prone to errors. With tight coupling, you have many data paths to keep track of, many chances for bad data to pass from one method to another, and many chances for one method to alter information needed by another method. **Loose coupling** occurs when methods do not depend on others. In general, you want to reduce coupling as much as possible because connections between methods make them more difficult to write, maintain, and reuse.

Imagine four cooks wandering in and out of a kitchen while preparing a stew. If each is allowed to add seasonings at will without the knowledge of the other cooks, you could end up with a culinary disaster. Similarly, if four payroll program methods can alter your gross pay without the "knowledge" of the other methods, you could end up with a financial disaster. A program in which several methods have access to your gross pay figure has methods that are tightly coupled. A superior program would control access to the payroll figure by limiting its passage to methods that need it.

You can evaluate whether coupling between methods is loose or tight by looking at how methods share data.

- Tight coupling occurs when methods have access to the same globally defined variables. When one method changes the value stored in a variable, other methods are affected. Because you should avoid tight coupling, all the examples in this book avoid using global variables. However, be aware that you might see them used in programs written by others.
- Loose coupling occurs when a copy of data that must be shared is passed from one method to another. That way, the sharing of data is always purposeful—variables must be explicitly passed to and from methods that use them. The loosest (best) methods pass single arguments rather than many variables or entire records, if possible.

Additionally, there is a time and a place for shortcuts. If you need a result from spreadsheet data in a hurry, you can type two values and take a sum rather than creating a formula with proper cell references. If a memo must go out in five minutes, you don't have time to change fonts or add clip art with your word processor. Similarly, if you need a quick programming result, you might very well use cryptic variable names, tight coupling, and minimal cohesion. When you create a professional application, however, you should keep professional guidelines in mind.

TWO TRUTHS & A LIE

Method Design Issues: Implementation Hiding, Cohesion, and Coupling

1. A calling method must know the interface to any method it calls.
2. You should try to avoid loose coupling, which occurs when methods do not depend on others.
3. Functional cohesion occurs when all operations in a method contribute to the performance of only one task.

The false statement is #2. You should aim for loose coupling so that methods are independent.

Understanding Recursion

Recursion occurs when a method is defined in terms of itself. A method that calls itself is a **recursive method**. Some programming languages do not allow a method to call itself, but those that do can be used to create recursive methods that produce interesting effects.

Figure 9-20 shows a simple example of recursion. The program calls an `infinity()` method, which displays *Help!* and calls itself again (see the shaded statement). The second call to `infinity()` displays *Help!* and generates a third call. The result is a large number of repetitions of the `infinity()` method. The output is shown in Figure 9-21.

```
start
    infinity()
stop

infinity()
    output "Help! "
    infinity()
return
```

Figure 9-20 A program that calls a recursive method

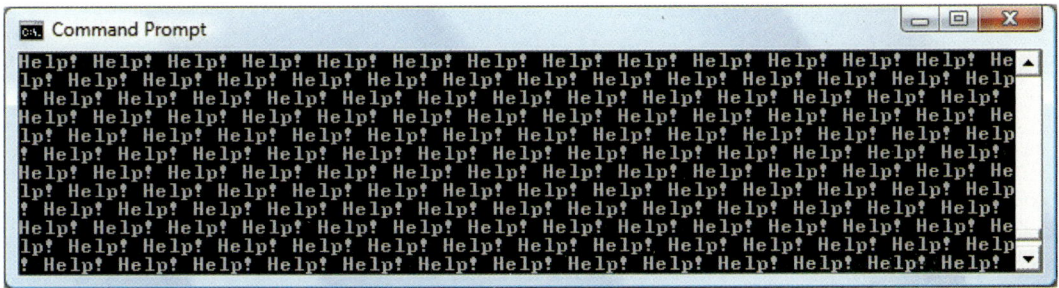

Figure 9-21 Output of program in Figure 9-20

Every time you call a method, the address to which the program should return at the completion of the method is stored in a memory location called the **stack**. When a method ends, the address is retrieved from the stack and the program returns to the location from which the method call was made. For example, suppose that a program calls methodA() and that methodA() calls methodB(). When the program calls methodA(), a return address is stored in the stack, and then methodA() begins execution. When methodA() calls methodB(), a return address in methodA() is stored in the stack and methodB() begins execution. When methodB() ends, the last entered address is retrieved from the stack and program control returns to complete methodA(). When methodA() ends, the remaining address is retrieved from the stack and program control returns to the main program method to complete it.

Like all computer memory, the stack has a finite size. When the program in Figure 9-20 calls the infinity() method, the stack receives so many return addresses that it eventually overflows. The recursive calls will end after an excessive number of repetitions and the program issues error messages.

Of course, there is no practical use for an infinitely recursive program. Just as you must be careful not to create endless loops, when you write useful recursive methods you must provide a way for the recursion to stop eventually.

CHAPTER 9   Advanced Modularization Techniques

 Using recursion successfully requires a thorough understanding of looping. You learned about loops in Chapter 5. An everyday example of recursion is printed on shampoo bottles: *Lather, rinse, repeat.*

Figure 9-22 shows an application that uses recursion productively. The program calls a recursive method that computes the sum of every integer from 1 up to and including the method's argument value. For example, the sum of every integer up to and including 3 is 1 + 2 + 3, or 6, and the sum of every integer up to and including 4 is 1 + 2 + 3 + 4, or 10.

```
start
    Declarations
        num LIMIT = 10
        num number
    number = 1
    while number <= LIMIT
        output "When number is ", number,
            " then cumulativeSum(number) is ",
            cumulativeSum(number)
        number = number + 1
    endwhile
return

num cumulativeSum(num number)
    Declarations
        num returnVal
    if number = 1 then
        returnVal = number
    else
        returnVal = number + cumulativeSum(number - 1)
    endif
return returnVal
```

Figure 9-22   Program that uses a recursive `cumulativeSum()` method

When thinking about cumulative summing relationships, remember that the sum of all the integers up to and including any number is that number plus the sum of the integers for the next lowest number. In other words, consider the following:

- The sum of the digits from 1, up to and including 1, is simply 1.
- The sum of the digits from 1 through 2 is the previous sum, plus 2.
- The sum of the digits from 1 through 3 is the previous sum, plus 3.
- The sum of the digits 1 through 4 is the previous sum, plus 4.
- And so on.

Understanding Recursion

The recursive cumulativeSum() method in Figure 9-22 uses this knowledge. For each number, its cumulative sum consists of itself plus the cumulative sum of all the previous lesser numbers.

The program in Figure 9-22 calls the cumulativeSum() method 10 times in a loop to show the cumulative sum of every integer from 1 through 10. Figure 9-23 shows the output.

```
Command Prompt
When number is 1 then cumulativeSum(number) is 1
When number is 2 then cumulativeSum(number) is 3
When number is 3 then cumulativeSum(number) is 6
When number is 4 then cumulativeSum(number) is 10
When number is 5 then cumulativeSum(number) is 15
When number is 6 then cumulativeSum(number) is 21
When number is 7 then cumulativeSum(number) is 28
When number is 8 then cumulativeSum(number) is 36
When number is 9 then cumulativeSum(number) is 45
When number is 10 then cumulativeSum(number) is 55
```

Figure 9-23 Output of program in Figure 9-22

If you examine Figures 9-22 and 9-23 together, you can see the following:

- When 1 is passed to the cumulativeSum() method, the if statement within the method determines that the argument is equal to 1, returnVal becomes 1, and 1 is returned for output.

- On the next pass through the loop, 2 is passed to the cumulativeSum() method. When the method receives 2 as an argument, the if statement within the method is false, and returnVal is set to 2 plus the value of cumulativeSum(1). This second call to cumulativeSum() using 1 as an argument returns a 1, so when the method ends, it returns 2 + 1, or 3.

- On the third pass through the loop within the calling program, 3 is passed to the cumulativeSum() method. When the method receives 3 as an argument, the if statement within the method is false and the method returns 3 plus the value of cumulativeSum(2). The value of this call is 2 plus cumulativeSum(1). The value of cumulativeSum(1) is 1. Ultimately, cumulativeSum(3) is 3 + 2 + 1.

Many sophisticated programs that operate on lists of items use recursive processing. However, following the logic of a recursive method can be difficult, and programs that use recursion are sometimes error-prone and hard to debug. Because such programs also can be hard for others to maintain, some business organizations forbid their programmers from using recursive logic in company programs. Many of the problems solved by recursive methods can be solved in a more straightforward way. For example, examine the program in Figure 9-24. This program produces the same result as the previous recursive program, but in a more straightforward fashion.

```
start
   Declarations
      num number
      num total
      num LIMIT = 10
   total = 0
   number = 1
   while number <= LIMIT
      total = total + number
      output "When number is ", number,
         " then the cumulative sum of 1 through",
         number, " is ", total
      number = number + 1
   endwhile
stop
```

Figure 9-24 Nonrecursive program that computes cumulative sums

 A humorous illustration of recursion is found in this sentence: "In order to understand recursion, you must first understand recursion." A humorous dictionary entry is "Recursion: See Recursion." These examples contain an element of truth, but useful recursion algorithms always have a point at which the infinite loop is exited. In other words, the base case, or exit case, is always reached at some point.

 Watch the video *Recursion*.

TWO TRUTHS & A LIE

Understanding Recursion

1. A method that calls itself is a recursive method.

2. Every time you call a method, the address to which the program should return at the completion of the method is stored in a memory location called the stack.

3. Following the logic of a recursive method is usually much easier than following the logic of an ordinary program, so recursion makes debugging easier.

The false statement is #3. Following the logic of a recursive method is difficult, and programs that use recursion are sometimes error-prone and hard to debug.

Chapter Summary

- A method is a program module that contains a series of statements that carry out a task. Any program can contain an unlimited number of methods, and each method can be called an unlimited number of times. A method must include a header, a body, and a `return` statement that marks the end of the method. Variables and constants are in scope within, or local to, only the method within which they are declared.

- When you pass a data item into a method, it is an argument to the method. When the method receives the data item, it is called a parameter. When you write the declaration for a method that can receive parameters, you must include the data type and a local name for each parameter within the method declaration's parentheses. You indicate that a method requires multiple arguments by listing their data types and local identifiers within the method header's parentheses. You can pass multiple arguments to a called method by listing the arguments within the method call and separating them with commas. When you call a method, the arguments you send to the method must match in order—both in number and in type—the parameters listed in the method declaration.

- When a method returns a value, the method must have a return type. A method's return type indicates the data type of the value that the method will send back to the location where the method call was made. The return type also is known as a method's type, and is indicated in front of the method name when the method is defined. When a method returns a value, you usually want to use the returned value in the calling method, although this is not required.

- You can pass a single array element to a method in exactly the same manner you would pass a variable or constant. Additionally, you can pass an entire array to a method. You can indicate that a method parameter must be an array by placing square brackets after the data type in the method's parameter list. When you pass an array to a method, it is passed by reference; that is, the method receives the actual memory address of the array and has access to the actual values in the array elements.

- When you overload a method, you write multiple methods with a shared name but different parameter lists. The compiler understands your meaning based on the arguments you use when you call the method. Overloading a method introduces the risk of creating ambiguous methods—a situation in which the compiler cannot determine which method to use. Methods can be overloaded correctly by providing different parameter lists for methods with the same name.

- All modern programming languages contain many built-in, prewritten methods to save you time and effort.

- With well-written methods, the implementation is hidden. To use a method, you need only know the name of the called method, what type of information to send to the method, and what type of return data to expect from the method. When writing methods, you should strive to achieve high cohesion and loose coupling.

- Recursion occurs when a method is defined in terms of itself. Following the logic of a recursive method is difficult, and programs that use recursion are sometimes error-prone and hard to debug.

Key Terms

A **method** is a program module that contains a series of statements that carry out a task.

A **method header** precedes a method; the header includes the method identifier and possibly other necessary identifying information.

A **method body** contains all the statements in the method.

Implementation describes the body of a method or the statements that carry out the tasks of a method.

A **method return statement** marks the end of a method and identifies the point at which control returns to the calling method.

Local describes data items that are only known to the method in which they are declared.

Global describes data items that are known to all the methods in a program.

An **argument to a method** is a value passed to a method in the call to the method.

A **parameter to a method** is a data item passed into the method from the outside.

A **parameter list** is all the data types and parameter names that appear in a method header.

A method's **signature** includes its name and parameter list.

A variable passed into a method is **passed by value**; that is, a copy of its value is sent to the method and stored in a new memory location accessible to the method.

Actual parameters are the arguments in a method call.

Formal parameters are the variables in the method declaration that accept the values from the actual parameters.

A method's **return type** indicates the data type of the value that the method will send back to the location where the method call was made.

A **void method** returns no value.

A **method's type** is the type of its return value.

Overhead refers to all the resources and time required by an operation.

An **IPO chart** identifies and categorizes each item needed within the method as pertaining to input, processing, or output.

When an item is **passed by reference** to a method, the method receives the actual memory address item. Arrays are passed by reference.

Overloading involves supplying diverse meanings for a single identifier.

Polymorphism is the ability of a method to act appropriately according to the context.

When you **overload a method,** you create multiple versions with the same name but different parameter lists.

Ambiguous methods are those that the compiler cannot distinguish because they have the same name and parameter types.

Implementation hiding is a programming principle that describes the encapsulation of method details.

The **interface to a method** includes the method's return type, name, and arguments. It is the part that a client sees and uses.

A method's **client** is a program or other method that uses the method.

A **black box** is the analogy programmers use to refer to hidden method implementation details.

Cohesion is a measure of how the internal statements of a method serve to accomplish the method's purpose.

Functional cohesion occurs when all operations in a method contribute to the performance of only one task. Functional cohesion is the highest level of cohesion; you should strive for it in all methods you write.

Coupling is a measure of the strength of the connection between two program methods.

Tight coupling occurs when methods excessively depend on each other; it makes programs more prone to errors.

Loose coupling occurs when methods do not depend on others.

Recursion occurs when a method is defined in terms of itself.

A **recursive method** is a method that calls itself.

The **stack** is a memory location that holds addresses to which methods should return.

Review Questions

1. Which of the following is true?
    a. A program can call one method at most.
    b. A program can contain a method that calls another method.
    c. A method can contain one or more other methods.
    d. All of the above are true.

CHAPTER 9 Advanced Modularization Techniques

2. Which of the following must every method have?
   a. a header
   b. a parameter list
   c. a return value
   d. all of the above

3. Which of the following is most closely related to the concept of *local*?
   a. abstract
   b. object-oriented
   c. in scope
   d. program level

4. Although the terms *parameter* and *argument* are closely related, the difference is that *argument* refers to _____.
   a. a passed constant
   b. a value in a method call
   c. a formal parameter
   d. a variable that is local to a method

5. A method's interface is its _____.
   a. signature
   b. return type
   c. identifier
   d. parameter list

6. When you write the declaration for a method that can receive a parameter, which of the following must be included in the method declaration?
   a. the name of the argument that will be used to call the method
   b. a local name for the parameter
   c. the return value for the method
   d. two of the above

7. When you use a variable name in a method call, it _____ as the variable in the method header.
   a. can have the same name
   b. cannot have the same name
   c. must have the same name
   d. cannot have the same data type

8. Assume that you have written a method with the header void myMethod(num a, string b). Which of the following is a correct method call?
   a. myMethod(12)
   b. myMethod(12, "Hello")
   c. myMethod("Goodbye")
   d. It is impossible to tell.

9. Assume that you have written a method with the header num yourMethod(string name, num code). The method's type is _____.
   a. num
   b. string
   c. num and string
   d. void

Review Questions

10. Assume that you have written a method with the header `string myMethod(num score, string grade)`. Also assume that you have declared a numeric variable named `test`. Which of the following is a correct method call?

    a. `myMethod()`
    b. `myMethod(test)`
    c. `myMethod(test, test)`
    d. `myMethod(test,"A")`

11. The value used in a method's `return` statement must _____.

    a. be numeric
    b. be a variable
    c. match the data type used before the method name in the header
    d. two of the above

12. When a method receives a copy of the value stored in an argument used in the method call, it means the variable was _____.

    a. unnamed
    b. passed by value
    c. passed by reference
    d. assigned its original value when it was declared

13. A void method _____.

    a. contains no statements
    b. requires no parameters
    c. returns nothing
    d. has no name

14. When an array is passed to a method, it is _____.

    a. passed by reference
    b. passed by value
    c. unnamed in the method
    d. unalterable in the method

15. When you overload a method, you write multiple methods with the same _____.

    a. name
    b. parameter list
    c. number of parameters
    d. return type

16. A program contains a method with the header `num calculateTaxes(num amount, string name)`. Which of the following methods can coexist in the same program with no possible ambiguity?

    a. `num calculateTaxes(string name, num amount)`
    b. `string calculateTaxes(num money, string taxpayer)`
    c. `num calculateTaxes(num annualPay, string taxpayerId)`
    d. All of these can coexist without ambiguity.

CHAPTER 9 Advanced Modularization Techniques

17. Methods in the same program with identical names and identical parameter lists are _____.

    a. overloaded
    b. overworked
    c. overwhelmed
    d. ambiguous

18. Methods in different programs with identical names and identical parameter lists are _____.

    a. overloaded
    b. illegal
    c. both of the above
    d. none of the above

19. The notion of _____ most closely describes the way a calling method is not aware of the statements within a called method.

    a. abstraction
    b. object-oriented
    c. implementation hiding
    d. encapsulation

20. Programmers should strive to _____.

    a. increase coupling
    b. increase cohesion
    c. both of the above
    d. neither a nor b

Exercises

1. Create an IPO chart for each of the following methods:

    a. The method that calculates the amount owed on a restaurant check, including tip

    b. The method that calculates your yearly education-related expenses

    c. The method that calculates your annual housing expenses, including rent or mortgage payment and utilities

2. Create the logic for a program that continuously prompts the user for a number of dollars until the user enters 0. Pass each entered amount to a conversion method that displays a breakdown of the passed amount into the fewest bills; in other words, the method calculates the number of 20s, 10s, 5s, and 1s needed.

3. Create the logic for a program that calculates and displays the amount of money you would have if you invested $5000 at 2 percent simple interest for one year. Create a separate method to do the calculation and return the result to be displayed.

Exercises

4. Create the logic for a program that accepts input values for the projected cost of a vacation and the number of months until vacation. Pass both values to a method that displays the amount you must save per month to achieve your goal.

5. a. Create the logic for a program that performs arithmetic functions. Design the program to contain two numeric variables, and prompt the user for values for the variables. Pass both variables to methods named sum() and difference(). Create the logic for the methods sum() and difference(); they compute the sum of and difference between the values of two arguments, respectively. Each method should perform the appropriate computation and display the results.

   b. Add a method named product() to the program in Exercise 5a. The product() method should compute the result when multiplying two numbers, but not display the answer. Instead, the method should return the answer to the calling program, which displays the answer.

6. Create the logic for a program that continuously prompts a user for a numeric value until the user enters 0. The application passes the value in turn to a method that computes the sum of all the whole numbers from 1 up to and including the entered number, and to a method that computes the product of all the whole numbers up to and including the entered number.

7. Create the logic for a program that calls a method that computes the final price for a sales transaction. The program contains variables that hold the price of an item, the salesperson's commission expressed as a percentage, and the customer discount expressed as a percentage. Create a calculatePrice() method that determines the final price and returns the value to the calling method. The calculatePrice() method requires three arguments: product price, salesperson commission rate, and customer discount rate. A product's final price is the original price plus the commission amount minus the discount amount. The customer discount is taken as a percentage of the total price after the salesperson commission has been added to the original price.

8. Create the logic for a program that continuously prompts the user for two numeric values that represent the dimensions of a room in feet. Include two overloaded methods that compute the room's area. One method takes two numeric parameters and calculates the area by multiplying the parameters. The other takes a single numeric parameter, which is squared to calculate area. Each method displays its calculated result. Accept input and respond as follows:

   - When the user enters zero for the first value, end the program.
   - If the user enters a negative number for either value, continue to reprompt the user until the value is not negative.
   - If both numbers entered are greater than 0, call the method version that accepts two parameters and pass it both values.
   - If the second value is zero, call the version of the method that accepts just one parameter and pass it the nonzero value.

CHAPTER 9 Advanced Modularization Techniques

9. a. Plan the logic for an insurance company program to determine policy premiums. The program continuously prompts the user for an insurance policy number. When the user enters an appropriate sentinel value, end the program. Call a method that prompts each user for the type of policy needed—health or auto. While the user's response does not indicate health or auto, continue to prompt the user. When the value is valid, return it from the method. Pass the user's response to a new method where the premium is set and returned—$550 for a health policy or $225 for an auto policy. Display the results for each policy.

   b. Modify Exercise 9a so that the premium-setting method calls one of two additional methods—one that determines the health premium or one that determines the auto premium. The health insurance method asks users whether they smoke; the premium is $550 for smokers and $345 for nonsmokers. The auto insurance method asks users to enter the number of traffic tickets they have received in the last three years. The premium is $225 for drivers with three or more tickets, $190 for those with one or two tickets, and $110 for those with no tickets. Each of these two methods returns the premium amount to the calling method, which returns the amount to be displayed.

10. Create the logic for a program that calculates the due date for a bill. Prompt the user for the month, day, and year a bill is received, and pass the data to a method that displays slashes between the parts of the date—for example, *6/24/2013*. Then pass the parts of the date to a method that calculates the bill's due date, which is 10 days after receipt. (A due date might be in the next month or even the next year.) This method displays the due date with slashes by calling the display method.

11. Create the logic for a program that computes hotel guest rates at Cornwall's Country Inn. Include two overloaded methods named `computeRate()`. One version accepts a number of days and calculates the rate at $99.99 per day. The other accepts a number of days and a code for a meal plan. If the code is *A*, three meals per day are included, and the price is $169.00 per day. If the code is *C*, breakfast is included, and the price is $112.00 per day. All other codes are invalid. Each method returns the rate to the calling program where it is displayed. The main program asks the user for the number of days in a stay and whether meals should be included; then, based on the user's response, the program either calls the first method or prompts for a meal plan code and calls the second method.

12. Create the logic for a program that prompts a user for five numbers and stores them in an array. Pass the array to a method that reverses the order of the numbers. Display the reversed numbers in the main program.

13. Create the logic for a program that prompts a user for six numbers and stores them in an array. Pass the array to a method that calculates the arithmetic average of the numbers and returns the value to the calling program. Display each number and how far it is from the arithmetic average. Continue to prompt the user for additional sets of six numbers until the user wants to quit.

Exercises

14. The Information Services Department at the Springfield Library has created methods with the following signatures:

Signature	Description
`num getNumber(num high, num low)`	Prompts the user for a number, and continues to prompt until the number falls between designated high and low limits; returns a valid number
`string getCharacter()`	Prompts the user for a character string and returns the entered string
`num lookUpISBN(string title)`	Accepts the title of a book and returns the ISBN; returns a 0 if the book cannot be found
`string lookUpTitle(num isbn)`	Accepts the ISBN of a book and returns a title; returns a space character if the book cannot be found
`string isBookAvailable(num isbn)`	Accepts an ISBN, searches the library database, and returns "Y" or "N" indicating whether the book is currently available

Table 9-1 Library methods

a. Design an interactive program that does the following, using the prewritten methods whenever they are appropriate.

- Prompt the user for and read a library card number, which must be between 1000 and 9999.

- Prompt the user for and read a search option—1 to search for a book by ISBN, 2 to search for a book by title, and 3 to quit. If the entry is invalid, repeat the request.

- While the user does not enter 3, prompt for an ISBN or title based on the user's previous selection. If the user enters an ISBN, get and display the book's title and ask the user to enter a "Y" or "N" to confirm whether the title is correct.

- If the user has entered a valid ISBN or a title that matches a valid ISBN, check whether the book is available, and display an appropriate message for the user.

- The user can continue to search for books until he or she enters 3 as the search option.

b. Develop the logic that implements each of the methods in Exercise 14a.

CHAPTER 9 Advanced Modularization Techniques

15. Each of the programs in Figure 9-25 uses a recursive method. Try to determine the output in each case.

a.
```
start
   output recursiveA(0)
stop
num recursiveA(num x)
   num result
   if x = 0 then
      result = x
   else
      result = x *
         (recursiveA(x - 1))
   endif
return result
```

b.
```
start
   output recursiveB(2)
stop
num recursiveB(num x)
   num result
   if x = 0 then
      result = x
   else
      result = x *
         (recursiveB(x - 1))
   endif
return result
```

c.
```
start
   output recursiveC(2)
stop
num recursiveC(num x)
   num result
   if x = 1 then
      result = x
   else
      result = x *
         (recursiveC(x - 1))
   endif
return result
```

Figure 9-25 Problems for Exercise 15

Find the Bugs

16. Your downloadable files for Chapter 9 include DEBUG09-01.txt, DEBUG09-02.txt, and DEBUG09-03.txt. Each file starts with some comments that describe the problem. Comments are lines that begin with two slashes (//). Following the comments, each file contains pseudocode that has one or more bugs you must find and correct.

Game Zone

17. In the Game Zone sections of Chapters 6 and 8, you designed the logic for a quiz that contains questions about a topic of your choice. Now, modify the program so it contains an array of five multiple-choice quiz questions related to the topic of your choice. Each question contains four answer choices. Also create a parallel array that holds the correct answer to each question—A, B, C, or D. In turn, pass each question to a method that displays the question and accepts the player's answer. If the player does not enter a valid answer choice, force the player to reenter the choice. Return the user's valid (but not necessarily correct) answer to the main program. After the user's answer is returned to the main program, pass it and the correct answer to a method that determines whether the values are equal and displays an appropriate message. After the user answers all five questions, display the number of correct and incorrect answers that the user chose.

Exercises

18. In the Game Zone section of Chapter 6, you designed the logic for the game Hangman, in which the user guesses letters in a hidden word. Improve the game to store an array of 10 words. One at a time, pass each word to a method that allows the user to guess letters continuously until the game is solved. The method returns the number of guesses it took to complete the word. Store the number in an array before returning to the method for the next word. After all 10 words have been guessed, display a summary of the number of guesses required for each word as well as the average number of guesses per word.

Up for Discussion

19. One advantage to writing a program that is subdivided into methods is that such a structure allows different programmers to write separate methods, thus dividing the work. Would you prefer to write a large program by yourself, or to work on a team in which each programmer produces one or more methods? Why?

20. In this chapter, you learned that hidden implementations are often said to exist in a black box. What are the advantages and disadvantages to this approach in both programming and real life?

CHAPTER 10

Object-Oriented Programming

In this chapter, you will learn about:

- The principles of object-oriented programming
- Classes
- Public and private access
- Ways to organize classes
- Instance methods
- Static methods
- Using objects

Principles of Object-Oriented Programming

Object-oriented programming (OOP) focuses on an application's data and the methods you need to manipulate that data. With OOP, you consider the objects that a program will manipulate—for example, a customer invoice, a loan application, or a menu from which a user selects an option. You define the characteristics of those objects and the methods that each object will use; you also define the information that must be passed to those methods.

OOP uses all of the familiar concepts of modular procedural programming, such as variables, methods, and passing arguments. Methods in object-oriented programs continue to use sequence, selection, and looping structures and make use of arrays. However, OOP adds several new concepts to programming and involves a different way of thinking. A considerable amount of new vocabulary is involved as well. First, you will read about OOP concepts in general, and then you will learn the specific terminology.

Five important features of object-oriented languages are:

- Classes
- Objects
- Polymorphism
- Inheritance
- Encapsulation

Classes and Objects

In object-oriented terminology, a **class** describes a group or collection of objects with common attributes. An **object** is one **instance** of a class. Object-oriented programmers sometimes say an object is one **instantiation** of a class; this word is just another form of *instance*. For example, your `redChevroletAutomobileWithTheDent` is an instance of the class that is made up of all automobiles, and your `goldenRetrieverDogNamedGinger` is an instance of the class that is made up of all dogs. A class is like a blueprint from which many houses might be constructed, or like a recipe from which many meals can be prepared. One house and one meal are each an instance of their class; countless instances might be created eventually. For example, Figure 10-1 depicts a `Dog` class and two instances of it.

Principles of Object-Oriented Programming

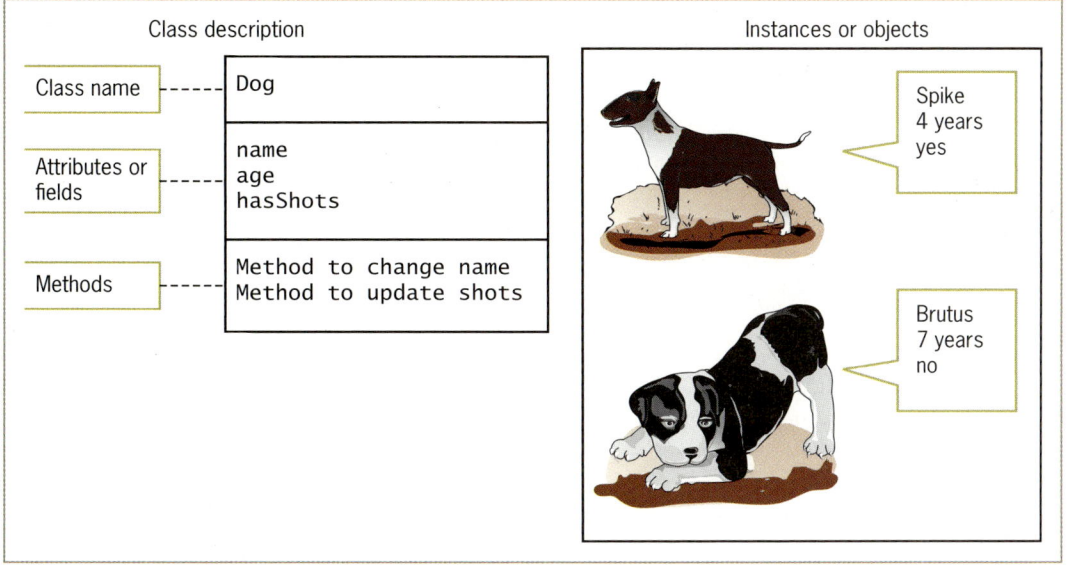

Figure 10-1 A Dog class and two instances

Since the beginning of this book, you have created application classes that could be used without creating instances. In this chapter, you will create additional types of classes that client programs will **instantiate**; that is, instances of the classes will be created.

Objects both in the real world and in object-oriented programming contain attributes and methods. **Attributes** are the characteristics that define an object as part of a class. For example, some of your automobile's attributes are its make, model, year, and purchase price. Other attributes include whether the automobile is currently running, its gear, its speed, and whether it is dirty. All automobiles possess the same attributes, but not the same values for those attributes. Similarly, your dog has the attributes of its breed, name, age, and whether its shots are current. Methods are the actions that can be taken on an object; often they alter, use, or retrieve the attributes. For example, an automobile has methods for changing and viewing its speed, and a dog has methods for setting and finding out its shot status.

Thinking of items as instances of a class allows you to apply your general knowledge of the class to its individual members. A particular instance of an object takes its attributes from the general category. If your friend purchases an `Automobile`, you know it has a model name, and if your friend gets a `Dog`, you know the dog has a breed. You might not know the current status of your friend's `Automobile`, such as its current speed, or the status of her `Dog`'s shots, but you do know what attributes exist for the `Automobile` and `Dog` classes, which allows you to imagine these objects reasonably well before you see them. You know enough to ask the `Automobile`'s model and not its breed; you know enough to ask the `Dog`'s name and not its engine size. As another example, when you use a new application on your computer, you expect each component to have specific, consistent

CHAPTER 10 Object-Oriented Programming

attributes, such as a button being clickable or a window being closable. Each component gains these attributes as a member of the general class of GUI (graphical user interface) components.

Most programmers employ the format in which class names begin with an uppercase letter and multiple-word identifiers are run together, such as `SavingsAccount` or `TemporaryWorker`. Each new word within the identifier starts with an uppercase letter. In Chapter 2, you learned that this format is known as *Pascal casing*.

Much of your understanding of the world comes from your ability to categorize objects and events into classes. As a young child, you learned the concept of *animal* long before you knew the word. Your first encounter with an animal might have been with the family dog, a neighbor's cat, or a goat at a petting zoo. As you developed speech, you might have used the same term for all of these creatures, gleefully shouting "Doggie!" as your parents pointed out cows, horses, and sheep in picture books or along the roadside on drives in the country. As you grew more sophisticated, you learned to distinguish dogs from cows; still later, you learned to distinguish breeds. Your understanding of the class `Animal` helps you see the similarities between dogs and cows, and your understanding of the class `Dog` helps you see the similarities between a Great Dane and a Chihuahua. Understanding classes gives you a framework for categorizing new experiences. You might not know the term *okapi*, but when you learn it's an animal, you begin to develop a concept of what an okapi might be like.

When you think in an object-oriented manner, everything is an object. You can think of any inanimate physical item as an object—your desk, your computer, and your house are all called *objects* in everyday conversation. You can think of living things as objects, too—your houseplant, your pet fish, and your sister are objects. Events also are objects—the stock purchase you made, the mortgage closing you attended, and your graduation party are all objects.

Everything is an object, and every object is a member of a more general class. Your desk is a member of the class that includes all desks, and your pet fish is a member of the class that contains all fish. An object-oriented programmer would say that the desk in your office is an instance, or one tangible example, of the `Desk` class, and your fish is an instance of the `Fish` class. These statements represent **is-a relationships** because you can say, "My oak desk with the scratch on top *is a* `Desk` and my goldfish named Moby *is a* `Fish`." Your goldfish, my guppy, and the zoo's shark each constitute one instance of the `Fish` class.

Object-oriented programmers also use the term *is-a* when describing inheritance. You will learn about inheritance later in this chapter and in Chapter 11.

The concept of a class is useful because of its reusability. For example, if you invite me to a graduation party, I automatically know many things about the party object. I assume that there will be attributes such as a starting time, a number of guests, some quantity of food, and gifts. I understand parties because of my previous knowledge of the `Party` class, of which all parties are members. I don't know the number of guests or the date or time of this particular party, but I understand that because all parties have a date and time, then this one must as well. Similarly, even though every stock purchase is unique, each must have a dollar amount and a number of shares. All objects have predictable attributes because they are members of certain classes.

The data components of a class that belong to every instantiated object are the class's **instance variables**. Also, object attributes often are called **fields** to help distinguish them from other variables you might use. The set of all the values or contents of an object's instance variables is known as its **state**. For example, the current state of a particular party might be 8 p.m. and Friday; the state of a particular stock purchase might be $10 and five shares.

In addition to their attributes, objects have methods associated with them, and every object that is an instance of a class possesses the same methods. For example, at some point you might want to issue invitations for a party. You might name the method issueInvitations(), and it might display some text as well as the values of the party's date and time fields. Your graduation party, then, might possess the identifier myGraduationParty. As a member of the Party class, it might have data members for the date and time, like all parties, and it might have a method to issue invitations. When you use the method, you might want to be able to send an argument to issueInvitations() that indicates how many copies to print. When you think of an object and its methods, it's as though you can send a message to the object to direct it to accomplish a particular task—you can tell the party object named myGraduationParty to print the number of invitations you request. Even though yourAnniversaryParty also is a member of the Party class, and even though it also has an issueInvitations() method, you will send a different argument value to yourAnniversaryParty's issueInvitations() method than I send to myGraduationParty's corresponding method. Within an object-oriented program, you continuously make requests to an object's methods, often including arguments as part of those requests.

In grammar, a noun is equivalent to an object and the values of a class's attributes are adjectives—they describe the characteristics of the objects. An object also can have methods, which are equivalent to verbs.

When you program in object-oriented languages, you frequently create classes from which objects will be instantiated. You also write applications to use the objects, along with their data and methods. Often, you will write programs that use classes created by others; at other times, you might create a class that other programmers will use to instantiate objects within their own programs. A program or class that instantiates objects of another prewritten class is a **class client** or **class user**. For example, your organization might already have a class named Customer that contains attributes such as name, address, and phoneNumber, and you might create clients that include arrays of thousands of Customers. Similarly, in a GUI operating environment, you might write applications that include prewritten components from classes with names like Window and Button.

Polymorphism

The real world is full of objects. Consider a door. A door needs to be opened and closed. You open a door with an easy-to-use interface known as a doorknob. Object-oriented programmers would say you are *passing a message* to the door when you tell it to open by turning its knob. The same message (turning a knob) has a different result when applied to your radio than when applied to a door. As depicted in Figure 10-2, the procedure you use to open something—call it the "open" procedure—works differently on a door than it does on a desk drawer, a bank account, a computer file, or your eyes. However, even though these procedures operate differently using the various objects, you can call each of these procedures "open."

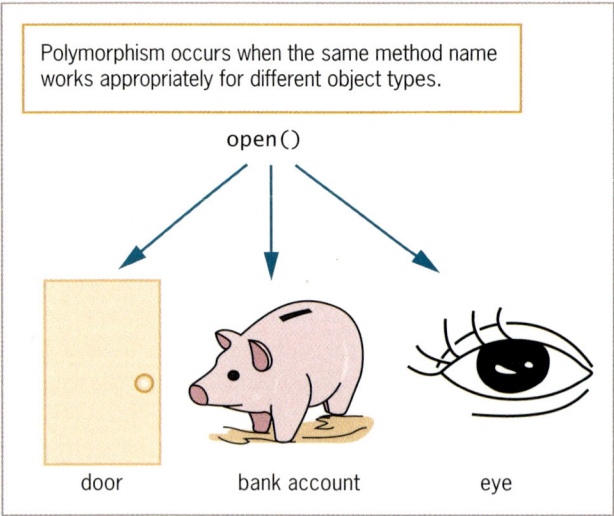

Figure 10-2   Examples of polymorphism

Within classes in object-oriented programs, you can create multiple methods with the same name, which will act differently and appropriately when used with different types of objects. In Chapter 9, you learned that this concept is called *polymorphism*, and you learned to overload methods. For example, you might use a method named `print()` to print a customer invoice, loan application, or envelope. Because you use the same method name to describe the different actions needed to print these diverse objects, you can write statements in object-oriented programming languages that are more like English; you can use the same method name to describe the same type of action, no matter what type of object is being acted upon. Using the method name `print()` is easier than remembering `printInvoice()`, `printLoanApplication()`, and so on. Object-oriented languages understand verbs in context, just as people do.

As another example of the advantages to using one name for a variety of objects, consider a screen you might design for a user to enter data into an application you are writing. Suppose that the screen contains a variety of objects—some forms, buttons, scroll bars, dialog boxes, and so on. Suppose also that you decide to make all the objects blue. Instead of having to memorize the method names that these objects use to change color—perhaps changeFormColor(), changeButtonColor(), and so on—your job would be easier if the creators of all those objects had developed a setColor() method that works appropriately with each type of object.

 Purists find a subtle difference between overloading and polymorphism. Some reserve the term *polymorphism* (or **pure polymorphism**) for situations in which one method body is used with a variety of arguments. For example, a single method that can be used with any type of object is polymorphic. The term *overloading* is applied to situations in which you define multiple methods with a single name—for example, three methods, all named display(), that display a number, an employee, and a student, respectively. Certainly, the two terms are related; both refer to the ability to use a single name to communicate multiple meanings. For now, think of overloading as a primitive type of polymorphism.

Inheritance

Another important concept in object-oriented programming is **inheritance**, which is the process of acquiring the traits of one's predecessors. In the real world, a new door with a stained glass window inherits most of its traits from a standard door. It has the same purpose, it opens and closes in the same way, and it has the same knob and hinges. As Figure 10-3 shows, the door with the stained glass window simply has one additional trait—its window. Even if you have never seen a door with a stained glass window, you know what it is and how to use it because you understand the characteristics of all doors. With object-oriented programming, once you create an object, you can develop new objects that possess all the traits of the original object plus any new traits you desire. If you develop a CustomerBill class of objects, there is no need to develop an OverdueCustomerBill class from scratch. You can create the new class to contain all the characteristics of the already developed one, and simply add necessary new characteristics. This not only reduces the work involved in creating new objects, it makes them easier to understand because they possess most of the characteristics of already developed objects.

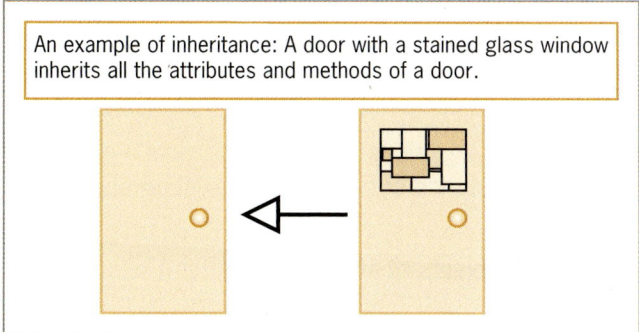

Figure 10-3 An example of inheritance

CHAPTER 10 — Object-Oriented Programming

 Watch the video *An Introduction to Object-Oriented Programming*.

Encapsulation

Real-world objects often employ encapsulation and information hiding. **Encapsulation** is the process of combining all of an object's attributes and methods into a single package; the package includes data that is frequently hidden from outside classes as well as methods that are available to outside classes to access and alter the data. **Information hiding** is the concept that other classes should not alter an object's attributes—only the methods of an object's own class should have that privilege. (The concept is also called **data hiding**.) Outside classes should only be allowed to make a request that an attribute be altered; then it is up to the class's methods to determine whether the request is appropriate. When using a door, you usually are unconcerned with the latch or hinge construction, and you don't have access to the interior workings of the knob. You care only about the functionality and the interface, the user-friendly boundary between the user and internal mechanisms of the device. When you turn a door's knob, you are interacting appropriately with the interface. Banging on the knob would be an inappropriate interaction, so the door would not respond. Similarly, the detailed workings of objects you create within object-oriented programs can be hidden from outside programs and modules if necessary, and the methods you write can control how the objects operate. When the details are hidden, programmers can focus on the functionality and the interface, as people do with real-life objects.

In summary, understanding object-oriented programming means that you must consider five of its integral components: classes, objects, polymorphism, inheritance, and encapsulation.

TWO TRUTHS & A LIE

Principles of Object-Oriented Programming

1. Learning about object-oriented programming is difficult because it does not use the concepts you already know, such as declaring variables and using modules.

2. In object-oriented terminology, a class describes a group or collection of objects with common attributes; an instance of a class is an existing object of a class.

3. A program or class that instantiates objects of another prewritten class is a class client or class user.

The false statement is #1. Object-oriented programming uses many features of procedural programming, including declaring variables and using modules.

Defining Classes and Creating Class Diagrams

A class is a category of things; an object is a specific instance of a class. A **class definition** is a set of program statements that list the characteristics of each object and the methods each object can use.

A class definition can contain three parts:

- Every class has a name.
- Most classes contain data, although this is not required.
- Most classes contain methods, although this is not required.

For example, you can create a class named Employee. Each Employee object will represent one employee who works for an organization. Data members, or attributes of the Employee class, include fields such as lastName, hourlyWage, and weeklyPay.

The methods of a class include all the actions you want to perform with the class. Appropriate methods for an Employee class might include setHourlyWage(), getHourlyWage(), and calculateWeeklyPay(). The job of setHourlyWage() is to provide values for an Employee's wage data field, the purpose of getHourlyWage() is to retrieve the wage value, and the purpose of calculateWeeklyPay() is to multiply the Employee's hourlyWage by the number of hours in a workweek to calculate a weekly salary. With object-oriented languages, you think of the class name, data, and methods as a single encapsulated unit.

Declaring a class does not create actual objects. A class is just an abstract description of what an object will be if any objects are actually instantiated. Just as you might understand all the characteristics of an item you intend to manufacture before the first item rolls off the assembly line, you can create a class with fields and methods long before you instantiate objects that are members of that class. After an object has been instantiated, its methods can be accessed using the object's identifier, a dot, and a method call. When you declare a simple variable that is a built-in data type, you write a statement such as one of the following:

```
num money
string name
```

When you write a program that declares an object that is a class data type, you write a statement such as the following:

```
Employee myAssistant
```

> In some object-oriented programming languages, you need to add more to the declaration statement to actually create an Employee object. For example, in Java you would write:
>
> ```
> Employee myAssistant = new Employee();
> ```
>
> You will understand more about the format of this statement when you learn about constructors in Chapter 11.

When you declare the myAssistant object, it contains all the data fields and has access to all the methods contained within its class. In other words, a larger section of memory is set aside than when you declare a simple variable, because an `Employee` contains several fields. You can use any of an `Employee`'s methods with the `myAssistant` object. The usual syntax is to provide an object name, a dot (period), and a method name. For example, you can write a program that contains statements such as those shown in Figure 10-4.

```
start
   Declarations
      Employee myAssistant
   myAssistant.setLastName("Reynolds")
   myAssistant.setHourlyWage(16.75)
   output "My assistant makes ",
      myAssistant.getHourlyWage(), " per hour"
stop
```

Figure 10-4 Application that declares and uses an `Employee` object

The program segment in Figure 10-4 is very short. In a more useful real-life program, you might read employee data from a data file before assigning it to the object's fields, each `Employee` might contain dozens of fields, and your application might create hundreds or thousands of objects.

Besides referring to `Employee` as a class, many programmers would refer to it as a **user-defined type**, but a more accurate term is **programmer-defined type**. Object-oriented programmers typically refer to a class like `Employee` as an **abstract data type** (ADT); this term implies that the type's data can be accessed only through methods.

When you write a statement such as `myAssistant.setHourlyWage(16.75)`, you are making a call to a method that is contained within the `Employee` class. Because `myAssistant` is an `Employee` object, it is allowed to use the `setHourlyWage()` method that is part of its class. You can tell from the method call that `setHourlyWage()` must accept a numeric parameter.

When you write the application in Figure 10-4, you do not need to know what statements are written within the `Employee` class methods, although you could make an educated guess based on the method names. Before you could execute the application in Figure 10-4, someone would have to write appropriate statements within the `Employee` class methods. If you wrote the methods, of course you would know their contents, but if another programmer has already written the methods, you could use the application without knowing the details contained in the methods. To use the methods, you only need to know their signatures—their names and parameter lists.

In Chapter 9, you learned that the ability to use methods as a black box without knowing their contents is a feature of encapsulation. The real world is full of many black-box devices. For example, you can use your television and microwave oven without knowing how they work internally—all you need to understand is the interface. Similarly, with well-written methods that belong to classes you use, you need not understand how they work internally to be able to use them; you need only understand the ultimate result when you use them.

Defining Classes and Creating Class Diagrams

In the client program segment in Figure 10-4, the focus is on the object—the `Employee` named `myAssistant`—and the methods you can use with that object. This is the essence of object-oriented programming.

In older object-oriented programming languages, simple numbers and characters are said to be **primitive data types**; this distinguishes them from objects that are class types. In the newest programming languages, every item you name, even one that is a numeric or string type, is an object that is a member of a class with both data and methods.

When you instantiate objects, their data fields are stored at separate memory locations. However, all members of the same class share one copy of the class's methods. You will learn more about this concept later in this chapter.

Creating Class Diagrams

A **class diagram** consists of a rectangle divided into three sections, as shown in Figure 10-5. The top section contains the name of the class, the middle section contains the names and data types of the attributes, and the bottom section contains the methods. This generic class diagram shows two attributes and three methods, but a given class might have any number of either, including none. Programmers often use a class diagram to plan or illustrate class features. Class diagrams also are useful for describing a class to nonprogrammers.

```
Class name
Attribute 1 : data type
Attribute 2 : data type
Method 1() : data type
Method 2() : data type
Method 3() : data type
```

Figure 10-5 Generic class diagram

Figure 10-6 shows the class diagram for the `Employee` class. By convention, a class diagram lists the names of the data items first; each name is followed by a colon and the data type. Method names are listed next, and each is followed by its data type (return type). Listing the names first and the data types last emphasizes the purposes of the fields and methods.

```
Employee
lastName: string
hourlyWage: num
weeklyPay: num
setLastName(name : string) : void
setHourlyWage(wage : num) : void
getLastName() : string
getHourlyWage() : num
getWeeklyPay() : num
calculateWeeklyPay() : void
```

Class diagrams are a type of Unified Modeling Language (UML) diagram. Chapter 13 covers the UML.

Figure 10-6 `Employee` class diagram

Figures 10-5 and 10-6 both show that a class diagram is intended to be only an overview of class attributes and methods. A class diagram shows *what* data items and methods the class will use, not the details of the methods nor *when* they will be used. It is a design tool that helps you see the big picture in terms of class requirements. Figure 10-6 shows the `Employee` class containing three data fields that represent an employee's name, hourly pay rate, and weekly pay amount. Every `Employee` object created in a program that uses this class will contain these three data fields. In other words, when you declare an `Employee` object, the single declaration statement allocates enough memory to hold all three fields.

Figure 10-6 also shows that the `Employee` class contains six methods. For example, the first method is defined as follows:

setLastName(name : string) : void

This notation means that the method name is `setLastName()`, that it takes a single `string` parameter named `name`, and that it returns nothing.

Various books, Web sites, and organizations use class diagrams that describe methods in different ways. For example, some developers use the method name only, and others omit parameter lists. This book will take the approach of being as complete as possible, so the class diagrams you see here will contain each method's identifier, parameter list with types, and return type.

The `Employee` class diagram shows that two of the six methods take parameters (`setLastName()` and `setHourlyWage()`). The diagram also shows the return type for each method—three void methods, two numeric methods, and one string method. The class diagram does not indicate what takes place inside the method, although you might be able to make an educated guess. Later, when you write the code that actually creates the `Employee` class, you include method implementation details. For example, Figure 10-7 shows some pseudocode you can use to list the details for the methods in the `Employee` class.

```
class Employee
    Declarations
        string lastName
        num hourlyWage
        num weeklyPay

    void setLastName(string name)
        lastName = name
    return

    void setHourlyWage(num wage)
        hourlyWage = wage
        calculateWeeklyPay()
    return

    string getLastName()
    return lastName

    num getHourlyWage()
    return hourlyWage

    num getWeeklyPay()
    return weeklyPay

    void calculateWeeklyPay()
        Declarations
            num WORK_WEEK_HOURS = 40
        weeklyPay = hourlyWage * WORK_WEEK_HOURS
    return
endClass
```

Figure 10-7 Pseudocode for `Employee` class described in the class diagram in Figure 10-6

In Figure 10-7, the `Employee` class attributes are identified with a data type and a field name. In addition to listing the required data fields, the figure shows the complete methods for the `Employee` class. The purposes of the methods can be divided into three categories:

- Two of the methods accept values from the outside world; these methods, by convention, have the prefix *set*. These methods are used to set the data fields in the class.

- Three of the methods send data to the outside world; these methods, by convention, have the prefix *get*. These methods return field values to a client program.

- One method performs work within the class; this method is named `calculateWeeklyPay()`. This method does not communicate with the outside; its purpose is to multiply `hourlyWage` by the number of hours in a week.

The Set Methods

In Figure 10-7, two methods begin with the word *set*; they are `setLastName()` and `setHourlyWage()`. The purpose of a **set method** or **mutator method** is to set the values of data fields within the class. There is no requirement that such methods start with *set*; the prefix is merely conventional and clarifies the intention of the methods. The method `setLastName()` is implemented as follows:

```
void setLastName(string name)
   lastName = name
return
```

In this method, a string `name` is passed in as a parameter and assigned to the field `lastName`. Because `lastName` is contained in the same class as this method, the method has access to the field and can alter it.

Similarly, the method `setHourlyWage()` accepts a numeric parameter and assigns it to the class field `hourlyWage`. This method also calls the `calculateWeeklyPay()` method, which sets `weeklyPay` based on `hourlyWage`. By writing the `setHourlyWage()` method to call the `calculateWeeklyPay()` method automatically, you guarantee that the `weeklyPay` field is updated any time `hourlyWage` changes.

When you create an `Employee` object with a statement such as `Employee mySecretary`, you can use statements such as the following:

```
mySecretary.setLastName("Johnson")
mySecretary.setHourlyWage(15.00)
```

Instead of literal constants, you could pass variables or named constants to the methods as long as they were the correct data type. For example, if you write a program in which you make the following declaration, then the assignment in the next statement is valid.

```
Declarations
   num PAY_RATE_TO_START = 8.00
mySecretary.setHourlyWage(PAY_RATE_TO_START)
```

> In some languages—for example, Visual Basic and C#—you can create a **property** instead of creating a set method. Using a property provides a way to set a field value using a simpler syntax. By convention, if a class field is `hourlyWage`, its property would be `HourlyWage`, and in a program you could make a statement similar to `mySecretary.HourlyWage = PAY_RATE_TO_START`. The implementation of the property `HourlyWage` (with an uppercase initial letter) would be written in a format very similar to that of the `setHourlyWage()` method.

Like other methods, the methods that manipulate fields within a class can contain any statements you need. For example, a more complicated `setHourlyWage()` method might be written as in Figure 10-8. In this version, the wage passed to the method is tested against minimum and maximum values, and is assigned to the class field `hourlyWage` only if it falls within the prescribed limits. If the wage is too low, the `MINWAGE` value is substituted, and if the wage is too high, the `MAXWAGE` value is substituted.

```
void setHourlyWage(num wage)
   Declarations
      num MINWAGE = 6.00
      num MAXWAGE = 70.00
   if wage < MINWAGE then
      hourlyWage = MINWAGE
   else
      if wage > MAXWAGE then
         hourlyWage = MAXWAGE
      else
         hourlyWage = wage
      endif
   endif
   calculateWeeklyPay()
return
```

Figure 10-8 More complex `setHourlyWage()` method

Similarly, if the set methods in a class required them, the methods could contain output statements, loops, array declarations, or any other legal programming statements. However, if the main purpose of a method is not to set a field value, then for clarity the method should not be named with the *set* prefix.

The Get Methods

The purpose of a **get method** or **accessor method** is to return a value to the world outside the class. In the `Employee` class in Figure 10-7, the three get methods have the prefix *get*: `getLastName()`, `getHourlyWage()`, and `getWeeklyPay()`. The methods are implemented as follows:

```
string getLastName()
return lastName

num getHourlyWage()
return hourlyWage

num getWeeklyPay()
return weeklyPay
```

Each of these methods simply returns the value in the field implied by the method name. Like set methods, any of these get methods could also contain more complex statements as needed. For example, in a more complicated class, you might return the hourly wage of an employee only if the user had also passed an appropriate access code to the method, or you might return the weekly pay value as a string with a dollar sign attached instead of as a numeric value. When you declare an `Employee` object such as

Employee mySecretary, you can then make statements in a program similar to the following:

```
Declarations
    string employeeName
employeeName = mySecretary.getLastName()
output "Wage is ", mySecretary.getHourlyWage()
output "Pay for half a week is ", mySecretary.getWeeklyPay() * 0.5
```

In other words, the value returned from a get method can be used as any other variable of its type would be used. You can assign the value to another variable, display it, perform arithmetic with it, or make any other statement that works correctly with the returned data type.

In some languages—for example, Visual Basic and C#—instead of creating a get method, you can add statements to the property to return a value using simpler syntax. For example, if you created an **HourlyWage** property, you could write a program that contains the statement `output mySecretary.HourlyWage`.

The work Methods

The **Employee** class in Figure 10-7 contains one method that is neither a get nor a set method. This method, `calculateWeeklyPay()`, is a **work method** within the class. A work method is also known as a **help method** or **facilitator**. It contains a locally named constant that represents the hours in a standard workweek, and it computes the weeklyPay field value by multiplying hourlyWage by the named constant. The method is written as follows:

```
void calculateWeeklyPay()
    Declarations
        num WORK_WEEK_HOURS = 40
    weeklyPay = hourlyWage * WORK_WEEK_HOURS
return
```

No values need to be passed into this method, and no value is returned from it because the method does not communicate with the outside world. Instead, this method is called only from another method in the same class (the `setHourlyWage()` method), and that method is called from the outside world. Each time a program uses the `setHourlyWage()` method to alter an Employee's hourlyWage field, `calculateWeeklyPay()` is called to recalculate the weeklyPay field. No `setWeeklyPay()` method is included in this Employee class because the intention is that weeklyPay is set only inside the `calculateWeeklyPay()` method each time the `setHourlyWage()` method calls it. If you wanted programs to be able to set the weeklyPay field directly, you would have to write a method to allow it.

Programmers who are new to class creation often want to pass the hourlyWage value into the `calculateWeeklyPay()` method so that it can use the value in its calculation. Although this technique would work, it is not required. The `calculateWeeklyPay()` method has direct access to the hourlyWage field by virtue of being a member of the same class.

Defining Classes and Creating Class Diagrams

For example, Figure 10-9 shows a program that declares an `Employee` object and sets the hourly wage value. The program displays the `weeklyPay` value. Then a new value is assigned to `hourlyWage`, and `weeklyPay` is displayed again. As you can see from the output in Figure 10-10, the `weeklyPay` value has been recalculated even though it was never set directly by the client program.

```
start
   Declarations
      num LOW = 9.00
      num HIGH = 14.65
      Employee myGardener
   myGardener.setLastName("Greene")
   myGardener.setHourlyWage(LOW)
   output "My gardener makes ",
      myGardener.getWeeklyPay(), " per week"
   myGardener.setHourlyWage(HIGH)
   output "My gardener makes ",
      myGardener.getWeeklyPay(), " per week"
stop
```

Figure 10-9 Program that sets and displays `Employee` data two times

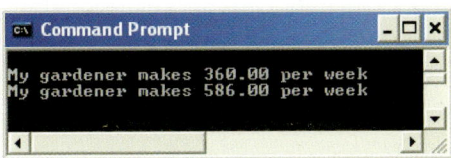

Figure 10-10 Execution of program in Figure 10-9

TWO TRUTHS & A LIE

Defining Classes and Creating Class Diagrams

1. Every class has a name, data, and methods.
2. After an object has been instantiated, its methods can be accessed using the object's identifier, a dot, and a method call.
3. A class diagram consists of a rectangle divided into three sections; the top section contains the name of the class, the middle section contains the names and data types of the attributes, and the bottom section contains the methods.

The false statement is #1. Most classes contain data and methods, although neither is required.

Understanding Public and Private Access

When you buy a new product, one of the usual conditions of its warranty is that the manufacturer must perform all repair work. For example, if your computer has a warranty and something goes wrong with its operation, you cannot open the system unit yourself, remove and replace parts, and then expect to get your money back for a device that does not work properly. Instead, when something goes wrong, you must take the computer to an approved technician. The manufacturer guarantees that your machine will work properly only if the manufacturer can control how the computer's internal mechanisms are modified.

Similarly, in object-oriented design, you do not want outside programs or methods to alter your class's data fields unless you have control over the process. For example, you might design a class that performs complicated statistical analysis on some data, and you would not want others to be able to alter your carefully crafted result. Or, you might design a class from which others can create an innovative and useful GUI screen object. In this case you would not want anyone altering the dimensions of your artistic design. To prevent outsiders from changing your data fields in ways you do not endorse, you force other programs and methods to use a method that is part of your class to alter data. (Earlier in this chapter, you learned that the principle of keeping data private and inaccessible to outside classes is called *information hiding* or *data hiding*.)

To prevent unauthorized field modifications, object-oriented programmers usually specify that their data fields will have **private access**—the data cannot be accessed by any method that is not part of the class. The methods themselves, like `setHourlyWage()` in the `Employee` class, support public access. When methods have **public access**, other programs and methods may use the methods to get access to the private data.

Figure 10-11 shows a complete `Employee` class to which access specifiers have been added to describe each attribute and method. An **access specifier** is the adjective that defines the type of access (`public` or `private`) outside classes will have to the attribute or method. In the figure, each access specifier is shaded.

Understanding Public and Private Access

```
class Employee
   Declarations
      private string lastName
      private num hourlyWage
      private num weeklyPay

   public void setLastName(string name)
      lastName = name
   return

   public void setHourlyWage(num wage)
      hourlyWage = wage
      calculateWeeklyPay()
   return

   public string getLastName()
   return lastName

   public num getHourlyWage()
   return hourlyWage

   public num getWeeklyPay()
   return weeklyPay

   private void calculateWeeklyPay()
      Declarations
         num WORK_WEEK_HOURS = 40
      weeklyPay = hourlyWage * WORK_WEEK_HOURS
   return
endClass
```

Figure 10-11 Employee class including public and private access specifiers

In many object-oriented programming languages, if you do not declare an access specifier for a data field or method, then it is private by default. This book will follow the convention of explicitly specifying access for every class member.

In Figure 10-11, each of the data fields is private, which means each field is inaccessible to an object declared in a program. In other words, if a program declares an Employee object, such as Employee myAssistant, then the following statement is illegal:

myAssistant.hourlyWage = 15.00

Don't Do It
You cannot assign a value to a private variable by using a statement in another class.

Instead, hourlyWage can be assigned only through a public method as follows:

myAssistant.setHourlyWage(15.00)

If you made hourlyWage public instead of private, then a direct assignment statement would work, but you would violate the important OOP principle of data hiding using encapsulation. Data fields should usually be private, and a client application should be able to access them only through the public interfaces—in other words, through the class's public methods. That way, if you have restrictions on the value of hourlyWage, those restrictions will be enforced by the public method that acts as an interface to the private data field. Similarly, a public get method might control how a private value is retrieved. Perhaps you do not want clients to have access to an Employee's hourlyWage if it is more than a specific value, or maybe you want to return the wage to the client as a string with a dollar sign attached. Even when a field has no data value requirements or restrictions, making data private and providing public set and get methods establishes a framework that makes such modifications easier in the future.

In the Employee class in Figure 10-11, only one method is not public; the calculateWeeklyPay() method is private. That means if you write a program and declare an Employee object such as Employee myAssistant, then the following statement is not permitted:

```
myAssistant.calculateWeeklyPay()
```

Don't Do It
The calculateWeeklyPay() method is not accessible outside the class.

Because it is private, the only way to call the calculateWeeklyPay() method is from another method that already belongs to the class. In this example, it is called from the setHourlyWage() method. This prevents a client program from setting hourlyWage to one value while setting weeklyPay to an incompatible value. By making the calculateWeeklyPay() method private, you ensure that the class retains full control over when and how it is used.

Classes usually contain private data and public methods, but as you have just seen, they can contain private methods. Classes can contain public data items as well. For example, an Employee class might contain a public constant data field named MINIMUM_WAGE; outside programs then would be able to access that value without using a method. Public data fields are not required to be named constants, but they frequently are.

In some object-oriented programming languages, such as C++, you can label a set of data fields or methods as public or private using the access specifier name just once, then following it with a list of the items in that category. In other languages, such as Java, you use the specifier *public* (+) or *private* (−) with each field or method. For clarity, this book will label each field and method as public or private.

Many programmers like to specify in class diagrams whether each component in a class is public or private. Figure 10-12 shows the conventions that are typically used. A minus sign (−) precedes the items that are private; a plus sign (+) precedes those that are public.

Understanding Public and Private Access

```
Employee
─────────────────────────────────
-lastName : string
-hourlyWage : num
-weeklyPay : num
─────────────────────────────────
+setLastName(name : string) : void
+setHourlyWage(wage : num) : void
+getLastName() : string
+getHourlyWage() : num
+getWeeklyPay() : num
-calculateWeeklyPay() : void
```

Figure 10-12 Employee class diagram with public and private access specifiers

When you learn more about inheritance in Chapter 11, you will learn about an additional access specifier—the protected access specifier. You use an octothorpe, also called a pound sign or number sign (#), to indicate protected access.

In object-oriented programming languages, the main program is most often written as a method named `main()` or `Main()`, and that method is virtually always defined as public.

Watch the video *Creating a Class*.

TWO TRUTHS & A LIE

Understanding Public and Private Access

1. Object-oriented programmers usually specify that their data fields will have private access.
2. Object-oriented programmers usually specify that their methods will have private access.
3. In a class diagram, a minus sign (−) precedes the items that are private; a plus sign (+) precedes those that are public.

The false statement is #2. Object-oriented programmers usually specify that their methods will have public access.

CHAPTER 10 — Object-Oriented Programming

Organizing Classes

The `Employee` class in Figure 10-12 contains just three data fields and six methods; most classes you create for professional applications will have many more. For example, in addition to a last name and pay information, real employees require an employee number, a first name, address, phone number, hire date, and so on, as well as methods to set and get those fields. As classes grow in complexity, deciding how to organize them becomes increasingly important.

Although it is not required, most programmers place data fields in some logical order at the beginning of a class. For example, an ID number is most likely used as a unique identifier for each employee, so it makes sense to list the employee ID number first in the class. An employee's last name and first name "go together," so it makes sense to store the two components adjacently. Despite these common-sense rules, you have considerable flexibility when positioning your data fields within a class. For example, depending on the class, you might choose to store the data fields alphabetically, or you might group together all the fields that are the same data type. Alternatively, you might choose to store all public data items first, followed by private ones, or vice versa.

In some languages, you can organize data fields and methods in any order within a class. For example, you could place all the methods first, followed by all the data fields, or you could organize the class so that data fields are followed by methods that use them. This book will follow the convention of placing all data fields first so that you can see their names and data types before reading the methods that use them. This format also echoes the way data and methods appear in standard class diagrams.

For ease in locating a class's methods, some programmers store them in alphabetical order. Other programmers arrange them in pairs of get and set methods, in the same order as the data fields are defined. Another option is to list all accessor (get) methods together and all mutator (set) methods together. Depending on the class, you might decide to create other logically functional groupings. Of course, if your company distributes guidelines for organizing class components, you must follow those rules.

TWO TRUTHS & A LIE

Organizing Classes

1. As classes grow in complexity, deciding how to organize them becomes increasingly important.

2. You have a considerable amount of flexibility in how you position your data fields within a class.

3. In a class, methods must be stored in the order in which they are used.

The false statement is #3. Methods can be stored in alphabetical order, in pairs of get and set methods, in the same order as the data fields are defined, or in any other logically functional groupings.

Understanding Instance Methods

Classes contain data and methods, and every instance of a class possesses the same data and has access to the same methods. For example, Figure 10-13 shows a class diagram for a simple `Student` class that contains just one private data field for a student's grade point average. The class also contains get and set methods for the field. Figure 10-14 shows the pseudocode for the `Student` class. This class becomes the model for a new data type named `Student`; when `Student` objects are created, eventually each will have its own `gradePointAverage` field and have access to methods to get and set it.

```
Student

-gradePointAverage : num

+setGradePointAverage(gpa: num) : void
+getGradePointAverage() : num
```

Figure 10-13 Class diagram for `Student` class

```
class Student
    Declarations
        private num gradePointAverage

    public void setGradePointAverage(num gpa)
        gradePointAverage = gpa
    return

    public num getGradePointAverage()
    return gradePointAverage
endClass
```

Figure 10-14 Pseudocode for the `Student` class

If you create multiple `Student` objects using the class in Figure 10-14, you need a separate storage location in computer memory to store each `Student`'s unique grade point average. For example, Figure 10-15 shows a program that creates three `Student` objects and assigns values to their `gradePointAverage` fields. It also shows how the `Student` objects look in memory after the values have been assigned.

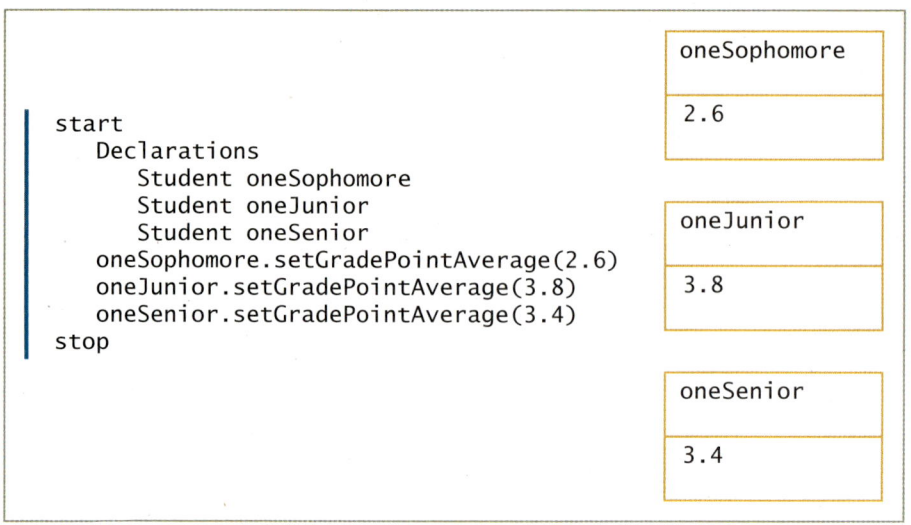

Figure 10-15   StudentDemo program and how Student objects look in memory

It makes sense for each Student object in Figure 10-15 to have its own gradePointAverage field, but it does not make sense for each Student to have its own copy of the methods that get and set gradePointAverage. Creating identical copies of a method for each instance would be inefficient. Instead, even though every Student has its own gradePointAverage field, only one copy of each of the methods getGradePointAverage() and setGradePointAverage() is stored in memory; however, each instantiated object of the class can use the single method copy. A method that works appropriately with different objects is an **instance method**.

Although the StudentDemo class contains only one copy of the get and set methods, they work correctly for any number of instances. Therefore, methods like getGradePointAverage() and setGradePointAverage() are instance methods. Because only one copy of each instance method is stored, the computer needs a way to determine which gradePointAverage is being set or retrieved when one of the methods is called. The mechanism that handles this problem is illustrated in Figure 10-16. When a method call such as oneSophomore.setGradePointAverage(2.6) is made, the true method call, which is invisible and automatically constructed, includes the memory address of the oneSophomore object. (These method calls are represented by the three narrow boxes in the center of Figure 10-16.)

Understanding Instance Methods

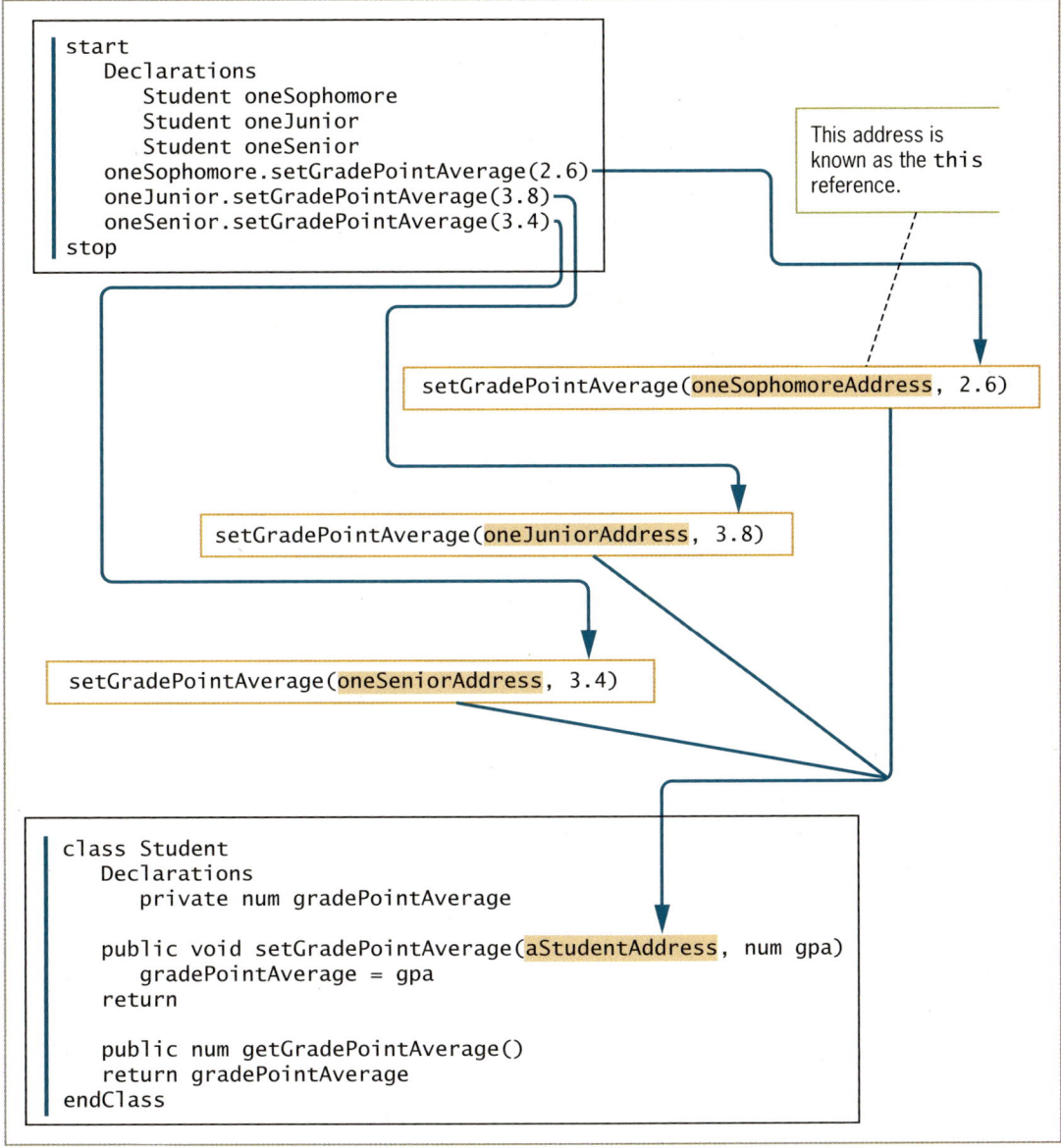

Figure 10-16 How `Student` addresses are passed from an application to an instance method of the `Student` class

Within the `setGradePointAverage()` method in the `Student` class, an invisible and automatically created parameter is added to the list. (For illustration purposes, this parameter is named `aStudentAddress` and is shaded in the `Student` class definition in Figure 10-16. In fact, no parameter is created with that name.) This parameter accepts the address of a `Student` object because the instance method belongs to the `Student` class; if this method belonged to another class—`Employee`, for example—then the method would accept an address for that type of object. The shaded addresses are not written as code in any program—they are "secretly" sent and received behind the scenes. The address variable in Figure 10-16 is called a `this` reference. A **this reference** is an automatically created variable that holds the address of an object and passes it to an instance method whenever the method is called. It is called a `this` reference because it refers to "this particular object" that is using the method at the moment. In other words, an instance method receives a `this` reference to a specific class instance. In the application in Figure 10-16, when `oneSophomore` uses the `setGradePointAverage()` method, the address of the `oneSophomore` object is contained in the `this` reference. Later in the program, when the `oneJunior` object uses the `setGradePointAverage()` method, the `this` reference will hold the address of that `Student` object.

Figure 10-16 shows each place the `this` reference is used in the `Student` class. It is implicitly passed as a parameter to each instance method. You never explicitly refer to the `this` reference when you write the method header for an instance method; Figure 10-16 just shows where it implicitly exists. Within each instance method, the `this` reference is implied any time you refer to one of the class data fields. For example, when you call `setGradePointAverage()` using a `oneSophomore` object, the `gradePointAverage` assigned within the method is the "*this* `gradePointAverage`", or the one that belongs to the `oneSophomore` object. The phrase "this gradePointAverage" usually is written as `this`, followed by a dot, followed by the field name—`this.gradePointAverage`.

The `this` reference exists throughout every instance method. You can explicitly use the `this` reference with data fields, but it is not required. Figure 10-17 shows two locations where the `this` reference can be used implicitly, or where you can (but do not have to) use it explicitly. Within an instance method, the following two identifiers mean exactly the same thing:

- any field name defined in the class
- `this`, followed by a dot, followed by the same field name

For example, within the `setGradePointAverage()` method, `gradePointAverage` and `this.gradePointAverage` refer to exactly the same memory location.

Understanding Instance Methods

```
class Student
   Declarations
      private num gradePointAverage

   public void setGradePointAverage(num gpa)
      this.gradePointAverage = gpa
   return

   public num getGradePointAverage()
      return this.gradePointAverage
endClass
```

You can write this as a reference in these locations.

Figure 10-17 Explicitly using this in the Student class

The this reference can be used only with identifiers that are field names. For example, in Figure 10-17 you can refer to this.gradePointAverage, but you cannot refer to this.gpa because gpa is not a class field—it is only a local variable.

The syntax for using this differs among programming languages. For example, within a class in C++, you can refer to the Student class gradePointAverage value as this->gradePointAverage or (*this).gradePointAverage, but in Java you refer to it as this.gradePointAverage. In Visual Basic, the this reference is named Me, so the variable would be Me.gradePointAverage.

Usually you do not need to use the this reference explicitly within the methods you write, but the this reference is always there, working behind the scenes, accessing the data field for the correct object.

Your organization might prefer that you explicitly use the this reference for clarity even though it is not required to create a workable program. It is the programmer's responsibility to follow the conventions established at work or by clients.

As an example of when you might use the this reference explicitly, consider the following setGradePointAverage() method and compare it to the version in the Student class in Figure 10-17.

```
public void setGradePointAverage(num gradePointAverage)
   this.gradePointAverage = gradePointAverage
return
```

In this version of the method, the programmer has used the variable name gradePointAverage as the parameter to the method and as the instance field within the class. Therefore, gradePointAverage is the name of a local variable within the method whose value is received by passing; it also is the name of a class field. To differentiate the two, you explicitly use the this reference with the copy of gradePointAverage that is a member of the class. Omitting the this reference in this case would result in the local parameter gradePointAverage being assigned to itself, and the class's instance variable would not be set.

Any time a local variable in a method has the same identifier as a field, the field is hidden; you must use a `this` reference to distinguish the field from the local variable.

 Watch the video *The `this` Reference*.

TWO TRUTHS & A LIE

Understanding Instance Methods

1. An instance method operates correctly yet differently for each separate instance of a class.

2. A `this` reference is a variable you must explicitly declare with each class you create.

3. When you write an instance method in a class, the following two identifiers within the method always mean exactly the same thing: any field name or `this` followed by a dot, followed by the same field name.

The false statement is #2. A `this` reference is an automatically created variable that holds the address of an object and passes it to an instance method whenever the method is called. You do not declare it explicitly.

Understanding Static Methods

Some methods do not require a `this` reference because it makes no sense for them either implicitly or explicitly. For example, the `displayStudentMotto()` method in Figure 10-18 does not use any data fields from the `Student` class, so it does not matter which `Student` object calls it. If you write a program in which you declare 100 `Student` objects, the `displayStudentMotto()` method executes in exactly the same way for each of them; it does not need to know whose motto is displayed and it does not need to access any specific object addresses. As a matter of fact, you might want to display the `Student` motto without instantiating any `Student` objects. Therefore, the `displayStudentMotto()` method can be written as a static method instead of an instance method.

Understanding Static Methods

```
public static void displayStudentMotto()
   output "Every student is an individual"
   output "in the pursuit of knowledge."
   output "Every student strives to be"
   output "a literate, responsible citizen."
return
```

Figure 10-18 Student class `displayStudentMotto()` method

When you write a class, you can indicate two types of methods:

- **Static methods**, also called **class methods**, are those for which no object needs to exist, like the `displayStudentMotto()` method in Figure 10-18. Static methods do not receive a `this` reference as an implicit parameter. Typically, static methods include the word `static` in the method header, as shown shaded in Figure 10-18.

- **Nonstatic methods** are methods that exist to be used with an object. These instance methods receive a `this` reference to a specific object. In most programming languages, you use the word `static` when you want to declare a static class member, but you do not use a special word when you want a class member to be nonstatic. In other words, methods in a class are nonstatic instance methods by default.

In everyday language, the word *static* means "stationary"; it is the opposite of *dynamic*, which means "changing." In other words, static methods are always the same for every instance of a class, whereas nonstatic methods act differently depending on the object used to call them.

In most programming languages, you use a static method with the class name, as in the following:

`Student.displayStudentMotto()`

In other words, no object is necessary with a static method.

In some languages, notably C++, besides using a static method with the class name, you also can use a static method with any object of the class, as in `oneSophomore.displayStudentMotto()`.

TWO TRUTHS & A LIE

Understanding Static Methods

1. Class methods do not receive a `this` reference.
2. Static methods do not receive a `this` reference.
3. Nonstatic methods do not receive a `this` reference.

The false statement is #3. Nonstatic methods receive a this reference automatically.

Using Objects

A class is a complex data type defined by a programmer, but in many ways you can use its instances like you use items of simpler data types. For example, you can create an array of objects, pass an object to a method, or return an object from a method.

```
class InventoryItem
    Declarations
        private string inventoryNumber
        private string description
        private num price

    public void setInventoryNumber(string number)
        inventoryNumber = number
    return

    public void setDescription(string description)
        this.description = description
    return

    public void setPrice(num price)
        if(price < 0)
            this.price = 0
        else
            this.price = price
    return

    public string getInventoryNumber()
    return inventoryNumber

    public string getDescription()
    return description

    public num getPrice()
    return price

endClass
```

Notice the uses of the this *reference to differentiate between the method parameter and the class field.*

Figure 10-19 InventoryItem class

Consider the `InventoryItem` class in Figure 10-19. The class represents items that a company manufactures and holds in inventory. Each item has a number, description, and price. The class contains a get and set method for each of the three fields.

Once you declare an `InventoryItem` object, you can use it in many of the ways you would use a simple numeric or string variable. For example, you could pass an `InventoryItem` object to a method or return one from a method. Figure 10-20 shows a program that declares

```
start
   Declarations
      InventoryItem oneItem
   oneItem.setInventoryNumber("1276")
   oneItem.setDescription("Mahogany chest")
   oneItem.setPrice(450.00)
   displayItem(oneItem)
stop

public static void displayItem(InventoryItem item)
   Declarations
      num TAX_RATE = 0.06
      num tax
      num pr
      num total
   output "Item #", item.getInventoryNumber()
   output item.getDescription()
   pr = item.getPrice()
   tax = pr * TAX_RATE
   total = pr + tax
   output "Price is $", pr, " plus $", tax, " tax"
   output "Total is $", total
return
```

Figure 10-20 Application that declares and uses an `InventoryItem` object

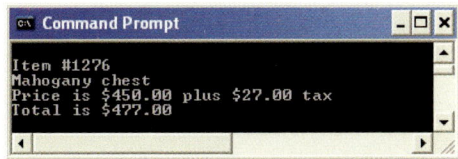

Figure 10-21 Execution of application in Figure 10-20

an `InventoryItem` object and passes it to a method for display. The `InventoryItem` is declared in the main program and assigned values. Then the completed item is passed to a method, where it is displayed. Figure 10-21 shows the execution of the program.

The `InventoryItem` declared in the main program in Figure 10-20 is passed to the `displayItem()` method in much the same way a numeric or string variable would be. The method receives a copy of the `InventoryItem` that is known locally by the identifier `item`. Within the method, the field values of the local item can be retrieved, displayed, and used in arithmetic statements in the same way they could have been in the main program where the `InventoryItem` was originally declared.

Figure 10-22 shows a more realistic application that uses `InventoryItem` objects. In the main program, an `InventoryItem` is declared and the user is prompted for a number. As long as the user does not enter the QUIT value, a loop is executed in which the entered inventory item number is passed to the `getItemValues()` method. Within that method, a local `InventoryItem` object is declared. This local object gathers and holds the user's input values. The user is prompted for a description and price, and then the passed item number and newly obtained description and price are assigned to the local `InventoryItem` object via its set methods. The completed object is returned to the program, where it

```
start
   Declarations
      InventoryItem oneItem
      string itemNum
      string QUIT = "0"
   output "Enter item number or ", QUIT, " to quit… "
   input itemNum
   while itemNum <> "0"
      oneItem = getItemValues(itemNum)
      displayItem(oneItem)
      output "Enter next item number or ", QUIT, " to quit… "
      input itemNum
   endwhile
stop

public static InventoryItem getItemValues(string number)
   Declarations
      InventoryItem inItem
      string desc
      num price
   output "Enter description… "
   input desc
   output "Enter price… "
   input price
   inItem.setInventoryNumber(number)
   inItem.setDescription(desc)
   inItem.setPrice(price)
return inItem

public static void displayItem(InventoryItem item)
   Declarations
      num TAX_RATE = 0.06
      num tax
      num pr
      num total
   output "Item #", item.getInventoryNumber()
   output item.getDescription()
   pr = item.getPrice()
   tax = pr * TAX_RATE
   total = pr + tax
   output "Price is $", pr, " plus $", tax, " tax"
   output "Total is $", total
return
```

Figure 10-22 Application that uses `InventoryItem` objects

```
Command Prompt
Enter item number or 0 to quit... 1276
Enter description... Mahogany chest
Enter price... 450.00

Item #1276
Mahogany chest
Price is $450.00 plus $27.00 tax
Total is $477.00

Enter next item number or 0 to quit... 1488
Enter description... Wicker chair
Enter price... 129.98

Item #1488
Wicker chair
Price is $129.98 plus $7.80 tax
Total is $137.78

Enter next item number or 0 to quit... 2215
Enter description... Decorator pillow
Enter price... 40.00

Item #2215
Decorator pillow
Price is $40.00 plus $2.40 tax
Total is $42.40

Enter next item number or 0 to quit... 0
```

Figure 10-23 Typical execution of program in Figure 10-22

is assigned to the `InventoryItem` object. That item is then passed to the `displayItem()` method. As in the previous example, the method calculates tax and displays results. Figure 10-23 shows a typical execution.

In Figure 10-22, notice that the return type for the `getItemValues()` method is `InventoryItem`. A method can return only a single value. Therefore, it is convenient that the `getItemValues()` method can encapsulate two strings and a number in a single `InventoryItem` object that it returns to the main program.

TWO TRUTHS & A LIE

Using Objects

1. You can pass an object to a method.
2. Because only one value can be returned from a method, you cannot return an object that holds more than one field.
3. You can declare an object locally within a method.

The false statement is #2. An object can be returned from a method.

CHAPTER 10 Object-Oriented Programming

Chapter Summary

- Classes are the basic building blocks of object-oriented programming. A class describes a collection of objects; each object is an instance of a class. A class's fields, or instance variables, hold its data, and every object that is an instance of a class has access to the same methods. A program or class that instantiates objects of another prewritten class is a class client or class user. In addition to classes and objects, three important features of object-oriented languages are polymorphism, inheritance, and encapsulation.

- A class definition is a set of program statements that list the characteristics of each object and the methods that each object can use. A class definition can contain a name, data, and methods. Programmers often use a class diagram to illustrate class features. The purposes of many methods contained in a class can be divided into three categories: set methods, get methods, and work methods.

- Object-oriented programmers usually specify that their data fields will have private access—that is, the data cannot be accessed by any method that is not part of the class. The methods frequently support public access, which means that other programs and methods may use the methods that control access to the private data. In a class diagram, a minus sign (−) precedes the items that are private; a plus sign (+) precedes those that are public.

- As classes grow in complexity, deciding how to organize them becomes increasingly important. Depending on the class, you might choose to store the data fields by listing a key field first. You also might list fields alphabetically, by data type, or by accessibility. Methods might be stored in alphabetical order or in pairs of get and set methods.

- An instance method operates correctly yet differently for every object instantiated from a class. When an instance method is called, a `this` reference that holds the object's memory address is automatically passed to the method.

- Some methods do not require a `this` reference. When you write a class, you can indicate two types of methods: static methods, which are also known as class methods and do not receive a `this` reference as an implicit parameter; and nonstatic methods, which are instance methods and do receive a `this` reference.

- You can use objects in many of the same ways you use simpler data types.

Key Terms

Object-oriented programming (OOP) is a style of programming that focuses on an application's data and the methods you need to manipulate that data.

A **class** describes a group or collection of objects with common attributes.

An **object** is one tangible example of a class; it is an instance of a class.

Key Terms

An **instance** is one tangible example of a class; it is an object.

An **instantiation** of a class is an instance.

To **instantiate** a class is to create an object from it.

Attributes are the characteristics that define an object as part of a class.

An **is-a relationship** exists between an object and its class.

A class's **instance variables** are the data components that belong to every instantiated object.

Fields are object attributes or data.

The **state** of an object is the set of all the values or contents of its instance variables.

A **class client** or **class user** is a program or class that instantiates objects of another prewritten class.

Pure polymorphism describes situations in which one method body is used with a variety of arguments.

Inheritance is the process of acquiring the traits of one's predecessors.

Encapsulation is the process of combining all of an object's attributes and methods into a single package.

Information hiding (or **data hiding**) is the concept that other classes should not alter an object's attributes—only the methods of an object's own class should have that privilege.

A **class definition** is a set of program statements that list the characteristics of the class's objects and the methods each object can use.

A **user-defined type**, or **programmer-defined type**, is a type that is not built into a language but is created by the programmer.

An **abstract data type** (ADT) is a programmer-defined type, such as a class.

Primitive data types are simple numbers and characters that are not class types.

A **class diagram** consists of a rectangle divided into three sections that show the name, data, and methods of a class.

A **set method** is an instance method that sets the value of a data field in a class.

A **mutator method** is an instance method that can modify one of an object's attributes.

A **property** provides methods that allow you to get and set a class field value using a simple syntax.

A **get method** is an instance method that returns a value from a class.

An **accessor method** gets values from class fields.

A **work method** performs tasks within a class.

A **help method** or **facilitator** is a work method.

Private access specifies that data or methods cannot be used by any method that is not part of the same class.

Public access specifies that other programs and methods may use the specified data or methods within a class.

An **access specifier** is the adjective that defines the type of access outside classes will have to the attribute or method.

An **instance method** operates correctly yet differently for each object. An instance method is nonstatic and receives a `this` reference.

A **this reference** is an automatically created variable that holds the address of an object and passes it to an instance method whenever the method is called.

Static methods are those for which no object needs to exist; they are not instance methods and they do not receive a `this` reference.

A **class method** is a static method; it is not an instance method and it does not receive a `this` reference.

Nonstatic methods are methods that exist to be used with an object; they are instance methods and receive a `this` reference.

Review Questions

1. Which of the following means the same as *object*?
   a. class
   b. field
   c. instance
   d. category

2. Which of the following means the same as *instance variable*?
   a. field
   b. instance
   c. category
   d. class

3. A program that instantiates objects of another prewritten class is a(n) _____.
   a. object
   b. client
   c. instance
   d. GUI

4. The relationship between an instance and a class is a(n) _____ relationship.
   a. has-a
   b. is-a
   c. polymorphic
   d. hostile

Review Questions

5. Which of these does not belong with the others?
   a. instance variable
   b. attribute
   c. object
   d. field

6. The process of acquiring the traits of one's predecessors is _____.
   a. inheritance
   b. encapsulation
   c. polymorphism
   d. orientation

7. When discussing classes and objects, *encapsulation* means that _____.
   a. all the fields belong to the same object
   b. all the fields are private
   c. all the fields and methods are grouped together
   d. all the methods are public

8. Every class definition must contain _____.
   a. a name
   b. data
   c. methods
   d. all of the above

9. Assume that a working program contains the following statement:
   myDog.setName("Bowser")
   Which of the following do you know?
   a. setName() is a public method.
   b. setName() accepts a string parameter.
   c. both of the above
   d. none of the above

10. Assume that a working program contains the following statement:
    name = myDog.getName()
    Which of the following do you know?
    a. getName() returns a string.
    b. getName() returns a value that is the same data type as name.
    c. both of the above
    d. none of the above

11. A class diagram _____.
    a. provides an overview of a class's data and methods
    b. provides method implementation details
    c. is never used by nonprogrammers because it is too technical
    d. all of the above

12. Which of the following is the most likely scenario for a specific class?
    a. Its data is private and its methods are public.
    b. Its data is public and its methods are private.
    c. Its data and methods are both public.
    d. Its data and methods are both private.

13. An instance method _____.
    a. is static
    b. receives a this reference
    c. both of the above
    d. none of the above

14. Assume that you have created a class named Dog that contains a data field named weight and an instance method named setWeight(). Further assume that the setWeight() method accepts a numeric parameter named weight. Which of the following statements correctly sets a Dog's weight within the setWeight() method?
    a. weight = weight
    b. this.weight = this.weight
    c. weight = this.weight
    d. this.weight = weight

15. A static method is also known as a(n) _____ method.
    a. instance
    b. public
    c. private
    d. class

16. By default, methods contained in a class are _____ methods.
    a. static
    b. nonstatic
    c. class
    d. public

17. Assume that you have created a class named MyClass, and that a working program contains the following statement:

    output MyClass.number

    Which of the following do you know?
    a. number is a numeric field.
    b. number is a static field.
    c. number is an instance variable.
    d. all of the above

18. Assume that you have created an object named myObject and that a working program contains the following statement:

    output myObject.getSize()

    Which of the following do you know?

    a. getSize() is a static method.
    b. getSize() returns a number.
    c. getSize() receives a this reference.
    d. all of the above

19. Assume that you have created a class that contains a private field named myField and a nonstatic public method named myMethod(). Which of the following is true?

    a. myMethod() has access to myField and can use it.
    b. myMethod() does not have access to myField and cannot use it.
    c. myMethod() can use myField but cannot pass it to other methods.
    d. myMethod() can use myField only if it is passed to myMethod() as a parameter.

20. An object can be _____.

    a. stored in an array
    b. passed to a method
    c. returned from a method
    d. all of the above

Exercises

1. Identify three objects that might belong to each of the following classes:

    a. Building
    b. Artist
    c. BankLoan

2. Identify three different classes that might contain each of these objects:

    a. William Shakespeare
    b. My favorite red sweater
    c. Public School 23 in New York City

3. Design a class named TermPaper that holds an author's name, the subject of the paper, and an assigned letter grade. Include methods to set the values for each data field and display the values for each data field. Create the class diagram and write the pseudocode that defines the class.

4. Design a class named `Automobile` that holds the vehicle identification number, make, model, and color of an automobile. Include methods to set the values for each data field, and include a method that displays all the values for each field. Create the class diagram and write the pseudocode that defines the class.

5. Design a class named `CheckingAccount` that holds a checking account number, name of account holder, and balance. Include methods to set values for each data field and a method that displays all the account information. Create the class diagram and write the pseudocode that defines the class.

6. Complete the following tasks:

    a. Design a class named `StockTransaction` that holds a stock symbol (typically one to four characters), stock name, and price per share. Include methods to set and get the values for each data field. Create the class diagram and write the pseudocode that defines the class.

    b. Design an application that declares two `StockTransaction` objects and sets and displays their values.

    c. Design an application that declares an array of 10 `StockTransactions`. Prompt the user for data for each of the objects, and then display all the values.

7. Complete the following tasks:

    a. Design a class named `Pizza`. Data fields include a string field for toppings (such as pepperoni) and numeric fields for diameter in inches (such as 12) and price (such as 13.99). Include methods to get and set values for each of these fields. Create the class diagram and write the pseudocode that defines the class.

    b. Design an application that declares two `Pizza` objects and sets and displays their values.

    c. Design an application that declares an array of 10 `Pizzas`. Prompt the user for data for each of the `Pizzas`, then display all the values.

8. Complete the following tasks:
    a. Design a class named `MagazineSubscription` that has fields for a subscriber's name, the magazine name, and number of months remaining in the subscription. Include methods to set and get the values for each data field. Create the class diagram and write the pseudocode that defines the class.

    b. Design an application that declares two `MagazineSubscription` objects and sets and displays their values.

    c. Design an application that declares an array of six `MagazineSubscriptions`. Prompt the user for data for each object, and then display all the values. Then subtract 1 from each "months remaining" field and display the objects again.

Exercises

Find the Bugs

9. Your downloadable student files for Chapter 10 include DEBUG10-01.txt, DEBUG10-02.txt, and DEBUG10-03.txt. Each file starts with some comments that describe the problem. Comments are lines that begin with two slashes (//). Following the comments, each file contains pseudocode that has one or more bugs you must find and correct.

Game Zone

10. a. Playing cards are used in many computer games, including versions of such classics as Solitaire, Hearts, and Poker. Design a `Card` class that contains a string data field to hold a suit (spades, hearts, diamonds, or clubs) and a numeric data field for a value from 1 to 13. Include get and set methods for each field. Write an application that randomly selects two playing cards and displays their values.

   b. Using two `Card` objects, design an application that plays a simple version of the card game War. Deal two `Cards`—one for the computer and one for the player. Determine the higher card, then display a message indicating whether the cards are equal, the computer won, or the player won. (Playing cards are considered equal when they have the same value, no matter what their suit is.) For this game, assume that the Ace (value 1) is low. Make sure that the two `Cards` dealt are not the same `Card`. For example, a deck cannot contain more than one Queen of Spades.

Up for Discussion

11. In this chapter, you learned that instance data and methods belong to objects (which are class members), but that static data and methods belong to a class as a whole. Consider the real-life class named `StateInTheUnitedStates`. Name some real-life attributes of this class that are static attributes and instance attributes. Create another example of a real-life class and discuss what its static and instance members might be.

12. Some programmers use a system called Hungarian notation when naming their variables and class fields. What is Hungarian notation, and why do many object-oriented programmers feel it is not a valuable style to use?

CHAPTER 11

More Object-Oriented Programming Concepts

In this chapter, you will learn about:

- Constructors
- Destructors
- Composition
- Inheritance
- GUI objects
- Exception handling
- The advantages of object-oriented programming

Understanding Constructors

In Chapter 10, you learned that you can create classes to encapsulate data and methods, and that you can instantiate objects from the classes you define. For example, you can create an `Employee` class that contains fields such as `lastName`, `hourlyWage`, and `weeklyPay`, and methods that set and return values for those fields. When you instantiate an object with a statement that uses the class type and an object identifier, such as `Employee chauffeur`, you are actually calling a method named `Employee()`. A method that has the same name as a class and that establishes an object is a constructor method, or more simply, a **constructor**. A **default constructor** is one that requires no arguments. If a constructor requires arguments, it is a **nondefault constructor**. In object-oriented programming (OOP) languages, you can write both default and nondefault constructors, but if you do not create either, then a default constructor is created automatically by the compiler for every class you write.

The constructor for the `Employee` class establishes one `Employee` object. Depending on the programming language, the automatically supplied default constructor might provide initial values for the object's data fields; for example, in many languages all numeric fields are set to zero by default. If you do not want an object's fields to hold default values, or if you want to perform additional tasks when you create an instance of a class, you can write your own constructor. Any constructor you write must have the same name as the class it constructs, and cannot have a return type. Normally, you declare constructors to be public so that other classes can instantiate objects that belong to the class. You can create a constructor to accept one or more parameters; when you do not include parameters for a constructor you write, your constructor becomes the default constructor for the class and the automatically supplied version is no longer usable. In other words, a class can have three types of constructors:

- A class can contain a default (parameterless) constructor that is created automatically.
- A class can contain a default (parameterless) constructor that you create explicitly. A class with an explicitly created default constructor no longer contains the automatically supplied version, but it can coexist with a nondefault constructor.
- A class can contain a nondefault constructor (with one or more parameters), which must be explicitly created. A class with a nondefault constructor no longer contains the automatically supplied default version, but it can coexist with an explicitly created default constructor.

Default Constructors

For example, if you want every `Employee` object to have a starting hourly wage of $10.00 as well as the correct weekly pay for that wage, then you could write the default constructor for the `Employee` class that appears in Figure 11-1. Any `Employee` object instantiated will have an `hourlyWage` field equal to 10.00 and a `weeklyPay` field equal to 400.00. The `lastName` field will hold the default value for strings in the programming language in which this class is implemented because `lastName` is not assigned in the constructor.

Understanding Constructors

```
class Employee
   Declarations
      private string lastName
      private num hourlyWage
      private num weeklyPay
   public Employee()
      hourlyWage = 10.00
      calculateWeeklyPay()
   return
   public void setLastName(string name)
      lastName = name
   return
   public void setHourlyWage(num wage)
      hourlyWage = wage
      calculateWeeklyPay()
   return
   public string getLastName()
   return lastName
   public num getHourlyWage()
   return hourlyWage
   public num getWeeklyPay()
   return weeklyPay
   private void calculateWeeklyPay()
      Declarations
         num WORK_WEEK_HOURS = 40
      weeklyPay = hourlyWage * WORK_WEEK_HOURS
   return
endClass
```

Figure 11-1 Employee class with a default constructor that sets hourlyWage and weeklyPay

The Employee constructor in Figure 11-1 calls the calculateWeeklyPay() method. You can write any statement you want in a constructor; it is just a method. Although you usually have no reason to do so, you could output a message from a constructor, accept input, declare local variables, or perform any other task. You can place a constructor anywhere inside the class, outside of any other method. Often, programmers list constructors first among the methods, because a constructor is the first method used when an object is created.

Figure 11-2 shows a program in which two Employee objects are declared and their hourlyWage values are displayed. In the output in Figure 11-3, you can see that even though the setHourlyWage() method is never called directly in the program, the Employees possess valid hourly wages as set by their constructors.

```
start
   Declarations
      Employee myPersonalTrainer
      Employee myInteriorDecorator
   output "Trainer's wage: ",
      myPersonalTrainer.getHourlyWage()
   output "Decorator's wage: ",
      myInteriorDecorator.getHourlyWage()
stop
```

Figure 11-2 Program that declares Employee objects using class in Figure 11-1

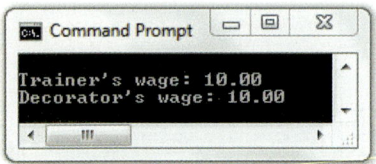

Figure 11-3 Output of program in Figure 11-2

The Employee class in Figure 11-1 sets an Employee's hourly wage to 10.00 at construction, but the class also contains a setHourlyWage() method that an application could use later to change the initial hourlyWage value. A potentially superior way to write the Employee class constructor is shown in Figure 11-4. In this version of the constructor, a named constant with the value 10.00 is passed to setHourlyWage(). Using this technique provides several advantages:

- The statement to call calculateWeeklyPay() is no longer required in the constructor because the constructor calls setHourlyWage(), which calls calculateWeeklyPay().

- In the future, if restrictions should be imposed on hourlyWage, the code will need to be altered in only one location. For example, if setHourlyWage() is modified to disallow rates that are too high and too low, the code will change only in the setHourlyWage() method and will not have to be modified in the constructor. This reduces the amount of work required and reduces the possibility for error.

```
public Employee()
   Declarations
      num DEFAULT_WAGE = 10.00
   setHourlyWage(DEFAULT_WAGE)
return
```

Figure 11-4 Alternate and efficient version of the Employee class constructor

Understanding Constructors

Of course, if different `hourlyWage` requirements are needed at initialization than are required when the value is set after construction, then different code statements will be written in the constructor than those written in the `setHourlyWage()` method.

Nondefault Constructors

You can write a nondefault constructor, which is one that accepts parameters. When you create a constructor, whether it is default or nondefault, the automatically supplied default constructor is no longer accessible.

For example, instead of forcing every `Employee` to be constructed with the same initial values, you might choose to create `Employee` objects that each have a unique `hourlyWage` by passing a numeric value for the wage to the constructor. Figure 11-5 shows an `Employee` constructor that receives an argument. With this constructor, an argument is passed using a declaration similar to one of the following:

```
Employee partTimeWorker(8.81)
Employee partTimeWorker(valueEnteredByUser)
```

When the constructor executes, the numeric value within the constructor call is passed to `Employee()`, where the parameter `rate` takes on the value of the argument. The value is assigned to `hourlyWage` within the constructor.

```
public Employee(num rate)
   hourlyWage = rate
   calculateWeeklyPay()
return
```

Figure 11-5   `Employee` constructor that accepts a parameter

If you create an `Employee` class with a constructor such as the one shown in Figure 11-5, and it is the only constructor in the class, then every `Employee` object you create must use a numeric argument in its declaration. In other words, with this new version of the class that contains a single nondefault constructor, the following declaration no longer works:

```
Employee partTimeWorker
```

Overloading Methods and Constructors

In Chapter 9, you learned that you can overload methods by writing multiple versions of a method with the same name but different argument lists. In the same way, you can overload instance methods and constructors. For example, Figure 11-6 shows a version of the `Employee` class that contains two constructors. Recall that a method's signature is its name and list of argument types. The constructors in Figure 11-6 have different signatures—one version requires no argument and the other requires a numeric argument. In other words, this version of the class contains both a default constructor and a nondefault constructor.

CHAPTER 11 More Object-Oriented Programming Concepts

```
class Employee
   Declarations
      private string lastName
      private num hourlyWage
      private num weeklyPay

   public Employee()                          ── Default constructor
      hourlyWage = 10.00
      calculateWeeklyPay()
   return

   public Employee(num rate)                  ── Nondefault constructor
      hourlyWage = rate
      calculateWeeklyPay()
   return

   public void setLastName(string name)
      lastName = name
   return

   public void setHourlyWage(num wage)
      hourlyWage = wage
      calculateWeeklyPay()
   return

   public string getLastName()
   return lastName

   public num getHourlyWage()
   return hourlyWage

   public num getWeeklyPay()
   return weeklyPay

   private void calculateWeeklyPay()
      Declarations
         num WORK_WEEK_HOURS = 40
      weeklyPay = hourlyWage * WORK_WEEK_HOURS
   return
endClass
```

Figure 11-6 Employee class with overloaded constructors

When you use the version of the class shown in Figure 11-6, then you can make statements like the following:

```
Employee deliveryPerson
Employee myButler(25.85)
```

Understanding Constructors

When you declare an `Employee` using the first statement, an `hourlyWage` of 10.00 is automatically set because the statement uses the parameterless version of the constructor. When you declare an `Employee` using the second statement, `hourlyWage` is set to the passed value. Any method or constructor in a class can be overloaded, and you can provide as many versions as you want as long as each version has a unique signature. For example, you could add a third constructor to the `Employee` class, as shown in Figure 11-7. This version can coexist with the other two because the parameter list is different from either existing version. With this version you can specify the hourly rate for the `Employee` as well as a name. If an application makes a statement similar to the following, then this two-parameter version would execute:

```
Employee myMaid(22.50, "Parker")
```

```
public Employee(num rate, string name)
    lastName = name
    hourlyWage = rate
    calculateWeeklyPay()
return
```

Figure 11-7 A third possible `Employee` class constructor

You might create an `Employee` class with several constructor versions to provide flexibility for client programs. For example, a particular client program might use only one version, and a different client might use another.

 Watch the video *Constructors*.

TWO TRUTHS & A LIE
Understanding Constructors

1. A constructor is a method that establishes an object.
2. A default constructor is defined as one that is created automatically.
3. Depending on the programming language, a default constructor might provide initial values for the object's data fields.

The false statement is #2. A default constructor is one that takes no arguments. Although the automatically created constructor for a class is a default constructor, not all default constructors are created automatically.

Understanding Destructors

A **destructor** contains the actions you require when an instance of a class is destroyed. Most often, an instance of a class is destroyed when the object goes out of scope. As with constructors, if you do not explicitly create a destructor for a class, one is provided automatically.

The most common way to declare a destructor explicitly is to use an identifier that consists of a tilde (~) followed by the class name. You cannot provide parameters to a destructor; it must have an empty parameter list. As a consequence, destructors cannot be overloaded; a class can have one destructor at most. Like a constructor, a destructor has no return type.

 The rules for creating and naming destructors vary among programming languages. For example, in Visual Basic classes, the destructor is called `Finalize`.

Figure 11-8 shows an `Employee` class that contains only one field (`idNumber`), a constructor, and a shaded destructor. Although it is unusual for a constructor or destructor to output anything, these display messages so you can see when the objects are created and destroyed. When you execute the program in Figure 11-9, you instantiate two `Employee` objects, each with its own `idNumber` value. When the program ends, the two `Employee` objects go out of scope, and the destructor for each object is called automatically. Figure 11-10 shows the output.

```
class Employee
    Declarations
        private string idNumber
    public Employee(string empID)
        idNumber = empId
        output "Employee ", idNumber, " is created"
    return
    public ~Employee()
        output "Employee ", idNumber, " is destroyed"
    return
endClass
```

Figure 11-8   `Employee` class with destructor

Understanding Destructors

```
start
   Declarations
      Employee aWorker("101")
      Employee anotherWorker("202")
stop
```

Figure 11-9   Program that declares two Employee objects

Figure 11-10   Output of program in Figure 11-9

The program in Figure 11-9 never explicitly calls the Employee class destructor, yet you can see from the output that the destructor executes twice. Destructors are invoked automatically; you usually do not explicitly call one, although in some languages you can. Interestingly, you can see from the output in Figure 11-10 that the last object created is the first object destroyed; the same relationship would hold true no matter how many objects the program instantiated if the objects went out of scope at the same time.

 An instance of a class becomes eligible for destruction when it is no longer possible for any code to use it—that is, when it goes out of scope. In many languages, the actual execution of an object's destructor might occur at any time after the object becomes eligible for destruction.

For now, you have little reason to create a destructor except to demonstrate how it is called automatically. Later, when you write more sophisticated programs that work with files, databases, or large quantities of computer memory, you might want to perform specific clean-up or close-down tasks when an object goes out of scope. Then you will place appropriate instructions within a destructor.

TWO TRUTHS & A LIE

Understanding Destructors

1. Unlike constructors, you must explicitly create a destructor if you want one for a class.
2. You cannot provide parameters to a destructor; it must have an empty argument list.
3. Destructors cannot be overloaded; a class can have one destructor at most.

The false statement is #1. As with constructors, if you do not explicitly create a destructor for a class, one is provided automatically.

Understanding Composition

A class can contain objects of another class as data fields. For example, you might create a class named `Date` that contains a month, day, and year, and add two `Date` fields to an `Employee` class to hold the `Employee`'s birth date and hire date. Then you might create a class named `Department` that represents every department in a company, and create the `Department` class to contain a supervisor, who is an `Employee`. Figure 11-11 contains a diagram of these relationships. When a class contains objects of another class, the relationship is called a **whole-part relationship** or **composition**. The relationship created is also called a **has-a relationship** because one class "has an" instance of another.

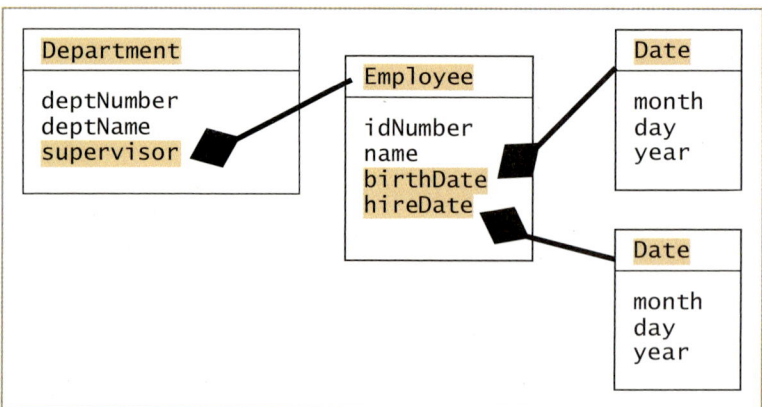

Figure 11-11 Diagram of typical composition relationships

Placing one or more objects within another object is often known as *composition* when the parts cease to exist if the whole ceases to exist, and *aggregation* when the parts can exist without the whole. For example, the relationship of a `Car` to its `Motor` might be called *composition*, but the relationship of a `UsedCarLot` to its `Cars` might be called *aggregation*. These terms are defined more precisely in Chapter 13.

When your classes contain objects that are members of other classes, your programming task becomes increasingly complex. For example, you sometimes must refer to a method by a very long name. Suppose you create a `Department` class that contains an array of `Employee` objects (those who work in the department), and a method named `getHighestPaidEmployee()` that returns a single `Employee` object. The `Employee` class contains a method named `getHireDate()` that returns a `Date` object—an `Employee`'s hire date. Further suppose the `Date` class contains a method that returns the year portion of the `Date`, and that you create a `Department` object named `sales`. An application might contain a statement such as the following, which outputs the year that the highest-paid employee in the sales department was hired:

```
output sales.getHighestPaidEmployee().getHireDate().getYear()
```

Additionally, when classes contain objects that are members of other classes, all the corresponding constructors and destructors execute in a specific order. As you work with object-oriented programming languages, you will learn to manage these complex issues.

TWO TRUTHS & A LIE

Understanding Composition

1. A class can contain objects of another class as data fields.
2. Composition occurs when you use an object as a field within another class.
3. Composition is called an is-a relationship because one class "is an" instance of another.

The false statement is #3. Composition is called a has-a relationship because one class "has an" instance of another.

Understanding Inheritance

Understanding classes helps you organize objects in real life. Understanding inheritance helps you organize them more precisely. Inheritance enables you to apply your knowledge of a general category to more specific objects. When you use the term *inheritance*, you might think of genetic inheritance. You know from biology that your blood type and eye color are the products of inherited genes. You might choose to own plants and animals based on their inherited attributes. You plant impatiens next to your house because they thrive in the shade; you adopt a poodle because you know poodles don't shed. Every plant and pet has slightly different characteristics, but within a species, you can count on many consistent inherited attributes and behaviors. In other words, you can reuse the knowledge you gain about general categories and apply it to more specific categories.

Similarly, the classes you create in object-oriented programming languages can inherit data and methods from existing classes. When you create a class by making it inherit from another class, the new class contains fields and methods automatically, allowing you to reuse fields and methods that are already written and tested.

You already know how to create classes and how to instantiate objects that are members of those classes. For example, consider the Employee class in Figure 11-12. The class contains two data fields, empNum and weeklySalary, as well as methods that get and set each field.

```
class Employee
    Declarations
        private string empNum
        private num weeklySalary

    public void setEmpNum(string number)
        empNum = number
    return

    public string getEmpNum()
    return empNum

    public void setWeeklySalary(num salary)
        weeklySalary = salary
    return

    public num getWeeklySalary()
    return weeklySalary
endClass
```

Figure 11-12   An Employee class

Suppose that you hire a new type of Employee who earns a commission as well as a weekly salary. You can create a class with a name such as CommissionEmployee, and provide this class with three fields (empNum, weeklySalary, and commissionRate) and six methods (to get and set each of the three fields). However, this work would duplicate much of the work that you already have done for the Employee class. The wise and efficient alternative is to create the CommissionEmployee class so it inherits all the attributes and methods of Employee. Then, you can add just the single field and two methods (the get and set methods for the new field) that are additions within the new class. Figure 11-13 depicts these relationships. The complete CommissionEmployee class is shown in Figure 11-14.

Understanding Inheritance

```
Employee
─────────────────────────────────
-empNum : string
-weeklySalary : num
─────────────────────────────────
+setEmpNum(number : string) : void
+getEmpNum() : string
+setWeeklySalary(salary : num) : void
+getWeeklySalary() : num
```
△
```
CommissionEmployee
─────────────────────────────────
-commissionRate : num
─────────────────────────────────
+setCommissionRate(rate : num) : void
+getCommissionRate() : num
```

Figure 11-13 CommissionEmployee inherits from Employee

Recall that a plus sign in a class diagram indicates public access and a minus sign indicates private access. Figure 11-13 and several other figures in this chapter are examples of UML diagrams. Chapter 13 describes UML diagrams in more detail.

```
class CommissionEmployee inheritsFrom Employee
   Declarations
      private num commissionRate

   public void setCommissionRate(num rate)
      commissionRate = rate
   return

   public num getCommissionRate()
   return commissionRate
endClass
```

Figure 11-14 CommissionEmployee class

The class in Figure 11-14 uses the phrase `inheritsFrom Employee` (see shading) to indicate inheritance. Each programming language uses its own syntax. For example, using Java you would write `extends`, in Visual Basic you would write `inherits`, and in C++ and C# you would use a colon between the new class name and the one from which it inherits.

When you use inheritance to create the `CommissionEmployee` class, you acquire the following benefits:

- You save time, because you need not re-create the `Employee` fields and methods.
- You reduce the chance of errors, because the `Employee` methods have already been used and tested.
- You make it easier for anyone who has used the `Employee` class to understand the `CommissionEmployee` class, because such users can concentrate on the new features only.
- You reduce the chance for errors and inconsistencies in shared fields. For example, if your company decides to change employee ID numbers from four digits to five, and you have code in the `Employee` class constructor that ensures valid ID numbers, then you can simply change the code in the `Employee` class; every `CommissionEmployee` object will automatically acquire the change. Without inheritance, not only would you make the change in multiple places, but the likelihood would increase that you would forget to make the change in one of the classes.

The ability to use inheritance makes programs easier to write, easier to understand, and less prone to errors. Imagine that besides `CommissionEmployee`, you want to create several other more specific `Employee` classes (perhaps `PartTimeEmployee`, including a field for hours worked, or `DismissedEmployee`, including a reason for dismissal). By using inheritance, you can develop each new class correctly and more quickly.

In part, the concept of class inheritance is useful because it makes class code reusable. However, you do not use inheritance simply to save work. When properly used, inheritance always involves a general-to-specific relationship.

Understanding Inheritance Terminology

A class that is used as a basis for inheritance, like `Employee`, is called a **base class**. When you create a class that inherits from a base class (such as `CommissionEmployee`), it is a **derived class** or **extended class**. When two classes have a base-derived relationship, you can distinguish the classes by using them in a sentence with the phrase *is a*. A derived class always "is a" case or instance of the more general base class. For example, a `Tree` class may be a base class to an `Evergreen` class. Every `Evergreen` *is a* `Tree`; however, it is not true that every `Tree` is an `Evergreen`. Thus, `Tree` is the base class and `Evergreen` is the derived class. Similarly, a `CommissionEmployee` *is an* `Employee`—not always the other way around—so `Employee` is the base class and `CommissionEmployee` is derived.

Understanding Inheritance

You can use the terms **superclass** and **subclass** as synonyms for base class and derived class. Thus, Evergreen can be called a subclass of the Tree superclass. You also can use the terms **parent class** and **child class**. A CommissionEmployee is a child to the Employee parent.

As an alternative way to discover which of two classes is the base class and which is the derived class, you can try saying the two class names together, although this technique might not work with every base-subclass pair. When people say their names in the English language, they state the more specific name before the all-encompassing family name, such as *Mary Johnson*. Similarly, with classes, the order that "makes more sense" is the child-parent order. Thus, because "Evergreen Tree" makes more sense than "Tree Evergreen," you can deduce that Evergreen is the child class. It also is convenient to think of a derived class as building upon its base class by providing the "adjectives" or additional descriptive terms for the "noun." Frequently, the names of derived classes are formed in this way, as in CommissionEmployee or EvergreenTree.

Finally, you usually can distinguish base classes from their derived classes by size. Although it is not required, a derived class is generally larger than its base class, in the sense that it usually has additional fields and methods. A subclass description may look small, but any subclass contains all of its base class's fields and methods as well as its own more specific fields and methods.

Do not think of a subclass as a *subset* of another class—in other words, as possessing only parts of its base class. In fact, a derived class usually contains more than its parent.

A derived class can be further extended. In other words, a subclass can have a child of its own. For example, after you create a Tree class and derive Evergreen, you might derive a Spruce class from Evergreen. Similarly, a Poodle class might derive from Dog, Dog from DomesticPet, and DomesticPet from Animal. The entire list of parent classes from which a child class is derived constitutes the **ancestors** of the subclass.

After you create the Spruce class, you might be ready to create Spruce objects. For example, you might create theTreeInMyBackYard, or you might create an array of 1000 Spruce objects for a tree farm. On the other hand, before you are ready to create objects, you might first want to create even more specific child classes such as ColoradoSpruce and NorwaySpruce.

A child inherits all the data fields and methods of all its ancestors. In other words, when you declare a Spruce object, it contains all the attributes and methods of both an Evergreen and a Tree, and a CommissionEmployee contains all the attributes and methods of an Employee. In other words, the components of Employee and CommissionEmployee are as follows:

- Employee contains two fields and four methods, as shown in Figure 11-12.
- CommissionEmployee contains three fields and six methods, even though you do not see all of them in Figure 11-14.

Although a child class contains all the data fields and methods of its parent, a parent class does not gain any child class data or methods. Therefore, when Employee and CommissionEmployee classes are defined as in Figures 11-12 and 11-14, the statements in

Figure 11-15 are all valid in an application. The `salesperson` object can use all the methods of its parent, and it can use its own `setCommissionRate()` and `getCommissionRate()` methods. Figure 11-16 shows the output of the program as it would appear in a command-line environment.

```
start
   Declarations
      Employee manager
      CommissionEmployee salesperson
   manager.setEmpNum("111")
   manager.setWeeklySalary(700.00)
   salesperson.setEmpNum("222")
   salesperson.setWeeklySalary(300.00)
   salesperson.setCommissionRate(0.12)
   output "Manager ", manager.getEmpNum(), manager.getWeeklySalary()
   output "Salesperson ", salesperson.getEmpNum(),
      salesperson.getWeeklySalary(), salesperson.getCommissionRate()
stop
```

Figure 11-15 `EmployeeDemo` application that declares two `Employee` objects

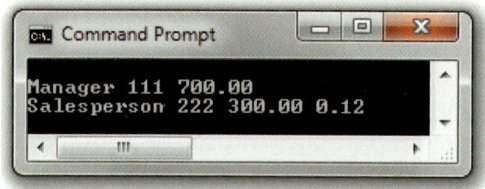

Figure 11-16 Output of the program in Figure 11-15

The following statements would not be allowed in the `EmployeeDemo` application in Figure 11-15 because `manager`, as an `Employee` object, does not have access to the methods of the `CommissionEmployee` child class:

```
manager.setCommissionRate(0.08)
output manager.getCommissionRate()
```

Don't Do It
These base class objects cannot use methods that belong to their class's child.

When you create your own inheritance chains, you want to place fields and methods at their most general level. In other words, a method named `grow()` rightfully belongs in a `Tree` class, whereas `leavesTurnColor()` does not because the method applies to only some of the `Tree` child classes. Similarly, a `leavesTurnColor()` method would be better located in a `DeciduousTree` class than separately within the `Oak` or `Maple` child classes.

Understanding Inheritance

It makes sense that a parent class object does not have access to its child's data and methods. When you create the parent class, you do not know how many future child classes might be created, or what their data or methods might look like. In addition, derived classes are more specific, so parent class objects cannot use them. For example, a `Cardiologist` class and an `Obstetrician` class are children of a `Doctor` class. You do not expect all members of the general parent class `Doctor` to have the `Cardiologist`'s `repairHeartValve()` method or the `Obstetrician`'s `performCaesarianSection()` method. However, `Cardiologist` and `Obstetrician` objects have access to the more general `Doctor` methods `takeBloodPressure()` and `billPatients()`. As with subclasses of doctors, it is convenient to think of derived classes as *specialists*. That is, their fields and methods are more specialized than those of the parent class.

In some programming languages, such as C#, Visual Basic, and Java, every class you create is a child of one ultimate base class, often called the `Object` class. The `Object` class usually provides basic functionality that is inherited by all the classes you create—for example, the ability to show its memory location and name.

Accessing Private Fields and Methods of a Parent Class

In Chapter 10 you learned that when you create classes, the most common scenario is for methods to be public but for data to be private. Making data private is an important concept in object-oriented programming. By making data fields private and allowing access to them only through a class's methods, you protect the ways in which data items can be altered and used.

When a data field within a class is private, no outside class can use it—including a child class. The principle of data hiding would be lost if you could access a class's private data merely by creating a child class. However, it can be inconvenient when the methods of a child class cannot directly access its own inherited data.

Watch the video *Inheritance*.

For example, suppose that some employees do not earn a weekly salary as defined in the `Employee` class, but are paid by the hour. You might create an `HourlyEmployee` class that descends from `Employee`, as shown in Figure 11-17. The class contains two new fields, `hoursWorked` and `hourlyRate`, and a get and set method for each.

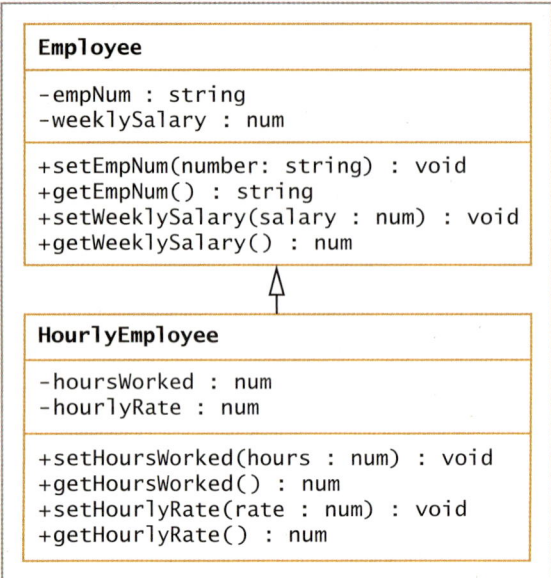

Figure 11-17 Class diagram for `HourlyEmployee` class

You can implement the new class as shown in Figure 11-18. Whenever you set either `hoursWorked` or `hourlyRate`, you want to modify `weeklySalary` based on the product of the hours and rate. The logic makes sense, but the code does not compile. The two shaded statements show that the `HourlyEmployee` class is attempting to modify the `weeklySalary` field. Although every `HourlyEmployee` *has* a `weeklySalary` field by virtue of being a child of `Employee`, the `HourlyEmployee` class methods do not have access to the `weeklySalary` field, because `weeklySalary` is private within the `Employee` class. In this case, the private `weeklySalary` field is **inaccessible** to any class other than the one in which it is defined.

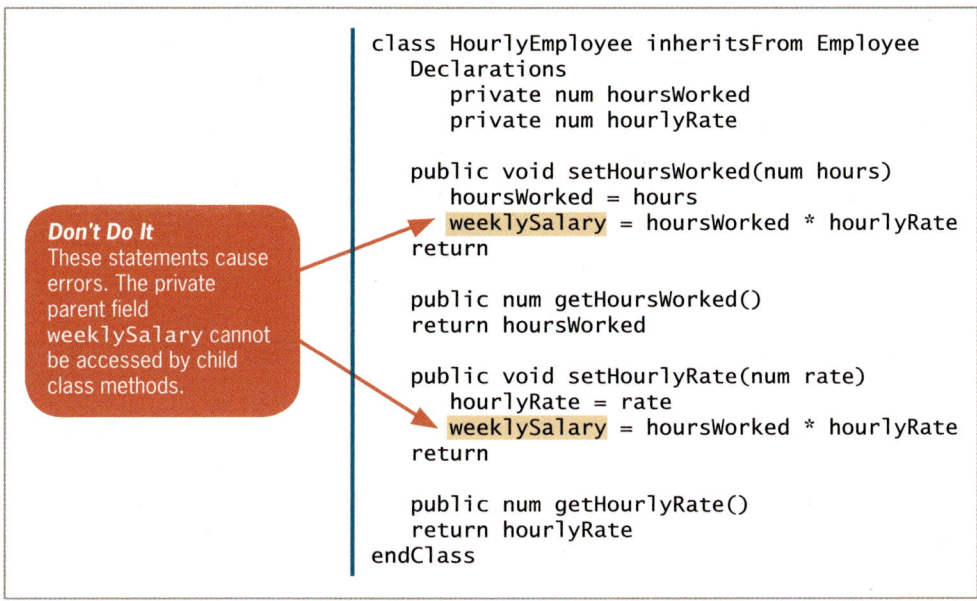

Figure 11-18 Implementation of `HourlyEmployee` class that attempts to access `weeklySalary`

One solution to this problem would be to make `weeklySalary` public in the parent `Employee` class. Then the child class could use it. However, that action would violate the important object-oriented principle of data hiding. Good object-oriented style dictates that your data should be altered only by the methods you choose and only in ways that you can control. If outside classes could alter an `Employee`'s private fields, then the fields could be assigned values that the `Employee` class could not control. In such a case, the principle of data hiding would be destroyed, causing the behavior of the object to be unpredictable.

Therefore, OOP languages allow a medium-security access specifier that is more restrictive than public but less restrictive than private. The **protected access specifier** is used when you want no outside classes to be able to use a data field, except classes that are children of the original class. Figure 11-19 shows a rewritten `Employee` class that uses the `protected` access specifier on one of its data fields (see shading). When this modified class is used as a base class for another class, such as `HourlyEmployee`, the child class's methods will be able to access any protected items (fields or methods) originally defined in the parent class. When the `Employee` class is defined with a protected `weeklySalary` field, as shown in Figure 11-19, the code in the `HourlyEmployee` class in Figure 11-18 works correctly.

```
class Employee
    Declarations
        private string empNum
        protected num weeklySalary

    public void setEmpNum(string number)
        empNum = number
    return

    public string getEmpNum()
    return empNum

    public void setWeeklySalary(num salary)
        weeklySalary = salary
    return

    public num getWeeklySalary()
    return weeklySalary
endClass
```

Figure 11-19 Employee class with a protected field

Figure 11-20 contains the class diagram for the version of the Employee class shown in Figure 11-19. Notice that the weeklySalary field is preceded with an octothorpe (#)—the character that conventionally is used in class diagrams to indicate protected class members.

```
Employee
───────────────────────────
-empNum : string
#weeklySalary : num
───────────────────────────
+setEmpNum(number: string) : void
+getEmpNum() : string
+setWeeklySalary(salary : num) : void
+getWeeklySalary() : num
```

Figure 11-20 Employee class with protected member

If weeklySalary is defined as protected instead of private in the Employee class, then either the creator of the class knew that a child class would want to access the field or the class was revised after it became known the child class would need access to the field.

If the Employee class's creator did not foresee that a field would need to be accessible, or if it is not preferable to revise the class, then weeklySalary will remain private. It is still possible to correctly set an HourlyEmployee's weekly pay—the HourlyEmployee is just required to use the same means as any other class would. That is, the HourlyEmployee class can use the public method `setWeeklySalary()` that already exists in the parent class. Any class, including a child, can use a public field or method of the base class. So, assuming that `weeklySalary` remains private in `Employee`, Figure 11-21 shows how `HourlyEmployee` could be written to correctly set `weeklySalary`.

```
class HourlyEmployee inheritsFrom Employee
    Declarations
        private num hoursWorked
        private num hourlyRate

    public void setHoursWorked(num hours)
        hoursWorked = hours
        setWeeklySalary(hoursWorked * hourlyRate)
    return

    public num getHoursWorked()
    return hoursWorked

    public void setHourlyRate(num rate)
        hourlyRate = rate
        setWeeklySalary(hoursWorked * hourlyRate)
    return

    public num getHourlyRate()
    return hourlyRate
endClass
```

Figure 11-21 The `HourlyEmployee` class when `weeklySalary` remains private

In the version of `HourlyEmployee` in Figure 11-21, the shaded statements within `setHoursWorked()` and `setHourlyRate()` assign a value to the corresponding child class field (`hoursWorked` or `hourlyRate`, respectively). Each method then calls the public parent class method `setWeeklySalary()`. In this example, no `protected` access specifiers are needed for any fields in the parent class, and the creators of the parent class did not have to foresee that a child class would eventually need to access any of its fields. Instead, any child classes of `Employee` simply follow the same access rules as any other outside class would. As an added benefit, if the parent class method `setWeeklySalary()` contained additional code (for example, to require a minimum base weekly pay for all employees), then that code would be enforced even for `HourlyEmployees`.

So, in summary, when a child class must access a private field of its parent's class, you can take one of several approaches:

- You can modify the parent class to make the field public. Usually, this is not advised because it violates the principle of data hiding.

- You can modify the parent class to make the field protected so that child classes have access to it, but other outside classes do not. This approach is necessary if you do not want public methods to be able to access the parent class field. Be aware that some programmers oppose making any data fields nonprivate. They feel that public methods should always control data access, even by a class's children.

- The child class can use a public method within the parent class that modifies the field, just as any other outside class would. This is frequently, but not always, the best option.

Using the `protected` access specifier for a field can be convenient, and it improves program performance a little by using a field directly instead of "going through" another method. Also, using the `protected` access specifier is occasionally necessary when no existing public method accesses a field in a way required by the child class. However, protected data members should be used sparingly. Whenever possible, the principle of data hiding should be observed, and even child classes should have to go through methods to "get to" their parent's private data.

The likelihood of future errors increases when child classes are allowed direct access to a parent's fields. For example, if the company decides to add a bonus to every `Employee`'s weekly salary, you might make a change in the `setWeeklySalary()` method. If a child class is allowed direct access to the `Employee` field `weeklySalary` without using the `setWeeklySalary()` method, then any child class objects will not receive the bonus. Classes that depend on field names from parent classes are said to be **fragile** because they are prone to errors—that is, they are easy to "break."

Some OOP languages, such as C++, allow a subclass to inherit from more than one parent class. For example, you might create an `InsuredItem` class that contains data fields such as value and purchase date for each insured possession, and an `Automobile` class with appropriate data fields (for example, vehicle identification number, make, model, and year). When you create an `InsuredAutomobile` class for a car rental agency, you might want to include information and methods for `Automobile`s and `InsuredItem`s, so you might want to inherit from both. The capability to inherit from more than one class is called **multiple inheritance**.

Sometimes, a parent class is so general that you never intend to create any specific instances of the class. For example, you might never create an object that is "just" an `Employee`; each `Employee` is more specifically a `SalariedEmployee`, `HourlyEmployee`, or `ContractEmployee`. A class such as `Employee` that you create only to extend from, but not to instantiate objects from, is an abstract class. An **abstract class** is one from which you cannot create any concrete objects, but from which you can inherit.

Using Inheritance to Achieve Good Software Design

When an automobile company designs a new car model, it does not build every component of the new car from scratch. The company might design a new feature; for example, at some point a carmaker designed the first air bag. However, many of a new car's features are simply modifications of existing features. The manufacturer might create a larger gas tank or more comfortable seats, but even these new features still possess many properties of their predecessors in the older models. Most features of new car models are not even modified; instead, existing components such as air filters and windshield wipers are included on the new model without any changes.

Understanding Inheritance

Similarly, you can create powerful computer programs more easily if many of their components are used either "as is" or with slight modifications. Inheritance makes your job easier because you don't have to create every part of a new class from scratch. Professional programmers constantly create new class libraries for use with OOP languages. Having these classes available to use and extend makes programming large systems more manageable. When you create a useful, extendable superclass, you and other future programmers gain several advantages:

- Subclass creators save development time because much of the code needed for the class has already been written.
- Subclass creators save testing time because the superclass code has already been tested and probably used in a variety of situations. In other words, the superclass code is **reliable**.
- Programmers who create or use new subclasses already understand how the superclass works, so the time it takes to learn the new class features is reduced.
- When you create a new subclass, neither the superclass source code nor the translated superclass code is changed. The superclass maintains its integrity.

When you consider classes, you must think about their commonalities, and then you can create superclasses from which to inherit. You might be rewarded professionally when you see your own superclasses extended by others in the future.

TWO TRUTHS & A LIE

Understanding Inheritance

1. When you create a class by making it inherit from another class, you save time because you need not re-create the base class fields and methods.
2. A class that is used as a basis for inheritance is called a base class, derived class, or extended class.
3. When a data field within a class is private, no outside class can use it—including a child class.

The false statement is #2. A class that is used as a basis for inheritance is called a base class, superclass, or parent class. A derived class is a subclass, extended class, or child class.

An Example of Using Predefined Classes: Creating GUI Objects

When you purchase or download a compiler for an object-oriented programming language, it comes packaged with many predefined, built-in classes. The classes are stored in **libraries** or **packages**—collections of classes that serve related purposes. Some of the most helpful are the classes you can use to create graphical user interface (GUI) objects such as frames, buttons, labels, and text boxes. You place these GUI components within interactive programs so that users can manipulate them using input devices—most frequently a keyboard and a mouse. For example, if you want to place a clickable button on the screen using a language that supports GUI applications, you instantiate an object that belongs to an existing class with a name similar to `Button`. You then create objects with names such as `yesButton` or `buyProductNowButton`. The `Button` class contains private data fields such as `text` and `height` and public methods such as `setText()` and `setHeight()` that allow you to alter the objects' fields. For example, you might write a statement such as the following to change the text on a `Button` object:

`buyProductNowButton.setText("Click here to buy now")`

If no predefined GUI object classes existed, you could create your own. However, this would present several disadvantages:

- It would be a lot of work. Creating graphical objects requires a substantial amount of code and at least a modicum of artistic talent.

- It would be repetitious work. Almost all GUI programs require standard components such as buttons and labels. If each programmer created the classes for these components from scratch, much of this work would be repeated unnecessarily.

- The components would look different in various applications. If each programmer created his or her own component classes, objects like buttons would look different and operate in slightly different ways. Users prefer standardization in their components—title bars on windows that are a uniform height, buttons that appear to be pressed when clicked, frames and windows that contain maximize and minimize buttons in predictable locations, and so on. By using standard component classes, programmers are assured that the GUI components in their programs have the same look and feel as those in other programs.

Programming languages that supply existing GUI classes often provide a **visual development environment** in which you can create programs by dragging components such as buttons and labels onto a screen and arranging them visually. (In several languages, the visual development environment is known by the acronym **IDE**, which stands for *integrated development environment*.) Then you write programming statements to control the actions that take place when a user manipulates the controls—by clicking them using a mouse, for example. Many programmers never create classes of their own from which they will instantiate objects, but only write application classes that use built-in GUI component classes. Some languages—for example, Visual Basic and C#—lend themselves very well to this type of programming. In Chapter 12, you will learn more about creating programs that use GUI objects.

Understanding Exception Handling

> **TWO TRUTHS & A LIE**
>
> **An Example of Using Predefined Classes: Creating GUI Objects**
>
> 1. Collections of classes that serve related purposes are called annals.
> 2. GUI components are placed within interactive programs so that users can manipulate them using input devices.
> 3. By using standard component classes, programmers are assured that the GUI components in their programs have the same look and feel as those in other programs.
>
> The false statement is #1. Collections of classes that serve related purposes are stored in libraries or packages.

Understanding Exception Handling

A great deal of the effort that goes into writing programs involves checking data items to make sure they are valid and reasonable. Professional data-entry operators who create the files used in business applications spend their entire working day entering facts and figures, so operators can and do make typing errors. When programs depend on data entered by average users who are not trained typists, the likelihood of errors is even greater.

 Programmers use the acronym *GIGO* to describe what happens when worthless or invalid input causes inaccurate or unrealistic results. GIGO is an acronym for "garbage in, garbage out."

In procedural programs, programmers handled errors in various ways that were effective, but the techniques had some drawbacks. The introduction of object-oriented programming has led to a new model called exception handling.

Drawbacks to Traditional Error-Handling Techniques

In traditional programming, probably the most common error-handling outcome was to terminate the program, or at least to terminate the method in which the offending statement occurred. For example, suppose that a program prompts a user to enter an insurance premium type from the keyboard, and that the entered value should be *A* or *H* for *Auto* or *Health*. Figure 11-22 shows a segment of pseudocode that causes the `determinePremium()` method to end if `policyType` is invalid; in the shaded `if` statement, the method ends abruptly when `policyType` is not *A* or *H*. This method of handling an error is not only unforgiving, it isn't even structured. Recall that a structured method should have one entry point and one exit point. The method in Figure 11-22 contains two exit points at the two `return` statements.

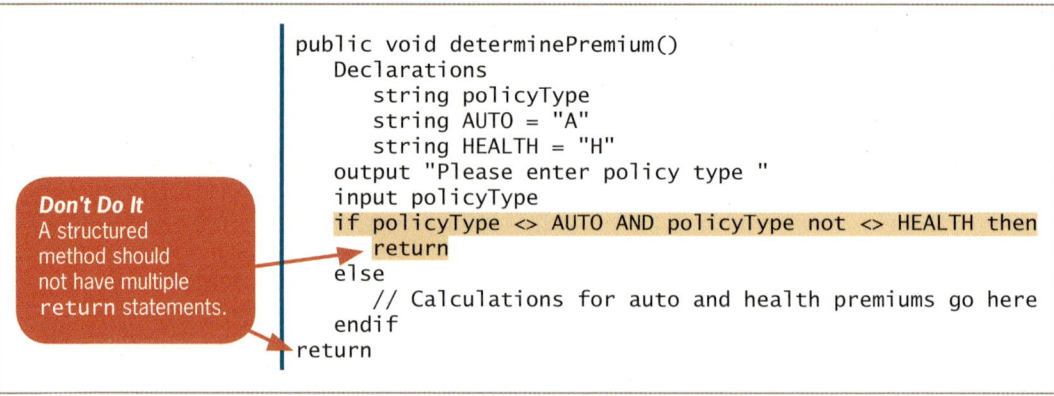

Figure 11-22 A method that handles an error in an unstructured manner

In the example in Figure 11-22, if `policyType` is an invalid value, the method in which the code appears is terminated. The client program might continue with an invalid value or it might stop working. If the program that contains this method is part of a business program or a game, the user may be annoyed. However, an early termination in a program that monitors a hospital patient's vital signs or navigates an airplane might have far more serious consequences.

Rather than ending a method prematurely just because it encounters a piece of invalid data, a more elegant solution involves looping until the data item becomes valid, as shown in the highlighted portion of Figure 11-23. As long as the value of `policyType` is invalid, the user is prompted continuously to enter a new value. Only when `policyType` is *A* or *H* does the method continue.

```
public void determinePremium()
   Declarations
      string policyType
      string AUTO = "A"
      string HEALTH = "H"
   output "Please enter policy type "
   input policyType
   while policyType <> AUTO AND policyType <> HEALTH
      output "You must enter ", AUTO, " or ", HEALTH
      input policyType
   endwhile
   // Calculations for auto and health premiums go here
return
```

Figure 11-23 Method that handles an error using a loop

Understanding Exception Handling

The error-handling logic shown in Figure 11-23 has at least two shortcomings:

- The method is not as reusable as it could be.
- The method is not as flexible as it might be.

One of the principles of modular and object-oriented programming is reusability. The method in Figure 11-23 is only reusable under limited conditions. The `determinePremium()` method allows the user to reenter policy data any number of times, but other programs in the insurance system may need to limit the number of chances the user gets to enter correct data, or may allow no second chance at all. A more flexible `determinePremium()` method would simply calculate the premium amount without deciding what to do about data errors. The `determinePremium()` method will be most flexible if it can detect an error and then notify the calling program or method that an error has occurred. Each client that uses the `determinePremium()` method then can handle the mistake appropriately for the current application.

The other drawback to forcing the user to reenter data is that the technique works only with interactive programs. A more flexible program accepts any kind of input, including data stored on a disk. Program errors can occur as a result of many factors—for example, a disk drive might not be ready, a file might not exist on the disk, or stored data items might be invalid. You cannot continue to reprompt a disk file for valid data the way you can reprompt a user in an interactive program; if stored data is invalid, it remains invalid.

In the next section, you will learn object-oriented exception-handling techniques that overcome the limitations of traditional error handling.

The Object-Oriented Exception-Handling Model

Object-oriented programs employ a group of techniques for handling errors called **exception handling**. The generic name used for errors in object-oriented languages is **exceptions** because errors are not usual occurrences; they are the "exceptions" to the rule.

In object-oriented terminology, you **try** some code that might **throw an exception**. If an exception is thrown, it is passed to a block of code that can **catch the exception**, which means to receive it in a way similar to how a parameter is received by a method. In some languages, the exception object that is thrown can be any data type—a number, a string, or a programmer-created object. Even when a language permits any data type to be thrown, most programmers throw an object of the built-in class `Exception`, or they derive a class from a built-in `Exception` class. For example, Figure 11-24 shows a `determinePremium()` method that throws an exception only if `policyType` is neither *H* nor *A*. If `policyType` is invalid, an object of type `Exception` named `mistake` is instantiated and thrown from the method by a `throw` statement. A **throw statement** is one that sends an `Exception` object out of the current code block or method so it can be handled elsewhere. If `policyType` is *H* or *A*, the method continues, the premium is calculated, and the method ends naturally.

```
public void determinePremium()
   Declarations
      string policyType
      string AUTO = "A"
      string HEALTH = "H"
   output "Please enter policy type "
   input policyType
   if policyType <> AUTO AND policyType <> HEALTH then
      Declarations
         Exception mistake
      throw mistake
   else
      // Calculations for auto and health premiums go here
   endif
return
```

Figure 11-24 A method that creates and throws an `Exception` object

When you create a segment of code in which something might go wrong, you place the code in a **try block**, which is a block of code you attempt to execute while acknowledging that an exception might occur. A `try` block consists of the keyword `try` followed by any number of statements, including some that might cause an exception to be thrown. If a statement in the block causes an exception, the remaining statements in the `try` block do not execute and the `try` block is abandoned. For pseudocode purposes, you can end a `try` block with a sentinel such as endtry.

You almost always code at least one `catch` block immediately following a `try` block. A **catch block** is a segment of code written to handle an exception that might be thrown by the `try` block that precedes it. Each `catch` block "catches" one type of exception—in many languages the caught object must be of type `Exception` or one of its child classes. You create a `catch` block using the following pseudocode elements:

- The keyword `catch`, followed by parentheses that contain an `Exception` type and an identifier
- Statements that take the action to handle the error condition
- An `endcatch` statement to indicate the end of the `catch` block in the pseudocode

Figure 11-25 shows a client program that calls the `determinePremium()` method. Because `determinePremium()` has the potential to throw an exception, the call to the method is contained in a `try` block. If `determinePremium()` throws an exception, the `catch` block in the program executes; if all goes well and `determinePremium()` does not throw an exception, the `catch` block is bypassed. A `catch` block looks like a method named `catch()` that takes an argument that is some type of `Exception`. However, it is not a method; it has no `return` type, and you can't call it directly.

Understanding Exception Handling

```
start
   try
      perform determinePremium()
   endtry
   catch(Exception mistake)
      output "A mistake occurred"
   endcatch
      // Other statements that would execute whether
      // or not the exception was thrown could go here
stop
```

Figure 11-25 A program that contains a try...catch pair

In the program in Figure 11-25, a message is displayed when the exception is thrown. Another application might take different actions. For example, you might write an application in which the `catch` block forces the `policyType` to *H* or to *A*, or reprompts the user for a valid value. Various programs can use the `determinePremium()` method and handle an error in the way that is considered most appropriate.

In the method in Figure 11-25, the variable `mistake` in the `catch` block is an object of type `Exception`. The object is not used within the `catch` block, but it could be. For example, depending on the language, the `Exception` class might contain a method named `getMessage()` that returns a string explaining the cause of the error. In that case, you could place a statement such as `output mistake.getMessage()` in the `catch` block.

Even when a program uses a method that throws an exception, the exceptions are created and thrown only occasionally, when something goes wrong. Programmers sometimes refer to a situation in which nothing goes wrong as the **sunny day case**.

The general principle of exception handling in object-oriented programming is that a method that uses data should be able to detect errors, but not be required to handle them. The handling should be left to the application that uses the object, so that each application can use each method appropriately.

Watch the video *Exception Handling*.

Using Built-in Exceptions and Creating Your Own Exceptions

Many OOP languages provide built-in `Exception` types. For example, Java, Visual Basic, and C# each provide dozens of categories of `Exceptions` that you can use in your programs. Every object-oriented language has an automatically created exception with a name like `ArrayOutOfBoundsException` that is thrown when you attempt to use an invalid subscript with an array. Similarly, an exception with a name like `DivideByZeroException` might be generated automatically if a program attempts to divide a number by zero.

Although some actions, such as dividing by zero, are errors in every programming situation, the built-in `Exceptions` in a programming language cannot cover *every* condition that might be an `Exception` in your applications. For example, you might want to declare an `Exception` when your bank balance is negative or when an outside party attempts to access your e-mail account. Most organizations have specific rules for exceptional data; for example, an employee number must not exceed three digits, or an hourly salary must not be less than the legal minimum wage. You can handle these potential error situations with `if` statements, but you also can create your own `Exceptions`.

To create your own throwable `Exception`, you usually extend a built-in `Exception` class. For example, you might create a class named `NegativeBankBalanceException` or `EmployeeNumberTooLargeException`. (When you create a class that derives from `Exception`, it is conventional, but not required, to use `Exception` in the name.) By inheriting from the `Exception` class, you gain access to methods contained in the parent class, such as those that display a default message describing the `Exception`.

Depending on the language you are using, you might be able to extend from other throwable classes as well as `Exception`.

In most object-oriented programming languages, a method can throw any number of exceptions. A `catch` block must be available for each type of exception that might be thrown.

TWO TRUTHS & A LIE

Understanding Exception Handling

1. In object-oriented terminology, you try some code that might throw an exception. The exception can then be caught and handled.

2. A `catch` block is a segment of code that can handle an exception that might be thrown by the `try` block preceding it.

3. The general principle of exception handling in object-oriented programming is that a method that uses data should be able to detect and handle most common errors.

The false statement is #3. The general principle of exception handling in object-oriented programming is that a method that uses data should be able to detect errors, but not be required to handle them.

Reviewing the Advantages of Object-Oriented Programming

In Chapter 10 and this chapter, you have been exposed to many concepts and features of object-oriented programming, which provide extensive benefits as you develop programs. Whether you instantiate objects from classes you have created or from those created by others, you save development time because each object automatically includes appropriate, reliable methods and attributes. When using inheritance, you can develop new classes more quickly by extending classes that already exist and work; you need to concentrate only on new features added by the new class. When using existing objects, you need to concentrate only on the interface to those objects, not on the internal instructions that make them work. By using polymorphism, you can use reasonable, easy-to-remember names for methods and concentrate on their purpose rather than on memorizing different method names.

TWO TRUTHS & A LIE

Reviewing the Advantages of Object-Oriented Programming

1. When you instantiate objects in programs, you save development time because each object automatically includes appropriate, reliable methods and attributes.

2. When using inheritance, you can develop new classes more quickly by extending existing classes that already work.

3. By using polymorphism, you can avoid the strict rules of procedural programming and take advantage of more flexible object-oriented methods.

The false statement is #3. By using polymorphism, you can use reasonable, easy-to-remember names for methods and concentrate on their purpose rather than on memorizing different method names.

Chapter Summary

- A constructor is a method that establishes an object. A default constructor is one that requires no arguments; in OOP languages, a default constructor is created automatically by the compiler for every class you write. If you want to perform specific tasks when you create an instance of a class, then you can write your own constructor. Any constructor you write must have the same name as the class it constructs, and cannot have a return type. Once you write a constructor for a class, you no longer receive the automatically written default constructor.

- A destructor contains the actions you require when an instance of a class is destroyed, most often when the instance goes out of scope. As with constructors, if you do not explicitly create a destructor for a class, one is automatically provided. The most common way to declare a destructor explicitly is to use an identifier that consists of a tilde (~) followed by the class name. You cannot provide parameters to a destructor; as a consequence, destructors cannot be overloaded. Like a constructor, a destructor has no return type.

- A class can contain objects of another class as data fields. Creating whole-part relationships is known as composition or aggregation.

- When you create a class by making it inherit from another class, you are provided with prewritten and tested data fields and methods automatically. Using inheritance helps you save time, reduces the chance of errors and inconsistencies, and makes it easier for readers to understand your classes. A class that is used as a basis for inheritance is called a base class. A class that inherits from a base class is a derived class or extended class. The terms *superclass* and *parent class* are synonyms for *base class*. The terms *subclass* and *child class* are synonyms for *derived class*.

- Some of the most useful classes packaged in language libraries are used to create graphical user interface (GUI) objects such as frames, buttons, labels, and text boxes. Programming languages that supply existing GUI classes often provide a visual development environment in which you can create programs by dragging components such as buttons and labels onto a screen and arranging them visually.

- Exception-handling techniques are used to handle errors in object-oriented programs. When you try a block of code, you attempt to use it, and if an exception occurs, it is thrown. A `catch` block of the correct type can receive the thrown exception and handle it. Many OOP languages provide built-in `Exception` types, and you can create your own types by extending the `Exception` class.

- When you use object-oriented programming techniques, you save development time because each object automatically includes appropriate, reliable methods and attributes. Efficiency is achieved through both inheritance and polymorphism.

Key Terms

A **constructor** is an automatically called method that establishes an object.

A **default constructor** is one that requires no arguments.

A **nondefault constructor** requires at least one argument.

A **destructor** is an automatically called method that contains the actions you require when an instance of a class is destroyed.

In a **whole-part relationship**, an object of one class is contained within an object of another class.

Composition is the technique of placing an object within an object of another class.

Key Terms

A **has-a relationship** describes a whole-part relationship.

A **base class** is one that is used as a basis for inheritance.

A **derived class** or **extended class** is one that is extended from a base class.

Superclass and **parent class** are synonyms for *base class*.

Subclass and **child class** are synonyms for *derived class*.

The **ancestors** of a derived class are the entire list of parent classes from which the class is derived.

Inaccessible describes any field or method that cannot be reached because of a logical error.

The `protected access specifier` is used when you want no outside classes to be able to use a data field, except classes that are children of the original class.

Fragile describes classes that depend on field names from parent classes. They are prone to errors—that is, they are easy to "break."

Multiple inheritance is the capability to inherit from more than one class.

An **abstract class** is one from which you cannot create concrete objects, but from which you can inherit.

Reliable describes code that has already been tested and used in a variety of situations.

Libraries are stored collections of classes that serve related purposes.

Packages are another name for libraries in some languages.

A **visual development environment** is one in which you can create programs by dragging components such as buttons and labels onto a screen and arranging them visually.

IDE is the acronym for *integrated development environment*, which is the visual development environment in some programming languages.

Exception handling is a set of techniques for handling errors in object-oriented programs.

Exception is the generic term used for an error in object-oriented languages. Presumably, errors are not usual occurrences; they are the "exceptions" to the rule.

In object-oriented terminology, you **try** a method that might throw an exception.

To **throw an exception** is to pass it out of a block where it occurs, usually to a block that can handle it.

To **catch an exception** is to receive it from a throw so it can be handled.

A **throw statement** is one that sends an `Exception` object out of a method so it can be handled elsewhere.

A **try block** is a block of code you attempt to execute while acknowledging that an exception might occur. A `try` block consists of the keyword `try` followed by any number of statements, including some that might cause an exception to be thrown.

A **catch block** is a segment of code written to handle an exception that might be thrown by the try block that precedes it.

A **sunny day case** is a case in which nothing goes wrong.

Review Questions

1. When you instantiate an object, the automatically created method that is called is a _____.

   a. creator
   b. initiator
   c. constructor
   d. architect

2. Every class has _____.

   a. exactly one constructor
   b. at least one constructor
   c. at least two constructors
   d. a default constructor and a programmer-written constructor

3. Which of the following can be overloaded?

   a. constructors
   b. instance methods
   c. both of the above
   d. none of the above

4. A default constructor is _____.

   a. another name that is used only for a class's automatically created constructor
   b. a constructor that requires no arguments
   c. a constructor that sets a value for every field in a class
   d. the only constructor that is explicitly written in a class

5. When you write a constructor that receives a parameter, _____.

   a. the parameter must be numeric
   b. the parameter must be used to set a data field
   c. the automatically created default constructor no longer exists
   d. the constructor body must be empty

6. When you write a constructor that receives no parameters, _____.

   a. the automatically created constructor no longer exists
   b. it becomes known as the default constructor
   c. both of the above
   d. none of the above

Review Questions

7. Most often, a destructor is called when _____.
   a. an object is created
   b. an object goes out of scope
   c. you make an explicit call to it
   d. a value is returned from a class method

8. Which of the following is not a similarity between constructors and destructors?
   a. Both can be called automatically.
   b. Both have the same name as the class.
   c. Both have no return type.
   d. Both can be overloaded.

9. Advantages of creating a class that inherits from another include all of the following *except*:
   a. You save time because subclasses are created automatically from those that come built in as part of a programming language.
   b. You save time because you need not re-create the fields and methods in the original class.
   c. You reduce the chance of errors because the original class's methods have already been used and tested.
   d. You make it easier for anyone who has used the original class to understand the new class.

10. Employing inheritance reduces errors because _____.
    a. the new classes have access to fewer data fields
    b. the new classes have access to fewer methods
    c. you can copy and paste methods that you already created
    d. many of the methods you need have already been used and tested

11. A class that is used as a basis for inheritance is called a _____.
    a. derived class
    b. subclass
    c. child class
    d. base class

12. Which of the following is another name for a derived class?
    a. base class
    b. child class
    c. superclass
    d. parent class

CHAPTER 11 — More Object-Oriented Programming Concepts

13. Which of the following is *not* another name for a derived class?
    a. extended class
    b. superclass
    c. child class
    d. subclass

14. Which of the following is true?
    a. A base class usually has more fields than its descendent.
    b. A child class can also be a parent class.
    c. A class's ancestors consist of its entire list of children.
    d. To be considered object oriented, a class must have a child.

15. Which of the following is true?
    a. A derived class inherits all the data and methods of its ancestors.
    b. A derived class inherits only the public data and methods of its ancestors.
    c. A derived class inherits only the private data and methods of its ancestors.
    d. A derived class inherits none of the data and methods of its ancestors.

16. Which of the following is true?
    a. A class's data fields usually are public.
    b. A class's methods usually are public.
    c. both of the above
    d. none of the above

17. A _____ is a collection of predefined, built-in classes that you can use when writing programs.
    a. vault
    b. black box
    c. library
    d. store

18. An environment in which you can develop GUI programs by dragging components to their desired positions is a(n) _____.
    a. visual development environment
    b. integrated compiler
    c. text-based editor
    d. GUI formatter

19. In object-oriented programs, errors are known as _____.
    a. faults
    b. gaffes
    c. exceptions
    d. omissions

Exercises

20. The general principle of exception handling in object-oriented programming is that a method that uses data should ——————.
    a. be able to detect errors, but not be required to handle them
    b. be able to handle errors, but not detect them
    c. be able to handle and detect errors
    d. not be able to detect or handle errors

Exercises

1. Complete the following tasks:
   a. Design a class named Circle with fields named radius, area, and diameter. Include a constructor that sets the radius to 1. Include get methods for each field, but include a set method only for the radius. When the radius is set, do not allow it to be zero or a negative number. When the radius is set, calculate the diameter (twice the radius) and the area (the radius squared times pi, which is approximately 3.14). Create the class diagram and write the pseudocode that defines the class.

   b. Design an application that declares two Circles. Set the radius of one manually, but allow the other to use the default value supplied by the constructor. Then, display each Circle's values.

2. Complete the following tasks:
   a. Design a class named PhoneCall with four fields: two strings that hold the 10-digit phone numbers that originated and received the call, and two numeric fields that hold the length of the call in minutes and the cost of the call. Include a constructor that sets the phone numbers to Xs and the numeric fields to 0. Include get and set methods for the phone number and call length fields, but do not include a set method for the cost field. When the call length is set, calculate the cost of the call at three cents per minute for the first 10 minutes, and two cents per subsequent minute. Create the class diagram and write the pseudocode that defines the class.

   b. Design an application that declares three PhoneCalls. Set the length of one PhoneCall to 10 minutes, another to 11 minutes, and allow the third object to use the default value supplied by the constructor. Then, display each PhoneCall's values.

   c. Create a child class named InternationalPhoneCall. Override the parent class method that sets the call length to calculate the cost of the call at 40 cents per minute.

   d. Create the logic for an application that instantiates a PhoneCall object and an InternationalPhoneCall object and displays the costs for both.

3. Complete the following tasks:
   a. The Rockford *Daily Clarion* wants you to design a class named `Issue`. Fields include the issue number, total number of advertisements sold in the issue, and total advertising revenue. Include get and set methods for each field. Include a static method that displays the newspaper's motto ("Everything you need to know"). Include three overloaded constructors as follows:

      - A default constructor that sets the issue number to 1 and the other fields to 0
      - A constructor that allows you to pass values for all three fields
      - A constructor that allows you to pass an issue number and a number of advertisements sold, but sets the advertising revenue to $50 per ad

      Create the class diagram and write the pseudocode that defines the class.

   b. Design an application that declares three `Issue` objects using a different constructor version with each object. Display each `Issue`'s values and then display the motto.

4. Complete the following tasks:
   a. Create a class named `BankAccount` that includes two numeric variables: a bank balance and an interest rate. Also create two overloaded methods named `computeInterest()`. The first method takes two numeric arguments representing balance and rate, multiplies them, and then displays the results. The second method takes a single argument representing balance. When this method is called, the interest rate is assumed to be 1.5 percent and the results are displayed.

   b. Create an application that declares two `BankAccount` objects and demonstrates how both method versions can be called.

5. Complete the following tasks:
   a. Create a class named `Pay` that includes five numeric variables: hours worked, hourly pay rate, withholding rate, gross pay, and net pay. Also create three overloaded `computeNetPay()` methods. When `computeNetPay()` receives values for hours, pay rate, and withholding rate, it computes the gross pay and reduces it by the appropriate withholding amount to produce the net pay. (Gross pay is computed as hours worked multiplied by hourly pay rate.) When `computeNetPay()` receives two arguments, they represent the hours and pay rate, and the withholding rate is assumed to be 15 percent. When `computeNetPay()` receives one argument, it represents the number of hours worked; the withholding rate is assumed to be 15 percent and the hourly rate is assumed to be 6.50.

   b. Create an application that demonstrates all the methods.

Exercises

6. Complete the following tasks:
   a. Design a class named `Book` that holds a stock number, author, title, price, and number of pages. Include methods to set and get the values for each data field. Also include a `displayInfo()` method that displays each of the `Book`'s data fields with explanations.

   b. Design a class named `TextBook` that is a child class of `Book`. Include a new data field for the grade level of the book. Override the `Book` class `displayInfo()` method to accommodate the new grade-level field.

   c. Design an application that instantiates an object of each type and demonstrates all the methods.

7. Complete the following tasks:
   a. Design a class named `Player` that holds a player number and name for a sports team participant. Include methods to set the values for each data field and output the values for each data field.

   b. Design two classes named `BaseballPlayer` and `BasketballPlayer` that are child classes of `Player`. Include a new data field in each class for the player's position. Include an additional field in the `BaseballPlayer` class for batting average. Include a new field in the `BasketballPlayer` class for free-throw percentage. Override the `Player` class methods that set and output the data so that you accommodate the new fields.

   c. Design an application that instantiates an object of each type and demonstrates all the methods.

8. Complete the following tasks:
   a. Create a class for a cell phone service named `Message` that includes a field for the price of the message. Create get and set methods for the field.

   b. Derive three subclasses—`VoiceMessage`, `TextMessage`, and `PictureMessage`. The `VoiceMessage` class includes a numeric field to hold the length of the message in minutes and a get and set method for the field. When a `VoiceMessage`'s length value is set, the price is calculated at 4 cents per minute. The `TextMessage` class includes a numeric field to hold the length of the message in words and a get and set method for the field. When a `TextMessage`'s length value is set, the price is calculated at 2 cents per word. The `PictureMessage` class includes a numeric field that holds the size of the picture in kilobytes and get and set methods for the field. When a `PictureMessage`'s length value is set, the price is calculated at 1 cent per kilobyte.

   c. Design a program that instantiates one object of each of the three classes, and demonstrate using all the methods defined for each class.

9. Complete the following tasks:
   a. Create a class named `Order` that performs order processing of a single item. The class has four fields: customer name, customer number, quantity ordered, and unit price. Include set and get methods for each field. The set methods

prompt the user for values for each field. This class also needs a `computePrice()` method to compute the total price (quantity multiplied by unit price) and a method to display the field values.

b. Create a subclass named `ShippedOrder` that overrides `computePrice()` by adding a shipping and handling charge of $4.00.

c. Create the logic for an application that instantiates an object of each of these two classes. Prompt the user for data for the `Order` object and display the results; then prompt the user for data for the `ShippedOrder` object and display the results.

d. Create the logic for an application that continuously prompts for order information until the user enters ZZZ for the customer name or 10 orders have been taken, whichever comes first. Ask the user whether each order will be shipped, and create an `Order` or a `ShippedOrder` appropriately. Store each order in an array. When the user finishes entering data, display all the order information taken as well as the total price that was computed for each order.

10. Complete the following tasks:
a. Design a method that calculates the cost of a weekly cleaning job for Molly's Maid Service. Variables include a job location code of B for business, which costs $200, or R for residential, which costs $140. The method should throw an exception if the location code is invalid.

b. Write a method that calls the method designed in Exercise 10a. If the method throws an exception, force the price of the job to 0.

c. Write a method that calls the method designed in Exercise 10a. If the method throws an exception, require the user to reenter the location code.

d. Write a method that calls the method designed in Exercise 10a. If the method throws an exception, force the location code to R and the price to $140.

11. Design a method that calculates the monthly cost to rent a roadside billboard. Variables include the size of the billboard (S, M, or L for small, medium, or large) and its location (H, M, or L for high-, medium-, or low-traffic areas). The method should throw an exception if the size or location code is invalid. The monthly rental cost is shown in Table 11-1.

	High Traffic	Medium Traffic	Low Traffic
Small size	100.00	65.00	35.00
Medium size	150.00	95.00	48.00
Large size	210.00	130.00	60.00

Table 11-1 Monthly billboard rental rates

Exercises

Find the Bugs

12. Your downloadable files for Chapter 11 include DEBUG11-01.txt, DEBUG11-02.txt, and DEBUG11-03.txt. Each file starts with some comments that describe the problem. Comments are lines that begin with two slashes (//). Following the comments, each file contains pseudocode that has one or more bugs you must find and correct.

Game Zone

13. a. Computer games often contain different characters or creatures. For example, you might design a game in which alien beings possess specific characteristics such as color, number of eyes, or number of lives. Create an `Alien` class. Include at least three data fields of your choice. Include a constructor that requires a value for each data field and a method named `toString()` that returns a string containing a complete description of the `Alien`.

    b. Create two classes—`Martian` and `Jupiterian`—that descend from `Alien`. Supply each with a constructor that sets the `Alien` data fields with values you choose. For example, you can decide that a `Martian` has four eyes but a `Jupiterian` has only two.

    c. Create an application that instantiates one `Martian` and one `Jupiterian`. Call the `toString()` method with each object and display the results.

14. In Chapter 2, you learned that in many programming languages you can generate a random number between 1 and a limiting value named `LIMIT` by using a statement similar to `randomNumber = random(LIMIT)`. In Chapters 4 and 5, you created and fine-tuned the logic for a guessing game in which the application generates a random number and the player tries to guess it. As written, the game should work as long as the player enters numeric guesses. However, if the player enters a letter or other nonnumeric character, the game throws an automatically generated exception. Improve the game by handling any exception so that the user is informed of the error and allowed to enter data again.

15. a. In Chapter 10, you developed a `Card` class that contains a string data field to hold a suit and a numeric data field for a value from 1 to 13. Now extend the class to create a class called `BlackjackCard`. In the game of Blackjack, each card has a point value as well as a face value. These two values match for cards with values of 2 through 10, and the point value is 10 for jacks, queens, and kings (face values 11 through 13). For a simplified version of the game, assume that the value of the ace is 11. (In the official version of Blackjack, the player chooses whether each ace is worth 1 or 11 points.)

b. Randomly assign values to 10 `BlackjackCard` objects, then design an application that plays a modified version of Blackjack. The objective is to accumulate cards whose total value equals 21, or whose value is closer to 21 than the opponent's total value without exceeding 21. Deal five `BlackjackCards` each to the player and the computer. Make sure that each `BlackjackCard` is unique. For example, a deck cannot contain more than one queen of spades.

Determine the winner as follows:

- If the player's first two, first three, first four, or all five cards have a total value of exactly 21, the player wins, even if the computer also achieves a total of 21.

- If the player's first two cards do not total exactly 21, sum as many as needed to achieve the highest possible total that does not exceed 21. For example, suppose that the player's five cards are valued as follows: 10, 4, 5, 9, 2. In that case, the player's total for the first three cards is 19; counting any more cards would cause the total to exceed 21.

- After you have determined the player's total, sum the computer's cards in sequence. For example, suppose that the computer's cards are 10, 10, 5, 6, 7. The first two cards total 20; you would not use the third card because it would cause the total to exceed 21.

- The winner has the highest total among the cards used. For example, if the player's total using the first three cards is 19 and the computer's total using the first two cards is 20, the computer wins.

Display a message that indicates whether the game ended in a tie, the computer won, or the player won.

Up for Discussion

16. Many programmers think object-oriented programming is a superior approach to procedural programming. Others think it adds a level of complexity that is not needed in many scenarios. Find and summarize arguments on both sides. With which side do you agree?

17. Many object-oriented programmers are opposed to using multiple inheritance. Find out why and decide whether you agree with this stance.

18. If you are completing all the programming exercises in this book, you can see how much work goes into planning a full-blown professional program. How would you feel if someone copied your work without compensating you? Investigate the magnitude of software piracy in our society. What are the penalties for illegally copying software? Are there circumstances in which it is acceptable to copy a program? If a friend asked you to copy a program for him, would you? What should we do about this problem, if anything?

… CHAPTER 12

Event-Driven GUI Programming, Multithreading, and Animation

In this chapter, you will learn about:

- The principles of event-driven programming
- User-initiated actions and GUI components
- Designing graphical user interfaces
- Developing an event-driven application
- Threads and multithreading
- Creating animation

Understanding Event-Driven Programming

From the 1950s, when businesses began to use computers, through the 1980s, almost all interactive dialogues between people and computers took place at the command prompt. (Programmers also call the command prompt the *command line*, and users of the Disk Operating System often call the command line the **DOS prompt**.) In Chapter 1, you learned that the command line is used to type entries to communicate with the computer's **operating system**—the software that you use to run a computer and manage its resources. In the early days of computing, interacting with an operating system was difficult because users had to know the exact syntax to use when typing commands, and they had to spell and type those commands accurately. (Syntax is the correct sequence of words and symbols that form the operating system's command set.) Figure 12-1 shows a command in the Windows operating system.

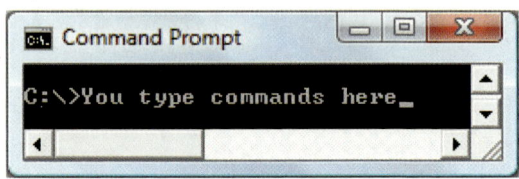

Figure 12-1 Command prompt screen

If you use the Windows operating system on a PC, you can locate the command prompt by clicking Start and pointing to the command prompt window shortcut on the Start menu. Alternatively, you can point to All Programs (or Programs in some earlier operating systems), then Accessories, and then click Command Prompt.

Fortunately for today's computer users, operating system software allows them to use a mouse or other pointing device to select pictures, or **icons**, on the screen. As you learned in Chapter 1, this type of environment is a graphical user interface, or GUI. Computer users can expect to see a standard interface in GUI programs. Rather than memorizing difficult commands that must be typed at a command line, GUI users can select options from menus and click buttons to make their preferences known to a program. Users can select objects that look like their real-world counterparts and get the expected results. For example, users may select an icon that looks like a pencil when they want to write a memo, or they may drag an icon shaped like a folder to a recycling bin icon to delete the files in the folder. Figure 12-2 shows a Windows program named Paint in which icons representing pencils, paint cans, and other objects appear on clickable buttons.

Figure 12-2 A GUI application that contains buttons and icons

Performing an operation on an icon (for example, clicking or dragging it) causes an **event**—an occurrence that generates a message sent to an object. GUI programs frequently are called **event-driven** or **event-based** because actions occur in response to user-initiated events such as clicking a mouse button. When you program with event-driven languages, the emphasis is on objects that users can manipulate, such as text boxes, buttons, and menus, and on events that users can initiate with those objects, such as typing, pointing, clicking, or double-clicking. The programmer writes instructions within modules that execute in response to each type of event.

Starting in Chapter 1, and throughout the rest of this book so far, the program logic you have developed has been procedural, and not event-driven; each step occurs in the order the programmer determines. In a procedural application, if you write statements that display a prompt and accept a user's response, the processing goes no further until the input is completed. When you write a procedural program and call `moduleA()` before calling `moduleB()`, you have complete control over the order in which all the statements will execute.

In contrast, with most event-driven programs, the user might initiate any number of events in any order. For example, when you use an event-driven word-processing program, you have dozens of choices at your disposal at any moment. You can type words, select text with the mouse, click a button to change text to bold or italics, choose a menu item such as *Save* or *Print*, and so on. With each word-processing document you create, the program must be ready to respond to any event you initiate. The programmers who created the word processor are not guaranteed that you will select *Bold* before you select *Italics*, or that you

CHAPTER 12 Event-Driven GUI Programming, Multithreading, and Animation

will select *Save* before you select *Quit*, so they must write programs that are more flexible than their procedural counterparts.

Within an event-driven program, a component from which an event is generated is the **source of the event**. A button that users can click to cause an action is an example of a source; a text box in which users enter typed characters is another source. An object that is "interested in" an event to which you want it to respond is a **listener**. It "listens for" events so it knows when to respond. Not all objects can receive all events—you probably have used programs in which clicking many areas of the screen has no effect. If you want an object such as a button to be a listener for an event such as a mouse click, you must write two types of appropriate program statements. You write the statements that define the object as a listener and the statements that constitute the event.

Although event-driven programming is newer than procedural programming, the instructions that programmers write to respond to events are still simply sequences, selections, and loops. Event-driven programs still have methods that declare variables, use arrays, and contain all the attributes of their procedural-program ancestors. The user's screen in an event-driven program might contain buttons or check boxes with labels like *Sort Records*, *Merge Files*, or *Total Transactions*, but each of these processes represents a method that uses the same logic you have learned throughout this book for programs that did not have a graphical interface. In object-oriented languages, the procedural modules that depend on user-initiated events are often called **scripts**. Writing event-driven programs involves thinking of possible events, writing scripts to execute actions, and writing the statements that link user-initiated events to the scripts.

TWO TRUTHS & A LIE

Understanding Event-Driven Programming

1. GUI programs are called event-driven or event-based because actions occur in response to user-initiated events such as clicking a mouse button.

2. With event-driven programs, the user might initiate any number of events in any order.

3. Within an event-driven program, a component from which an event is generated, such as a button, is a listener. An object that is "interested in" an event is the source of the event.

The false statement is # 3. Within an event-driven program, a component from which an event is generated is the source of the event, and an object that is "interested in" an event to which you want it to respond is a listener.

User-Initiated Actions and GUI Components

To understand GUI programming, you need to have a clear picture of the possible events a user can initiate. A partial list is shown in Table 12-1. Most languages allow you to distinguish between many additional events. For example, you might be able to initiate different events when a mouse key is pressed, during the time it is held down, and when it is released.

Event	Description of User's Action
Key press	Pressing a key on the keyboard
Mouse point or mouse over	Placing the mouse pointer over an area on the screen
Mouse click or left mouse click	Pressing the left mouse button
Right mouse click	Pressing the right mouse button
Mouse double-click	Pressing the left mouse button two times in rapid sequence
Mouse drag	Holding down the left mouse button while moving the mouse over the desk surface

Table 12-1 Common user-initiated events

You also need to be able to picture common GUI components. Table 12-2 describes some common GUI components, and Figure 12-3 shows how they look on a screen.

Component	Description
Label	A rectangular area that displays text
Text box	A rectangular area into which the user can type text
Check box	A label placed beside a small square; you can click the square to display or remove a check mark, which selects or deselects an option
Option buttons	A group of options that are similar to check boxes. When the options are square, users typically can select any number of them; such options are called a *check box group*. When the options are round, they are often mutually exclusive and are called *radio buttons*.
List box	When the user clicks a list box, a menu of items appears. Depending on the options the programmer sets, you might be able to make only one selection, or you might be able to make multiple selections.
Button	A rectangular object you can click; when you do, its appearance usually changes to look pressed

Table 12-2 Common GUI components

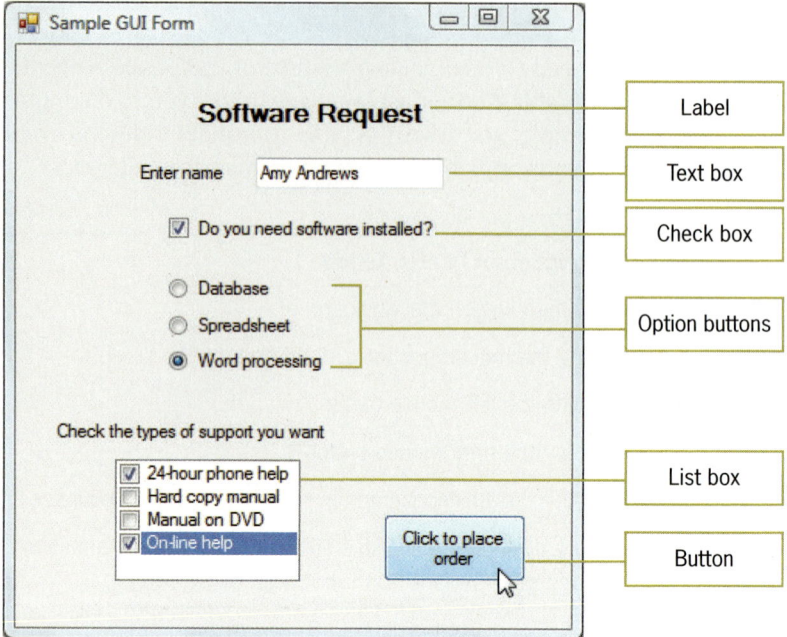

Figure 12-3 Common GUI components

When you program in a language that uses GUI components, you do not create them from scratch. Instead, you call prewritten methods that draw the GUI components on the screen for you. The components themselves are constructed using existing classes complete with names, attributes, and methods. In some programming languages, you can work in a text environment and write statements that instantiate GUI objects. In other languages, you can work in a graphical environment, drag GUI objects onto your screen from a toolbox, and arrange them appropriately for your application. Some languages offer both options. Either way, you do not think about the details of constructing the components. Instead, you concentrate on the actions that should occur when a user initiates an event from one of the components. Thus, GUI components are excellent examples of the best principles of object-oriented programming—they represent objects with attributes and methods that operate like black boxes, making them easy for you to use.

When you use existing GUI components, you instantiate objects, each of which belongs to a prewritten class. For example, you might use a `Button` object when you want the user to click a button to make a selection. Depending on the programming language, the `Button` class might contain attributes or properties such as the text on the `Button` and its position on the screen. The class might also contain methods such as `setText()` and `setPosition()`. For example, Figure 12-4 shows how a built-in `Button` class might be written.

User-Initiated Actions and GUI Components

```
class Button
   Declarations
      private string text
      private num x_position
      private num y_position

   public void setText(string messageOnButton)
      text = messageOnButton
   return

   public void setPosition(num x, num y)
      x_position = x
      y_position = y
   return
endClass
```

Figure 12-4 Button class

The x_position and y_position of the Button object in Figure 12-4 refer to horizontal and vertical coordinates where the Button appears on an object, such as a window that appears on the screen during program execution. A **pixel** is one of the tiny dots of light that form a grid on your screen. The term *pixel* derives from combining the first syllables of *picture* and *element*. You will use x- and y-positions again when you learn about animation later in this chapter.

Watch the video *GUI Components*.

The Button class shown in Figure 12-4 is an abbreviated version so you can easily see its similarity to a class such as Employee, which you read about in Chapter 11. The figure shows three fields and two set methods. A working Button class in most programming languages would contain many more fields and methods. For example, a full-blown class might also contain get methods for the text and position, and other fields and methods to manipulate a Button's font, color, size, and so on.

To create a Button object in a client program, you would write a statement similar to the following:

`Button myProgramButton`

In this statement, Button is the type and myProgramButton is the name of the object you create. To use a Button's methods, you would write statements such as the following:

```
myProgramButton.setText("Click here")
myProgramButton.setPosition(10, 30)
```

Different GUI classes support different attributes and methods. For example, a CheckBox class might contain a method named getCheckedStatus() that returns true or false, indicating whether the CheckBox object has been checked. A Button, however, would have no need for such a method.

An important advantage of using GUI data-entry objects is that you often can control what users enter by limiting their options. When you provide a finite set of buttons to click or a limited number of menu items, the user cannot make unexpected, illegal, or bizarre choices. For example, if you provide only two buttons so the user must click Yes or No, you can eliminate writing code to handle invalid entries.

TWO TRUTHS & A LIE

User-Initiated Actions and GUI Components

1. In a GUI program, a key press is a common user-initiated event and a check box is a typical GUI component.

2. When you program in a language that supports event-driven logic, you call prewritten methods that draw GUI components on the screen for you.

3. An advantage of using GUI objects is that each class you use to create the objects supports identical methods and attributes.

The false statement is # 3. Different GUI classes support different attributes and methods.

Designing Graphical User Interfaces

You should consider several general design principles when creating a program that will use a GUI:

- The interface should be natural and predictable.
- The interface should be attractive, easy to read, and nondistracting.
- To some extent, it's helpful if the user can customize your applications.
- The program should be forgiving.
- The GUI is only a means to an end.

The Interface Should Be Natural and Predictable

The GUI program interface should represent objects like their real-world counterparts. In other words, it makes sense to use an icon that looks like a recycling bin to let a user drag files or other components to the bin and delete them. Using a recycling bin icon is "natural" in that people use one in real life when they want to discard actual items; dragging files to the bin is also "natural" because that's what people do with real items they discard. Using a recycling bin for discarded items is also predictable, because users are already familiar

Designing Graphical User Interfaces

with the icon in other programs. Some icons may be natural, but if they are not predictable as well, then they are not as effective. An icon that depicts a recycling truck seems natural, but because other programs do not use such imagery, it is not as predictable.

GUIs should also be predictable in their layout. For example, when a user must enter personal information in text boxes, the street address is expected to come before the city and state. Also, a menu bar appears at the top of the screen in most GUI programs, and the first menu item is almost always *File*. If you design a program interface in which the menu runs vertically down the right side of the screen, or in which *File* is the last menu option instead of the first, you will confuse users. Either they will make mistakes when using your program or they may give up using it entirely. It doesn't matter if you can prove that your layout plan is more efficient than the standard one—if you do not use a predictable layout, your program will be rejected in the marketplace.

Many studies have proven that the Dvorak keyboard layout is more efficient for typists than the QWERTY keyboard layout that most of us use. The QWERTY keyboard layout gets its name from the first six letter keys in the top row. With the Dvorak layout, which is named for its inventor, the most frequently used keys are in the home row, allowing typists to complete many more keystrokes per minute. However, the Dvorak keyboard has not caught on because it is not predictable to users who know the QWERTY keyboard.

Stovetops often have an unnatural interface, making unfamiliar stoves more difficult for you to use. Most stovetops have four burners arranged in two rows, but the knobs that control the burners frequently are placed in a single horizontal row. Because there is not a natural correlation between the placement of a burner and its control, you are likely to select the wrong knob when adjusting the burner's flame or heating element.

The Interface Should Be Attractive, Easy to Read, and Nondistracting

If your interface is attractive, people are more likely to use it. If it is easy to read, users are less likely to make mistakes. When it comes to GUI design, fancy fonts and weird color combinations are the signs of amateur designers. In addition, you should make sure that unavailable screen options are either dimmed (also called *grayed*) or removed, so the user does not waste time clicking components that aren't functional. An excellent way to learn about good GUI design is to pay attention to the design features used in popular applications and in Web sites you visit. Notice that the designs you like to use feel more "natural."

Screen designs should not be distracting. When a screen has too many components, users can't find what they're looking for. When a component is no longer needed, it should be removed from the interface. GUI programmers sometimes refer to screen space as *real estate*. Just as a plot of land becomes unattractive when it supports no open space, your screen becomes unattractive when you fill the limited space with too many components.

You also want to avoid distracting users with overly creative design elements. When users click a button to open a file, they might be amused the first time a filename dances across the screen or the speakers play a tune. However, after one or two experiences with your creative additions, users find that intruding design elements hamper the actual work of the program. Also, creative embellishments might consume extensive memory and CPU time, slowing an application's performance.

To Some Extent, It's Helpful If the User Can Customize Your Applications

All users work in their own way. If you are designing an application that will use numerous menus and toolbars, it's helpful if users can position components in the order that's easiest for them. Users appreciate being able to change features like color schemes. Allowing a user to change the background color in your application may seem frivolous to you, but to users who are color blind or visually impaired, it might make the difference in whether they use your application at all. Making programs easier to use for people with physical limitations is known as enhancing **accessibility**.

Don't forget that many programs are used internationally. If you can allow the user to work with a choice of languages, you might be able to market your program more successfully in other countries. If you can allow the user to convert prices to multiple currencies, you might be able to make sales in more markets.

The Program Should Be Forgiving

Perhaps you have had the inconvenience of accessing a voice mail system in which you selected several sequential options, only to find yourself at a dead end with no recourse but to hang up and redial the number. Good program design avoids similar problems. You should always provide an escape route to accommodate users who make bad choices or change their minds. By providing a Back button or a working Escape key, you provide more functionality to your users. It also can be helpful to include an option for the user to revert to the default settings after making changes. Some users might be afraid to alter an application's features if they are not sure they can easily return to the original settings.

Users also appreciate being able to perform tasks in a variety of ways. For example, you might allow a user to select a word on a screen by highlighting it using a mouse or by holding down the Ctrl and Shift keys while pressing the right arrow key. A particular technique might be easier for people with disabilities, and it might be the only one available after the mouse batteries fail or the user accidentally disables the keyboard by spilling coffee on it.

The GUI Is Only a Means to an End

The most important principle of GUI design is to remember that a GUI is only an interface. Using a mouse to click items and drag them around is not the point of any business programs except those that train people how to use a mouse. Instead, the point of a graphical interface is to help people be more productive. To that end, the design should help the user see what options are available, allow the use of components in the ordinary way, and not force the user to concentrate on how to interact with your application. The real work of a GUI program is done after the user clicks a button or makes a list box selection. Actual program tasks then take place.

TWO TRUTHS & A LIE

Designing Graphical User Interfaces

1. To keep the user's attention, a well-designed GUI interface should contain unique and creative controls.
2. To be most useful, a GUI interface should be attractive, easy to read, and nondistracting.
3. To avoid frustrating users, a well-designed program should be forgiving.

The false statement is #1. A GUI interface should be natural and predictable.

Developing an Event-Driven Application

In Chapter 1, you first learned the steps to developing a computer program. They are:

1. Understanding the problem
2. Planning the logic
3. Coding the program
4. Translating the program into machine language
5. Testing the program
6. Putting the program into production
7. Maintaining the program

When you develop an event-driven application, you expand on Step 2 (planning the logic) and include three new substeps as follows:

2a. Creating storyboards

2b. Defining the objects

2c. Defining the connections between the screens the user will see

For example, suppose that you want to create a simple, interactive program that determines premiums for prospective insurance customers. A graphical interface will allow users to select a policy type—health or auto. Next, users answer pertinent questions about their age, driving record, and whether they smoke. Although most insurance premiums would be based on more characteristics than these, assume that policy rates are determined using the factors shown in Table 12-3. The final output of the program is a second screen that shows the semiannual premium amount for the chosen policy.

CHAPTER 12 Event-Driven GUI Programming, Multithreading, and Animation

Health Policy Premiums	Auto Policy Premiums
Base rate: $500	Base rate: $750
Add $100 if over age 50	Add $400 if more than 2 tickets
Add $250 if smoker	Subtract $200 if over age 50

Table 12-3 Insurance premiums based on customer characteristics

Creating Storyboards

A **storyboard** represents a picture or sketch of a screen the user will see when running a program. Filmmakers have long used storyboards to illustrate key moments in the plots they are developing; similarly, GUI storyboards represent "snapshot" views of the screens the user will encounter during the run of a program. If the user could view up to four screens during the insurance premium program, then you would draw four storyboard cells, or frames.

Figure 12-5 shows two storyboard sketches for the insurance program. They represent the introductory screen at which the user selects a premium type and answers questions, and the final screen, which displays the semiannual premium.

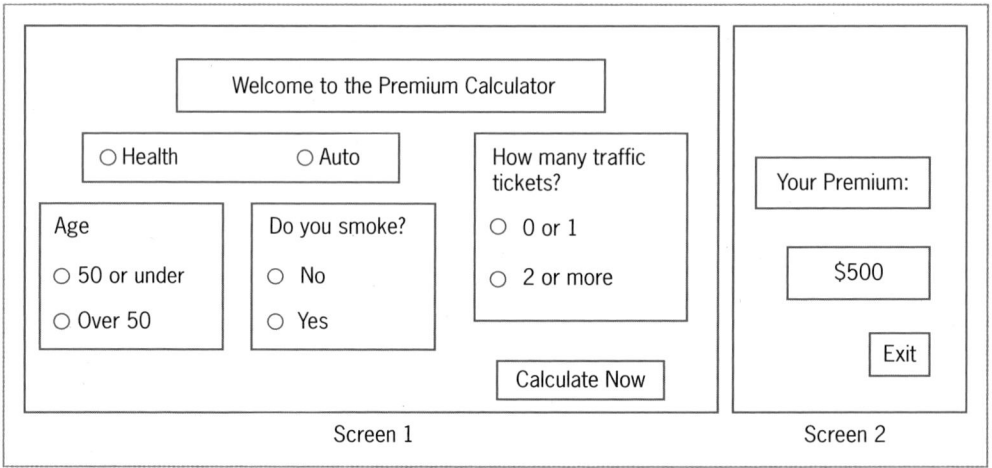

Figure 12-5 Storyboard for insurance program

Defining the Storyboard Objects in an Object Dictionary

An event-driven program may contain dozens or even hundreds of objects. To keep track of them, programmers often use an object dictionary. An **object dictionary** is a list of the objects used in a program, including which screens they are used on and whether any code, or script, is associated with them.

Figure 12-6 shows an object dictionary for the insurance premium program. The type and name of each object to be placed on a screen are listed in the two left columns. The third column shows the screen number on which the object appears. The next column names any variables that are affected by an action on the object. The right column indicates whether any code or script is associated with the object. For example, the label named welcomeLabel appears on the first screen. It has no associated actions—it does not call any methods or change any variables; it is just a label. The calcButton, however, does cause execution of a method named calcRoutine(). This method calculates the semiannual premium amount and stores it in the premiumAmount variable. Depending on the programming language, you might need to name calcRoutine() something similar to calcButton.click(). In languages that use this format, a standard method named click() holds the statements that execute when the user clicks the calcButton.

Object Type	Name	Screen Number	Variables Affected	Script?
Label	welcomeLabel	1	none	none
RadioButton	healthRadioButton	1	premiumAmount	none
RadioButton	autoRadioButton	1	premiumAmount	none
Label	ageLabel	1	none	none
RadioButton	lowAgeRadioButton	1	premiumAmount	none
RadioButton	highAgeRadioButton	1	premiumAmount	none
Label	smokeLabel	1	none	none
RadioButton	smokeNoRadioButton	1	premiumAmount	none
RadioButton	smokeYesRadioButton	1	premiumAmount	none
Label	ticketsLabel	1	none	none
RadioButton	lowTicketsRadioButton	1	premiumAmount	none
RadioButton	highTicketsRadioButton	1	premiumAmount	none
Button	calcButton	1	premiumAmount	calcRoutine()
Label	premiumLabel	2	none	none
Label	premAmtLabel	2	none	none
Button	exitButton	2	none	exitRoutine()

Figure 12-6   Object dictionary for insurance premium program

Defining Connections Between the User Screens

The insurance premium program is small, but with larger programs you may need to draw the connections between the screens to show how they interact. Figure 12-7 shows an interactivity diagram for the screens used in the insurance premium program.

An **interactivity diagram** shows the relationship between
screens in an interactive GUI program. Figure 12-7
shows that the first screen calls the second screen,
and the program ends.

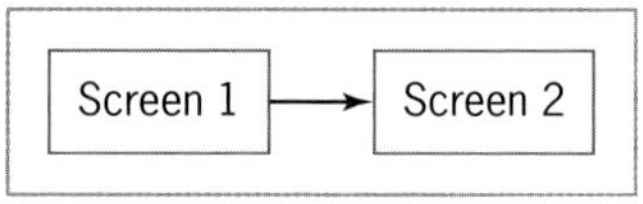

Figure 12-8 shows how a diagram might look for a
more complicated program in which the user has several
options available at Screens 1, 2, and 3. Notice how each
of these three screens may lead to different screens,
depending on the options the user selects at a previous screen.

Figure 12-7 Interactivity diagram for insurance premium program

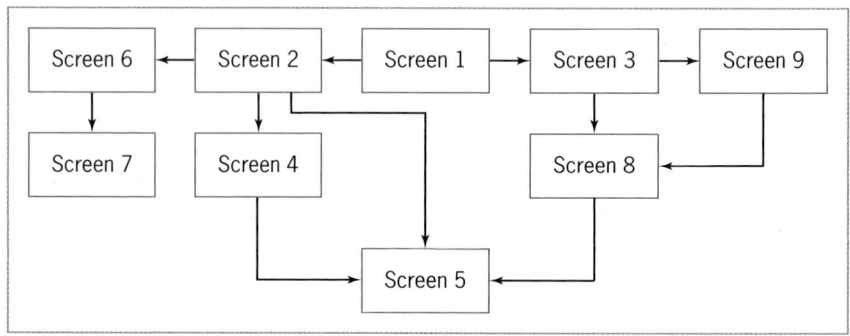

Figure 12-8 Interactivity diagram for a complicated program

Planning the Logic

In an event-driven program, you design the screens, define the objects, and define how the screens will connect. Then you can start to plan the program class. For example, following the storyboard plan for the insurance program (see Figure 12-5), you need to create the first screen, which contains four labels, four sets of radio buttons, and a button. Figure 12-9 shows the pseudocode that creates these components.

```
Declarations
   Label welcomeLabel
   RadioButton healthRadioButton
   RadioButton autoRadioButton
   Label ageLabel
   RadioButton lowAgeRadioButton
   RadioButton highAgeRadioButton
   Label smokeLabel
   RadioButton smokeNoRadioButton
   RadioButton smokeYesRadioButton
   Label ticketsLabel
   RadioButton lowTicketsRadioButton
   RadioButton highTicketsRadioButton
   Button calcButton
welcomeLabel.setText("Welcome to the Premium Calculator")
welcomeLabel.setPosition(30, 10)

healthRadioButton.setText("Health")
healthRadioButton.setPosition(15, 40)

autoRadioButton.setText("Auto")
autoRadioButton.setPosition(50, 40)

ageLabel.setText("Age")
ageLabel.setPosition(5, 60)

lowAgeRadioButton.setText("50 or under")
lowAgeRadioButton.setPosition(5, 70)

highAgeRadioButton.setText("Over 50")
highAgeRadioButton.setPosition(5, 80)

smokeLabel.setText("Do you smoke?")
smokeLabel.setPosition(40, 60)

smokeNoRadioButton.setText("No")
smokeNoRadioButton.setPosition(40, 70)

smokeYesRadioButton.setText("Yes")
smokeYesRadioButton.setPosition(40, 80)

ticketsLabel.setText("How many traffic tickets?")
ticketsLabel.setPosition(60, 50)

lowTicketsRadioButton.setText("0 or 1")
lowTicketsRadioButton.setPosition(60, 70)

highTicketsRadioButton.setText("2 or more")
highTicketsRadioButton.setPosition(60, 90)

calcButton.setText("Calculate Now")
calcButton.setPosition(60, 100)
calcButton.registerListener(calcRoutine())
```

When you use an integrated development environment to create applications, you can drag components like those in Figure 12-9 onto a screen without explicitly writing all the statements shown in the pseudocode. In that case, the coding statements will be generated for you. It's beneficial to understand these statements so that you can more easily modify and debug your programs.

In Figure 12-9, the statement `calcButton.registerListener(calcRoutine())` specifies that `calcRoutine()` executes when a user clicks the `calcButton`. The syntax of this statement varies among programming languages. With most object-oriented programming (OOP) languages, you must **register components**, or sign them up so that they can react to events initiated by other components. The details vary among languages, but the basic process is to write a statement that links the appropriate method (such as the `calcRoutine()` or `exitRoutine()` method) with an event such as a user's button click. In many development environments, the statement that registers a component to react to a user-initiated event is written for you automatically when you click components while designing your screen.

In reality, you might generate more code than that shown in Figure 12-9 when you create the insurance program components. For example, each component might require a color and font. You also might want to initialize some components with default values to indicate they are selected. For example, you might want one radio button in a group to be selected already, which allows the user to click a different option only if he does not want the default value.

You also need to create the component that holds all the GUI elements in Figure 12-9. Depending on the programming language, you might use a class with a name such as `Screen`, `Form`, or `Window`. Each of these generically is a **container**, or a class of objects whose main purpose is to hold other elements. The container class contains methods that allow you to set physical properties such as height and width, as well as methods that allow you to add the appropriate components to a container. Figure 12-10 shows how you would define a `Screen` class, set its size, and add the necessary components.

```
Declarations
    Screen screen1
screen1.setSize(150, 150)
screen1.add(welcomeLabel)
screen1.add(healthRadioButton)
screen1.add(autoRadioButton)
screen1.add(ageLabel)
screen1.add(lowAgeRadioButton)
screen1.add(highAgeRadioButton)
screen1.add(smokeLabel)
screen1.add(smokeNoRadioButton)
screen1.add(smokeYesRadioButton)
screen1.add(ticketsLabel)
screen1.add(lowTicketsRadioButton)
screen1.add(highTicketsRadioButton)
screen1.add(calcButton)
```

Figure 12-10 Statements that create `screen1`

Similarly, Figure 12-11 shows how you can create and define the components for the second screen in the insurance program and how to add the components to the container. Notice the label that holds the user's insurance premium is not filled with text, because the amount is not known until the user makes all the selections on the first screen.

```
Declarations
    Screen screen2
    Label premiumLabel
    Label premAmtLabel
    Button exitButton

screen2.setSize(100, 100)

premiumLabel.setText("Your Premium:")
premiumLabel.setPosition(5, 30)

premAmtLabel.setPosition(20, 50)

exitButton.setText("Exit")
exitButton.setPosition(60, 80)
exitButton.registerListener(exitRoutine())

screen2.add(premiumLabel)
screen2.add(premAmtLabel)
screen2.add(exitButton)
```

Figure 12-11   Statements that define and create `screen2` and its components

After the GUI components are designed and arranged, you can plan the logic for each of the methods or scripts that the program will use. For example, given the program requirements shown earlier in Table 12-3, you can write the pseudocode for the `calcRoutine()` method of the insurance premium program, as shown in Figure 12-12. The `calcRoutine()` method does not execute until the user clicks the `calcButton`. At that point, the user's choices are sent to the method and used to calculate the premium amount.

```
public void calcRoutine()
   Declarations
      num HEALTH_AMT = 500
      num HIGH_AGE = 100
      num SMOKER = 250
      num AUTO_AMT = 750
      num HIGH_TICKETS = 400
      num HIGH_AGE_DRIVER_DISCOUNT = 200
      num premiumAmount
   if healthRadioButton.getChecked() then
      premiumAmount = HEALTH_AMT
      if highAgeRadioButton.getChecked() then
         premiumAmount = premiumAmount + HIGH_AGE
      endif
      if smokeYesRadioButton.getChecked() then
         premiumAmount = premiumAmount + SMOKER
      endif
   else
      premiumAmount = AUTO_AMT
      if highTicketsRadioButton.getChecked() then
         premiumAmount = premiumAmount + HIGH_TICKETS
      endif
      if highAgeRadioButton.getChecked() then
         premiumAmount = premiumAmount - HIGH_AGE_DRIVER_DISCOUNT
      endif
   endif
   premAmtLabel.setText(premiumAmount)
   screen1.remove()
   screen2.display()
return
```

Figure 12-12 Pseudocode for `calcRoutine()` method of insurance premium program

The pseudocode in Figure 12-12 should look very familiar to you—it declares numeric constants and a variable and uses decision-making logic you have used since the early chapters of this book. After the premium is calculated based on the user's choices, it is placed in the label that appears on the second screen. The basic structures of sequence, selection, and looping will continue to serve you well, whether you are programming in a procedural or event-driven environment.

The last two statements in the `calcRoutine()` method indicate that after the insurance premium is calculated and placed in its label, the first screen is removed and the second screen is displayed. Screen removal and display are accomplished differently in different languages; this example assumes that the appropriate methods are named `remove()` and `display()`.

Two more program segments are needed to complete the insurance premium program. These segments include the main program that executes when the program starts and the last method that executes when the program ends. In many GUI languages, the process is slightly more complicated, but the general logic appears in Figure 12-13. The final method in the program is associated with the `exitButton` object on `screen2`. In Figure 12-13, this method is called `exitRoutine()`. In this example, the main program sets up the first screen and the last method removes the last screen.

```
start
    screen1.display()
stop

public void exitRoutine()
    screen2.remove()
return
```

Figure 12-13 The main program and `exitRoutine()` method for the insurance program

---

TWO TRUTHS & A LIE
Developing an Event-Driven Application

1. A storyboard represents a diagram of the logic used in an interactive program.
2. An object dictionary is a list of the objects used in a program, including which screens they are used on and whether any code, or script, is associated with them.
3. An interactivity diagram shows the relationship between screens in an interactive GUI program.

The false statement is #1. A storyboard represents a picture or sketch of a screen the user will see when running a program.

Understanding Threads and Multithreading

A **thread** is the flow of execution of one set of program statements. When you execute a program statement by statement, from beginning to end, you are following a thread. Many applications follow a single thread; this means that the application executes only a single program statement at a time. If a computer has more than one central processing unit (CPU), then each can execute a thread at the same time. However, if a computer has a single CPU and the system supports only single threading, then tasks must occur one at a time. For example, Figure 12-14 shows how three tasks might execute in a single thread in a computer with a single CPU. Each task must end before the next task starts.

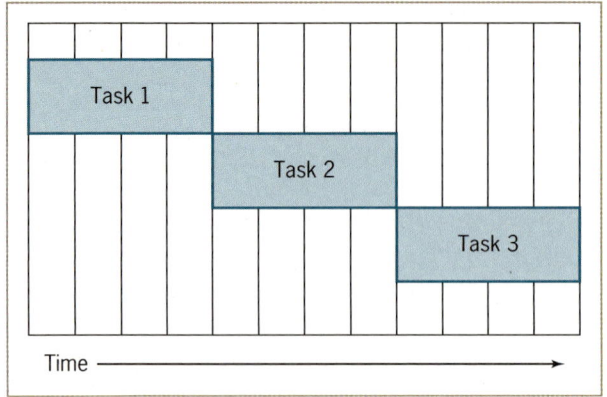

Figure 12-14 Executing multiple tasks as single threads in a single-processor system

Even if the computer has only one CPU, all major OOP languages allow you to launch, or start, multiple threads of execution by using a technique known as **multithreading**. With multithreading, threads share the CPU's time, as shown in Figure 12-15. The CPU devotes a small amount of time to one task, and then devotes a small amount of time to another. The CPU never actually performs two tasks at the same instant. Instead, it performs a piece of one task and then part of another. The CPU performs so quickly that each task seems to execute without interruption.

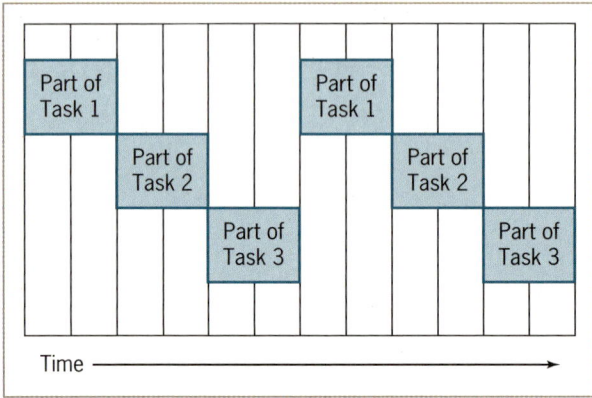

Figure 12-15 Executing multiple threads in a single-processor system

Perhaps you have seen an expert chess player participate in games with several opponents at once. The expert makes a move on the first chess board, and then moves to the second board against a second opponent while the first opponent analyzes his next move. The master can move to the third board, make a move, and return to the first board before the first opponent is even ready to respond. To the first opponent, it might seem as though the expert is devoting all of his time to the first game. Because the expert is so fast, he can play other opponents while the first opponent contemplates his next move. Executing multiple threads on a single CPU is a similar process. The CPU transfers its attention from thread to thread so quickly that the tasks don't even "miss" the CPU's attention.

You use multithreading to improve the performance of your programs. Multithreaded programs often run faster, but more importantly, they are more user-friendly. With a multithreaded program, a user can continue to make choices by clicking buttons while the program is reading a data file. An animated figure can appear on one part of the screen while the user makes menu selections elsewhere on the screen. When you use the Internet, the benefits of multithreading increase. For example, you can begin to read a long text file, watch a video, or listen to an audio file while the file is still downloading. Web users are likely to abandon a site if they cannot use it before a lengthy downloading process completes. When you use multithreading to perform concurrent tasks, you are more likely to retain visitors to your Web site—this is particularly important if your site sells a product or service.

Programmers sometimes describe thread execution as a *lightweight process* because it is not a full-blown program. Rather, a thread must run within the context of a full, heavyweight program.

Writing good code to execute multithreading requires skill. Without careful coding, problems can arise such as **deadlock**, in which two or more threads wait for each other to execute, and **starvation**, in which a thread is abandoned because other threads occupy all the computer's resources.

When threads share an object, special care is needed to avoid unwanted results. For example, consider a customer order program in which two clerks are allowed to fill orders concurrently. Imagine the following scenario:

- The first clerk accesses an inventory file and tells a customer that one item is left.
- A second clerk accesses the file and tells a different customer that one item is left.
- The first customer places an order, and inventory is reduced to 0.
- The second customer places an order, and inventory is reduced to −1.

Two items have been ordered, but only one exists, and the inventory file is now incorrect. There will be confusion in the warehouse, problems in the Accounting department, and one unsatisfied customer. Similar problems can occur in programs that reserve airline seats or concert tickets. OOP languages provide sophisticated techniques, known as **thread synchronization**, that help avoid these potential problems.

Object-oriented languages often contain a built-in `Thread` class that contains methods to help handle and synchronize multiple threads. For example, a `sleep()` method is frequently used to pause program execution for a specified amount of time. Computer processing speed is so rapid that sometimes you have to slow down processing for human consumption. The next section describes one application that frequently requires a `sleep()` method—computer animation.

Watch the video *Threads and Multithreading*.

> **TWO TRUTHS & A LIE**
>
> Understanding Threads and Multithreading
>
> 1. In the last few years, few programs that follow a single thread have been written.
> 2. Single-thread programs contain statements that execute in very rapid sequence, but only one statement executes at a time.
> 3. When you use a computer with multiple CPUs, the computer can execute multiple instructions simultaneously.
>
> The false statement is #1. Many applications follow a single thread; this means that at any one time the application executes only a single program statement.

Creating Animation

Animation is the rapid sequence of still images, each slightly different from the previous one, that produces the illusion of movement. Cartoonists create animated films by drawing a sequence of frames or cells. These individual drawings are shown to the audience in rapid succession to create the sense of natural movement. You create computer animation using the same techniques. If you display computer images as fast as your CPU can process them, you might not be able to see anything. Most computer animation employs a `Thread` class `sleep()` method to pause for short intervals between animation cells so the human brain has time to absorb each image's content.

Many object-oriented languages offer built-in classes that contain methods you can use to draw geometric figures. The methods typically have names like `drawLine()`, `drawCircle()`, `drawRectangle()`, and so on. You place figures on the screen based on a graphing coordinate system. Each component has a horizontal, or **x-axis**, position as well as a vertical, or **y-axis**, position on the screen. The upper-left corner of a display is position 0, 0. The first, or **x-coordinate**, value increases as you travel from left to right across the window. The second, or **y-coordinate**, value increases as you travel from top to bottom. Figure 12-16 shows four screen coordinate positions.

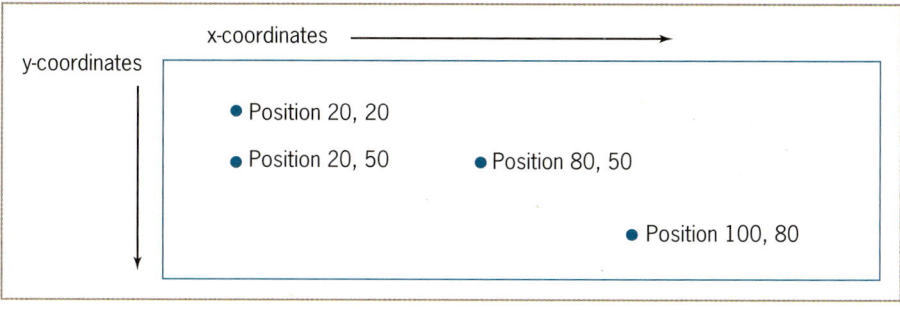

Figure 12-16 Selected screen coordinate positions

Artists often spend a great deal of time creating the exact images they want to use in an animation sequence. As a simple example, Figure 12-17 shows pseudocode for a MovingCircle class. As its name implies, the class moves a circle across the screen. The class contains data fields to hold x- and y-coordinates that identify the location at which a circle appears. The constants SIZE and INCREASE define the size of the first circle drawn and the relative increase in size and position of each subsequent circle. The MovingCircle class assumes that you are working with a language that provides a drawCircle() method, which creates a circle when given parameters for horizontal and vertical positions and radius. Assuming you are working with a language that provides a sleep() method to accept a pause time in milliseconds, the SLEEP_TIME constant provides a 100-millisecond gap before the production of each new circle.

```
public class MovingCircle
    Declarations
        private num x = 20
        private num y = 20
        private num SIZE = 40
        private num INCREASE = SIZE / 10
        private num SLEEP_TIME = 100

    public void main()
        while true
            repaintScreen()
        endwhile
    return

    public void repaintScreen()
        drawCircle(x, y, SIZE)
        x = x + INCREASE
        y = y + INCREASE
        SIZE = SIZE + INCREASE
        Thread.sleep(SLEEP_TIME)
    return
endClass
```

Figure 12-17 The MovingCircle class

In most object-oriented languages, a method named `main()` executes automatically when a class object is created. The `main()` method in the `MovingCircle` class executes a continuous loop. A similar technique is used in many languages that support GUI interfaces. Program execution will cease only when the user quits the application—by clicking a window's Close button, for example. In the `repaintScreen()` method of the `MovingCircle` class, a circle is drawn at the `x,y` position, then x, y, and the circle size are increased. The application sleeps for one-tenth of a second (the `SLEEP_TIME` value), and then the `repaintScreen()` method draws a new circle more to the right, further down, and a little larger. The effect is a moving circle that leaves a trail of smaller circles behind as it moves diagonally across the screen. Figure 12-18 shows the output as a Java version of the application executes.

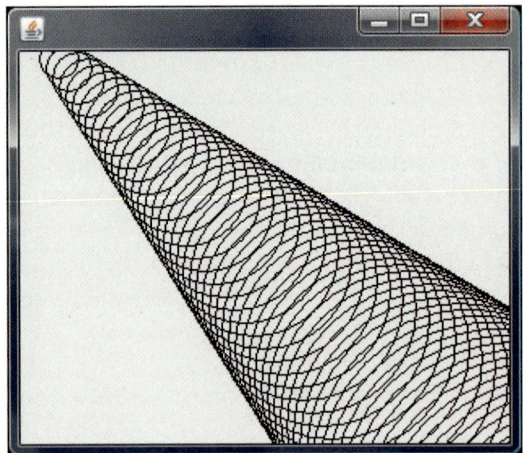

Figure 12-18 Output of the `MovingCircle` application

Although an object-oriented language might make it easy to draw geometric shapes, you also can substitute a variety of more sophisticated, predrawn animated images to achieve the graphic effects you want within your programs. An image is loaded in a separate thread of execution, which allows program execution to continue while the image loads. This is a significant advantage because loading a large image can be time-consuming.

 Many animated images are available on the Web for you to use freely. Use your search engine and keywords such as *gif files*, *jpeg files*, and *animation* to find sources for shareware and freeware files.

TWO TRUTHS & A LIE

Creating Animation

1. Each component you place on a screen has a horizontal, or x-axis, position as well as a vertical, or y-axis, position.
2. The x-coordinate value increases as you travel from left to right across a window.
3. You almost always want to display animation cells as fast as your processor can handle them.

The false statement is #3. If you display computer images as fast as your CPU can process them, you might not be able to see anything. Most computer animation employs a method to pause for short periods of time between animation cells.

Chapter Summary

- Interacting with a computer operating system from the command line is difficult; it is easier to use an event-driven graphical user interface (GUI), in which users manipulate objects such as buttons and menus. Within an event-driven program, a component from which an event is generated is the source of the event. A listener is an object that is "interested in" an event to which you want it to respond.

- A user can initiate many events, such as a key press, mouse point, click, right-click, double-click, and drag. Common GUI components include labels, text boxes, buttons, check boxes, check box groups, option buttons, and list boxes. GUI components are excellent examples of the best principles of object-oriented programming; they represent objects with attributes and methods that operate like black boxes.

- When you create a program that uses a GUI, the interface should be natural, predictable, attractive, easy to read, and nondistracting. It's helpful if the user can customize your applications. The program should be forgiving, and you should not forget that the GUI is only a means to an end.

- Developing event-driven applications requires more steps than developing other programs. The steps include creating storyboards, defining objects, and defining the connections between the screens the user will see.

- A thread is the flow of execution of one set of program statements. Many applications follow a single thread; others use multithreading so that diverse tasks can execute concurrently.

- Animation is the rapid sequence of still images that produces the illusion of movement. Many object-oriented languages contain built-in classes that contain methods you can use to draw geometric figures on the screen. Each component has a horizontal, or x-axis, position as well as a vertical, or y-axis, position on the screen.

Key Terms

The **DOS prompt** is the command line in the DOS operating system.

An **operating system** is the software that you use to run a computer and manage its resources.

Icons are small pictures on the screen that the user can select with a mouse.

An **event** is an occurrence that generates a message sent to an object.

In **event-driven** or **event-based** programs, actions occur in response to user-initiated events such as clicking a mouse button.

The **source of an event** is the component from which the event is generated.

A **listener** is an object that is "interested in" an event to which you want it to respond.

A **script** is a term in object-oriented programming used to describe procedural modules that depend on user-initiated events.

A **pixel** is a picture element, or one of the tiny dots of light that form a grid on your screen.

Accessibility describes the screen design concerns that make programs easier to use for people with physical limitations.

A **storyboard** represents a picture or sketch of a screen the user will see when running a program.

An **object dictionary** is a list of the objects used in a program, including which screens they are used on and whether any code, or script, is associated with them.

An **interactivity diagram** shows the relationship between screens in an interactive GUI program.

Registering components is the act of signing them up so they can react to events initiated by other components.

A **container** is a class of objects whose main purpose is to hold other elements—for example, a window.

A **thread** is the flow of execution of one set of program statements.

Multithreading is using multiple threads of program execution.

Deadlock is a flaw in multithreaded programs in which two or more threads wait for each other to execute.

Starvation is a flaw in multithreaded programs in which a thread is abandoned because other threads occupy all the computer's resources.

Thread synchronization is a set of techniques that coordinates threads of execution to help avoid potential multithreading problems.

Animation is the rapid sequence of still images, each slightly different from the previous one, that produces the illusion of movement.

The **x-axis** represents horizontal positions in a screen window.

The **y-axis** represents vertical positions in a screen window.

The **x-coordinate** value increases as you travel from left to right across a window.

The **y-coordinate** value increases as you travel from top to bottom across a window.

Review Questions

1. Compared to using a command line, an advantage to using an operating system that employs a GUI is _____.
   a. you can interact directly with the operating system
   b. you do not have to deal with confusing icons
   c. you do not have to memorize complicated commands
   d. all of the above

2. When users can initiate actions by clicking the mouse on an icon, the program is _____-driven.
   a. event
   b. prompt
   c. command
   d. incident

3. A component from which an event is generated is the _____ of the event.
   a. base
   b. icon
   c. listener
   d. source

4. An object that responds to an event is a _____.
   a. source
   b. listener
   c. transponder
   d. snooper

5. All of the following are user-initiated events except a _____.
   a. key press
   b. key drag
   c. right mouse click
   d. mouse drag

6. All of the following are typical GUI components except a _____.
   a. label
   b. text box
   c. list box
   d. button box

7. GUI components operate like _____.
   a. black boxes
   b. procedural functions
   c. looping structures
   d. command lines

8. Which of the following is *not* a principle of good GUI design?
   a. The interface should be predictable.
   b. The fancier the screen design, the better.
   c. The program should be forgiving.
   d. The user should be able to customize applications.

9. Which of the following aspects of a GUI layout is most predictable and natural for the user?
   a. A menu bar runs down the right side of the screen.
   b. *Help* is the first option on a menu.
   c. A dollar sign icon represents saving a file.
   d. Pressing *Esc* allows the user to cancel a selection.

10. In most GUI programming environments, the programmer can change all of the following attributes of most components except their _____.
    a. color
    b. screen location
    c. size
    d. You can change all of these attributes.

11. Depending on the programming language, you might _____ to change a screen component's attributes.
    a. use an assignment statement
    b. call a module
    c. enter a value into a list of properties
    d. all of the above

Review Questions

12. When you create an event-driven application, which of the following must be done before defining objects?
    a. Translate the program.
    b. Create storyboards.
    c. Test the program.
    d. Code the program.

13. A ———— is a sketch of a screen the user will see when running a program.
    a. flowchart
    b. hierarchy chart
    c. storyboard
    d. tale timber

14. An object ———— is a list of objects used in a program.
    a. thesaurus
    b. glossary
    c. index
    d. dictionary

15. A(n) ———— diagram shows the connections between the various screens a user might see during a program's execution.
    a. interactivity
    b. help
    c. cooperation
    d. communication

16. The flow of execution of one set of program statements is a ————.
    a. thread
    b. string
    c. path
    d. route

17. When a computer contains a single CPU, it can execute ———— computer instruction(s) at a time.
    a. one
    b. several
    c. an unlimited number of
    d. from several to thousands of

18. Multithreaded programs usually ———— than their procedural counterparts.
    a. run faster
    b. are harder to use
    c. are older
    d. all of the above

19. An object's horizontal position on the computer screen is its ————.
    a. a-coordinate
    b. h-coordinate
    c. x-coordinate
    d. y-coordinate

20. You create computer animation by ————.
    a. drawing an image and setting its animation property to true
    b. drawing a single image and executing it on a multiprocessor system
    c. drawing a sequence of frames that are shown in rapid succession
    d. Animation is not used in computer applications.

Exercises

1. Take a critical look at three GUI applications you have used—for example, a spreadsheet, a word-processing program, and a game. Describe how well each conforms to the GUI design guidelines listed in this chapter.

2. Select one element of poor GUI design in a program you have used. Describe how you would improve the design.

3. Select a GUI program that you have never used before. Describe how well it conforms to the GUI design guidelines listed in this chapter.

4. Design the storyboards, interactivity diagram, object dictionary, and any necessary scripts for an interactive program for customers of Sanderson's Ice Cream Sundaes.

    Allow customers the option of choosing a three-scoop, two-scoop, or one-scoop creation at a base price of $4.00, $3.00, or $2.20, respectively. Let the customer choose chocolate, strawberry, or vanilla as the primary flavor. If the customer adds nuts, whipped cream, or cherries to the order, add $0.50 for each to the base price. After the customer clicks an Order Now button, display the price of the order.

5. Design the storyboards, interactivity diagram, object dictionary, and any necessary scripts for an interactive program for customers of Carrie's Custom T-Shirts.

    Allow customers the option of five T-shirt sizes and styles—for example, *XL long sleeve* or *M short sleeve*. Assume that each product has a unique price that is displayed when the user clicks a Buy Now button.

6. Design the storyboards, interactivity diagram, object dictionary, and any necessary scripts for an interactive program for customers of the Dharma Day Spa.

    Allow customers the option of choosing a manicure ($10), pedicure ($25), or both ($32). After the customer clicks a Select button, display the price of the service.

Find the Bugs

7. Your downloadable files for Chapter 12 include DEBUG12-01.txt, DEBUG12-02.txt, and DEBUG12-03.txt. Each file starts with some comments that describe the problem. Comments are lines that begin with two slashes (//). Following the comments, each file contains pseudocode that has one or more bugs you must find and correct.

Exercises

 Game Zone

8. Design the storyboards, interactivity diagram, object dictionary, and any necessary scripts for an interactive program that allows a user to play a card game named Lucky Seven. In real life, the game can be played with seven cards, each containing a number from 1 through 7, that are shuffled and dealt number-side down. To start the game, a player turns over any card. The exposed number on the card determines the position (reading from left to right) of the next card that must be turned over. For example, if the player turns over the first card and its number is 7, the next card turned must be the seventh card (counting from left to right). If the player turns over a card whose number denotes a position that was already turned, the player loses the game. If the player succeeds in turning over all seven cards, the player wins.

   Instead of cards, you will use seven buttons labeled 1 through 7 from left to right. Randomly associate one of the seven values 1 through 7 with each button. (In other words, the associated value might or might not be equivalent to the button's labeled value.) When the player clicks a button, reveal the associated hidden value. If the value represents the position of a button already clicked, the player loses. If the revealed number represents an available button, force the user to click it—that is, do not take any action until the user clicks the correct button. After a player clicks a button, remove the button from play.

   For example, a player might click Button 7, revealing a 4. Then the player clicks Button 4, revealing a 2. Then the player clicks Button 2, revealing a 7. The player loses because Button 7 is already "used."

9. In the Game Zone sections of Chapters 6 and 9, you designed and fine-tuned the logic for the game Hangman, in which the user guesses letters in a series of hidden words. Design the storyboards, interactivity diagram, object dictionary, and any necessary scripts for a version of the game in which the user clicks lettered buttons to fill in the secret words. Draw a "hanged" person piece by piece with each missed letter. For example, when the user chooses a correct letter, place it in the appropriate position or positions in the word, but the first time the user chooses a letter that is not in the target word, draw a head for the "hanged" man. The second time the user makes an incorrect guess, add a torso. Continue with arms and legs. If the complete body is drawn before the user has guessed all the letters in the word, display a message indicating that the player has lost the game. If the user completes the word before all the body parts are drawn, display a message that the player has won. Assume that you can use built-in methods named `drawCircle()` and `drawLine()`. The `drawCircle()` method requires three parameters—the x- and y-coordinates of the center, and a radius size. The `drawLine()` method requires four parameters—the x- and y-coordinates of the start of the line, and the x- and y-coordinates of the end of the line.

 *Up for Discussion*

10. Making exciting, entertaining, professional-looking GUI applications becomes easier once you learn to include graphics images. You can copy these images from many locations on the Web. Should there be any restrictions on their use? Does it make a difference if you are writing programs for your own enjoyment as opposed to putting them on the Web where others can see them? Is using photographs different from using drawings? Does it matter if the photographs contain recognizable people? Would you impose any restrictions on images posted to your organization's Web site?

11. Playing computer games has been shown to increase the level of dopamine in the human brain. High levels of this substance are associated with addiction to drugs. Suppose that you work for a computer game company that decides to research how its products can produce more dopamine in the brains of players. Would you support the company's decision?

12. When people use interactive programs on the Web, do you feel it is appropriate to track which buttons they click or to record the data they enter? When is it appropriate, and when is it not? Does it matter how long the data is stored? Does it matter if a profit is made from using the data?

13. Should there be limits on Web content? Consider sites that might display pornography, child abuse, suicide, or the assassination of a political leader. Does it make a difference if the offensive images are shown as animation?

CHAPTER 13

System Modeling with the UML

In this chapter, you will learn about:

- System modeling
- The Unified Modeling Language (UML)
- UML use case diagrams
- UML class and object diagrams
- Other UML diagrams
- Deciding when to use the UML and which UML diagrams to use

Understanding System Modeling

Computer programs often stand alone to solve a user's specific problem. For example, a program might exist only to print paychecks for the current week. Most computer programs, however, are part of a larger system. Your company's payroll system might consist of dozens of programs, including programs that produce employee paychecks, apply raises to employee salaries, alter employee deduction options, and create federal and state tax forms at the end of the year. Each program you write as part of a system might be related to several others. Some programs depend on input from other programs in the system or produce output to be fed into other programs. Similarly, an organization's accounting, inventory, and customer ordering systems all consist of many interrelated programs. Producing a set of programs that operate together correctly requires careful planning. **System design** is the detailed specification of how all the parts of a system will be implemented and coordinated. Usually, system design refers to computer system design, but even a noncomputerized, manual system can benefit from good design techniques. Planning the parts of a system before creating them is also called **modeling**.

Many textbooks cover the theories and techniques of system design and modeling. If you continue to study in a Computer Information Systems program at a college or university, you probably will be required to take a semester-long course in system design. Explaining all the techniques of system design is beyond the scope of this book. However, some basic principles parallel those you have used throughout this book in designing individual programs:

- Large systems are easier to understand when you break them down into subsystems.
- Good modeling techniques are increasingly important as the size and complexity of systems increase.
- Good models promote communication among technical and nontechnical workers while ensuring professional and efficient business solutions.

In other words, developing a model for a single program or an entire business system requires organization and planning. In this chapter, you learn the basics of one popular design tool, the **Unified Modeling Language (UML)**, which is based on the preceding principles. The UML allows you to envision systems with an object-oriented perspective: breaking a system into subsystems, focusing on the big picture, and hiding the implementation details. In addition, the UML provides a means for programmers and businesspeople to communicate about system design. It also provides a way to divide responsibilities for large systems. Understanding the principles of the UML helps you design a variety of system types and talk about systems with the people who will use them.

In addition to modeling a system before creating it, system analysts sometimes model an existing system to get a better picture of its operation. Scrutinizing an existing system and creating an improved one is called **reverse engineering**.

TWO TRUTHS & A LIE

Understanding System Modeling

1. Large systems are easier to understand when you break them down into subsystems.
2. Good modeling techniques are most important in small systems.
3. Good models often lead to superior business solutions.

The false statement is #2. Good modeling techniques are increasingly important as the size and complexity of systems increase.

What Is the UML?

The UML is a standard way to specify, construct, and document systems that use object-oriented methods. The UML is a modeling language, not a programming language. The systems you develop using the UML probably will be implemented later in object-oriented programming languages such as Java, C++, C#, or Visual Basic. As with flowcharts, pseudocode, hierarchy charts, and class diagrams, the UML has its own notation that consists of a set of specialized shapes and conventions. You can use UML shapes to construct different kinds of software diagrams and model different kinds of systems. Just as you can use a flowchart or hierarchy chart to diagram real-life activities or organizational relationships as well as computer programs, you can also use the UML for many purposes, including modeling business activities, organizational processes, or software systems.

You can purchase compilers for most programming languages from a variety of manufacturers, and you can purchase several different flowcharting programs. Similarly, you can purchase a variety of tools to help you create UML diagrams, but the UML itself is vendor-independent.

The UML was created at Rational Software by Grady Booch, Ivar Jacobson, and Jim Rumbaugh. The Object Management Group (OMG) adopted the UML as a standard for software modeling in 1997. The OMG includes more than 800 software vendors, developers, and users who seek a common architectural framework for object-oriented programming. The UML is in its second major version; the current version is UML 2.4. You can view or download the entire UML specification and usage guidelines from the OMG at *www.uml.org*.

When you draw a flowchart or write pseudocode, your purpose is to illustrate the individual steps in a process. When you draw a hierarchy chart, you use more of a "big picture" approach. As with a hierarchy chart, you use the UML to create top-view diagrams of business processes that let you hide details and focus on functionality. This approach lets you start with a generic view of an application and introduce details and complexity later. UML diagrams are useful as you begin designing business systems, when customers who are not technically oriented must accurately communicate with the technical staff members who will create the actual systems. The UML was intentionally designed to be nontechnical so that developers, customers, and implementers (programmers) could all "speak the same language." If business and technical people can agree on what a system should do, the chances improve that the final product will be useful.

The UML is very large; its documentation is more than 800 pages, and new diagram types are added frequently. Currently, the UML provides 14 diagram types that you can use to model systems. Each of the diagram types lets you see a business process from a different angle, and each type appeals to a different type of user. Just as an architect, interior designer, electrician, and plumber use different diagram types to describe the same building, different computer users appreciate different perspectives. For example, a business user most values a system's use case diagrams because they illustrate who is doing what. On the other hand, programmers find class and object diagrams more useful because they help explain details of how to build classes and objects into applications.

The UML superstructure groups the diagram types into two broad categories—structure diagrams and behavior diagrams. A subcategory of behavior diagrams is interaction diagrams. The UML diagram types are listed below.

- **Structure diagrams** emphasize the "things" in a system, and include:
  - Class diagrams
  - Object diagrams
  - Component diagrams
  - Composite structure diagrams
  - Package diagrams
  - Deployment diagrams
  - Profile diagrams
- **Behavior diagrams** emphasize what happens in a system, and include:
  - Use case diagrams
  - Activity diagrams
  - State machine diagrams
- **Interaction diagrams** emphasize the flow of control and data among the system elements being modeled, and include:
  - Sequence diagrams
  - Communication diagrams
  - Timing diagrams
  - Interaction overview diagrams

Using UML Use Case Diagrams

An alternate way to categorize UML diagrams is to divide them into diagrams that illustrate the static, or steady, aspects of a system and those that illustrate the dynamic, or changing, aspects of a system. For example, the static elements of a restaurant system might include the menu and employees, and the dynamic elements would include how the restaurant reacts to a customer. Static diagrams include class, object, component, deployment, and profile diagrams. Dynamic diagrams include use case, sequence, communication, state machine, and activity diagrams.

Each UML diagram type supports multiple variations, and explaining them all would require an entire textbook. This chapter presents an overview and simple examples of several diagram types, which provides a good foundation for further study of the UML. You also can find several tutorials on the UML at *www.uml.org*.

 Watch the video *The UML*.

TWO TRUTHS & A LIE
What Is the UML?

1. The UML is a standard way to specify, construct, and document systems that use object-oriented methods; it is a modeling language.

2. The UML provides an easy-to-learn alternative to complicated programming languages such as Java, C++, C#, or Visual Basic.

3. The UML documentation is more than 800 pages and provides more than 10 diagram types.

The false statement is #2. The systems you develop using the UML probably will be implemented later in object-oriented programming languages such as Java, C++, C#, or Visual Basic.

Using UML Use Case Diagrams

The **use case diagram** shows how a business works from the perspective of those who actually interact with the business, such as employees, customers, and suppliers. Although users can also be governments, private organizations, machines, or other systems, it is easiest to think of them as people, so users are called actors and are represented by stick figures in use case diagrams. The actual use cases are represented by ovals.

Use cases do not necessarily represent all the functions of a system; they are the system functions or services that are visible to the system's actors. In other words, they represent the cases by which an actor uses and presumably benefits from the system. Determining all the cases for which users interact with systems helps you divide a system logically into functional parts.

Establishing use cases usually follows from analyzing the main events in a system. For example, from a librarian's point of view, two main events are `acquireNewBook()` and `checkOutBook()`. Figure 13-1 shows a use case diagram for these two events.

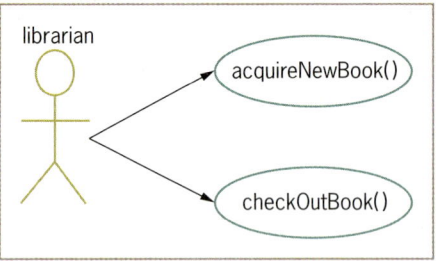

Figure 13-1 Use case diagram for librarian

 Many system developers would use the standard English form to describe activities in their UML diagrams— for example, **check out book** instead of **checkOutBook()**, which looks like a programming method call. Because you are used to seeing method names in camel casing and with trailing parentheses throughout this book, this discussion of the UML continues with the same format.

Many systems have variations in use cases. The three possible types of variations are:

- Extend
- Include
- Generalization

An **extend variation** is a use case variation that shows functions beyond those found in a base case. In other words, an extend variation is usually an optional activity. For example, checking out a book for a new library patron who doesn't have a library card is slightly more complicated than checking out a book for an existing patron. Each variation in the sequence of actions required in a use case is a **scenario**. Each use case has at least one main scenario, but the case might have several more that are extensions or variations of the main one. Figure 13-2 shows how you would diagram the relationship between the use case `checkOutBook()` and the more specific scenario `checkOutBookForNewPatron()`. Extended use cases are shown in an oval with a dashed arrow pointing to the more general base case.

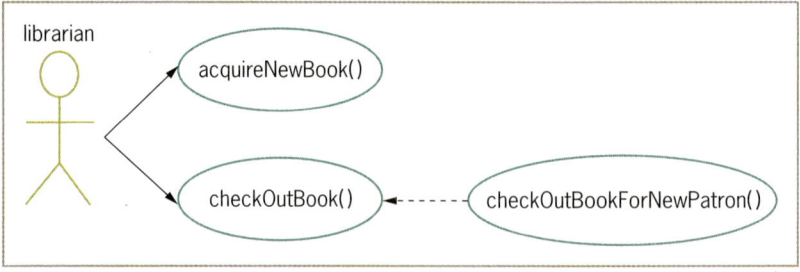

Figure 13-2 Use case diagram for librarian with scenario extension

Using UML Use Case Diagrams

For clarity, you can add <<extend>> near the line that shows a relationship extension. Such a feature, which adds to the UML vocabulary of shapes to make them more meaningful, is called a **stereotype**. Figure 13-3 includes a stereotype.

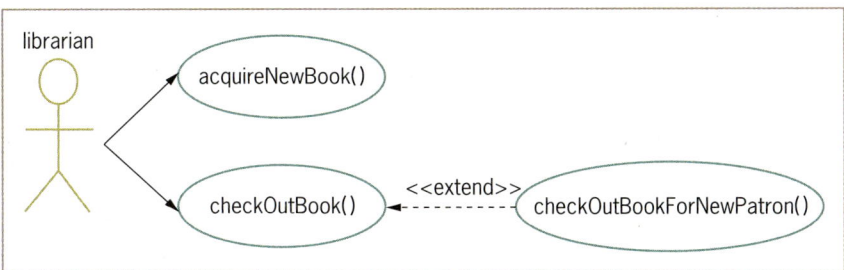

Figure 13-3 Use case diagram for librarian using stereotype

In addition to extend relationships, use case diagrams can also show include relationships. You use an **include variation** when a case can be part of multiple use cases. This concept is very much like that of a subroutine or submodule. You show an include use case in an oval with a dashed arrow pointing to the subroutine use case. For example, `issueLibraryCard()` might be a function of `checkOutBook()` used when a new patron checks out a book, but it might also be a function of `registerNewPatron()`, which occurs when a patron registers at the library but does not want to check out books yet. See Figure 13-4.

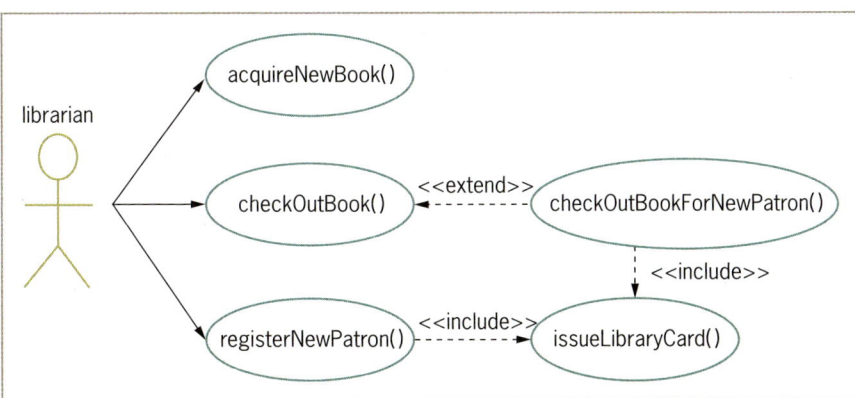

Figure 13-4 Use case diagram for librarian using include relationship

You use a **generalization variation** when a use case is less specific than others and you want to be able to substitute the more specific case for a general one. For example, a library has certain procedures for acquiring new materials, whether they are videos, tapes, CDs, hardcover books, or paperbacks. However, the procedures might become more specific during a particular acquisition—perhaps the librarian must procure plastic cases for circulating videos or assign locked storage locations for CDs. Figure 13-5 shows the generalization `acquireNewItem()` with two more specific situations: acquiring videos and acquiring CDs. The more specific scenarios are attached to the general scenario with open-headed dashed arrows.

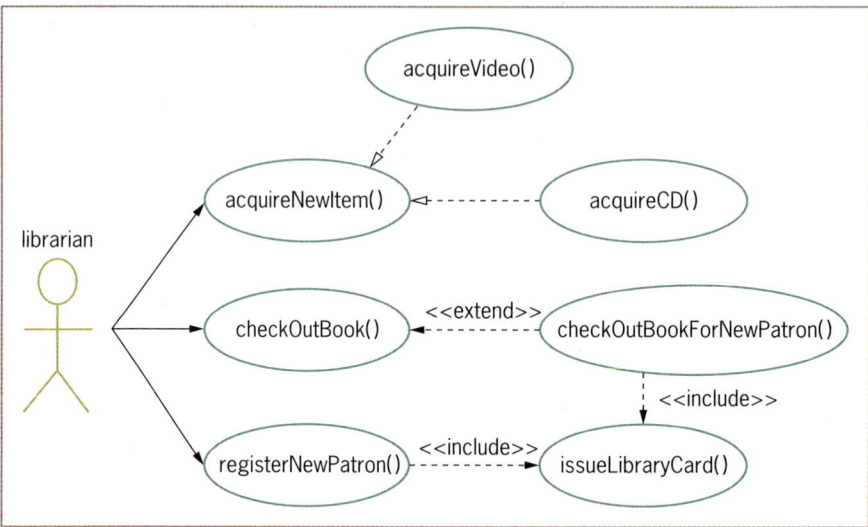

Figure 13-5 Use case diagram for librarian with generalizations

Many use case diagrams show multiple actors. For example, Figure 13-6 shows that a library clerk cannot perform as many functions as a librarian; the clerk can check out books and register new patrons but cannot acquire new materials.

Using UML Use Case Diagrams

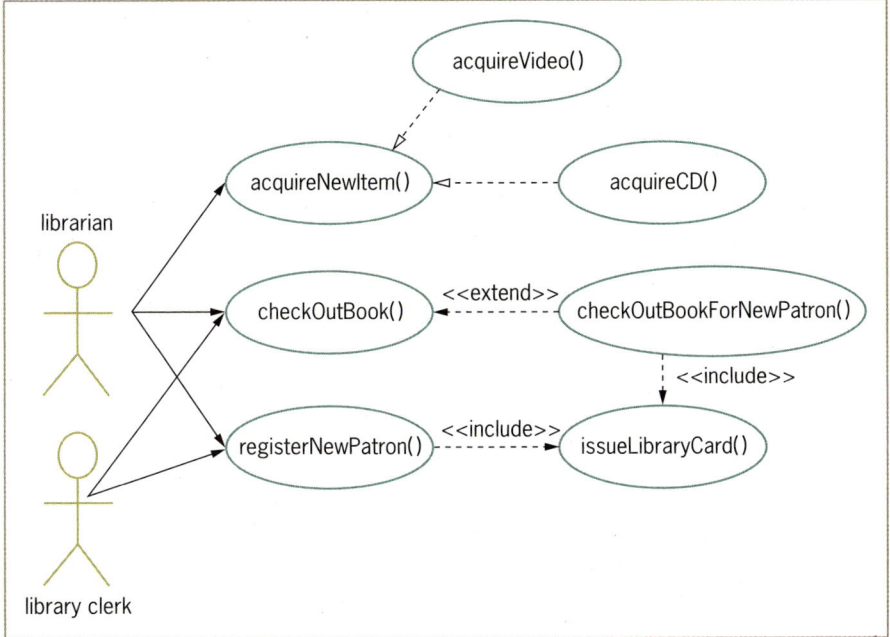

Figure 13-6 Use case diagram for librarian with multiple actors

While designing an actual library system, you could add many more use cases and actors to the use case diagram. The purpose of such a diagram is to encourage discussion between the system developer and the library staff. Library staff members do not need to know the technical details of the system that the analysts will eventually create, and they certainly do not need to understand computers or programming. However, by viewing the use cases, the library staff can visualize activities they perform while doing their jobs and correct the system developer if inaccuracies exist. The final software products developed for such a system are far more likely to satisfy users than those developed without this design step.

A use case diagram is only a tool to aid communication. No single "correct" use case diagram exists; you might correctly represent a system in several ways. For example, you might choose to emphasize the actors in the library system, as shown in Figure 13-7, or to emphasize system requirements, as shown in Figure 13-8. Diagrams that are too crowded are neither visually pleasing nor very useful. Therefore, the use case diagram in Figure 13-7 shows all the specific actors and their relationships, but purposely omits more specific system functions. By comparison, Figure 13-8 shows many actions that are often hidden from users, but purposely omits more specific actors. For example, the activities carried out to manageNetworkOutage(), if done properly, should be invisible to library patrons checking out books.

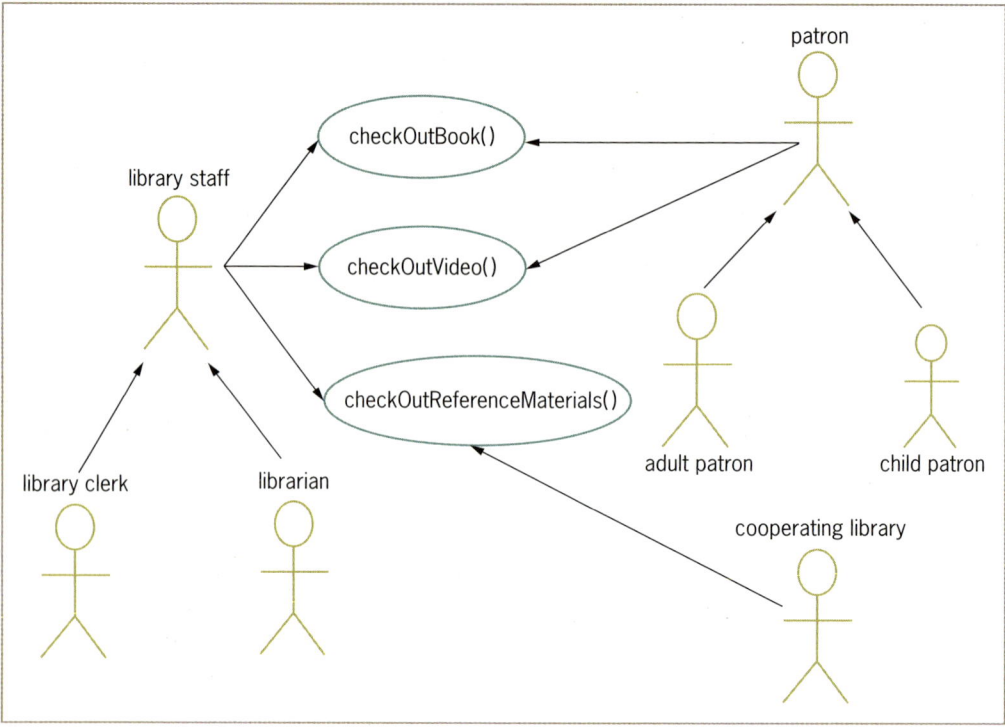

Figure 13-7 Use case diagram emphasizing actors

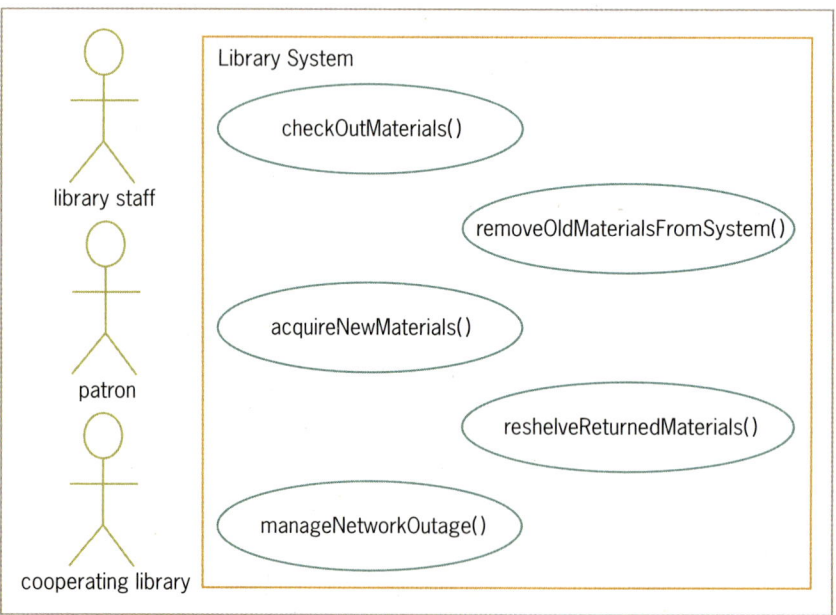

Figure 13-8 Use case diagram emphasizing system requirements

Using UML Class and Object Diagrams

In Figure 13-8, the relationship lines between the actors and use cases have been removed because the emphasis is on the system requirements, and too many lines would make the diagram confusing. When system developers omit parts of diagrams for clarity, they refer to the missing parts as **elided**. For the sake of clarity, eliding extraneous information is perfectly acceptable. The main purpose of UML diagrams is to facilitate clear communication.

TWO TRUTHS & A LIE

Using UML Use Case Diagrams

1. A use case diagram shows how a business works from the perspective of those who actually interact with the business.
2. Users are called actors and are represented by stick figures in use case diagrams. The actual use cases are represented by ovals.
3. Use cases are important because they describe all the functions of a system.

The false statement is #3. Use cases do not necessarily represent all the functions of a system; they are the system functions or services that are visible to the system's actors.

Using UML Class and Object Diagrams

You use a class diagram to illustrate the names, attributes, and methods of a class or set of classes. (You saw some examples in Chapter 10.) Class diagrams are more useful to a system's programmers than to its users because they closely resemble code the programmers will write. A class diagram illustrating a single class contains a rectangle divided into three sections: The top section contains the name of the class, the middle section contains the names of the attributes, and the bottom section contains the names of the methods. Figure 13-9 shows the class diagram for a Book class. Each Book object contains an idNum, title, and author. Each Book object also contains methods to create a Book when it is acquired, and to retrieve or get title and author information when the Book object's idNum is supplied.

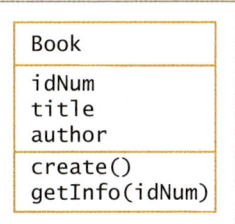

Figure 13-9 Book class diagram

In the preceding section, you learned how to use generalizations with use case diagrams to show general and more specific use cases. With use case diagrams, you drew an open-headed arrow from the more specific case to the more general one. Similarly, you can use generalizations with class diagrams to show more general (or parent) classes and more specific (or child) classes that inherit attributes from parents. (You learned about parent and child classes in Chapter 11.) For example, Figure 13-10 shows Book and Video classes that are more specific than the general LibraryItem class. All LibraryItem objects contain an idNum and title, but each Book item also contains an author, and each Video item also contains a runningTime. Child classes contain all the attributes of their parents and usually contain additional attributes not found in the parent.

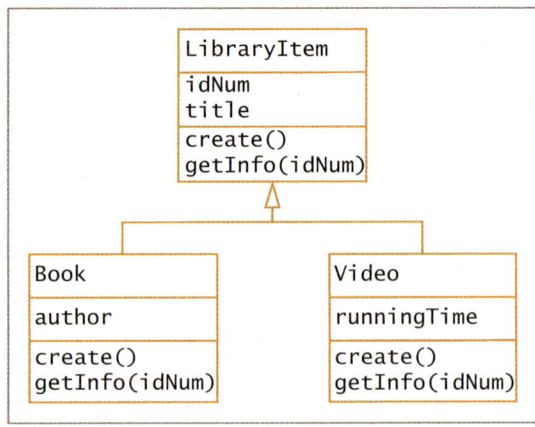

Figure 13-10   LibraryItem class diagram showing generalization

 When a child class contains a method with the same signature as one in the parent class, the child class version **overrides** the version in the parent class. That is, by default, the child class version is used with any child class object. The create() and getInfo() methods in the Book and Video classes override the versions in the LibraryItem class.

Class diagrams can include symbols that show the relationships between objects. You can show two types of relationships:

- An association relationship
- A whole-part relationship

An **association relationship** describes the connection or link between objects. You represent an association relationship between classes with a straight line. Frequently, you include information about the arithmetical relationship or ratio (called **cardinality** or **multiplicity**) of the objects. For example, Figure 13-11 shows the association relationship between a Library and the LibraryItems it lends. Exactly one Library object exists, and it can be associated with any number of LibraryItems from 0 to

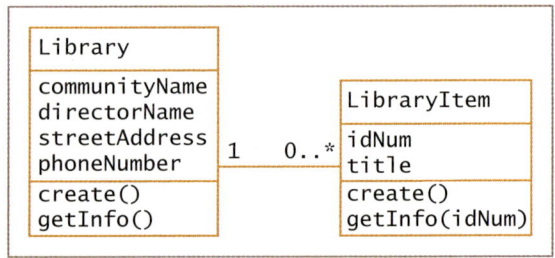

Figure 13-11   Class diagram with association relationship

infinity, which is represented by an asterisk. Figure 13-12 adds the `Patron` class to the diagram and shows how you indicate that any number of `Patrons` can be associated with the `Library`, but that each `Patron` can borrow only up to five `LibraryItems` at a time, or currently might not be borrowing any. In addition, each `LibraryItem` can be associated with one `Patron` at most, but at any given time might not be on loan.

As you learned in Chapter 11, a whole-part relationship describes an association that uses composition. In other words, it is a relationship in which one or more classes make up the parts of a larger whole class. For example, 50 states make up the United States, and 10 departments might make up a company. This type of relationship is represented by a filled diamond at the "whole part"

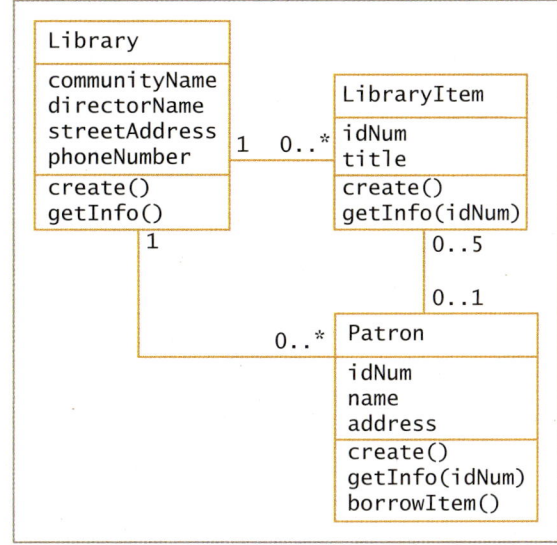

Figure 13-12 Class diagram with several association relationships

end of the line that indicates the relationship. You can also call a whole-part relationship a *has-a relationship* because the phrase describes the association between the whole and one of its parts; for example, "The library has a Circulation Department." Figure 13-13 shows a whole-part relationship for a `Library`.

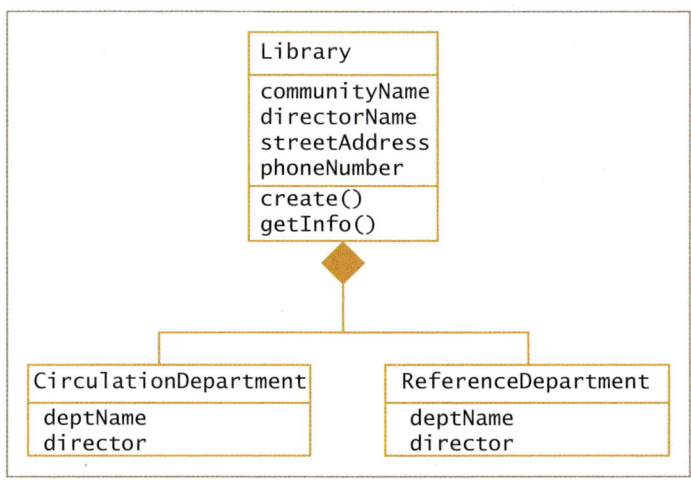

Figure 13-13 Class diagram with whole-part relationship

When a part is completely owned by a whole and ceases to exist without the whole, then the relationship is called composition, and the diamond in the UML diagram is filled as in Figure 13-13. For example, composition describes the relationship between a `Hotel` and its `Lobby`. When the part also exists without the whole or belongs to other wholes, then the relationship is called an **aggregation**, and the diamond is open. For example, aggregation describes the relationship between a `Customer` and a `Hotel` if the `Customer` is also part of a `CarRental` and `Restaurant` class.

Object diagrams are similar to class diagrams, but they model specific instances of classes. You use an object diagram to show a snapshot of an object at one point in time, so you can more easily understand its relationship to other objects. Imagine looking at the travelers in a major airport. If you try to watch them all at once, you see a flurry of activity, but it is hard to understand all the tasks a traveler must accomplish, such as buying a ticket and checking luggage. However, if you concentrate on one traveler and follow his or her actions through the airport from arrival to takeoff, you get a clearer picture of the required activities. An object diagram serves the same purpose; you concentrate on a specific instance of a class to better understand how a class works.

Figure 13-14 contains an object diagram showing the relationship between one `Library`, `LibraryItem`, and `Patron`. Notice the similarities between Figures 13-12 and 13-14. If you need to describe the relationships among three classes, you can use either model—a class diagram or an object diagram—interchangeably. You simply use the model that seems clearer to you and your intended audience.

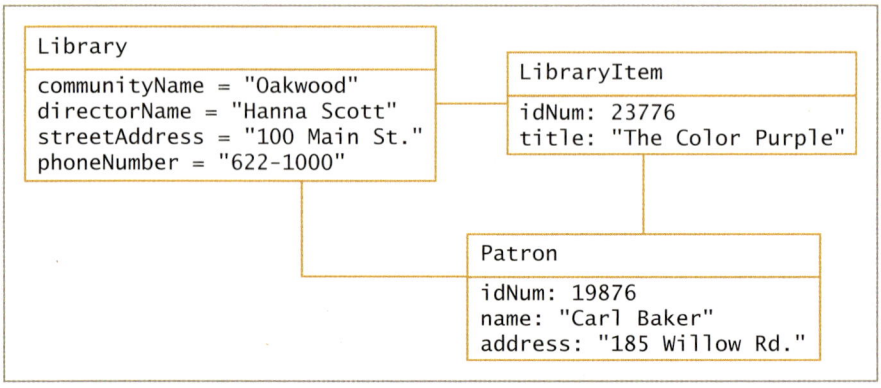

Figure 13-14 Object diagram for `Library`

Watch the video *Class and Object Diagrams*.

> **TWO TRUTHS & A LIE**
>
> Using UML Class and Object Diagrams
>
> 1. Class diagrams are most useful to a system's users because they are much easier to understand than program code.
>
> 2. A class diagram illustrating a single class contains a rectangle divided into three sections: The top section contains the name of the class, the middle section contains the names of the attributes, and the bottom section contains the names of the methods.
>
> 3. A whole-part relationship describes an association in which one or more classes make up the parts of a larger whole class; this type of relationship is also called an aggregation.
>
> The false statement is #1. Class diagrams are more useful to a system's programmers than to its users because they closely resemble the code the programmers will write.

Using Other UML Diagrams

The wide variety of UML diagrams allow you to illustrate systems from many perspectives. You have already read about use case diagrams, class diagrams, and object diagrams. This section provides a brief overview of other UML diagram types.

Sequence Diagrams

You use a **sequence diagram** to show the timing of events in a single use case. A sequence diagram makes it easier to see the order in which activities occur. The horizontal axis (x-axis) of a sequence diagram represents objects, and the vertical axis (y-axis) represents time. You create a sequence diagram by placing objects that are part of an activity across the top of the diagram along the x-axis, starting at the left with the object or actor that begins the action. Beneath each object on the x-axis, you place a vertical dashed line that represents the period of time the object exists. Then, you use horizontal arrows to show how the objects communicate with each other over time.

In a sequence diagram, time increases vertically down the diagram. A *timing diagram* is a type of sequence diagram in which the time axis is represented horizontally.

For example, Figure 13-15 shows a sequence diagram for a scenario that a librarian can use to create a book check-out record. The librarian begins a `create()` method with `Patron idNum` and `Book idNum` information. The `BookCheckOutRecord` object requests additional `Patron` information (such as `name` and `address`) from the `Patron` object with the correct `Patron idNum`, and additional `Book` information (such as `title` and `author`) from the `Book` object with the correct `Book idNum`. When `BookCheckOutRecord` contains all the data it needs, a completed record is returned to the librarian.

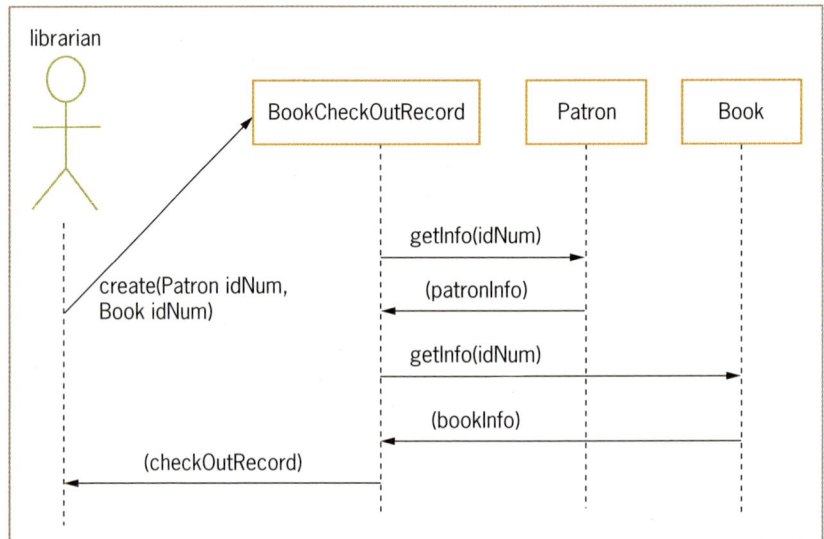

Figure 13-15 Sequence diagram for checking out a `Book` for a `Patron`

 In Figures 13-15 and 13-16, `patronInfo` and `bookInfo` represent group items that contain all of a `Patron`'s and `Book`'s data. For example, `patronInfo` might contain `idNum`, `lastName`, `firstName`, `address`, and `phoneNumber`, all of which have been defined as attributes of that class.

Communication Diagrams

A **communication diagram** emphasizes the organization of objects that participate in a system. It is similar to a sequence diagram, except that it contains sequence numbers to represent the precise order in which activities occur. Communication diagrams focus on object roles instead of the times that messages are sent. Figure 13-16 shows the same

Using Other UML Diagrams

sequence of events as Figure 13-15, but the steps to creating a `BookCheckOutRecord` are clearly numbered. Decimal numbered steps (1.1, 1.2, and so on) represent substeps of the main steps. Checking out a library book is a fairly straightforward event, so a sequence diagram sufficiently illustrates the process. Communication diagrams become more useful with more complicated systems.

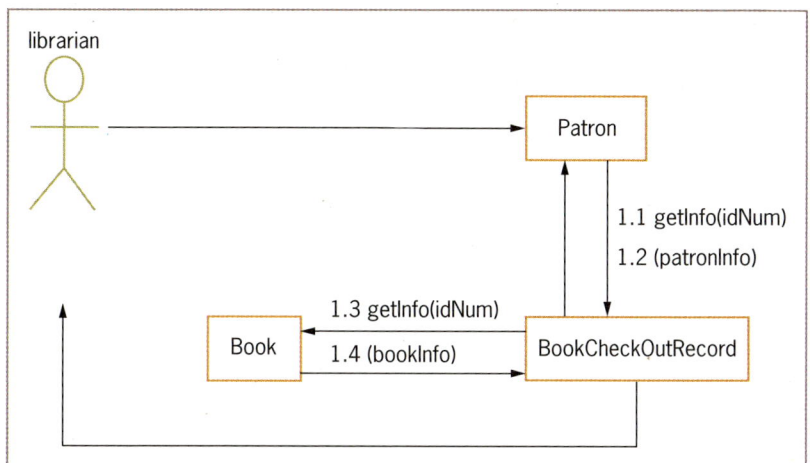

Figure 13-16 Communication diagram for checking out a `Book` for a `Patron`

State Machine Diagrams

Like use case diagrams, state machine and activity diagrams both illustrate the behavior of a system.

A **state machine diagram** shows the different statuses of a class or object at different points in time. You use a state machine diagram to illustrate aspects of a system that show interesting changes in behavior as time passes. Conventionally, you use rounded rectangles to represent each state and labeled arrows to show the sequence in which events affect the states. A solid dot indicates the start and stop states for the class or object. Figure 13-17 contains a state machine diagram that describes the states of a `Book`.

 To make sure that your diagrams are clear, you should use the correct symbol in each UML diagram you create, just as you should use the correct symbol in each program flowchart. However, if you create a flowchart and use a rectangle for an input or output statement where a parallelogram is conventional, others will still understand your meaning. Similarly, with UML diagrams, the exact shape you use is not nearly as important as the sequence of events and relationships between objects.

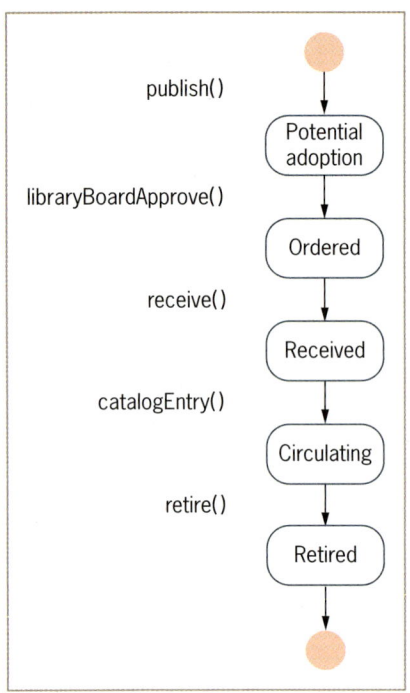

Figure 13-17 State machine diagram for states of a Book

Activity Diagrams

The UML diagram that most closely resembles a conventional flowchart is an activity diagram. In an **activity diagram**, you show the flow of actions of a system, including branches that occur when decisions affect the outcome. Conventionally, activity diagrams use flowchart start and stop symbols (called lozenges) to describe actions and solid dots to represent start and stop states. Like flowcharts, activity diagrams use diamonds to describe decisions. Unlike the diamonds in flowcharts, the diamonds in UML activity diagrams usually are empty; the possible outcomes are documented along the branches emerging from the decision symbol.

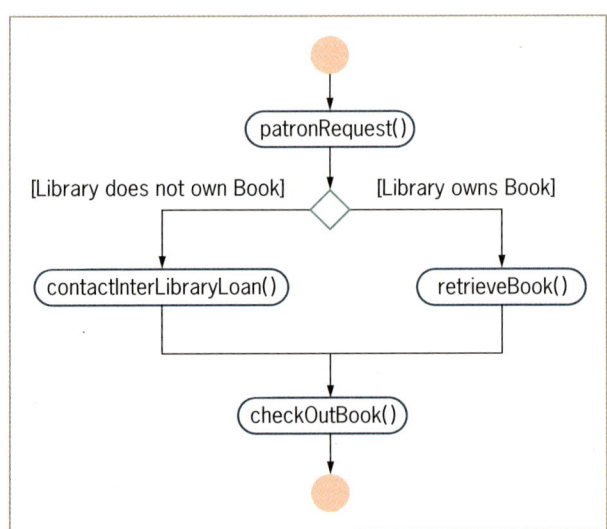

Figure 13-18 Activity diagram showing branch

As an example, Figure 13-18 shows a simple activity diagram with a single branch.

Many real-life systems contain actions that are meant to occur simultaneously. For example, when you apply for a home mortgage with a bank, a bank officer might perform a credit or background check while an appraiser determines the value of the house you are buying. When both actions are complete, the loan process continues. UML activity diagrams use forks and joins to show simultaneous activities. A **fork** is similar to a decision, but whereas the flow of control follows only one path after a decision, a fork defines a branch in which all paths are followed simultaneously or concurrently. A **join**, as its name implies, reunites the flow of control after a fork. You indicate forks and joins with thick straight lines. Figure 13-19 shows how you might model the way an interlibrary loan system processes book requests. When a request is received, simultaneous searches begin at three local libraries that are part of the library system.

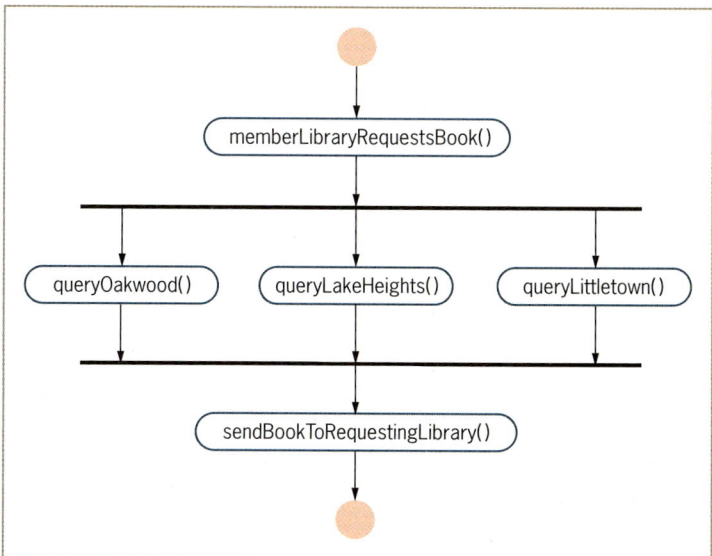

Figure 13-19 Activity diagram showing fork and join

An activity diagram can contain a time signal. A **time signal** indicates that a specific amount of time should pass before an action starts. The time signal looks like two stacked triangles (resembling the shape of an hourglass). Figure 13-20 shows a time signal indicating that if a patron requests a book checked out to another patron, then only if the book's due date has passed should a request be issued to return the book. In activity diagrams for other systems, you might see explanations at time signals, such as "10 hours have passed" or "at least January 1." If an action is time-dependent, whether by a fraction of a second or by years, using a time signal is appropriate.

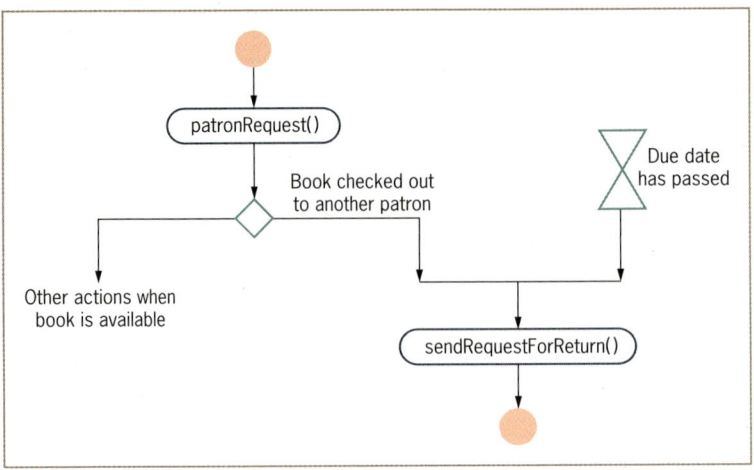

Figure 13-20 A time signal starting an action

Component and Deployment Diagrams

Component and deployment diagrams model the physical aspects of systems. You use a **component diagram** when you want to emphasize the files, database tables, documents, and other components used by a system's software. You use a **deployment diagram** when you want to focus on a system's hardware. You can use a variety of icons in each type of diagram, but each icon must convey meaning to the reader. Figures 13-21 and 13-22 show component and deployment diagrams, respectively, that illustrate aspects of a library system. Figure 13-21 contains icons that symbolize paper and Internet requests for library items, the library database, and two tables that constitute the database. Figure 13-22 shows some commonly used icons that represent hardware components.

A **communication diagram** is a UML diagram that emphasizes the organization of objects that participate in a system.

A **state machine diagram** is a UML diagram that shows the different statuses of a class or object at different points in time.

An **activity diagram** is a UML diagram that shows the flow of actions of a system, including branches that occur when decisions affect the outcome.

A **fork** is a feature of a UML activity diagram; it is similar to a decision, but whereas the flow of control follows only one path after a decision, a fork defines a branch in which all paths are followed simultaneously or concurrently.

A **join** is a feature of a UML activity diagram; it reunites the flow of control after a fork.

A **time signal** is a UML diagram symbol indicating that a specific amount of time has passed before an action is started.

A **component diagram** is a UML diagram that emphasizes the files, database tables, documents, and other components used by a system's software.

A **deployment diagram** is a UML diagram that focuses on a system's hardware.

A **profile diagram** is used to extend a UML model for a particular domain or platform.

A **protected node** is the UML diagram name for an exception-throwing try block.

A **handler body node** is the UML diagram name for an exception-handling catch block.

Review Questions

1. The detailed specification of how all the parts of a system will be implemented and coordinated is called _____.

    a. programming
    b. paraphrasing
    c. system design
    d. structuring

2. The primary purpose of good modeling techniques is to _____.

    a. promote communication
    b. increase functional cohesion
    c. reduce the need for structure
    d. reduce dependency between modules

3. The UML provides standard ways to do all of the following to business systems except _____ them.

    a. construct
    b. document
    c. describe
    d. destroy

CHAPTER 13 System Modeling with the UML

4. The UML is commonly used to model all of the following except _____.

    a. computer programs
    b. business activities
    c. organizational processes
    d. software systems

5. The UML was intentionally designed to be _____.

    a. low-level, detail-oriented
    b. used with Visual Basic
    c. nontechnical
    d. inexpensive

6. The UML diagrams that show how a business works from the perspective of those who actually interact with the business, such as employees or customers, are _____ diagrams.

    a. communication
    b. use case
    c. state machine
    d. class

7. Which of the following would be portrayed as an extend relationship in a use case diagram for a hospital?

    a. the relationship between the head nurse and the floor nurses
    b. admitting a patient who has never been admitted before
    c. serving a meal
    d. scheduling the monitoring of patients' vital signs

8. The people shown in use case diagrams are called _____.

    a. workers
    b. clowns
    c. actors
    d. relatives

9. One aspect of use case diagrams that makes them difficult to learn is that _____.

    a. they require programming experience to understand
    b. they use a technical vocabulary
    c. there is no single right answer for any case
    d. all of the above

10. The arithmetic association relationship between a college student and college courses would be expressed as _____.

    a. 1   0
    b. 1   1
    c. 1   0..*
    d. 0..* 0..*

Review Questions

11. In the UML, object diagrams are most similar to _____ diagrams.
    a. use case
    b. activity
    c. class
    d. sequence

12. In any given situation, you should choose the type of UML diagram that is _____ .
    a. shorter than others
    b. clearer than others
    c. more detailed than others
    d. closest to the programming language you will use to implement the system

13. A whole-part relationship can be described as a(n) _____ relationship.
    a. parent-child
    b. has-a
    c. is-a
    d. creates-a

14. The timing of events is best portrayed in a(n) _____ diagram.
    a. sequence
    b. use case
    c. communication
    d. association

15. A communication diagram is closest to a(n) _____ diagram.
    a. activity
    b. use case
    c. deployment
    d. sequence

16. A(n) _____ diagram shows the different statuses of a class or object at different points in time.
    a. activity
    b. state machine
    c. sequence
    d. deployment

17. The UML diagram that most closely resembles a conventional flowchart is a(n) _____ diagram.
    a. activity
    b. state machine
    c. sequence
    d. deployment

18. You use a _____ diagram when you want to emphasize the files, database tables, documents, and other components used by a system's software.
    a. state machine
    b. component
    c. deployment
    d. use case

19. The UML diagram that focuses on a system's hardware is a(n) _____ diagram.

   a. deployment
   b. sequence
   c. activity
   d. use case

20. When using the UML to describe a single system, most designers would use _____.

   a. a single type of diagram
   b. at least three types of diagrams
   c. most of the available types of diagrams
   d. all the types of diagrams

Exercises

1. Complete the following tasks:

   a. Develop a use case diagram for a convenience food store. Include an actor representing the store manager and use cases for orderItem(), stockItem(), and sellItem().

   b. Add more use cases to the diagram you created in Exercise 1a. Include two generalizations for stockItem() called stockPerishable() and stockNonPerishable(). Also include an extension to sellItem() called checkCredit() for cases in which a customer purchases items using a credit card.

   c. Add a customer actor to the use case diagram you created in Exercise 1b. Show that the customer participates in sellItem(), but not in orderItem() or stockItem().

2. Develop a use case diagram for a department store credit card system. Include at least two actors and four use cases.

3. Develop a use case diagram for a college registration system. Include at least three actors and five use cases.

4. Develop a class diagram for a Yard class that describes objects serviced by a landscaping maintenance company. Include at least four attributes and three methods.

5. Develop a class diagram for a Shape class. Include generalizations for child classes Rectangle, Circle, and Triangle.

6. Develop a class diagram for a Message class for a cell phone company. Include generalizations for child classes TextMessage, VideoMessage, and VoiceMessage.

Exercises

7. Develop a class diagram for a college registration system. Include at least three classes that cooperate to register students.

8. Develop a sequence diagram that shows how a clerk at a mail-order company places a customer `Order`. The `Order` accesses `Inventory` to check availability. Then, the `Order` accesses `Invoice` to produce a customer invoice that returns to the clerk.

9. Develop a state machine diagram that shows the states of an `Employee` from `Applicant` to `Retiree`.

10. Develop a state machine diagram that shows the states of a `Movie` from `Concept` to `Production`.

11. Develop an activity diagram that illustrates how to throw a party.

12. Develop an activity diagram that illustrates how to clean a room.

13. Develop the UML diagram of your choice that illustrates some aspect of your life.

14. Complete the following tasks:

    a. Develop the UML diagram of your choice that best illustrates some aspect of a place you have worked.

    b. Develop a different UML diagram type that illustrates the same functions as the diagram you created in Exercise 14a.

Find the Bugs

15. Your downloadable student files for Chapter 13 include DEBUG13-01.doc, DEBUG13-02.doc, and DEBUG13-03.doc. Each file contains some comments that describe a problem and a UML diagram that has one or more bugs you must find and correct.

Game Zone

16. Develop a use case diagram for a baseball game. Include actors representing a player and an umpire. Create use cases for `hitBall()`, `runBases()`, and `makeCallAtBase()`. Include two generalizations for `makeCallAtBase()` named `callSafe()` and `callOut()`.

17. Develop a class diagram for a `CardGame` class. Include generalizations for child classes `SolitaireCardGame` and `OpponentCardGame`.

18. Choose a child's game such as Hide and Seek or Duck, Duck, Goose and describe it using UML diagrams of your choice.

Up for Discussion

19. Which do you think you would enjoy more on the job—designing large systems that contain many programs, or writing the programs themselves? Why?

20. In earlier chapters, you considered ethical dilemmas in writing programs that select candidates for organ transplants. Are the ethical responsibilities of a system designer different from those of a programmer? If so, how?

CHAPTER 14

Using Relational Databases

In this chapter, you will learn about:

- Relational database fundamentals
- Creating databases and table descriptions
- Primary keys
- Database structure notation
- Working with records within a table
- Creating queries
- Relationships between tables
- Poor table design
- Anomalies, normal forms, and normalization
- Database performance and security issues

CHAPTER 14 Using Relational Databases

Understanding Relational Database Fundamentals

In Chapter 7, you learned that when you store data items for use within computer systems, they are often stored in a data hierarchy that is organized as follows:

- **Characters** are the smallest usable units of data—for example, a letter, digit, or punctuation mark is a character. When characters are stored in a computer, they are created from smaller pieces called bits, which represent computer circuitry, but human users seldom care about bits; characters have meaning to users.

- **Fields** are formed from groups of characters and represent a piece of information, such as firstName, lastName, or socialSecurityNumber.

- **Records** are formed from groups of related fields. The fields go together because they represent attributes of some entity, such as an employee, a customer, an inventory item, or a bank account.

- **Files** are composed of associated records; for example, a file might contain a record for each employee in a company or each account at a bank.

Most organizations store many files that contain the data they need to operate their businesses; for example, businesses often need to maintain files of data about employees, customers, inventory items, and orders. Many organizations use a database to organize and coordinate the information in these files. A **database** holds a group of files that an organization needs to support its applications. In a database, the files often are called **tables** because you can arrange their contents in rows and columns. Real-life examples of these tables abound. For example, consider the listings in a telephone book. Each listing might contain four columns, as shown in Figure 14-1—last name, first name, street address, and phone number. You can see that each column represents a field and that each row represents one record. You can picture a table within a database in the same way.

Last Name	First Name	Address	Phone
Abbott	William	123 Oak Lane	490-8920
Ackerman	Kimberly	467 Elm Drive	787-2781
Adams	Stanley	8120 Pine Street	787-0129
Adams	Violet	347 Oak Lane	490-8912
Adams	William	12 Second Street	490-3667

Figure 14-1 A telephone book table

Arrays (stored in memory) and tables (stored in databases) are similar in that both contain rows and columns. In an array, each element must have the same data type. The same is not true for tables stored in databases.

Understanding Relational Database Fundamentals

 Sometimes, one record or row is also called an **entity**; however, many definitions of *entity* exist in database texts. For example, some developers refer to a table as an entity. One column (field) can also be called an **attribute**.

Figure 14-1 includes five records, each representing a unique person. It is relatively easy to scan this short list of names to find a person's phone number; of course, telephone books contain many more records. The records are in alphabetical order by last name. Some users might prefer alternate orders. For example, telemarketers or phone company employees might prefer to have records organized in telephone-number order, and door-to-door salespeople might prefer street-address order. Using a computerized database is convenient because the stored data can easily be sorted and displayed to fit each user's needs.

Unless you are using a telephone book for a very small town, a last name alone often is not sufficient to identify a person. In the example in Figure 14-1, three people have the last name of Adams. For these records, you need to examine the first name before you can determine the correct phone number. In a large city, many people might have the same first and last names; in that case, you might also need to examine the street address to identify a person. As with the telephone book, most computerized database tables need to have a way to identify each record uniquely, even if it means using multiple columns. A value that uniquely identifies a record is called a **primary key**, or a **key** for short. Key fields often are defined as a single table column, but as with the telephone book, keys can be constructed from multiple columns; such a key is a **compound key**, or **composite key**.

Telephone books are republished periodically because changes have occurred—people have left or moved into the city, canceled service, or changed phone numbers. With computerized database tables, you also need to add, delete, and modify records, although usually with more frequency than phone books are published.

Computerized database tables frequently contain thousands of records, or rows, and each row might contain entries in dozens of columns. Handling and organizing all the data in an organization's tables requires sophisticated software. **Database management software** is a set of programs that allows users to:

- Create table descriptions.
- Identify keys.
- Add, delete, and update records within a table.
- Arrange records within a table so they are sorted by different fields.
- Write questions that select specific records from a table for viewing.
- Write questions that combine information from multiple tables. This is possible because the database management software establishes and maintains relationships between the columns in the tables. A group of database tables from which you can make these connections is a **relational database**.
- Create reports for interpreting data, and create forms for viewing and entering data using interactive screens.
- Keep data secure by employing sophisticated security measures.

Each database management software package operates differently; however, with each, you perform the same types of tasks.

> **TWO TRUTHS & A LIE**
>
> Understanding Relational Database Fundamentals
>
> 1. Files are composed of associated records, and records are composed of fields.
> 2. In a database, files often are called tables because you can arrange their contents in rows and columns.
> 3. Key fields always are defined as a single table column.
>
> The false statement is #3. Key fields often are defined as a single table column, but keys can be constructed from multiple columns; such a key is a compound key.

Creating Databases and Table Descriptions

Creating a useful database requires planning and analysis. You must decide what data will be stored, how that data will be divided between tables, and how the tables will interrelate. Before you create any tables, you must create the database itself. With most database software packages, creating the database that will hold the tables requires nothing more than naming it and indicating the physical location, perhaps a hard disk drive, where the database will be stored. When you save a table, it is conventional to provide a name that begins with the prefix *tbl*—for example, `tblCustomers`. Your databases often become filled with a variety of objects—tables, forms for data entry, reports that organize the data for viewing, queries that select subsets of data for viewing, and so on. Using naming conventions, such as beginning each table name with a prefix that identifies it as a table, helps you keep track of the objects in your system.

When you save a table description, many database management programs suggest a default, generic table name such as `Table1`. Usually, a more descriptive name is more useful as you create objects.

Before you can enter data into a database table, you must design the table. It is important to think carefully about the original design of a database. After the database has been created and data has been entered, it could be difficult and time consuming to make changes.

At minimum, designing a table requires that you choose columns for it and then provide names and data types for each column. A table description closely resembles the list of variables that you have used with every program throughout this book. For example, assume you are designing a customer database table. Figure 14-2 shows some column names and data types you might use.

Creating Databases and Table Descriptions

Column	Data Type
customerID	text
lastName	text
firstName	text
streetAddress	text
balanceOwed	numeric

Figure 14-2 Customer table description

The table description in Figure 14-2 uses just two data types—text and numeric. Text columns can hold any type of characters—letters or digits. Numeric columns can hold numbers only. Depending on the database management software, you might have many more sophisticated data types at your disposal. For example, some database software divides the numeric data type into several subcategories such as integer values (whole number only) and double-precision numbers (which contain decimals). Other options might include special categories for currency numbers (representing dollars and cents), dates, and Boolean columns (representing true or false). At the least, all database software recognizes the distinction between text and numeric data.

Throughout this book, you have been aware of the distinction that computers make between text and numeric data. Because of the way computers handle data, every type of software observes this distinction. Throughout this book, the term *string* has been used to describe text fields. The term *text* is used in this chapter only because popular database packages use this term.

Unassigned variables within computer programs might be empty (containing a null value), or they might contain unknown or garbage values. Similarly, columns in database tables might also contain null or unknown values. When a field in a database contains a null value, it does not mean that the field holds a 0 or a space; it means that no data has been entered for the field at all. Although *null* and *empty* are used synonymously by many database developers, the terms have slightly different meanings to some professionals, such as Visual Basic programmers.

The table description in Figure 14-2 uses one-word column names and camel casing, in the same way that variable names have been defined throughout this book. Many database software packages allow multiple-word column names with embedded spaces, but many database table designers prefer single-word names because they resemble variable names in programs. In addition, when you write programs that access a database table, the single-word field names can be used "as is," without special syntax to indicate the names that represent a single field. Also, when you use a single word to label each database column, it is easier to understand whether one column or several are being referenced.

The `customerID` column in Figure 14-2 is defined as text. If `customerID` numbers are composed entirely of digits, this column could also be defined as numeric. However, many database designers feel that columns should be defined as numeric only if necessary—that is, only if they might be used in arithmetic calculations. The description in Figure 14-2 follows this convention by declaring `customerID` as text.

 Watch the video *Creating Databases*.

Many database management software packages allow you to add a narrative description of each data column to a table. These comments become part of the table, but do not affect the way it operates; they simply serve as documentation for those who are reading a table description. For example, you might want to make a note that `customerID` should consist of five digits, or that `balanceOwed` should not exceed a given limit. Some software allows you to specify that values for a certain column are required—the user cannot create a record without providing data for these columns. In addition, you might be able to indicate range limits for a column—high and low values between which the column contents must fall. In some database programs, the comments fields are called *memos*.

> **TWO TRUTHS & A LIE**
>
> **Creating Databases and Table Descriptions**
>
> 1. When you save a table, it is conventional to provide a name that begins with the prefix *table*.
>
> 2. Designing a table involves deciding what columns your table needs, providing names for them, and providing a data type for each column.
>
> 3. Many database table designers prefer single-word column names because they resemble variable names in programs, they can be easily used in programs, and they make it easier to understand whether one column or several are being referenced.
>
> The false statement is # 1. When you save a table, it is conventional to provide a name that begins with the prefix *tbl*.

Identifying Primary Keys

In most tables you create for a database, you want to identify a column or a combination of columns as the table's key column or field (or primary key). The primary key in a table is the column that makes each record different from all others. For example, in the customer table in Figure 14-2, the logical choice for a primary key is the `customerID` column—each record entered into the customer table has a unique value in this column.

Identifying Primary Keys

Many customers might have the same first name or last name (or both), and multiple customers might have the same street address or balance due. However, each customer possesses a unique ID number.

Other typical examples of primary keys include:

- A student ID number in a table that contains college student information
- A part number in a table that contains inventory items
- A state abbreviation in a table that contains sales information for each state in the United States

In some database software packages, such as Microsoft Access, you indicate a primary key simply by selecting a column name and clicking a button that is labeled with a key icon.

In each of these examples, the primary key uniquely identifies the row. For example, each student has a unique ID number assigned by the college. Other columns in a student table would not be adequate keys—many students have the same last name, first name, hometown, or major. Often, keys are numbers. Usually, assigning a number to each row in a table is the simplest and most efficient method of obtaining a useful key. However, a table's key can be a text field, as in the state abbreviation example.

Sometimes, several columns could serve as the key. For example, if an employee record contains both a company-assigned employee ID and a Social Security number, then both columns are **candidate keys**. After you choose a primary key from candidate keys, the remaining candidate keys become **alternate keys**. (Many database developers would object to using a Social Security number as a primary key because of privacy issues.)

The primary key is important for several reasons:

- You can configure your database software to prevent multiple records from containing the same value in this column, thus avoiding data-entry errors.
- You can sort your records in this order before displaying or printing them.
- You use the primary key column when setting up relationships between this table and others that will become part of the same database.
- You need to understand the concept of the primary key when you normalize a database—a concept you will learn more about later in this chapter.

In some tables, when no identifying number has been assigned to the rows, a primary key must be constructed from multiple columns, making it a compound key. For example, consider Figure 14-3, which might be used by a residence hall administrator to store data about students living on a university campus. Each room in a building has a number and two students, each assigned to either bed A or bed B.

hall	room	bed	lastName	firstName	major
Adams	101	A	Fredricks	Madison	Chemistry
Adams	101	B	Garza	Lupe	Psychology
Adams	102	A	Liu	Jennifer	CIS
Adams	102	B	Smith	Crystal	CIS
Browning	101	A	Patel	Sarita	CIS
Browning	101	B	Smith	Margaret	Biology
Browning	102	A	Jefferson	Martha	Psychology
Browning	102	B	Bartlett	Donna	Spanish
Churchill	101	A	Wong	Cheryl	CIS
Churchill	101	B	Smith	Madison	Chemistry
Churchill	102	A	Patel	Jennifer	Psychology
Churchill	102	B	Jones	Elizabeth	CIS

Figure 14-3 Table containing residence hall student records

In Figure 14-3, no single column can serve as a primary key. Many students live in the same residence hall, and the same room numbers exist in the different residence halls. In addition, some students have the same last name, first name, or major. It is even possible that two students with the same first name, last name, or major are assigned to the same room. In this case, the best primary key is a multicolumn key that combines residence hall, room number, and bed number (hall, room, and bed). "Adams 101 A" identifies a single room and student, as does "Churchill 102 B". A primary key should be **immutable**, meaning that a value does not change during normal operation. In other words, in Figure 14-3, "Adams 102 A" will always pertain to a fixed location, even though the resident or her major might change. Of course, the school might choose to change the name of a residence hall—for example, to honor a benefactor—but that action would fall outside the range of "normal operation."

As an alternative to selecting three columns to create the compound key in Figure 14-3, many database designers would prefer that the college uniquely number every bed on campus and add a new column to the database for the ID number. Many database designers feel that a primary key should be short to minimize the amount of required storage in all the tables that refer to it.

Even if only one student was named Smith, for example, or only one Psychology major was listed in Figure 14-3, those fields still would not be good primary key candidates because of the potential for future Smiths and Psychology majors within the database. Analyzing existing data is not a foolproof way to select a good key; you must also consider likely future data.

Usually, after you have identified the necessary fields, data types, and the primary key, you are ready to save your table description and begin to enter data.

TWO TRUTHS & A LIE
Identifying Primary Keys

1. The primary key in a table is the record that has different data in its columns from all other records.
2. A multicolumn key is needed when no single column in a table contains unique data for a record.
3. You usually enter database data after all the fields and keys have been determined.

The false statement is #1. The primary key in a table is the column that makes each record different from all others.

Understanding Database Structure Notation

A shorthand way to describe a table is to use the table name followed by parentheses that contain all the field names, with the primary key underlined. (Some database designers insert an asterisk after the key instead of underlining it.) Thus, when a table is named **tblStudents** and contains columns named `idNumber`, `lastName`, `firstName`, and `gradePointAverage`, and `idNumber` is the key, you can reference the table using the following notation:

tblStudents(<u>idNumber</u>, lastName, firstName, gradePointAverage)

Although this shorthand notation does not provide information about data types or range limits on values, it does provide a quick overview of the table's structure. The key does not have to be the first attribute listed in a table reference, but frequently it is.

TWO TRUTHS & A LIE
Understanding Database Structure Notation

1. A shorthand way to describe a table is to use the table name followed by parentheses that contain all the field names.
2. Typically, when you describe a table using database structure notation, the primary key is underlined.
3. Database structure notation provides information about column names, their data types, and their range limits.

The false statement is #3. Although this shorthand notation does not provide information about data types or range limits on values, it does provide a quick overview of the table's structure.

Working with Records within Tables

The records in most databases are continuously changing. Personnel must frequently add, delete, update, and sort database records.

Entering data into an existing table is not difficult, but it can require a good deal of time and accurate typing. Depending on the application, the contents of the tables might be entered over the course of months or years by many data-entry personnel. Entering data of the wrong type is not allowed by most database applications. In addition, you might set up your table to prevent duplicate data in specific fields, or to prevent data entry outside of specified bounds in certain fields. With some database software, you type data into rows representing each record and columns representing each field in each record, much as you would enter data into a spreadsheet. With other software, you can create on-screen forms to make data entry more user-friendly. Some software does not allow you to enter a partial record; that is, you might not be allowed to leave fields blank.

In some organizations, data values are not entered manually but are scanned from an original source, greatly reducing the chances for error. For example, purchases can be scanned at the point of sale in a retail store, and patient wristbands and medicines can be scanned by healthcare workers in a hospital.

Deleting and modifying records in a database table are also relatively easy tasks. Products are discontinued, customers change addresses, and so on. Keeping data records up to date is a vital part of any database management system.

In many database systems, some "deleted" records are not physically removed. Instead, they are just marked as deleted so that they will not be used to process active records. For example, a company might want to retain data about former employees, but not process them with current personnel reports. On the other hand, an employee record that was entered by mistake would be permanently removed from the database.

Database management software generally allows you to sort a table based on any column, letting you view the data in the way that is most useful to you. For example, you might want to view inventory items in alphabetical order, or from the most to the least expensive. You also can sort by multiple columns—for example, you might sort employees by first name within last name (so that Aaron Black is listed before Andrea Black), or by department within first name within last name (so that Aaron Black in Department 1 is listed before another Aaron Black in Department 6). When sorting records on multiple fields, the software first uses a primary sort—for example, by last name. After all records with the same primary sort key are grouped, the software sorts by the secondary key—for example, first name.

After rows are sorted, they usually can be grouped. For example, you might want to sort customers by their zip code, or employees by the department in which they work; in addition, you might want counts or subtotals at the end of each group. Database software allows you to create displays in the formats that suit your needs.

> **TWO TRUTHS & A LIE**
>
> **Working with Records within Tables**
>
> 1. Depending on the application, the contents of tables in a database system might be entered over the course of months or years by many data-entry personnel.
> 2. In most organizations, much of the important data is permanent.
> 3. Database management software generally allows you to sort and group data, letting you view the data in the way that is most useful to you.
>
> The false statement is #2. In most organizations, much of the important data is in a constant state of change. Keeping data records up to date is a vital part of any database management system.

Creating Queries

Data tables often contain hundreds or thousands of rows; making sense out of that much information is a daunting task. Frequently, you want to view subsets of data from a table you have created. For example, you might want to examine only those customers with an address in a specific state, only those inventory items whose quantity in stock has fallen below the normal reorder point, or only those employees who participate in an insurance plan. Besides limiting records, you might also want to limit the columns that you view. For example, student records might contain dozens of fields, but a school administrator might only be interested in looking at names and grade point averages. The questions you use to extract the appropriate records from a table and specify the fields to be viewed are called queries; a **query** is a question using syntax that the database software can understand.

Depending on the software, you might create a query by filling in blanks (a process called **query by example**) or by writing statements similar to those in many programming languages. The most common language that database administrators use to access data in their tables is **Structured Query Language**, or **SQL**. The basic form of the SQL statement that retrieves selected records from a table is **SELECT-FROM-WHERE**. This statement:

- *Selects* the columns you want to view
- *From* a specific table
- *Where* one or more conditions are met

SQL frequently is pronounced *sequel*; however, several SQL product Web sites insist that the official pronunciation is *S-Q-L*. Similarly, some people pronounce *GUI* as *gooey* and others insist that it should be *G-U-I*. In general, a preferred pronunciation evolves in an organization. The TLA, or three-letter abbreviation, is the most popular type of abbreviation in technical terminology.

For example, suppose that a customer table named `tblCustomer` contains data about your business customers and that the structure of the table is as follows:

`tblCustomer(custId, lastName, state)`

Then, a statement such as the following would display a new table containing two columns—`custId` and `lastName`—and only as many rows as needed to hold those customers whose `state` column contains "WI":

`SELECT custId, lastName FROM tblCustomer WHERE state = "WI"`

Besides using = to mean *equal to*, you can use the comparison operators > (greater than), < (less than), >= (greater than or equal to), and <= (less than or equal to). As you have already learned from working with programming variables throughout this book, text field values are contained within quotation marks, but numeric values are not.

Conventionally, SQL keywords such as SELECT appear in uppercase; this book follows that convention.

In database management systems, a particular way of looking at a database by selecting specific fields and records, or placing records in a selected order, is sometimes called a **view**. The different views provided by database software are virtual; they do not affect the physical organization or contents of the database.

To create a view that contains all fields for each record in a table, you can use the asterisk as a wildcard; a **wildcard** is a symbol that means "any" or "all." For example, the following statement would select all columns for every customer whose state is "WI", not just specifically named columns:

`SELECT * FROM tblCustomer WHERE state = "WI"`

To select all customers from a table, you can omit the WHERE clause in a SELECT-FROM-WHERE statement. The following statement selects all columns for all customers:

`SELECT * FROM tblCustomer`

You learned about making selections in computer programs much earlier in this book, and you have probably noticed that SELECT-FROM-WHERE statements serve the same purpose as programming decisions. As with decision statements in programs, SQL allows you to create compound conditions using AND or OR operators. In addition, you can precede any condition with a NOT operator to achieve a negative result. In summary, Figure 14-4 shows a database table named `tblInventory` with the following structure:

`tblInventory(itemNumber, description, quantityInStock, price)`

The table contains five records. Figure 14-5 lists several typical SQL SELECT statements you might use with `tblInventory` and explains each.

itemNumber	description	quantityInStock	price
144	Pkg 12 party plates	250	$14.99
231	Helium balloons	180	$2.50
267	Paper streamers	68	$1.89
312	Disposable tablecloth	20	$6.99
383	Pkg 20 napkins	315	$2.39

Figure 14-4 The `tblInventory` table

SQL Statement	Explanation
SELECT itemNumber, price FROM tblInventory	Shows only the item number and price for all five records.
SELECT * FROM tblInventory WHERE price > 5.00	Shows all fields from only those records where price is over $5.00– items 144 and 312.
SELECT itemNumber FROM tblInventory WHERE quantityInStock > 200 AND price > 10.00	Shows item number 144–the only record that has a quantity greater than 200 as well as a price greater than $10.00.
SELECT description, price FROM tblInventory WHERE description = "Pkg 20 napkins" OR itemNumber < 200	Shows the description and price fields for the package of 12 party plates and the package of 20 napkins. Each selected record must satisfy only one of the two criteria.
SELECT itemNumber FROM tblInventory WHERE NOT price < 14.00	Shows the item number for the only record where the price is not less than $14.00–item 144.

Figure 14-5 Sample SQL statements and explanations

> **TWO TRUTHS & A LIE**
>
> **Creating Queries**
>
> 1. A query is a question you use to extract appropriate fields and records from a table.
> 2. The most common language that database administrators use to access data in their tables is Structured Query Language, or SQL.
> 3. The basic form of the SQL command that retrieves selected records from a table is RETRIEVE-FROM-SELECTION.
>
> The false statement is # 3. The basic form of the SQL command that retrieves selected records from a table is SELECT-FROM-WHERE.

Understanding Relationships between Tables

Most database applications require many tables, and require that the tables be related. The connection between two tables is a **relationship**, and the database containing the relationships is a *relational database*. Connecting two tables based on the values in a common column is called a **join operation**, or more simply, a **join**; the column on which they are connected is the **join column**. The table displayed as the result of the query provides a virtual view—it uses data from each joined table without disrupting the contents of the originals. For example, in Figure 14-6, the customerNumber column is the join column that could produce a virtual view when a user asks to see the name of a customer associated with a specific order number. Three types of relationships can exist between tables:

- One-to-many
- Many-to-many
- One-to-one

tblCustomers

customerNumber	customerName
214	Kowalski
215	Jackson
216	Lopez
217	Thompson
218	Vitale

tblOrders

orderNumber	customerNumber	orderQuantity	orderItem	orderDate
10467	215	2	HP203	10/15/2013
10468	218	1	JK109	10/15/2013
10469	215	4	HP203	10/16/2013
10470	216	12	ML318	10/16/2013
10471	214	4	JK109	10/16/2013
10472	215	1	HP203	10/16/2013
10473	217	10	JK109	10/17/2013

Figure 14-6 Sample customers and orders

Understanding One-To-Many Relationships

In a **one-to-many relationship**, one row in a table can be related to many rows in another table. It is the most common type of relationship between tables. Consider the following tables:

```
tblCustomers(customerNumber, customerName)
tblOrders(orderNumber, customerNumber, orderQuantity, orderItem, orderDate)
```

The tblCustomers table contains one row for each customer, and customerNumber is the primary key. The tblOrders table contains one row for each order, and each order is assigned an orderNumber, which is the primary key in this table.

In most businesses, a single customer can place many orders. In the sample data in Figure 14-6, customer 215 has placed three orders. One row in the tblCustomers table can correspond to, and be related to, many rows in the tblOrders table. This means there is a one-to-many relationship between the two tables tblCustomers and tblOrders. The "one" table (tblCustomers) is the **base table** in this relationship, and the "many" table (tblOrders) is the **related table**.

When two tables have a one-to-many relationship, it is based on the values in one or more columns in the tables. In this example, the column, or attribute, that links the two tables together is the customerNumber attribute. In the tblCustomers table, customerNumber is the primary key, but in the tblOrders table, customerNumber is not a key—it is a **nonkey attribute**. When a column that is not a key in a table contains an attribute that is a key in a related table, the column is called a **foreign key**. When a base table is linked to a related table in a one-to-many relationship, the primary key of the base table is always related to the foreign key in the related table. In the example in Figure 14-6, customerNumber in the tblOrders table is a foreign key.

A key in a base table and the foreign key in the related table do not need to have the same name; they only need to contain the same type of data. Some database management software programs automatically create a relationship if the columns in two tables you select have the same name and data type. However, if this is not the case (for example, if the column is named customerNumber in one table and custID in another), you can explicitly instruct the software to create the relationship.

Understanding Many-To-Many Relationships

Another example of a one-to-many relationship is depicted with the following tables:

```
tblItems(itemNumber, itemName, itemPurchaseDate, itemPurchasePrice, itemCategoryId)
tblCategories(categoryId, categoryName, categoryInsuredAmount)
```

Assume that you are creating these tables to keep track of all the items in your household for insurance purposes. You want to store data about your sofa, stereo, refrigerator, and so on. The tblItems table contains the item number, name, purchase date, and purchase price of each item. In addition, this table contains the ID number of the category (Appliance, Jewelry, Antique, and so on) to which the item belongs. You need these categories because your insurance policy has specific coverage limits for different types of property. For example, with many insurance policies, antiques might have a different coverage limit than appliances, or jewelry might have a different limit than furniture. Sample data for these tables is shown in Figure 14-7.

tblItems

itemNumber	itemName	itemPurchaseDate	itemPurchasePrice	itemCategoryId
1	Sofa	1/13/2003	$6,500	5
2	Stereo	2/10/2005	$1,200	6
3	Refrigerator	5/12/2005	$750	1
4	Diamond ring	2/12/2006	$42,000	2
5	TV	7/11/2006	$285	6
6	Rectangular pine coffee table	4/21/2007	$300	5
7	Round pine end table	4/21/2012	$200	5

tblCategories

categoryId	categoryName	categoryInsuredAmount
1	Appliance	$30,000
2	Jewelry	$15,000
3	Antique	$10,000
4	Clothing	$25,000
5	Furniture	$5,000
6	Electronics	$2,500
7	Miscellaneous	$5,000

Figure 14-7   Sample items and categories: a one-to-many relationship

The primary key of the tblItems table is itemNumber, a unique identifying number that you have assigned to each item you own. (You might even prepare labels with these numbers and stick a label on each item in an inconspicuous place.) The tblCategories table contains the category names and the maximum insured amounts for the specific categories. For example, one row in this table has a categoryName of "Jewelry" and a categoryInsuredAmount of $15,000. The primary key for the tblCategories table is categoryId, a uniquely assigned value for each property category.

The two tables in Figure 14-7 have a one-to-many relationship. Which is the "one" table and which is the "many" table? Or, asked in another way, which is the base table and which is the related table? You have probably determined that tblCategories is the base table (the "one" table) because one category can describe many items that you own. Therefore, tblItems is the related table (the "many" table); that is, many items fall into each category. The two tables are linked with the category ID attribute, which is the primary key in the base table (tblCategories) and a foreign key in the related table (tblItems).

In Figure 14-7, one row in the tblCategories table relates to multiple items you own. The opposite is not true—one item in the tblItems table cannot relate to multiple categories in the tblCategories table. The row in the tblItems table that describes the "rectangular pine coffee table" relates to one specific category in the tblCategories table—the Furniture

Understanding Relationships between Tables

category. However, what if you own a rectangular pine coffee table that has a built-in refrigerator, or a diamond ring that is an antique?

The structure of the tables shown in Figure 14-7 and the relationship between those tables are designed to keep track of possessions for insurance purposes. If you needed help categorizing your sofa with a built-in DVD player, you might call your insurance agent. If the agent says that the item is considered a piece of furniture for insurance purposes, then the existing table structures and relationships are adequate. If the agent says the sofa is considered a special type of hybrid item that has a specific maximum insured amount, you could create a new row in the `tblCategories` table to describe this special hybrid category—perhaps Electronic Furniture. This new category would acquire a category number, and you could associate the DVD-sofa with the new category using the foreign key in the `tblItems` table.

However, if your insurance agent didn't know whether to categorize the sofa as furniture or electronics, the item would present a problem to your database. You may want to categorize your new sofa as both a furniture item *and* an electronic item. The existing table structures, with their one-to-many relationship, would not support this because the current design limits any specific item to only one category. When you insert a row into the `tblItems` table to describe the new DVD-sofa, you can assign the Furniture code to the foreign key `itemCategoryId`, or you can assign the Electronics code, but not both.

If you want to assign the new DVD-sofa to both categories (Furniture and Electronics), you have to change the design of the table structures and relationships, because there is no longer a one-to-many relationship between the two tables. Now, there is a **many-to-many relationship**—one in which multiple rows in each table can correspond to multiple rows in the other. In this example, one row in the `tblCategories` table (for example, Furniture) can relate to many rows in the `tblItems` table (for example, sofa and coffee table), *and* one row in the `tblItems` table (for example, the sofa with the built-in DVD player) can relate to multiple rows in the `tblCategories` table.

The `tblItems` table contains a foreign key named `itemCategoryId`. If you want to change the application so that one specific row in the `tblItems` table can link to many rows (and, therefore, many `categoryIds`) in the `tblCategories` table, you cannot continue to maintain the foreign key `itemCategoryId` in the `tblItems` table, because one item may be assigned to many categories. You could change the structure of the `tblItems` table so that you can assign multiple `itemCategoryIds` to one specific row in that table, but as you will learn later in this chapter, that approach leads to many problems using the data. Therefore, it is not an option.

The simplest way to support a many-to-many relationship between the `tblItems` and `tblCategories` tables is to remove the `itemCategoryId` attribute (what was once the foreign key) from the `tblItems` table, producing:

tblItems(itemNumber, itemName, itemPurchaseDate, itemPurchasePrice)

The `tblCategories` table structure remains the same:

tblCategories(categoryId, categoryName, categoryInsuredAmount)

CHAPTER 14 Using Relational Databases

With just the preceding two tables, there is no way to know that any specific rows in the tblItems table link to any specific rows in the tblCategories table, so you create a new table called tblItemsCategories that contains the primary keys from the two tables you want to link in a many-to-many relationship. This table is depicted as:

tblItemsCategories(itemNumber, categoryId)

Notice that this new table contains a compound primary key—both itemNumber and categoryId are underlined. The itemNumber value of 1 might be associated with many categoryIds. Therefore, itemNumber alone cannot be the primary key because the same value may occur in many rows. Similarly, a categoryId might relate to many different itemNumbers; this would disallow using just the categoryId as the primary key. However, combining the two attributes itemNumber and categoryId results in a unique primary key value for each row of the tblItemsCategories table.

A table such as tblItemsCategories that contains common fields from multiple tables is known by several terms, including *junction table*, *bridge table*, *join table*, *map table*, *cross-reference table*, *linking table*, *many-to-many resolver*, and *association table*. Junction tables can also contain additional fields.

The purpose of all this is to create a many-to-many relationship between the tblItems and tblCategories tables. The tblItemsCategories table contains two attributes; together, these attributes are the primary key. In addition, each of these attributes separately is a foreign key to one of the two original tables. The itemNumber attribute in the tblItemsCategories table is a foreign key that links to the primary key of the tblItems table. The categoryId attribute in the tblItemsCategories table links to the primary key of the tblCategories table. Now, there is a one-to-many relationship between the tblItems table (the "one," or base table) and the tblItemsCategories table (the "many," or related table), and a one-to-many relationship between the tblCategories table (the "one," or base table) and the tblItemsCategories table (the "many," or related table). This, in effect, implies a many-to-many relationship between the two base tables (tblItems and tblCategories).

Figure 14-8 shows the new tables holding a few items. The sofa (itemNumber 1) in the tblItems table is associated with the Furniture category (categoryId 5) in the tblCategories table because the first row of the tblItemsCategories table contains a 1 and a 5. Similarly, the stereo (itemNumber 2) in the tblItems table is associated with the Electronics category (categoryId 6) in the tblCategories table because the tblItemsCategories table has a row containing the values 2, 6.

tblItems

itemNumber	itemName	itemPurchaseDate	itemPurchasePrice
1	Sofa	1/13/2003	$6,500
2	Stereo	2/10/2005	$1,200
3	Sofa with DVD player	5/24/2010	$8,500
4	Coffee table with built-in refrigerator	6/24/2007	$12,000
5	Grandpa's pocket watch	4/7/1925	$100

tblItemsCategories

itemNumber	categoryId
1	5
2	6
3	5
3	6
4	1
4	5
5	2
5	3

tblCategories

categoryId	categoryName	categoryInsuredAmount
1	Appliance	$30,000
2	Jewelry	$15,000
3	Antique	$10,000
4	Clothing	$25,000
5	Furniture	$5,000
6	Electronics	$2,500
7	Miscellaneous	$5,000

Figure 14-8 Sample items, categories, and item categories: a many-to-many relationship

The fancy sofa with the built-in DVD player (itemNumber 3 in the tblItems table) occurs in two rows in the tblItemsCategories table: once with a categoryId of 5 (Furniture) and once with a categoryId of 6 (Electronics). Similarly, the coffee table with the built-in refrigerator (a piece of furniture that is an appliance) and Grandpa's pocket watch (an antique piece of jewelry) both belong to multiple categories. The tblItemsCategories table, then, allows the establishment of a many-to-many relationship between the two base tables, tblItems and tblCategories.

Understanding One-To-One Relationships

In a **one-to-one relationship**, a row in one table corresponds to exactly one row in another table. This type of relationship is easy to understand, but is the least frequently encountered. When one row in a table corresponds to a row in another table, the columns could be combined into a single table. A common reason you create a one-to-one relationship is security. For example, Figure 14-9 shows two tables, tblEmployees and tblSalaries. Each employee in the tblEmployees table has exactly one salary in the tblSalaries table. The salaries could have been added to the tblEmployees table as another column; the salaries are separate because you want some clerks to be allowed to view only names, addresses, and other nonsensitive data, so you give them permission to access only the tblEmployees table. Others who work in payroll or administration can create queries and view joined tables that include the salary information.

tblEmployees

empId	empLast	empFirst	empDept	empHireDate
101	Parker	Laura	3	4/07/2000
102	Walters	David	4	1/19/2001
103	Shannon	Ewa	3	2/28/2012

tblSalaries

empId	empSalary
101	$42,500
102	$28,800
103	$36,000

Figure 14-9   Employees and salaries tables: a one-to-one relationship

Another reason to create tables with one-to-one relationships is to avoid extensive empty columns, or **nulls**, if a subset of columns is applicable only to specific types of rows in the main table.

TWO TRUTHS & A LIE

Understanding Relationships Between Tables

1. In a one-to-many relationship, one row in a table can be related to many rows in another table; this is the most common type of relationship between tables.

2. In a many-to-many relationship, multiple rows in a table each correspond to a single row in many different tables.

3. In a one-to-one relationship, a row in one table corresponds to exactly one row in another table; this type of relationship is easy to understand, but is the least frequently encountered.

The false statement is #2. A many-to-many relationship is one in which multiple rows in each table can correspond to multiple rows in the other.

Recognizing Poor Table Design

As you create database tables to hold the data used by an organization, you will often find the table design, or structure, inadequate to support the needs of the application. In other words, even if a table contains all the attributes required by a specific application, the structural design of the table may make the application cumbersome to use and prone to data errors.

Recognizing Poor Table Design

For example, assume that you have been hired by an Internet-based college to design a database to keep track of its students. After meeting with the college administrators, you determine that you need to know the following information:

- Students' names
- Students' addresses
- Students' cities
- Students' states
- Students' zip codes
- ID numbers for classes in which students are enrolled
- Titles for classes in which students are enrolled

In a real-life example, you could think of many other data requirements for the college. The number of attributes is small in this example for simplicity.

Figure 14-10 contains the Students table. Assume that because the Internet-based college is new, only three students have already enrolled. Besides the columns you identified as being necessary, notice the addition of the studentId attribute. Given the earlier discussions, you probably recognize that this is the best choice for a primary key, because many students can have the same names and even the same addresses. Although the table in Figure 14-10 contains a column for each data requirement from the preceding list, the table is poorly designed and will create many problems.

studentId	name	address	city	state	zip	class	classTitle
1	Rodriguez	123 Oak	Schaumburg	IL	60193	CIS101 PHI150 BIO200	Computer Literacy Ethics Genetics
2	Jones	234 Elm	Wild Rose	WI	54984	CHM100 MTH200	Chemistry Calculus
3	Mason	456 Pine	Dubuque	IA	52004	HIS202	World History

Figure 14-10 Students table before normalization

What if a college administrator wanted to view a list of courses offered by the Internet-based college? You can see six courses listed for the three students, so you can assume that at least six courses are offered. But, could there also be a Psychology course, or a class whose code is CIS102? You can't tell from the table because no students have enrolled in those classes. It would be good to know all the classes offered by your institution, regardless of whether any students have enrolled in them.

Consider another potential problem: What if student Mason withdraws from the school, and his row is deleted from the table? You would lose some valuable information that has nothing to do with student Mason, but is important for running the college. For instance, if Mason's row is deleted, you no longer know from the remaining data in the table whether the college offers any History classes, because Mason was the only student enrolled in a class with the HIS prefix (the HIS202 class).

Why is it so important to discuss the deficiencies of the existing table structure? You have probably heard the saying, "Pay me now or pay me later." This is especially true for table design. If you do not take the time to ensure well-designed table structures during the initial database design, users will spend plenty of time later fixing data errors, typing the same information multiple times, and being frustrated by the inability to cull important subsets of information from the database. If you had created this table structure as a solution to the college's needs, you probably would not be hired for future database projects.

TWO TRUTHS & A LIE

Recognizing Poor Table Design

1. The structural design of a table is excellent when the table contains all the attributes required by a specific application.

2. In a poorly designed database, you might risk losing important data when specific records are deleted.

3. If you do not take the time to ensure well-designed table structures during the initial database design, users will spend plenty of time later fixing data errors, typing the same information multiple times, and being frustrated by the inability to cull important subsets of information from the database.

The false statement is #1. Even if a table contains all the attributes required by a specific application, the structural design of the table may make the application cumbersome to use and prone to data errors.

Understanding Anomalies, Normal Forms, and Normalization

Database management programs can maintain all the relationships you need. As you add, delete, and modify records within your database tables, the software keeps track of all the relationships you have established, so that you can view any needed joins any time you want. The software, however, can only maintain useful relationships if you have planned ahead to create a set of database tables that satisfies the users' needs, supports all the applications you will need, and avoids potential problems. This process is called **normalization**.

Understanding Anomalies, Normal Forms, and Normalization

The normalization process helps you reduce data redundancies and anomalies. **Data redundancy** is the unnecessary repetition of data. An **anomaly** is an irregularity in a database's design that causes problems and inconveniences. Three common types of anomalies are:

- Update anomalies
- Delete anomalies
- Insert anomalies

If you look ahead to the college database table in Figure 14-11, you will see an example of an **update anomaly**, or a problem that occurs when the data in a table needs to be altered. Because the table contains redundant data, if student Rodriguez moves to a new residence, you have to change the address, city, state, and zip values in more than one location. Of course, this table example is small; imagine if additional data were stored about Rodriguez, such as birth date, e-mail address, major field of study, and previous schools attended.

The database table in Figure 14-10 contains a **delete anomaly**, or a problem that occurs when a row is deleted. If student Jones withdraws from the college and his entries are deleted from the table, important data regarding the classes CHM100 and MTH200 are lost.

With an **insert anomaly**, problems occur when new rows are added to a table. In the table in Figure 14-10, if a new student named Reed has enrolled in the college but has not yet registered for specific classes, then you can't insert a complete row for student Reed; the only way to do so would be to "invent" at least one phony class for him. (Some database software allows incomplete rows.) It would be valuable to the college to be able to maintain data on all enrolled students, regardless of whether they have registered for specific classes—for example, the college might want to send catalogs and registration information to these students.

When you normalize a database table, you walk through a series of steps that allows you to remove redundancies and anomalies. Normalization involves altering a table so that it satisfies one or more of three **normal forms**, or sets of rules for constructing a well-designed database. The three normal forms are:

- **First normal form**, also known as **1NF**, in which you eliminate repeating groups
- **Second normal form**, or **2NF**, in which you eliminate partial key dependencies
- **Third normal form**, or **3NF**, in which you eliminate transitive dependencies

Each normal form is structurally better than the one preceding it. In any well-designed database, you almost always want to convert all tables to 3NF.

In a 1970 paper titled "A Relational Model of Data for Large Shared Data Banks," Dr. E. F. Codd listed seven normal forms. For business applications, 3NF is usually sufficient, and so only 1NF through 3NF are discussed in this chapter.

First Normal Form

A table that contains repeating groups is **unnormalized**. A **repeating group** is a subset of rows in a database table that all depend on the same key. A table in 1NF contains no repeating groups of data.

The table in Figure 14-10 violates this 1NF rule. The class and classTitle attributes repeat multiple times for some of the students. For example, student Rodriguez is taking three classes; her class attribute contains a repeating group. To remedy this situation, and to transform the table to 1NF, you simply repeat the rows for each repeating group of data. Figure 14-11 contains the revised table.

studentId	name	address	city	state	zip	class	classTitle
1	Rodriguez	123 Oak	Schaumburg	IL	60193	CIS101	Computer Literacy
1	Rodriguez	123 Oak	Schaumburg	IL	60193	PHI150	Ethics
1	Rodriguez	123 Oak	Schaumburg	IL	60193	BIO200	Genetics
2	Jones	234 Elm	Wild Rose	WI	54984	CHM100	Chemistry
2	Jones	234 Elm	Wild Rose	WI	54984	MTH200	Calculus
3	Mason	456 Pine	Dubuque	IA	52004	HIS202	World History

Figure 14-11 Students table in 1NF

The repeating groups have been eliminated from the table in Figure 14-11. However, there is still a problem—the primary key, studentId, is no longer unique for each row in the table. For example, the table now contains three rows in which studentId equals 1. You can fix this problem and create a primary key simply by adding the class attribute to the primary key, creating a compound key. (Other problems still exist, as you will see later in this chapter.) The table's key then becomes a combination of studentId and class. By knowing the studentId and class, you can identify one, and only one, row in the table—for example, a combination of studentId 1 and class BIO200 identifies a single row. Using the notation discussed earlier in this chapter, the table in Figure 14-11 can be described as:

tblStudents(<u>studentId</u>, name, address, city, state, zip, <u>class</u>, classTitle)

Both the studentId and class attributes are underlined, showing that they are both part of the key. When you combine two columns to create a compound key, you are **concatenating the columns**.

The table in Figure 14-11 is now in 1NF because there are no repeating groups and the primary key attributes are defined. Satisfying the "no repeating groups" condition is also called making the columns **atomic attributes**—making them as small as possible to contain an undividable piece of data. In 1NF, all values for an intersection of a row and column must be atomic. Recall the table in Figure 14-10, in which the class attribute for studentId 1 (Rodriguez) contained three entries: CIS101, PHI150, and BIO200. This violated the 1NF atomicity rule because these three classes represented a set of values rather than one specific

Understanding Anomalies, Normal Forms, and Normalization

value. The table in Figure 14-11 does not repeat this problem because, for each row in the table, the `class` attribute contains one and only one value. The same is true for the other attributes that were part of the repeating group.

Database developers also refer to series of operations or transactions as **atomic transactions** when they execute completely or not at all. Making actions atomic guarantees that no actions will be only partially completed, which could cause more problems than if the tasks were not started at all.

Think back to the earlier discussion about why we normalize tables in the first place. Does Figure 14-11 still have redundancies? Are there still anomalies? The answer is *Yes* to both questions. Recall that you want to have the tables in 3NF before actually defining them to the database. Currently, the table in Figure 14-11 is only in 1NF.

In Figure 14-11, notice that Student 1, Rodriguez, is taking three classes. If you were responsible for typing data into this table, would you want to type this student's name, address, city, state, and zip code for each of the three classes? For one of her classes, you might mistype her name as "Rodrigues." Or, you might misspell the city of Schaumburg as "Schamburg" for one of Rodriguez's classes. A college administrator might look at the table and not know the correct spelling for the name or city, and if the administrator queried the database to select or count the number of classes being taken by students residing in Schaumburg, one of Rodriguez's classes would be missed.

Misspellings are examples of data integrity errors. You learn more about this type of error later in this chapter.

Consider the student Jones, who is taking two classes. If Jones changes his residence, how many times will you need to retype his new address, state, city, and zip code? What if Jones is taking six classes?

Second Normal Form

To improve the design of the table in Figure 14-11 and bring the table to 2NF, you need to eliminate all **partial key dependencies**; that is, no column should depend on only part of the key. For a table to be in 2NF, it must be in 1NF and all nonkey attributes must be dependent on the entire primary key.

In the table in Figure 14-11, the key is a combination of `studentId` and `class`. Consider the `name` attribute. Does the `name` "Rodriguez" depend on the entire primary key? In other words, do you need to know that the `studentId` is 1 *and* that the `class` is CIS101 to determine that the `name` is "Rodriguez"? No, it is sufficient to know that the `studentId` is 1 to know that the `name` is "Rodriguez". Therefore, the `name` attribute is only partially dependent on the primary key, and so the table violates 2NF. The same is true for the other attributes of `address`, `city`, `state`, and `zip`. If you know, for example, that `studentId` is 3, then you also know that the student's `city` is "Dubuque"; you do not need to know any `class` codes.

Similarly, examine the `classTitle` attribute in the first row of the table in Figure 14-11. This attribute has a value of "Computer Literacy". In this case, you do not need to know both the `studentId` and the `class` to predict the `classTitle` "Computer Literacy". Rather, just the `class` attribute, which is only part of the compound key, is required. Also, class "PHI150" will always have the associated `classTitle` "Ethics", regardless of the particular students who are taking that class. So, `classTitle` represents a partial key dependency.

You bring a table into 2NF by eliminating the partial key dependencies. To accomplish this, you create multiple tables so that each nonkey attribute of each table is dependent on the *entire* primary key for the specific table within which the attribute occurs. If the resulting tables are still in 1NF and there are no partial key dependencies, then those tables will also be in 2NF.

Figure 14-12 contains three tables: `tblStudents`, `tblClasses`, and `tblStudentClasses`. To create the `tblStudents` table, you simply take the attributes from the original table that depend on the `studentId` attribute and group them into a new table—name, address, city, state, and zip all can be determined by the `studentId` alone. The primary key to the `tblStudents` table is `studentId`. Similarly, you can create the `tblClasses` table simply by grouping the attributes from the 1NF table that depend on the `class` attribute. In this application, only one attribute from the original table, the `classTitle` attribute, depends on the `class` attribute. The first two tables in Figure 14-12 can be notated as:

`tblStudents(studentId, name, address, city, state, zip)`
`tblClasses(class, classTitle)`

tblStudents

studentId	name	address	city	state	zip
1	Rodriguez	123 Oak	Schaumburg	IL	60193
2	Jones	234 Elm	Wild Rose	WI	54984
3	Mason	456 Pine	Dubuque	IA	52004

tblClasses

class	classTitle
CIS101	Computer Literacy
PHI150	Ethics
BIO200	Genetics
CHM100	Chemistry
MTH200	Calculus
HIS202	World History

tblStudentClasses

studentId	class
1	CIS101
1	PHI150
1	BIO200
2	CHM100
2	MTH200
3	HIS202

Figure 14-12 Students table in 2NF

Understanding Anomalies, Normal Forms, and Normalization

The `tblStudents` and `tblClasses` tables contain all the attributes from the original table. Remember the prior redundancies and anomalies. Several improvements have occurred:

- You have eliminated the update anomalies. The name "Rodriguez" occurs just once in the `tblStudents` table. The same is true for Rodriguez's address, city, state, and zip code. The original table contained three rows for student Rodriguez. By eliminating the redundancies, you have fewer anomalies. If Rodriguez changes her residence, you only need to update one row in the `tblStudents` table.

- You have eliminated the insert anomalies. With the new configuration, you can insert a complete row into the `tblStudents` table even if the student has not yet enrolled in any classes. Similarly, you can add a complete row to the `tblClasses` table for a new class offering even though no students are currently taking the class.

- You have eliminated the delete anomalies. Recall from the original table that Mason was the only student taking HIS202. This caused a delete anomaly because the HIS202 class would disappear if Mason was removed. Now, if you delete Mason from the `tblStudents` table in Figure 14-12, the HIS202 class remains in the `tblClasses` list.

If you create the first two tables shown in Figure 14-12, you have eliminated many of the problems associated with the original version. However, if you have those two tables alone, you have lost some important information that you originally had while at 1NF—specifically, which students are taking which classes or which classes are being taken by which students. When breaking up a table into multiple tables, you need to consider the type of relationship among the resulting tables—you are designing a *relational* database, after all.

You know that the Internet-based college application requires that you keep track of which students are taking which classes. This implies a relationship between the `tblStudents` and `tblClasses` tables. Your job is to determine what type of relationship exists between the two tables. Recall from earlier in the chapter that the two most common types of relationships are one-to-many and many-to-many. This application requires that one specific student can enroll in many different classes, and that one specific class can be taken by many different students. Therefore, a many-to-many relationship exists between the tables `tblStudents` and `tblClasses`.

As you learned in the earlier example of categorizing insured items, you create a many-to-many relationship between two tables by creating a third table that contains the primary keys from the two tables that you want to relate. In this case, you create the `tblStudentClasses` table in Figure 14-12 as:

`tblStudentClasses(studentId, class)`

If you examine the rows in the `tblStudentClasses` table, you can see that the student with `studentId` 1, Rodriguez, is enrolled in three classes; `studentId` 2, Jones, is taking two classes; and `studentId` 3, Mason, is enrolled in only one class. Finally, the table requirements for the Internet-based college have been fulfilled.

Or have they? Earlier, you saw the many redundancies and anomalies that were eliminated by structuring the tables into 2NF, and the 2NF table structures certainly result in a much better database than the 1NF structures. But look again at the `tblStudents` table in Figure 14-12. As the college expands, what if you need to add 50 new students to this table, and all of the new students reside in Schaumburg, IL? If you were the data-entry person, would you want to type the city of "Schaumburg", the state of "IL", and the zip code of "60193" 50 times? This data is redundant, and you can improve the design of the tables to eliminate this redundancy.

Third Normal Form

3NF requires that a table be in 2NF and that it have no transitive dependencies. A **transitive dependency** occurs when the value of a nonkey attribute determines, or predicts, the value of another nonkey attribute. Clearly, the `studentId` attribute of the `tblStudents` table in Figure 14-12 is a determinant—if you know a particular `studentId` value, you can also know that student's `name`, `address`, `city`, `state`, and `zip`. However, this is not considered a transitive dependency because the `studentId` attribute is the primary key for the `tblStudents` table, and, after all, the primary key's job is to determine the values of the other attributes in the row.

A problem arises, however, if a nonkey attribute determines another nonkey attribute. The `tblStudents` table in Figure 14-12 has five nonkey attributes: `name`, `address`, `city`, `state`, and `zip`.

The name is a nonkey attribute. If you know the value of `name` is "Rodriguez", do you also know the one specific address where Rodriguez resides? In other words, is this a transitive dependency? No, it isn't. Even though only one student is named Rodriguez now, there may be more in the future. So, though it may be tempting to consider that the `name` attribute is a determinant of `address`, it isn't. If your boss said, "Look at the `tblStudents` table and tell me Jones's address," you couldn't if you had 10 students named Jones.

The `address` attribute is a nonkey attribute. Does it predict anything? If you know that the value of `address` is "20 N. Main Street", can you determine which student is associated with that address? No, because in the future, many students might live at 20 N. Main Street, but they might live in different cities, or two students might live at the same address in the same city. Therefore, `address` does not cause a transitive dependency.

Similarly, the `city` and `state` attributes are not keys, but they also are not determinants because knowing their values alone is not sufficient to predict another nonkey attribute value. You might argue that if you know a city's name, you know the state, but many states contain cities named Union or Springfield, for example.

What about the nonkey attribute `zip`? If you know that the zip code is 60193, can you determine the value of any other nonkey attributes? Yes, a zip code of 60193 indicates that the `city` is Schaumburg and the `state` is IL. This is the "culprit" that is causing the redundancies in the `city` and `state` attributes. The attribute `zip` is a determinant because it determines `city` and `state`; therefore, the `tblStudents` table contains a transitive dependency and is not in 3NF.

To convert the `tblStudents` table to 3NF, simply remove the attributes that are determined by, or are **functionally dependent** on, the `zip` attribute. For example, if attribute `zip` determines attribute `city`, then attribute `city` is considered to be functionally dependent on attribute `zip`. So, as Figure 14-13 shows, the new `tblStudents` table is defined as:

`tblStudents(studentId, name, address, zip)`

Key Terms

Characters are the smallest usable units of data—for example, a letter, digit, or punctuation mark.

Fields are formed from groups of characters and represent a piece of information, such as `firstName`, `lastName`, or `socialSecurityNumber`.

Records are formed from groups of related fields. The fields go together because they represent attributes of an entity, such as an employee, a customer, an inventory item, or a bank account.

Files are composed of associated records; for example, a file might contain a record for each employee in a company or each account at a bank.

A **database** holds a group of files, or tables, that an organization needs to support its applications.

A database **table** contains data in rows and columns.

An **entity** is one record or row in a database table.

An **attribute** is one field or column in a database table.

A **primary key**, or **key** for short, is a field or column that uniquely identifies a record.

A **compound key**, also known as a **composite key**, is a key constructed from multiple columns.

Database management software is a set of programs that allows users to create and manage data.

A **relational database** contains a group of tables from which you can make connections to produce virtual tables.

Candidate keys are columns or attributes that could serve as a primary key in a table.

Alternate keys are the remaining candidate keys after you choose a primary key.

Immutable means not changing during normal operation.

A **query** is a question using syntax that the database software can understand. Its purpose is often to display a subset of data.

Query by example is the process of creating a query by filling in blanks.

Structured Query Language, or **SQL**, is a commonly used language for accessing data in database tables.

The **SELECT-FROM-WHERE** SQL statement is the command that selects the fields you want to view from a specific table where one or more conditions are met.

A **view** is a particular way of looking at a database.

A **wildcard** is a symbol that means "any" or "all."

A **relationship** is a connection between two tables.

A **join operation**, or a **join**, connects two tables based on the values in a common column.

A **join column** is the column on which two tables are connected.

A **one-to-many relationship** is one in which one row in a table can be related to many rows in another table. It is the most common type of relationship among tables.

The **base table** in a one-to-many relationship is the "one" table.

The **related table** in a one-to-many relationship is the "many" table.

A **nonkey attribute** is any column in a table that is not a key.

A **foreign key** is a column that is not a key in a table, but it contains an attribute that is a key in a related table.

A **many-to-many relationship** is one in which multiple rows in one table can correspond to multiple rows in another table.

In a **one-to-one relationship**, a row in one table corresponds to exactly one row in another table.

Nulls are empty columns in a database.

Normalization is the process of designing and creating a set of database tables that satisfies the users' needs and avoids redundancies and anomalies.

Data redundancy is the unnecessary repetition of data.

An **anomaly** is an irregularity in the design of a database that causes problems and inconveniences.

An **update anomaly** is a problem that occurs when the data in a table needs to be altered; the result is repeated data.

A **delete anomaly** is a problem that occurs when a row in a table is deleted; the result is loss of related data.

An **insert anomaly** is a problem that occurs when new rows are added to a table; the result is incomplete rows.

Normal forms are rules for constructing a well-designed database.

First normal form, also known as **1NF**, is the normalization form in which you eliminate repeating groups.

Second normal form, or **2NF**, is the normalization form in which you eliminate partial key dependencies.

Third normal form, or **3NF**, is the normalization form in which you eliminate transitive dependencies.

An **unnormalized** table contains repeating groups.

A **repeating group** is a subset of rows in a database table that all depend on the same key.

To **concatenate columns** is to combine columns to produce a compound key.

Atomic attributes or columns are as small as possible so as to contain an undividable piece of data.

Atomic transactions appear to execute completely or not at all.

A **partial key dependency** occurs when a column in a table depends on only part of the table's key.

A **transitive dependency** occurs when the value of a nonkey attribute determines, or predicts, the value of another nonkey attribute.

Functionally dependent describes an attribute's relationship to another if it can be determined by the other attribute.

To **denormalize** a table is to place it in a lower normal form by putting some repeated information back into it.

Data integrity is the database condition that results when a set of rules is followed to make data accurate and consistent.

Recovery is the process of returning the database to a correct form that existed before an error occurred.

A **concurrent update problem** occurs when two database users need to modify the same record at the same time.

A **lock** is a mechanism that prevents changes to a database for a period of time.

A **persistent lock** is a long-term database lock required when users want to maintain a consistent view of their data while making modifications over a long transaction.

A **batch** is a group of transactions applied all at once.

Authentication techniques include storing and verifying passwords or even using physical characteristics, such as fingerprints or voice recognition, before users can view data.

The **permissions** assigned to a user indicate which parts of the database the user can view, modify, and delete.

Encryption is the process of coding data into a format that human beings cannot read.

Review Questions

1. A field or column that uniquely identifies a row in a database table is a(n) _____ .
    a. variable
    b. identifier
    c. principal
    d. key

CHAPTER 14   Using Relational Databases

2. Which of the following is *not* a feature of most database management software?
   a. sorting records in a table
   b. creating reports
   c. preventing poorly designed tables
   d. relating tables

3. Before you can enter data into a database table, you must do all of the following except _____ .
   a. determine the attributes the table will hold
   b. provide names for each attribute
   c. provide data types for each attribute
   d. determine maximum and minimum values for each attribute

4. Which of the following is the best key for a table containing a landlord's rental properties?
   a. numberOfBedrooms
   b. amountOfMonthlyRent
   c. streetAddress
   d. tenantLastName

5. A table's notation is:
   tblClients(socialSecNum, lastName, firstName, <u>clientNumber</u>, balanceDue).
   You know that _____ .
   a. the primary key is socialSecNum
   b. the primary key is clientNumber
   c. there are four candidate keys
   d. there is at least one numeric attribute

6. You can extract subsets of data from database tables using a(n) _____ .
   a. query
   b. sort
   c. investigation
   d. subroutine

7. A database table has the structure
   tblPhoneOrders(<u>orderNum</u>, custName, custPhoneNum, itemOrdered, quantity).
   Which SQL statement could be used to extract all attributes for orders for item AB3333?
   a. SELECT * FROM tblPhoneOrders WHERE itemOrdered = "AB3333"
   b. SELECT tblPhoneOrders WHERE itemOrdered = "AB3333"
   c. SELECT itemOrdered FROM tblPhoneOrders WHERE = "AB3333"
   d. Two of the above are correct.

8. Connecting two database tables based on the value of a column (producing a virtual view of a new table) is a _____ operation.
   a. merge
   b. concatenate
   c. join
   d. met

Review Questions

9. Heartland Medical Clinic maintains a database to keep track of patients. One table can be described as:
   `tblPatients(patientId, name, address, primaryPhysicianCode)`. Another table contains physician codes along with other physician data; it is described as `tblPhysicians(physicianCode, name, officeNumber, phoneNumber, daysOfWeekInOffice)`. In this example, the relationship is _____ .

   a. one-to-one
   b. one-to-many
   c. many-to-many
   d. impossible to determine

10. Edgerton Insurance Agency sells life, home, health, and auto insurance policies. The agency maintains a database containing a table that holds policy data—each record contains the policy number, the customer's name and address, and the type of policy purchased. For example, customer Michael Robertson is referenced in two records because he holds life and auto policies. Another table contains information on each type of policy the agency sells—coverage limits, term, and so on. In this example, the relationship is _____ .

    a. one-to-one
    b. one-to-many
    c. many-to-many
    d. impossible to determine

11. Kratz Computer Repair maintains a database that contains a table of information about each repair job the company agrees to perform. The jobs table is described as: `tblJobs(jobId, dateStarted, customerId, technicianId, feeCharged)`. Each job has a unique ID number that serves as a key to this table. The `customerId` and `technicianId` columns in the table each link to other tables of customer information, such as name, address, and phone number, and technician information, such as name, office extension, and hourly rate. When the `tblJobs` and `tblCustomers` tables are joined, which is the base table?

    a. tblJobs
    b. tblCustomers
    c. tblTechnicians
    d. a combination of two tables

12. When a column that is not a key in a table contains an attribute that is a key in a related table, the column is called a _____ .

    a. foreign key
    b. merge column
    c. internal key
    d. primary column

13. The most common reason to construct a one-to-one relationship between two tables is _____ .

    a. to save money
    b. to save time
    c. for security purposes
    d. so that neither table is considered "inferior"

CHAPTER 14   Using Relational Databases

14. The process of designing and creating a set of database tables that satisfies the users' needs and avoids potential problems is _____ .
    a. purification
    b. normalization
    c. standardization
    d. structuring

15. The unnecessary repetition of data is called data _____ .
    a. amplification
    b. echoing
    c. redundancy
    d. mining

16. Problems with database design are caused by irregularities known as _____ .
    a. glitches
    b. anomalies
    c. bugs
    d. abnormalities

17. When you place a table into first normal form, you have eliminated _____ .
    a. transitive dependencies
    b. partial key dependencies
    c. repeating groups
    d. all of the above

18. When you place a table into third normal form, you have eliminated _____ .
    a. transitive dependencies
    b. partial key dependencies
    c. repeating groups
    d. all of the above

19. If a table contains no repeating groups, but a column depends on part of the table's key, the table is in _____ normal form.
    a. first
    b. second
    c. third
    d. fourth

20. Which of the following is not a database security issue?
    a. providing data integrity
    b. recovering lost data
    c. providing normalization
    d. providing encryption

Exercises

1. The Lucky Dog Grooming Parlor maintains data about each of its clients in a table named `tblClients`. Attributes include each dog's name, breed, and owner's name, all of which are text attributes. The only numeric attributes are an ID number assigned to each dog and the balance due on services. The table structure is `tblClients(dogId, name, breed, owner, balanceDue)`. Write the SQL statement that would select each of the following:

Exercises

   a. names and owners of all Great Danes
   b. owners of all dogs with balances due of more than $100
   c. all attributes of dogs named Fluffy
   d. all attributes of poodles whose balance is no greater than $50

2. Consider the following table with the structure
   tblRecipes(recipeName, timeToPrepare, ingredients). If necessary, redesign the table so it satisfies 1NF, 2NF, and 3NF.

recipeName	timeToPrepare	ingredients
Baked lasagna	1 hour	1 pound lasagna noodles ½ pound ground beef 16 ounces tomato sauce ½ pound ricotta cheese ½ pound parmesan cheese 1 onion
Fruit salad	10 minutes	1 apple 1 banana 1 bunch grapes 1 pint blueberries
Marinara sauce	30 minutes	16 ounces tomato sauce ¼ pound parmesan cheese 1 onion

3. Consider the following table with the structure
   tblFriends(lastName, firstName, address, birthday, phoneNumbers, emailAddresses). If necessary, redesign the table so it satisfies 1NF, 2NF, and 3NF.

lastName	firstName	address	birthday	phoneNumbers	emailAddresses
Gordon	Alicia	34 Second St.	3/16	222-4343 349-0012	agordon@mail.com
Washington	Edward	12 Main St.	12/12	222-7121	ewash@mail.com coolguy@earth.com
Davis	Olivia	55 Birch Ave.	10/3	222-9012 333-8788 834-0112	olivia@abc.com

4. You have created the following table to keep track of your DVD collection. The structure is tblDVDs(<u>movie</u>, year, stars). If necessary, redesign the table so it satisfies 1NF, 2NF, and 3NF.

movie	year	stars
The Departed	2006	Leonardo DiCaprio Matt Damon
Hairspray	2007	John Travolta Michelle Pfeiffer Christopher Walken
Catch Me If You Can	2002	Leonardo DiCaprio Tom Hanks Christopher Walken
True Grit	2010	Jeff Bridges Matt Damon

5. The Midtown Ladies Auxiliary is sponsoring a scholarship for local high school students. They have constructed a table with the structure tblScholarshipApplicants(<u>appId</u>, lastName, hsAttended, hsAddress, gpa, honors, clubsActivities). The hsAttended and hsAddress attributes represent the high school attended and its street address, respectively. The gpa attribute is a grade point average. The honors attribute holds awards received, and the clubsActivities attribute holds the names of clubs and activities in which the student participated. If necessary, redesign the table so it satisfies 1NF, 2NF, and 3NF.

Exercises

appId	lastName	hsAttended	hsAddress	gpa	honors	clubsActivities
1	Wong	Central	1500 Main	3.8	Citizenship award	Future teachers
						Class officer
						Model airplane
						Soccer MVP
						Newspaper
2	Jefferson	Central	1500 Main	4.0	Valedictorian	Pep
					Citizenship award	Yearbook
						Homecoming court
						Football MVP
3	Mitchell	Highland	200 Airport	3.6	Class officer	Pep
						Homecoming court
						Future teachers
4	O'Malley	St. Joseph	300 Fourth	4.0	Valedictorian	Pep
						Chess
5	Abel	Central	1500 Main	3.7	Citizenship award	Yearbook
						Class officer

6. Assume that you want to create a database to store information about your music collection. You want to be able to query the database for each of the following attributes:

- A particular title (for example, *Tapestry* or Beethoven's Fifth Symphony)
- Artist (for example, Carole King or the Chicago Symphony Orchestra)
- Format of the recording (for example, CD or MP3 file)
- Style of music (for example, rock or classical)
- Year recorded
- Year acquired as part of your collection
- Recording company
- Address of the recording company

Design the tables you would need so they are all in third normal form. Create at least five sample data records for each table you create.

7. Design a collection of database tables for the Springfield Town Council. The council is made up of representatives from each of the town's 15 precincts. The data you need to store includes the following attributes:

- Precinct number
- Precinct population
- Council representative's last name
- Council representative's first name
- Council representative's phone number
- Council representative's political party
- Political party chairperson's name
- Political party headquarters address

Design the tables you would need so they are all in third normal form. Create at least five sample data records for each table you create.

Find the Bugs

8. Your downloadable student files for Chapter 14 include DEBUG14-01.doc, DEBUG14-02.doc, and DEBUG14-03.doc. Each file starts with some comments that describe the problem. Following the comments, each file contains a table that is not in 3NF. Create tables as needed to put the data in 3NF.

Game Zone

9. Massively Multiplayer Online Role-Playing Games (MMORPG) are online computer role-playing games in which a large number of players interact with one another in a virtual world. Players assume the role of a fictional character and control that character's actions. MMORPGs are distinguished from smaller RPGs by the number of players and by the game's persistent world, usually hosted by the game's publisher, which continues to exist and evolve while the player is away from the game. Design the database you would use to host an MMORPG, including at least three tables.

Up for Discussion

10. In this chapter, a phone book was mentioned as an example of a database you use frequently. Name some other examples.

Exercises

11. Suppose that you have authority to browse your company's database. The company keeps information on each employee's past jobs, health insurance claims, and any criminal record. Also suppose that you want to ask a coworker out on a date. Should you use the database to obtain information about the person? If so, are there any limits on the data you should use? If not, should you be allowed to pay a private detective to discover similar data?

12. The FBI's National Crime Information Center (NCIC) is a computerized database of criminal justice information, including data on criminal histories, fugitives, stolen property, and missing persons. Such large systems almost inevitably contain inaccuracies. Various studies have indicated that perhaps less than half the records in this database are complete, accurate, and unambiguous. Do you approve of this system or object to it? Would you change your mind if there were no inaccuracies? Is there a level of inaccuracy you would find acceptable to realize the benefits of such a system?

13. What type of data might be useful to a community in the wake of a natural disaster? Who should pay for the expense of gathering, storing, and maintaining this data?

APPENDIX A

Understanding Numbering Systems and Computer Codes

The numbering system you know best is the **decimal numbering system**—the system based on 10 digits, 0 through 9. Mathematicians call decimal-system numbers **base 10** numbers. When you use the decimal system, no other symbols are available; if you want to express a value larger than 9, you must use multiple digits from the same pool of 10, placing them in columns.

When you use the decimal system, you analyze a multicolumn number by mentally assigning place values to each column. The value of the far right column is 1, the value of the next column to the left is 10, the next column is 100, and so on; the column values are multiplied by 10 as you move to the left. There is no limit to the number of columns you can use; you simply keep adding columns to the left as you need to express higher values. For example, Figure A-1 shows how the value 305 is represented in the decimal system. You simply sum the value of the digit in each column after it has been multiplied by the value of its column.

```
   Column value
  100    10    1
 ┌─────┬─────┬─────┐
 │  3  │  0  │  5  │
 └─────┴─────┴─────┘

  3 * 100 = 300
  0 *  10 =   0
  5 *   1 =   5
            ───
            305
```

Figure A-1 Representing 305 in the decimal system

The **binary numbering system** works in the same way as the decimal numbering system, except that it uses only two digits, 0 and 1. Mathematicians call these numbers **base 2** numbers. When you use the binary system, you must use multiple columns if you want to express a value greater than 1 because no single symbol is available that represents any value other than 0 or 1. However, instead of each new column to the left being 10 times greater than the previous column, each new column in the binary system is only two times the value of the previous column. For example, Figure A-2 shows how the numbers 9 and 305 are represented in the binary system. Notice that in both the binary system and the decimal system, it is perfectly acceptable—and often necessary—to create numbers with 0 in one or more columns. As with the decimal system, there is no limit to the number of columns used in a binary number—you can use as many as it takes to express a value.

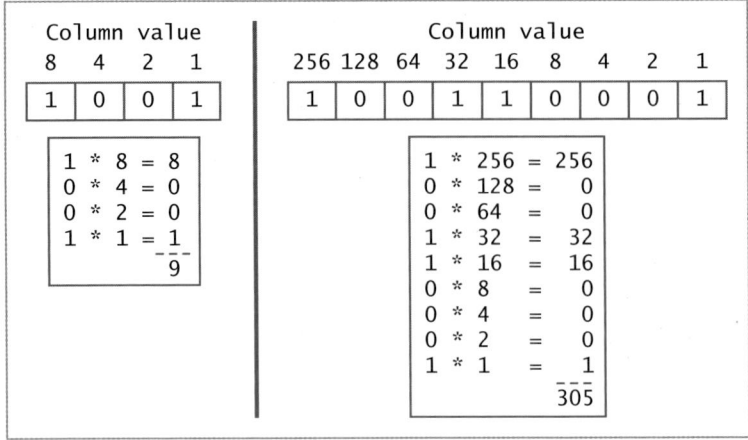

Figure A-2 Representing decimal values 9 and 305 in the binary system

A computer stores every piece of data it uses as a set of 0s and 1s. Each 0 or 1 is known as a **bit**, which is short for *binary digit*. Every computer uses 0s and 1s because all values in a computer are stored as electronic signals that are either on or off. This two-state system is most easily represented using just two digits.

Computers use a set of binary digits to represent stored characters. If computers used only one binary digit to represent characters, then only two different characters could be represented, because the single bit could be only 0 or 1. If computers used only two digits, then only four characters could be represented—the four codes 00, 01, 10, and 11, which in decimal values are 0, 1, 2, and 3, respectively. Many computers use sets of eight binary digits to represent each character they store, because using eight binary digits provides 256 different combinations. A set of eight bits is a **byte**. One byte combination can represent an *A*, another a *B*, still others *a* and *b*, and so on. Two hundred fifty-six combinations are enough so that each capital letter, small letter, digit, and punctuation mark used in English has its own code; even a space has a code. For example, in the system named the **American Standard Code for Information Interchange** (**ASCII**), 01000001 represents the character *A*. The binary number 01000001 has a decimal value of 65, but this numeric value is not important to ordinary computer users; it is simply a code that stands for *A*.

The ASCII code is not the only computer code, but it is typical, and it is used in most personal computers. The **Extended Binary Coded Decimal Interchange Code**, or **EBCDIC**, is an eight-bit code that is used in IBM mainframe computers. In these computers, the principle is the same—every character is stored in a byte as a series of binary digits. However, the actual values used are different. For example, in EBCDIC, an *A* is 11000001, or 193. Another code used by languages such as Java and C# is **Unicode**; with this code, 16 bits are used to represent each character. The character *A* in Unicode has the same decimal value as the ASCII *A*, 65, but it is stored as 0000000001000001. Using two bytes provides many more possible

Understanding Numbering Systems and Computer Codes

combinations than using only eight bits—65,536 to be exact. With Unicode, enough codes are available to represent all English letters and digits, as well as characters from many international alphabets.

Ordinary computer users seldom think about the numeric codes behind the letters, numbers, and punctuation marks they enter from their keyboards or see displayed on a monitor. However, they see the consequence of the values behind letters when they see data sorted in alphabetical order. When you sort a list of names, *Andrea* comes before *Brian*, and *Caroline* comes after *Brian* because the numeric code for *A* is lower than the code for *B*, and the numeric code for *C* is higher than the code for *B*, no matter whether you use ASCII, EBCDIC, or Unicode.

Table A-1 shows the decimal and binary values behind the most commonly used characters in the ASCII character set—the letters, numbers, and punctuation marks you can enter from your keyboard using a single key press. (Other values not shown in Table A-1 also have specific purposes. For example, when you display the character that holds the decimal value 7, nothing appears on the screen, but a bell sounds. Programmers often use this character when they want to alert a user to an error or some other unusual condition.)

Each binary number in Table A-1 is shown containing two sets of four digits; this convention makes the eight-digit numbers easier to read. Four digits, or a half byte, is a **nibble**.

Decimal Number	Binary Number	ASCII Character	
32	0010 0000		Space
33	0010 0001	!	Exclamation point
34	0010 0010	"	Quotation mark, or double quote
35	0010 0011	#	Number sign, also called an octothorpe or a pound sign
36	0010 0100	$	Dollar sign
37	0010 0101	%	Percent
38	0010 0110	&	Ampersand
39	0010 0111	'	Apostrophe, single quote
40	0010 1000	(	Left parenthesis
41	0010 1001	)	Right parenthesis
42	0010 1010	*	Asterisk

Table A-1 Decimal and binary values for common ASCII characters

APPENDIX A: Understanding Numbering Systems and Computer Codes

Decimal Number	Binary Number	ASCII Character	
43	0010 1011	+	Plus sign
44	0010 1100	,	Comma
45	0010 1101	-	Hyphen or minus sign
46	0010 1110	.	Period or decimal point
47	0010 1111	/	Slash or front slash
48	0011 0000	0	
49	0011 0001	1	
50	0011 0010	2	
51	0011 0011	3	
52	0011 0100	4	
53	0011 0101	5	
54	0011 0110	6	
55	0011 0111	7	
56	0011 1000	8	
57	0011 1001	9	
58	0011 1010	:	Colon
59	0011 1011	;	Semicolon
60	0011 1100	<	Less-than sign
61	0011 1101	=	Equal sign
62	0011 1110	>	Greater-than sign
63	0011 1111	?	Question mark
64	0100 0000	@	At sign
65	0100 0001	A	
66	0100 0010	B	
67	0100 0011	C	
68	0100 0100	D	
69	0100 0101	E	
70	0100 0110	F	

Table A-1 Decimal and binary values for common ASCII characters (*continued*)

Understanding Numbering Systems and Computer Codes

Decimal Number	Binary Number	ASCII Character	
71	0100 0111	G	
72	0100 1000	H	
73	0100 1001	I	
74	0100 1010	J	
75	0100 1011	K	
76	0100 1100	L	
77	0100 1101	M	
78	0100 1110	N	
79	0100 1111	O	
80	0101 0000	P	
81	0101 0001	Q	
82	0101 0010	R	
83	0101 0011	S	
84	0101 0100	T	
85	0101 0101	U	
86	0101 0110	V	
87	0101 0111	W	
88	0101 1000	X	
89	0101 1001	Y	
90	0101 1010	Z	
91	0101 1011	[	Opening or left bracket
92	0101 1100	\	Backslash
93	0101 1101	]	Closing or right bracket
94	0101 1110	^	Caret
95	0101 1111	_	Underline or underscore
96	0110 0000	`	Grave accent
97	0110 0001	a	
98	0110 0010	b	

Table A-1 Decimal and binary values for common ASCII characters (*continued*)

APPENDIX A — Understanding Numbering Systems and Computer Codes

Decimal Number	Binary Number	ASCII Character	
99	0110 0011	c	
100	0110 0100	d	
101	0110 0101	e	
102	0110 0110	f	
103	0110 0111	g	
104	0110 1000	h	
105	0110 1001	i	
106	0110 1010	j	
107	0110 1011	k	
108	0110 1100	l	
109	0110 1101	m	
110	0110 1110	n	
111	0110 1111	o	
112	0111 0000	p	
113	0111 0001	q	
114	0111 0010	r	
115	0111 0011	s	
116	0111 0100	t	
117	0111 0101	u	
118	0111 0110	v	
119	0111 0111	w	
120	0111 1000	x	
121	0111 1001	y	
122	0111 1010	z	
123	0111 1011	{	Opening or left brace
124	0111 1100	|	Vertical line or pipe
125	0111 1101	}	Closing or right brace
126	0111 1110	~	Tilde

Table A-1 Decimal and binary values for common ASCII characters (*continued*)

The Hexadecimal System

The **hexadecimal numbering system** is the **base 16** system; it uses 16 digits. As shown in Table A-2, the digits are 0 through 9 and A through F. Computer professionals often use the hexadecimal system to express addresses and instructions as they are stored in computer memory because hexadecimal provides convenient shorthand expressions for groups of binary values. In Table A-2, each hexadecimal value represents one of the 16 possible combinations of four-digit binary values. Therefore, instead of referencing memory contents as a 16-digit binary value, for example, programmers can use a 4-digit hexadecimal value.

Decimal Value	Hexadecimal Value	Binary Value (shown using four digits)
0	0	0000
1	1	0001
2	2	0010
3	3	0011
4	4	0100
5	5	0101
6	6	0110
7	7	0111
8	8	1000
9	9	1001
10	A	1010
11	B	1011
12	C	1100
13	D	1101
14	E	1110
15	F	1111

Table A-2 Values in the decimal and hexadecimal systems

In the hexadecimal system, each column is 16 times the value of the column to its right. Therefore, column values from right to left are 1, 16, 256, 4096, and so on. Figure A-3 shows how 78, 171, and 305 are expressed in hexadecimal.

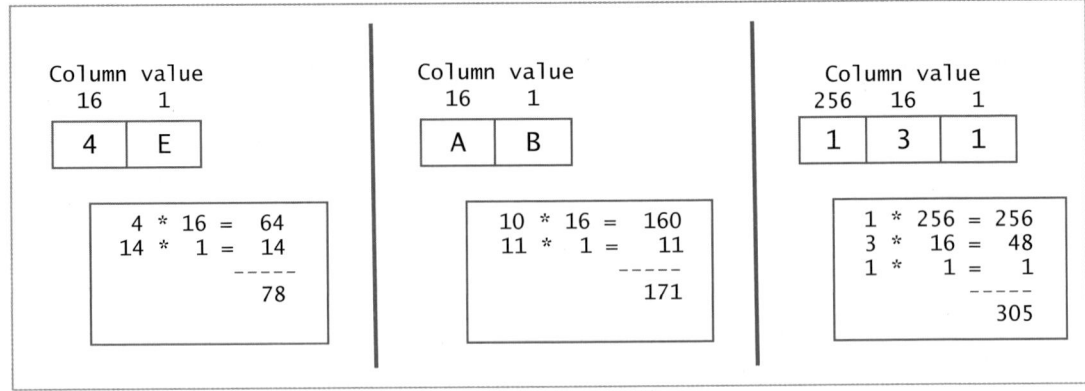

Figure A-3　Representing decimal values 78, 171, and 305 in the hexadecimal system

Measuring Storage

In computer systems, both internal memory and external storage are measured in bits and bytes. Eight bits make a byte, and a byte frequently holds a single character (in ASCII or EBCDIC) or half a character (in Unicode). Because a byte is such a small unit of storage, the size of memory and files is often expressed in thousands or millions of bytes. Table A-3 describes some commonly used terms for storage measurement.

Measuring Storage

Term	Abbreviation	Number of Bytes Using Binary System	Number of Bytes Using Decimal System	Example
Kilobyte	KB or kB	1024	one thousand	This appendix occupies about 85 kB on a hard disk.
Megabyte	MB	1,048,576 (1024 × 1024 kilobytes)	one million	One megabyte can hold an average book in text format. A 3½ inch diskette you might have used a few years ago held 1.44 megabytes.
Gigabyte	GB	1,073,741,824 (1,024 megabytes)	one billion	The hard drive on a fairly new laptop computer is at least 250 gigabytes. A DVD_R can hold about 5 gigabytes.
Terabyte	TB	1024 gigabytes	one trillion	Some hard drives are 1 terabyte. The entire Library of Congress occupied about 300 terabytes when this book was published.
Petabyte	PB	1024 terabytes	one quadrillion	The Google Web site processes about 24 petabytes per day.
Exabyte	EB	1024 petabytes	one quintillion	A popular expression claims that all words ever spoken by humans could be stored in text form in 5 exabytes.
Zettabyte	ZB	1024 exabytes	one sextillion	A popular expression claims that all words ever spoken by humans could be stored in audio form in 42 zettabytes.
Yottabyte	YB	1024 zettabytes	one septillion (a 1 followed by 24 zeros)	The combined space on all hard drives in the world is less than 1 yottabyte.

Table A-3 Commonly used terms for computer storage

APPENDIX A — Understanding Numbering Systems and Computer Codes

In the metric system, *kilo* means 1000. However, in Table A-3, notice that a kilobyte is 1024 bytes. The discrepancy occurs because everything stored in a computer is based on the binary system, so multiples of two are used in most measurements. If you multiply 2 by itself 10 times, the result is 1024, which is a little over 1000. Similarly, a gigabyte is 1,073,741,824 bytes, which is more than a billion.

Confusion arises because many hard-drive manufacturers use the decimal system instead of the binary system to describe storage. For example, if you buy a hard drive that holds 10 gigabytes, it holds exactly 10 billion bytes. However, in the binary system, 10 GB is 10,737,418,240 bytes, so when you check your hard drive's capacity, your computer will report that you don't quite have 10 GB, but only 9.31 GB.

Key Terms

The **decimal numbering system** is the numbering system based on 10 digits and in which column values are multiples of 10.

Base 10 describes numbers created using the decimal numbering system.

The **binary numbering system** is the numbering system based on 2 digits and in which column values are multiples of 2.

Base 2 describes numbers created using the binary numbering system.

A **bit** is a binary digit; it is a unit of storage equal to one-eighth of a byte.

A **byte** is a storage measurement equal to eight bits.

American Standard Code for Information Interchange (ASCII) is an eight-bit character coding scheme used on many personal computers.

Extended Binary Coded Decimal Interchange Code (EBCDIC) is an eight-bit character coding scheme used on many larger computers.

Unicode is a 16-bit character coding scheme.

A **nibble** is a storage measurement equal to four bits, or a half byte.

The **hexadecimal numbering system** is the numbering system based on 16 digits and in which column values are multiples of 16.

Base 16 describes numbers created using the hexadecimal numbering system.

APPENDIX B

Flowchart Symbols

This appendix contains the flowchart symbols used in this book.

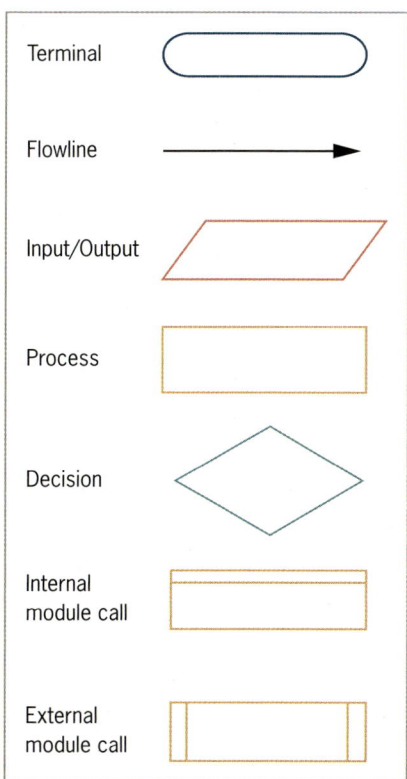

Figure B-1 Flowchart symbols

APPENDIX C

Structures

This appendix contains diagrams of the structures allowed in structured programming. Although all logical problems can be solved using the three fundamental structures, the additional structures provide convenience in some situations. Every structure has one entry point and one exit point. At these points, structures can be stacked and nested.

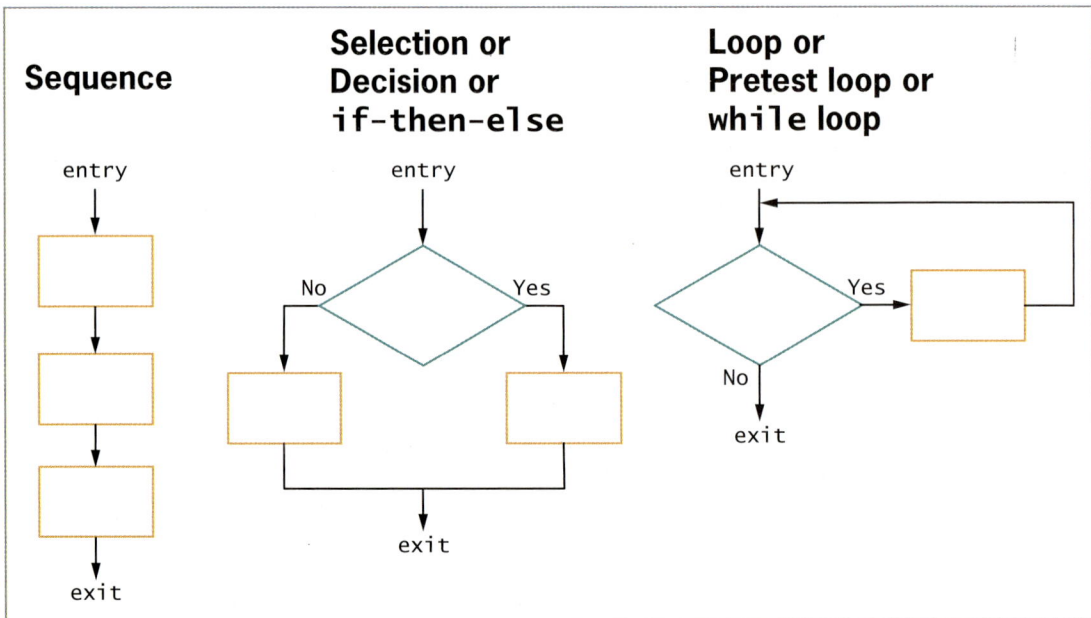

Figure C-1   Three fundamental structures

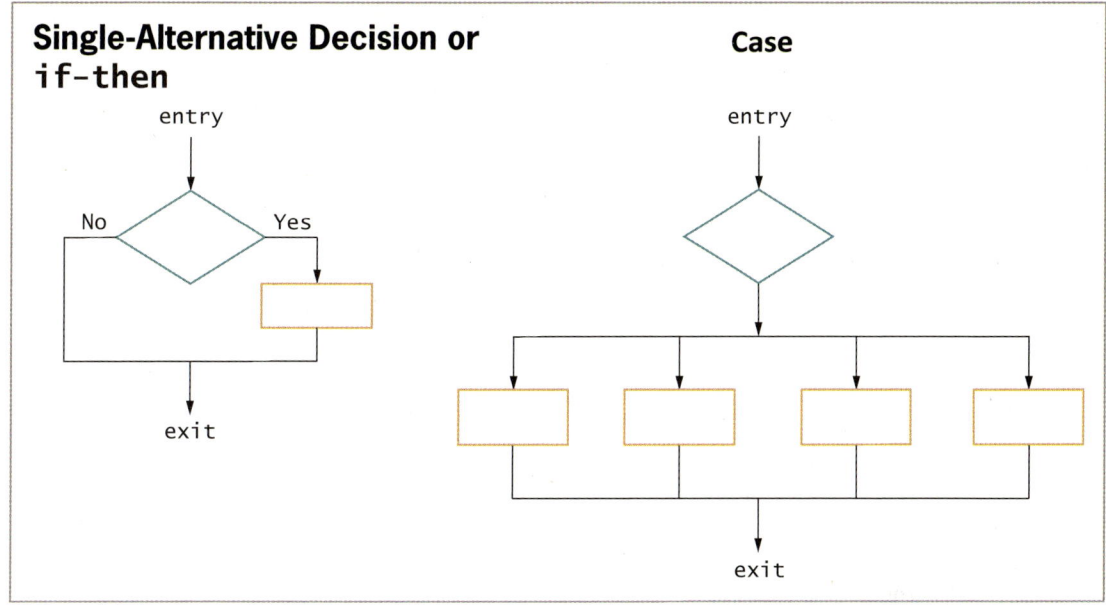

Figure C-2 Additional selection structures

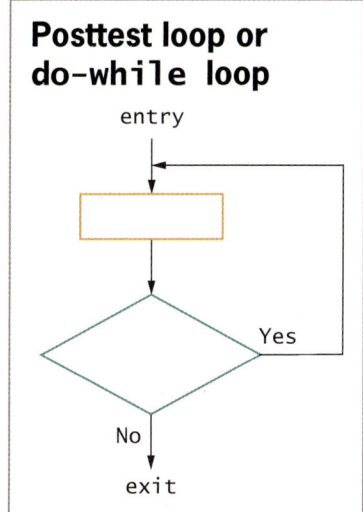

Figure C-3 Additional loop structure

APPENDIX D

Solving Difficult Structuring Problems

In Chapter 3, you learned that you can solve any logical problem using only the three standard structures—sequence, selection, and loop. Modifying an unstructured program to make it adhere to structured rules often is a simple matter. Sometimes, however, structuring a more complicated program can be challenging. Still, no matter how complicated, large, or poorly structured a problem is, the same tasks can *always* be accomplished in a structured manner.

Consider the flowchart segment in Figure D-1. Is it structured?

No, it is not structured. To straighten out the flowchart segment, making it structured, you can use the "spaghetti" method. Untangle each path of the flowchart as if you were attempting to untangle strands of spaghetti in a bowl. The objective is to create a new flowchart segment that performs exactly the same tasks as the first, but using only the three structures—sequence, selection, and loop.

To begin to untangle the unstructured flowchart segment, you start at the beginning with the decision labeled A, shown in Figure D-2. This step must represent the beginning of either a selection or a loop, because a sequence would not contain a decision.

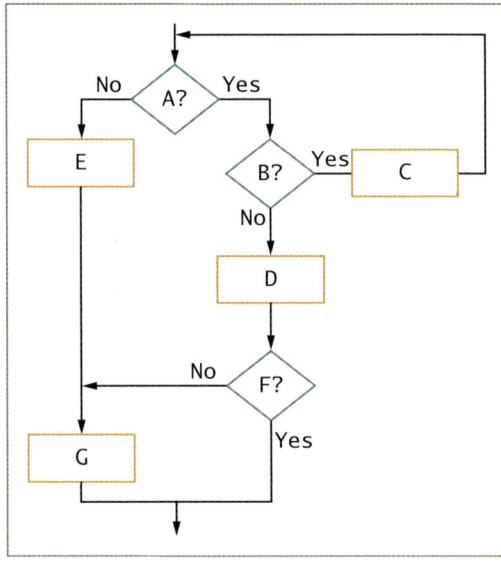

Figure D-1 Unstructured flowchart segment

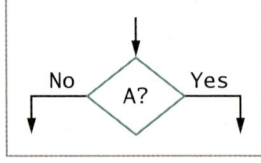

Figure D-2 Structuring, Step 1

If you follow the logic on the *No*, or left, side of the question in the original flowchart, you can pull up on the left branch of the decision. You encounter process E, followed by G, followed by the end, as shown in Figure D-3. Compare the *No* actions after Decision A in the first flowchart (Figure D-1) with the actions after Decision A in Figure D-3; they are identical.

Now continue on the right, or *Yes*, side of Decision A in Figure D-1. When you follow the flowline, you encounter a decision symbol labeled B. Pull on B's left side, and a process, D, comes up next. See Figure D-4.

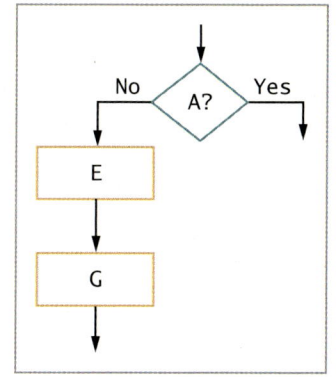

Figure D-3 Structuring, Step 2

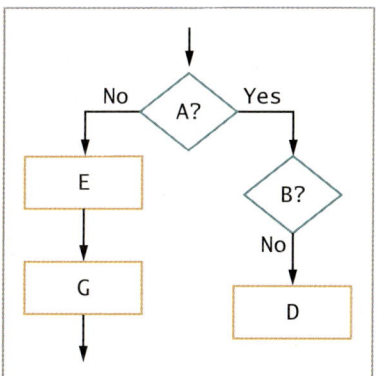

Figure D-4 Structuring, Step 3

After Step D in the original diagram, a decision labeled F comes up. Pull on its left, or *No*, side and you get a process, G, and then the end. When you pull on F's right, or *Yes*, side in the original flowchart, you simply reach the end, as shown in Figure D-5. Notice in Figure D-5 that the G process now appears in two locations. When you improve unstructured flowcharts so that they become structured, you often must repeat steps to eliminate crossed lines and spaghetti logic that is difficult to follow.

APPENDIX D — Solving Difficult Structuring Problems

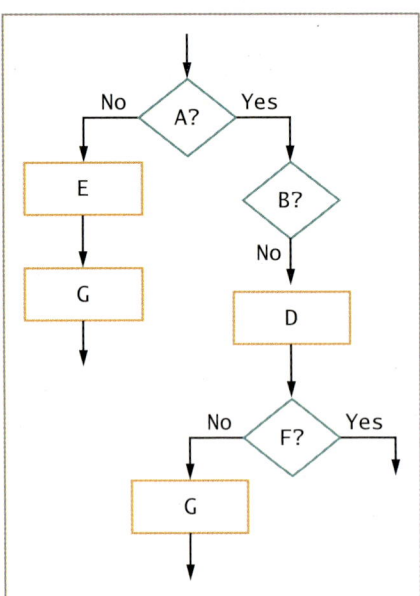

Figure D-5 Structuring, Step 4

The biggest problem in structuring the original flowchart segment from Figure D-1 follows the right, or *Yes*, side of the B decision. When the answer to B is *Yes*, you encounter process C, as shown in Figures D-1 and D-6. The structure that begins with Decision C looks like a loop because it doubles back, up to Decision A. However, a structured loop must have the appearance shown in Figure D-7: a question followed by a structure, returning right back to the question. In Figure D-1, if the path coming from C returned directly to B, there would be no problem; it would be a simple, structured loop. However, as it is, Question A must be repeated. The spaghetti technique requires that if lines of logic are tangled up, start repeating the steps in question. So, you repeat an A decision after C, as Figure D-6 shows.

Solving Difficult Structuring Problems

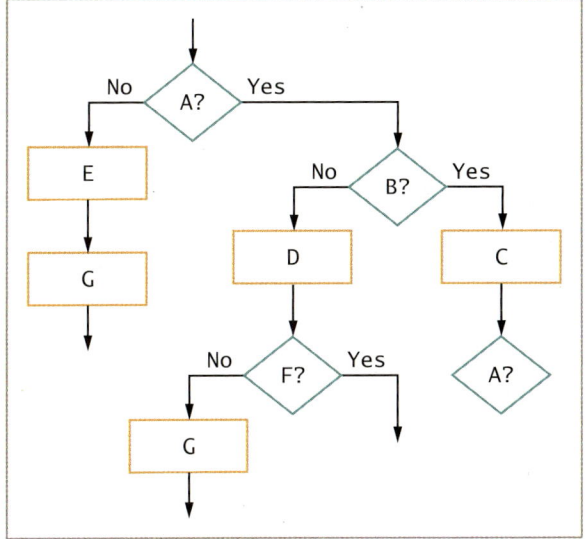

Figure D-6 Structuring, Step 5

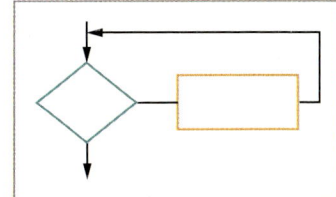

Figure D-7 A structured loop

In the original flowchart segment in Figure D-1, when A is *Yes*, Question B always follows. So, in Figure D-8, after A is *Yes* and B is *Yes*, Step C executes, and A is asked again; when A is *Yes*, B repeats. In the original, when B is *Yes*, C executes, so in Figure D-8, on the right side of B, C repeats. After C, A occurs. On the right side of A, B occurs. On the right side of B, C occurs. After C, A should occur again, and so on. Soon you should realize that, to follow the steps in the same order as in the original flowchart segment, you will repeat these same steps forever.

APPENDIX D — Solving Difficult Structuring Problems

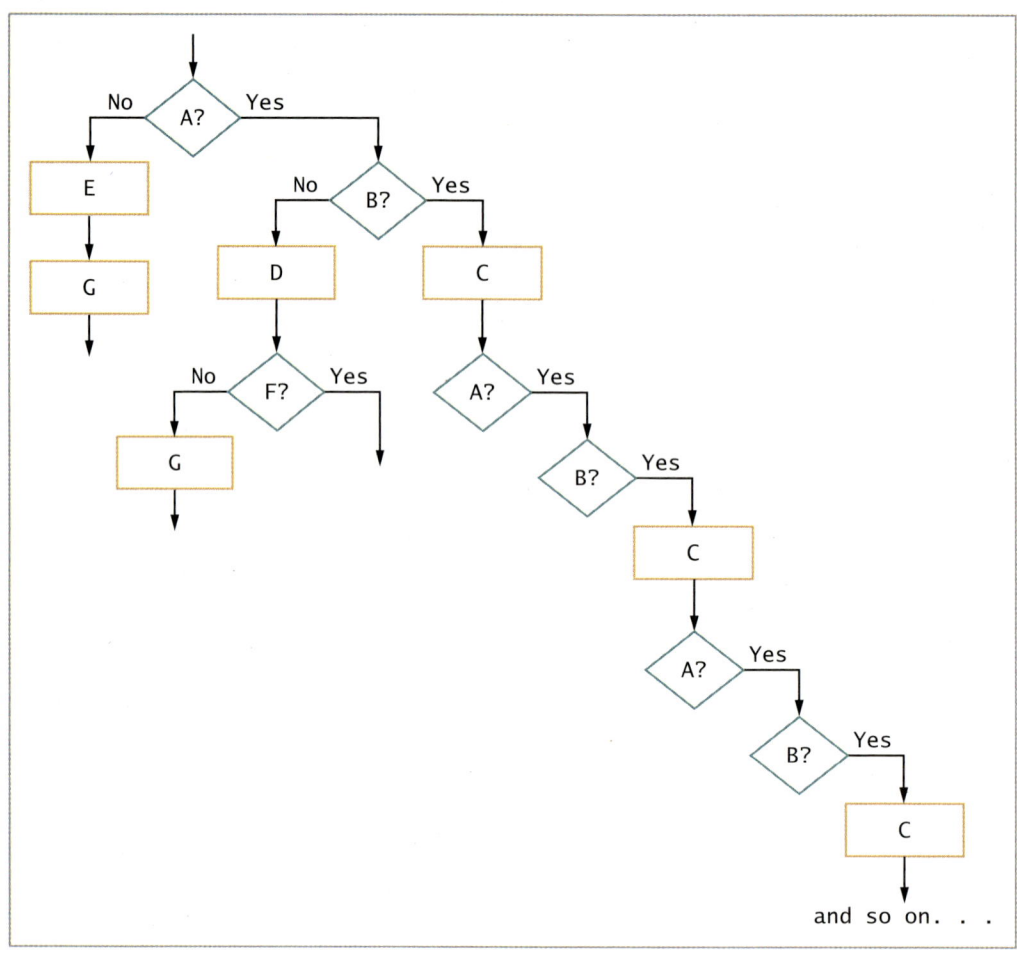

Figure D-8 Structuring, Step 6

If you continue with Figure D-8, you will never be able to finish the flowchart; every C is always followed by another A, B, and C. Sometimes, to make a program segment structured, you have to add an extra flag variable to get out of an infinite mess. A flag is a variable that you set to indicate a true or false state. Typically, a variable is called a flag when its only purpose is to tell you whether some event has occurred. You can create a flag variable named `shouldRepeat` and set its value to *Yes* or *No*, depending on whether it is appropriate to repeat Decision A. When A is *No*, the `shouldRepeat` flag should be set to *No* because, in this situation, you never want to repeat Question A again. See Figure D-9.

Solving Difficult Structuring Problems

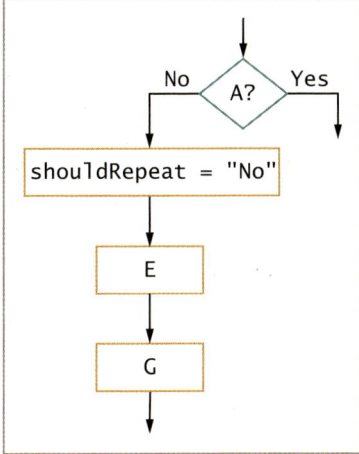

Figure D-9 Adding a flag to the flowchart

Similarly, after A is *Yes*, but when B is *No*, you never want to repeat Question A again. Figure D-10 shows that you set `shouldRepeat` to *No* when the answer to B is *No*. Then you continue with D and the F decision that executes G when F is *No*.

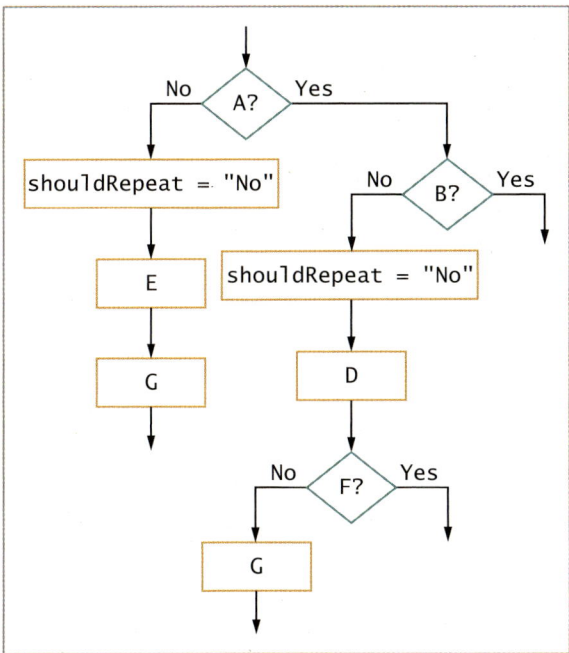

Figure D-10 Adding a flag to a second path in the flowchart

APPENDIX D Solving Difficult Structuring Problems

However, in the original flowchart segment in Figure D-1, when the B decision result is *Yes*, you *do* want to repeat A. So, when B is *Yes*, perform the process for C and set the shouldRepeat flag equal to *Yes*, as shown in Figure D-11.

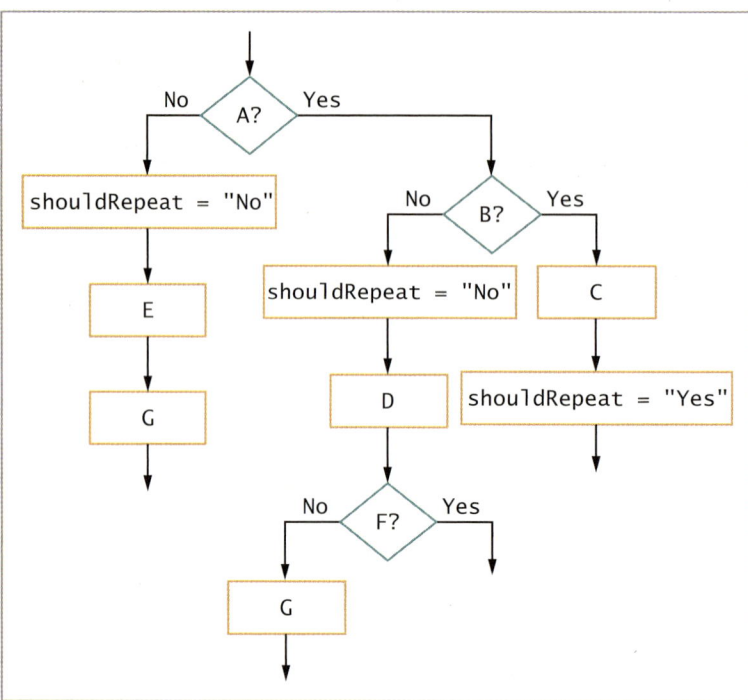

Figure D-11 Adding a flag to a third path in the flowchart

Now all paths of the flowchart can join together at the bottom with one final question: Is shouldRepeat equal to *Yes*? If it isn't, exit; but if it is, extend the flowline to go back to repeat Question A. See Figure D-12. Take a moment to verify that the steps that would execute following Figure D-12 are the same steps that would execute following Figure D-1.

Solving Difficult Structuring Problems

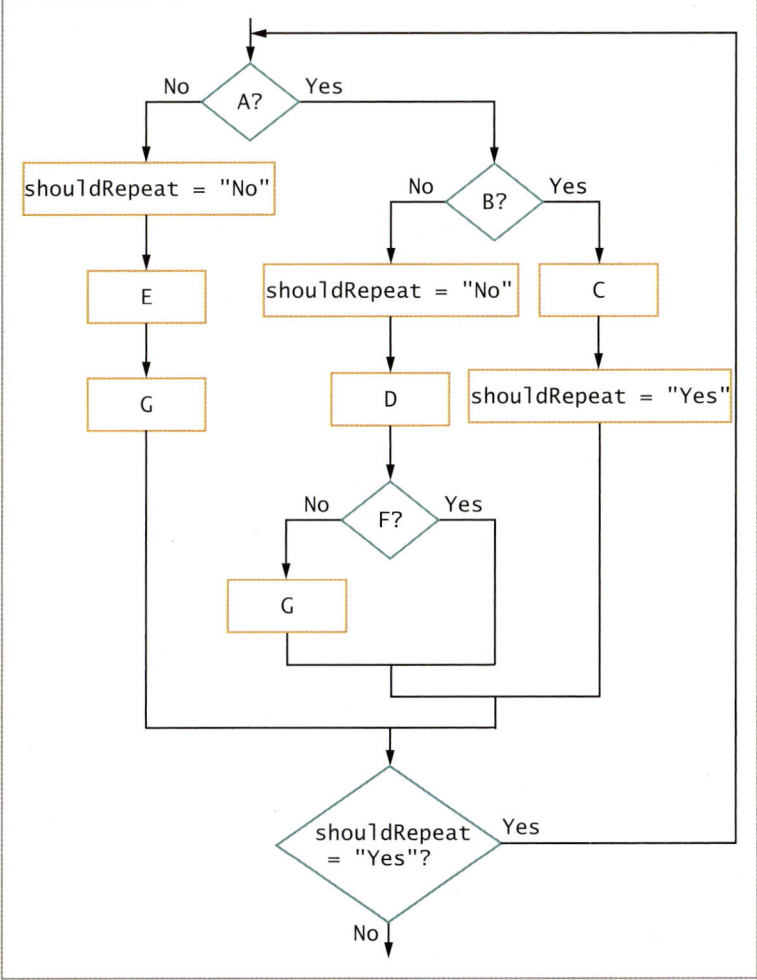

Figure D-12 Tying up the loose ends

- When A is *No*, E and G always execute.
- When A is *Yes* and B is *No*, D and decision F always execute.
- When A is *Yes* and B is *Yes*, C always executes and A repeats.

 Figure D-12 contains three nested selection structures. Notice how the F decision begins a complete selection structure whose *Yes* and *No* paths join together when the structure ends. This F selection structure is within one path of the B decision structure; the B decision begins a complete selection structure whose *Yes* and *No* paths join at the bottom. Likewise, the B selection structure resides entirely within one path of the A selection structure.

The flowchart segment in Figure D-12 performs identically to the original spaghetti version in Figure D-1. However, is this new flowchart segment structured? There are so many steps in

APPENDIX D Solving Difficult Structuring Problems

the diagram, it is hard to tell. You may be able to see the structure more clearly if you create a module named aThroughG(). If you create the module shown in Figure D-13, then the original flowchart segment can be drawn as in Figure D-14.

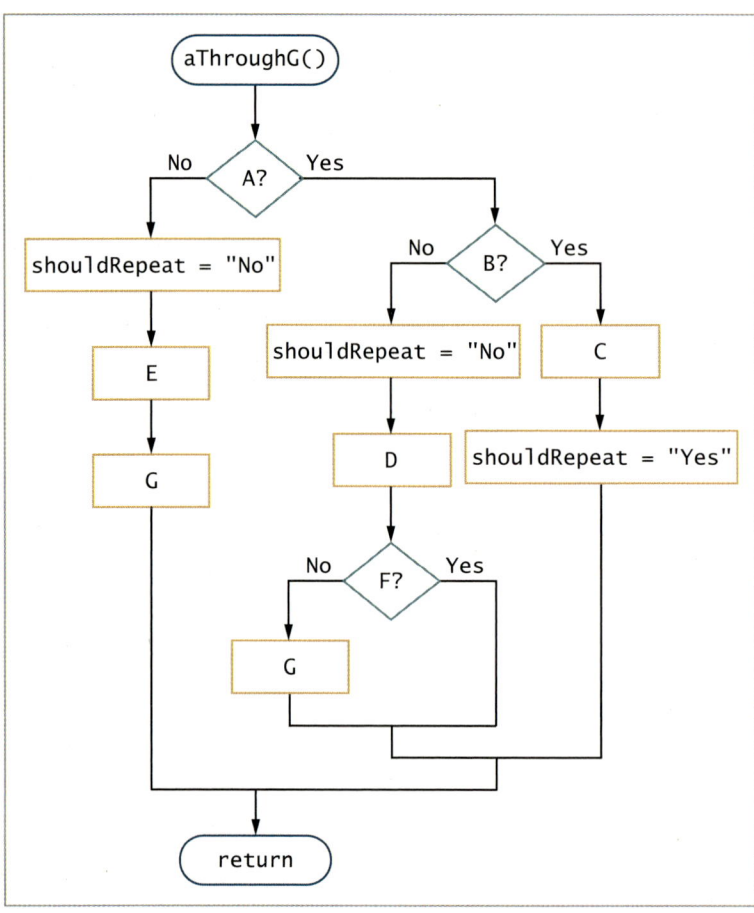

Figure D-13 The aThroughG() module

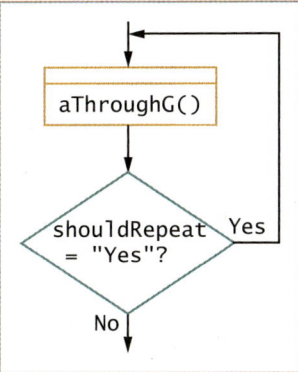

Figure D-14 Logic in Figure D-12, substituting a module for steps A through G

Now you can see that the completed flowchart segment in Figure D-14 is a do-until loop. If you prefer to use a while loop, you can redraw Figure D-14 to perform a sequence followed by a while loop, as shown in Figure D-15.

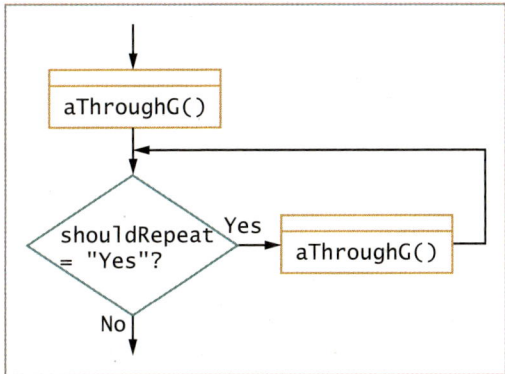

Figure D-15 Logic in Figure D-14, substituting a sequence and while loop for the do-until loop

It has taken some extra effort, including repeating specific steps and using some flag variables, but every logical problem can be solved and made to conform to structured rules by using the three structures: sequence, selection, and loop.

APPENDIX E

Creating Print Charts

A printed report is a very common type of output. You can design a printed report on a printer spacing chart, which also is called a print chart or a print layout. Many modern-day programmers use various software tools to design their output, but you also can create a print chart by hand. This appendix provides some of the details for creating a traditional handwritten print chart. Even if you never design output on your own, you might see print charts in the documentation of existing programs.

Figure E-1 shows a printer spacing chart, which basically looks like graph paper. The chart has many boxes, and in each box the designer places one character that will be printed. The rows and columns in the chart usually are numbered for reference.

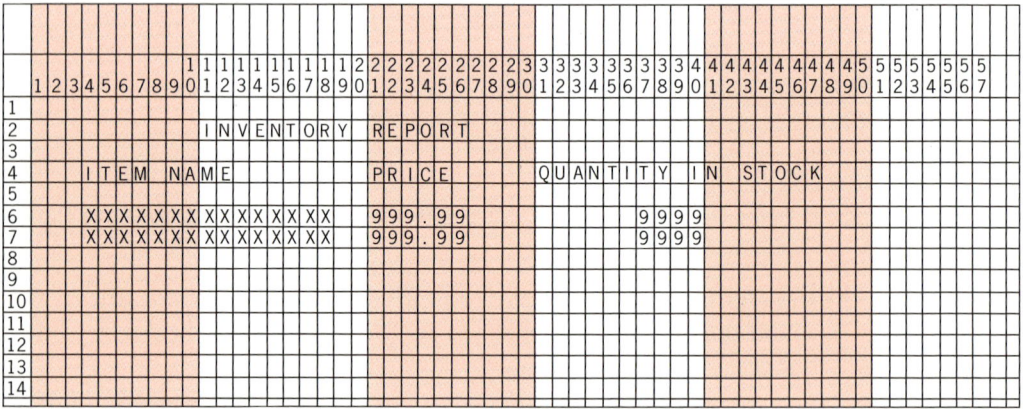

Figure E-1   A printer spacing chart

Creating Print Charts

For example, suppose that you want to create a printed report with the following features:

- A printed title, INVENTORY REPORT, that begins 11 spaces from the left edge of the page and one line down
- Column headings for ITEM NAME, PRICE, and QUANTITY IN STOCK, two lines below the title and placed over the actual data items that are displayed
- Variable data appearing below each of the column headings

The exact spacing and the use of uppercase or lowercase characters in the print chart make a difference. Notice that the constant data in the output—the items that remain the same in every execution of the report—do not need to follow the same rules as variable names in the program. Within a report, constants like INVENTORY REPORT and ITEM NAME can contain spaces. These headings exist to help readers understand the information presented in the report, not for a computer to interpret; there is no need to run the names together, as you do when choosing identifiers for variables.

A print layout typically shows how the variable data will appear on the report. Of course, the data will probably be different every time the program is executed. Thus, instead of writing in actual item names and prices, the users and programmers usually use Xs to represent generic variable characters, and 9s to represent generic variable numeric data. (Some programmers use Xs for both character and numeric data.) Each line containing Xs and 9s is a detail line, or a line that displays the data details. Detail lines typically appear many times per page, as opposed to heading lines, which contain the title and any column headings, and usually appear only once per page.

Even though an actual inventory report might eventually go on for hundreds or thousands of detail lines, writing two or three rows of Xs and 9s is sufficient to show how the data will appear. For example, if a report contains employee names and salaries, those data items will occupy the same print positions on output for line after line, whether the output eventually contains 10 employees or 10,000. A few rows of identically positioned Xs and 9s are sufficient to establish the pattern.

APPENDIX F

Two Variations on the Basic Structures—case and do-while

You can solve any logic problem you might encounter using only the three structures: sequence, selection, and loop. However, many programming languages allow two more structures: the case structure and the do-while loop. These structures are never *needed* to solve a problem—you can always use a series of selections instead of the case structure, and you can always use a sequence plus a while loop in place of the do-while loop. However, sometimes these additional structures are convenient. Programmers consider them all to be acceptable, legal structures.

The case Structure

You can use the **case structure** when there are several distinct possible values for a single variable, and each value requires a different subsequent action. Suppose that you work at a school at which tuition varies per credit hour, depending on whether a student is a freshman, sophomore, junior, or senior. The structured flowchart and pseudocode in Figure F-1 show a series of decisions that assigns different tuition values depending on the value of year.

The case Structure

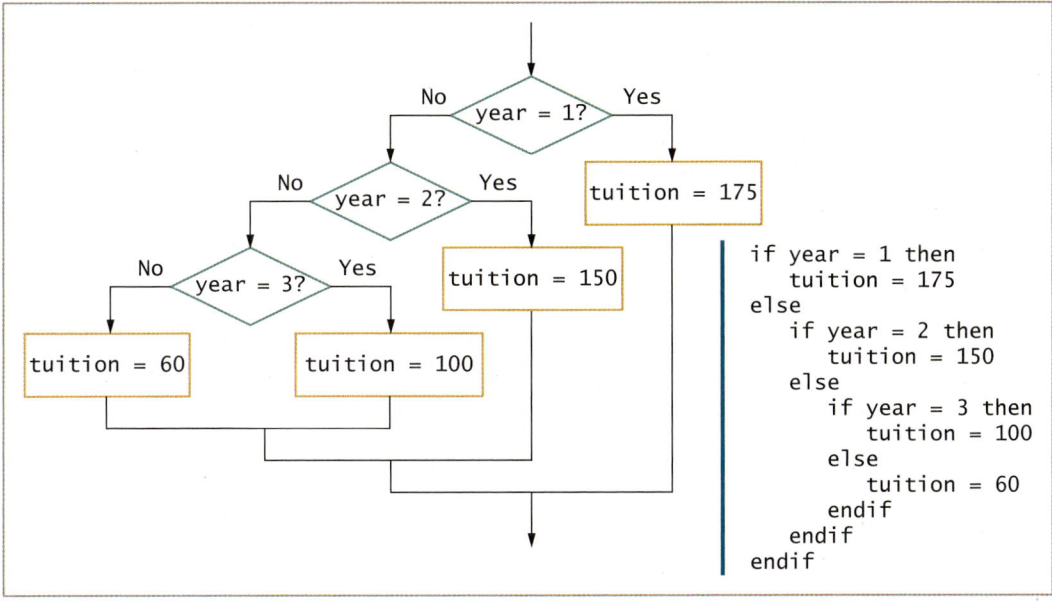

Figure F-1 Flowchart and pseudocode of tuition decisions

The logic shown in Figure F-1 is correct and completely structured. The year = 3? selection structure is contained within the year = 2? structure, which is contained within the year = 1? structure. (This example assumes that if year is not 1, 2, or 3, the student receives the senior tuition rate.)

Even though the program segments in Figure F-1 are correct and structured, many programming languages permit using a case structure, as shown in Figure F-2. When using the case structure, you compare a variable to a series of test values, taking appropriate action when a match is found. Many people feel programs that contain the case structure are easier to read than a program with a long series of decisions, and the case structure is allowed because the same results *could* be achieved with a series of structured selections (thus making the program structured). That is, if the first program is structured and the second one reflects the first one point by point, then the second one must be structured as well.

APPENDIX F — Two Variations on the Basic Structures—case and do-while

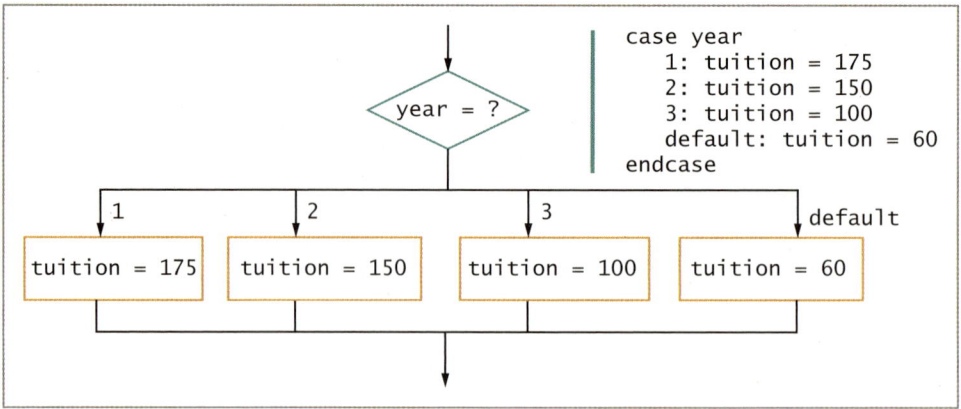

Figure F-2 Flowchart and pseudocode of case structure that determines tuition

 The term *default* in Figure F-2 means *if none of the other cases is true*. Various programming languages use different syntaxes for the default case.

You use the case structure only when a series of decisions is based on different values stored in a single variable. If multiple variables are tested, then you must use a series of decisions.

Even though a programming language permits you to use the case structure, you should understand that the case structure is just a convenience that might make a flowchart, pseudocode, or actual program code easier to understand at first glance. When you write a series of decisions using the case structure, the computer still makes a series of individual decisions, just as though you had used many if-then-else combinations. In other words, you might prefer looking at the diagram in Figure F-2 to understand the tuition fees charged by a school, but a computer actually makes the decisions as shown in Figure F-1—one at a time. When you write your own programs, it is always acceptable to express a complicated decision-making process as a series of individual selections.

The do-while Loop

Recall that a structured loop (often called a while loop) looks like Figure F-3. A special-case loop called a do-while loop looks like Figure F-4.

The do-while Loop

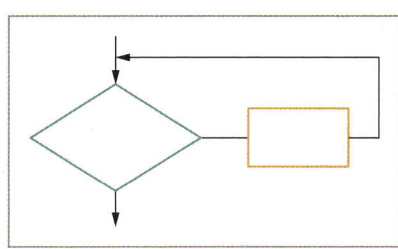

Figure F-3 The while loop, which is a pretest loop

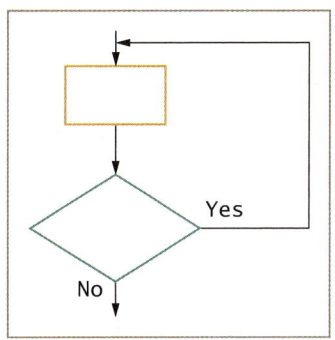

Figure F-4 Structure of a do-while loop, which is a posttest loop

An important difference exists between these two structures. In a while loop, you ask a question and, depending on the answer, you might or might not enter the loop to execute the loop's procedure. Conversely, in a **do-while loop**, you ensure that the procedure executes at least once; then, depending on the answer to the controlling question, the loop may or may not execute additional times.

Notice that the word *do* begins the name of the do-while loop. This should remind you that the action you "do" precedes testing the condition.

In a while loop, the question that controls a loop comes at the beginning, or "top," of the loop body. A while loop is a pretest loop because a condition is tested before entering the loop even once. In a do-while loop, the question that controls the loop comes at the end, or "bottom," of the loop body. Do-while loops are posttest loops because a condition is tested after the loop body has executed.

You encounter examples of do-while looping every day. For example:

do
    pay a bill
while more bills remain to be paid

As another example:

do
    wash a dish
while more dishes remain to be washed

In these examples, the activity (paying bills or washing dishes) must occur at least one time. With a do-while loop, you ask the question that determines whether you continue only after the activity has been executed at least once.

You never are required to use a posttest loop; you can duplicate the same series of actions by creating a sequence followed by a standard, pretest while loop. Consider the flowcharts and pseudocode in Figure F-5.

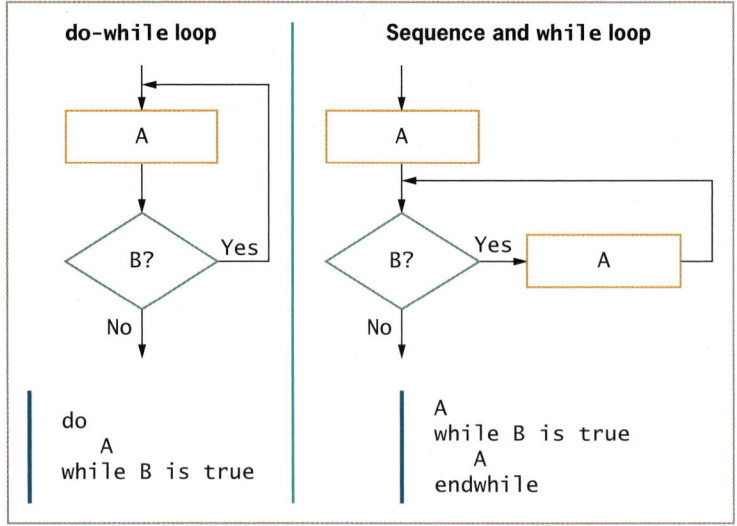

Figure F-5 Flowchart and pseudocode for do-while loop and while loop that do the same thing

On the left side of Figure F-5, A executes, and then B is asked. If B is yes, then A executes and B is asked again. On the right side of the figure, A executes, and then B is asked. If B is yes, then A executes and B is asked again. In other words, both sets of flowchart and pseudocode segments do exactly the same thing.

Because programmers understand that any posttest loop (do-while) can be expressed with a sequence followed by a while loop, most languages allow at least one version of the posttest loop for convenience.

Recognizing the Characteristics Shared by All Structured Loops

As you examine Figures F-3 and F-4, notice that in the while loop, the loop-controlling question is placed at the beginning of the steps that repeat. In the do-while loop, the loop-controlling question is placed at the end of the sequence of steps that repeat.

All structured loops, both pretest and posttest, share these two characteristics:

- The loop-controlling question must provide either the entry to or exit from the repeating structure.
- The loop-controlling question provides the *only* entry to or exit from the repeating structure.

In other words, there is exactly one loop-controlling value, and it provides either the only entrance to or the only exit from the loop.

Recognizing Unstructured Loops

 Some languages support a **do-until loop**, which is a posttest loop that iterates until the loop-controlling question is false. The `do-until` loop follows structured loop rules.

Recognizing Unstructured Loops

Figure F-6 shows an unstructured loop. It is not a `while` loop, which begins with a decision and, after an action, returns to the decision. It is also not a `do-while` loop, which begins with an action and ends with a decision that might repeat the action. Instead, it begins like a posttest loop (a `do-while` loop), with a process followed by a decision, but one branch of the decision does not repeat the initial process. Instead, it performs an additional new action before repeating the initial process.

If you need to use the logic shown in Figure F-6—performing a task, asking a question, and perhaps performing an additional task before looping back to the first process—then the way to make the logic structured is to repeat the initial process within the loop at the end of the loop. Figure F-7 shows the same logic as Figure F-6, but now it is structured logic, with a sequence of two actions occurring within the loop.

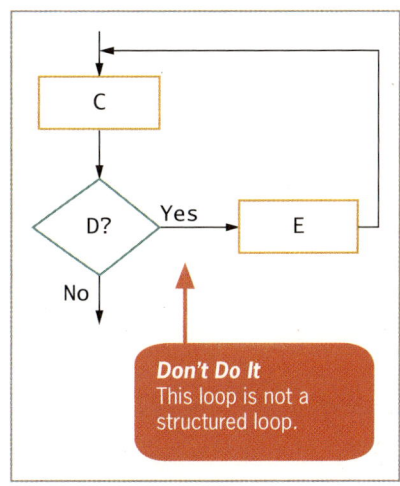

Figure F-6 Unstructured loop

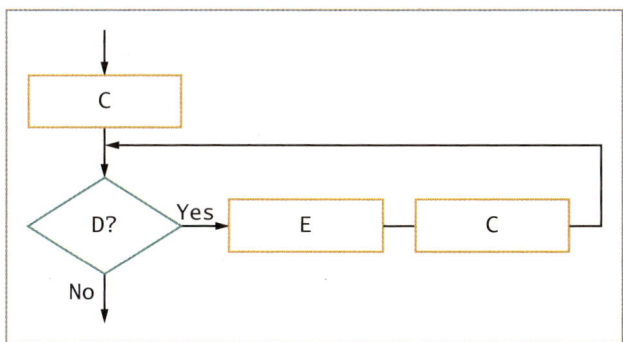

Figure F-7 Sequence and structured loop that accomplish the same tasks as Figure F-6

 Especially when you are first mastering structured logic, you might prefer to use only the three basic structures—sequence, selection, and `while` loop. Every logical problem can be solved using only these three structures, and you can understand all of the examples in this book using only these three structures.

APPENDIX F: Two Variations on the Basic Structures—case and do-while

Key Terms

A **case structure** tests a single variable against multiple values, providing separate actions for each logical path.

A **do-while loop** is a posttest loop in which the body executes before the loop control variable is tested.

A **do-until loop** is a posttest loop that iterates until the loop-controlling question is false.

Glossary

A

abstract class A class from which concrete objects cannot be created, but which can serve as a basis for inheritance.

abstract data type (ADT) A programmer-defined type, such as a class.

abstraction The process of paying attention to important properties while ignoring nonessential details.

access specifier The adjective that defines the type of access outside classes will have to the attribute or method.

accessibility Describes screen design issues that make programs easier to use for people with physical limitations.

accessor method A method that gets values from class fields.

accumulator A variable used to gather or accumulate values.

activity diagram A UML diagram that shows the flow of actions of a system, including branches that occur when decisions affect the outcome.

actual parameters The arguments in a method call.

addresses Numbers that identify computer memory and storage locations.

aggregation A whole-part relationship, specifically when the part can exist without the whole.

algorithm The sequence of steps necessary to solve any problem.

alphanumeric values The set of values that include alphabetic characters, numbers, and punctuation.

alternate keys In a database, the remaining candidate keys after a primary key is chosen.

ambiguous methods Methods that the compiler cannot distinguish because they have the same name and parameter types.

American Standard Code for Information Interchange (ASCII) An eight-bit character coding scheme used on many personal computers.

ancestors The entire list of parent classes from which a class is derived.

AND decision A decision in which two conditions must both be true for an action to take place.

animation The rapid sequence of still images, each slightly different from the previous one, that produces the illusion of movement.

GLOSSARY

annotation symbol A flowchart symbol used to hold comments; it is most often represented by a three-sided box connected with a dashed line to the step it explains.

anomaly An irregularity in a database's design that causes problems and inconveniences.

application software Programs that carry out a task for the user, in contrast to *system software*.

argument to a method A value passed to a method in the method call.

array A series or list of variables in computer memory, all of which have the same name but are differentiated with subscripts.

ascending order Describes the arrangement of data items from lowest to highest.

assignment operator The equal sign; it always requires the name of a memory location on its left side.

assignment statement A statement that stores the result of any value on its right side to the named location on its left side.

association relationship Describes the connection or link between objects in a UML diagram.

atomic attributes In a database, describes columns that are as small as possible so that they contain undividable pieces of data.

atomic transactions A series of transactions that execute completely or not at all, avoiding partial completion of a task.

attribute One field or column in a database table or a characteristic that defines an object as part of a class.

authentication techniques Security techniques that include storing and verifying passwords and using physical characteristics, such as fingerprints or voice recognition, before users can be authorized to view data.

B

backup file A copy that is kept in case values need to be restored to their original state.

base 2 Describes numbers created using the binary numbering system.

base 10 Describes numbers created using the decimal numbering system.

base 16 Describes numbers created using the hexadecimal numbering system.

base class A class that is used as a basis for inheritance.

base table The "one" table in a one-to-many relationship in a database.

batch A group of transactions applied all at once.

batch processing Processing that performs the same tasks with many records in sequence.

behavior diagrams UML diagrams that emphasize what happens in a system.

binary decision A yes-or-no decision; so called because there are two possible outcomes.

binary files Files that contain data that has not been encoded as text.

binary language A computer language represented using a series of 0s and 1s.

binary numbering system The numbering system based on two digits; column values are multiples of 2.

binary operator An operator that requires two operands—one on each side.

GLOSSARY

binary search A search that starts in the middle of a sorted list, and then determines whether it should continue higher or lower to find a target value.

bit A binary digit; a unit of storage equal to one-eighth of a byte.

black box The analogy that programmers use to refer to the details of hidden methods.

block A group of statements that execute as a single unit.

Boolean expression An expression that represents only one of two states, usually expressed as true or false.

bubble sort A sorting algorithm in which list elements are arranged in ascending or descending order by comparing items in pairs and swapping them when they are out of order.

byte A unit of computer storage equal to eight bits.

C

call a module To use a module's name to invoke it, causing it to execute.

camel casing A naming convention in which the initial letter is lowercase, multiple-word names are run together, and each new word within the name begins with an uppercase letter.

candidate keys Columns or attributes that could serve as a primary key in a table.

cardinality Describes an arithmetic relationship between objects.

cascading if statement A series of nested if statements.

case structure A structure that tests a single variable against multiple values, providing separate actions for each logical path.

catch an exception To receive an exception from a throw so it can be handled.

catch block A segment of code written to handle an exception that might be thrown by the try block that precedes it.

central processing unit (CPU) The piece of hardware that processes data.

character A letter, number, or special symbol such as *A*, *7*, or *$*.

child class A derived class.

child file A copy of a file after revision.

class A group or collection of objects with common attributes.

class client or **class user** A program or class that instantiates objects of another prewritten class.

class definition A set of program statements that define the characteristics of a class's objects and the methods that can be applied to its objects.

class diagram A tool for describing a class that consists of a rectangle divided into three sections that show the name, data, and methods of a class.

class method A static method; class methods are not instance methods and they do not receive a this reference.

client A program or other method that uses a method.

closing a file An action that makes a file no longer available to an application.

coding the program The act of writing the statements of a program in a programming language.

cohesion A measure of how a method's internal statements are focused to accomplish the method's purpose.

GLOSSARY

command line The location on a computer screen where entries are typed to communicate with the computer's operating system.

communication diagram A UML diagram that emphasizes the organization of objects that participate in a system.

compiler Software that translates a high-level language into machine language and identifies syntax errors. A compiler is similar to an interpreter; however, a compiler translates all the statements in a program prior to executing them.

component diagram A UML diagram that emphasizes the files, database tables, documents, and other components used by a system's software.

composition The technique of placing an object within an object of another class.

compound condition A condition constructed when multiple decisions are required before determining an outcome.

compound key or **composite key** In a database, a key constructed from multiple columns.

computer file A collection of data stored on a nonvolatile device in a computer system.

computer memory The temporary, internal storage within a computer.

computer system A combination of all the components required to process and store data using a computer.

concatenate columns To combine database table columns to produce a compound key.

concurrent update problem A problem that can occur when two database users revise the same record at the same time.

conditional AND operator A symbol used to combine decisions so that two or more conditions must be true for an action to occur. Also called an *AND operator*.

conditional OR operator A symbol used to combine decisions when any one condition can be true for an action to occur. Also called an *OR operator*.

constructor An automatically called method that establishes an object.

container One of a class of objects whose main purpose is to hold other elements—for example, a window.

control break A temporary detour in the logic of a program for special group processing.

control break field A variable that holds the value that signals a special processing break in a program.

control break program A program in which a change in the value of a variable initiates special actions or processing.

control break report A report that lists items in groups. Frequently, each group is followed by a subtotal.

conversion The set of actions an organization must take to switch over to using a new program or system.

counter Any numeric variable used to count the number of times an event has occurred.

coupling A measure of the strength of the connection between two program methods.

D

data dictionary A list of every variable name used in a program, along with its type, size, and description.

GLOSSARY

data hierarchy Represents the relationship of databases, files, records, fields, and characters.

data integrity Describes a database that follows a set of rules to make its data accurate and consistent.

data redundancy The unnecessary repetition of data.

data type The characteristic of a variable that describes the kind of values the variable can hold and the types of operations that can be performed with it.

database A logical container that holds a group of files, often called tables, that together serve the information needs of an organization.

database management software A set of programs that allows users to create and manage data.

dead path A logical path that can never be traveled.

deadlock A flaw in multithreaded programs in which two or more threads wait for each other to execute.

debugging The process of finding and correcting program errors.

decimal numbering system The numbering system based on 10 digits; column values are multiples of 10.

decision structure A program structure in which a question is asked, and, depending on the answer, one of two courses of action is taken. Then, no matter which path is followed, the paths join and the next task executes.

decision symbol A symbol that represents a decision in a flowchart; it is shaped like a diamond.

declaration A statement that names a variable and its data type.

declaring variables The process of naming program variables and assigning a type to them.

decrement To change a variable by decreasing it by a constant value, frequently 1.

default constructor A constructor that requires no arguments.

default input and output devices Hardware devices that do not require opening; usually they are the keyboard and monitor, respectively.

defensive programming A technique in which programmers try to prepare for all possible errors before they occur.

definite loop A loop for which the number of repetitions is a predetermined value.

delete anomaly A problem that occurs when a row is deleted from a database table; the result is loss of related data.

denormalize To place a database table in a lower normal form by repeating information.

deployment diagram A UML diagram that focuses on a system's hardware.

derived class An extended class.

descending order Describes the arrangement of data items from highest to lowest.

desk-checking The process of walking through a program solution on paper.

destructor An automatically called method that contains the actions required when an instance of a class is destroyed.

detail loop tasks The steps that are repeated for each set of input data.

direct access files Random access files.

GLOSSARY

directories Organization units on storage devices; each can contain multiple files as well as additional directories. In a graphical interface system, directories are often called *folders*.

documentation All of the supporting material that goes with a program.

DOS prompt The command line in the DOS operating system.

do-until loop A posttest loop that iterates until the loop-controlling question is false.

do-while loop A posttest loop in which the body executes before the loop control variable is tested.

dual-alternative if or **dual-alternative selection** A selection structure that defines one action to be taken when the tested condition is true, and another action to be taken when it is false.

dummy value A preselected value that stops the execution of a program.

E

echoing input The act of repeating input back to a user either in a subsequent prompt or in output.

element A separate array variable.

elided Describes the omitted parts of UML diagrams that are edited for clarity.

else clause A part of a decision that holds the action or actions that execute only when the Boolean expression in the decision is false.

encapsulation The act of containing a task's instructions and data in the same method.

encryption The process of coding data into a format that human beings cannot read.

end-of-job task A step at the end of a program to finish the application.

end-structure statement A statement that designates the end of a pseudocode structure.

entity One record or row in a database table.

eof An end-of-data file marker, short for *end of file*.

event An occurrence that generates a message sent to an object.

event-driven or **event-based** Describes programs and actions that occur in response to user-initiated events such as clicking a mouse button.

exception The generic term used for an error in object-oriented languages. Presumably, errors are not usual occurrences; they are the "exceptions" to the rule.

exception-handling techniques The techniques for managing errors in object-oriented programs.

executing To have a computer use a written and compiled program; also called *running*.

extend variation A UML use case variation that shows functions beyond those found in a base case.

Extended Binary Coded Decimal Interchange Code (EBCDIC) An eight-bit character coding scheme used on many larger computers.

extended class A derived class.

external documentation All the external material that programmers develop to support a program; contrast with *program comments*, which are internal program documentation.

GLOSSARY

F

facilitator A work method.

field A single data item, such as `lastName`, `streetAddress`, or `annualSalary`.

file A group of records that go together for some logical reason.

first normal form, or **1NF** The normalization form in which repeating groups are eliminated from a database.

flag A variable that indicates whether some event has occurred.

floating-point value A fractional, numeric variable that contains a decimal point.

flowchart A pictorial representation of the logical steps it takes to solve a problem.

flowline An arrow that connects the steps in a flowchart.

folders Organization units on storage devices; each can contain multiple files as well as additional folders. Folders are graphic directories.

for statement A statement that can be used to code definite loops; also called a *for loop*. The statement contains a loop control variable that it automatically initializes, evaluates, and alters.

foreign key A column that is not a key in a table but contains an attribute that is a key in a related table.

fork A feature of a UML activity diagram that defines a logical branch in which all paths are followed simultaneously.

formal parameters The variables in a method declaration that accept values from the actual parameters.

fragile Describes classes that depend on field names from parent classes and are prone to errors.

functional cohesion The extent to which all operations in a method contribute to the performance of only one task.

functional dependence A relationship in which an attribute can be determined by another.

G

garbage Describes the unknown value stored in an unassigned variable.

generalization variation A variation used in a UML diagram when a use case is less specific than others and the more specific case should be substituted for a general one.

get method An instance method that returns a value from a class.

gigabyte A billion bytes.

GIGO Acronym for *garbage in, garbage out*; it means that if input is incorrect, output is worthless.

global Describes variables that are known to an entire program.

goto-less programming A name to describe structured programming, because structured programmers do not use a "go to" statement.

graphical user interface (GUI) A program interface that uses screens to display program output and allows users to interact with a program in a graphical environment.

H

hardware The equipment of a computer system.

has-a relationship A whole-part relationship; the type of relationship that exists when using composition.

help method A work method.

GLOSSARY

hexadecimal numbering system The numbering system based on 16 digits; column values are multiples of 16.

hierarchy chart A diagram that illustrates modules' relationships to each other.

high-level programming language A programming language that is English-like, as opposed to a low-level programming language.

housekeeping tasks Tasks that must be performed at the beginning of a program to prepare for the rest of the program.

Hungarian notation A variable-naming convention in which a variable's data type or other information is stored as part of its name.

I

I/O symbol An input/output symbol.

icons Small pictures on a screen that a user can select with a mouse.

identifier A program component's name.

IDE The acronym for Integrated Development Environment, which is the visual development environment in some programming languages.

if-then A structure similar to an if-then-else, but no alternative or "else" action is necessary.

if-then clause The part of a decision that holds the resulting action when the Boolean expression in the decision is true.

if-then-else Another name for a selection structure.

immutable Not changing during normal operation.

implementation The body of a method; the statements that carry out the tasks of a method.

implementation hiding A programming principle that describes the encapsulation of method details.

in scope The characteristic of variables and constants declared within a method that apply only within that method.

inaccessible Describes any field or method that cannot be reached because of a logical error.

include variation A UML use case variation in which a case can be part of multiple use cases.

increment To change a variable by adding a constant value to it, frequently 1.

indefinite loop A loop for which the number of executions cannot be predicted when the program is written.

index A list of key fields paired with the storage address for the corresponding data record.

indirect relationship Describes the relationship between parallel arrays in which an element in the first array does not directly access its corresponding value in the second array.

infinite loop A repeating flow of logic without an ending.

information Processed data.

information hiding or **data hiding** The concept that other classes should not alter an object's attributes—only the methods of an object's own class should have that privilege.

inheritance The process of acquiring the traits of one's predecessors.

initializing a variable The act of assigning the first value to a variable, often at the same time the variable is created.

GLOSSARY

inner loop When loops are nested, the loop that is contained within the other loop.

input Describes the entry of data items into computer memory using hardware devices such as keyboards and mice.

input symbol A symbol that indicates an input operation and is represented in flowcharts as a parallelogram.

input/output symbol A parallelogram in flowcharts.

insert anomaly A problem that occurs in a database when new rows are added to a table; the result is incomplete rows.

insertion sort A sorting algorithm in which each list element is examined one at a time; if an element is out of order relative to any of the items earlier in the list, each earlier item is moved down one position and then the tested element is inserted.

instance An existing object or tangible example of a class.

instance method A method that operates correctly yet differently for each class object; an instance method is nonstatic and receives a `this` reference.

instance variables The data components that belong to every instantiated object.

instant access files Random access files in which records must be accessed immediately.

instantiate To create an object.

instantiation An instance of a class.

integer A whole number.

integrated development environment (IDE) A software package that provides an editor, compiler, and other programming tools.

interaction diagrams UML diagrams that emphasize the flow of control and data among the system elements being modeled.

interactive program A program in which a user makes direct requests, as opposed to one in which input comes from a file.

interactivity diagram A diagram that shows the relationship between screens in an interactive GUI program.

interface to a method A method's return type, name, and arguments; the part of a method that a client sees and uses.

internal documentation Documentation within a program. See also *program comments*.

IPO chart A program development tool that delineates input, processing, and output tasks.

is-a relationship The relationship between an object and each of the classes in its ancestry.

iteration Another name for a loop structure.

J

join A feature of a UML activity diagram that reunites the flow of control after a fork.

join column The column on which two tables are connected in a database.

join operation, or **join** The operation that connects two tables based on the values in a common column.

K

key A field or column that uniquely identifies a record.

key field The field whose contents make a record unique among all records in a file.

GLOSSARY

keywords The limited word set that is reserved in a language.

kilobyte Approximately 1000 bytes.

L

left-to-right associativity Describes operators that evaluate the expression to the left first.

libraries Stored collections of classes that serve related purposes.

linear search A search through a list from one end to the other.

linked list A list that contains an extra field in every record that holds the physical address of the next logical record.

listener An object that is prepared to respond to events from specified sources.

local Describes variables that are declared within the method that uses them.

lock A mechanism that prevents changes to a database for a period of time.

logic Instructions given to the computer in a specific sequence, without omitting any instructions or adding extraneous instructions.

logical error An error that occurs when incorrect instructions are performed, or when instructions are performed in the wrong order.

logical NOT operator A symbol that reverses the meaning of a Boolean expression.

logical order The order in which a list is used, even though it is not necessarily stored in that physical order.

loop A structure that repeats actions while a condition continues.

loop body The set of actions that occur within a loop.

loop control variable A variable that determines whether a loop will continue.

loop structure A structure that repeats actions while a test condition remains true.

loose coupling A relationship that occurs when methods do not depend on others.

low-level language A programming language not far removed from machine language, as opposed to a high-level programming language.

lvalue The memory address identifier to the left of an assignment operator.

M

machine language A computer's on/off circuitry language; the low-level language made up of 1s and 0s that the computer understands.

magic number An unnamed numeric constant.

main program A program that runs from start to stop and calls other modules; also called a *main program method*.

mainline logic The overall logic of the main program from beginning to end.

maintenance All the improvements and corrections made to a program after it is in production.

making a decision Testing a value to determine a logical path.

making declarations The process of naming program variables and assigning a type to them.

many-to-many relationship A relationship in which multiple rows in a database table can correspond to multiple rows in another table.

master file A file that holds complete and relatively permanent data.

GLOSSARY

matrix A term sometimes used by mathematicians to describe a two-dimensional array.

mean The arithmetic average.

median The value in the middle position of a list when the values are sorted.

megabyte A million bytes.

merging files The act of combining two or more files while maintaining the sequential order.

method A series of statements that carry out a task.

method body The set of all the statements in a method.

method header A program component that precedes a method's implementation; the header includes the method identifier and possibly other necessary information.

method return statement A statement that marks the end of the method and identifies the point at which control returns to the calling method.

method type The data type of a method's return value.

Microsoft Visual Studio IDE A software package that contains useful tools for creating programs in Visual Basic, C++, and C#.

modeling The process of designing an application before writing code.

modularization The process of breaking down a program into modules.

module A small program unit used with other modules to make a program. Programmers also refer to modules as subroutines, procedures, functions, and methods.

module's body The part of a module that contains all the statements in the module.

module's header The part of a module that includes the module identifier and possibly other necessary identifying information.

module's return statement The part of a module that marks its end and identifies the point at which control returns to the program or module that called the module.

multidimensional arrays Lists with more than one dimension.

multiple inheritance The ability to inherit from more than one class.

multiplicity An arithmetic relationship between objects.

multithreading Using multiple threads of execution.

mutator method An instance method that can modify an object's attributes.

N

named constant A named memory location, similar to a variable, except its value never changes during the execution of a program. Conventionally, constants are named using all capital letters.

nested decision A decision within the if-then or else clause of another decision; also called a *nested if*.

nested loop A loop structure within another loop structure; nesting loops are loops within loops.

nesting structures Placing a structure within another structure.

nibble A storage measurement equal to four bits, or a half byte.

nondefault constructor A constructor that requires at least one argument.

GLOSSARY

nonkey attribute Any column in a database table that is not a key.

nonstatic methods Methods that exist to be used with an object; they are instance methods and they receive a `this` reference.

nonvolatile Describes storage whose contents are retained when power is lost.

normal forms Rules for constructing a well-designed database.

normalization The process of designing and creating a set of database tables that satisfies the users' needs and avoids redundancies and anomalies.

null case The branch of a decision in which no action is taken.

nulls Empty columns in a database.

numeric Describes data that consists of numbers.

numeric constant A specific numeric value.

numeric variable A variable that holds numeric values.

O

object One tangible example of a class; an instance of a class.

object code Code that has been translated to machine language.

object diagrams UML diagrams that are similar to class diagrams, but that model specific instances of classes.

object dictionary A list of the objects used in a program, including which screens they are used on and whether any code, or script, is associated with them.

object-oriented programming (OOP) A programming technique that focuses on objects, or "things," and describes their attributes and behaviors.

one-dimensional array A list accessed using a single subscript.

one-to-many relationship The relationship in which one row in a table can be related to many rows in another table. It is the most common type of relationship among tables.

one-to-one relationship The relationship in which a row in one table corresponds to exactly one row in another table.

opening a file The process of locating a file on a storage device, physically preparing it for reading, and associating it with an identifier inside a program.

operating system The software that runs a computer and manages its resources.

OR decision A decision that contains two or more conditions; if at least one condition is met, the resulting action takes place.

order of operations Describes the rules of precedence.

out of bounds Describes an array subscript that is not within the range of acceptable subscripts.

outer loop The loop that contains a nested loop.

output Describes the operation of retrieving information from memory and sending it to a device, such as a monitor or printer, so people can view, interpret, and work with the results.

output symbol A symbol that indicates an output operation and is represented as a parallelogram in flowcharts.

overhead All the resources and time required by an operation.

overload a method To create multiple methods with the same name but different parameter lists.

GLOSSARY

overloading Supplying diverse meanings for a single identifier.

overrides The action that occurs when a method is used by default in place of another method with the same signature.

P

packages Another name for libraries in some languages.

parallel arrays Two or more arrays in which each element in one array is associated with the element in the same relative position in the other array or arrays.

parameter list All the data types and parameter names that appear in a method header.

parameter to a method A data item passed into a method from the outside.

parent class A base class.

parent file A copy of a file before revision.

partial key dependency The condition that occurs when a column in a database table depends on only part of the table's key.

Pascal casing A naming convention in which the initial letter is uppercase, multiple-word names are run together, and each new word within the name begins with an uppercase letter.

passed by reference Describes a method parameter that represents the item's memory address.

passed by value Describes a variable that has a copy of its value sent to a method and stored in a new memory location accessible to the method.

path The combination of a file's disk drive and the complete hierarchy of directories in which the file resides.

permanent storage devices Hardware devices that hold nonvolatile data; examples include hard disks, DVDs, Zip disks, USB drives, and reels of magnetic tape.

permissions Attributes assigned to a user to indicate which parts of a database the user can view, change, or delete.

persistent lock A long-term database lock required when users want to maintain a consistent view of their data while making modifications over a long transaction.

physical order The order in which a list is actually stored even though it might be accessed in a different logical order.

pixel A picture element; one of the tiny dots of light that form a grid on a monitor.

polymorphism The ability of a method to act appropriately depending on the context.

populating an array To assign values to array elements.

portable Describes a module that can more easily be reused in multiple programs.

posttest loop A loop that tests its loop control variable after each iteration, meaning that the loop body executes at least one time.

precedence The quality of an operation that determines the order in which it is evaluated.

pretest loop A loop that tests its loop control variable before each iteration, meaning that the loop body might never execute.

primary key A field or column that uniquely identifies a record or database object.

priming input or **priming read** The statement that reads the first input data record prior to starting a structured loop.

GLOSSARY

primitive data types In a programming language, simple number and character types that are not class types.

private access A privilege of class members in which data or methods cannot be used by any method that is not part of the same class.

procedural programming A programming technique that focuses on the procedures that programmers create.

processing To organize data items, check them for accuracy, or perform mathematical operations on them.

processing symbol A symbol represented as a rectangle in flowcharts.

program Sets of instructions for a computer.

program code The set of instructions a programmer writes in a programming language.

program comment A nonexecuting statement that programmers place within code to explain program statements in English. See also *internal program documentation*.

program development cycle The steps that occur during a program's lifetime, including planning, coding, translating, testing, producing, and maintaining the program.

program level The level at which global variables are declared.

programming The act of developing and writing programs.

programming language A language such as Visual Basic, C#, C++, Java, or COBOL, used to write programs.

prompt A message that is displayed on a monitor, asking the user for a response.

property A method that gets and sets a field value using simple syntax.

protected access specifier A specifier used when outside classes should not be able to use a data field unless they are children of the original class.

protected node The UML diagram name for an exception-throwing `try` block.

pseudocode An English-like representation of the logical steps it takes to solve a problem.

public access A privilege of class members in which other programs and methods may use the specified data or methods within a class.

pure polymorphism The situation in which one method implementation can be used with a variety of arguments in object-oriented programming.

Q

query A question used to access values in a database; its purpose is often to display a subset of data.

query by example The process of creating a database query by filling in blanks.

R

random access files Files that contain records that can be located in any order.

random access memory (RAM) Temporary, internal computer storage.

random-access storage device A storage device, such as a disk, from which records can be accessed in any order.

range check The comparison of a variable to a series of values that mark the limiting ends of ranges.

GLOSSARY

reading from a file The act of copying data from a file on a storage device into RAM.

real numbers Floating-point numbers.

real-time Describes applications that require a record to be accessed immediately while a client is waiting.

record A group of fields stored together as a unit because they hold data about a single entity.

recovery The process of returning a database to a correct form that existed before an error occurred.

recursion A programming event that occurs when a method is defined in terms of itself.

recursive method A method that calls itself.

registering components The act of signing up components so they can react to events initiated by other components.

related table The "many" table in a one-to-many relationship in a database.

relational comparison operator A symbol that expresses Boolean comparisons. Examples include =, >, <, >=, <=, and <>.

relational database A group of tables from which connections can be made to produce virtual tables.

relationship A connection between two tables in a database.

reliability The feature of modular programs that ensures a module has been tested and proven to function correctly.

repeating group A subset of rows in a database table that all depend on the same key.

repetition Another name for a loop structure.

return type The data type for any value a method returns.

reusability The feature of modular programs that allows individual modules to be used in a variety of applications.

reverse engineering The process of creating an improved model of an existing system.

right-associativity and **right-to-left associativity** Descriptions of operators that evaluate the expression to the right first.

running To have a computer use a written and compiled program. Also called *executing*.

S

scenario A variation in the sequence of actions required in a UML use case diagram.

script A procedural module that depends on user-initiated events in object-oriented programs.

scripting language A language such as Python, Lua, Perl, or PHP used to write programs that are typed directly from a keyboard and are stored as text rather than as binary executable files. Also called *scripting programming languages* or *script languages*.

second normal form, or **2NF** The normalization form in which partial key dependencies are eliminated from a database.

SELECT-FROM-WHERE An SQL statement that selects fields to view from a table where one or more conditions are met.

selection structure A program structure that contains a question and takes one of two courses of action depending on the answer. Then, no matter which path is followed, program logic continues with the next task.

GLOSSARY

self-documenting Describes programs that contain meaningful and descriptive data, method, and class names.

semantic error An error that occurs when a correct word is used in an incorrect context.

sentinel value A value that represents an entry or exit point.

sequence diagram A UML diagram that shows the timing of events in a single use case.

sequence structure A program structure that contains steps that execute in order. A sequence can contain any number of tasks, but there is no chance to branch off and skip any of the tasks.

sequential file A file in which records are stored one after another in some order.

sequential order The arrangement of records when they are stored one after another on the basis of the value in a particular field.

set method An instance method that sets the values of a data field within a class.

short-circuit evaluation A logical feature in which each part of a larger expression is evaluated only as far as necessary to determine the final outcome.

signature A method's name and parameter list.

single-alternative `if` or **single-alternative selection** A selection structure in which action is required for only one branch of the decision. This form of the selection structure is also called an `if-then`, because no "else" action is necessary.

single-dimensional array A list accessed using a single subscript.

single-level control break A break in the logic of a program based on the value of a single variable.

sinking sort A bubble sort.

size of the array The number of elements an array can hold.

software Programs that tell the computer what to do.

sorting The process of placing records in order by the value in a specific field or fields.

source code The readable statements of a program, written in a programming language.

source of an event The component from which an event is generated.

spaghetti code Snarled, unstructured program logic.

stack A memory location that holds the memory addresses to which method calls should return.

stacking structures To attach program structures end to end.

starvation A flaw in multithreaded programs in which a thread is abandoned because other threads occupy all the computer's resources.

state The set of all the values or contents of a class's instance variables.

state machine diagram A UML diagram that shows the different statuses of a class or object at different points in time.

static methods Methods for which no object needs to exist; static methods are not instance methods and they do not receive a `this` reference.

step value A number used to increase a loop control variable on each pass through a loop.

stereotype A feature that adds to the UML vocabulary of shapes to make them more meaningful for the reader.

storage device A hardware apparatus that holds information for later retrieval.

storyboard A picture or sketch of screens the user will see when running a program.

string Describes data that is nonnumeric.

string constant or **literal string constant** A specific group of characters enclosed within quotation marks.

string variable A variable that can hold text that includes letters, digits, and special characters such as punctuation marks.

structure A basic unit of programming logic; each structure is a sequence, selection, or loop.

structure diagrams UML diagrams that emphasize the "things" in a system.

structured programs Programs that follow the rules of structured logic.

Structured Query Language (SQL) A commonly used language for accessing data in database tables.

stub A method without statements that is used as a placeholder.

subclass A derived class.

subscript A number that indicates the position of an element within an array.

summary report A report that lists only totals, without individual detail records.

sunny day case A program execution in which nothing goes wrong.

superclass A base class.

swap values To exchange the values of two variables.

syntax The rules of a language.

syntax error An error in language or grammar.

system design The detailed specification of how all the parts of a system will be implemented and coordinated.

system software The programs that manage a computer, in contrast to *application software*.

T

table A database file that contains data in rows and columns; also, a term sometimes used by mathematicians to describe a two-dimensional array.

temporary variable A working variable that holds intermediate results during a program's execution.

terminal symbol A symbol used at each end of a flowchart; its shape is a lozenge. Also called a *start/stop symbol*.

text editor A program used to create simple text files; it is similar to a word processor, but without as many features.

text files Files that contain data that can be read in a text editor.

third normal form, or **3NF** The normalization form in which transitive dependencies are eliminated from a database.

this reference An automatically created variable that holds the address of an object and passes it to an instance method whenever the method is called.

thread The flow of execution of one set of program statements.

thread synchronization A set of techniques that coordinates threads of execution to help avoid potential multithreading problems.

GLOSSARY

three-dimensional arrays Arrays in which each element is accessed using three subscripts.

throw an exception To pass an exception out of a block where it occurs, usually to a block that can handle it.

throw statement A programming statement that sends an `Exception` object out of a method or code block to be handled elsewhere.

tight coupling A problem that occurs when methods excessively depend on each other; it makes programs more prone to errors.

time signal A UML diagram symbol that indicates a specific amount of time has passed before an action is started.

TOE chart A program development tool that lists tasks, objects, and events.

transaction file A file that holds temporary data used to update a master file.

transitive dependency A database condition in which the value of a nonkey attribute determines or predicts the value of another nonkey attribute.

trivial expression An expression that always evaluates to the same value.

truth table A diagram used in mathematics and logic to help describe the truth of an entire expression based on the truth of its parts.

try To execute code that might throw an exception.

try block A block of code that attempts to execute while acknowledging that an exception might occur.

two-dimensional arrays Arrays that have rows and columns of values accessed using two subscripts.

type-safety The feature of programming languages that prevents assigning values of an incorrect data type.

U

Unicode A 16-bit character coding scheme.

Unified Modeling Language (UML) A standard way to specify, construct, and document systems that use object-oriented methods.

unnamed constant A literal numeric or string value.

unnormalized Describes a database table that contains repeating groups.

unstructured programs Programs that do *not* follow the rules of structured logic.

update a master file To modify the values in a master file based on transaction records.

update anomaly A problem that occurs when the data in a database table needs to be altered; the result is repeated data.

use case diagrams UML diagrams that show how a business works from the perspective of those who actually interact with the business.

user-defined type or **programmer-defined type** A type that is not built into a language but is created by the programmer.

users or **end users** People who work with and benefit from computer programs.

V

validating data Ensuring that data falls within an acceptable range.

variable A named memory location of a specific data type, whose contents can vary or differ over time.

view A way of looking at a database.

visible A characteristic of data items that means they "can be seen" only within the method in which they are declared.

visual development environment A programming environment in which programs are created by dragging components such as buttons and labels onto a screen and arranging them visually.

void method A method that returns no value.

volatile A characteristic of internal memory in which its contents are lost every time the computer loses power.

W

while loop or **while...do loop** A loop in which a process continues while some condition continues to be true.

whole-part relationship An association in which an object of one class is part of an object of a larger whole class.

wildcard A symbol that means *any* or *all*.

work method A method that performs tasks within a class.

writing to a file The act of copying data from RAM to persistent storage.

X

x-axis An imaginary line that represents horizontal positions in a screen window.

x-coordinate A position value that increases from left to right across a window.

Y

y-axis An imaginary line that represents vertical positions in a screen window.

y-coordinate A position value that increases from top to bottom across a window.

Index

Note: Page numbers in **boldface** type indicate where key terms are defined.

Special Characters
> (greater-than operator), 126
< (less-than operator), 126
() (parentheses), 52
<> (not-equal-to operator), 126
* (asterisk), 47
+ (plus sign), 47
- (minus sign), 47
/ (slash), 47
= (equal sign), 47, 126
>= (greater-than or equal-to operator), 126
<= (less-than or equal-to operator), 126

A
abstract classes, **470**
abstract data types, **416**
abstraction, **49**
   modularization, 49–50
access specifiers, **424**
accessibility, **500**
accessor methods, **421,** 421–422
accumulators, **195,** 195–198
activity diagrams, **540,** 540–542
actual parameters, **364**
addition operator (+), 47
addresses, **341**
aggregations, **536**
algorithms, **9, 308**
   bubble sort. *See* bubble sort
   insertion sort, 329–332

alphanumeric values, **38**
alternate keys, **561**
ambiguous methods, **383**
   avoiding, 383–385
American Standard Code for Information
     Interchange (ASCII),
   306, 307–310
ancestors, **463**
AND decisions, **129,** 129–138
   common errors, 136–138
   nested decisions, 129–132
   nesting for efficiency, 132–134
   AND operator. *See* AND operator
AND operator, **124,** 134–136
   combining with OR operator,
     precedence, 154–157
   short-circuit evaluation, 135
   truth tables, 135
animation, **512,** 512–515
annotation symbols, **64,** 64–65
application software, **2**
argument to the method, **358**
arithmetic operations, 45–48
arrays, 213–245, **214**
   constants, 224–225
   elements, 214–215
   multidimensional, 333–340
   one-dimensional (single-dimensional),
     333, 335
   parallel. *See* parallel arrays

arrays (*continued*)
  passing to methods, 373–380
  populating, 215
  processing using `for` loops, 244–245
  remaining within array bounds, 241–243
  replacing nested decisions, 216–224
  searching for exact matches, 226–229
  searching for range matches, 237–241
  size, 214
  storing data, 214–216
  three-dimensional, 338–339
  two-dimensional, 334–338
ascending order, **273**
ASCII (American Standard Code for Information Interchange), **306,** 307–310
assignment operator (=), 47
assignment operators, **42**
assignment statements, **42**
association relationships, **534,** 534–535
asterisk (*), multiplication operator, 47
atomic attributes, **578,** 578–579
atomic transactions, **579**
attributes, **409, 557**
  nonkey, 569
authentication techniques, **586,** 586–587

B

backup files, **266**
base classes, **462,** 462–463
base 16, **311**
base table, **569**
base 10, **305**
base 2, **305**
batch(es), **586**
batch processing, **290**
behavior diagrams, **526**
binary files, **258**
binary language, **3**
binary numbering system, **305,** 305–312
binary operators, **42**
bits, **306**

black box, **388**
Booch, Grady, 525
Boolean expressions, **122.** *See also* AND decisions; OR decisions
  logical NOT operator, 147
bubble sort, **307,** 307–326
  eliminating unnecessary passes, 324–326
  lists of variable size, 318–322
  reducing unnecessary comparisons, 322–323
  swapping values, 308–309
bytes, **258, 306**

C

calling a module, **48,** 48–49, 52
camel casing, **41**
candidate keys, **561**
cardinality, **534**
cascading `if` statements, **130,** 130–132
`case` selection structure, 317, **330,** 330–332
`catch` blocks, **476**
catching an exception, **475,** 476
central processing unit (CPU), **2**
characters, **260, 556**
child classes, **463**
child files, **266,** 282
class(es), **408**
  abstract, 470
  base, 462–463
  child, 463
  class diagrams, 417–419
  derived (extended), 462–463
  fragile, 470
  instantiation, 408–409
  methods, 415. *See also* method(s)
  organizing, 428
  parent. *See* parent classes
  predefined, 472–473
  types, 415–417
class clients, **411**
class definitions, **415**

INDEX

class diagrams, **417,** 417–419
   UML, 533–536
class methods, 434–435, **435**
class users, **411**
clients, **388**
   class, 411
closing a file, **264**
Codd, E. F., 577
coding a program, **3,** 10
cohesion, **389**
   increasing, 388–389
command lines, **24**
communication diagrams,
   538, 538–539
compilers, **3,** 4
component diagrams, **542,** 543
composite keys, **557**
composition, **458,** 458–459
compound condition, **129**
compound keys, **557**
computer files, **258,** 258–260
   backup, 266
   binary files, 258
   child, 266, 282
   closing, 264
   declaring, 261–262
   master and transaction file processing,
      281–289
   merging, 273
   opening, 262
   organizing, 259
   parent, 266, 282
   programs performing file operations,
      264–267
   random access, 290–291
   reading data, 262–264
   sequential. *See* sequential files
   text files, 258
   writing data, 264
computer memory, **3**
computer systems, **2,** 2–4
concatenating the columns, **578**
concurrent update problem, **586**

conditional AND operator, **124.** *See also*
   AND operator
conditional OR operator, **141.** *See also* OR
   operator
constants
   as array element values, 225
   as array subscripts, 225
   declaring within modules, 55–57
   as size of array, 224
constructors, **450,** 450–455
   default, 450–453
   nondefault, 450, 453
   overloading, 453–455
containers, **506**
control break(s), **268**
   single-level, 269
control break fields, **269**
control break programs, **268**
control break reports, **268,** 268–269
conversion, **13**
counted loops, **172**
counter(s), **173**
counter-controlled loops, **172**
coupling, **389**
   reducing, 389–390
CPU (central processing unit), **2**

D

data dictionaries, **67**
data hiding, **414,** 424
data hierarchy, **260,** 260–261
data integrity, **585**
data items, **2**
data redundancy, **577**
data types, **39,** 40, 43–44
database(s), **261,** 556
   relational. *See* relational databases
database management software, **557**
dead paths, **150,** 150–152
deadlock, **511**
debugging, **13**
decimal numbering system, **305,** 307–312
decision flowchart symbol, **20,** 315

655

INDEX

decision structure. *See* selection structure
declarations, **39,** 39–41
   within modules, 55–57
declaring files, 261–262
decrementing, **173**
default constructors, **450,** 450–453
default input and output devices, **264**
defensive programming, **198**
definite loops, **172**
   with counters, 172–173
delete anomalies, **577**
denormalization, **584**
deployment diagrams, **542,** 544
derived classes, **462,** 462–463
descending order, **273**
desk-checking, **10**
destructors, **456,** 456–458
detail loop tasks, **58**
`didSwap` flag, 324–325
direct access files, **290**
directories, **259**
`displayArray()` method, 317, 318, 320, 321
displaying, 266
division operator (/), 47
documentation, **9**
   internal and external, 64
DOS prompt, **492**
`do-until` loops, 335
`do-while` loops (posttest loops), 193, 317, 332–334, **333**
dual-alternative `ifs` (dual-alternative selections), **88**
dummy values, **21**
Dvorak keyboard, 499

E

EBCDIC (Extended Binary Coded Decimal Interchange Code), **306**
echoing input, **70,** 70–71
elegance, 189
elements, **214,** 214–215
   constants as array element values, 225

eliding, **533**
`else` clauses, **125**
encapsulated modules, **55**
encapsulation, **414**
encryption, **587**
end users, **8**
`endif` statement, 87
end-of-job tasks, **58**
end-structure statement, **87**
entities, **557**
`eof`, 21
equal sign (=)
   assignment operator, 47
   equivalency operator, 126
event(s), **493**
event-based programs, **493**
event-driven applications, 501–509
   defining connections between user screens, 503–504
   planning logic, 504–509
   storyboards, 502–503
event-driven programming, 492–494, **493**
exabytes, 313
exact matches, searching arrays, 226–229
exception(s), **475**
   built-in, 477–478
   catching, 475, 476
   creating your own, 478
   throwing, 475
exception handling, 473–478, **475**
   built-in exceptions, 477–478
   creating your own exceptions, 478
   drawbacks to traditional error-handling techniques, 473–475
   object-oriented exception-handling model, 475–477
   UML, diagraming, 544–545
executing a program, **3**
Extended Binary Coded Decimal Interchange Code (EBCDIC), **306**
extended classes, **462,** 462–463
extended variations, **528**

external documentation, **64**
external module call flowchart symbol, 315

F

facilitators, **422,** 422–423
fields, **260, 411, 556**
   key, 340–341
   private, of parent classes, accessing, 465–470
files, **260, 556.** *See also* computer files
   indexed, 340–342, 345
`fillArray()` method, 310, 318, 319, 321, 322
first normal form (1NF), **577,** 578–579
floating-point variables, **38**
flowcharts, **14**
   drawing, 16–17
   modules, 52–54
   symbols, 315
flowline(s), **16**
flowline flowchart symbol, 315
folders, **259**
`for` loops, processing arrays, 244–245
`for` statements (`for` loops), **192,** 192–194
forcing, **201**
foreign keys, **569**
forks, **541**
formal parameters, **364**
forward slash (/), division operator, 47
fragile classes, **470**
function(s). *See* modularization; module(s)
functional cohesion, **55, 389**
functional decomposition. *See* modularization
functional dependence, **582,** 582–583

G

garbage, **40**
garbage in, garbage out (GIGO), **200**
generation variations, **529,** 529–530
get methods, **421,** 421–422
gigabytes, **258,** 313

GIGO (garbage in, garbage out), **200**
global data items, **356**
global program level, **57**
goto-less programming, **101**
graphical user interfaces (GUIs), **24**
   accessibility, 500
   designing, 498–501
   GUI components, 495–498
greater-than operator (>), 126
greater-than or equal-to operator (>=), 126
GUI(s). *See* graphical user interfaces (GUIs)
GUI components, 495–498

H

handler body nodes, **544**
hardware, **2**
has-a relationships, **458,** 458–459, 535
help methods, **422,** 422–423
hexadecimal numbering system, **311,** 311–312
hierarchy charts, **61,** 61–63
high-level programming languages, **10**
housekeeping tasks, **57**
Hungarian notation, **41**
icons, **492**
IDE (integrated development environment), **23,** 23–24, **472**

I

identifiers, **39,** 40
   choosing, 66–67
`if-then` clauses, **125**
`if-then` (single-alternative decision) structure, 317
`if-then-else` structure, **87,** 316
immutability, **562**
implementation, **356**
implementation hiding, **388**
in scope, **57**
inaccessibility, **466,** 466–467
include variations, **529**

INDEX

incrementing, **173**
indefinite loops, **173**, 173–175
index(es), **214**
indexed files, 340–342, 345
indexing, **341**
indirect relationships, **234**
infinite loops, **18**, 18–19
information, **3**
information hiding, **414**, 424
inheritance, **413**, 459–471
    accessing private fields and methods of a parent class, 465–470
    multiple, 470
    terminology, 462–465
    using to achieve good software design, 470–471
initializing the loop control variable, neglecting, 183–184
initializing the variable, **40**
inner loops, **177**
input, **2**
    echoing, 70–71
input devices, default, 264
input symbols, **16**
input/output flowchart (I/O) symbol, **16**, 315
insert anomalies, **577**
insertion sort, **329**, 329–332
`insertionSort()` method, 330
instance methods, 429–434, **430**
instance variables, **411**
instant access files, **290**
instantiation, **408**, 408–409
instructions, repeating, 17–18
integer variables, **38**
integrated development environment (IDE), **23**, 23–24, **472**
interaction diagrams, **526**
interactive programs, **290**
interactivity diagrams, **504**
interface to the method, **388**
internal documentation, **64**
internal module call flowchart symbol, 315
interpreters, **3**, 4
I/O (input/output) flowchart symbol, **16**, 315
IPO charts, **9**, **372**
IPV4 exhaustion, 13
is-a relationships, **410**
iteration, **88**. *See also* loop structure

J

Jacobson, Ivar, 525
join(s), **541**, **568**
join column, **568**
join operations, **568**

K

key(s), **557**
    alternate, 561
    candidate, 561
    composite (compound), 557
    foreign, 569
    partial key dependencies, 579–580
    primary, 557, 560–563
key field, **340**, 340–341
keyboards, 499
keywords, **41**
kilobytes, **258**, 313

L

left-to-right associativity, **47**
less-than operator (<), 126
less-than or equal-to operator (<=), 126
libraries, **472**
line breaks, confusing, avoiding, 68
linear searches, **226**
linked lists, **342**, 342–344
list(s)
    linked, 342–344
    variable size, sorting, 318–322
listeners, **494**
literal numeric constants, **38**
literal string constants, **38**
local data items, **356**
local variables and constants, **57**

locks, **586**
logic, **5,** 5–7
   mainline, 51
   planning, 9–10
logical errors, **5**
logical NOT operator, **147**
logical order, **340**
loop(s), **18,** 169–205
   accumulating totals, 194–198
   advantages, 170–171
   common mistakes, 183–191
   counted (counter-controlled), 172
   definite, 172–173
   `do-until`, 335
   `do-while` (posttest), 193, 317, 332–334, **333**
   indefinite, 173–175
   infinite, 18–19
   loop control variables, 171–177
   `for` loops, 192–194
   nested, 177–182
   pretest, 193
   reprompting, limiting, 200–202
   structured, characteristics shared by, 334–335
   understanding in program's mainline logic, 175–177
   unstructured, recognizing, 335
   validating data, 198–200
   validating data types, 202–203
   validating reasonableness and consistency of data, 203–204
loop body, **88**
loop control variables, **171,** 171–177
   decrementing, 173
   definite loops with counters, 172–173
   including statements that belong outside loop, 187–191
   incorrect comparison, 186–187
   incrementing, 173
   indefinite loops with sentinel values, 173–175
   neglecting to alter, 185
   neglecting to initialize, 183–184
   understanding loops program's mainline logic, 175–177
loop structure, **88,** 88–89, 96–97
   selection structure compared, 96
loose coupling, **389**
lost data, recovering, 586
Lovelace, Ada Byron, 26
low-level programming languages, **10**

M

machine language, **3**
   translating programs into, 10–11
magic numbers, **44**
main program, **51**
mainline logic, **51**
   understanding loops in, 175–177
maintenance, **13,** 13–14
making a decision, **20**
many-to-many relationships, 569–573, **571**
master files, **281**
   updating, 281
matrices, **336**
mean, **306**
median, **306**
megabytes, **258,** 313
memory, occupation by arrays, 214–215
merging files, **273**
method(s), **356.** *See also* modularization; module(s); *specific method names*
   ambiguous, avoiding, 383–385
   arguments (parameters) to, **358**
   get (accessor), 421–422
   implementation, **356**
   implementation hiding, 388
   increasing cohesion, 388–389
   instance, 429–434
   interface to, 388
   names, conventions in C++ and Java, 387
   with no parameters, 356–358
   overloading, 380–386, 453–455

method(s) (*continued*)
  parameter list, 359
  of parent classes, accessing, 465–470
  passing arrays to, 373–380
  predefined, 386–387
  recursive, 390
  reducing coupling, 389–390
  requiring parameters, creating, 358–366
  returning values, creating, 366–372
  set (mutator), 420–421
  signature, 359
  static (class), 434–435
  work (help method or facilitator), 422–423
method body, **356**
method headers, **356**
method `return` statements, **356**
method's type, **367**
Microsoft Visual Studio IDE, **23**
minus sign (-), subtraction operator, 47
modeling, **524**
modularization, 48–61, 355–397
  abstraction, 49–50
  creating methods that require parameters, 358–366
  creating methods that return a value, 366–372
  declaring variables and constants within modules, 55–57
  method design issues, 388–390
  methods with no parameters, 356–358
  most common configuration for mainline logic, 57–61
  multiple programmers, 50
  overloading methods, 380–386
  passing a array to a method, 373–380
  predefined methods, 386–387
  process, 51–61
  recursion, 390–394
  reusability of work, 50–51
  unstructured logic, 105–110

module(s), **48**
  calling, 48–49, 52
  encapsulation, 55
  flowcharts, 52–54
  functional cohesion, 55
  naming, 52
  portability, 57
module body, **51**
module headers, **51**
module `return` statements, **51**
multidimensional arrays, 333–340, **339**
multifield records, sorting. *See* sorting multifield records
multiple inheritance, **470**
multiplication operator (*), 47
multiplicity, **534**
multithreading, **510**, 510–512
mutator methods, **420**, 420–521

N

named constants, **44**, 44–45
naming
  modules, 52
  variables, 41–42
nested decisions (nested `if`s), **129**, 129–132
  replacing with arrays, 216–224
nested loops, **177**, 177–182
nesting structures, **90**, 90–92
nondefault constructors, **450**, 453
nonkey attributes, **569**
nonstatic methods, **435**
nonvolatile storage, **3**
normal forms, **577**
  first normal form, 577, 578–579
  second normal form, 577, 579–582
  third normal form, 577, 582–584
normalization, **576**, 576–585
  first normal form, 577, 578–579
  second normal form, 577, 579–582
  third normal form, 577, 582–584
not-equal-to operator (<>), 126
null case, **88**

numbering systems, 305–312
  binary, 307–312
  decimal, 307–312
  hexadecimal, 311–312
numeric constants, **38**
numeric data type, **38**
numeric variables, **43**

O

object(s), **408**
  attributes, 409
  using, 436–439
object code, **3**
object diagrams, **536**
object dictionaries, **502**, 502–503
Object Management Group (OMG), 525
object-oriented programming, **26**, 407–442, **408**, 449–482
  advantages, 479
  classes and objects, 408–411. *See also* class(es); object(s)
  composition, 458–459
  constructors. *See* constructors
  destructors, 456–458
  encapsulation, 414
  exception handing. *See* exception handling
  inheritance. *See* inheritance
  instance methods, 429–434
  polymorphism, 412–413
  predefined classes, 472–473
  public and private access, 424–427
  static methods, 434–435
OMG (Object Management Group), 525
one-dimensional arrays, **333**, 335
1NF (first normal form), **577**, 578–579
one-to-many relationships, **569**
one-to-one relationships, **573**, 573–574
opening a file, **262**
operating systems, **492**
operators, 47

OR decisions, **138**, 138–147
  common errors, 143–147
  efficiency, 140–141
  OR operator. *See* OR operator
OR operator, **141**, 141–142
  combining with AND operator, precedence, 154–157
order of operations, **46**
out of bounds, 243
outer loops, **177**
output, **3**
output devices, default, 264
output symbols, **16**
overhead, **45**, 369
overloading, **380**
overloading a method, **380**, 380–386
  avoiding ambiguous methods, 383–385
overriding, **534**

P

packages, **472**
parallel arrays, **230**, 230–237
  sorting records, 326–327
parameter(s), actual and formal, 364
parameter list, **359**
parameter to the method, **358**
parent classes, **463**
  accessing private fields and methods, 465–470
parent files, **266**, 282
parentheses (()), module names, 52
partial key dependencies, **579**, 579–580
Pascal casing, **41**
passed by reference, **376**
passed by value, **362**
passing a message, 412
paths, **259**
permanent storage devices, **258**
permissions, **587**
persistent locks, **586**
petabytes, 313
physical order, **340**
pixels, **497**

INDEX

plus sign (+), addition operator, 47
polymorphism, **380,** 412–413
populating the array, 215
portable modules, **57**
posttest loop (`do-while`), 193, 317, 332–334, **333**
precedence, **154**
  combining AND and OR operators, 154–157
predefined classes, 472–473
predefined methods, 386–387
pretest loops, **193**
primary keys, **557,** 560–563
priming input (priming read), **98**
  structuring programs, 95–101
primitive data types, **417**
printer spacing charts, 328–329
printing, 266
private access, **424,** 424–427
procedural programming, **26**
procedures. *See* modularization; module(s)
process flowchart symbol, 315
processing, **2**
processing symbols, **16**
profile diagrams, **544**
program(s), **2**
  coding, 3, 10
  ending with a sentinel value, 19–22
  good design features, 63–72
  maintaining, 13–14
  putting into production, 13
  structured, 84
  testing, 12–13
  translating into machine language, 10–11
  unstructured, 84–86
program code, **3**
program comments, **64,** 64–66
program development cycle, **7,** 7–14
  coding step, 10
  maintenance step, 13–14
  planning the logic step, 9–10
  production step, 13
  testing step, 12–13
  translating program into machine language step, 10–11
  understanding program step, 8–9
programmer-defined types, **416**
programming, **2**
programming environments, 22–24
programming languages, **3**
programming models, evolution, 25–27
prompts, **69**
  clear, writing, 69–70
properties, **420**
`protected` access specifier, **467**
protected nodes, **544**
pseudocode, **14**
  writing, 15
public access, **424,** 424–427
pure polymorphism, **413**

Q

queries, **565,** 565–568
query by example, **565**
QWERTY keyboard, 499

R

random access files, **290,** 290–291
random access memory (RAM), **3**
random-access storage devices, **341**
range checks, **148,** 148–154
  common errors, 150–154
range matches, searching arrays, 237–241
reading from a file, **262,** 262–264
real numbers, **38**
real-time applications, **290**
records, **260, 556**
  multifield, sorting. *See* sorting multifield records
recovery, **586**
recursion, **390,** 390–394
recursive methods, **390**
registering components, **506**
related table, **569**

relational comparison operators, **126,** 126–129
  common error using, 129
  list, 126
relational databases, 555–591, **557**
  authentication and permissions, 586–587
  characters, 556
  compound (composite) key, 557
  concurrent update problems, 586
  creating database and table descriptions, 558–560
  data integrity, 585
  encryption, 587
  fields, 556
  files, 556
  normalization. *See* normalization
  primary keys, 557, 560–563
  queries, 565–568
  records, 556, 564–565
  recovering lost data, 586
  relationships between tables. *See* relationships
  structure notation, 563
  tables. *See* tables
relationships, **568,** 568–574
  many-to-many, 569–573
  one-to-many, 569
  one-to-one, 573–574
reliability, **50,** 50–51, **471**
repeating groups, **578**
repetition, **88.** *See also* loop structure
`return` statements, module, 51
return types, **366,** 367
reusability, **50**
  modularization, 50–51
reverse engineering, **524**
right-associativity, **42**
right-to-left associativity, **42,** 42–43
rules of precedence, **46**
Rumbaugh, Jim, 525
running a program, 3

S

scenarios, **528**
script(s), **494**
scripting languages (scripting programming languages or script languages), **3**
searches
  improving efficiency, 234–236
  parallel arrays, 230–237
searching arrays
  exact matches, 226–229
  range matches, 237–241
second normal form (2NF), **577,** 579–582
SELECT-FROM-WHERE statement, **565**
selection structure, **87,** 87–88, 122–125
  `case`, 317, **330,** 330–332
  diagram, 316
  loop structure compared, 96
  single-alternative decision (`if-then`), 317
self-documenting names, **66**
sentinel values, 19–22, **21**
sequence diagrams, **537,** 537–538
sequence structure, **86,** 86–87
  diagram, 316
sequential files, **267,** 267–281
  control break logic, 268–272
  merging, 273–281
sequential order, **306**
set methods, **420,** 420–521
short-circuit evaluation, **135**
signatures, **359**
single-alternative decision structure (`if-then`), 317
single-alternative `if`s (single-alternative selections), **88**
single-dimensional arrays, **333,** 335
single-level control breaks, **269**
sinking sort, **308**
size of the array, **214**

INDEX

slash (/), division operator, 47
software, **2**
   inheritance to achieve good design, 470–471
`sortArray()` method, 311–312, 314–316, 320, 321, 323
sorting, **267,** 306–333
   bubble sort algorithm. *See* bubble sort
   insertion sort algorithm, 329–332
   multifield records. *See* sorting multifield records
   need for sorting data, 306–307
   sequential order, 306
   sinking sort, 308
sorting multifield records, 326–328
   data stored in parallel arrays, 326–327
   sorting records as a whole, 328
source code, **3**
source of the event, **494**
spaghetti code, **84,** 84–86
SQL (Structured Query Language), **565**
stack, **55, 391**
stacking structures, **89,** 89–90
starvation, **511**
state, **411**
state machine diagrams, **539,** 539–540
statements. *See also specific statements*
   clear, designing, 68–69
   long, clarifying with temporary variables, 68–69
static methods, 434–435, **435**
step values, **192**
stereotypes, **529**
storage, measuring, 312–314
storage devices, **3**
storing data in arrays, 214–216
storyboards, **502**
   defining storyboard objects in object dictionary, 502–503
string constants, **38**
string data type, **38**

string variables, **43**
structure(s), 83–111, **86,** 316–317. *See also* structured programs
   advantages, 84–86
   case, 317, 330–332
   `if-then-else`, 87, 316
   loop, 88–89, 96–97, 316
   nesting, 90–92
   posttest loop (`do-while`), 193, 317, 332–334, **333**
   reasons for using, 101–102
   recognizing, 102–105
   selection (decision). *See* selection structure
   sequence, 86–87, 316
   solving difficult structuring problems, 318–327
   stacking, 89, 91
   structuring and modularizing unstructured logic, 105–110
structure diagrams, **526**
structured programs, 84. *See also* structure(s)
   characteristics, 94
   priming input to structure, 95–101
Structured Query Language (SQL), **565**
stubs, **181**
subclasses, **463**
   ancestors, 463
subroutines. *See* modularization; module(s)
subscripts, **214**
   constants, 225
   out of bounds, 243
subtraction operator (-), 47
summary reports, **198**
sunny day case, **477**
superclasses, **463**
`swap()` method, 312–313, 320, 321
swap values, **308,** 308–309
syntax, **3**
syntax errors, **3**

INDEX

system design, **524**
system modeling, 524–525. *See also* Unified Modeling Language (UML)
system software, **2**

T

tables, **261, 336, 556**
  base, 569
  descriptions, 558–560
  poorly designed, recognizing, 574–576
  records, 564–565
  related, 569
  relationships. *See* relationships
  structure notation, 563
temporary variables, **68**
  clarifying long statements using, 68–69
terabytes, 313
terminal flowchart symbol, **16,** 315
testing
  programs, 12–13
  values, 20
text editors, **22,** 22–23
text files, **258**
third normal form (3NF), **577,** 582–584
`this` reference, **432,** 432–433
thread(s), **509,** 509–512
  multithreading, 510–512
thread synchronization, **511**
three-dimensional arrays, **338,** 338–339
3NF (third normal form), **577,** 582–584
throw statements, **475**
throwing an exception, **475**
tight coupling, **389**
time signals, **541**
TOE charts, **9**
totals, loops to accumulate, 194–198
transaction files, **281**
transitive dependencies, **582**
translating programs into machine language, 10–11
trivial expressions, **126**
truth tables, **135**
`try` blocks, **476**
trying code, **475**
Turing, Alan, 26
two-dimensional arrays, **334,** 334–338
2NF (second normal form), **577,** 579–582
type-safety, **44**

U

Unicode, **306**
Unified Modeling Language (UML), 523–549, **524**
  activity diagrams, 540–542
  behavior diagrams, 526
  class and object diagrams, 533–537
  communication diagrams, 538–539
  component diagrams, 542, 543
  creation, 525
  deciding which diagrams to use, 546
  deployment diagrams, 542, 544
  exception handling, 544–545
  interaction diagrams, 526
  overview, 525–527
  profile diagrams, 544
  sequence diagrams, 537–538
  state machine diagrams, 539–540
  structure diagrams, 526
  use case diagrams, 527–533
  when to use, 546
unnamed constants, **38**
unnormalized tables, **578**
unreachable paths, **150,** 150–152
unstructured logic, structuring and modularizing, 105–110
unstructured programs, **84,** 84–86
update anomalies, **577**
updating a master file, **281**
use case diagrams, **527,** 527–533
user(s), **8**
user environments, 24–25

INDEX

user-defined types, **416**
user-initiated actions, 495

V

validating
  data. *See* validating data
  data types, 202–203
validating data, **198**
  loops, 198–200
  reasonableness and consistency of data, 203–204
values, **43**
variables, **6,** 38–44
  assigning values, 42–43
  data types, 43–44
  declaring, 39–41
  declaring within modules, 55–57
  floating-point, 38
  initializing, 40
  integer, 38
  naming, 41–42
  passed by value, 362
views, **566**
visible data items, **57**
visual development environment, **472**
void methods, **366,** 366–367
volatile storage, **3**

W

while...do (while loop), **88,** 88–89
  diagram, 316
whole-part relationships, **458,** 458–459, 535
wildcards, **566**
work methods, **422,** 422–423

X

writing to a file, **264**
x-axis, **512**
x-coordinate, **512**

Y

y-axis, **512**
y-coordinate, **512**
yottabytes, 313

Z

zettabytes, 313

PART II

A Guide to Working With Visual Logic, 1st Edition

Crews/Murphy

TABLE OF CONTENTS

PREFACE ... IX

CHAPTER 1 INPUT, PROCESS, OUTPUT ... 1
INTRODUCTION ... 1
LOGIC AND SYNTAX ... 2
YOUR FIRST PROGRAM: HELLO WORLD ... 3
YOUR SECOND PROGRAM: HELLO NAME ... 5
   Simple Programming Formats ... 6
WEEKLY PAYCHECK PROGRAM ... 7
   Step 1: Input ... 7
   Step 2: Processing ... 8
   Step 3: Output ... 9
HOW TO WRITE ARITHMETIC EXPRESSIONS ... 11
QUICK CHECK 1-A ... 12
QUICK CHECK 1-B ... 12
   Strategies for Doing Conversions ... 12
INTRINSIC FUNCTIONS ... 13
DEBUGGING WITH VISUAL LOGIC ... 14
CHAPTER SUMMARY ... 16
   Key Terms ... 16
   Review Questions ... 16
   Programming Exercises ... 16

CHAPTER 2 MAKING DECISIONS ... 19
MAKING DECISIONS ... 19
THE IF STATEMENT ... 20
QUICK CHECK 2-A ... 21
   Simple IF Statements ... 21
   Solving the Overtime Problem ... 22
NESTED IF STATEMENTS ... 23
   Long-Distance Billing Problem ... 24
COMPOUND CONDITIONS ... 25
QUICK CHECK 2-B ... 27
CHAPTER SUMMARY ... 33
   Key Terms ... 33
   Review Questions ... 33
   Programming Exercises ... 33

CHAPTER 3 WHILE LOOPS   37
CONSOLE INPUT AND OUTPUT   37
   Console End-of-Output Character   38
WHILE LOOPS   40
QUICK CHECK 3-A   45
WHILE LOOPS AND SENTINEL VALUES   46
EXIT LOOP   49
CHAPTER SUMMARY   53
   Key Terms   53
   Review Questions   53
   Programming Exercises   54

CHAPTER 4 FOR LOOPS AND NESTED LOOPS   59
FOR LOOPS   59
   Comparing While Loops and For Loops   60
   Working with Final and Step Values   61
NESTED LOOPS   63
CHAPTER SUMMARY   69
   Key Terms   69
   Review Questions   69
   Programming Exercises   69

CHAPTER 5 ARRAYS   73
ARRAYS   74
   Creating an Array   74
   Accessing Individual Elements of an Array   74
BENEFITS OF USING AN ARRAY   75
SAMPLE PROGRAM #1: EVENS AND ODDS   78
   Analysis and Design   79
SAMPLE PROGRAM #2: DICE ROLL SIMULATION   81
   Analysis and Design   81
SAMPLE PROGRAM #3: PARALLEL ARRAYS (USERNAME AND PASSWORD)   83
   Reading Data from a Text File   83
   Analysis and Design   84
CHAPTER SUMMARY   91
   Key Terms   91
   Review Questions   91
   Programming Exercises   91

CHAPTER 6 GRAPHICS AND PROCEDURES   97
GRAPHICS   98
   Forward and Turn Right   98
QUICK CHECK 6-A   101
   Using Loops   102

WORKING WITH COLORS	103
Set Color and Pen Width	104
Color Forward	105
QUICK CHECK 6-B	105
STRUCTURED DESIGN USING PROCEDURES	106
Rotating Flags Problem	106
Creating a Procedure	107
QUICK CHECK 6-C	110
PROCEDURES WITH PARAMETERS	110
Rotating Shapes Program	110
Visual Logic Implementation	111
RECURSION	114
CHAPTER SUMMARY	121
Key Terms	121
Review Questions	121
Programming Exercises	121
APPENDIX A VISUAL LOGIC RESERVED WORDS	**125**
APPENDIX B DEBUGGING IN VISUAL LOGIC	**126**
COMMON MISTAKE #1: CHECK FOR MISSPELLED VARIABLE NAMES	126
COMMON MISTAKE #2: MULTIPLE VARIABLE NAMES	127
DEBUGGING–PENCIL AND PAPER	127
DEBUGGING–BREAKPOINTS AND VARIABLE WATCH	127
APPENDIX C USING MULTIMEDIA	**129**
INDEX	**130**

PREFACE

A Guide to Working with Visual Logic is the perfect companion for use with the software package "Visual Logic," a tool that combines the graphics of flowcharts (visual representations of algorithms) and the utility of pseudo-code (a minimal syntax description of an algorithm) into a single simulation tool. In combination with the software, *A Guide to Working with Visual Logic* will provide novice programming students with a minimal-syntax introduction to essential programming concepts including variables, input, assignment, output, conditions, loops, procedures, arrays, and files. Research has shown that students have more success when they initially focus on concepts rather than syntax, and our approach allows instructors to present material in a clear and illustrated manner that empowers rather than overwhelms the student.

ORGANIZATION AND COVERAGE

A Guide to Working with Visual Logic provides a hands-on, minimal syntax introduction to programming fundamentals. Chapter 1 covers input, assignment, and output statements. These three commands are sufficient for students to write a variety of simple but interesting programs. This chapter also introduces variables and expressions. Chapter 2 explains the role of conditional statements and the decision-making ability programs can have when conditions are used. This chapter also uses a case study to illustrate that there is more than one correct solution to a problem.

Chapters 3 and 4 present the concept of loops or iterative actions. Sequential (Chapter 1), conditional (Chapter 2), and iterative (Chapter 3) actions are sufficient to write any computer program. Students are also introduced to Console I/O which provides a full, persistent history of the input and output for a program's execution. Sentinel values, as well as nested loops, are introduced and numerous examples are presented in both chapters to help students develop a strong understanding of these critical control structures.

Chapter 5 introduces the power of arrays for holding and manipulating structured data. The chapter emphasizes the way that For loops and arrays are often used together, and there are again numerous examples to help students solidify their understanding of the power of arrays. The notion of File I/O is also introduced in this chapter, giving students yet another way to get data to and from their program.

Chapter 6 introduces both Graphics and Procedures. Our experience has been that these two topics are complementary and that presenting them together is beneficial to students. Using procedures to repeatedly call a series of related graphical commands gives the student a visual confirmation of the power and utility of procedures. Arguments and parameters are used to specify the location and size of the graphical objects being drawn. The chapter also includes an example of a recursive graphical procedure to visual demonstration how code can be used to call itself.

Finally, three appendices identify a list of Visual Logic reserved words, provide debugging strategies and techniques, and open the door to more creative problem solving using multimedia elements in a Visual Logic solution file.

FEATURES OF THE TEXT

Case Study Scenario and Solution—The Case Study Scenarios are used to promote problem-based learning. Scenarios present the student with a challenging programming problem whose solution requires skills the student has not yet developed. These skills are presented as the chapter unfolds, and then the Case Study Solution is presented that solves the scenario problem. The scenarios all involve a creative and fun-loving instructor, Mr. Taylor, and his interactions with students in his introductory programming class.

Ask the Author—Common student questions are asked and answered in the appropriate learning context. These questions help the student stay engaged with the material and are used to identify and dispel common areas of misconception.

Quick Checks—Quick check problems appear throughout the text to provide readers with an opportunity to apply their knowledge.

Tell Me More—These elements provide a business or applied perspective on the current topic.

Tips—These provide additional information or clarification to improve the student's learning experience.

Figures—Screen shots of programs during execution are frequently included. Students see GUI and console sample screens to show just how input and output will look.

Topic Summary—Following each major topic is a summary that recaps the programming concepts and techniques students should remember for that topic. This feature reinforces key ideas before moving on to new material.

Chapter Summary—Each chapter concludes with a complete summary of the terms and ideas introduced in the chapter. This feature provides a concise means for students to review and check their understanding of the main points in each chapter.

Key Terms—Each chapter lists key terms. Along with the chapter summary, the list of key terms provides a snapshot overview of a chapter's main ideas.

Review Questions—Review questions appear at the end of every chapter to allow students to test their comprehension of the major ideas and techniques presented.

Programming Exercises—Exercises are included so students have more opportunities for hands-on programming practice of concepts they have learned in that chapter.

VISUAL LOGIC™

This book is a guide to the software program called **Visual Logic**™. Visual Logic is a simple but powerful tool for teaching programming logic and design without traditional high-level programming language syntax. Visual Logic uses flowcharts to explain essential programming concepts, including variables, input, assignment, output, conditions, loops, procedures, graphics, arrays, and files. It also has the ability to interpret and execute flowcharts, providing students with immediate and accurate feedback about their solutions. By executing student solutions, Visual Logic combines the power of a high-level language with the ease and simplicity of flowcharts.

Visual Logic runs on any of the following Windows operating systems: 98, NT, 2000, ME, XP, or Vista. The minimum requirements for Windows also satisfy the minimum requirements for Visual Logic. Visual Logic may be purchased along with your text. Please contact your Course Technology sales representative for more information.

PREFACE

ACKNOWLEDGMENTS

First of all, we want to thank you, the students and instructors who use our book. We are honored that you chose us.

We would also like to thank the fine people at Course Technology. In particular, Managing Editor Tricia Coia and Acquisitions Editor Amy Jollymore both provided excellent vision and direction, always providing valuable insight when surveying the forest as well as when inspecting the individual trees. Others who stand out include Marie Lee, Jill Braiewa, Chris Scriver, and Danielle Shaw. We are delighted to be working with Course Technology on this (and other) projects.

We are also very grateful to the instructors who have used Visual Logic as a stand-alone product while this Guide was under development. We knew this book would eventually be available to complement the software, but things often take longer than anticipated. Thank you for your patience and we hope you will find this book to be worth the wait.

We also acknowledge the development team at VisualLogic.org and appreciate their support with this book. They have set up an e-mail address that you can use to comment on this book, including what you like and what we can do better in future editions. Please send e-mail to Guide@VisualLogic.org. We look forward to hearing from you.

Finally, we dedicate this book to our families for their unfailing love and support, and who join with us in thanking God for His many blessings.

— Thad Crews

— Chip Murphy

CHAPTER ONE

INPUT, PROCESS, OUTPUT

> **»CASE STUDY SCENARIO**
>
> **Grocery Checkout**
>
> Mr. Marion Taylor's programming course is one of the most popular classes on campus: students appreciate Mr. Taylor's knowledge of the material and passion for teaching. In the minutes before the first class begins, Mr. Taylor and his students discuss movies, sports, and the parking problem on campus.
>
> At the first class meeting, Mr. Taylor takes roll and hands out the syllabus, then asks, "How many of you have ever written a computer program before?" A few students raise their hands. "How many of you are ready to learn how to program?" Most of the class raises their hands. Looking around the room, Mr. Taylor smiles and says, "Well, the best way to learn programming is to program. Today we will cover input, processing, and output statements. After discussing these three statements, we will develop a working grocery checkout program. Our solution will input the purchase price of three items in the store. The program will determine the total price of all three items, add 6 percent sales tax, and display the resulting total." After a short pause for effect, he adds, "Oh yeah, and we will finish the program with enough time left in class for me to tell a bad joke."
>
> Mr. Taylor's solution is presented later this chapter.

INTRODUCTION

A **computer program** is a solution to a problem, such as, "How can customers view and purchase products over the Internet?" or "How can sales representatives have immediate and accurate access to inventory data?"

Most useful computer programs typically do at least three things: input data, process data, and output resulting information (see Figure 1-1).

INPUT, PROCESS, OUTPUT

Figure 1-1 Input-Process-Output

For example, an online catalog information system might have input that includes the product ID for the items a customer wishes to purchase, along with the customer's mailing address and credit card number. The processing could include referencing a database to determine the cost of each item, calculating the sales tax, computing the shipping charge based on the customer's mailing address, and billing the customer's credit card the appropriate amount. The output might include a customer receipt and reports for the sales department and the warehouse (see Figure 1-2).

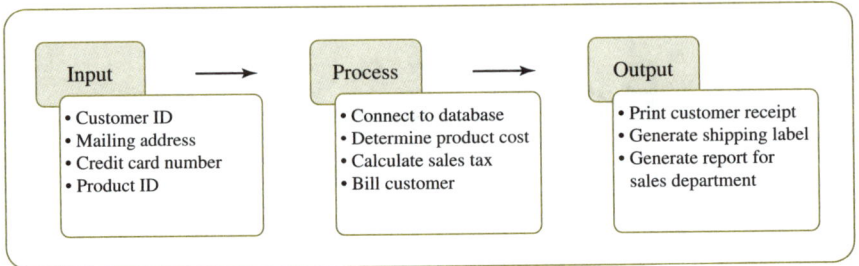

Figure 1-2 Input-Process-Output for an Internet shopping cart system

LOGIC AND SYNTAX

Building a software application is often compared to building a house. First you decide what kind of house you want (ranch, A-frame, tri-level, etc.) and what features you want (privacy, lots of sunlight, good for entertaining, etc.). Then you design a house blueprint that achieves all of the objectives. The blueprint design must be detailed, not only containing the complete floor plan, but also containing a description of all electrical and plumbing information. When the design is finalized, then the construction can begin. If you have a good design being worked on by skilled professionals (carpenters, plumbers, electricians, brick layers, etc.), the house should turn out great.

Would you consider building a house without a blueprint? Of course not! (What a terrible house that would be.) The same is true for programming. Software professionals would never build an important piece of software (such as an air traffic control system or an online banking system) without first having a blueprint for the software. An **algorithm** is the logical blueprint for software. Various tools for representing computing algorithms are available, the two most common being flowcharts and pseudocode. In this book we will use **Visual Logic™**, which combines the graphics of flowcharts (graphical representations of algorithms) and the utility of pseudocode (a minimal syntax description of an algorithm) into a single simulation tool. Using Visual Logic, you will create computer algorithms that can be saved, edited, executed, and debugged.

Once an algorithm has been developed, it must be communicated in an appropriate language. To communicate actions to a computer, developers use a programming language like Visual Basic, C#, C++, Java, Pascal, or COBOL (among others). Syntax refers to the specific rules of a programming language. There are literally hundreds of programming languages to choose from, each with its own unique syntax. Therefore, writing a computer program involves first creating a logical solution to solve a problem and then implementing that solution in an appropriate syntax.

»TELL ME MORE

An algorithm is not limited to computer programs. Driving directions, a cooking recipe, and the rules to play Monopoly are all everyday examples of algorithms.

Consider the instructions to bake a cake. The algorithm (or steps) include adding eggs, mixing ingredients, and cooking at a specific temperature. These basic steps can be stated in various languages. For example, the step of adding two eggs can be stated in English ("Add two eggs"), Spanish ("Agregue dos huevos"), or French ("Ajouter deux oeufs"). The result is the same regardless of the language.

Likewise, the logic of an Internet shopping cart remains essentially the same regardless of its implementation language (Visual Basic, C#, C++, Java, Pascal, COBOL, etc.).

Of course the process (e.g., algorithm) for selling products over the Internet is more complicated than baking a cake, but it is still eventually broken down to a series of steps to accomplish the objective.

ASK THE AUTHOR

Q: What is the difference between data and information?

A: From an information system perspective, data refers to numbers, characters, or images without context. Data by itself has no meaning. When data is processed in a context (either by a human or a computer system) it becomes information. As information is collected, it can also be processed for patterns and insights, thus creating knowledge. Finally, wisdom is appropriate behavior guided by knowledge. Consider the following example as it applies to a screen-printing company's online purchasing system.

- "5000" is data.
- "A 5000 percent increase in T-shirt orders by Gizmo Company" is information.
- "A 5000 percent increase in T-shirt orders by any company is an unusually large increase" is knowledge.
- "We had better confirm the numbers on this order before we manufacture and ship the T-shirts, just to make sure it was not a human or system mistake" is wisdom.

YOUR FIRST PROGRAM: HELLO WORLD

It is a time-honored tradition that your first program in any language be the output message "Hello World." We will follow suit and write a Hello World program using Visual Logic.

Begin by running the Visual Logic program contained on the CD-ROM included with this text. When the program begins, you will see two flowcharting elements, Begin and End, connected by a flow-arrow. Click the left mouse button on the flow-arrow; the Flowchart Elements menu should pop up (Figure 1-3).

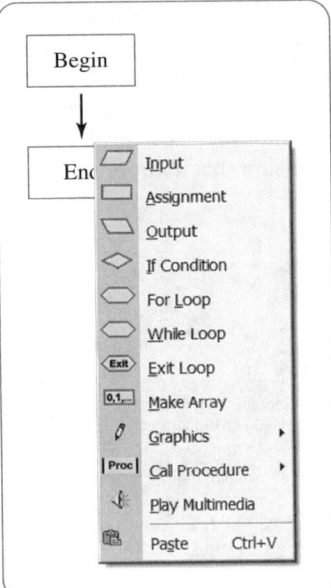

Figure 1-3 Flowchart Elements menu

Select Output from the pop-up menu to add an output element to your flowchart. Then double-click on the newly added output element, opening the output dialog box. Type **"Hello World"** (make sure that you include the double quotes) in the text box, and then click the OK button. Figure 1-4 shows how your flowchart should look after closing the dialog box.

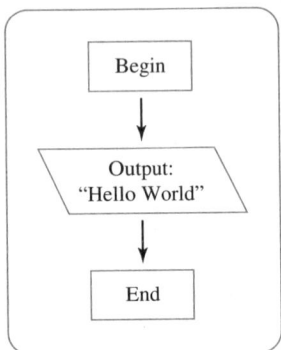

Figure 1-4 Hello World solution

Press F5 to run the program. The program executes, generating an output dialog box that appears with the text "Hello World" (Figure 1-5). Congratulations! You have just written your first computer program!

Figure 1-5 Hello World simulation output

ASK THE AUTHOR

Q: Adobe Illustrator and Microsoft Visio can also create flowcharts. Can those programs execute their flowcharts as well?

A: No. Those programs' flowcharts cannot be executed. Flowcharts without execution are of limited value because students have no way of knowing if they are on the right track. Visual Logic flowcharts are executable, providing immediate and accurate feedback to the student, combining the benefits of a high-level language with the simplicity of the classic flowcharting tool.

YOUR SECOND PROGRAM: HELLO NAME

Remember that an information system must input data, process data, and output resulting information. The first of those three tasks, inputting data into the system, is accomplished by means of an input statement. An **input statement** accepts data from the user and stores that data into a variable. A **variable** is a storage location that can be accessed and changed by developer code. A variable has a name (which does not change) and an associated data value (which may change during execution).

To understand the input statement, consider the following modification to the Hello World program you just wrote. Click on the flow-arrow above the output statement and add an input element. Double-click on the input element, opening the input element dialog box. Type **Name** (without quotes) in the variable text box and press OK. Then double-click on the output element and edit the text in the dialog box to read **"Hello " & Name** (being sure to include quotes around "Hello " followed by the ampersand [&] symbol followed by the unquoted Name variable). Your solution should now look like Figure 1-6.

INPUT, PROCESS, OUTPUT

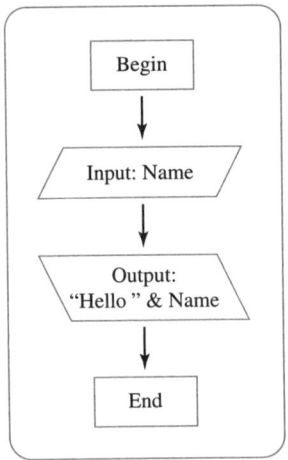

> **TIP**
> The ampersand (&) is a concatenation operator, meaning it links items together.

Figure 1-6 Hello Name solution

Run the program. You will be prompted to type a value for Name. Enter your name inside double quotes (e.g., "Dave"). The program will then display a message box with the appropriate greeting (e.g., "Hello Dave"; see Figure 1-7).

> **TIP**
> Text contained inside double quotes is called a string literal, and it appears literally as typed. Notice there is a space inside the double quotes following the word "Hello " which makes the output more readable.

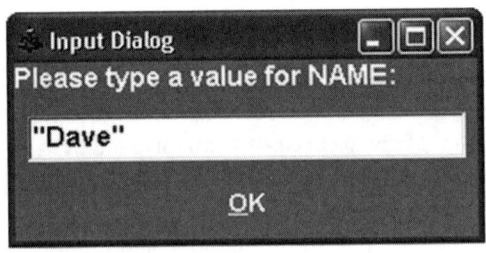 

Figure 1-7 One possible output of the Hello Name program

SIMPLE PROGRAMMING FORMATS

The Hello Name program uses an input statement to prompt the user for a value that is stored and then reused in an output statement. The value entered at the input prompt can be either numeric (e.g., 42 or 3.14159) or a string (e.g., "Abraham Lincoln" or "Merry Christmas"). Be aware that string input data must be contained within quotes.

There are some constraints with numeric data as well. Most programming languages do not allow numeric input to include symbols such as the percent symbol (%) or dollar sign ($) or even commas (,). Numeric input should consist of only digits and possibly one decimal point. You will quickly get used to using proper numeric notations for programming. Table 1-1 summarizes some common numeric notations and the correct programming format.

CHAPTER ONE

Value	Written format	Programming format	Comment
String	Hello World	`"Hello World"`	Use quotes to delimit strings
Percent	15%	`0.15`	Use decimal format
Dollars	$300	`300`	Dollar signs not allowed
Large numbers	12,345,678	`12345678`	Commas not allowed

Table 1-1 Common notations with correct programming formats

VARIABLE SUMMARY
» Variables are storage locations used for holding data and information.
» Each variable has two components: its name (which does not change) and its value (which may change during execution).

INPUT STATEMENT SUMMARY
» Input statements are used to get data into variables.
» In Visual Logic, the input flowchart element is a parallelogram with the keyword Input followed by the variable name.
» When the input statement is executed, the user is prompted to enter a value using the keyboard. The value typed is then stored in the variable for later use.
» String input must be placed inside quotes.
» Numeric input must contain only digits and possibly one decimal point. Percent symbols (%), dollar signs ($), and commas (,), among other symbols, are not allowed.

WEEKLY PAYCHECK PROGRAM

You have now written your first two computer programs, Hello World and Hello Name. Your third program will be a bit more complicated. You will now write a weekly paycheck program that accepts the hours worked and the hourly rate for an employee, and the program will calculate and display the appropriate pay amount due to the employee for the current week. This weekly paycheck program will use all three basics of an information system—input, processing, and output—and will be developed in steps.

STEP 1: INPUT
The weekly paycheck program has two input variables, *Hours* and *Rate*. Start Visual Logic. (If it is already running, under the menu click File, then New.) Click on the flow-arrow and select the input element. Repeat to add a second input element. Then double-click on each element to add the variable names Hours and Rate (Figure 1-8). These two elements are the input for the weekly paycheck program.

INPUT, PROCESS, OUTPUT

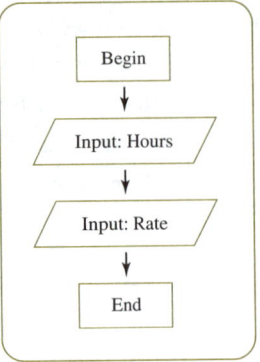

Figure 1-8 Partial weekly paycheck solution (input only)

> **ASK THE AUTHOR**
>
> Q: You used **Hours** and **Rate** as variable names. Could you have chosen different names?
>
> A: Yes. You have a great deal of freedom when it comes to naming variables. However, below are some suggestions and rules to remember:
>
> 1. A variable name should be descriptive of the data it holds.
> 2. A variable name must begin with a letter.
> 3. Only letters, digits, or the underscore character (_) may be used in variable names. Uppercase and lowercase do not matter. This means that **HOURS**, **hours**, and **Hours** are all interchangeable. In this book we will use the convention of starting each word in a variable name with an uppercase letter (e.g., **Cost**, **MailingAddress**, **ZipCode**).
> 4. The variable name must not be a word that is reserved by the programming language for other special uses. A list of reserved words can be found in Appendix A.

STEP 2: PROCESSING

The assignment statement can be used to perform a calculation and store the result. Addition (+), subtraction (−), multiplication (*), and division (/) are common arithmetic operations found in almost every high-level programming language. Note that the multiplication operator is typically an asterisk (*) rather than the traditional times operator (x), because X could be mistaken as a variable name.

To illustrate the use of the assignment statement, we return to the weekly paycheck program. You have already used two input statements to accept the data Hours and Rate. You will now add an assignment statement to process that data. The required calculation is straightforward. Hours times rate produces the pay amount due.

Returning to Visual Logic, click on a flow-arrow below the two input statements, and then select an assignment element from the menu. Double-click the assignment element to open the assignment edit dialog. The text box on the left is labeled *Variable*, and the text box on the right is labeled *Expression*. An **expression** is a value-returning code element, such as a variable or mathematical formula. Most programming languages follow this tradition of specifying the expression on the right-hand side (RHS) of the assignment statement, and specifying the variable to store the result on the left-hand side (LHS) of the assignment statement. When executed, the right-hand side expression is evaluated first. The result of the expression is then stored into the left-hand side variable.

Enter **Hours * Rate** in the right-hand expression text box and **Pay** in the left-hand text box. When finished, your solution should look like Figure 1-9. Your program now accepts two input values and performs an appropriate calculation based on those input values.

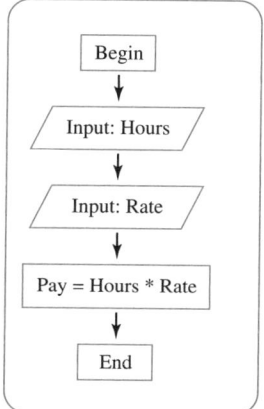

Figure 1-9 Partial weekly paycheck solution (input and assignment)

ASSIGNMENT STATEMENT SUMMARY
» Assignment statements are used to perform calculations and store the result.
» In Visual Logic, the assignment flowchart element is a rectangle with a variable on the left-hand side (LHS) and an expression on the right-hand side (RHS).
» When executed, the expression is evaluated, and the result is stored in the variable.

STEP 3: OUTPUT
Output can occur in many forms. Two common types of output are screen output and printed (i.e., hardcopy) output, both of which are visual. Sound output is common through speakers. Output involving the other senses (touch, smell, and taste) are possible as well. Information saved to a storage device such as a floppy disk, hard disk, or CD is also considered to be a form of output.

We conclude the paycheck program by adding an output dialog that displays an appropriate message to the user. Add an output element to your flowchart, and then double-click the element to enter the output expression. In the text box, type:

"Pay amount due is " & FormatCurrency(Pay)

Your completed flowchart should look like Figure 1-10.

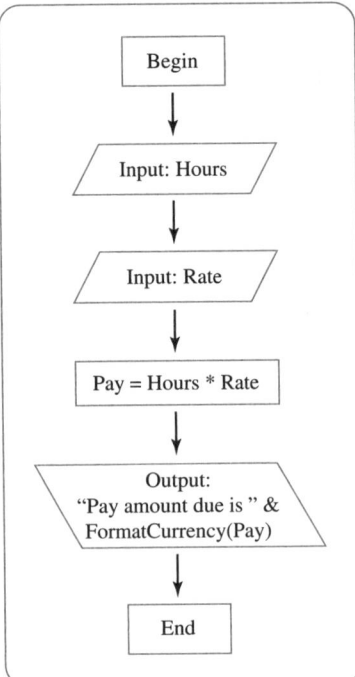

Figure 1-10 Weekly paycheck solution

Press F5 to run the program. The program prompts the user to enter a value for hours, then prompts the user again for a value for rate. The calculation is made and the information is displayed to the user in an output dialog box. For example, Figure 1-11 shows the output generated by input values of 30 hours and 8 dollars per hour rate.

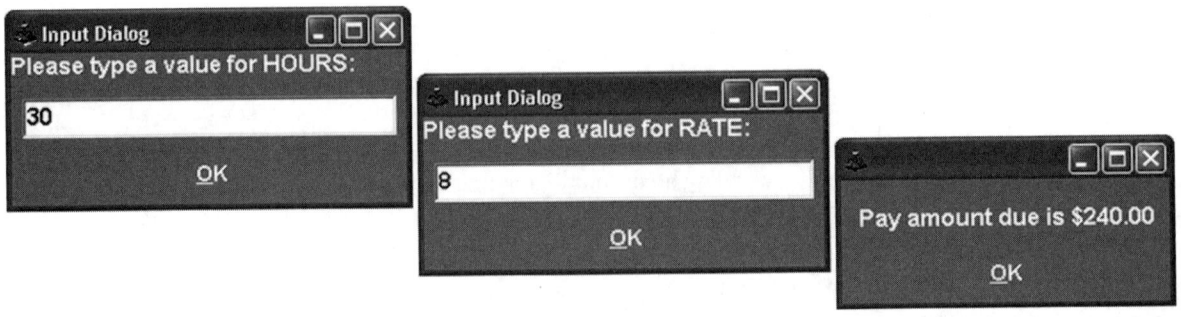

Figure 1-11 Weekly paycheck solution output

Congratulations! You have just written your third computer program! Save this program, as we will revise it in Chapter 2. (To save the file, select the menu option File | Save to create a .vls file, which is the Visual Logic solution file format.)

CHAPTER ONE

> **»TIP** When you create an output statement, you can combine string literals and variables in any combination, connected by the ampersand (&). For example, all of the following are valid Output messages:
>
> "You are " & Feet & " feet " & Inches & " inches tall"
> "The Area of the yard is " & Area & " and the perimeter is " & Perimeter

> **ASK THE AUTHOR**
>
> Q: You mentioned touch, smell, and taste output. Are you serious? If so, who is doing these kinds of things?
>
> A: Yes, full sensory output is a real area of exploration. Various tactile (e.g., touch) output is already available, such as force-feedback game controllers or dynamic Braille.
>
> As for the "Who?" part of your question, there are traditionally two groups. First are the scientists and inventors who are trying to do new and different things just to see if it can be done. Then there are the entrepreneurs who use new technologies to create business opportunities. For example, a perfume company may want to make samples of their products available online. Likewise, a clothing company may want to give Internet visitors the opportunity to feel the texture of the products as they shop. Most of these technologies are still experimental. Nonetheless, it is a real possibility that you will use all five senses when you browse the Internet in 2020.

HOW TO WRITE ARITHMETIC EXPRESSIONS

The calculation in the weekly paycheck program is rather straightforward (hours times rate). As a developer, you will often have to perform calculations that are significantly more complex. Visual Logic supports seven arithmetic operators, evaluated in the order of operator precedence shown in Table 1-2. Operators of the same precedence are evaluated left to right. Parentheses can be used to override the default precedence order.

There are three operators related to division. Regular division (/) produces a decimal value if necessary. Integer division (\) and integer remainder (Mod) require integer arguments and produce an integer answer. Integer division is the integer result, throwing away any remainder. Integer remainder is the amount left over after taking out as many whole occurrences of the numerator from the divisor as possible.

Operation	Operator	Expression1	Result1	Expression2	Result2
Exponentiation	^	5 ^ 2 + 1	26	5 ^ (2 + 1)	125
Multiplication and division	* /	1 + 3 * 7	22	17 / 3	5.667
Integer division	\	12 \ 4	3	17 \ 3	5
Integer remainder	Mod	12 Mod 4	0	17 Mod 3	2
Addition and subtraction	+ -	4 - 5 + 2	1	4 - (5 + 2)	-3

Table 1-2 Numeric operator precedence, highest to lowest

> **»TELL ME MORE**
>
> Integer division and integer remainder are new operators to most students. Once you understand them, you will find they can be used in a variety of situations. For example, you can determine if a number is even or odd using the integer remainder operator. If **N Mod 2** is 0, then N is even. If not, then N is odd.
>
> For another example, consider the everyday task of giving correct change. If you were owed 82 cents in change, you typically would not expect 82 pennies. Instead, you would expect 3 quarters, 1 nickel, and 2 pennies. A developer can use an expression like **Amount \ 25** to determine how many quarters are appropriate, and **Amount MOD 25** would calculate the change remaining after the quarters have been given. Additional integer division and integer remainder expressions could calculate the number of dimes, nickels, and pennies.

QUICK CHECK 1-A

Evaluate each of the following mathematical expressions. Assume A = 3, B = 5.

1. A + B * 5
2. (2 * 3) ^ 2
3. 11 \ A
4. 2 * 3 ^2
5. 11 / A
6. 11 Mod A

QUICK CHECK 1-B

Write Visual Logic expressions for each of the following.

1. The average of Exam 1, Exam 2, and Exam 3
2. $1 + \frac{1}{2} + \frac{1}{4}$
3. $\frac{4A^2B}{C}$

STRATEGIES FOR DOING CONVERSIONS

One area where it is easy to make a mistake is when performing a calculation to convert from one unit of measurement to another. Consider the seemingly simple task of converting inches to feet. Below are the incorrect and correct versions of this calculation.

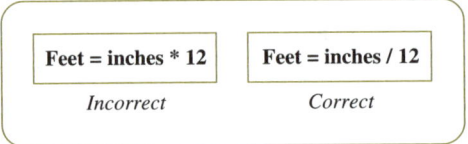

To understand why the first assignment is incorrect and the second is correct, consider the situation where inches has the value of 24. Since 24 inches is 2 feet, the correct value for feet should be 2. The first example above would calculate 24 * 12 and assign the result (288) to feet, which is almost the size of a football field. The second example would calculate 24/12 and assign the result (2) to feet, which is of course the correct answer.

CHAPTER ONE

> **» TELL ME MORE**
>
> When converting inches to feet, the correct action is to divide. In other situations the correct action is to multiply. How do you know when to divide and when to multiply? Here is the general rule:
>
> You should divide when you are moving to relatively "bigger" units, such as converting from inches to feet, e.g., Feet = Inches / 12
>
> You should multiply when you are moving to relatively "smaller" units, such as converting from yards to feet, e.g., Feet = Yards * 3

INTRINSIC FUNCTIONS

The weekly paycheck solution uses the intrinsic function FormatCurrency to display a numeric value in a currency format, including a leading dollar sign, two decimal places, and delimiting commas as necessary. Intrinsic functions are predefined commands that provide developers with common, helpful functionality. Intrinsic functions are divided into several categories, including math functions, business functions, string functions, time and date functions, conversion functions, file access functions, and so on. Another intrinsic function is FormatPercent, which takes a decimal percent value and converts it to its equivalent value with a percent symbol and two decimal places. Abs accepts a numeric value and produces the absolute value equivalent. Int accepts a decimal value and produces the integer whole value. Round accepts a decimal value and produces the nearest integer value. Finally, Random accepts an integer value N and produces a random integer between 0 and (N−1). Table 1-3 shows examples of these intrinsic functions.

Example	Result
FormatCurrency(12345)	$12,345.00
FormatCurrency(.02)	$0.02
FormatPercent(0.0625)	6.25%
FormatPercent(0.75)	75.00%
Abs(-3.3)	3.3
Abs(5.67)	5.67
Int(3.8)	3
Int(7.1)	7
Round(3.8)	4
Round(7.1)	7
Random(5)	A random integer between 0 and 4
Random(100) + 1	A random integer between 1 and 100

Table 1-3 Intrinsic functions for Visual Logic

OUTPUT STATEMENT SUMMARY

» Output statements are used to display information.

» In Visual Logic, the output flowchart element is a parallelogram with the keyword Output followed by an output expression.

INPUT, PROCESS, OUTPUT

» When executed, string literals are displayed exactly as typed inside the containing quotes.
» When executed, expressions are evaluated and the result is displayed.
» The ampersand (&) operator may be used to concatenate a series of string literals, variables, and expressions into one large expression.
» Carriage returns in the output expression appear as carriage returns in the displayed output.

DEBUGGING WITH VISUAL LOGIC

Even the best developers will eventually make mistakes. A programming mistake is often called a **bug** (see Tell Me More box, below), although the term error is probably more appropriate. Visual Logic provides debugging support to help you track down and fix your errors. Figure 1-12 shows the execution and debugging portion of the Visual Logic standard toolbar. Note that these functions are also available under the Debug menu item. *Run* is the command that executes the simulator. *Pause* stops the simulation on the current command. *Terminate* ends the execution of the current program.

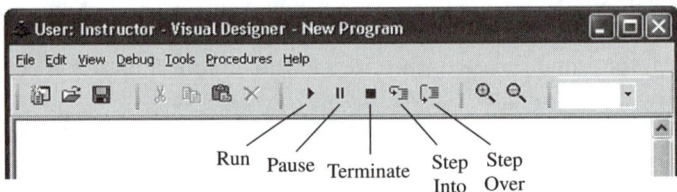

Figure 1-12 Execution and debugging in the Visual Logic toolbar

The last two options, *Step Into* and *Step Over*, allow a paused program to execute one step at a time. When the program is paused, the Variable Watch window appears displaying the current values for all program variables. Step Into takes you to the next command and will go into a structure like a condition or a loop (which we discuss in the following chapters). Step Over takes you to the next command at the same level as the current command. Using the step commands to study the program variable values as each statement executes can be helpful in determining why your program is generating an error. For more information about debugging, see Appendix B.

» TELL ME MORE

There is an interesting history behind the term **bug**. The term may have arisen as early as the fourteenth century to mean "an object of dread" derived from the Welsh word *bwg* for hobgoblin. Thomas Edison is quoted as using the term bugs for flaws in a system in 1878.

The term became particularly popular in 1947 when a moth was found in a relay of the Harvard Mark II machine. Grace Murray Hopper (who later helped design COBOL and is affectionately knows as the "Mother of Modern Computing") was involved in the project. She once related the events as follows, "Things were going badly; there was something wrong in one of the circuits of the long glass-enclosed computer.

Finally, someone located the trouble spot and, using ordinary tweezers, removed the problem, a two-inch moth. From then on, when anything went wrong with a computer, we said it had bugs in it."

The moth was taped in the computer log, with the following entry: *"First actual case of bug being found."* The logbook, now in the collection of Naval Surface Weapons Center, still contains the remains of the moth.

(Additional Source: The AFU and Urban Legends Archive. "Have Some Grace and Don't Let it Bug You," http://www.tafkac.org/faq2k/compute_86.html)

CHAPTER ONE

≫ CASE STUDY SOLUTION

Grocery Checkout

"Now it's time to put our new knowledge to the test," Mr. Taylor says 10 minutes before the class ends. "We have discussed how Visual Logic can be used to do input, processing, and output. Our grocery checkout problem requires three input values (the prices of the three items), three calculations (the subtotal of the three items, the appropriate sales tax, and the resulting total), and a single output (the resulting total). Let me show you how this can be done in Visual Logic." Below are the steps Mr. Taylor follows when demonstrating the solution for the class.

1. From the Visual Logic menu, select File | New to start a new program. Add three input elements to your flowchart. Enter the variable names **Item1**, **Item2**, and **Item3** respectively.
2. Add an assignment element to your flowchart. Enter **SubTotal** as the result variable, and enter **Item1 + Item2 + Item3** as the expression.
3. Add a second assignment element to your flowchart. Set the variable **SalesTax** to be the result of the expression **SubTotal * 0.06**.
4. Add a third assignment element that sets **Total** to be the sum of **SubTotal + SalesTax**.
5. Display the Total with an appropriate output statement. Your solution should look something like Figure 1-13.
6. Run your program to see if it works. If the input values are 10, 20, and 30, the output should be "Your purchase total is $63.60."

The class works on their programs getting help from Mr. Taylor as needed. Finally, just as class is about to end, a student from the back of the class shouts, "What about the bad joke?"

Mr. Taylor considers for a moment, then says "What did the termite say when he went into the bar?" (pause) "Where is the bar tender?"

A couple of students laugh and explain the joke to their neighbors. Others are confused, not sure if it was supposed to be funny or not. "Don't quit your day job," one student says.

"Not a chance," Mr. Taylor says, smiling.

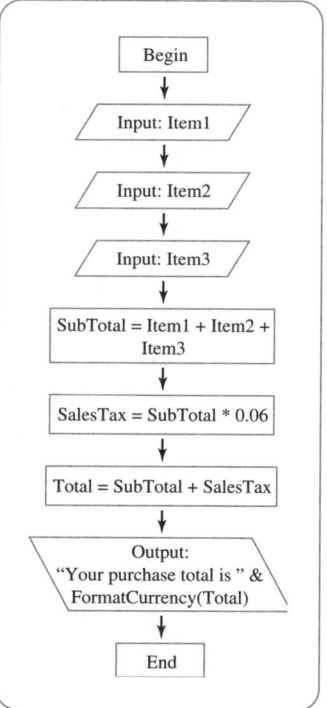

Figure 1-13 Grocery Checkout solution

CHAPTER SUMMARY

» Variables are storage locations used for holding data and information.
» Each variable has two components: its name (which does not change) and its value (which may change during execution).
» Input statements are used to get data into variables. When executed, the user is prompted to enter a value using the keyboard. The value typed is then stored in the variable for later use.
» Expressions are value-returning code elements, such as a variable or mathematical formula.
» Assignment statements are used to perform calculations and store the result. When an assignment statement is executed, the expression is evaluated and the result is stored in the variable.
» Output statements are used to display information. When an output statement is executed, string literals are displayed exactly as typed inside the containing quotes, and expressions are evaluated and the result is displayed. The ampersand (&) operator may be used to concatenate a series of string literals and expressions into one large expression.
» Input, assignment, and output statements are sufficient to write small but interesting computer programs.

KEY TERMS

algorithm
assignment statement
bug
computer program
data

expression
input statement
intrinsic function
knowledge
operator precedence

output statement
syntax
variable
wisdom

REVIEW QUESTIONS

1. Consider the similarities and differences between developing an algorithm and developing syntax. What skills are required for each activity? What is the added value for each activity?
2. Identify possible input, processing, and output for a video store's rental checkout system.
3. Imagine you are an entrepreneur with access to some of the innovative output technologies regarding smell, touch, and taste. Identify some business uses of these technologies that you think might become profitable.

PROGRAMMING EXERCISES

1-1. A Rose by Any Other Name. Paulette has just planted a large rose garden that she wants to fertilize. She knows the area of her rose garden in square feet, but the fertilizer is measured by the square yard. Write a program that converts square feet to square yards. (*Hint*: Make sure you are using the correct conversion ratio. Most everyone knows 3 feet makes 1 yard. Are square feet and square yards any different?)

Input Variable	Process/Output Variable
SquareFeet	SquareYards

CHAPTER ONE

1-2. Twenty Thousand Leagues Under the Sea. Jules Verne's book <u>Twenty Thousand Leagues Under the Sea</u> is the story of Captain Nemo and his fantastic submarine *Nautilus*. The story is told from the perspective of Professor Aronnax, who entered the Nautilus as a prisoner but later is treated as a guest. At one point the professor writes, "I have crossed 20,000 leagues in that submarine tour of the world, which has revealed so many wonders." Write a program that will input a distance in leagues and then calculate and display that same distance in nautical miles. (*Hint*: Perform an Internet search to find the conversion ratio between leagues and nautical miles.)

Input Variable	Process/Output Variable
Leagues	NauticalMiles

1-3. Run the Numbers. Write a program with two input values. The program should display the sum, difference, quotient, product, and average of the two numbers.

Input Variables	Process/Output Variables
Num1, Num2	Sum, Difference, Quotient, Product, Average

1-4. Gross and Net Pay. Write a program with two input values, Hours and Rate. The program should first calculate Gross pay, which is your pay before deductions. The program should then calculate the following three deduction amounts: Federal Tax (20% of Gross), State Tax (5% of Gross), Social Security Tax (6.2% of Gross). Then your program should calculate Net pay, which is your Gross pay minus the three deductions. The output should be all five of the calculated values.

Input Variables	Process/Output Variables
Hours, Rate	GrossPay, FederalTax, StateTax, SocialSecurity, NetPay

1-5. "As I was going to St. Ives . . . " Consider the following nursery rhyme:

As I was going to St. Ives, I met a man with seven wives. Every wife had seven sacks, every sack had seven cats, and every cat had seven kittens. Kittens, cats, sacks, and wives, how many were going to St. Ives?

The question at the end of the rhyme is a trick question because only the narrator is going to St. Ives. Write a program to determine the total number of things (including people, animals, and sacks) that were met by the narrator.

Input Variable	Process/Output Variables
(none required; it is all provided in the rhyme)	Man, Wives, Sacks, Cats, Kittens

1-6. Correct Change. Write a program to assist a cashier with determining correct change. The program should have one input, the number of cents to return to the customer. The output should be the appropriate change in quarters, dimes, nickels and cents.

INPUT, PROCESS, OUTPUT

(*Hint*: Consider how integer division (\) and integer remainder (Mod) can be used as part of your solution.)

Input Variable	Process/Output Variables
Change	Quarters, Dimes, Nickels, Pennies

1-7. Jake's Problem. Jake has a car with an 8-gallon fuel tank. Jake fills his tank with gas and then drives 60 miles to a friend's house. When he gets to his friend's house, he has 6 gallons left in his fuel tank. Write a program that uses three input elements to enter values for tank size, miles traveled, and gallons left. The program should calculate and display how many miles Jake can drive on a full tank of gas. (*Note*: Be sure to use input elements to accept the values 8, 60, and 6 rather than hard-coding them into your solution.)

Input Variables	Process/Output Variables
TankSize, MilesTraveled, GallonsLeft	*(left to the reader)*

CHAPTER **TWO**

MAKING DECISIONS

> **»CASE STUDY SCENARIO**
>
> **Smallest Number**
>
> Dr. Taylor begins class by discussing some of the programs the students wrote as homework from Chapter 1. He presents a solution to Jake's problem (Chapter 1) that contains some unusual logic. This discussion triggers questions about the difference between a good solution and a correct solution. Dr. Taylor explains, "A correct solution generates the appropriate information, but a good solution is a correct solution that is also easy to understand and maintain."
>
> A student sitting near the middle of the room raises her hand and asks, "Can there be multiple good solutions to the same problem?"
>
> "Absolutely. Consider the problem of finding the smallest (or largest) value from a series of input data. Finding such a value is an essential step for many activities, including sorting or calculating weighted grades," Dr. Taylor explains. "In fact, today we will examine multiple solutions to this problem. You can then decide which solutions are most clear."
>
> Dr. Taylor's solutions are presented later in this chapter.

MAKING DECISIONS

In the previous chapter we developed a program for calculating a weekly paycheck. The amount due was calculated using a simple assignment statement:

Pay = Hours * Rate

MAKING DECISIONS

This calculation works fine under normal circumstances. However, it is a common practice for many businesses to give overtime pay to employees who work more than 40 hours in a week. The formula for calculating pay with overtime is 40 hours at regular pay plus hours over 40 at one-and-a-half times regular pay. This can be easily expressed in an assignment statement, as follows:

$$\text{Pay} = 40 * \text{Rate} + (\text{Hours} - 40) * \text{Rate} * 1.5$$

The "Normal" formula works for regular pay, and the "Overtime" formula works for overtime pay. Unfortunately, neither formula works in all situations. What is needed, therefore, is a way for the program to choose which formula is appropriate. In other words, the program needs to make a decision.

ASK THE AUTHOR

Q: What kind of decisions can a computer make?

A: A computer's decision-making process is limited because each of the computer's possible actions must be specified in advance. Humans have the ability to be creative, but a computer can only select between predefined actions based on the result of some evaluation. Those with an interest in the history of computing may find it interesting that Edward Dijkstra used the term "selection" when referring to the computer's ability to make decisions (see the following Tell Me More entry).

»TELL ME MORE

Edward Dijkstra was one of the most influential persons in the history of computer programming. His article "Structured programming" (first published in *Software Engineering Techniques*, 1970) demonstrated that any logical programming solution might be expressed using only three control flow constructs: sequential, selection, and repetition. Sequential commands (e.g., input, assignment, and output) were presented in Chapter 1 of this textbook. This chapter is about Selection, and Chapter 3 is about Repetition. By mastering these three constructs, programmers can create code in which the logical design is evident on inspection, thus making solutions easier to develop, test, and maintain.

THE IF STATEMENT

The most common selection (or "decision") structure is the **IF statement**. The IF statement begins with a condition, followed by a block of statements that execute only when the condition evaluates to true, and an optional block of statements that execute only when the condition evaluates to false. The two blocks are called the true block and the false block (for obvious reasons). The IF statement ends where the two blocks reconnect.

A **condition** is a boolean expression that evaluates to either true or false. Conditions typically involve one of the six **relational operators** shown in Table 2-1.

CHAPTER TWO

Operator	Description	Expression	Result (assume x = 2, y = 3)
=	Equal	x = 2	True
		x = y	False
<>	Not Equal	y <> 5	True
		y <> 3	False
>	Greater Than	x > 1	True
		x > y	False
<	Less Than	x < y	True
		x < 2	False
>=	Greater Than Or Equal	x >= 2	True
		x >= y	False
<=	Less Than Or Equal	x <= 2	True
		x <= 1	False

Table 2-1 Relational operators

QUICK CHECK 2-A

Evaluate each of the following conditions. Assume A = 2, B = 6.

1. A < B
2. A = B
3. 17 Mod B <> 5
4. (A - B) = (B - A)
5. B + A * B = 18

SIMPLE IF STATEMENTS

To understand how an IF statement is used in Visual Logic, consider the simple problem of reading two values and determining if they are equal or not. Our solution will use two input statements followed by an IF statement to compare the two values. Add an output statement inside the true branch to display the message: **The values are equal**. Likewise, add an output statement inside the false branch to display the message: **The values are not equal** (see Figure 2-1). Run this solution multiple times with different input values to verify its behavior.

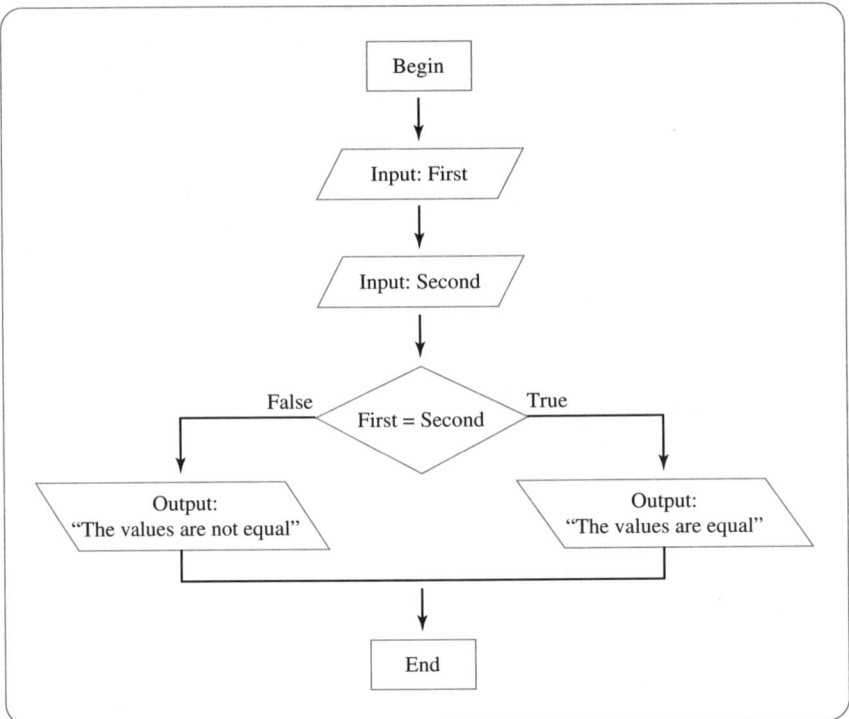

Figure 2-1 A simple IF statement

SOLVING THE OVERTIME PROBLEM

An IF statement can be used to solve the overtime problem. Specifically, the solution will make a decision about which formula is appropriate based on the number of hours worked by the employee.

From the Visual Logic menu, select File | Open. Open the file containing the paycheck program you saved from the previous chapter (see Figure 1-8). Click on the flow-arrow above the assignment statement, and add a condition element to your flowchart. Then double-click the element to enter the condition. In the text box, type the following condition:

Hours < 40

Press OK to close the condition edit dialog box. Drag the existing assignment statement to the true branch and drop it there. Click the false branch and add a new assignment statement with the overtime formula. Your flowchart should now look like Figure 2-2. Run the program multiple times to ensure that the condition is working properly.

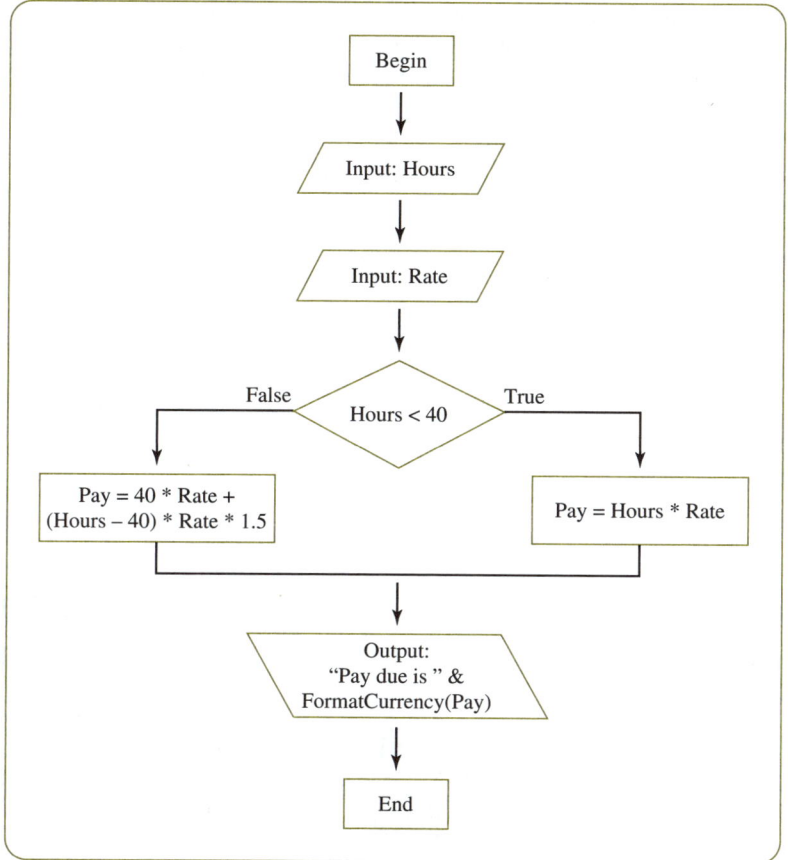

Figure 2-2 Weekly paycheck program with overtime

IF STATEMENT SUMMARY
» IF statements are used to choose between actions.
» In Visual Logic, the IF flowchart element is a diamond containing a condition and two exit arrows labeled True and False.
» A condition is a boolean expression, typically involving one of six relational operators.
» When executed, the condition is evaluated. If the condition is true, control flows along the true arrow. If the condition is false, control flows along the false arrow.
» An IF statement ends where the true and false branches reconnect.

NESTED IF STATEMENTS

The true and false branches of an IF statement may contain any number of statements of any type, including other IF statements. The term nested IF refers to an IF statement contained within the true or false branch of another IF statement.

MAKING DECISIONS

To understand nested IF statements, consider the simple problem of reading two values and determining if they are equal, if the first is greater than the second, or if the first is smaller than the second. The three possible results are properly handled by the nested IF solution in Figure 2-3.

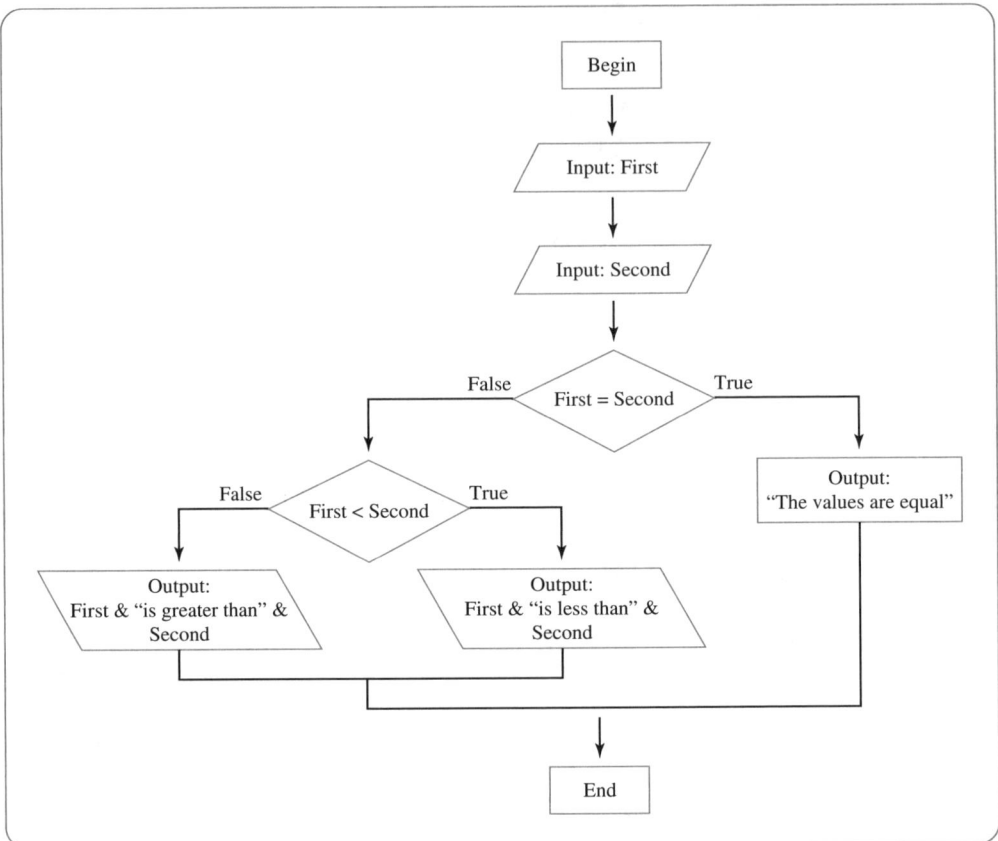

Figure 2-3 A nested IF solution

LONG-DISTANCE BILLING PROBLEM

Consider the problem of determining the billing rate for a long distance phone call. According to one billing plan, if a call is made between 6:00 a.m. and 6:00 p.m., then the billing rate should be 10 cents per minute. Nights and mornings are free. One possible solution to the billing requirement is shown in Figure 2-4. The problem assumes a military time format is being used (e.g., "1800" refers to 6:00 p.m.).

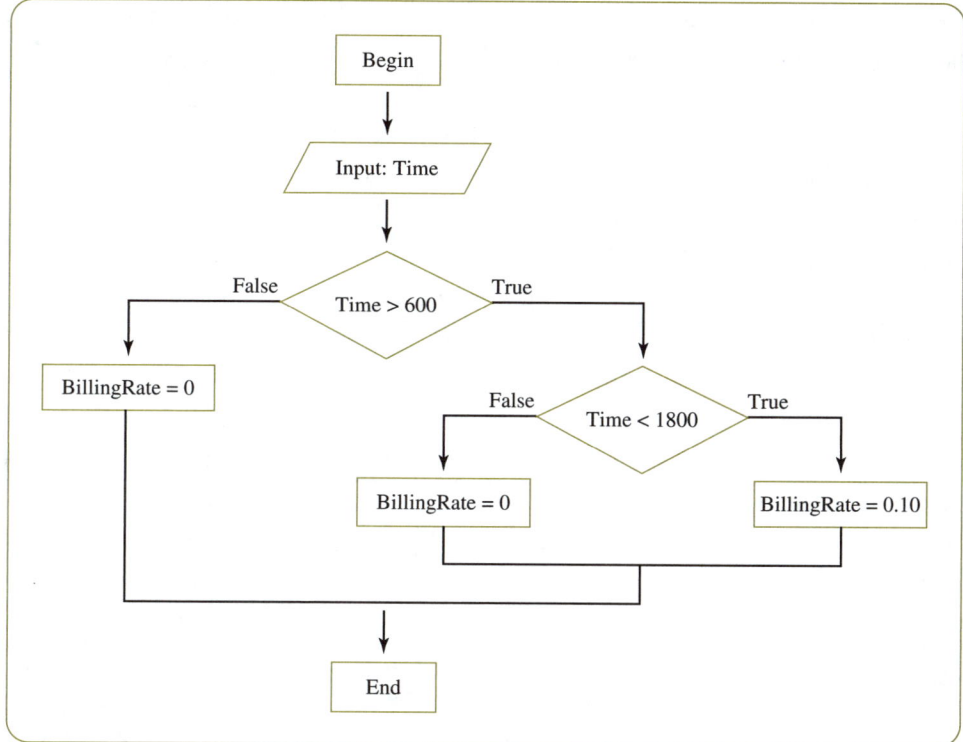

Figure 2-4 Nested IF solution to determine long-distance billing rate

COMPOUND CONDITIONS

When it comes to making decisions, developers are often faced with complex conditions that require multiple comparisons. A compound condition consists of two conditions within parentheses joined by a logical operator. The four most common logical operators are NOT, AND, OR, and XOR. Table 2-2 illustrates these four logical operators.

MAKING DECISIONS

Operator	Description	Example	Result (assume A = 5, B = 8)
NOT	Returns the opposite of the condition	NOT (A < 3) NOT (B = 8)	True False
AND	Returns true if and only if both conditions are true	(A = 1) AND (B = 9) (A = 5) AND (B = 9) (A = 1) AND (B = 8) (A = 5) AND (B = 8)	False False False True
OR	Returns true if at least one condition is true	(A = 1) OR (B = 9) (A = 5) OR (B = 9) (A = 1) OR (B = 8) (A = 5) OR (B = 8)	False True True True
XOR	Returns true if the conditions have opposite values	(A = 1) XOR (B = 9) (A = 5) XOR (B = 9) (A = 1) XOR (B = 8) (A = 5) XOR (B = 8)	False True True False

Table 2-2 Logical operators with results

> **»TIP** Be sure to use parentheses around each condition when writing compound conditions. The parentheses make the conditions evaluate before the relational operator. If you do not use parentheses, then the result may not be what you expect. For example, the condition
>
> (5 > 4) AND (4 > 3)
>
> evaluates to True if you use parentheses; but it may evaluate incorrectly to False if you omit the parentheses.

To understand how compound conditions may be used, consider an automobile insurance company that charges a premium for male drivers under the age of 25. The condition that tests for this could be the following compound condition:

(Gender = "Male") AND (Age < 25)

Another example would be a test to see if a student is a senior (90 or more hours) with a grade point average at or above 3.25. The compound condition that tests for this would be:

(HoursEarned > 90) AND (GPA > 3.25)

There are times when a single compound condition can be used in place of a nested IF. For example, consider again the long-distance billing algorithm previously shown in Figure 2-4. This can be rewritten using a single compound condition, as shown in Figure 2-5. Both solutions are right because they both produce the correct result. It is a subjective opinion as to which, if either, is the better (e.g., more clear) solution.

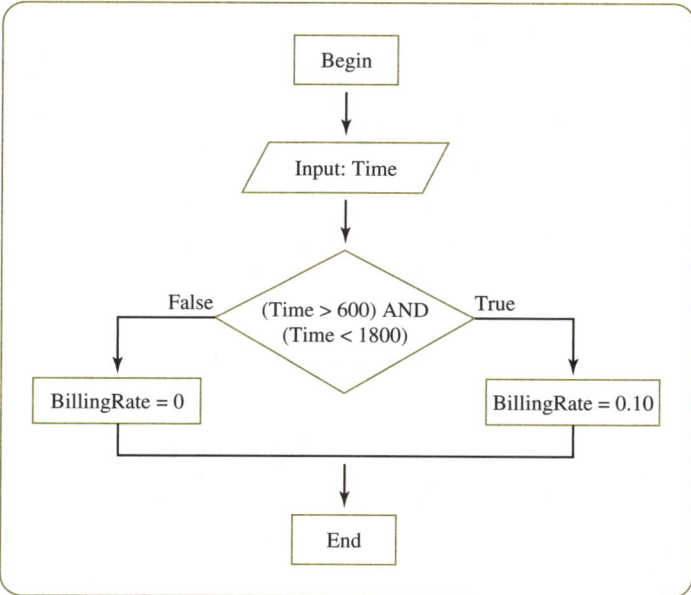

Figure 2-5 Compound condition solution to determine long-distance billing rate

ASK THE AUTHOR

Q: Are you saying there is no difference between the nested IF solution (Figure 2-4) and the compound condition solution (Figure 2-5) to the long-distance billing problem?

A: There are advantages and disadvantages with both. If the night and morning billing rate were to change, you would have to change two assignments in Figure 2-4 but only one in Figure 2-5, meaning the compound condition reduces the likelihood of a simple oversight error. On the other hand, using compound conditions requires caution because it is easy to use OR when AND is required and vice versa. What would happen in Figure 2-5 if the logical operator OR had been used instead of AND? (*Hint*: Customers would be unhappy.)

Generally speaking, it is a good idea to consider multiple solutions and choose the one that is clearest to you. The Case Study Solution will further illustrate this point.

QUICK CHECK 2-B

Evaluate each of the following compound conditions. Assume X = 3, Y = 7.

1. (X = 1) AND (Y = 7)
2. (X = 1) OR (Y = 7)
3. (X < Y) AND (Y > 10)
4. (X ^ 3 = 27) AND (Y Mod 2 = 1)
5. (X ^ 3 = 27) XOR (Y Mod 2 = 1)

MAKING DECISIONS

⟫ CASE STUDY SOLUTION

Smallest Number

Dr. Taylor continues, "Now that we have looked at IF statements, nested IF statements, and compound conditions, we can use these structures to write interesting programs. Consider the problem of inputting three unduplicated values and displaying the smallest value. We will examine four different solutions to this problem, all of which are correct. However, they are not necessarily equal."

John Paul speaks up, asking "If they are all correct, doesn't that make them equal?"

"Not necessarily. If, for example, one of the solutions is much easier to understand than the others, then that solution would be better. Given the choice, you should use the algorithm you understand best. In addition, some solutions lend themselves to modification better than others. Sometimes it is beneficial to consider alternative solutions rather than always using the first idea that comes to your mind."

Solution 1: Nested Conditions

Dr. Taylor hands out the first solution (Figure 2-6). "This first solution uses nested conditions. The first condition determines which is the smaller of A and B. The smaller of A and B is then compared with C via a nested condition. The smaller value of the second comparison is then displayed."

Solution 2: Compound Conditions

"This second solution (Figure 2-7) uses a series of compound conditions. The first compound condition checks to see if A holds the smallest value and, if so, prints A. Similar compound conditions are used for testing B and C. These conditions are sequential, not nested."

Solution 3: Nested and Compound Condition

"The third solution (Figure 2-8) to the smallest number problem begins with a compound condition. In this case, however, the program contains a nested condition in the false branch. Since A is not the smallest, the nested condition need only compare B and C to determine the smallest value."

Solution 4: Placeholder Variable

"Our fourth and final solution (Figure 2-9) takes a different approach than the first three. This solution makes use of an extra variable, **Smallest**, to serve as a placeholder for the smallest value. The placeholder is initially given the value of the first input number. Then each remaining input number is individually compared with the placeholder value. If a smaller number is found, the placeholder becomes the same as the newer, smaller value. After all values have been compared, the placeholder will hold the smallest of the input values."

Wrap-up

"All four of these solutions for finding the smallest number are correct. Which one is most clear?" The ensuing discussion is lively with a variety of opinions presented. The solutions are evaluated for how well they would handle slight variations on the problem. For example, what if duplicate values were allowed? What if the middle value were required instead of the smallest value? What if the size of the input was more than three values? The general consensus is that each solution has its advantages and that different solutions lend themselves better to different variations of the original problem. Looking at his watch, Dr. Taylor wraps up the conversation. "Comparing the strengths and weaknesses of multiple solutions is a key skill for writing great software. I think you are all doing an excellent job."

ASK THE AUTHOR

Q: In both Figures 2-7 and 2-8 you have a condition that reads:

$$(A < B) \text{ AND } (A < C)$$

Could this have also been written as: $(A < B < C)$?

A: No. The condition $(A < B < C)$ will not evaluate correctly. For your program to work properly, you need two explicit tests $(A < B)$ and $(A < C)$, and you need to join those two tests using the compound AND operator, as shown in Figure 2-6 and Figure 2-7. Also remember to include parentheses around the two conditions to ensure the AND evaluates properly.

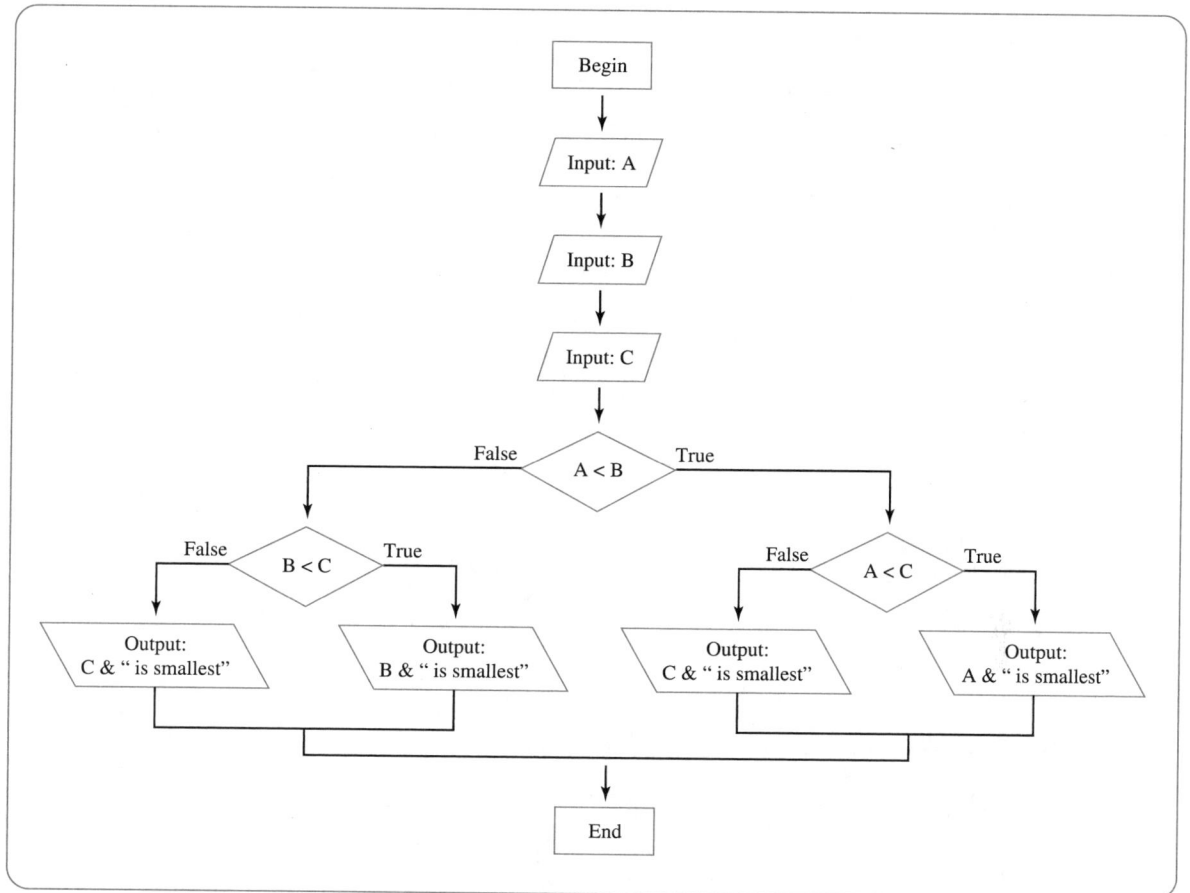

Figure 2-6 Smallest number solution #1 - Using nested conditions

MAKING DECISIONS

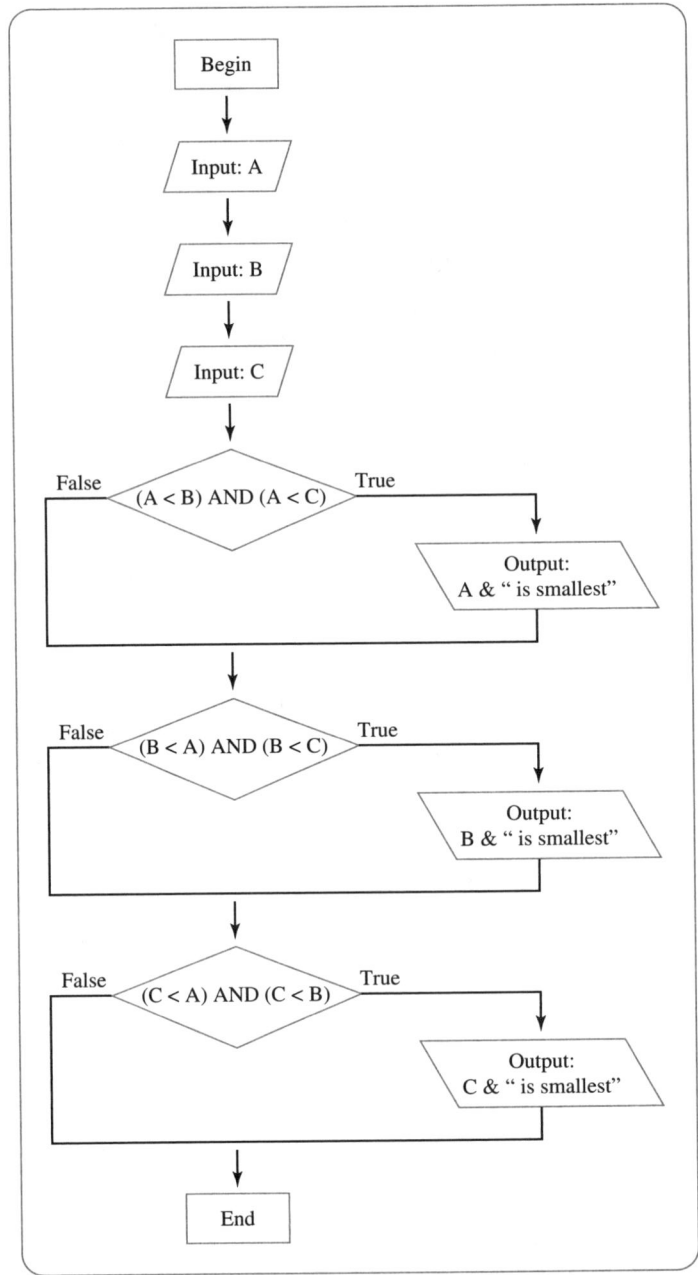

Figure 2-7 Smallest number solution #2 - Using sequential compound conditions

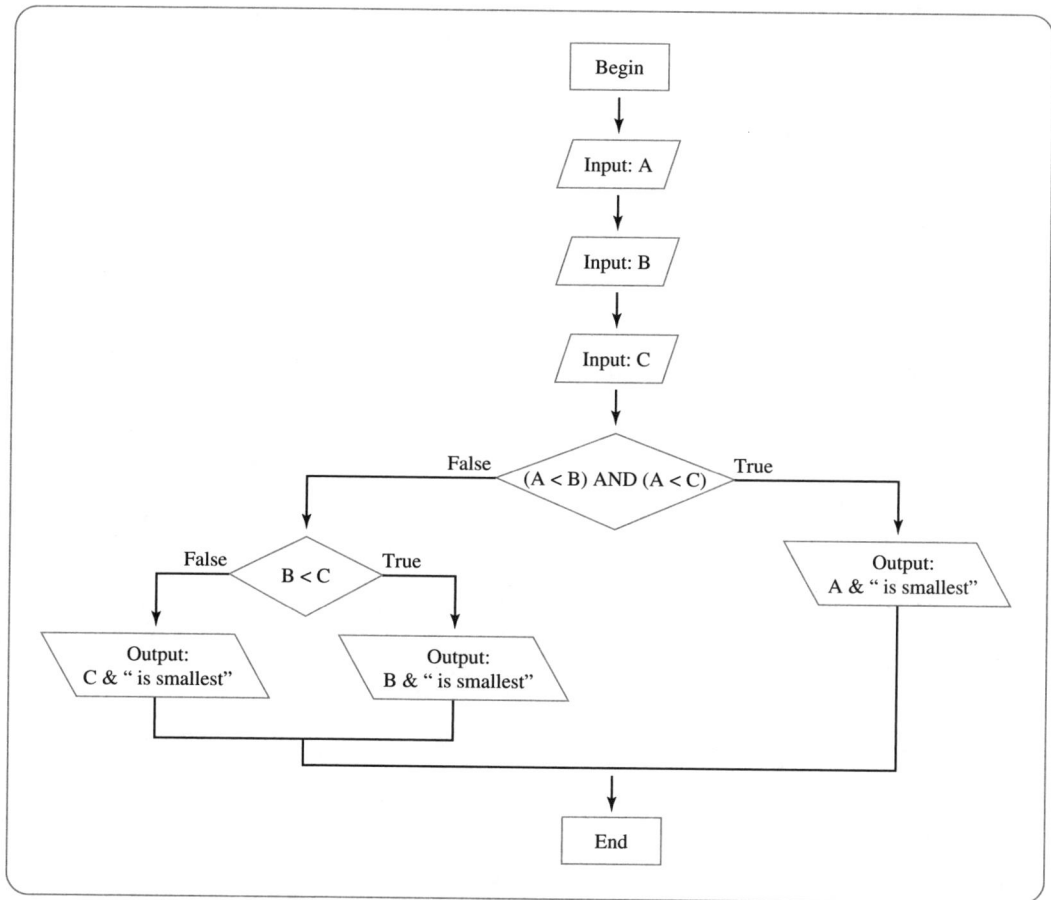

Figure 2-8 Smallest number solution #3 - Using nested and compound conditions

MAKING DECISIONS

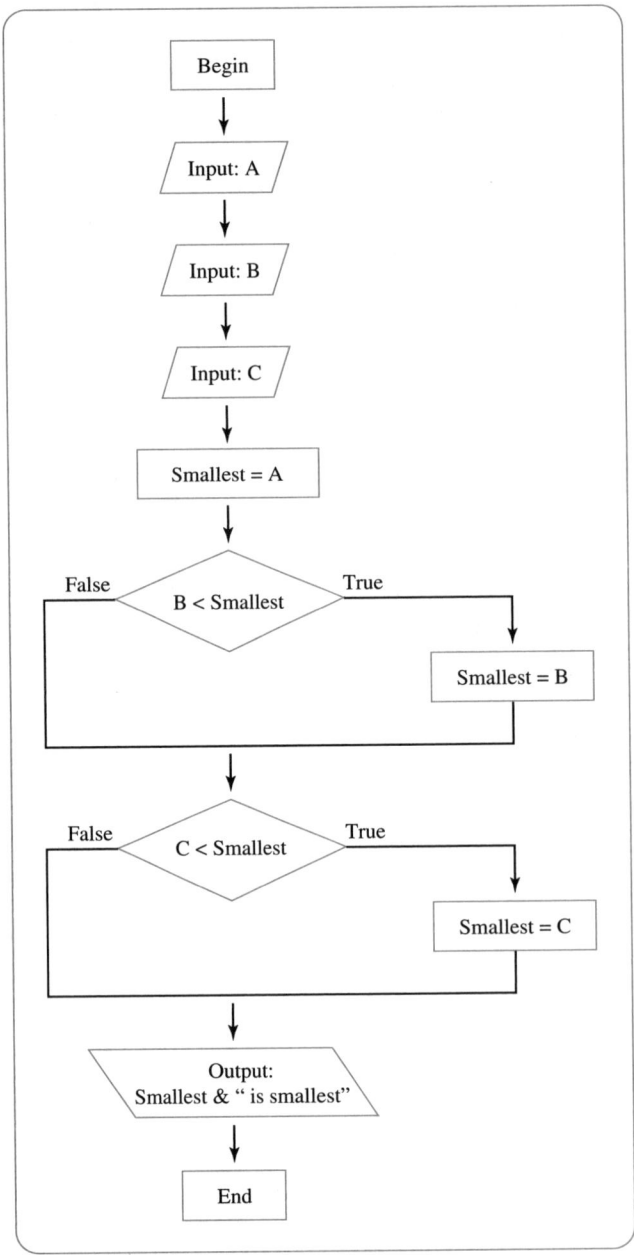

Figure 2-9 Smallest number solution #4 - Using a placeholder variable

CHAPTER TWO

CHAPTER SUMMARY

» A condition is an expression that evaluates to either true or false. Conditions typically use one of six relational operators: =, >, <, >=, <=, <>.

» IF statements use conditions to choose between actions. When executed, the condition is evaluated. If the condition is true, control flows to the true branch. If the condition is false, control flows to the false branch.

» The true and false branches of an IF statement may contain any valid statement, including other IF statements. An IF statement within the true or false branch of another IF statement is referred to as a nested IF.

» A compound condition is two or more conditions joined by a logical operator. The four most common logical operators are AND, OR, NOT, and XOR.

KEY TERMS

compound condition
condition
IF statement
logical operators
nested IF
relational operators

REVIEW QUESTIONS

1. What is the difference between a correct program solution and a good program solution? Why is it important for solutions to be not only correct but also good?

2. Identify possible uses of decision statements (IF statements) for a video store's rental checkout system.

3. The long-distance billing problem has a nested IF solution (Figure 2-4). This solution was rewritten as a compound condition solution (Figure 2-5). Can all nested IF solutions be rewritten as compound condition solutions? As part of your answer, consider the problem of inputting two values and displaying if the first is smaller than, equal to, or greater than the second (Figure 2-3). If it can be rewritten, include the new solution with your answer. If it cannot be rewritten, explain why not.

4. Consider the four solutions in Figures 2-6 through 2-9. These solutions assume the input data contains unduplicated numbers. Determine if each solution would work if duplicate input values were allowed (e.g., 3, 5, 3 as input).

PROGRAMMING EXERCISES

2-1. Positive Difference. Write a program that inputs two values and displays their positive difference. For example, if the first input is 6 and the second input is 9, then the positive difference is 3. Likewise, if the first input is 9 and the second input is 6, the output is still a positive 3.

Input Variable
Num1, Num2

2-2. All's Well That Ends Well. Write a program that inputs a number between 1 and 10 and displays the number with the appropriate two-letter ending (e.g., 1st, 2nd, 3rd, 4th, 5th, . . .).

Input Variable
Number

2-3. Middle Value. Write a program that displays the middle value of three unduplicated input values. *Hint*: Review the four solutions in the smallest number case study in this chapter. Consider how easy or hard it would be to modify each of those algorithms to find the middle value rather than the smallest value. Then modify the algorithm you consider most appropriate for this problem.

Input Variable
A, B, C

2-4. Smallest of Five. Write a program that displays the smallest of five input values that may include duplicate values (e.g., 6, 4, 8, 6, 7). *Hint*: Review the four solutions in the smallest number case study in this chapter. Consider how easy or hard it would be to modify each of those algorithms to find the smallest of five rather than three values. Then modify the algorithm you consider most appropriate for this problem.

Input Variable
A, B, C, D, E

2-5. Grade Determination. Write a program that will input three test scores. The program should determine and display their average. The program should then display the appropriate letter grade based on the average. The letter grade should be determined using a standard 10-point scale (A = 90–100; B = 80–89.999; C = 70–79.999, etc.)

Input Variable
Score1, Score2, Score3

2-6. All's Well That Ends Well, Part II. Write a program that inputs a number between 1 and 1000 and displays the number with the appropriate two-letter ending (e.g., 1st, 2nd, 3rd, 4th, 5th, . . .). *Hint*: This problem is harder than it sounds. The most common ending is th, but there are many exceptions. You might want to start by finding all the exceptions and looking for patterns. You might then find integer division (\) and integer remainder (Mod) helpful in testing for those patterns.

Input Variable
Number

2-7. The Perfect Fit. Write a program with three input variables, RW (for rectangle width), RH (for rectangle height), and SS (for square side). The program should output two sentences. The first sentence will be one of the following.

> "The object with the greatest area is the square."
>
> "The object with the greatest area is the rectangle."
>
> "The square and the rectangle have the same area."

The second sentence will be one of the following.

> "The square fits inside the rectangle."
>
> "The rectangle fits inside the square."
>
> "Neither shape fits inside the other."

Note: A 5 × 3 rectangle does not fit inside a 5 × 5 square; however, a 4.9 × 3 rectangle does fit inside a 5 × 5 square.

Input Variable	Process/Output Variable
RW, RH, SS	*(two sentences)*

CHAPTER THREE

WHILE LOOPS

CONSOLE INPUT AND OUTPUT

Sometimes you may want the input and output interactions with the user to be maintained for later inspection. This can be done through the use of **console** input and output statements. Figure 3-1 shows the input edit dialog window with the console input option button selected. (Click the "More >>" button to show the Console option button. A similar console option exists inside the output edit dialog window.) Figure 3-1 also shows a prompt to the user. This prompt will be used in place of the default prompt.

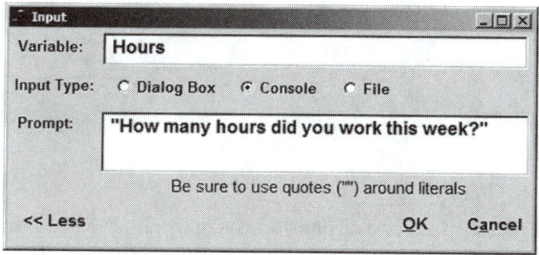

Figure 3-1 Input edit dialog window with the Console input option selected

The flowchart elements for console input and output have a console screen icon at the top of the flowchart element (see Figure 3-2).

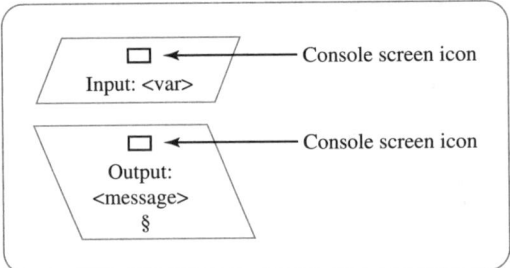

Figure 3-2 Console Input and Output elements

Console I/O is persistent, meaning each line of input and output remains in the console window for the lifetime of the program. The programs in Figure 3-3 illustrate the differences between Dialog I/O and Console I/O.

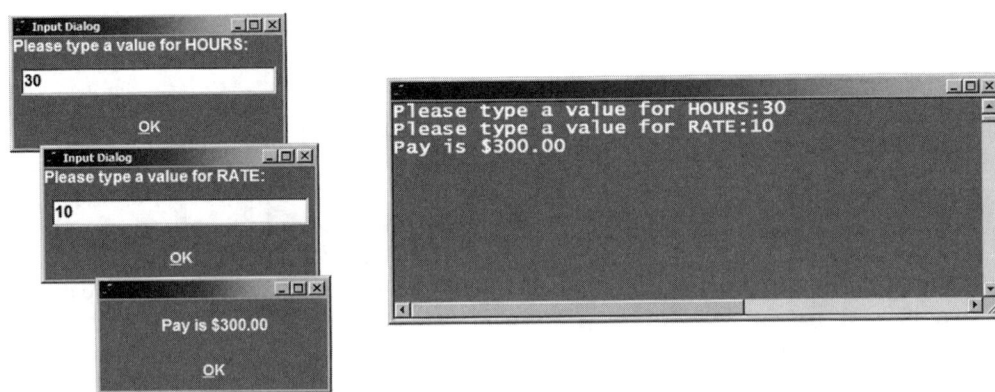

Figure 3-3 Dialog I/O (left) versus Console I/O (right)

> **TIP** When you run a Visual Logic program that uses the console window, Visual Logic creates a second task in the Taskbar (at the bottom of your desktop). The console window may be hidden behind other open windows, so you may have to click on the second task to bring the console window to the front.

CONSOLE END-OF-OUTPUT CHARACTER

Because console output is persistent, multiple outputs can appear on the same line. The ending position of the current output (and therefore the starting position of the next console I/O) is indicated with the **end-of-output symbol (§)**. Figure 3-4 illustrates how the end-of-output symbol determines the starting location of the *next* line of I/O.

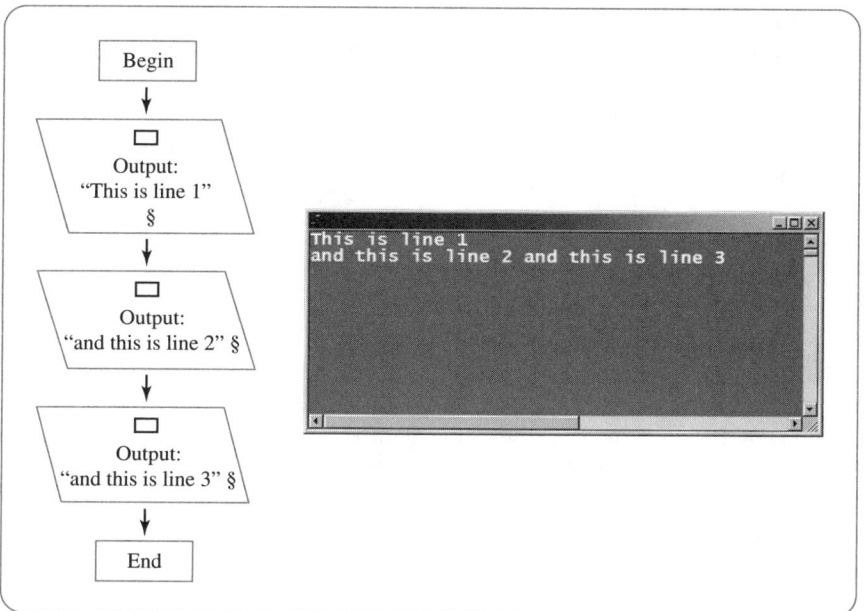

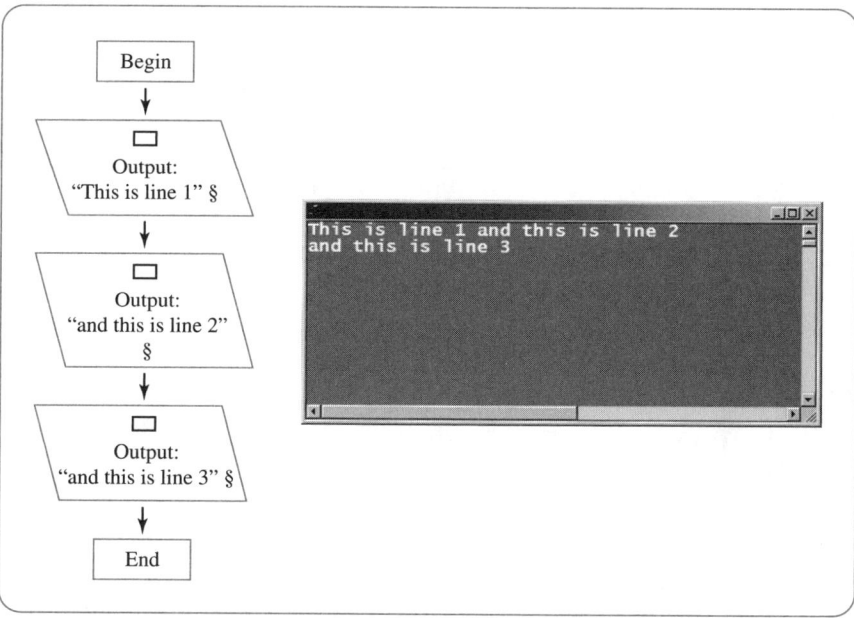

Figure 3-4 The console end-of-output symbol determines the starting location of the next line of console input or output

WHILE LOOPS

CONSOLE INPUT/OUTPUT SUMMARY
» Console I/O is persistent, meaning each line of input and output remains in the console window for the lifetime of the program.
» In Visual Logic, console input and output options are under the "More >>" button in the edit dialog, and console I/O is indicated by the presence of the console screen icon at the top of the flowchart element.
» The end-of-output (§) symbol always appears at the end of the console output expression. The position of the end-of-output symbol determines the starting location for the next console I/O.

WHILE LOOPS

While loops are used to repeat actions. As long as the condition inside the loop element evaluates to True, the body of the loop is executed and then control returns to the condition to be tested again. When the condition evaluates to False, the loop is complete and control flows to the element after the loop.

Figure 3-5 shows a common template for a While loop. In this example there is a **Loop Control Variable** (LCV) that is initialized before the loop begins, tested as part of the loop condition and updated as the last step inside the body of the loop.

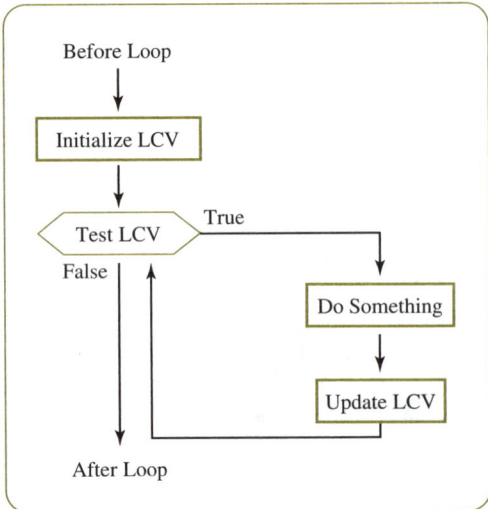

Figure 3-5 A common template for a While loop

A simple counting loop is shown in Figure 3-6. The variable "Count" is the Loop Control Variable, and it is initialized to 1, tested if less than or equal to 5, and updated by 1 each pass through the loop body.

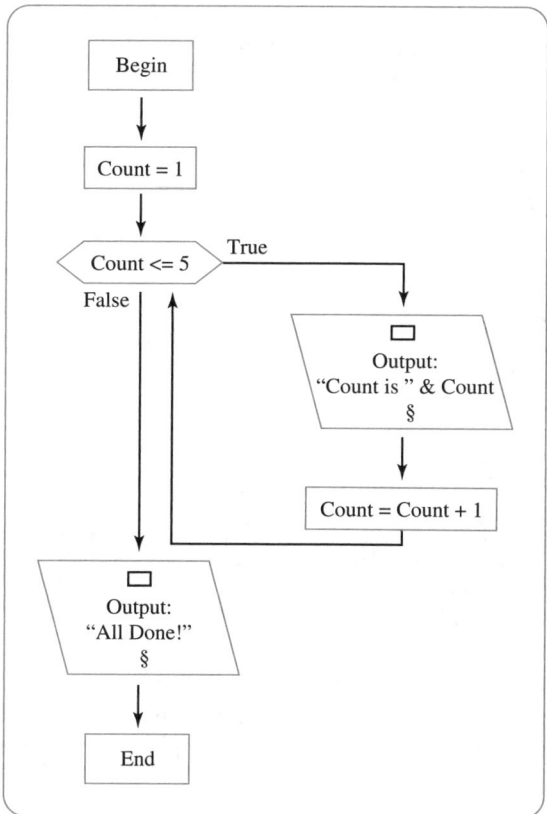

Figure 3-6 Counting While loop

Create the program shown in Figure 3-6 and then press F5 to run the program.

The initialization statement assigns the value 1 to Count. The program then flows into the Loop Test, which evaluates if Count <= 5. It evaluates to True and control flows into the body of the loop, generating the output:

Count is 1

The Count variable is updated (becoming 2) and the control flows back to the Loop Test. Because Count is still less than 5, the body of the loop executes again, generating the output:

Count is 2

This process of executing the body and then updating the loop variable repeats three more times, generating the following output:

Count is 3
Count is 4
Count is 5

After the fifth pass the loop variable is updated to the value 6. Because the loop variable is now greater than the final value, the loop is finished, and control leaves the loop and moves to the next element, which displays the message "Loop finished." Notice that console input and output are used, creating a record of I/O activity in the console window as shown in Figure 3-7.

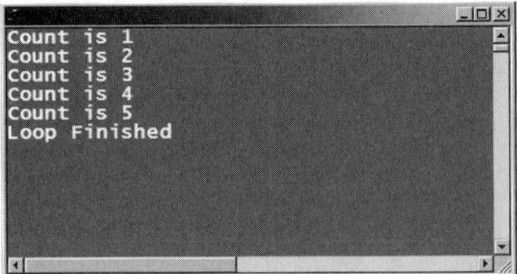

Figure 3-7 Output from program shown in Figure 3-6

> **TIP** An **infinite loop** is what you get if there is no way for the loop to end. For example, if the "Count = Count + 1" statement was removed from Figure 3-6, then the resulting loop would be an infinite loop because the variable Count would always remain its initial value of 1, never becoming > 5, which is necessary to end the loop. (If you accidentally write an infinite loop when using Visual Logic, you can click the Terminate button on the toolbar or select Terminate from the Debug menu.)

Loops are simple but powerful ideas. Consider what happens when we slightly modify the program in Figure 3-6 by changing the condition and the output statements as shown in Figure 3-8. The resulting output, shown in Figure 3-9, seems much more complex but in fact the flowchart still follows the same simple design.

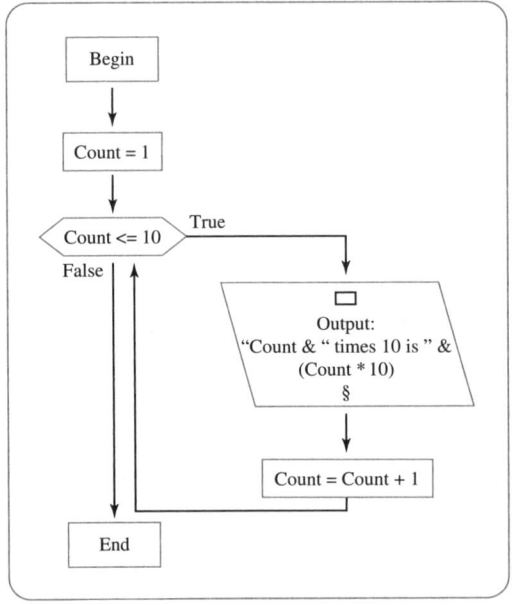

Figure 3-8 Another simple While loop

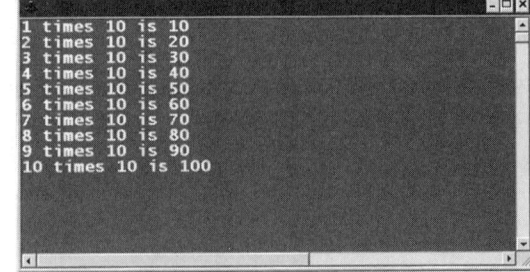

Figure 3-9 Output generated by Figure 3-8

CHAPTER THREE

> **TIP** While loops come in two forms, **pre-test loop** and **post-test loop**. The only difference is that a pre-test loop tests the looping condition before executing the body of the loop. If the condition is initially false, then the loop body is never executed. When using the post-test loop, the body executes one time before the looping condition is ever tested, thus guaranteeing at least one execution of the loop body regardless of the condition. After one pass through the loop, there is no difference between the pre-test and post-test forms.

PROGRAM: COUNTING BACKWARDS

Let's get more practice with While loops by solving the following problem:

Write a program that uses only one loop to print the even numbers from 60 down to 20, except for the value 40, which does not print, but instead two # symbols are printed in its place (e.g., 60, 58, 56. , . . . , 42, ##, 38, . . . , 24, 22, 20).

A first attempt to solve this problem is shown in Figure 3-10, which starts by setting the loop variable to an initial value of 60 and decrementing the loop variable by 1. Each time through the body of the loop, the loop variable is tested to see if it is an even value using the condition "Number MOD 2 = 0", which is true for even values (e.g., values divisible by 2.) Finally, when an even value is found, it is tested against the value 40 and if so, the "##" are printed instead of the value. This solution works and the output is shown in Figure 3-11.

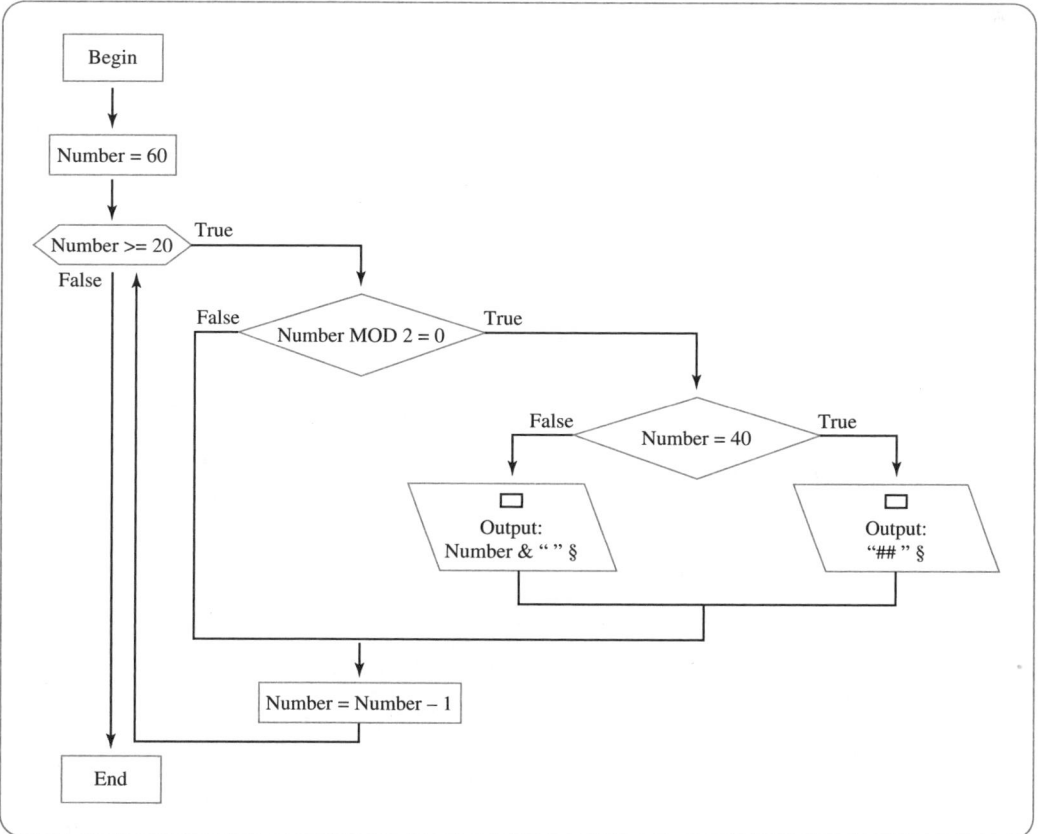

Figure 3-10 First solution for counting backwards problem

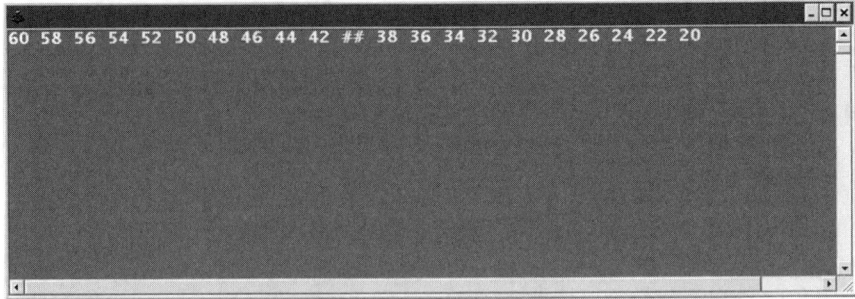

Figure 3-11 Output for counting backwards problem

A second, and better, solution to the counting backwards problem appears in Figure 3-12. In this solution the initial value is still 60, but the decrement is always -2. This eliminates the need to test for even values because the loop variable is always even. This is a simple change that makes the program much easier to read, while producing the same output (Figure 3-11).

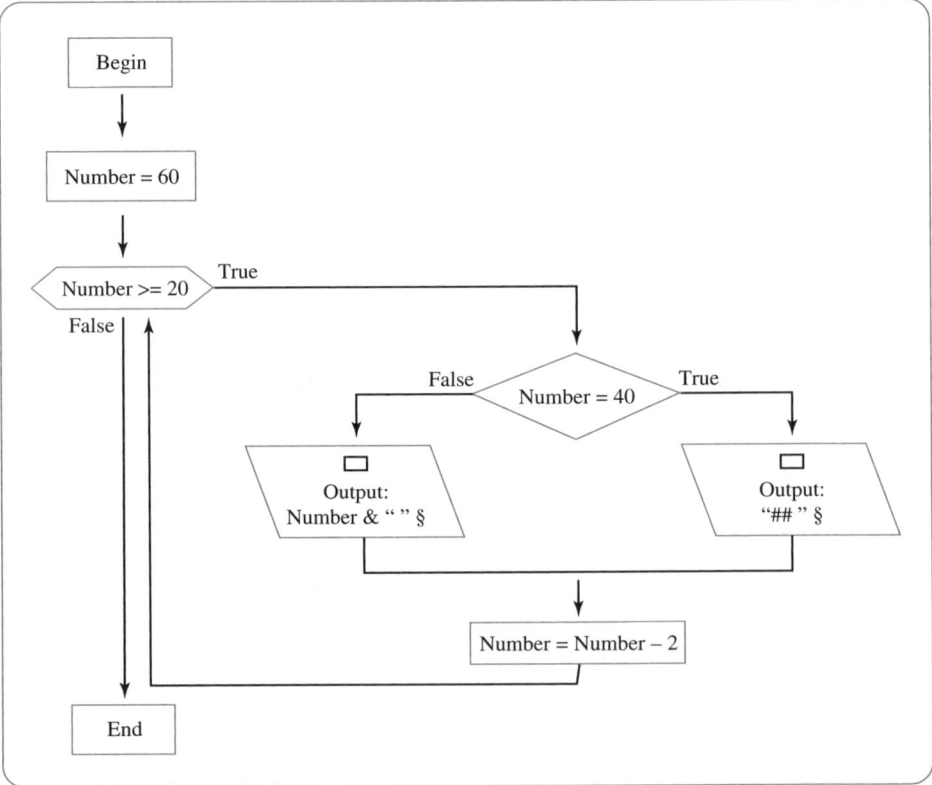

Figure 3-12 Second (and better) solution for counting backwards problem

QUICK CHECK 3-A

1. Use a While loop to display the squares of the numbers 1 to 10 (e.g., 1, 4, 9, 16, 25, etc.) in a console output window.

```
1 squared is 1
2 squared is 4
3 squared is 9
4 squared is 16
5 squared is 25
6 squared is 36
7 squared is 49
8 squared is 64
9 squared is 81
10 squared is 100
```

2. Use a While loop to display the numbers between 42 and 87 at intervals of 5 (e.g., 42, 47, 52, 57, etc.) in a console output window. (*Hint*: Use a statement like "Number = Number + 5" inside the body of your loop.)

```
Number is now 42
Number is now 47
Number is now 52
Number is now 57
Number is now 62
Number is now 67
Number is now 72
Number is now 77
Number is now 82
Number is now 87
```

WHILE LOOP SUMMARY

» While loops are used to repeat actions.

» In Visual Logic, the While loop flowchart element is a six-sided figure with a condition and two exit arrows, True and False.

» When control flows to the While loop, the condition is evaluated. If the condition is True, then control flows out through the True arrow into the body of the loop. At the end of the body of the loop the control flows back to the While loop and the condition is evaluated again. This process repeats until the condition eventually evaluates to False, at which time the control flows out through the False arrow to the statement after the While loop.

» When using the pre-test version of the While loop, the condition is tested first, and the loop body only executes if the initial test is true. When using the post-test version of the While loop, the loop body executes before the condition is tested; thus, the loop always executes at least one time. Both loops terminate when the condition evaluates to False.

WHILE LOOPS AND SENTINEL VALUES

There are many instances where you want to use a loop but you do not know how many times a loop will repeat. For example, a program that helps customers check out at a grocery store cannot assume how many items the person will have. One customer might have three items, and the next customer might have 42 items. It is necessary for the checkout program to work for both customers. A special value called a **sentinel value** (or signaling value) can be used to indicate all the data has been entered and the program should move on to the next phase of processing.

PROGRAM: GROCERY CHECKOUT REVISED

Consider again the grocery checkout program from Chapter 1. At that time we assumed the customer would purchase exactly three items, no more, no less.

An improved solution algorithm would be to allow the user to purchase as many items as desired. After the price of the last item is entered, a sentinel value is entered to indicate the end of input and to exit the loop. Sales tax would then be calculated and added to determine the total amount due. The solution flowchart for this algorithm is shown in Figure 3-13, and the program trace is shown in Figure 3-14.

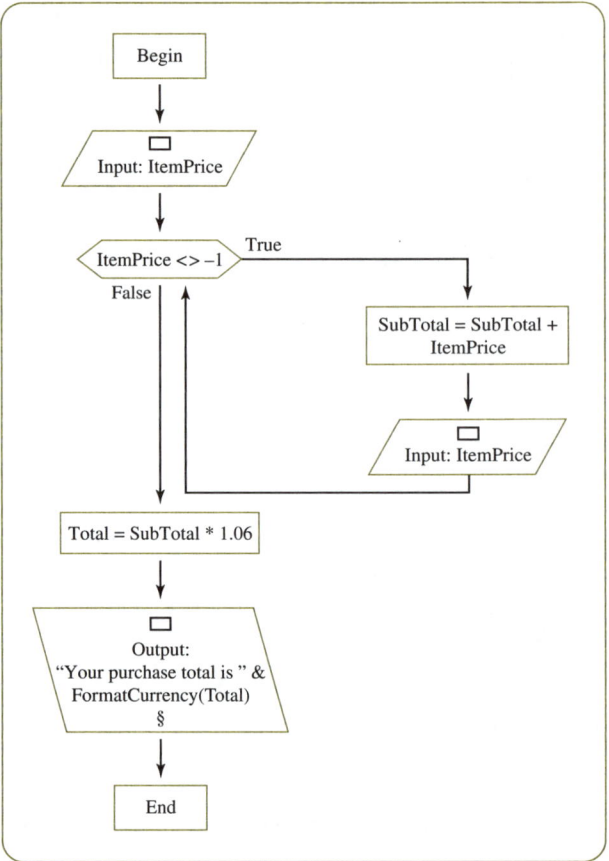

Figure 3-13 While loop with sentinel values used to solve grocery checkout problem

```
Please type a value for ITEMPRICE:9.95
Please type a value for ITEMPRICE:14.49
Please type a value for ITEMPRICE:3.75
Please type a value for ITEMPRICE:8.99
Please type a value for ITEMPRICE:10.50
Please type a value for ITEMPRICE:-1
Your purchase total is $50.54
```

Figure 3-14 Output for Figure 3-13

> **TIP** The sentinel value can change from one program to the next. A sentinel value for a program should be a value that cannot be valid data. For example, negative one (−1) is a common sentinel value that works for many input types such as item price or exam scores, because −1 is not a valid price or exam score. (If something did cost negative one dollar, then you should buy a million of them and retire. Likewise, no matter how poorly a student does on an exam, the score will not be negative.) However, −1 is not a good sentinel value when working with weather temperatures because −1° Celsius is a valid temperature in many places around the globe. If the input is temperature values, then a good sentinel value might be 9999, which is well above the hottest weather temperature on Earth.

PROGRAM: DETERMINE THE AVERAGE

Let's get more practice with sentinel values by solving the following problem:

Write a program that reads a list of values terminated by the sentinel value −1. After the sentinel value is read, the program should display the average of the values entered (not including the sentinel value).

To calculate an average, you need to know two things: how many numbers are there and what is their total. Counter and accumulator variables can be used for this purpose. **Counters** are variables used to keep track of how many times a statement has executed. Counters update themselves by a constant value, typically 1. **Accumulators** are variables used to maintain a running total. Accumulators update themselves by the value of another variable or expression. Counters and accumulators are typically used inside the body of a loop to build up and maintain summary data on the information being processed. In Figure 3-15 the variable "Count" is a counter and the variable "Sum" is an accumulator.

Each time a non-sentinel value is read, that value is added to the Sum variable and the Count variable is updated by 1. After the sentinel value is entered, the loop finishes and the average is calculated based on the sum and count. (The sentinel value is not added or counted.) Figure 3-16 shows a sample run with three input values plus the sentinel value. Note that the sentinel value is not included in the count or the sum, and therefore is not part of the average.

WHILE LOOPS

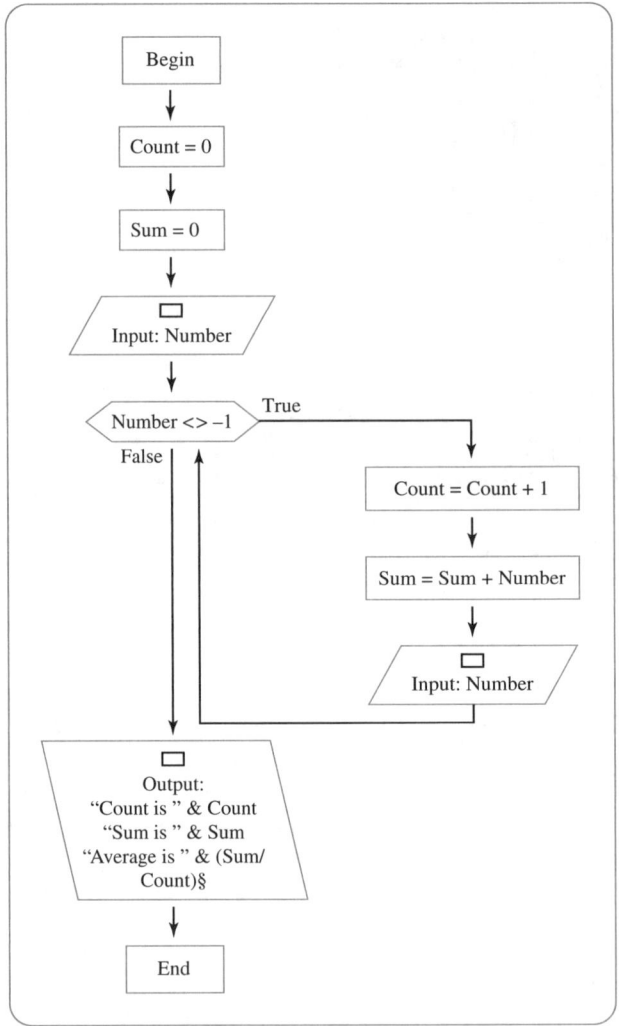

Figure 3-15 Sentinel value used to calculate the average

> **TIP**
> Figure 3-15 includes the statements **Count=0** and **Sum=0** before those variables are used for counting and accumulation. While not required, it is common practice to initialize counters and accumulators directly above the loop where they are used.

```
Please type a value for NUMBER:10
Please type a value for NUMBER:20
Please type a value for NUMBER:30
Please type a value for NUMBER:-1
Count is 3
Sum is 60
Average is 20
```

Figure 3-16 Output for Figure 3-15

SENTINEL VALUE, COUNTER, AND ACCUMULATOR SUMMARY

» Sentinel values are "end of data" values that indicate that all the data has been processed. Sentinel values are not part of the data set and should not be processed.

» Counters and accumulators are variables typically used inside a loop to help calculate counts, totals, and averages. Counters are typically incremented by one, and accumulators are typically updated by the value of a variable.

EXIT LOOP

An **Exit loop** causes control to jump out of the loop to the statement immediately below the loop. When using an Exit loop, the loop condition is typically set to the constant True, making sure the test always sends the control flow back into the body of the loop. The body of the loop begins with an input statement followed by a test to see if the input is the sentinel value. If so, then the Exit loop statement is executed, terminating the loop. If the input is not the sentinel value, then the remainder of the loop body is used to process the non-sentinel value. Figure 3-17 shows a template for a While loop with a sentinel input and an Exit loop.

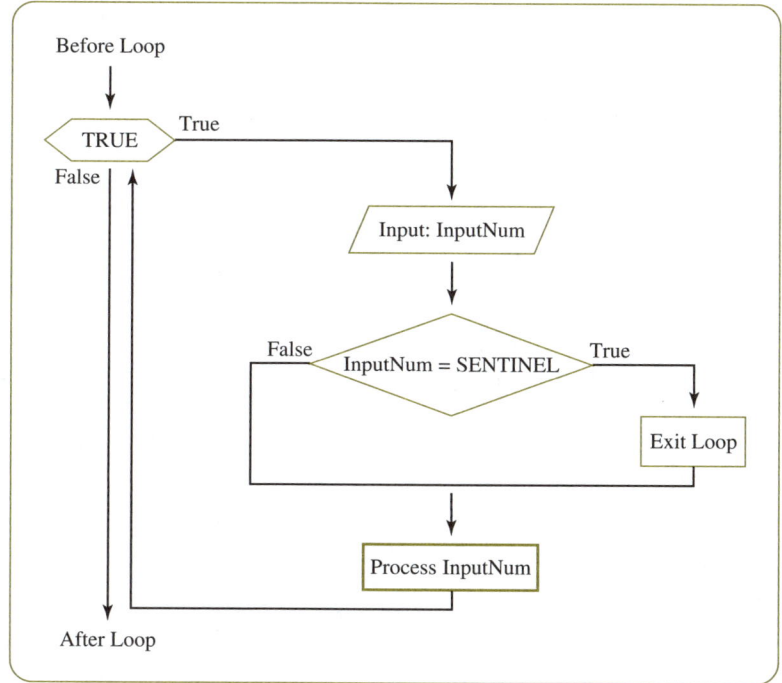

Figure 3-17 A template for a While loop with a sentinel input and an Exit loop

To illustrate how an Exit loop statement can be used, consider Figure 3-18 as a valid alternative to Figure 3-13. In this solution, the While loop condition is set to the constant True (so that the loop always repeats) and the first line in the loop body is the input statement. Immediately after inputting a value, the input is tested to see if it is the sentinel value. If it is, the Exit loop

WHILE LOOPS

> **TIP**
> The While loop condition should only be set to the constant "TRUE" when you are using an Exit loop inside the loop body; otherwise you will create an infinite loop.

statement is used to terminate the loop immediately. If the input is not the sentinel value, then the remainder of the loop body is executed to process the data in some appropriate manner. Both Figure 3-13 and Figure 3-18 produce exactly the same output, and there is no general consensus among developers about which sentinel solution is better. You are encouraged to understand both solutions.

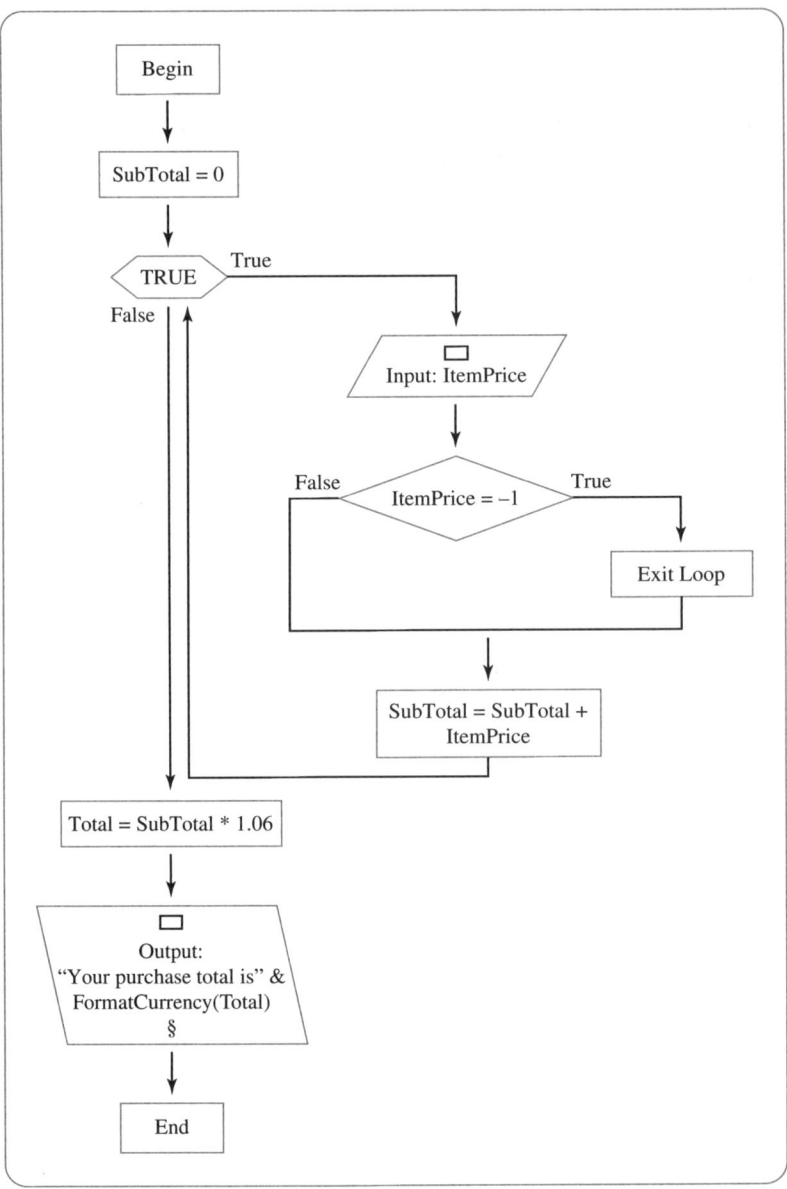

Figure 3-18 Alternative grocery checkout solution using Exit loop

PROGRAM: HIGH-LOW GAME

On the TV Show "The Price is Right" there is a game called "High-Low" where the contestant tries to guess a number (the price of an item) and the host tells the contestant "Higher" or "Lower" until the contestant guesses the number. We will now examine a program that plays a similar game. Rather than racing against the clock, the user will try to guess the number in the fewest number of guesses possible. Figure 3-19 shows a solution to this problem. A sample run of the program appears in Figure 3-20.

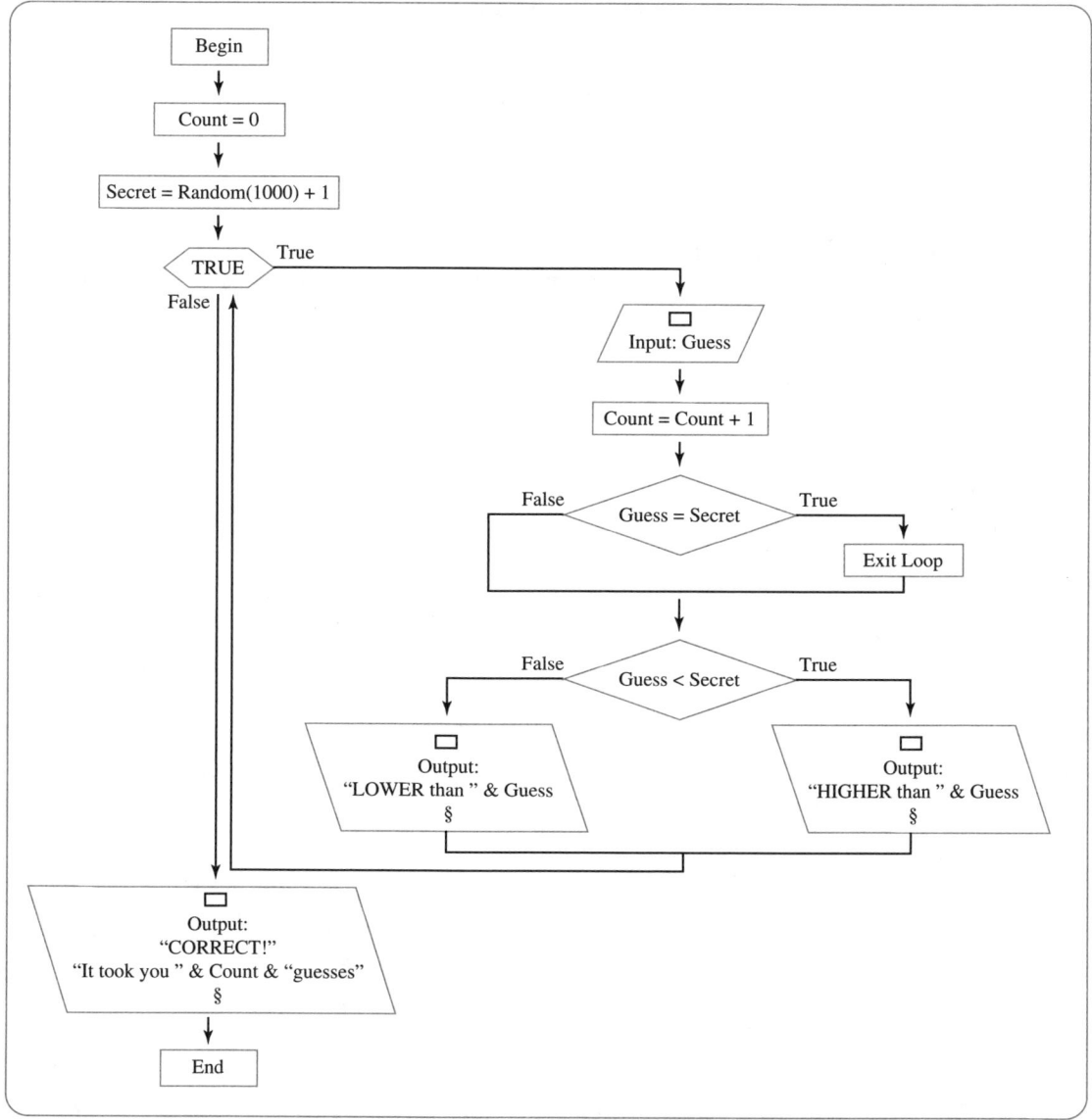

Figure 3-19 Solution to High-Low game

WHILE LOOPS

```
Please type a value for GUESS:500
HIGHER than 500
Please type a value for GUESS:700
LOWER than 700
Please type a value for GUESS:600
HIGHER than 600
Please type a value for GUESS:650
HIGHER than 650
Please type a value for GUESS:675
HIGHER than 675
Please type a value for GUESS:685
LOWER than 685
Please type a value for GUESS:680
HIGHER than 680
Please type a value for GUESS:682
CORRECT!
It took you 8 guesses
```

Figure 3-20 Sample run of Figure 3-19

EXIT LOOP SUMMARY

» The Exit loop statement causes control to jump directly to the statement following the current loop.

CHAPTER THREE

CHAPTER SUMMARY

- Console I/O is persistent, meaning each line of input and output remains in the console window for the lifetime of the program.
- In Visual Logic, console input and output options are under the "More >>" button in the edit dialog, and console I/O is indicated by the presence of the console screen icon at the top of the flowchart element.
- The end-of-output (§) symbol always appears at the end of the console output expression. The position of the end-of-output symbol determines the starting location for the next console I/O.
- While loops are used to repeat actions.
- In Visual Logic, the While loop flowchart element is a six-sided figure with a condition and two exit arrows, True and False.
- When control flows to the While loop, the condition is evaluated. If the condition is True, then control flows out through the True arrow into the body of the loop. At the end of the body of the loop, the control flows back to the While loop and the condition is evaluated again. This process repeats until the condition eventually evaluates to False, at which time the control flows out through the False arrow to the statement after the While loop.
- When using the pre-test version of the While loop, the condition is tested first, and the loop body only executes if the initial test is true. When using the post-test version of the While loop, the loop body executes before the condition is tested; thus, the loop always executes at least one time. Both loops terminate when the condition evaluates to False.
- Sentinel values are "end of data" values that indicate that all the data has been processed. Sentinel values are not part of the data and should not be processed.
- Counters and accumulators are variables typically used inside a loop to help calculate counts, totals, and averages. Counters are typically incremented by one, and accumulators are typically updated by the value of a variable.
- The Exit loop statement causes control to jump directly to the statement following the current loop.

KEY TERMS

accumulator
console input
console output
counter
end-of-output symbol (§)
Exit loop
Loop Control Variable (LCV)
sentinel value
While loop

REVIEW QUESTIONS

1. What are the three things that happen to a Loop Control Variable (LCV) in a simple While loop?
2. What is the difference between an accumulator variable and a counter variable?
3. What is the difference between a While loop with a pre-test and a While loop with a post-test?
4. Consider the solution to the High-Low game shown in Figure 3-19. If the assignment statement **Secret = Random(1000) + 1** was moved into the body of the loop, would the solution still work correctly? Why or why not?

5. Consider the solution to the High-Low game shown in Figure 3-19. If the assignment statement **Count = Count + 1** was moved to the False branch of the "Guess = Secret" condition, would the solution still work correctly? Why or why not?

6. Consider the solution to the High-Low game shown in Figure 3-19. If the assignment statement **Count = Count + 1** was moved to the bottom of the loop body, would the solution still work correctly? Why or why not?

PROGRAMMING EXERCISES

3-1. Merry Christmas. Write a program that uses a While loop to display "Ho Ho Ho Merry Christmas" to console output. *Note*: Your program should use the word "Ho" only once.

```
Ho Ho Ho Merry Christmas
```

3-2. Cubed. Write a program that uses a While loop to display the cubes of the numbers 1 to 10 to console output.

```
1 cubed is 1
2 cubed is 8
3 cubed is 27
4 cubed is 64
5 cubed is 125
6 cubed is 216
7 cubed is 343
8 cubed is 512
9 cubed is 729
10 cubed is 1000
```

3-3. I'll Raise You Ten. Write a program that uses a While loop to display the value of 10 raised to the power of X where X is 1 through 5. (*Hint*: You can use the intrinsic function Power as part of your solution. Power(10,3) returns the value 1000.)

```
10 to the power of 1 is 10
10 to the power of 2 is 100
10 to the power of 3 is 1000
10 to the power of 4 is 10000
10 to the power of 5 is 100000
```

3-4. Four by Four. Write a program that uses a While loop to display the numbers between 37 and 77 at intervals of 4 (e.g., 37, 41, 45, 49, etc.) to console output.

```
Number is now 37
Number is now 41
Number is now 45
Number is now 49
Number is now 53
Number is now 57
Number is now 61
Number is now 65
Number is now 69
Number is now 73
Number is now 77
```

3-5. Please Try Again. Write a program that asks the user to respond to a question by entering either 1 for yes or 2 for no. Use a While loop to continue prompting the user until a valid response is entered. Upon entering a valid response, the program should display an appropriate message to the user.

```
Are you happy? (1=yes, 2=no) 5
Please try again. Are you happy? (1=yes, 2=no) "Hello"
Please try again. Are you happy? (1=yes, 2=no) -1
Please try again. Are you happy? (1=yes, 2=no) 2
I'm sorry to hear that
```

3-6. Even-Odd Average. Write a program that reads a list of values from the user until the user enters the sentinel value –1. The program should then calculate and display the average of the even input values and the average of the odd input values, not including the sentinel. (*Hint*: Use two counters and two accumulators.)

```
Please type a value for NUMBER:20
Please type a value for NUMBER:30
Please type a value for NUMBER:55
Please type a value for NUMBER:77
Please type a value for NUMBER:-1
Even Average = 25
Odd Average = 66
```

WHILE LOOPS

3-7. King of the Hill. Write a program that reads in a list of positive integers from the user until the user enters the value –1 as a sentinel. At that time the program should display the largest value in the input list.

```
Please type a value for NUM:45
Please type a value for NUM:41
Please type a value for NUM:51
Please type a value for NUM:54
Please type a value for NUM:53
Please type a value for NUM:38
Please type a value for NUM:-1
Largest value was 54
```

3-8. Payment Plan. You have been hired to work for 10 days and you are given two payment options. The first option is to get paid $100 the first day and have your daily total increase by $100 each day. The second option is to get paid $2 the first day and have your daily total double each day. Write a program that determines your Day 10 payment for both options.

```
Day 1 Results: Plan1 = $100.00 and Plan2 = $2.00
Day 2 Results: Plan1 = $200.00 and Plan2 = $4.00
Day 3 Results: Plan1 = $300.00 and Plan2 = $8.00
Day 4 Results: Plan1 = $400.00 and Plan2 = $16.00
Day 5 Results: Plan1 = $500.00 and Plan2 = $32.00
Day 6 Results: Plan1 = $600.00 and Plan2 = $64.00
Day 7 Results: Plan1 = $700.00 and Plan2 = $128.00
Day 8 Results: Plan1 = $800.00 and Plan2 = $256.00
Day 9 Results: Plan1 = $900.00 and Plan2 = $512.00
Day 10 Results: Plan1 = $1,000.00 and Plan2 = $1,024.00
```

3-9. High-Low Redux. Write a solution to the High-Low game problem without using the Exit loop statement.

```
Please type a value for GUESS:500
HIGHER than 500
Please type a value for GUESS:700
LOWER than 700
Please type a value for GUESS:600
HIGHER than 600
Please type a value for GUESS:650
HIGHER than 650
Please type a value for GUESS:675
HIGHER than 675
Please type a value for GUESS:685
LOWER than 685
Please type a value for GUESS:680
HIGHER than 680
Please type a value for GUESS:682
CORRECT!
It took you 8 guesses
```

CHAPTER THREE

3-10. Account Balancer. Write a Visual Logic program to help balance a customer's bank account. The program should read numeric values that represent banking transactions. Special sentinel values will be read to indicate display-current-balance (8888) and end-of-the-month (9999) activities. In addition, the program solution should conform to the following requirements:

» The first value read is the starting balance.
» The program will then read integer values one at a time until the end-of-the-month sentinel value (9999) is read.
» Negative numbers are **checks** that reduce the account balance.
» Positive numbers (except for sentinel values) are **deposits** that add to the account balance.
» Any time a check is processed and the resulting balance is negative, the check bounces and there is a $10 fee assessed to the account (e.g., the balance is reduced by an additional 10 dollars).
» When the user inputs the special (sentinel) value 8888, the program should NOT treat this as a deposit, but instead should display the current account balance with a message formatted similar to:

```
The current balance is ####
```

» When the user inputs the special (sentinel) value 9999, the program should NOT treat this as a deposit, but instead should calculate the monthly service fee, which is either $10 or 10 percent of the account balance, whichever is smaller. Then the program should display the monthly service fee and the end-of-the-month balance with two messages formatted similar to the following lines:

```
The monthly service fee is ####
The account balance at the end of the month is ####
```

» The program ends after displaying the end-of-the-month account balance.

Two sample runs are shown below:

```
Please type a value for BALANCE:300
Please type a value for AMOUNT:500
Please type a value for AMOUNT:400
Please type a value for AMOUNT:9999
The monthly service fee is $10.00
The account balance at the end of the month is $1,190.00
```

```
Please type a value for BALANCE:100
Please type a value for AMOUNT:-50
Please type a value for AMOUNT:-30
Please type a value for AMOUNT:8888
The current balance is $20.00

Please type a value for AMOUNT:-40
Please type a value for AMOUNT:70
Please type a value for AMOUNT:8888
The current balance is $40.00

Please type a value for AMOUNT:20
Please type a value for AMOUNT:-30
Please type a value for AMOUNT:9999
The monthly service fee is $3.00
The account balance at the end of the month is $27.00
```

CHAPTER **FOUR**

FOR LOOPS AND NESTED LOOPS

FOR LOOPS

For loops are used to automate the initialize, test, and update process. The best way to understand how For loops work is to look at a simple example. Start a new solution and add a For loop element from the element menu. Double-click the element to open the For Loop edit dialog window. Enter the following values (as shown in Figure 4-1): variable name **Count**; initial value **1**; final value **5**; and step **1**.

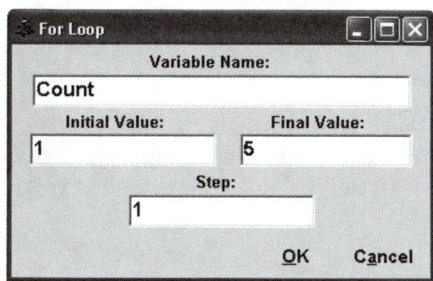

Figure 4-1 For Loop dialog window

Click OK to close the edit dialog box, and then add the two output statements as shown in Figure 4-2. Run the program and you will get the output shown in Figure 4-3.

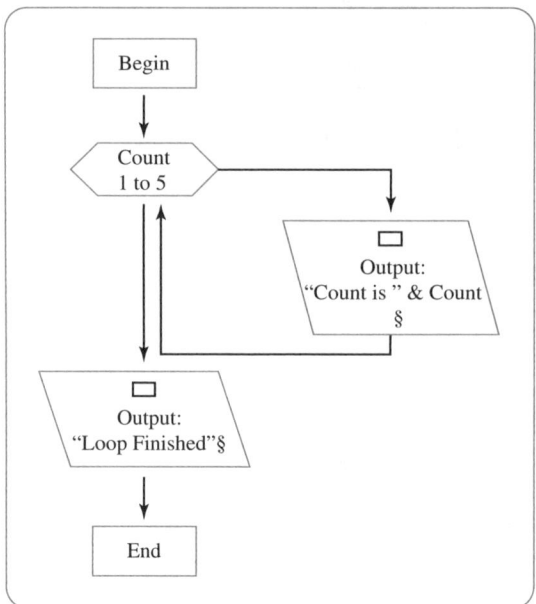

Figure 4-2 Simple For loop program

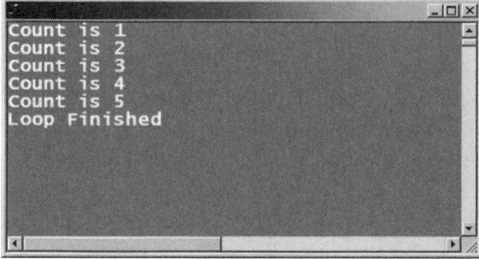

Figure 4-3 Output from program shown in Figure 4-2

COMPARING WHILE LOOPS AND FOR LOOPS

You probably recognize that there are numerous similarities between the While loop introduced last chapter and the For loop. Figure 4-4 shows a side-by-side comparison of two equivalent While and For loops.

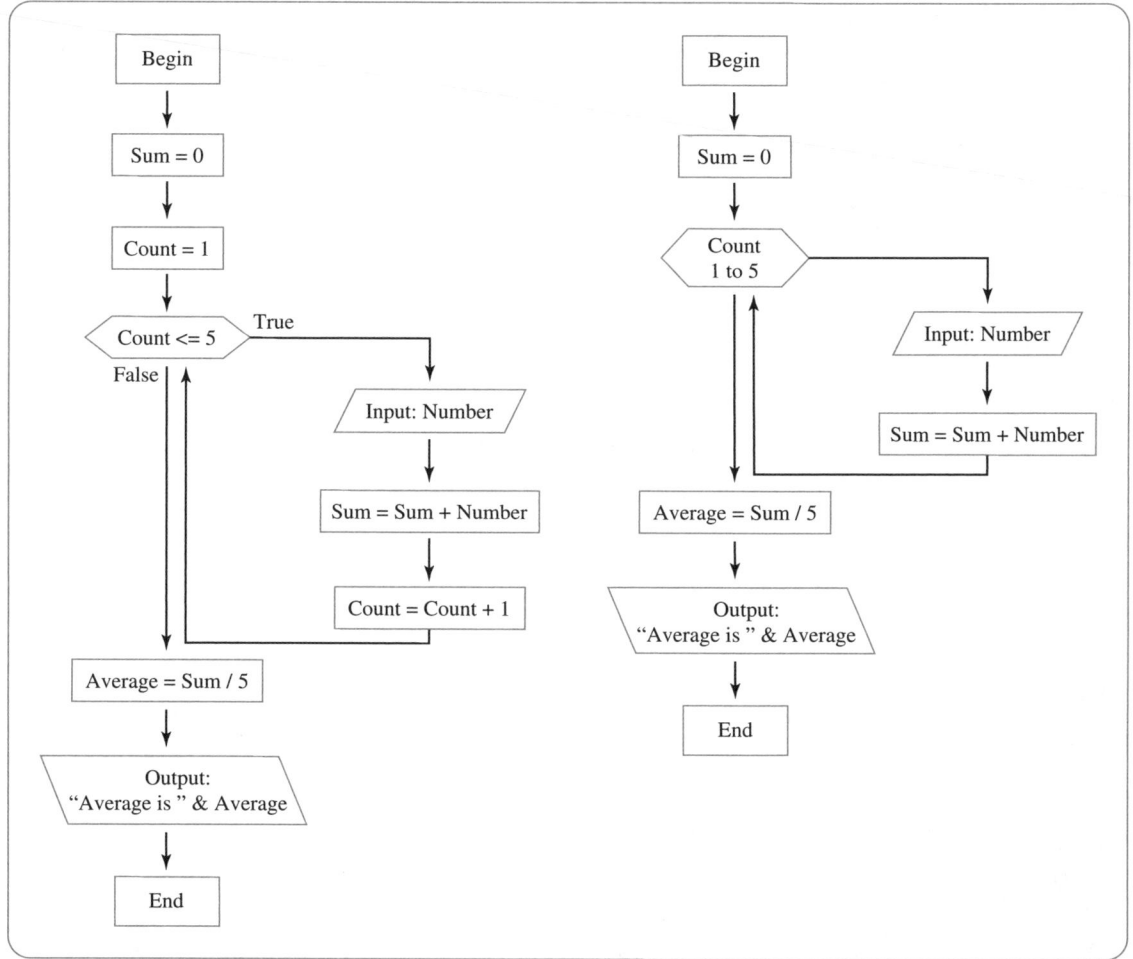

Figure 4-4 Side-by-side comparison of equivalent While Loop and For Loop

In the While loop version of Figure 4-4, there is an explicit initialization statement that sets the "Count = 1", an explicit test condition to test if "Count <= 5", and an explicit update statement inside the loop that sets "Count = Count + 1". The For loop performs these three actions (initialize, test, update) automatically based on the loop's *initial value*, *final value*, and *step value*. When control first flows to the For loop, the loop variable is assigned the initial value. The For loop then repeats the body of the loop as long as the loop variable is less than or equal to the final value. Each time the body of the loop is executed, the For loop automatically updates the loop variable by adding the step value, and the process repeats.

>>> **TIP**
As Figure 4-4 illustrates, a For loop can be easier to read and understand than an equivalent While loop.

WORKING WITH FINAL AND STEP VALUES

Figure 4-5 shows a program with a step value equal to 5. The output for this program appears in Figure 4-6. The loop variable starts with the value 42 and increments by 5 after each pass through the loop (e.g., 42, 47, 52, 57, 62). After the fifth pass through the loop, the loop variable is incremented and becomes 67. Because the value of the loop variable now exceeds the loop's "final value" of 66, the loop terminates. This illustrates an important point, which is that the loop variable does not have to exactly match the final value, but rather that the final value is a threshold that, when crossed, terminates the loop.

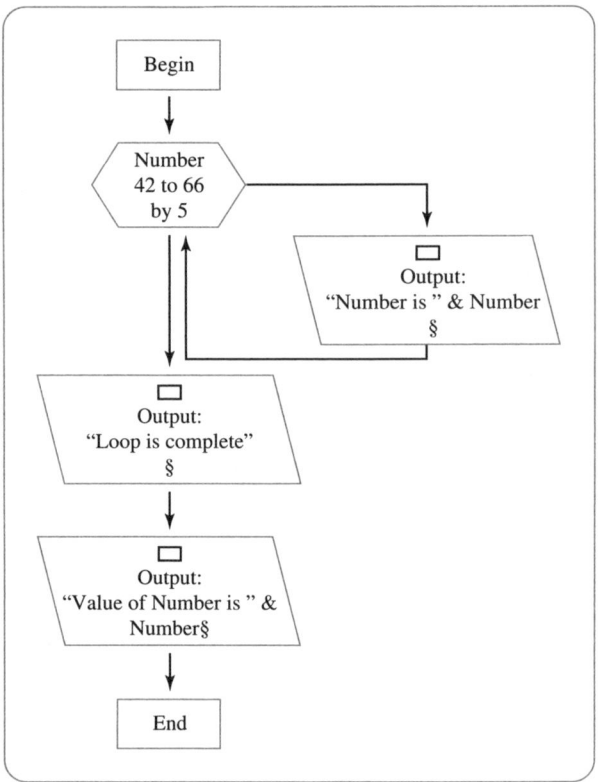

>> TIP
The Visual Logic flowchart element for a For Loop does not show the step value when the step value is 1. When the step value is something other than 1, it will also appear in the flowchart element.

Figure 4-5 For Loop with step value equal to 5

```
Number is 42
Number is 47
Number is 52
Number is 57
Number is 62
Loop is complete
Value of Number is 67
```

Figure 4-6 Output generated by program in Figure 4-5

Figure 4-7 shows a For loop with a negative step value. When the step value is negative, the loop continues until the loop variable becomes smaller than the final value. The loop variable N has an initial value of 16 and is decremented by 2 after each pass through the loop until it exceeds (falls below) the final value of 4. Therefore the loop variable has the values 16, 14, 12, 10, 8, 6, and 4. The sum of those numbers is 70.

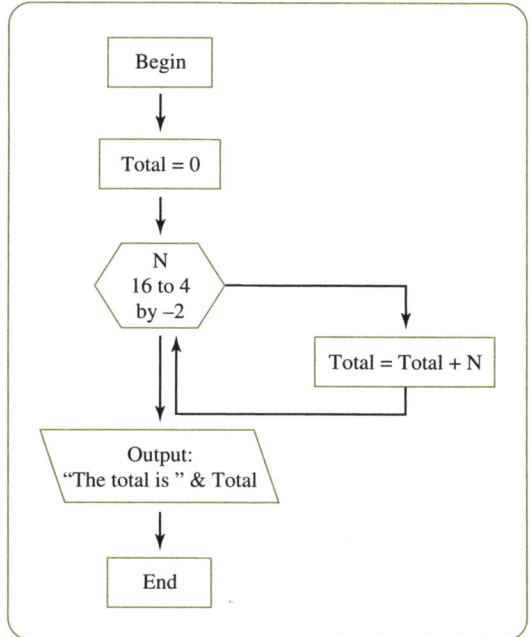

Figure 4-7 For loop with negative step value

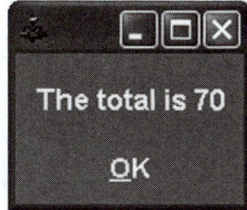

Figure 4-8 Dialog output generated by program in Figure 4-7

FOR LOOP SUMMARY

» For loops are used to automate the initialize, test, and update process.
» In Visual Logic, the For loop flowchart element appears as a six-sided figure with a loop variable, a start value, an end value, and two exit arrows. (The step value also appears if the step value is something other than 1.) The body of the loop is to the right and below the element.
» When executed, the first action is to initialize the loop variable to the start value.
» The body of the loop executes as long as the value of the loop variable does not exceed the final value. (*Note*: If the step value is negative, then the body of the loop executes as long as the value of the loop variable is not smaller than the final value.) After the body of the loop executes, the loop variable is updated by the step value, and the process is repeated.

NESTED LOOPS

For loops and While loops are similar in that any valid statements can occur inside the body of a loop, including input, assignment, output, conditions, and even other loops. A ***nested loop*** refers to a loop contained inside the body of another loop. Figure 4-9 shows two examples of nested loops. Figure 4-9(a) shows a For loop nested inside a While loop. Figure 4-9(b) shows a While loop nested inside a For loop. Both programs produce the same output, which is shown in Figure 4-10.

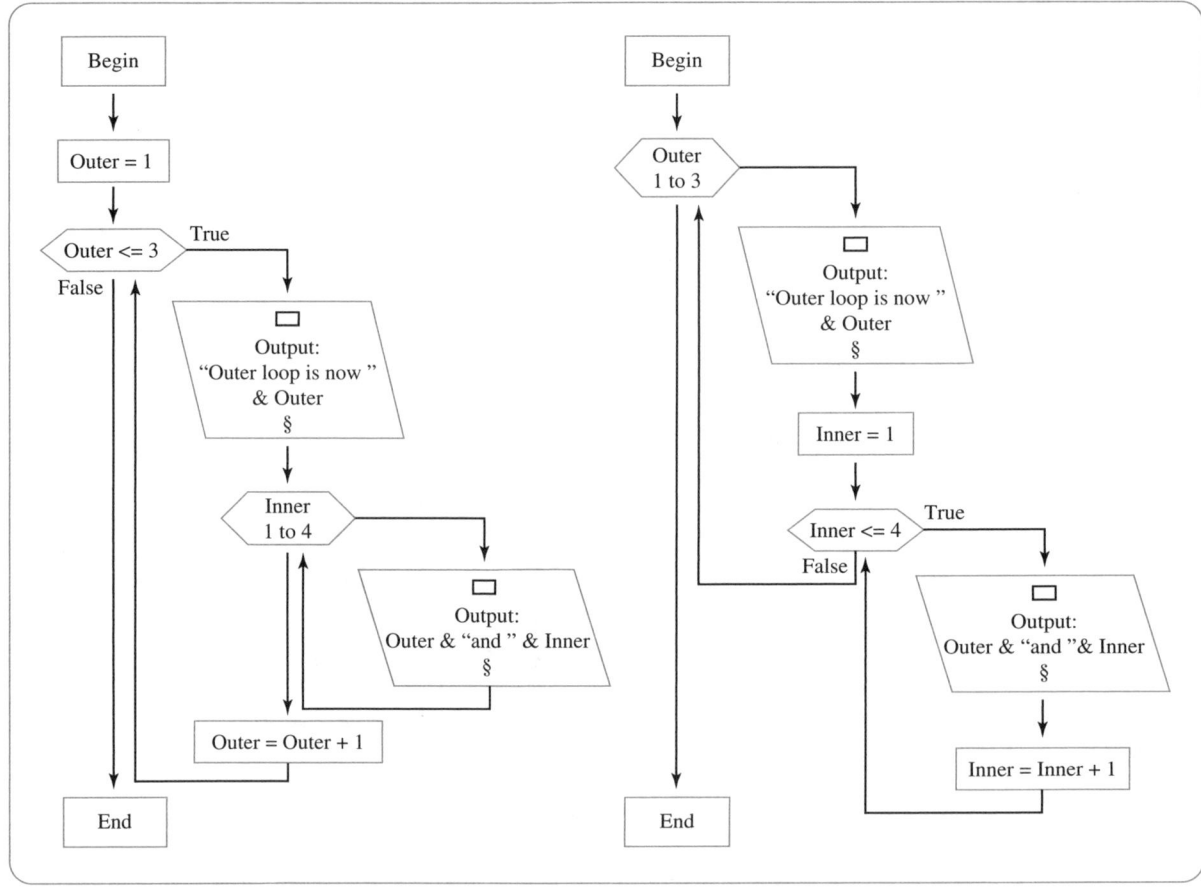

Figure 4-9 Two nested loop examples

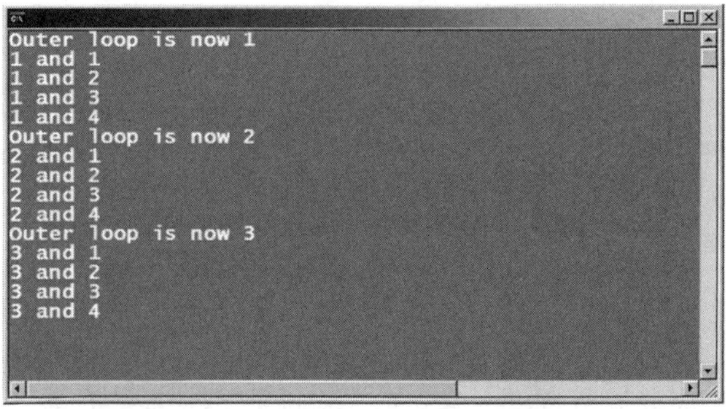

Figure 4-10 Output generated by program in Figure 4-9

CHAPTER FOUR

When working with nested loops, it is important to remember that the inner (nested) loop will be executed many times. Specifically, because the nested loop is part of the body of the outside loop, the nested loop executes in full each pass through the outside loop. Figure 4-11 shows three different programs that all have the same result, which is to display "Hello" 16 times.

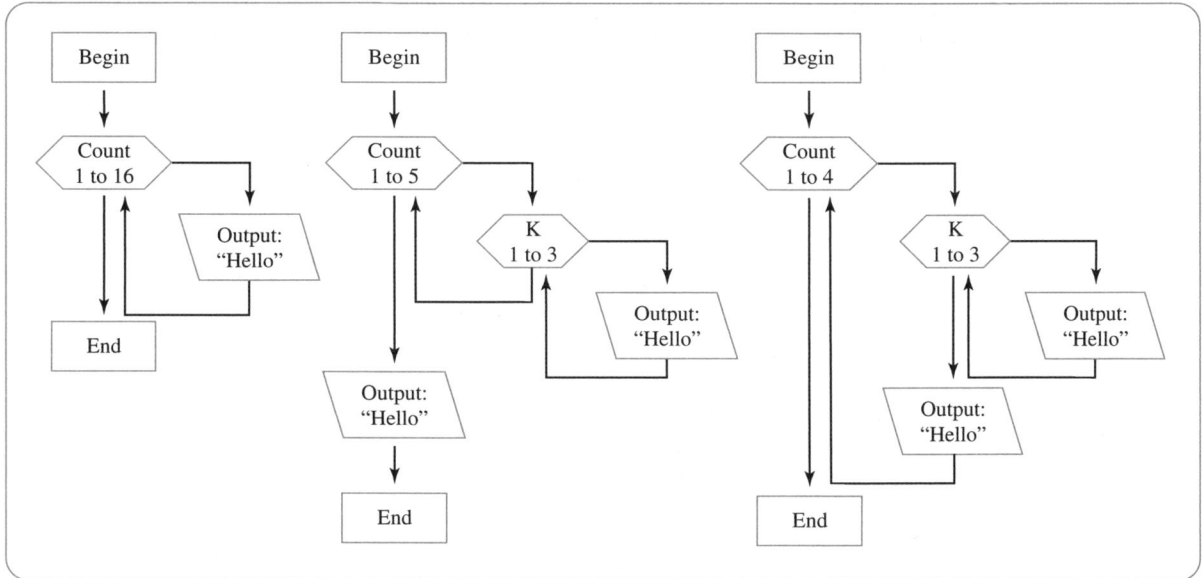

Figure 4-11 Three different programs that each output "Hello" 16 times

PROGRAM: MULTIPLICATION TABLE

Let's get more practice with nested loops by considering the problem of creating a multiplication table where each number in the table is the product of the row value multiplied by the column value. A 9 × 10 version of the table would look similar to the following:

```
 1   2   3   4   5   6   7   8   9
 2   4   6   8  10  12  14  16  18
 3   6   9  12  15  18  21  24  27
 4   8  12  16  20  24  28  32  36
 5  10  15  20  25  30  35  40  45
 6  12  18  24  30  36  42  48  54
 7  14  21  28  35  42  49  56  63
 8  16  24  32  40  48  56  64  72
 9  18  27  36  45  54  63  72  81
10  20  30  40  50  60  70  80  90
```

Figure 4-12 shows a solution for this problem. The left-hand line number is the value of a loop variable 1 to 10. Inside this loop there is a second loop that displays the nine values for that line. This inner loop therefore runs from 1 to 9. Each pass through the inner loop will multiply the row and column values and display the resulting product to console output. To help keep the output vertically aligned, we can add a test to see if the product is only a single digit and, if so, to print a leading space before displaying the number. Finally, after the inner loop completes and all nine values have been displayed on the same line, the program displays an output statement with the end-of-output character on the next line. This causes the console output to move to the next line in preparation for the next pass through the outer loop. The resulting output is shown in Figure 4-13.

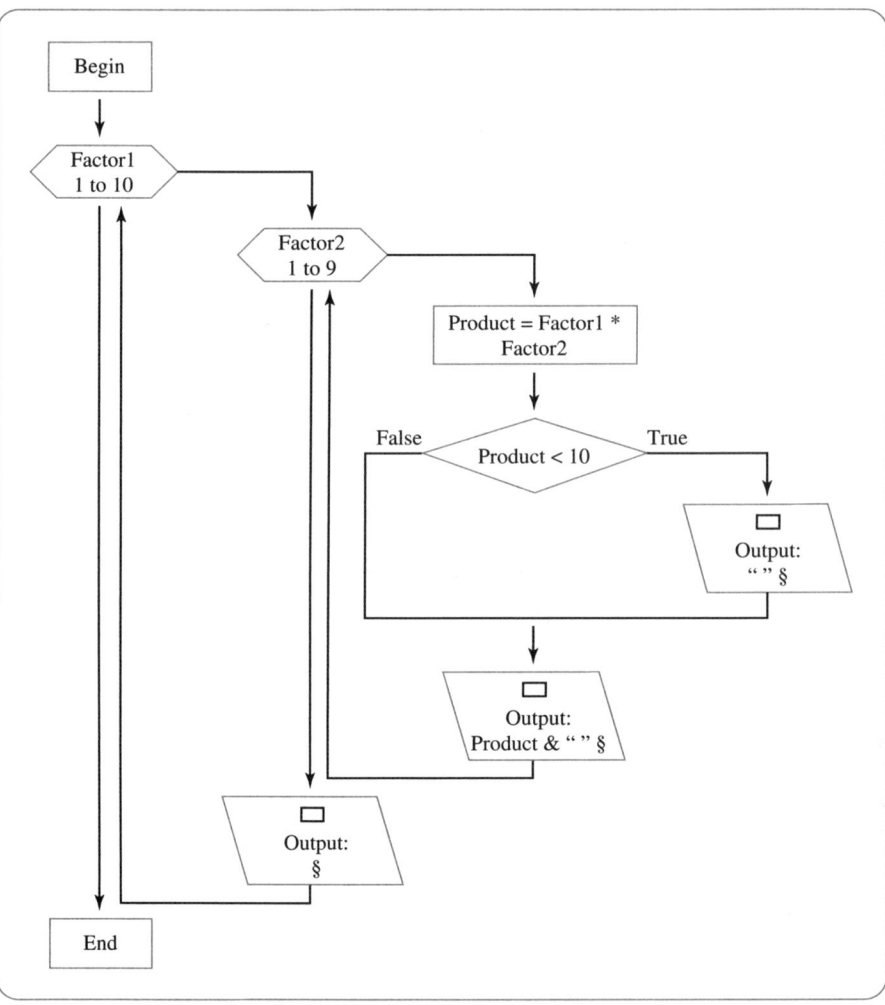

Figure 4-12 Solution to the multiplication table problem

CHAPTER FOUR

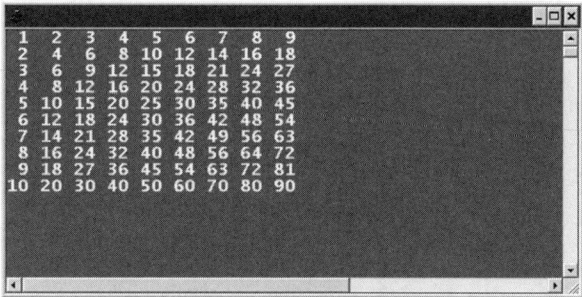

Figure 4-13 Output generated by the program in Figure 4-12

PROGRAM: TRIANGLE PROBLEM

Let's get more practice with nested loops by considering the problem of displaying a series of circles that form a right triangle like the following:

o
oo
ooo
oooo
ooooo
oooooo
ooooooo
oooooooo
ooooooooo
oooooooooo

This triangle has 10 lines of output. This suggests the solution should use a loop **LineCount** from 1 to 10 in which each pass through the loop generates one line of output.

When examining each line of output, we realize that each line contains the same number of circles as the line number (e.g., line four has four circles, line five has five circles, etc.). The solution therefore also has an inner loop **CircleCount** from 1 to **LineCount** for printing each line of circles.

Each horizontal line of circles can be generated by outputting one circle many times. This is done using a series of console output statements, each containing a single circle followed immediately by the end-of-output symbol (§). After the line is complete, an additional console output statement can be used to move the end-of-output symbol (§) to the beginning of the next line.

Figure 4-14 shows an implementation of the solution described above. Note that the nested CircleCount loop uses a variable, LineCount, as the final value, which causes the nested loop to have a different final value each time it is initialized. Also note that the output statement inside the nested loop prints one circle followed immediately by the end-of-output character on the same line. This causes the next circle to appear immediately after the previous circle. It is the output statement below the nested loop that moves the end-of-output character to a new line in preparation for the next line to begin (e.g., the next pass through the main LineCount loop.) The resulting output is shown in Figure 4-15.

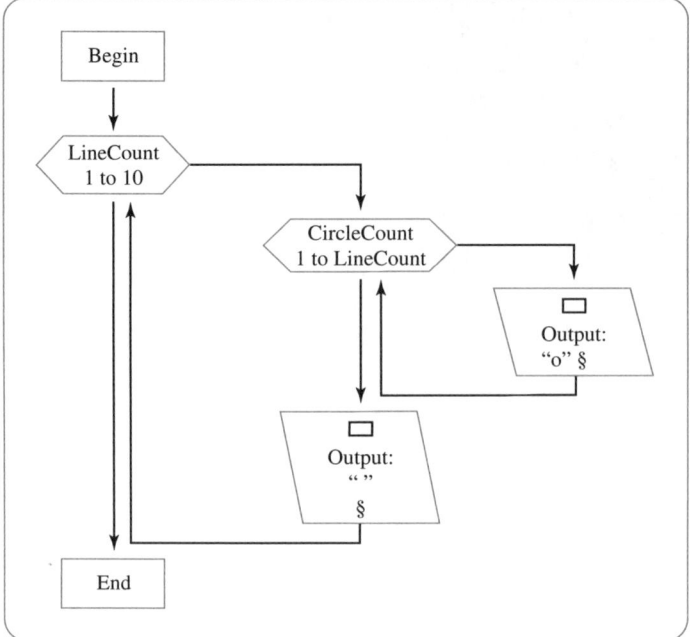

Figure 4-14 Solution to triangle problem

Figure 4-15 Output generated by program in Figure 4-14

NESTED LOOP SUMMARY

» Any valid statements can occur inside the body of a loop, including input, assignment, output, conditions, and even other loops.

» A nested loop refers to a loop that appears inside the body of another loop.

CHAPTER FOUR

CHAPTER SUMMARY

» For loops are used to automate the initialize, test, and update process.
» In Visual Logic, the For loop flowchart element appears as a six-sided figure with a loop variable, a start value, an end value, and two exit arrows. (The step value also appears if the step value is something other than 1.) The body of the loop is to the right and below the element.
» When executed, the first action is to initialize the loop variable to the start value.
» The body of the loop executes as long as the value of the loop variable does not exceed the final value. (*Note*: If the step value is negative, then the body of the loop executes as long as the value of the loop variable is not smaller than the final value.) After the body of the loop executes, the loop variable is updated by the step value, and the process is repeated.
» Any valid statements can occur inside the body of a loop, including input, assignment, output, conditions, and even other loops.
» A nested loop refers to a loop that appears inside the body of another loop.

KEY TERMS
final value   initial value   step value
For loop   nested loop

REVIEW QUESTIONS
1. What is the difference between a For loop and a While loop?
2. When using a For loop, what happens when the loop variable is equal to the final value? What happens when the loop variable exceeds the final value?
3. Consider two For loops, one with a positive step value and one with a negative step value. How are these two loops similar? How are these two loops different?
4. When writing a program that reads input terminated by a sentinel value, which loop is more appropriate to use, a For loop or a While loop? Explain your answer.
5. Consider the following statement: "An infinite loop is more likely to occur when using a While loop than when using a For loop." Do you agree or disagree with the statement? Explain your answer.

PROGRAMMING EXERCISES
4-1. Blast Off! Write a program that uses a For loop to generate the output shown below. The text "Rocket launch" should appear only once in your program.

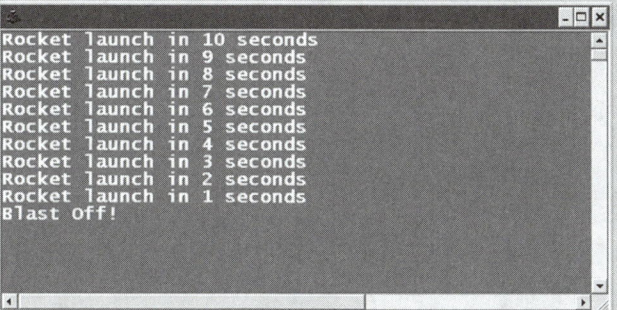

4-2. Pass It Around. Write a program that uses a For loop to generate the output shown below. Note that the program should only show the text for 99, 98, 97, and 96 bottles (*Hint*: Have a start value of 99 and a final value of 96, with a step value of –1).

```
99 bottles of rootbeer on the wall
99 bottles of rootbeer
Take one down and pass it around
One less bottle of rootbeer on the wall

98 bottles of rootbeer on the wall
98 bottles of rootbeer
Take one down and pass it around
One less bottle of rootbeer on the wall

97 bottles of rootbeer on the wall
97 bottles of rootbeer
Take one down and pass it around
One less bottle of rootbeer on the wall

96 bottles of rootbeer on the wall
96 bottles of rootbeer
Take one down and pass it around
One less bottle of rootbeer on the wall
```

4-3. Very Merry Christmas. Write a program that uses a nested loop to display "Ho Ho Ho Merry Christmas" five times to console output. *Note*: Your program should use the word "Ho" only once.

```
Ho Ho Ho Merry Christmas
Ho Ho Ho Merry Christmas
Ho Ho Ho Merry Christmas
Ho Ho Ho Merry Christmas
Ho Ho Ho Merry Christmas
```

4-4. Number Stack Different. Write a program that uses a nested loop to generate the output shown below. Be sure that the value on the line changes with each digit displayed. For example, line 5 has the values "1", "2", "3", "4", and "5".

```
1
1 2
1 2 3
1 2 3 4
1 2 3 4 5
1 2 3 4 5 6
1 2 3 4 5 6 7
1 2 3 4 5 6 7 8
1 2 3 4 5 6 7 8 9
```

4-5. Number Stack Same. Write a program that uses a nested loop to generate the output shown below. Be sure that all the values on a single line are the same. For example, line 5 has the values "5", "5", "5", "5", and "5".

4-6. Right Triangle. Write a program that generates the following triangle to console output. Note that the number of blank spaces decreases each line. (*Hint*: Modify the solution in Figure 4-14 by adding a "SpaceCount" loop above the "CircleCount" loop. Both the SpaceCount and CircleCount loops should be nested inside the LineCount loop.)

4-7. Tree. Write a program that generates the following tree shape to console output. Note that every line contains an odd number of circles.

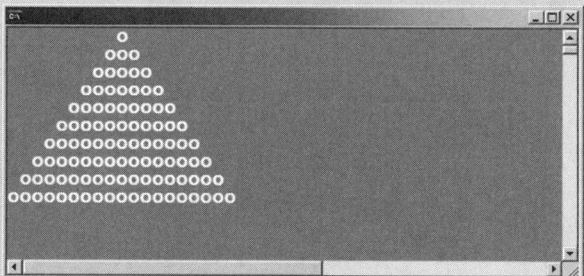

4-8. Diamond. Write a program that generates the following diamond shape to console output. Note that every line has an odd number of circles.

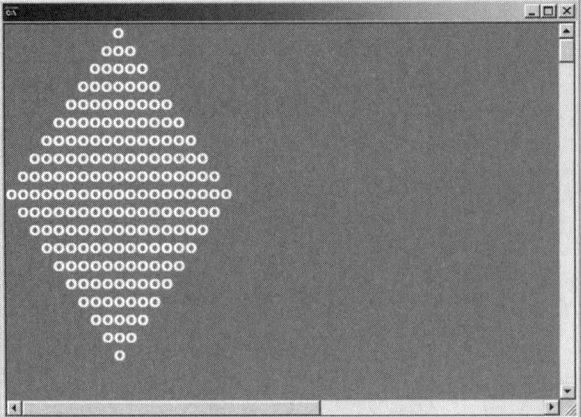

CHAPTER FIVE

5

ARRAYS

»CASE STUDY SCENARIO

Sorting Data

A dozen umbrellas lie on the ground just inside the classroom door when Dr. Taylor begins his lecture. "A cold, rainy day like today makes me want to stay in and order pizza for delivery rather than go out myself." Handing a phone book to a student in the front row, Dr. Taylor says, "Gail, please look up the phone number for Domino's Pizza on Main Street, and if you don't mind, I will time how long it takes you to find the number." Gail flips through a few pages while Dr. Taylor looks at his watch. "Here it is . . . 555-8275," she says.

"Seven seconds. Thank you Gail." Dr. Taylor presses some keys on his cell phone while continuing his conversation. "Now please look up the name of the person with the phone number 555-5982, and again I will time you." Dr. Taylor's focus returns to his watch even as he speaks into the phone. Gail slowly flips a couple of pages, then stops just about the same time Dr. Taylor ends his call. "I assure you the number is in there, Gail. We will wait while you look it up."

"You will probably wait a long time," she says, "because there is no fast way to find a number."

"Why not? It's the same data."

"But the phone book is sorted by names, so finding a name is easy. Finding a number is very difficult because a phone book is not sorted by numbers."

Dr. Taylor takes the phone book from Gail. "Exactly! The sorting process does not change the data, but it organizes the data in a context, making it useful information. Sorting is a fundamental processing activity, and we will discuss it very soon."

"But first, we need to discuss arrays, which are a useful means to hold large amounts of data, sorted or unsorted."

Dr. Taylor's sorting solution is presented later in this chapter.

ARRAYS

Sometimes it is beneficial to work with related data items as a single group. For example, all the scores from an entire class of students, all the names of employees for a company, or all the batting averages of the players on a baseball team. The easiest and most common way to store such related data is with an array.

An **array** is a variable that holds a collection of related data values. Each of the values in an array is called an **element**. Each element is like a separate variable, capable of storing and recalling a value as needed. Elements are uniquely identified by an integer value called its **index**, which indicates the position of the element in the array. The lowest index value is zero, and the largest index value is called the **upper bound**. Each element of an array is like a separate variable, capable of storing and recalling a value. To reference an element, you must specify both the array name and the specific index value.

CREATING AN ARRAY

In Visual Logic you create, or declare, an array using the **Make Array command**. The Make Array edit dialog contains text boxes for entering the name of the array and its upper bound. Figure 5-1 shows the Visual Logic Make Array dialog box for creating an array named "Scores" with an upper bound of 8. The resulting array is shown in Figure 5-2.

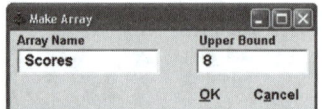

Figure 5-1 An example of the Make Array edit dialog box

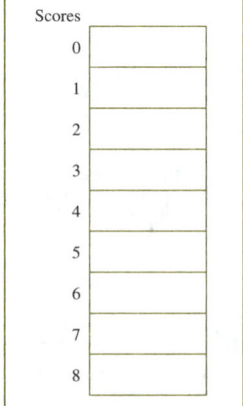

Figure 5-2 The Scores array created by the Make Array command in Figure 5-1

ACCESSING INDIVIDUAL ELEMENTS OF AN ARRAY

To access individual array elements, you specify the array name and follow it with an index expression enclosed in parentheses. The value of the expression determines which element to access. The index to an array can be a constant, a variable, or an expression. For example, Scores(5) references the element with index value 5 in the array named Scores. Likewise, if K has the value 5, then Scores(K) also references the same element. Finally, if A is 2 and B is 3, then Scores(A + B) would also reference the index 5 element. Figure 5-3 includes a flowchart that creates an array and then assigns four values to that array. The resulting state of the array after the flowchart code is complete is also shown in Figure 5-3.

CHAPTER FIVE

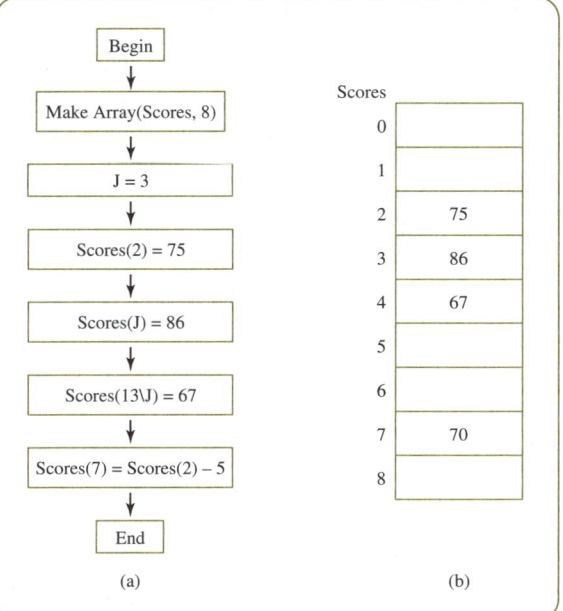

Figure 5-3 A flowchart with four array assignments and the resulting array elements

> **TIP** Each element of an array is like a separate variable, capable of storing and recalling a value.

> **TIP** Whenever you reference an element, you must specify the array name followed by the index value inside parentheses.

> **TIP** Arrays contain a finite number of elements, each of which is referenced by a unique index. If you attempt to reference an array with an index value greater than the upper bound of the array, the result will be an out-of-bounds error. For example, a reference to Scores(9) in the Figure 5-3 array would generate an out-of-bounds error because the index value 9 is greater than the upper bound for this array.

ARRAY SUMMARY
» An array is a storage location that holds a collection of related data.
» The values in the array are called the array elements.
» Individual elements in an array are identified by means of an index. Index values are integer values from 0 to the upper bound of the array.
» When referencing an element of an array, start with the array name and then specify the desired index inside parentheses.
» The index value that references an array can be provided by an integer constant, an integer variable, or an integer expression. This gives a great deal of power to developers when using arrays.

BENEFITS OF USING AN ARRAY

Arrays are valuable tools for developers. But what exactly is it about arrays that make them so helpful? One answer is that arrays combine the power of loops with the power of multiple storage locations. Consider briefly the following two problems:

(Problem #1) Input five numbers and output their average.

(Problem #2) Input five numbers and display the numbers in reverse order.

ARRAYS

These two problems can both be solved without using arrays, but the two solutions will be very different. Figure 5-4 shows a common solution to both. The first problem would most likely be solved using a loop to minimize the inputs and allow the program to easily be modified to handle 50 or 500 inputs. The second problem requires five different storage locations and therefore a loop cannot be used. Furthermore, the second solution would be time consuming and monotonous to modify to handle 12 or 500 inputs.

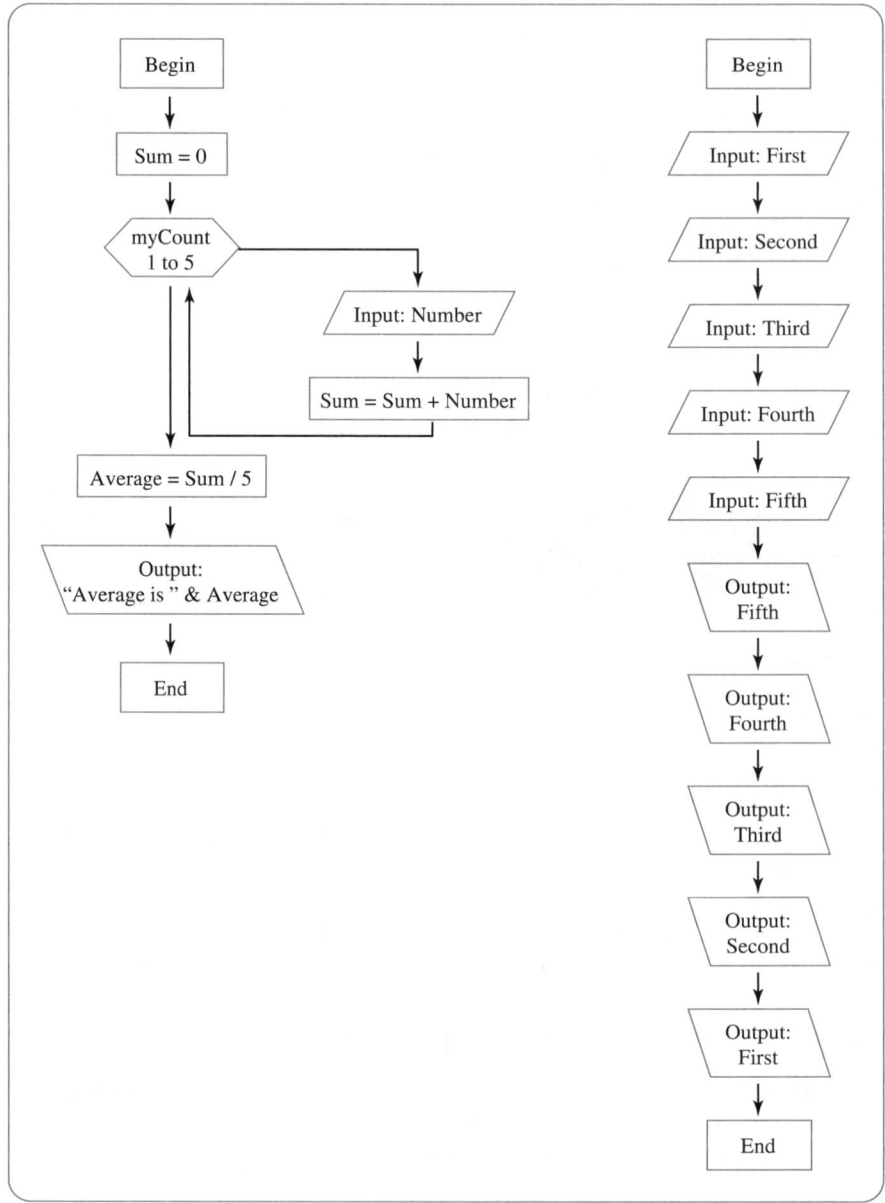

Figure 5-4 A loop solution to calculate average and a multi-variable solution to reverse order

CHAPTER FIVE

The point of Figure 5-4 is to show that there are times when loops are desirable and there are times when separate storage locations are desirable. Now imagine a third problem that combines both of the previous problems. To make the problem even more interesting, assume there are 12 input values (rather than just five).

(Problem #3) Input 12 numbers and output their average and then display the input numbers in reverse order.

Neither solution in Figure 5-4 will solve this problem. (Take a few minutes if necessary to convince yourself that the previous statement is true.) However, this problem is easily solved using an array, as shown in Figure 5-5. The array solution combines the best features of the two programs from Figure 5-4, including having only a single input statement inside a loop, while also storing all the input values in separate storage locations so nothing is lost.

>> TIP
In this book, we will not use the array element at index 0, and instead will store the first array value at index 1, the second array value at index 2, the third array value at index 3, and so on. This will make the programs easier to read and understand.

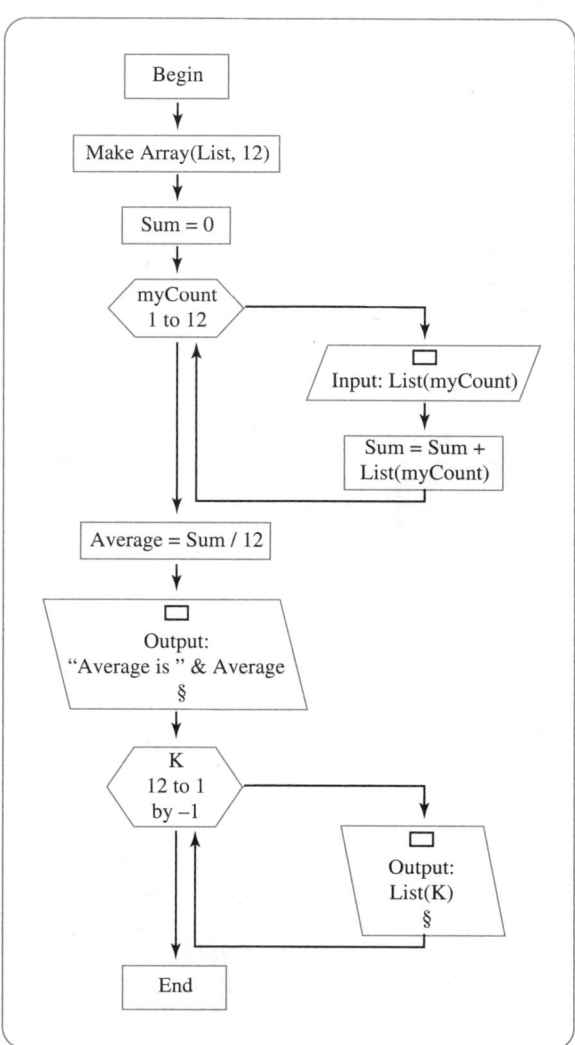

Figure 5-5 An array solution that calculates average and displays values in reverse order

When referencing an array inside the body of a loop, the loop variable is often used as the array's index value. As the loop variable changes from 1 to 2 to 3 to 4 (and so on), so also the array index changes from 1 to 2 to 3 to 4 (and so on). This allows the loop to process each element of the array.

```
Please type a value for LIST:41
Please type a value for LIST:42
Please type a value for LIST:43
Please type a value for LIST:44
Please type a value for LIST:45
Please type a value for LIST:50
Please type a value for LIST:60
Please type a value for LIST:70
Please type a value for LIST:80
Please type a value for LIST:90
Please type a value for LIST:98
Please type a value for LIST:99

Average is 63.5

99
98
90
80
70
60
50
45
44
43
42
41
```

Figure 5-6 Sample output from Figure 5-5

> **TIP** Many programs that utilize arrays will also employ For loops, with the For loop variable used as the index value for the array. Notice in Figure 5-5 that the first loop has the loop variable myCount and the first loop body uses myCount as the index value for the array in both the input and assignment statement. Then notice that the second loop has the loop variable K and the second loop body uses K as the index value for the array in the output statement. The general principle illustrated here is that when using a For loop to process an array, inside the body of that loop the For Loop variable is often used as the array index value.

BENEFITS OF USING AN ARRAY SUMMARY

» An array can be used to store multiple values in a single storage location. This makes the code easy to read and easy to work with.
» Arrays get their full power when used in conjunction with loops, where the body of the loop containing a reference to the array and the loop variable is used as the index value for the array.

SAMPLE PROGRAM #1: EVENS AND ODDS

Write a program that declares an array named List with an upper bound of 10. The program should prompt the user for 10 values and store them into the array. The program should then calculate and display the average of the 10 values. The program should then display the even values and their average, and the program should display the odd values and their average.

CHAPTER FIVE

ANALYSIS AND DESIGN

Let's break this problem apart into separate requirements:

1. Write a program that declares an array named List with an upper bound of 10.
2. The program should prompt the user for 10 values and store them into the array.
3. The program should then calculate and display the average of the 10 values.
4. The program should then display the even values and their average.
5. The program should then display the odd values and their average.

Now that the problem has been broken into separate steps, these smaller pieces can be solved individually. Solving all the smaller pieces will therefore solve the larger problem. This technique is sometimes called "Divide and Conquer" and it works well for this problem. Figure 5-7 shows the solution to this problem, with the code for the individual requirements indicated.

The first requirement is satisfied by an appropriate Make Array command, being sure to use the required array name and upper bound value.

The second requirement is satisfied by an Input statement inside of a For loop. Note that the For loop variable, J, is used as the array index value List(J) in the Input statement.

The third requirement involves calculating an average, which means the program needs a total and a count. The count is known (it will be the average for all 10 values) and the total can be calculated inside a loop. Once the total has been generated, the average can be determined with a simple calculation.

The fourth requirement is to display the even values and their average. This requires a conditional test on each value in the array to see if the value is even (e.g., divisible by 2 with no remainder). If the value is even, it should be displayed, counted, and added to the appropriate total. After all even values have been found, the appropriate total and count values can be used to calculate and display the even average.

The fifth requirement is similar to the fourth and also requires testing each element in the array to see if the value is odd, and updating appropriate count and total values if so. After all odd values have been found and displayed, the appropriate count and total values are used to calculate and display the odd average.

By breaking the problem up into separate requirements and solving the individual pieces, we can solve the entire problem. Note that Figure 5-7 contains four loops and that the loop variable is different each time (J, K, M, N). Because these are not nested loops, we could have reused the same variable name each time. However, separate loop variables are used intentionally in Figure 5-7 to point out that the array index variable depends on the loop in which the statement appears. In other words, inside the K loop the array index is List(K), and inside the M loop the array index is List(M). Figure 5-8 shows the output generated by this program.

> **TIP** The idea of breaking a problem down into smaller parts and solving those smaller parts individually is one of the main reasons for the use of procedures, which is discussed in Chapter 6.

ARRAYS

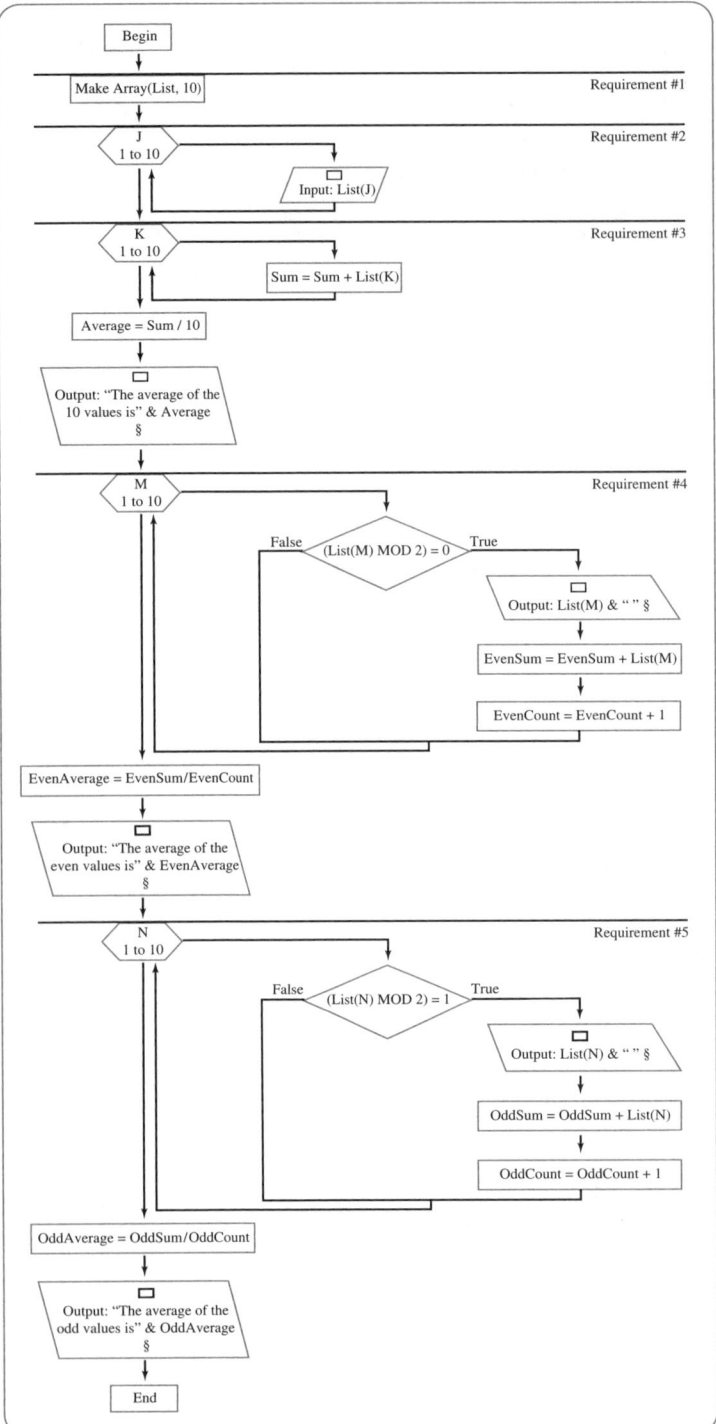

Figure 5-7 Solution to Sample Program #1: Even and Odds

Figure 5-8 Sample output from Figure 5-7

CHAPTER FIVE

SAMPLE PROGRAM #2: DICE ROLL SIMULATION

Computer simulations are powerful tools for studying the behavior of certain types of systems. In fact, today's engineer would never consider launching a satellite or producing a new automobile design without first creating computer simulations to model the product's behavior and functionality. While satellite and automobile performance simulations are beyond the scope of this book, a simple simulation such as rolling a single dice is something we can explore. Consider the following:

> A single die is equally likely to roll a 1, 2, 3, 4, 5, or 6. While no single roll can be predicted, if the die is rolled many times, the roll values should move toward an even distribution. Specifically, as the number of rolls increases, the distributions should become closer to one-sixth, or 16.67%. Write a program that simulates rolling a single die many times. The program should maintain a count of how many times each of the six values was rolled. After all the rolls have been made, the program should display the totals of how many times each value was rolled.

Write a program that performs a simulation of a single die rolled many times. The program should keep a running total of how many times each of the six values have been rolled. This running total should be kept in an array with an upper bound of 6. For example, every time the roll value is 3, the program should increment (or increase by 1) the value in the array at index 3. After the simulation is done rolling and counting, the program should display the total number of times each die value was rolled. Additionally, the program could present the simulation results in a visual manner as a histogram.

ANALYSIS AND DESIGN

This simulation requires a means to approximate the rolling of a die. This can be done using the expression **Random(6) + 1**. Random(6) produces a random integer between 0 and 5, and adding 1 to the result produces random values between 1 and 6, which is exactly what this simulation needs.

The problem also requires six different counter variables to keep up with how many times each of the six values was rolled. Using an array to hold the six counter values has the benefit that the random value can be used as the index of the array. In other words, Counters(5) holds a count of how many times 5 was rolled, and each time the random roll value is 5, the Counters(5) value is updated to be increased by 1.

Finally, after all the values have been rolled and counted, the program displays the totals and their percentages as well as a histogram of the data. The histogram is generated using nested loops. The inner loop generates a horizontal line of circles whose length is determined by the counter value (one circle for each time the die value was rolled). Following the loop to print the circles is an output with a carriage return to terminate the line. The outer loop then repeats the inner loop process for each of the six roll values.

The complete solution is shown in Figure 5-9. Two sample outputs with 400 rolls are presented in Figure 5-10. Each run will be slightly different because random values will generate different totals.

ARRAYS

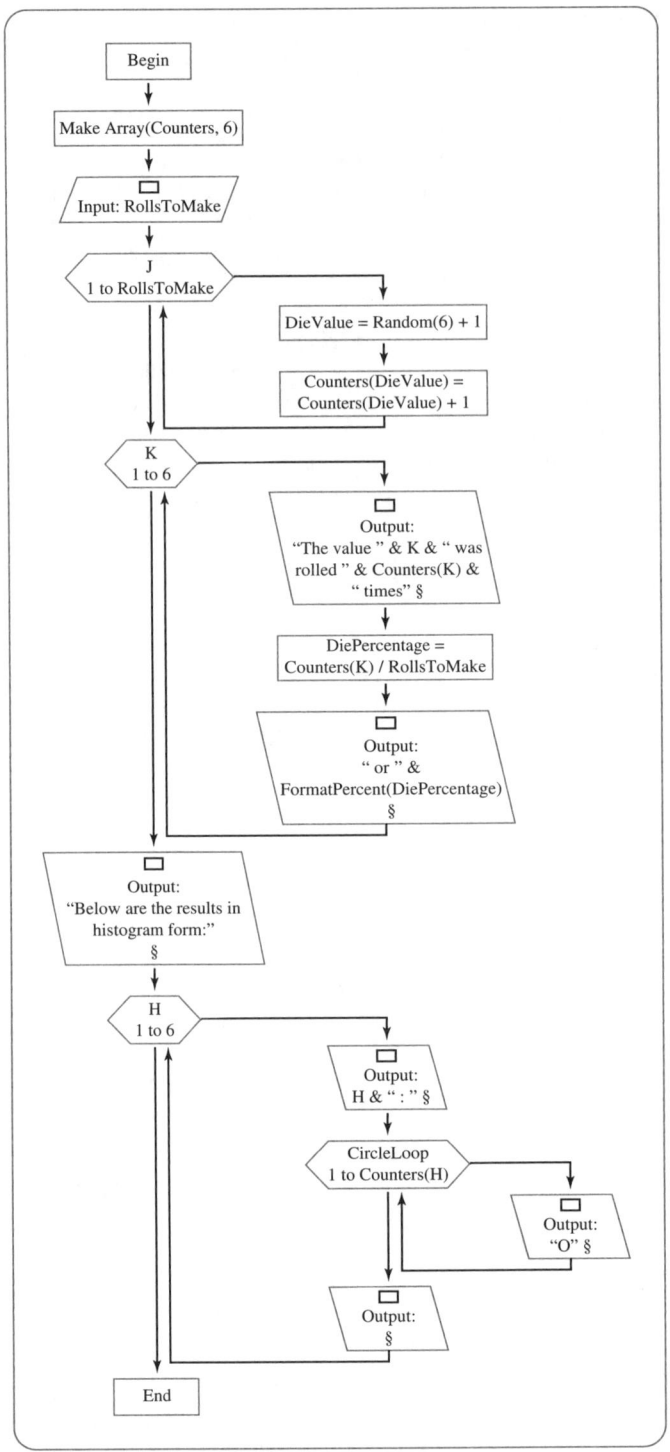

Figure 5-9 Solution to Sample Program #2: Dice Roll Solution

```
Please type a value for ROLLSTOMAKE:400
The value 1 was rolled 66 times   or    16.50%
The value 2 was rolled 73 times   or    18.25%
The value 3 was rolled 59 times   or    14.75%
The value 4 was rolled 73 times   or    18.25%
The value 5 was rolled 66 times   or    16.50%
The value 6 was rolled 63 times   or    15.75%

Below are the results in histogram form:

1 : OOOOOOOOOOOOOOOOOOOOOOOOOOOOOOOOOOOOOOOOOOOOOOOOOOOOOOOOOOOOOOOOOO
2 : OOOOOOOOOOOOOOOOOOOOOOOOOOOOOOOOOOOOOOOOOOOOOOOOOOOOOOOOOOOOOOOOOOOOOOOOO
3 : OOOOOOOOOOOOOOOOOOOOOOOOOOOOOOOOOOOOOOOOOOOOOOOOOOOOOOOOOOOOO
4 : OOOOOOOOOOOOOOOOOOOOOOOOOOOOOOOOOOOOOOOOOOOOOOOOOOOOOOOOOOOOOOOOOOOOOOOOO
5 : OOOOOOOOOOOOOOOOOOOOOOOOOOOOOOOOOOOOOOOOOOOOOOOOOOOOOOOOOOOOOOOOOO
6 : OOOOOOOOOOOOOOOOOOOOOOOOOOOOOOOOOOOOOOOOOOOOOOOOOOOOOOOOOOOOOOO
```

```
Please type a value for ROLLSTOMAKE:400
The value 1 was rolled 71 times   or    17.75%
The value 2 was rolled 67 times   or    16.75%
The value 3 was rolled 60 times   or    15.00%
The value 4 was rolled 73 times   or    18.25%
The value 5 was rolled 62 times   or    15.50%
The value 6 was rolled 67 times   or    16.75%

Below are the results in histogram form:

1 : OOOOOOOOOOOOOOOOOOOOOOOOOOOOOOOOOOOOOOOOOOOOOOOOOOOOOOOOOOOOOOOOOOOOOOO
2 : OOOOOOOOOOOOOOOOOOOOOOOOOOOOOOOOOOOOOOOOOOOOOOOOOOOOOOOOOOOOOOOOOOO
3 : OOOOOOOOOOOOOOOOOOOOOOOOOOOOOOOOOOOOOOOOOOOOOOOOOOOOOOOOOOOO
4 : OOOOOOOOOOOOOOOOOOOOOOOOOOOOOOOOOOOOOOOOOOOOOOOOOOOOOOOOOOOOOOOOOOOOOOOOO
5 : OOOOOOOOOOOOOOOOOOOOOOOOOOOOOOOOOOOOOOOOOOOOOOOOOOOOOOOOOOOOOO
6 : OOOOOOOOOOOOOOOOOOOOOOOOOOOOOOOOOOOOOOOOOOOOOOOOOOOOOOOOOOOOOOOOOOO
```

Figure 5-10 Sample outputs from running Figure 5-9 twice (Notice how the random values produce different results)

SAMPLE PROGRAM #3: PARALLEL ARRAYS (USERNAME AND PASSWORD)

In this section we examine a problem that involves maintaining two parallel arrays. The first array holds usernames and the second array holds passwords. The two arrays are separate but related, each having the same number of elements, and the values in one correspond to the values in the other. For example, the seventh element in the username array and the seventh element in the password array together form a valid username/password combination that would grant authentication to the system.

Write a program that reads 10 username and password pairs and stores those username and password values into parallel arrays. After the arrays have been loaded, the program should behave as a login screen, prompting for a username and a password. Based on the data entered for username and password, the program should respond appropriately with one of three output messages. If the username does not match one of the values in the username array, then the message should be *"Username not found."* If the username is found in the username array, but the password does not match the parallel value in the password array, then the message should be *"Username and password do not match."* If the username is found and the password matches the parallel value in the password array, the message should be *"Access granted."*

READING DATA FROM A TEXT FILE

In addition to Dialog and Console input, there is a third input option called File input, which allows the input data to come from a text file rather than being manually typed in each time the program is executed. In this program, for example, the 10 username and password pairs can be entered one time into a simple text file and those values can then be read from the text file into the parallel arrays each time the program is executed. This will eliminate redundant typing and reduce the likelihood of a typing error.

To perform file I/O, double-click on the Input (or Output) element to show the edit dialog, click "More >>", select the File option button, and then specify the appropriate text file name.

> **TIP** The authors have created a **usernames.txt** input file for this program, which may be made available to you, or your instructor may have created an input file for you to use. At the same time, you can create your own input file as well using Notepad or a similar tool to create a simple .txt file. When creating an input file, remember that each line in the file corresponds to one input value. You should therefore keep the input file to one input item per line, being sure to include quotes around string input, just like with console or dialog input.

Four tips to remember when doing file I/O:

1. First, when creating your input text file, DO use quotes around string data inside the text file. (Note that File input works the same as Console input in that strings must have delimiting quotes, and that the delimiters can be either single or double quotes, just so long as you use the same delimiter to start and stop the string.)
2. Second, do NOT use quotes around the text file name in the I/O dialog.
3. Third, if your file name in the I/O dialog box uses a relative reference (without the full path name), the text file needs to be in the same folder as the Visual Logic.exe executable (which is not necessarily the same folder as the *.vls solution file).
4. Fourth, if you have both FileInput and FileOutput in the same program, you must use different file names for the Input and Output files.

> **ASK THE AUTHOR**
> Q: Are usernames and passwords typically saved as text files?
> A: No. (Thank goodness.) A text file with usernames and passwords would not be very secure and you certainly would not want your bank account information stored in this format. An enterprise system would most likely store username and password data in a password-protected database.

ANALYSIS AND DESIGN

We begin our implementation of the username and password solution by confirming that we have a valid text file with username and password pairs. Figure 5-11 shows the username and password pairs from the username.txt file. Note that the first four username and password pairs are "peanut butter"/"jelly," "sunrise"/"sunset," "light"/"dark," and "forward"/"reverse." Those values are read and stored into parallel arrays that will look like Figure 5-12.

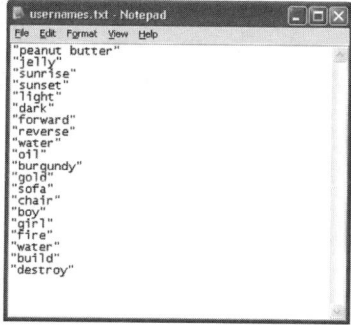

Figure 5-11 Usernames.txt input file

Username			Password	
0			0	
1	"peanut butter"		1	"jelly"
2	"sunrise"		2	"sunset"
3	"light"		3	"dark"
4	"forward"		4	"reverse"
5	"water"		5	"oil"
6	"burgundy"		6	"gold"
7	"sofa"		7	"chair"
8	"boy"		8	"girl"
9	"fire"		9	"water"
10	"build"		10	"destroy"

Figure 5-12 Parallel arrays after reading data from input file

Once the parallel arrays have their data, the program prompts the user for a username. The program checks the user's input against the Username array, looking for a match. If the entire array is searched and no match is found, then the program gives the "Username not found" error message. If the username is found, the program prompts the user to input the associated password. The program then looks in the Password array at the same index value location where the Username was found. If the user-entered password matches the associated password in the parallel array, then the program gives the "Access granted" message; otherwise the program gives the "Username and password do not match" error message. The solution to this problem is shown in Figure 5-13, and three sample runs are shown in Figure 5-14.

ARRAYS

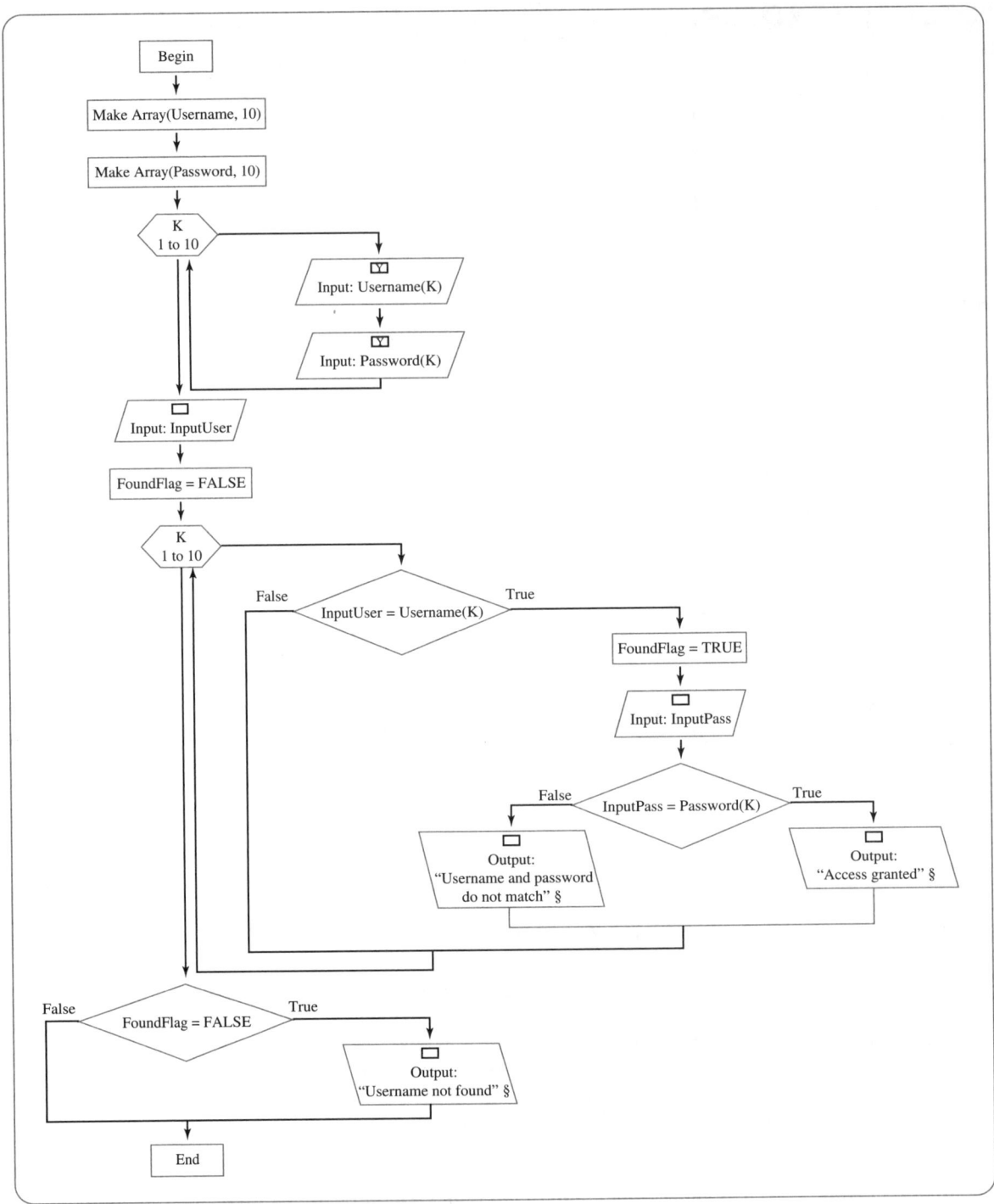

Figure 5-13 Solution to Sample Program #3: Parallel Arrays

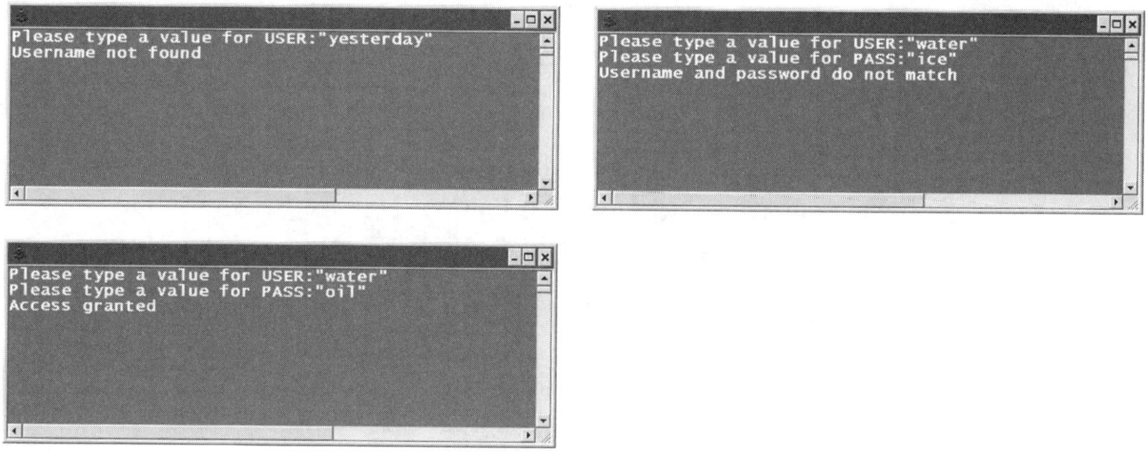

Figure 5-14 Output from Figure 5-13

▶▶CASE STUDY SOLUTION

Sorting Data

"Probably the simplest way to sort an array is a technique called bubble sort. The basic idea is to repeatedly compare two adjacent values and swap them if they are in the wrong order. The bigger values flow in one direction, and the smaller values flow in the other direction." Dr. Taylor turns to the blackboard, draws an array with nine elements, and fills them with apparently random values.

"The heart of the solution is a loop from the start to the end of the array. The loop swaps adjacent elements if necessary as it goes. After one pass through the array, the largest value will have moved to the end of the array." Dr. Taylor makes a few marks on the chalkboard to illustrate the eight comparisons needed to pass through the entire array and the resulting location of the largest element in the final position (see Figure 5-15).

"If you repeat the loop a second time, the second largest element will be placed in its proper location." Dr. Taylor makes additional marks on the chalkboard to represent the second pass through the array (see Figure 5-16).

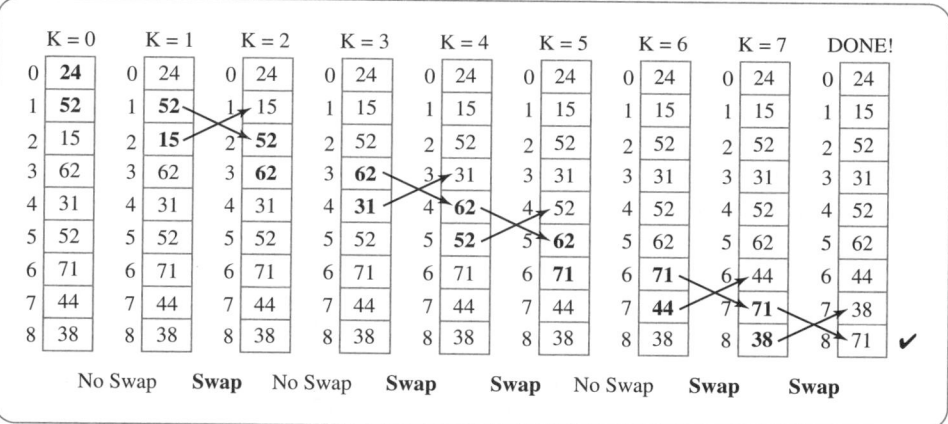

Figure 5-15 Array after one pass (one value guaranteed to be in proper location)

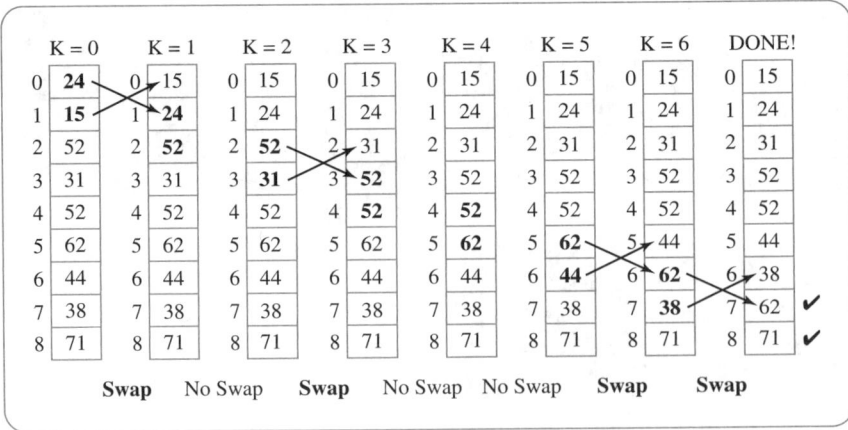

Figure 5-16 Array after two passes (two values guaranteed to be in proper locations)

Dr. Taylor continues, "After two passes, there are two elements that are certain to be in their proper locations. Three passes ensure three elements are in the proper location and so on. Sorting the array, therefore, requires N–1 passes where N is the number of elements in the array. If N–1 elements are in the proper location, the Nth element must also be in the proper location."

He then begins handing out a sheet with a solution similar to Figure 5-17 printed on it. "This handout shows a simple implementation of bubble sort. Notice the two loops we just discussed. The solution also includes code to display the sorted values." Figure 5-18 shows the output generated by the solution in Figure 5-17.

"Are there other sorting algorithms?" Leslie asks.

"Absolutely, and almost all of them run faster than bubble sort. But bubble sort is the easiest to understand, and it works fine with arrays of size 5,000 or less. If the size of the array is significantly bigger than that, you will probably need to consider one of the faster, more complex sorting algorithms."

A few more aspects of the bubble sort algorithm are discussed in the remaining few moments of the class. Finally, there is a knock on the classroom door by a Domino's delivery person holding a flat, cardboard box. Dr. Taylor smiles, as the aroma of pepperoni and sausage pizza fills the room. Glancing at his watch, he announces, "My lunch has arrived with perfect timing. Class dismissed."

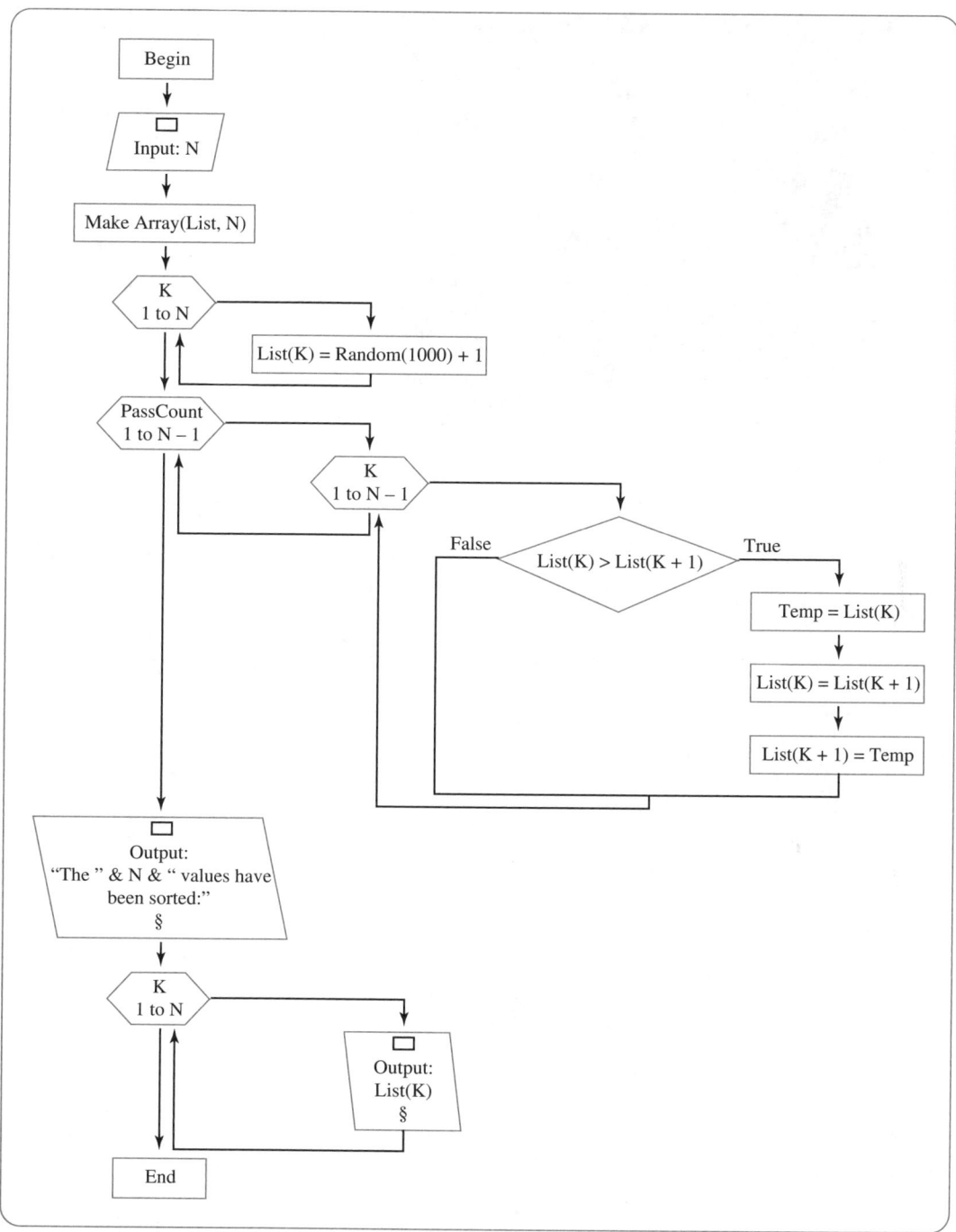

Figure 5-17 Case Study solution: bubble sort

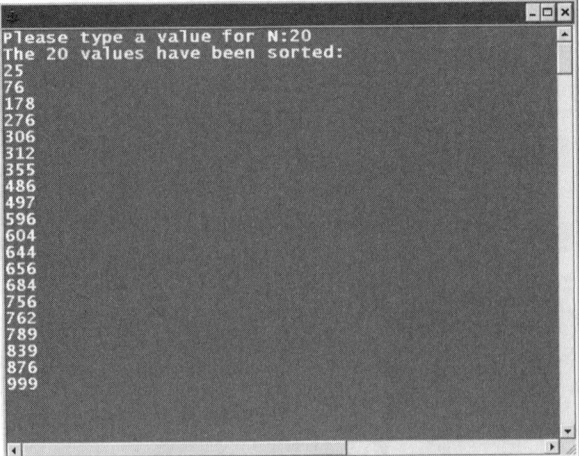

Figure 5-18 Sample output for Figure 5-17

CHAPTER FIVE

CHAPTER SUMMARY

» An array is a variable that holds a collection of related data values. Each of the values in an array is called an element. Each element in the array is identified by an integer value called its index, which indicates the position of the element in the array.

» Most modern programming languages implement zero-based arrays, meaning that array index values begin with 0. The length of an array is the number of elements in the array. The upper bound of an array is the index of the last element.

» To access individual array elements, you specify the array name and follow it with an index expression enclosed in parentheses. The value of the expression determines which element to access.

» Arrays contain a finite number of elements, each of which is referenced by a unique index. If you attempt to reference an array with an index value greater than the upper bound of the array, the result will be an out-of-bounds error.

» Parallel arrays are two or more arrays whose elements are related by their positions in the arrays.

» Bubble sort is a simple sorting technique involving multiple passes through the array, each pass comparing adjacent elements and swapping them if necessary.

KEY TERMS

array	index	upper bound
array length	Make Array command	zero-based arrays
bubble sort	out-of-bounds error	
element	parallel arrays	

REVIEW QUESTIONS

1. How is an array with five elements similar to having five different variables?
2. How is an array with five elements better than having five different variables?
3. What is the difference between an array index and an array element?
4. What is the difference between an array length and an array upper bound?
5. In Visual Logic, how is an array declared?
6. The index value for an array can be a variable. Explain how this is helpful when writing programs.
7. Identify some general recommendations for when an array should be used.
8. Consider the bubble sort solution in Figure 5-17. What is the purpose of the Temp variable? Explain why swapping two values could not be done without a third storage location.

PROGRAMMING EXERCISES

5-1. Reverse. Write a program that uses an array to accept 10 input values and store them into an array. The program should then display those 10 numbers in reverse order.

ARRAYS

```
Please type a value for LIST:10
Please type a value for LIST:20
Please type a value for LIST:30
Please type a value for LIST:31
Please type a value for LIST:32
Please type a value for LIST:33
Please type a value for LIST:34
Please type a value for LIST:35
Please type a value for LIST:40
Please type a value for LIST:50

The values in reverse order are:

50
40
35
34
33
32
31
30
20
10
```

5-2. Above Average. Write a program that accepts five input values and stores them into an array. The program should then display the average of the five numbers. Finally, the program should display all the numbers in the array that are larger than the average of the five numbers.

```
Please type a value for LIST:10
Please type a value for LIST:45
Please type a value for LIST:35
Please type a value for LIST:20
Please type a value for LIST:30

The average is 28

The following are greater than the average:
45
35
30
```

5-3. Target Value. Write a program that accepts 10 input values and stores them into an array. After reading the 10 values, the program should then input one more value, which is called the target value. The program should then search through the array to calculate and display how many times the target value appears inside the array.

```
Please type a value for LIST:7
Please type a value for LIST:7
Please type a value for LIST:4
Please type a value for LIST:5
Please type a value for LIST:3
Please type a value for LIST:2
Please type a value for LIST:3
Please type a value for LIST:7
Please type a value for LIST:5
Please type a value for LIST:7
Please type a value for TARGETVALUE:7

The target value appears 4 times in the array.
```

5-4. Batting Average. Write a program that uses parallel arrays to determine the batting average for a baseball team by position. There are nine positions on a baseball team and your program should have parallel arrays with an upper bound of 9. Your program will read data in pairs; the first number will be between 1 and 9 and will represent the batter's position, and the second number will be either 0 or 1 and will represent an out (0) or a hit (1). The program will continue to input data pairs until the sentinel value −1 is read. At that point, the program should output the batting average for each of the nine positions. (*Note*: Batting average is the number of hits divided by the number of at bats. Therefore, hits and at bats may be good values to store in parallel arrays.) The output shown below was generated using the input file "battingaverage.txt," which may be available from your instructor.

```
424 pairs of data were read from a file.
The batting average for each position was:
Position 1 batting average is 0.346938775510204
Position 2 batting average is 0.240740740740741
Position 3 batting average is 0.274509803921569
Position 4 batting average is 0.268292682926829
Position 5 batting average is 0.234042553191489
Position 6 batting average is 0.222222222222222
Position 7 batting average is 0.322033898305085
Position 8 batting average is 0.304347826086957
Position 9 batting average is 0.219512195121951
```

5-5. Batting Average and Slugging Percentage. Write a program that uses parallel arrays to determine the batting average and slugging percentage for a baseball team by position. There are nine positions on a baseball team and your program should have parallel arrays with an upper bound of 9. Your program will read data in pairs; the first number will be between 1 and 9 and will represent the batter's position, and the second number will be either a 0 (for an out) or a 1 (for a single) or a 2 (for a double) or a 3 (for a triple) or a 4 (for a home run). The program will continue to input data pairs until the sentinel value −1 is read. At that point, the program should output the batting average and slugging percentage for each of the nine positions. (*Note*: Batting average is the number of hits divided by the number of at bats and slugging percentage is the total number of bases divided by the number of at bats. You might want to have three parallel arrays in your solution.) The output shown below was generated using the input file "battingandslugging.txt," which may be available from your instructor. (*Hint*: You will probably need parallel arrays for Hits, AtBats, and Bases.)

```
424 pairs of data were read from a file.
The batting average for each position was:
Position 1 batting average is 0.346938775510204
Position 2 batting average is 0.240740740740741
Position 3 batting average is 0.274509803921569
Position 4 batting average is 0.268292682926829
Position 5 batting average is 0.234042553191489
Position 6 batting average is 0.222222222222222
Position 7 batting average is 0.322033898305085
Position 8 batting average is 0.304347826086957
Position 9 batting average is 0.219512195121951
The slugging percentage for each position was:
Position 1 batting average is 0.530612244897959
Position 2 batting average is 0.37037037037037
Position 3 batting average is 0.509803921568627
Position 4 batting average is 0.292682926829268
Position 5 batting average is 0.25531914893617
Position 6 batting average is 0.388888888888889
Position 7 batting average is 0.627118644067797
Position 8 batting average is 0.434782608695652
Position 9 batting average is 0.268292682926829
```

ARRAYS

5-6. Two Dice Simulation. Write a program that simulates the rolling of two dice many times. Each of the two dice should have a separate "Random(6) + 1" and the two random values should be added together to get the total of the two dice roll. After rolling the two dice, the total rolled should be updated in an array of counters. For example, if the random values were 3 and 4, then the dice total is 7, and the index 7 element should be incremented by 1. Because the maximum roll possible for two dice is 12, your array of counters should have an upper bound of 12. Your program should simulate rolling the two dice many times (400 rolls is the number used in the figure below) and then display how many times each total was rolled and the percentage for each total. Finally, the program should display the roll totals visually by creating a histogram. *Note*: Each time you run your program you will get different totals and therefore a different histogram. In general the middle totals (such as 6, 7, 8) should be rolled more often than the extremes (2, 3, 4 on the low end and 10, 11, 12 on the high end) because there are more combinations of two dice that result in those middle values.

```
Please type a value for ROLLSTOMAKE:400
The value 2 was rolled 13 times   or   3.25%
The value 3 was rolled 21 times   or   5.25%
The value 4 was rolled 34 times   or   8.50%
The value 5 was rolled 42 times   or  10.50%
The value 6 was rolled 58 times   or  14.50%
The value 7 was rolled 70 times   or  17.50%
The value 8 was rolled 49 times   or  12.25%
The value 9 was rolled 45 times   or  11.25%
The value 10 was rolled 31 times  or   7.75%
The value 11 was rolled 28 times  or   7.00%
The value 12 was rolled 9 times   or   2.25%

Below are the results in histogram form:

2  : OOOOOOOOOOOOO
3  : OOOOOOOOOOOOOOOOOOOOO
4  : OOOOOOOOOOOOOOOOOOOOOOOOOOOOOOOOOO
5  : OOOOOOOOOOOOOOOOOOOOOOOOOOOOOOOOOOOOOOOOOO
6  : OOOOOOOOOOOOOOOOOOOOOOOOOOOOOOOOOOOOOOOOOOOOOOOOOOOOOOOOOO
7  : OOOOOOOOOOOOOOOOOOOOOOOOOOOOOOOOOOOOOOOOOOOOOOOOOOOOOOOOOOOOOOOOOOOOOO
8  : OOOOOOOOOOOOOOOOOOOOOOOOOOOOOOOOOOOOOOOOOOOOOOOOO
9  : OOOOOOOOOOOOOOOOOOOOOOOOOOOOOOOOOOOOOOOOOOOOO
10 : OOOOOOOOOOOOOOOOOOOOOOOOOOOOOOO
11 : OOOOOOOOOOOOOOOOOOOOOOOOOOOO
12 : OOOOOOOOO
```

5-7. Access Granted. Write a program that reads 10 username and password pairs and stores those username and password values into parallel arrays. After the arrays have been loaded, the program should behave as a login screen, continuously prompting for a username and password until a valid combination is entered and access is granted. Each time the user enters username and password data, the program should respond appropriately with one of three output messages. If the username does not match one of the values in the username array, then the message should be *"Username not found."* If the username is found in the username array, but the password does not match the parallel value in the password array, then the message should be *"Username and password do not match."* If the username is found and the password matches the parallel value in the password array, the message should be *"Access granted."* The program should use a loop and continue to prompt the user for a valid username and password pair until a valid pair is entered and access is granted.

```
Please type a value for INPUTUSER:"yesterday"
Username not found

Please type a value for INPUTUSER:"water"
Please type a value for INPUTPASS:"ice"
Username and password do not match

Please type a value for INPUTUSER:"water"
Please type a value for INPUTPASS:"oil"
Access granted
```

5-8. Olympic Judging. When judging an Olympic event, the highest and lowest judges' scores are often dropped, and the remaining judges' scores are averaged. Write a program that accepts six numeric values as input representing scores from six Olympic judges. The program should store those six values into an array. Your program should then use bubble sort to sort the scores in the array. Finally, your program should output the highest score, the lowest score, and the average of the other four scores.

```
Please type a value for SCORES:3
Please type a value for SCORES:2
Please type a value for SCORES:1
Please type a value for SCORES:4
Please type a value for SCORES:9
Please type a value for SCORES:5
Highest score : 9
Lowest score : 1
Olympic Average : 3.5
```

CHAPTER SIX

GRAPHICS AND PROCEDURES

»CASE STUDY SCENARIO

Drawing Houses

"The materials we have covered so far in this course, including expressions, conditions, loops, and arrays are foundational concepts essential to most any programming language," Dr. Taylor says at the beginning of class. "Visual Basic, C#, C++, Java, Cobol, Pascal, and other popular languages all use these commands in their solutions. Even graphical languages use these commands."

"What's a graphical language?" one student asks.

"Graphical languages contain graphics commands that allow developers to create programs that generate a variety of interesting, pictorial outputs." Dr. Taylor turns on the overhead projector and shows a series of images, including geometric figures and colorful designs. "For example, all these images were created with Visual Logic graphics commands combined with expressions, conditions, and loops."

Dr. Taylor walks away from the projector to the desk at the front of the room. "In addition to graphics, we will also discuss a common strategy for solving complex problems, which is to break the problem down into smaller pieces, solve the smaller pieces individually, and then put the pieces back together to solve the original problem."

"Kind of like divide-and-conquer?" asks Stephanie.

"Yes, exactly. We write solutions to the small pieces in blocks called procedures. We then call the procedures as necessary to solve the original problem."

Jay raises his hand. "Did you say we will write programs that generate all those images?" he asks, pointing to the screen that is still showing various graphics outputs.

"Yes. We will soon be making the images you see on the screen. That last image, the one with multiple houses, requires both graphics and procedures. But we start with simple geometric shapes."

Dr. Taylor's solution to the house graphics appears later in this chapter.

GRAPHICS

Visual Logic graphics are a variation on **Logo Programming Language**, which has been used in educational settings for over three decades. The graphics commands are based on the idea that a pen can be instructed to move over a drawing board, leaving a mark as it moves. The drawing board is illustrated in Figure 6-1. Note that the coordinates (0, 0) are at the center of the screen and that north, east, south, and west are 0 degrees, 90 degrees, 180 degrees, and 270 degrees respectively. These are absolute positions and directions that do not change.

The 14 graphics commands available in the Visual Logic system can be accessed through the Element menu, as shown in Figure 6-2. Each command is described in Table 6-1. These graphics commands can be combined with other Visual Logic commands to create many interesting programs, as we will see shortly.

FORWARD AND TURN RIGHT

The first two graphics commands we examine are **Forward** and **Turn Right**. The Forward command moves the pen a specified number of units. If the pen is down, a line is drawn. If the pen is up, it moves without making a mark. The Turn Right command rotates the drawing direction a specified number of degrees. The pen does not move and does not make any marks.

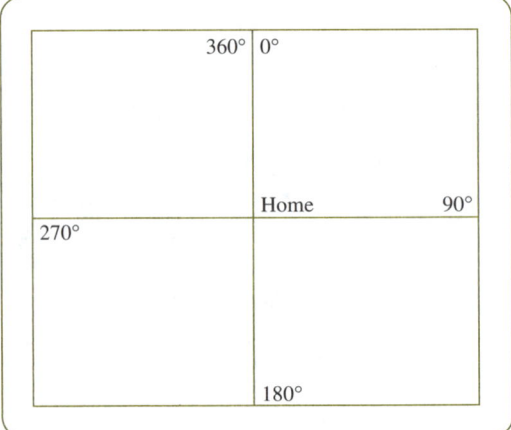

Figure 6-1 Absolute graphics positions

> **TELL ME MORE**
>
> In the early 1970s, Semore Papert and others at MIT developed Logo as an exploratory learning environment that would be understood by children and adults alike. The Logo Programming Language originally utilized a turtle-sized robot that moved around on the floor with a pen attached to its belly. As personal computers became available, the turtle and pen migrated to the computer screen. However, the idea of a turtle remains popular as a tribute to Logo's history. For more information about Logo, visit the Logo Foundation at http://el.media.mit.edu/logo-foundation/index.html.

CHAPTER SIX

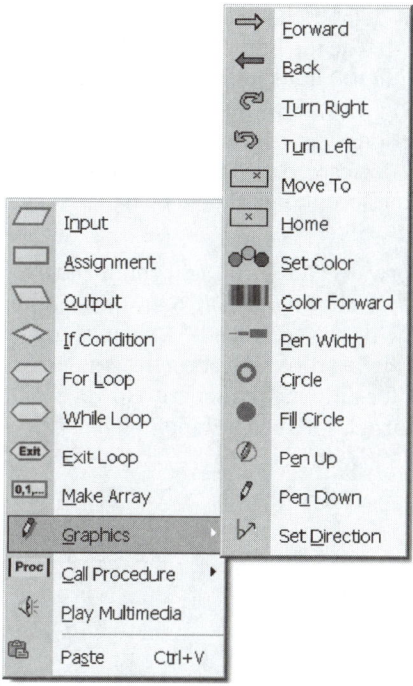

Figure 6-2 Visual Logic graphics commands

Command	Description
Forward **N**	Move the turtle N units forward (in the current direction)
Back **N**	Move the turtle N units backward (opposite the current direction)
Turn Right **D**	Turn the turtle D degrees to the right (clockwise)
Turn Left **D**	Turn the turtle D degrees to the left (counterclockwise)
Move to **X**, **Y**	Move the turtle to specified X, Y screen position
Go Home	Move the turtle to the center of the screen, facing up (north)
Set Color **C**	Set the pen color to the specific color C
Color Forward **F**	Step through a fixed color palette by F
Pen Width **N**	Set the pen width to N units
Circle **N**	Draw a circle with a center at the current location and a radius of N units
Fill Circle **N**	Draw a circle with a center at the current location and a radius of N units; fill the circle using the current pen color
Pen Up	Lift the turtle pen so that no lines are drawn as the turtle moves
Pen Down	Lower the turtle pen so that a line is drawn as the turtle moves
Set Direction **D**	Rotate the turtle so it faces D degree

Table 6-1 Descriptions of Turtle Graphic Commands

GRAPHICS AND PROCEDURES

Consider the graphics program shown in Figure 6-3a. By default, the pen begins at the home position, which is at the center of the screen facing north (the top of the screen). The first graphics command is Forward 100, which results in a line 100 units long drawn north, the initial drawing direction. The second command, Turn Right 90, turns the drawing direction right by 90 degrees. There is no movement, but its direction is now due east. The final command, Forward 50, causes the pen to move forward (in this case, east) 50 units. The exact length of the units will vary from screen to screen, but the second line should be half as long as the first line. The output is shown in Figure 6-3b.

Many interesting designs can be made using only the Forward and Turn Right commands. A program that draws a small square (sides 50 units in length) is shown in Figure 6-4a. Figure 6-4b shows the step-by-step actions of the turtle when following the commands. A small turtle icon has been included in the images to illustrate the drawing direction at each stage. Note that the last command, Turn Right 90, is not necessary for drawing the square. However, it does return the drawing direction to exactly where it started. This can be helpful when drawing multiple figures.

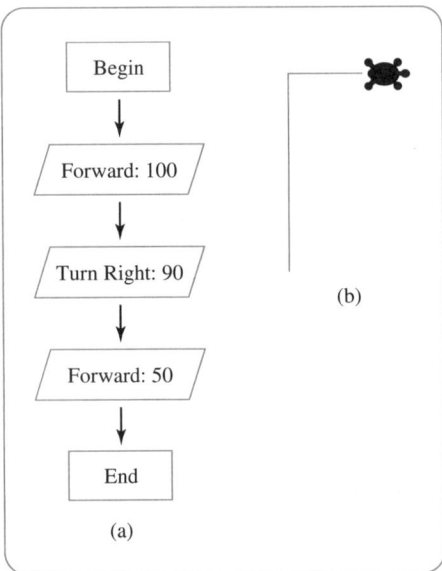

Figure 6-3 A graphics right angle

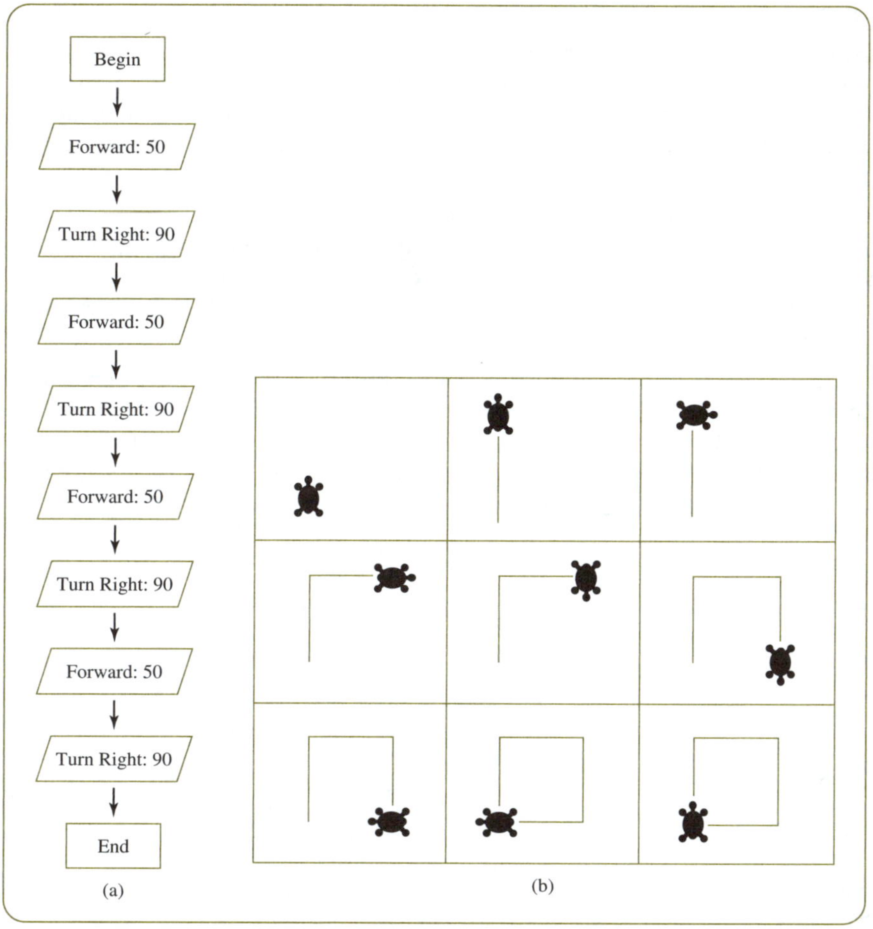

CHAPTER SIX

> **TIP**
> The commands Turn Right and Turn Left do not move the pen. They only rotate the drawing direction.

Figure 6-4 Drawing a square with Visual Logic graphics

QUICK CHECK 6-A

Using only Forward and Turn Right commands, draw the shapes in Figure 6-5. (*Hint*: The drawing must rotate a total of 360 degrees to return to its original direction.)

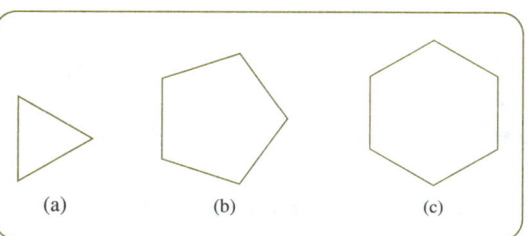

Figure 6-5 Forward and Turn Right Quick Check problem

USING LOOPS

At this point you should have successfully drawn the four shapes (triangle, square, pentagon, and hexagon) from the previous section. In doing so, you probably noticed a couple of patterns about the shape-drawing process. The first pattern is the repetition of the commands Forward and Turn Right. These two commands appear the same number of times as the sides of the figure. The second pattern is not so obvious.

The degrees the drawing direction must turn right are different for each shape and are based on the number of sides in the shape. Since the drawing direction will end up facing the same direction it started, the sum of all the right turns should be 360 degrees. The drawing direction should therefore rotate right 360 / N degrees after every turn, where N is the number of sides on the figure.

Determining patterns can make it easier to write programs because a pattern can be expressed once and repeated many times with a loop. The program shown in Figure 6-6a illustrates how a loop can be used to make a shape-drawing solution. The user enters the number of sides desired for the shape, and then a loop is used to draw the sides of the shapes. Inputs of 3, 5, and 6 would draw the shapes shown in Figure 6-5. An input of 10 would generate a decagon (10 sides), as shown in Figure 6-6b.

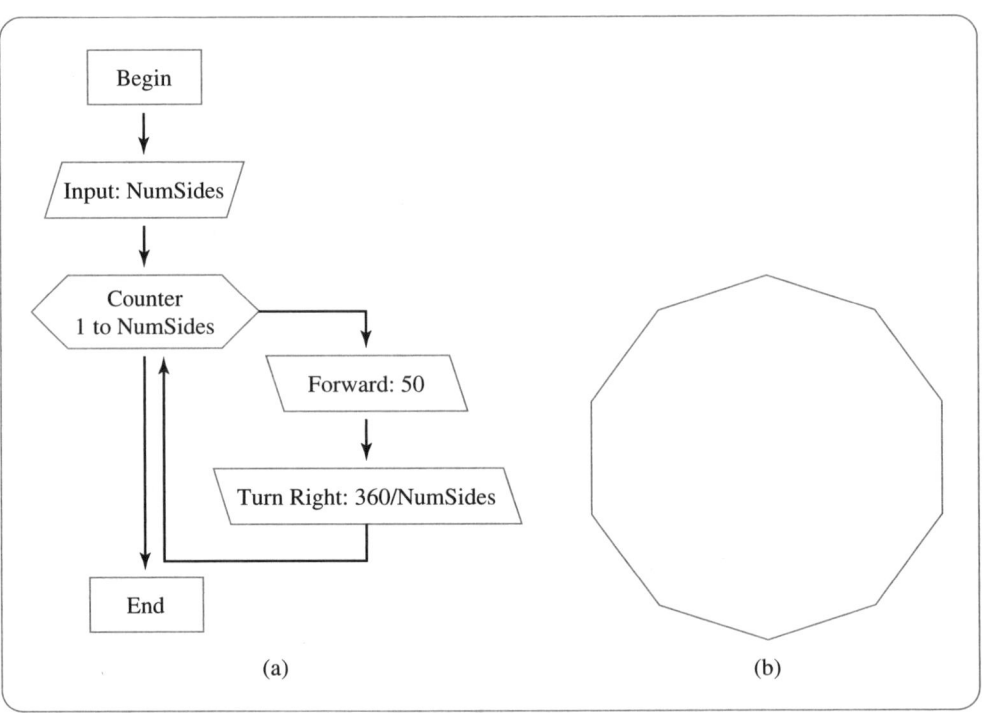

Figure 6-6 A shape-drawing program with a sample decagon output

When the loop variable is included inside the body of the loop, the output can be interesting. For example, Figure 6-7 creates a spiral by drawing increasingly longer lines after each turn. Figure 6-8 shows the same program with a 91-degree rotation.

CHAPTER SIX

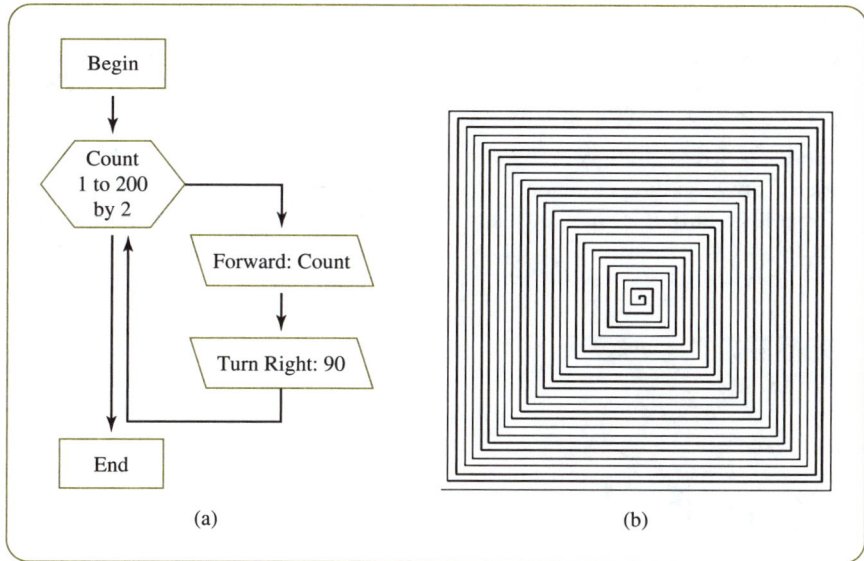

Figure 6-7 A spiral program and output

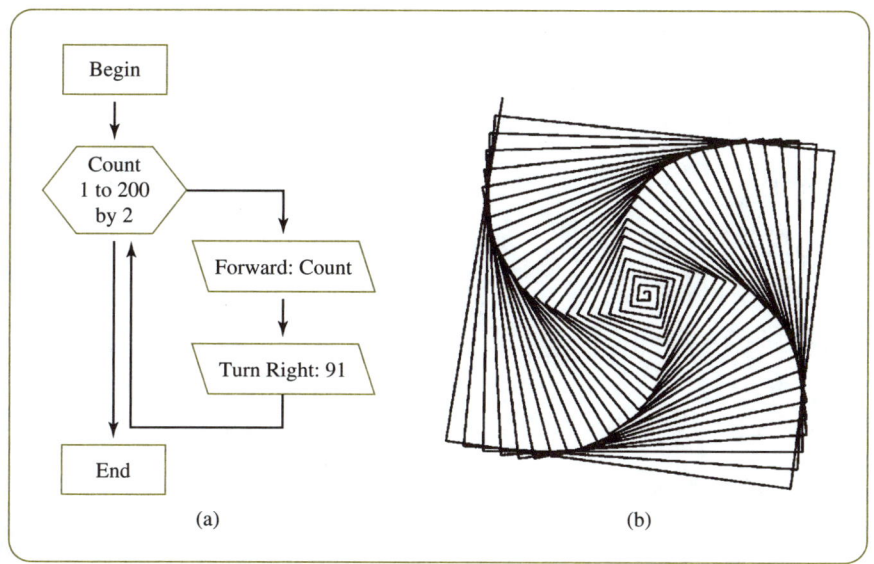

Figure 6-8 A spiral program with a 91-degree rotation

WORKING WITH COLORS

By default, the pen draws with black ink and is 1 unit in width. Visual Logic provides commands for changing the pen's color and width. The ability to manipulate the pen gives developers even greater opportunity to be creative in their designs.

SET COLOR AND PEN WIDTH

The **Set Color** command allows the developer to select any color from the standard Color dialog box. Figure 6-9 shows the Color dialog with custom colors expanded. The **Pen Width** command changes the thickness of the drawing pen.

A yellow circle and a series of thick yellow lines combine to look like a sun as shown in Figure 6-10. Notice that when the pen color is changed to yellow, it stays yellow for the rest of the program (or at least until it is changed again later). *Note*: When you select a Pen Color from the color pallet, the flowchart will give the RGB color breakdown. Thus, when you select Yellow, it appears as (255, 255, 0).

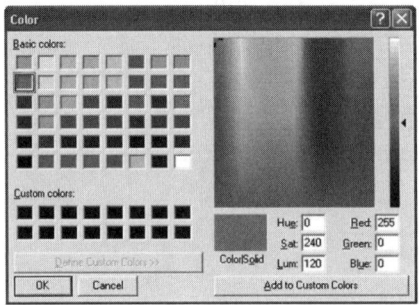

Figure 6-9 The Color dialog box (expanded)

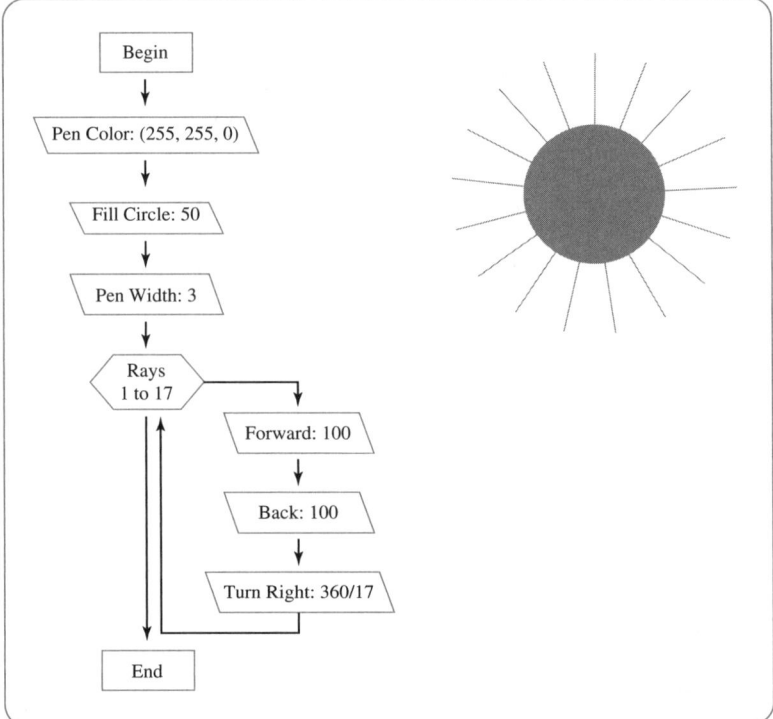

Figure 6-10 Sun algorithm and output

CHAPTER SIX

COLOR FORWARD

Another way of changing the pen color is to use the **Color Forward** command. This command moves the pen through the three base colors of red, green, and blue. There are 256 color variations between blue and green, 256 color variations between green and red, and 256 color variations between red and blue, at which point the color cycle begins again. The Color Forward command typically occurs inside a loop.

Figure 6-11 shows one use of the Color Forward command. The program draws increasingly larger circles with the pen color rotating through shades of blue, green, and red. If the default pen width of 1 is used, some pixels are left uncolored because of mathematical rounding. The slightly thicker pen width of 2 makes the colors solid between the concentric circles.

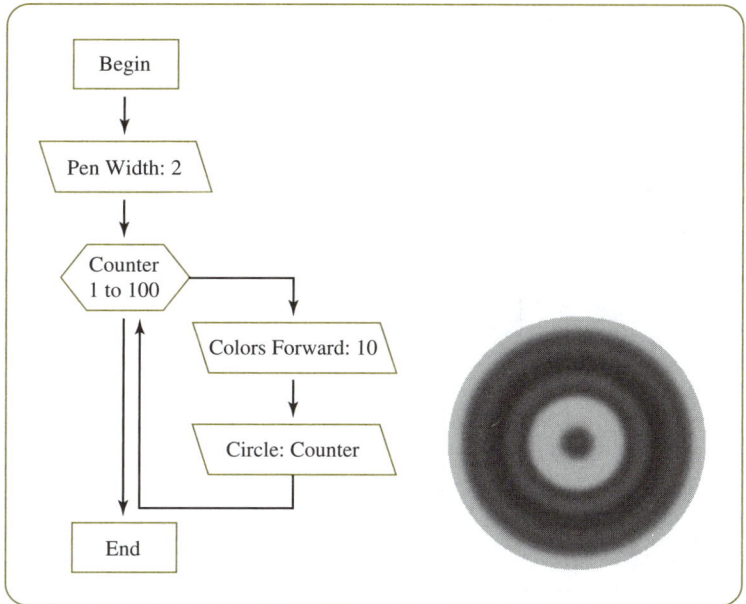

Figure 6-11 Colored concentric circles program and output

QUICK CHECK 6-B

Modify the solution in Figure 6-11 in the following ways and see how the image changes.

1. Change the Color Forward value to 5.
2. Change the Color Forward value to 256.
3. Change the Color Forward back to 10, then set the pen width to the default value 1. Notice how small mathematical rounding errors affect the image with this smaller pen size.

STRUCTURED DESIGN USING PROCEDURES

As problems become larger and more complicated, it becomes necessary to design solutions in a systematic manner. One common approach is called **structured design**. When structured design is used, a problem is broken into smaller pieces, each of which is solved individually. The solution to an individual piece of the problem is often stored in a procedure.

A **procedure** is a series of instructions that are grouped together and treated as a single unit. The procedure can be called from elsewhere in the solution by referencing the procedure's name. When the procedure is called, control flows to the statements inside the procedure. When the procedure is finished, control returns to the calling statement (Figure 6-12).

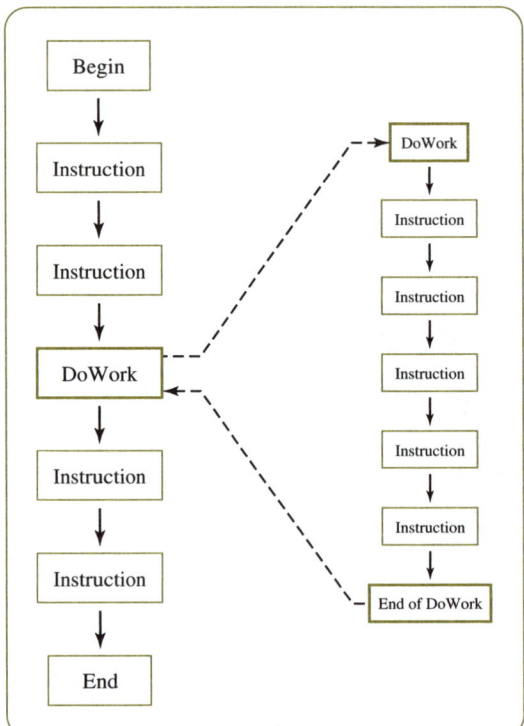

Figure 6-12 Flow of a procedure call

ROTATING FLAGS PROBLEM

To understand how procedures are created and used, consider the problem of drawing eight rotating flags. There is no single command for drawing a flag, but if there was such a command, the solution to this problem would probably look like Figure 6-13.

CHAPTER SIX

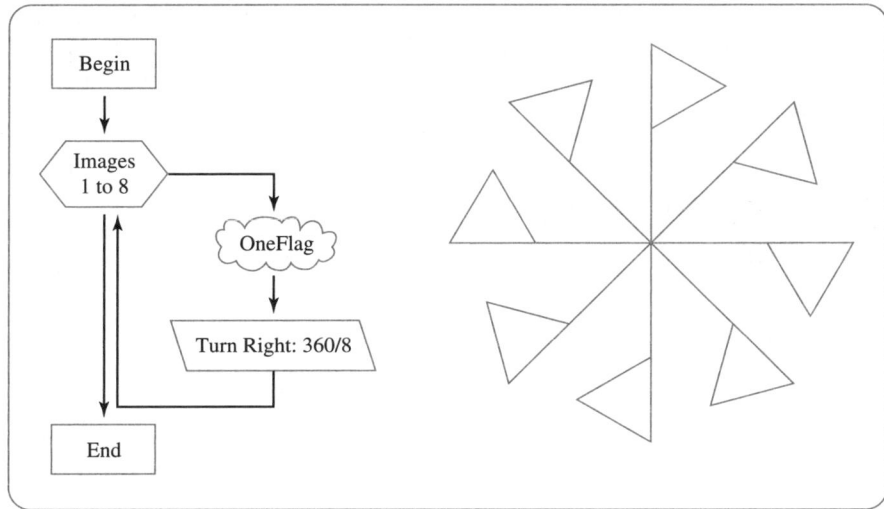

Figure 6-13 Desired program and output for rotating flags

> **TIP** Procedures allow programs to be divided into logical units. For example, Figure 6-13 shows how the Rotating Flags program would work if "OneFlag" were a single command. Creating a "OneFlag" procedure will give the user a single command to perform all the work necessary to draw a single flag, thus making the flowchart in Figure 6-13 a valid solution.

The flowchart in Figure 6-13 represents the highest level of our structured design. The details of how a flag is drawn are not important at this level. When considering the solution at this highest level, it is assumed the OneFlag procedure will do what it is supposed to do (e.g., draw one flag).

CREATING A PROCEDURE

To create a procedure in Visual Logic, select "Procedures | Add New Procedure" from the main menu (Figure 6-14).

Figure 6-14 Menu option to add new procedure

The Procedure Edit dialog box appears, containing a text box for the name of the procedure and a list box for the parameters. (Parameters allow communication between the procedure and the calling program. Parameters are discussed later in this chapter.) Enter **OneFlag** into the text box (Figure 6-15) and press OK.

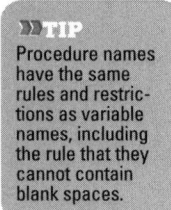

> **TIP**
> Procedure names have the same rules and restrictions as variable names, including the rule that they cannot contain blank spaces.

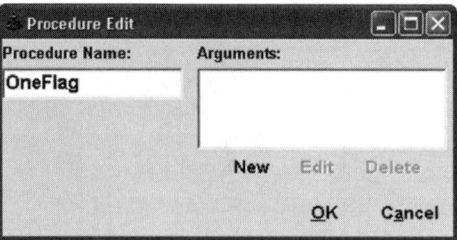

Figure 6-15 The Procedure Edit dialog box

After you press OK, Visual Logic creates an empty procedure stub with the name you specified (Figure 6-16).

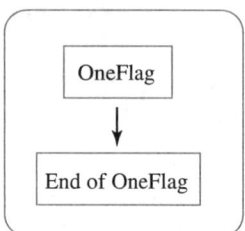

Figure 6-16 The OneFlag procedure stub

Commands are added to the procedure exactly the same as they are in the main routine. Drawing the flag begins by drawing the pole (70 units long) on which the flag flies. The flag itself is a triangle with sides of 50 units. After the triangle is drawn, the procedure moves the pen back to the initial starting location. The full implementation of the OneFlag procedure is shown in Figure 6-17.

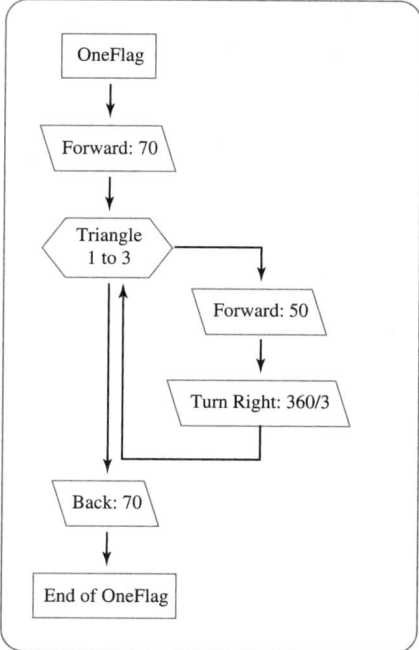

Figure 6-17 The complete OneFlag procedure

The OneFlag procedure is now finished. Return to the main procedure by selecting from the main menu "Procedures | Main." You may use the Call Procedure submenu as shown in Figure 6-18 to create a call to the OneFlag procedure. Use the OneFlag procedure to implement the Main level solution shown in Figure 6-19. The output for this program matches the desired output originally presented in Figure 6-13.

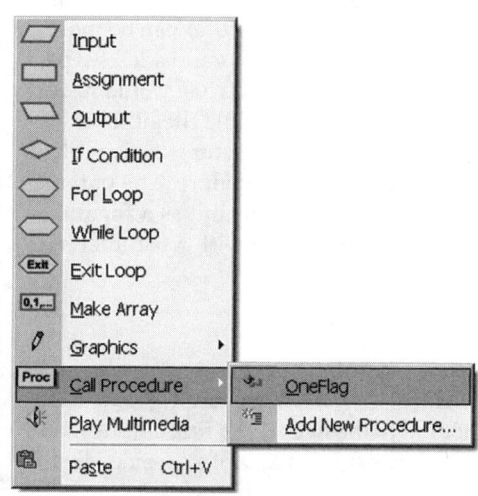

Figure 6-18 Calling a flag procedure

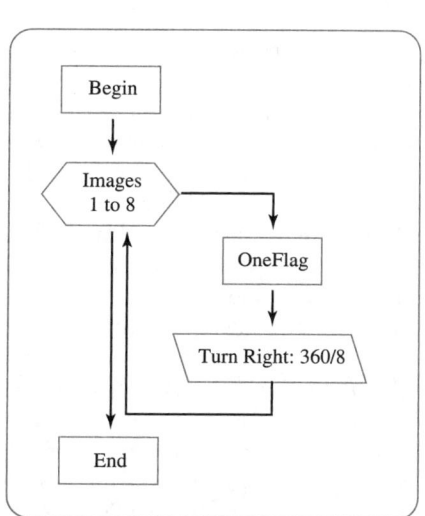

Figure 6-19 The solution for the rotating flags problem

GRAPHICS AND PROCEDURES

> ### QUICK CHECK 6-C
> Using the OneFlag procedure, write programs that generate the output shown in Figure 6-20.

Figure 6-20 Output for two different programs, each utilizing the OneFlag procedure

PROCEDURES WITH PARAMETERS

> **TIP**
> Parameters appear in parentheses after the procedure name.

Consider again the OneFlag procedure from the previous section. Whenever that procedure is called, the result is always the same, drawing a single flag shape. Procedures can be more flexible than this. For example, a procedure could be written that draws a multisided shape, and the number of sides could change from drawing to drawing. To do this, we would need to call the procedure and also provide additional information, for example the number of sides the shape should have. This can be done using parameters. A parameter is a piece of information that is communicated between the calling code and the procedure. The parameter is referred to as an **actual parameter** when calling the procedure and as a **formal parameter** inside the procedure body. To illustrate using a procedure with a parameter, consider the following rotating shapes program.

ROTATING SHAPES PROGRAM

If there was a procedure that would draw an AnySided figure (where the number of sides in the figure to be drawn is specified when calling the procedure) then the flowchart in Figure 6-21 would be able to produce the outputs shown in the bottom of the figure. The first output shows three rotations of a six-sided figure. The second output shows six rotations of a six-sided figure. (*Note*: The second output looks like a stack of blocks, but it is actually six hexagons.) Finally, the third output in Figure 6-21 is the result of rotating 10 pentagons.

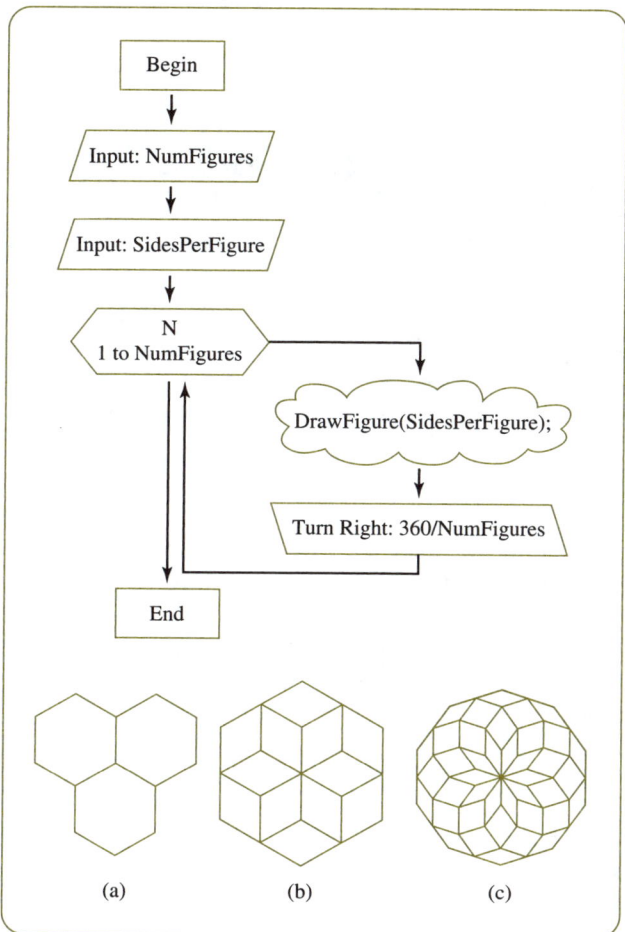

Figure 6-21 Various outputs generated by rotating shapes around 360 degrees

VISUAL LOGIC IMPLEMENTATION

Now consider the challenge of implementing the high-level solution design shown in Figure 6-21. We begin by implementing the conceptual action DrawFigure(NumSides) as a procedure. Select Add New Procedure from the Procedures menu. In the Procedure Edit dialog box, give the procedure the name **DrawFigure**. Then click the New button under the Arguments (or Parameters) box, and name the formal parameter **NumSides** (Figure 6-22a). Press OK to accept the new argument and your Procedure Edit dialog will look like Figure 6-22b. Press OK to close the Edit dialog window.

>> **TIP**
Parameters are also known as *"arguments,"* which is the term used in the Procedure Edit dialog box.

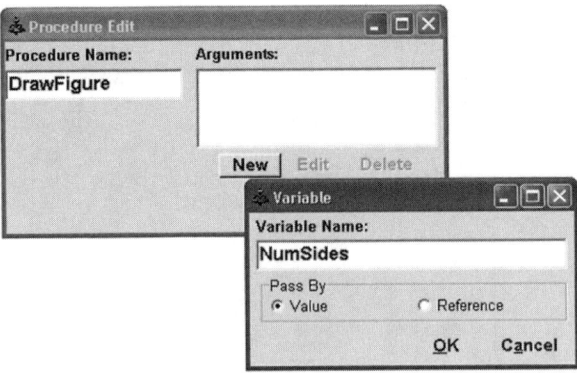
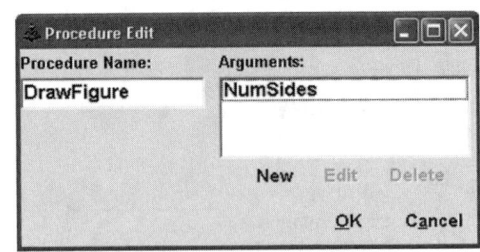

(a) Click "New" and enter argument

(b) New argument appears in Arguments list

Figure 6-22 Creating a procedure argument

Notice that the DrawFigure header and footer elements include the formal argument NumSides in parentheses. In most high-level programming languages, the parameters appear inside of parentheses after the procedure name.

Write the body of the procedure as follows. First add a For loop that iterates from 1 to the value of the formal argument **NumSides**. The body of the loop should draw one side of the image and rotate an appropriate amount so that the entire figure covers 360 degrees. Figure 6-23 shows the completed DrawFigure procedure.

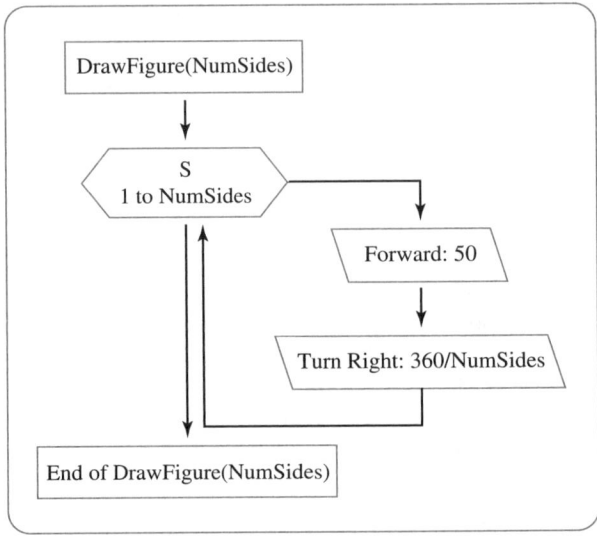

Figure 6-23 The DrawFigure procedure

The DrawFigure procedure is now finished. Return to the main procedure, where you should implement the high-level solution design shown in Figure 6-21. After you add the procedure call for DrawFigure, you should double-click on the procedure call to open the Arguments dialog box. Notice that you cannot edit either the procedure name ("DrawFigure") or the formal argument name ("NumSides") from this window. However, you can (and should!) edit the actual argument value that appears to the right of the formal argument. Enter **SidesPerFigure** as the actual argument as shown in Figure 6-24. (Remember that the actual argument is a variable or expression provided when calling the procedure, and the actual argument value is copied as the initial value for the formal argument during the current pass through the procedure code. In this case, the user's input value SidesPerFigure is passed to the procedure to become the initial value for the NumSides parameter.)

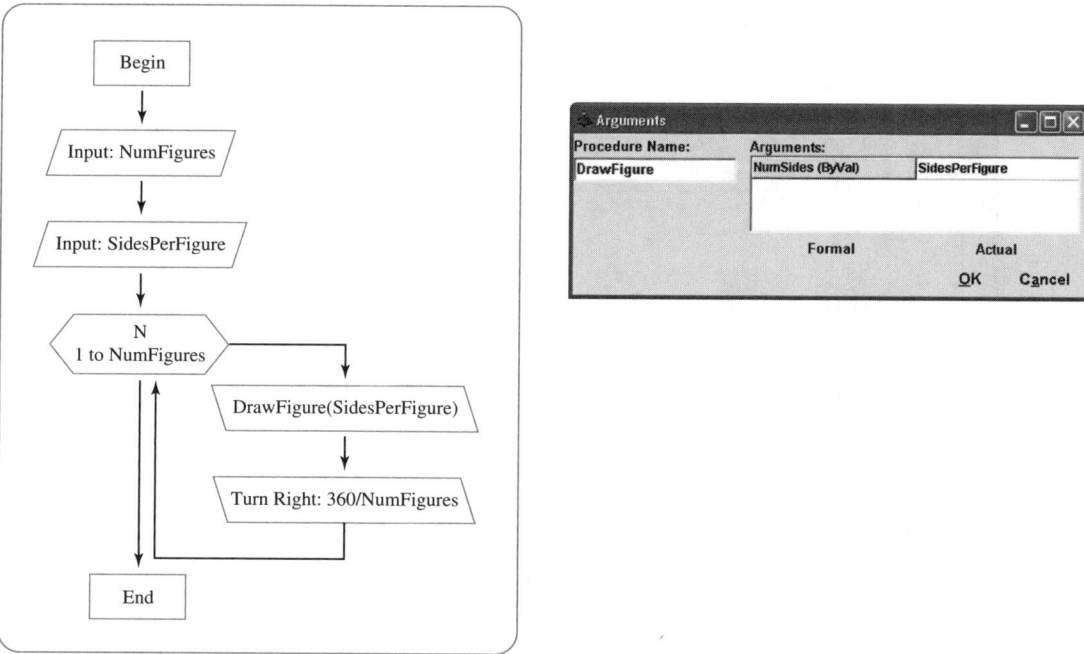

Figure 6-24 Rotating shapes solution with SidesPerFigure as an actual argument

When Figure 6-23 and Figure 6-24 are complete as shown, you can test the program by running it three times. The input pairs of {3, 6}, {6, 6}, and {10, 10} should generate the three outputs shown in Figure 6-21. Continue running the program using different input values, and see what kind of interesting drawings you can create.

PROCEDURES WITH PARAMETERS SUMMARY

» A parameter is a means of sharing information between the calling program and a procedure.

» Formal parameters are declared in the Procedure Edit dialog box at the same time as the procedure name. Formal parameters are displayed in parentheses after the procedure name in the procedure's header and footer elements.

» The calling program specifies the actual parameters at the time of the procedure call. Actual parameters are displayed in parentheses after the procedure name in the procedure call element.

RECURSION

The rotating shapes solution from the previous section involved a procedure with a single parameter. Procedures can contain as many parameters as necessary to pass all the desired information between the calling program and the procedure. To illustrate the use of multiple parameters, start a new application and create a procedure named **BentLine**. Under the Arguments list box, click the New button to add the parameter **Size**, and click OK. Then click the New button again to add a second parameter **Count** and then click OK. Your Procedure Edit dialog box should have two arguments, Size and Count, as shown in Figure 6-25.

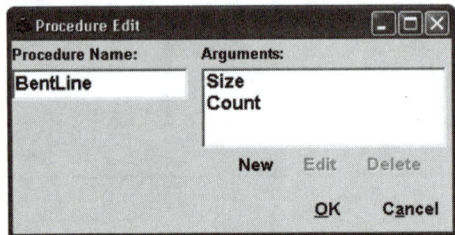

Figure 6-25 BentLine procedure declaration with two arguments

Close the Procedure Edit dialog box. Visual Logic creates a procedure stub for BentLine containing the two parameters Size and Count in the parameter list. Add the code for the BentLine procedure as shown in Figure 6-26, including the formal versus actual values that you should specify when editing (double-clicking) the Call Procedure flowchart elements.

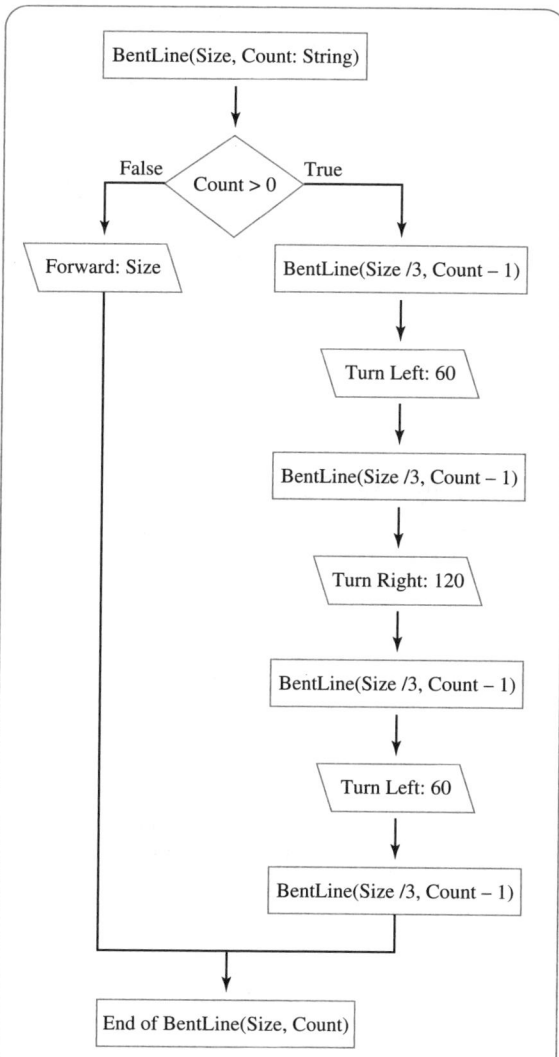
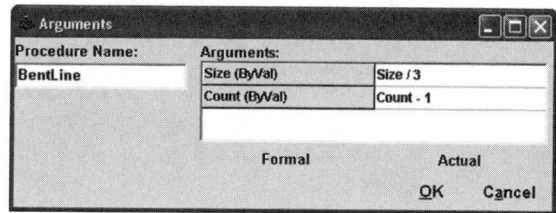

Figure 6-26 A recursive procedure for drawing a bent line

Notice that inside the BentLine procedure there is a call to the BentLine procedure itself. (Actually, there are four calls to itself inside the procedure.) BentLine is therefore a **recursive procedure**, meaning it is a procedure that calls itself. A recursive procedure is similar to a loop in that the code inside the procedure will be repeated many times. You must be cautious when writing recursive procedures to avoid infinite recursion. A recursive procedure therefore typically begins by performing a test on one of its parameters to check for a base case. If the base case is satisfied, then the procedure does not call itself. If the base case is not satisfied, then the procedure does some processing that includes a recursive call. In Figure 6-26, the base case test is Count > 0. If the test is True, then the procedure recursively calls itself and draws a smaller (e.g., Size / 3) line with a lower (e.g., Count − 1) base value. Eventually, the value for Count will be zero, at which time the procedure will simply draw a line of length Size without making a recursive call. (This is how the procedure avoids an infinite loop.)

After writing the BentLine procedure, return to the main procedure and add a call to BentLine. Double-click on the procedure element and enter actual parameter values of 200 and 1 to the formal parameters of Size and Count respectively.

When you close the Parameters dialog box, the main program will look like Figure 6-27.

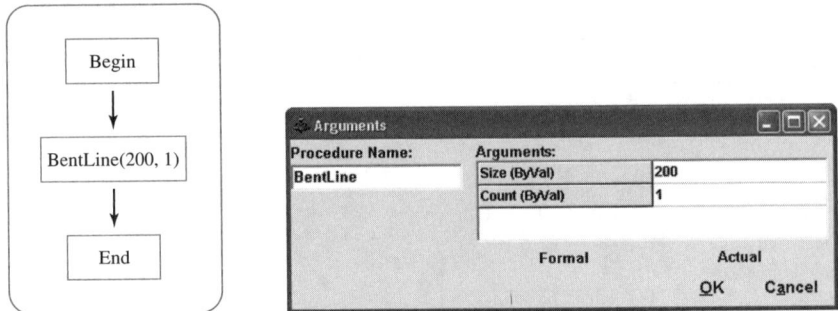

Figure 6-27 The main body with a call to the recursive BentLine procedure

Run the solution. You should get a line with a single bend. Edit the Count parameter to 2 and rerun the solution. Then change the Count value to 3 and 4, running the solution after each change. You should generate outputs similar to Figure 6-28.

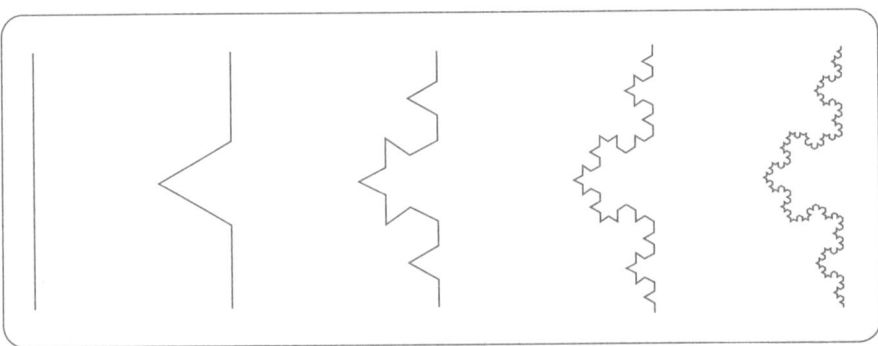

Figure 6-28 BentLine output results for runs with Count being 0, 1, 2, 3, and 4

CHAPTER SIX

»CASE STUDY SOLUTION

Drawing Houses

Problem: Write a program to generate a series of houses similar to the image shown in Figure 6-29.

Analysis: The image contains 45 houses, each drawn using a random pen color. The design for each house is the same: a square base with a triangle roof and two windows. The final figure will contain 45 houses and 90 windows. To help handle the complexity and to avoid repeating code, procedures are used.

The **DrawWindow** procedure (Figure 6-30) draws a window as four contiguous squares. The position of the window is specified by the arguments passed to the procedure.

The **DrawHouse** procedure (Figure 6-31) draws the house as a square frame under a triangle roof. The position of the house is specified by the arguments passed to the procedure. Additionally, the DrawHouse procedure calls the DrawWindow procedure twice to add the two windows at the proper position.

The high-level solution for this problem (Figure 6-32) specifies the maximum house size and, based on that value, determines the yard size for each house (so the houses do not overlap with each other.) The high-level solution then draws the 45 houses at different horizontal and vertical positions on the screen based on changing X and Y values. Each house has a random size and a random color, and the drawing of the house is done by calling the DrawHouse procedure.

Figure 6-29 Houses output

GRAPHICS AND PROCEDURES

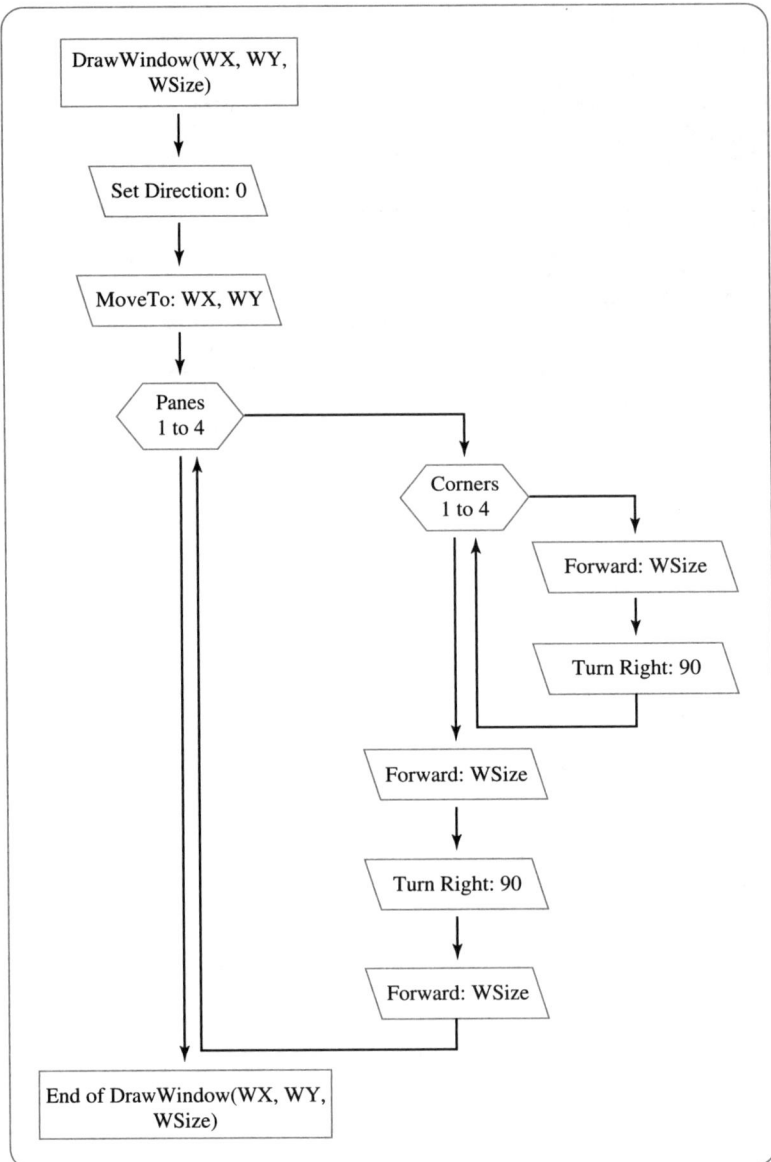

Figure 6-30 DrawWindow procedure

CHAPTER SIX

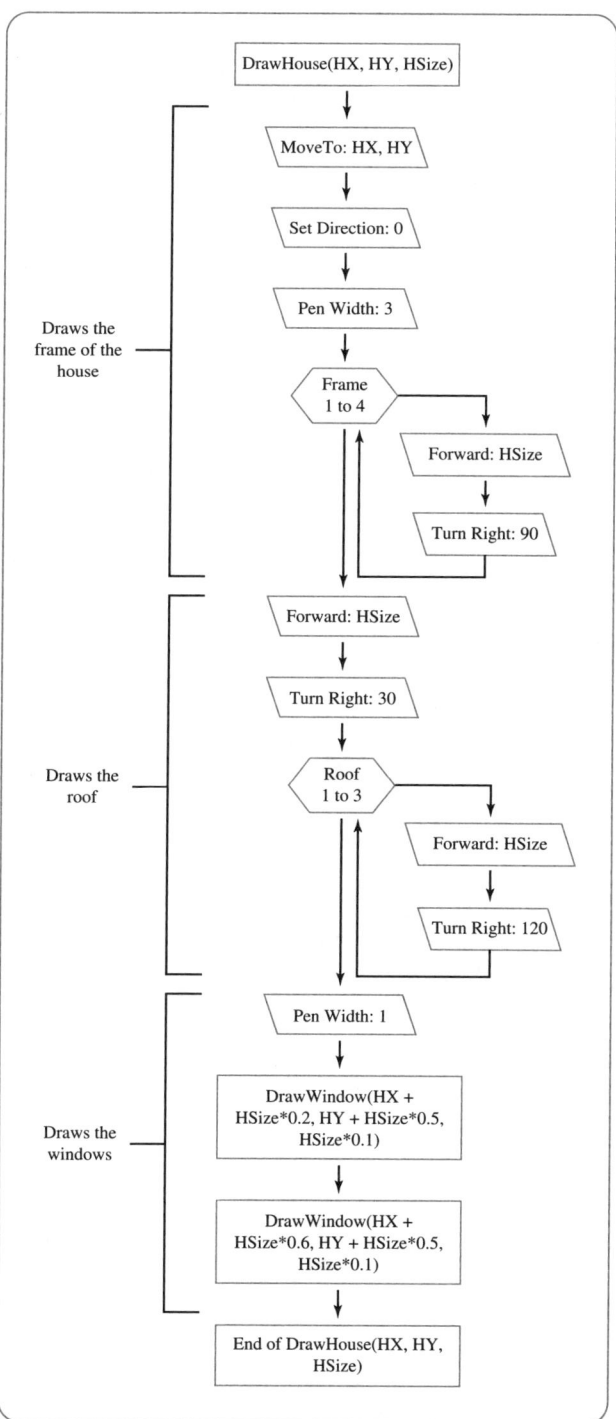

Figure 6-31 DrawHouse procedure

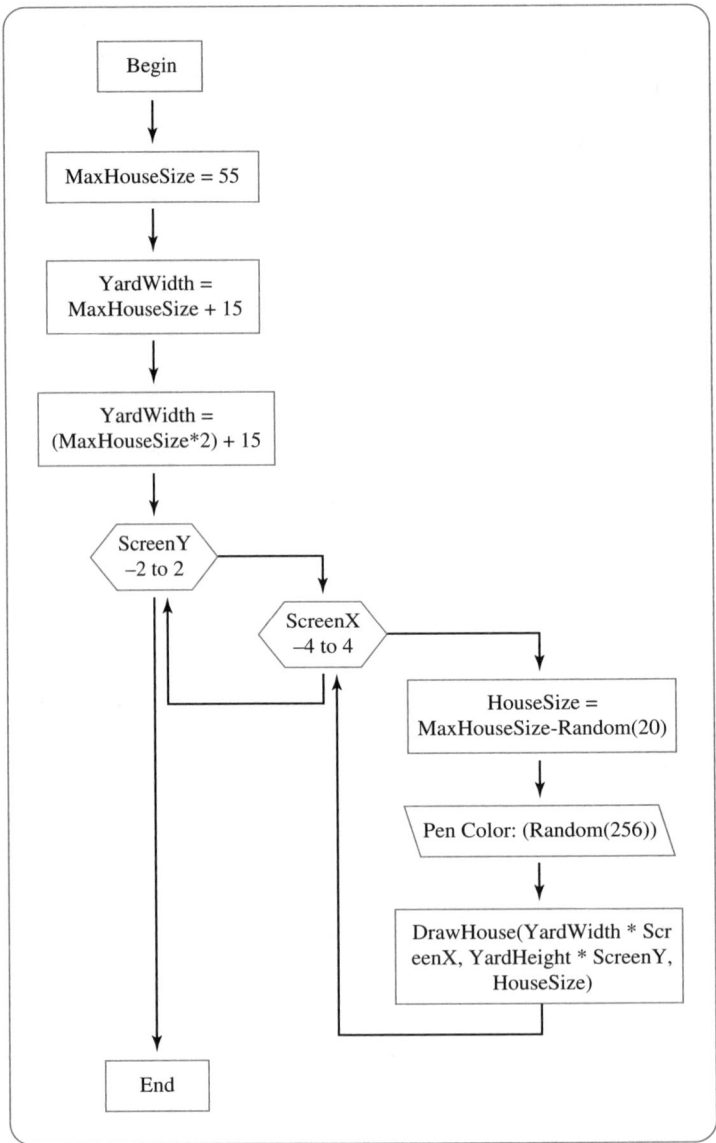

Figure 6-32 High-level solution to draw house problem

CHAPTER SIX

CHAPTER SUMMARY

» Visual Logic graphics include commands, such as Forward and Right. These commands move a virtual pen across the screen.

» Procedures allow code to be written once and called many times. Procedures also allow for code to be organized by logical function.

» An actual parameter is a value or reference passed from the calling code to a procedure. A formal parameter is the corresponding variable in the procedure that receives the value or reference.

KEY TERMS

actual parameter	Logo Programming Language	recursive procedure
Color Forward	parameter	Set Color
formal parameter	Pen Width	structured design
Forward	procedure	Turn Right

REVIEW QUESTIONS

1. What is the Visual Logic graphics pen, and how is it related to the Logo Programming Language turtle?
2. If the current pen drawing direction is north and you want to draw a line from the current position to a point 100 units to the east, what graphics command(s) would you use?
3. Explain the difference between the Set Color command and the Color Forward command.
4. Explain the difference between the Circle command and the Fill Circle command.
5. What is structured design? How does it benefit developers when solving large problems?
6. What is a procedure? What happens when a procedure is called? What happens when a procedure is finished executing?
7. What is the purpose of a parameter? What is the difference between a formal parameter and an actual parameter?
8. What is a recursive procedure? How does a recursive procedure avoid infinite recursion?

PROGRAMMING EXERCISES

6-1. Raising Flags. Draw four flags of increasing sizes.

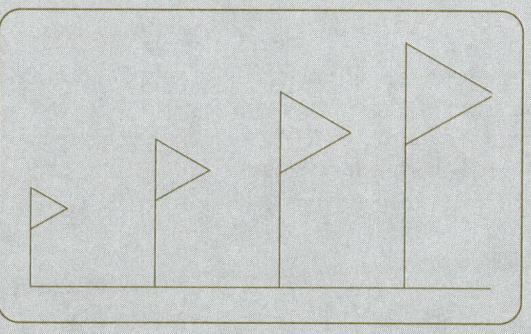

6-2. Rotating Rectangles. Write a graphics program with three inputs: rectangle height, rectangle width, and number of rectangles. The program should then display the specified rectangles rotated around a center point. Two sample runs are shown below. In the first output shown, the input values were 100, 50, 5. In the second sample run shown below, the input values were 50, 200, 7. (Only one set of rotating rectangles should appear each time you run the program, and the shape and number of rectangles will depend on the three input values.)

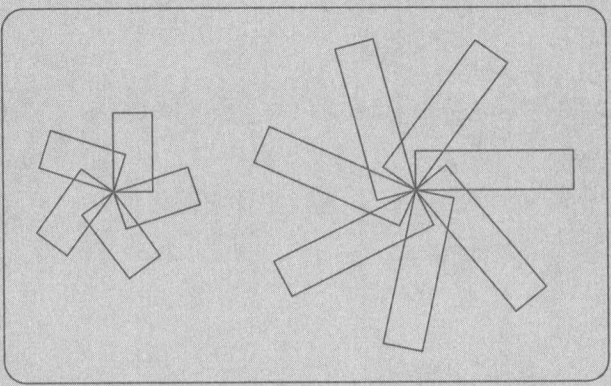

6-3. Concentric Squares. Use the Color Forward command to generate a series of concentric squares similar to the following figure.

6-4. CD Burn. It is always a good idea to back up your files on a regular basis, and this process has been made easier by affordable CD burners. Generate an image similar to the following to remind others that frequently backing up your hard drive on CD is a good idea. (*Hint*: This can be drawn similar to sun rays in Figure 6-10 only with color changes.)

CHAPTER SIX

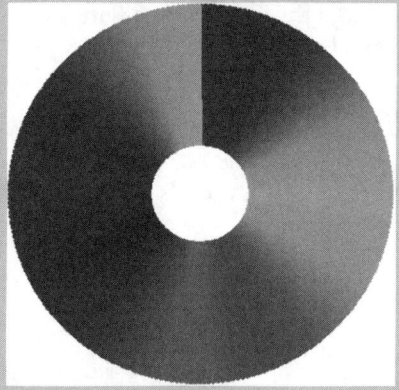

6-5. Random Flags. Write a program that uses a flag-drawing procedure to draw 10 flags at random locations. Every time you run the program, the flags should show up at different locations on the screen. Therefore, the position of your 10 flags will be different than those shown in the figure below.

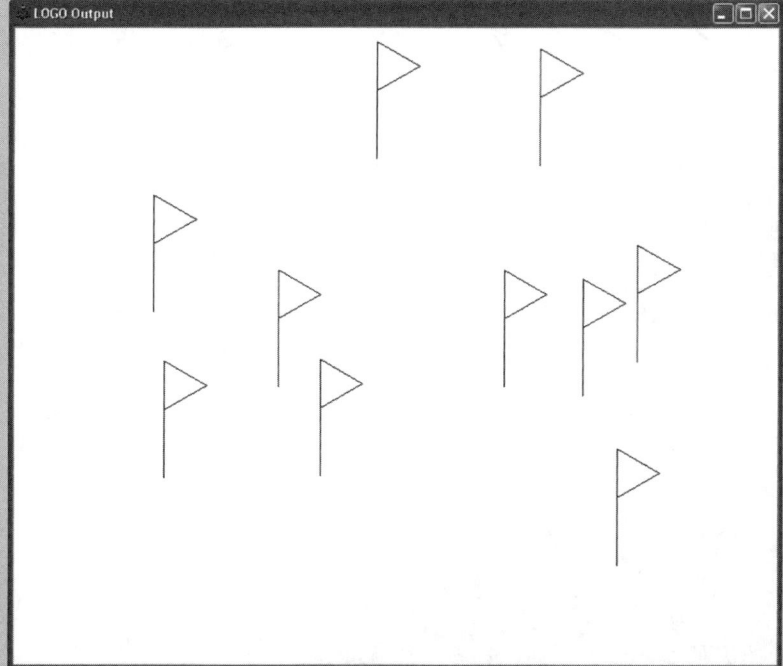

6-6. Random Other. Write a program with a procedure that draws a shape of your choice. (In the example below, the shape is a stickman figure.) Your program should then call the procedure 10 times to draw the shape at 10 random locations. Every time you run the program, your shape should show up at different locations on the screen. Therefore, the position of your 10 shapes will be different than those shown in the figure below.

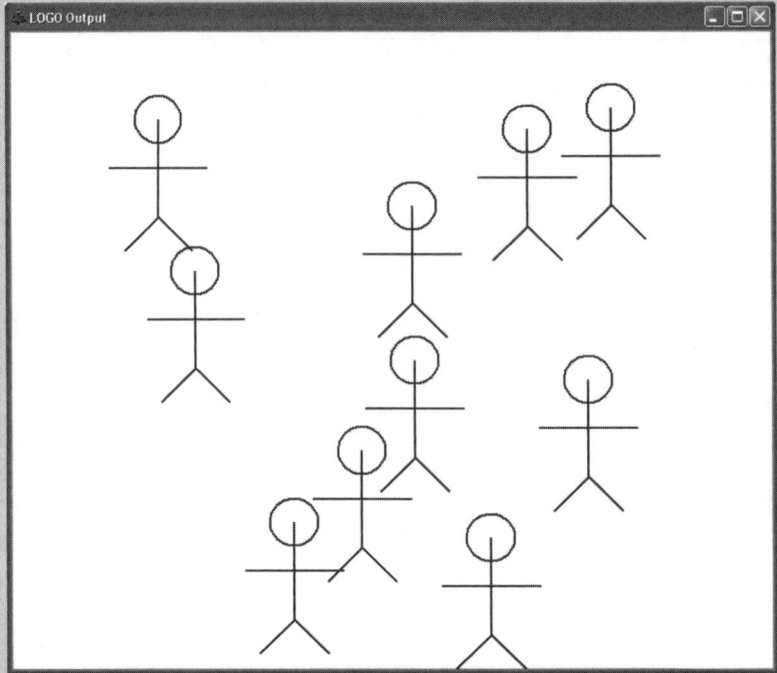

6-7. Fireworks. Consider the image of fireworks in a nighttime sky. Write a procedure called Burst that moves the pen to a random location on the screen, moves the pen color forward 256, and then draws a firework burst with a random size and number of rays. (*Hint*: You may want to add a minimum value to the random size and random number of rays to avoid having bursts that are too small or have too few rays.) The main procedure should call Burst multiple times to generate an image similar to the image below. *Note*: Because of the random values, your solution image will be different each time you run your program. (*Hint*: You can create a nighttime background by setting the pen color to black and then calling Fill Circle with a sufficiently large value, such as 2000.)

APPENDIX A

VISUAL LOGIC RESERVED WORDS

The following are reserved words that Visual Logic uses for special purposes and therefore these cannot (or should not) be used as variable or procedure names.

And	Except	Not	Shr
Array	File	Object	String
As	Finally	Of	Then
Begin	For	On	ThreadVar
Case	Function	Or	To
Class	Goto	Packed	Try
Const	If	Procedure	Type
Constructor	Implementation	Program	Unit
Destructor	In	Property	Until
Div	Inherited	Raise	Uses
Do	Interface	Record	Var
DownTo	Is	Repeat	While
Else	Length	Set	With
End	Mod	Shl	Xor

APPENDIX B

DEBUGGING IN VISUAL LOGIC

Eventually, all developers write programs that contain errors. This appendix contains some suggestions on how to identify and fix errors in your program.

COMMON MISTAKE #1: CHECK FOR MISSPELLED VARIABLE NAMES

One of the most common errors that novice students will make is mistyping their variable names. For example, if you input "Height" and then later perform a calculation "Area = Width * Heigth", your Area value will be zero (0). This is because "Height" and "Heigth" are different variable names. The first holds the input value and the second is a different, unassigned variable and therefore has the default value of zero. So the assignment statement is basically "Area = Width * 0" which gives the zero result.

Strangely enough, consistent spelling is more important than correct spelling. If you misspell "Heigth" in both instances above, the program will work. Of course, correct and consistent spelling is best!

APPENDIX B

COMMON MISTAKE #2: MULTIPLE VARIABLE NAMES

This is similar to the first common mistake, but rather than having a typing error, your program might have two different variables for the same value. Consider two inputs for "Height" and "Width", then the assignment "Area = Height * Size". This would also produce a zero (0) result because the input value "Width" is not used in the calculation, but instead an unassigned new variable "Size" is used. Other example would be to use both "Max" and "Maximum" when referencing the same value.

The thing to remember here is to pick one descriptive variable name and stick with it.

DEBUGGING—PENCIL AND PAPER

If the common mistakes above did not solve your problem, you will need to examine your solution logic more closely. A pencil and paper remains one of the most powerful tools of engineers and inventors, which is good because programming involves a little of both. A "desk check" is a manual (pencil and paper) technique for checking the logic of an algorithm. Your goal is to carefully mimic exactly what the computer will do when executing the program, writing down each variable name and how the values for each variable changes while the program executes. When the variable's values change, simply cross out the old values and write down the new values below the variable name. By stepping through the entire program this way you are likely to determine why your program is not working, and hopefully it will be clear what needs to change to fix the problem.

DEBUGGING—BREAKPOINTS AND VARIABLE WATCH

Finally, if you still cannot figure out why your program is not working, you can try debugging your program by stepping through your program one element at a time. The main menu contains a "Debug" menu option with six options. The "Step Into" option will cause a Variable Watch window to appear and will move through your program one element at a time. (*Note*: You can also hit the F8 key as a shortcut for "Step Into".) When running your program like this you are said to be in Debug mode and you can monitor how the variable values change as you step through the solution.

Note that the current flowchart element is highlighted by a flashing background. Also note that an Input dialog box might appear in the background when running in debug mode (so that you have to click on the item in the Taskbar at the bottom of the screen.) Finally, when doing input, be sure to click in the input window text box so that your input value appears in the proper window.

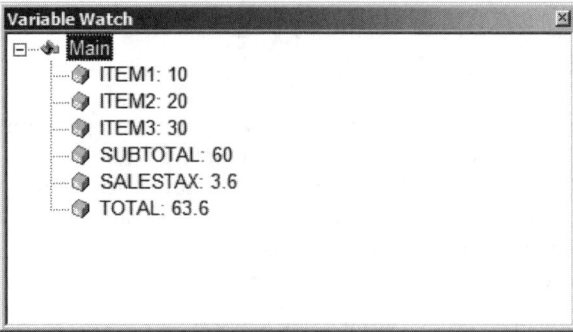

By examining the program variables and watching their values change as each step of the program executes, hopefully you will better understand what is happening when your program runs, and therefore be better able to fix any problems that exist.

APPENDIX C

USING MULTIMEDIA

One feature of Visual Logic that is not directly covered in this Guide is the last menu element "Play Multimedia". This is an optional element that can be introduced in the first chapter, or can be ignored for the entire book. However it is very easy to use and is something that can dramatically change the look and feel of your solutions.

Visual Logic can support .wav audio and .mp3 video formats, and may support other formats as well depending on the encoding used. By placing the "Play Multimedia" element in the proper, logical location you can give the use a richer audio-video experience when running your solution.

The possibilities are limited only by your imagination. Have fun being creative!

INDEX

Special Characters
\- (back slash), 11
\> (greater than operator), 21
\> (less than operator), 21
( ) (parentheses), 26
<> (not equal operator), 21
" (quotation mark), 6
§ (console end-of-output symbol), 38–39
& (ampersand), 6
* (asterisk), 8, 11
\+ (plus sign), 8, 11
− (minus sign), 8, 11
/ (slash), 8, 11
\>= (greater than or equal operator), 21
<= (less than or equal operator), 21
^ (caret), 11
= equal sign, 21

A
accumulator, 47, 48, 49
actual parameter, 110
addition operator (+), 8, 11
algorithm, 2–3
ampersand (&), concatenation operator, 6
AND operator, 26
argument. *See* parameter
arithmetic expression, 11–13
array, 73–91
   accessing individual elements, 74–75
   benefits of using, 75–78
   creating, 74
   dice roll simulation program, 81–83
   elements, 74
   evens and odds program, 78–80
   index, 74, 75, 78
   For loop, 78
   parallel arrays program, 83–90
   sorting, 87–89
   upper bound, 74
assignment statement, 8–9
asterisk (*), multiplication operator, 8, 11

B
back slash (, integer division operator, 11
bubble sort, 87–89
bug, 14

C
caret (^), exponentiation operator, 11
color, graphics, 103–105
Color dialog box, 104
Color Forward command, 105
command. *See also specific commands*
   sequential, 20
compound condition, 25–27, 28, 30, 31
computer program, 1
concatenation operator, 6
condition, 20
   nested, 28, 29
console end-of-output symbol (§), 38–39
console input, 37–38
console output, 37–39
conversion, units of measurement, 12–13
counter, 47, 48, 49
counting backwards program, 43–44

D
debugging, 14
decision making, 19–33
   compound conditions, 25–27, 28, 30, 31
   computer capability, 20
   IF statement, 20–23
   nested IF statements, 23–25
determine the average program, 47–48
dice roll simulation program, 81–83
Dijkstra, Edward, 20
division, 11
division operator (/), 8, 11
double quote ("), string literals, 6
drawing houses program, 117–120

INDEX

E

Edison, Thomas, 14
element, array, 74
   accessing, 74–75
   index, 74, 75, 78
   referencing, 75
end-of-output symbol (§), 38–39
equal operator (=), 21
equal sign (=), equal operator, 21
evens and odds program, 78–80
Exit loop, 49–52
   high-low game program, 51–52
exponentiation, 11
exponentiation operator (^), 11
expression, 8

F

final value, For loop, 59, 61–63
flowchart, 3–5
   without execution, 5
Flowchart Elements menu, 3–4
For loop, 59–63
   arrays, 78
   final value, 59, 61–63
   initial value, 59, 61
   step value, 59, 61–63
   While loops compared, 60–61
formal parameter, 110
format
   programming, 6–7
   username and password storage, 84
Forward command, 98–101
function, intrinsic, 13–14

G

graphics, 98–103
   colors, 103–105
   commands, 98, 99
   Forward command, 98–101
   loops, 102–103
   Turn Left command, 101
   Turn Right command, 98–101
greater than operator (>), 21
greater than or equal operator (>=), 21

H

Hello Name program, 5–7
Hello World program, 3–5
high-low game program, 51–52
Hopper, Grace Mary, 14

I

IF statement, 20–23
   nested, 23–25
index, array elements, 74, 75, 78

infinite loop, 42
initial value, For loop, 59, 61
input
   console, 37–38
   weekly paycheck program, 7–8
input statement, 5
integer division, 11
integer division operator (, 11
integer remainder, 11
intrinsic function, 13–14

L

less than operator (>), 21
less than or equal operator (<=), 21
Logo Programming Language, 98
loop
   Exit loop, 49–52
   graphics, 102–103
   infinite, 42
   For loop. *See* For loop
   nested. *See* nested loop
   While. *See* While loop
Loop Control Variable, 40

M

Make Array command, 74
measurement units, conversion, 12–13
minus sign (−), subtraction operator, 8, 11
multiplication, 11
multiplication operator (*), 8, 11
multiplication table program, 65–67

N

nested condition, 28, 29
nested IF statement, 23–25
nested loop, 63–68
   multiplication table program, 65–67
   triangle problem program, 67–68
not equal operator (<>), 21
NOT operator, 26
numeric input, 6

O

OR operator, 26
output
   console, 37–39
   format for statements, 9, 11
   forms, 9, 11
   weekly paycheck program, 9–11

P

Papert, Semore, 98
parallel arrays program, 83–90
parameter, 110–114
   actual, 110

INDEX

parameter (*continued*)
  formal, 110
  rotating shapes program, 110–111
  Visual Logic implementation, 111–113
parentheses (( )), compound conditions, 26
password, parallel arrays program, 83–90
Pen Width command, 104
placeholder variable, 28, 32
plus sign (+), addition operator, 8, 11
post-test loop, 43
pre-test loop, 43
procedure, 106. *See also* structured design using procedures
  calling, 109
  creating, 107–109
  names, 108
  parameters, 110–114
  recursive, 114–116
processing, weekly paycheck program, 8–9
program, 1
programming format, 6–7

Q

quotation mark ("), string literals, 6

R

random integer, 81
reading data from a text file, 83–84
recursive procedure, 114–116
relational operator, 20–21
repetition, 20
rotating flags program, 106–107
rotating shapes program, 110–111

S

selection, 20
sentinel value, 46–49
  determine the average program, 47–48
sequential command, 20
Set Color command, 104
signaling value, 46–49
slash (/), division operator, 8, 11
sorting an array, 87–89
step value, For loop, 59, 61–63
string literal, 6
structured design using procedures, 106–109
  creating procedures, 107–109
  procedures with parameters, 110–114

recursion, 114–116
  rotating flags program, 106–107
  rotating shapes program, 110–111
  Visual Logic implementation, 111–113
"Structured Programming" (Dijkstra), 20
subtraction operator (−), 8, 11
syntax, 3

T

text file, reading data, 83–84
triangle problem program, 67–68
Turn Left command, 101
Turn Right command, 98–101

U

units of measurement, conversion, 12–13
upper bound, 74
username, parallel arrays program, 83–90

V

value
  final, 59, 61–63
  initial, 59, 61
  sentinel (signaling), 46–49
  step, 59, 61–63
variable, 5
  Loop Control Variable, 40
  placeholder, 28, 32
Visual Logic, 2

W

weekly paycheck program, 7–11
  input, 7–8
  output, 9–11
  processing, 8–9
While loop, 40–49
  counting backwards program, 43–44
  Exit loops with, 49, 50
  For loops compared, 60–61
  post-test, 43
  pre-test, 43
  sentinel values, 46–49

X

XOR operator, 26